Prelude to Patterns in Computer Science Using Java

BETA EDITION

Ed C. Epp

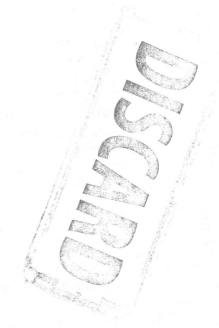

Franklin, Beedle & Associates
8536 SW St. Helens Drive, Ste. D
Wilsonville, OR 97070
(503) 682–7668

President and Publisher	Jim Leisy
Developmental Editor	Sue Page
Cover	Ian Shadburne
Marketing	Chris Collier
Order Processing	Krista Hall
	Lois Allison

Dedication

I would like to dedicate this book to my wife Marilyn Johnson and my children Dietrich Epp, Elizabeth Johnson, and Olivia Johnson, who should have thrown me out of the house years ago.

BOOK MAP

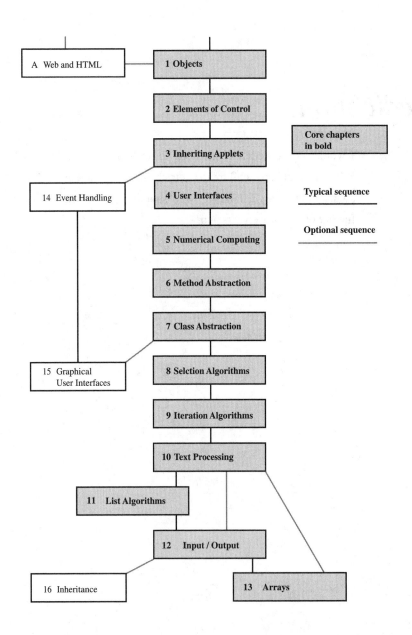

A Web and HTML

1 Objects

2 Elements of Control

3 Inheriting Applets

14 Event Handling

4 User Interfaces

5 Numerical Computing

6 Method Abstraction

7 Class Abstraction

15 Graphical
User Interfaces

8 Selction Algorithms

9 Iteration Algorithms

10 Text Processing

11 List Algorithms

12 Input / Output

16 Inheritance

13 Arrays

Core chapters
in bold

Typical sequence

Optional sequence

CHAPTER MAP

Christopher Alexander, a designer of great buildings, says that a good design is composed of patterns of living units. His ideas have been applied to software and certainly can be applied to books as well. Creating a book is like designing a building. A book must be designed so that each chapter is a useful place to live for a while. Because each of us is different, a book must be designed to serve many learning styles.

Concepts

The first part of each chapter focuses on a key topic. These topics are pulled from many areas of computer science with the goal of providing us with an appreciation of the breadth of computer science. Some of the topics have to do with software development topics such as object-oriented programming. Others come from economics. We talk about how chaos influences the way we model the world. We use lists to organize movie titles. We make images dance across the screen.

Patterns

In each chapter we introduce and solve a programming problem that directly relates to the key topic of the chapter. Careful analysis of the solution reveals bits of code, algorithms, and design constructs that will appear again and again in the solution of many problems. Patterns capture these bits of code and design and provide us with problem-solving tools that can be used for a lifetime. They transcend programming languages. That is their power.

Java Skills

Finally, we need a canvas, paint, and brushes with which to paint our ideas. That is the function of a programming language. It provides us with a mechanism for expressing our ideas in such a way that a computer understands them. Java is a good programming language to learn. It has a richness that allows us to paint expressive programs.

Supplementary Materials

Some topics are less central, but too fun to ignore. Other times there are ideas that some will not have time to explain. This material is placed in the supplementary section. If there is time for it, great. If not, we can catch it in a later course.

WHERE DO WE START?

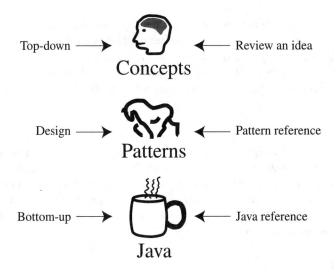

Top-down ⟶ **Concepts** ⟵ Review an idea

Design ⟶ **Patterns** ⟵ Pattern reference

Bottom-up ⟶ **Java** ⟵ Java reference

A good living space has many points of entry. We may enter our living room from the kitchen, the dining room, or the hallway. We enter a room based on what we know about the house, what we need to do, and where we happen to be.

A chapter may also have different entry points. Some of us are top-down learners. We learn better by looking at the world and then studying the people, indoor plumbing, and valleys that comprise it. We need to see how the pieces fit into the world before we understand the details. We need to place our knowledge in a context.

Others of us are bottom-up learners. We learn better by creating a strong foundation of fundamentals. We begin with gears, wires, and sewing needles. We start with the small details and put them together to create more complex ideas. We keep building until we have all the knowledge we need to understand the entire system.

As in the room analogy, we as learners do not always enter through the same door. Sometimes we learn more effectively top-down, other times bottom-up, and often we jump back and forth between the two. Sometimes we need to enter a room to find a lost item. If we have forgotten a piece of syntax, the Java section of each chapter is a good place to enter. For program design, enter the Patterns section. It is not necessary to read each chapter from front to back or to read the chapters in order. Feel free to jump around and revisit chapters.

Table of Contents

1

Objects   1

2

Elements

of Control   37

3

Inheriting Applets   89

4

User Interfaces   *121*

5

Numeric Computing   *159*

6

Method Abstraction   209

7

Class Abstraction   275

8

Selection Algorithms   339

9

Iteration

Algorithms   391

10   *Text Processing*   *435*

11 *List Algorithms* 483

12 *Input /Output* 535

13

Arrays   597

14

Event Handling   659

15 *User Interfaces   683*

16 *Inheritance   755*

A

HTML 807

B

Java Class Reference 843

C

Vista Reference 911

Glossary   *925*

Index   *933*

Preface

Patterns

Much of what we do in life is based on patterns of behavior we have learned. We learn strategies that help us merge our car into traffic, we learn organizations for buildings that make them valuable living spaces, we learn patterns of social behavior that help us make friends, we learn patterns for cooking that maximize flavor, and we learn patterns for constructing our day so we minimize effort and maximize fun.

Learning about computer science and software engineering is no different. It is important to learn patterns that maximize utility and minimize effort. At the micro level we learn about language syntax patterns and how single elements can be organized to achieve a small task. At higher levels we learn how these small tasks can be organized to achieve larger functions. There are patterns that delineate effective ways to assemble software components into software architectures. There are algorithmic patterns that delineate the sequence of steps required to accomplish a task. Software engineering utilizes patterns that help us manage large software projects. Analysis patterns help us determine which algorithms and software architectures are most suitable for a particular task.

The purpose of this book is to help us understand the role of patterns and introduce us to some of the patterns used by computer scientists and software engineers. It is not possible within a single text to introduce more than a handful of patterns; and it is not possible to look at any pattern in depth. As a result, this book is a prelude to patterns. A future volume will build on these ideas and focus much more deeply on patterns.

Computing is a rapidly changing discipline. New patterns are constantly being discovered. Programming languages come and go. We have a lifetime of learning ahead of us. So read this book with the understanding that we are only getting our feet wet and the world around us will change. The patterns we learn in this book are not new to Java. They have served us in languages such as Pascal, C++, Ada, and Smalltalk. The patterns introduced within this book are designed to form a foundation in computing that will weather change.

The Approach

When we walk into our first physics class we know more about physics than we know about computer science when we walk into our first computer science class. We have experienced gravity since we began to walk. We have seen the refraction of light through water droplets that creates rainbows. We have thrown Frisbees. Thus, when we enter a physics class, we have a lifetime of experience to build upon.

Many of us have also worked with computers since we learned to walk. We know what a disk drive is and that more RAM is good. However, computer science is an artificial science. Unlike nature, the science of computers has been carefully hidden away within a box to make them easier to use. The algorithms that drive these boxes are so prized that they are carefully hidden from competing commercial enterprises. As a result, when we walk into our first class we may think that computer science is synonymous with using a spreadsheet or surfing the Web. But this is not computer science. Because we have so little experience with computer science, we must start from the very beginning. We must assume we know nothing about it.

In physics we start with theory on the first day. There is a lifetime of experience from which to reap examples that put that theory in context. Since we have little experience with computer science, it is important to build that context first before we can spend much time on theory. This text begins by teaching us how to write programs. Theory is added slowly. But this does not mean it is not important.

Imagine growing up in a small town with the goal of being an architect of large buildings. There is little in our experience to prepare us for the forces that make high-rises livable. First, we need a trained eye to walk us through our own homes. We must be shown how the organization and relationships of rooms govern how our families interact. Next, we need to take these patterns of living units and see how they change and expand when we visit large buildings.

In this book we will begin by looking at small programs. Our first programs will be composed of a single programming unit that is called a class. We can think of it like a single room of a house. We will study snippets of code that organize classes into functioning units.

Next we will look at programs with multiple classes and see how these classes can be organized to create a good program. The programs will be small like a small house. For example, we learn that placing a garage entry close to the kitchen makes it easier to haul in groceries from the car. Placing the family room next to the kitchen makes it easier to serve snacks at a party. However, not all design decisions are this easy. We cannot place every room next to the kitchen. We must also learn to prioritize our goals and look at the trade-offs in our designs. This book will start that process by looking at a couple of object-design patterns that meet import and design criteria.

When we learn to program we are both designer and builder. Each chapter contains a program that demonstrates key organizational patterns and Java construction techniques. Our programs start small and slowly grow. They will teach us many of the fundamentals.

However, we must remember our goal to build large software systems. We cannot get there by looking at small programs. Some of the programs we look at will contain more detail than we can master in a single week. We must learn how to focus on the details that will help us in the task at hand. Although we may study how several classes fit together to create a program, we may only have the skills and time to visit one or two of the classes in a larger program. This is the same with junior architects. No architect needs to know every detail down to the baseboard in each conference room. We must have a master architect who understands how the pieces fit together and many teams of junior architects who understand the intricacies of several small rooms and how these rooms fit into a larger picture.

We will look at our first programs and wonder why is the word "static" here, or why is the word "public" there. We cannot answer these questions on the first day, or even in the first week. We must learn to focus on central ideas while temporarily accepting some of the details without full understanding. Learning to focus on important details and learning what details can be temporarily ignored is a critical skill. All the programs in this book are small and yet contain more detail than we can master in a semester. However, the word processors, spreadsheet programs, language compilers, and web navigators we use everyday contain hundreds of thousands to tens of millions of lines of code partitioned into many hundreds of classes. If we do not learn how to focus, we will not be able to contribute.

The Organization

This text strives to capture the joy of computer science by looking at interesting problems. As a result, most chapters contain three major themes (see page v.) The first theme focuses on an idea. These ideas are pulled from many areas of computer science with the goal of providing us with an appreciation for the breadth and variety of programs.

The second theme focuses on an important pattern. A piece of design that can be used over and over again. Patterns can be applied to many projects and many programming languages.

The third theme of each chapter focuses on the Java programming skills needed to represent an idea. It has been said that scientists build so that they may learn and engineers learn so that they may build. Currently, computer science is both science and engineering. So we must learn to build and build to learn. Unfortunately, most of us have no experience building software systems. There are no software Lego sets on department store shelves. We do not wake up one birthday morning with Java class libraries in brightly covered boxes. As a result, we must work hard to master Java skill but never lose sight of our goal of learning computer science.

Since we all approach learning differently the text is organized so we have a choice of approaches. Each chapter begins with an idea and an example program. This appeals to those who learn by doing. It provides a context. However, some of us may do better by first learning all the details. If the first part of the chapter does not make sense, skip to the Java section and read it first.

Icons

Table 0.1 Book Icons and Their Meaning

icon	meaning
	An exclamation point is used whenever an important point is stated that might otherwise get lost.
	A Clydesdale horse is displayed whenever a pattern is being introduced. A Clydesdale is a symbol of a powerful tool used to get work done.
	A wrench is displayed when a process is described to accomplish an important task. It symbolizes a mechanism or a set of steps.

FOR THE INSTRUCTOR

An important idea presented in this text is choice. Each of us belongs to different colleges and universities. Our students are different: some are computer science majors, some are education or mathematics majors, some have had several programming language experiences, some have never touched a computer, some breeze through analysis, others cloud over at a fleeting hint of mathematics, many may be headed for industry, and some may be headed for graduate school. For some of us, learning the skills of programming is most important. For others, learning how to analyze algorithms or to design software is most important. This section will help customize the text for our courses.

Chapter Organization

Each chapter follows a pattern. It is partitioned into several components. The first page describes the objectives of a chapter and how those objectives will be realized. This is followed with material that focuses on a key idea and an example that illustrates it. Next we come to a section that captures important patterns. Next comes a Java section that describes the Java syntax and semantics that supports the key idea and patterns. Some chapters have a supplementary section that contains material for which there is not time to teach, or that may be beyond the scope of the traditional CS1 course. This supplementary material sharpens earlier ideas or adds fun. Finally, typical summaries and problem sets are presented.

When choosing how to present the material within a chapter, several strategies can be followed:

- Focus on key ideas and examples in the lecture. Projects can be assigned that expand the ideas presented. Laboratories or recitation periods can be used to practice Java syntax and semantic skills.

- Focus on Java syntax and semantics in lectures. Projects can be assigned that develop Java skills. Laboratory or recitation periods can be used to reinforce classroom activities.

- For students who have other languages under their belt it may be prudent to focus lectures on key chapter ideas and examples, while leaving much of the responsibility for learning Java syntax to the student.

One problem with computer science texts is that they are often highly readable but difficult to use as a reference, or easy to use as a reference but difficult to use for learning. The first part of each chapter is designed to be readable. The Java section is designed to work as a Java reference.

As stated above, each chapter begins with an example. Most examples are so small that they can be completely explained. In a few cases this is not possible. These examples are carefully partitioned in order to focus on key ideas. Key ideas are centralized in one or two classes. Lectures, projects, and laboratories should focus on these classes.

Ideas that are not the focus of a chapter are hidden within other classes. It is typically not desirable, or possible, to completely explain the detail in these other classes. This should be viewed as a positive rather than a negative attribute. It is the way of life and the sooner students learn how to focus on key ideas the better they are served. We must learn to tell our students that here is a class that we need to use to accomplish a task. Learn how to use it, but wait for a later time to understand how it works.

For example, the stock market program in Chapter 9 and the movie review program in Chapter 11 rely on file IO. We do not cover file IO until Chapter 12. Thus, the details of the file IO class cannot be discussed until we reach Chapter 12. The focus of Chapter 9 is iteration and the focus of Chapter 11 is lists. We can concentrate on this material and tell our students how to use the provided classes to do file IO.

In another example, the movie review program in Chapter 11 uses a more sophisticated GUI than can be discussed before reaching Chapter 15. Because the focus in Chapter 11 is on lists, concentrate on the movie list class and do not discuss the user interface. However, the code for the user interface is provided at the end of the chapter. It is there for further reference if students wish to see how it works.

The traffic example in Chapter 13 uses a class in which mouse-event details are hidden. Mouse events are discussed in Chapter 14. Hiding a language feature in a program before that feature is explained has multiple benefits. It allows us to work with programs that do interesting things. It provides a motivation for moving to a new chapter. It provides examples of the benefits of information hiding.

Hiding implementation is not new. We have been hiding detail since we began teaching Fortran in the 1950s. User IO and floating point arithmetic are typically hidden in all beginning courses. An advantage of Java and other OO languages is that instructors can more easily hide details of their choice.

In all the examples listed above unknown language detail is carefully hidden in a class, allowing us to completely ignore it. In two cases language detail is seen before it is explained. This is unavoidable in many programming languages and in particular Java.

The example program in Chapter 1 uses the public, class, void, import, and extends keywords. The function of each of these keywords cannot be explained in the first chapter. However, by Chapter 7, each of these keywords is explained. In Java it is simply necessary to tell our students to be patient and focus on other ideas that can be explained completely.

There is one situation within a later chapter in which a snippet of code contains an undiscussed language feature. A listing shows how to create a buffer using an array before we cover arrays in Chapter 13. The example is timely and because the discussion of arrays follows in the next chapter, a circumstance was created that the author could simply not resist. However, the purpose of the example is to demonstrate the importance of a buffer, not how to implement one.

Book Organization

Choosing a book for a course is hard. Java has made the process more difficult. Applying several classifications is an attempt to make that process easier. Books are classified as objects or algorithms early, applets or applications early, graphics or text early, and so forth. These categorization techniques may or may not be helpful.

Objects vs. Algorithms Early

Chapter 1 and Chapter 2 show us how to use a predefined class to control a robot butler. Within these two chapters we learn how to use objects and simple control constructs (sequence, selection, and iteration). The early patterns in this text are primarily algorithmic. However, once we learn how to use objects, we learn how to create them in Chapter 6 and Chapter 7. Learning to create objects is followed by expanding our knowledge of control flow in Chapter 8 and Chapter 9. Learning about objects early is important. However, before we can do interesting things with objects it is important to know some control flow. This text balances objects and algorithms rather than playing them off of each other.

Applets vs. Applications Early

Applets are used in the first two chapters and discussed in Chapter 3. They require less code to create windows and can be attached to web pages, which is a great motivator. However, the introduction of applications is not delayed for long. Applications are introduced in Chapter 4. After Chapter 4 there is often a choice about whether to use an applet or an application.

Graphics vs. Text Early

Most of the programs in this book have graphics. Graphics are important, motivating, and visually pleasing. Text processing is equally important. Numeric computing is discussed in depth in Chapter 5 and text (strings) in depth in Chapter 10. Java has provided us with a good opportunity to teach graphics and text output.

GUI vs. Text Based

Chapter 4 introduces a simplified GUI and a simplified text-based interface. Thus, many projects can be programmed either way. Many of the examples given utilize GUIs. However, several of those examples have text-based solutions in the supplementary chapter sections. For example, the story-writing program at the beginning of Chapter 10 uses a GUI. An equivalent text-based solution can be found at the end of the chapter. Chapter 10 and Chapter 12 focus on text-based interfaces in detail, while Chapter 14 and Chapter 15 focus on event-based interfaces in more detail. Thus, an instructor can choose to focus on GUIs, text-based interfaces, or a combination of both. The author teaches the event-based chapters immediately after Chapter 7 because it allows students to write full-blown GUI programs early. Students are used to interacting with GUI programs and expect to learn how to program them. The result of moving GUIs early is that arrays and IO are covered during the second semester in the author's course.

Inheritance Early, Late, or Never

Since the introduction of C++ in the CS curriculum, a burning question has been when to introduce inheritance: early or later. This text strives for a middle ground. Java is an object-oriented language that uses inheritance extensively. As a result, we learn how to inherit applets in Chapter 3. We learn to talk about it early but we wait until Chapter 16 to create our own inheritance hierarchy.

Vector Early or Never

A number of reviewers felt strongly that arrays should come before vectors, or that vectors should not be taught at all. I have chosen to cover vectors early because I find them easier to use and teach than arrays. It is easy to insert and delete in the middle of vectors, and their syntax matches the syntax of methods (no messy square brackets). However, vectors require a messy type cast. If you feel more comfortable or are constrained to teach arrays before, or rather than vectors, then do Chapter 13 earlier.

Theory and Mathematics or Programming

Various views exist on how much mathematics should be presented in a beginning course. Some feel that the early course should concentrate on theory with programming introduced late in a student's tenure. Others feel that the algebraic example of chaos in the Numerics chapter will turn students off to computers. This book strives for balance, although it does fall heavily on the software side. However, there are supplementary sections that introduce algorithmic analysis for those interested in more theory. Computers have their roots in computation. Thus, it is hard to avoid mathematics all together. For those who think the numerics chapter is too heavily mathematical, the chaos example can be skipped and the instructor can focus on minimal Java mathematics constructs. For that matter, the instructor should feel free to skip any of the examples. Their goal is to provide context for the material in the rest of the other chapters.

To Loop and a Half or Not

The usage of the loop and a half pattern, beginning in Chapter 4, is liberating for some of us and blasphemy for others. The author agrees with Eric Robert's analysis of the pattern. See reference in that chapter. The author considered providing counter examples for people who are strongly opposed to the loop. There are alternate examples in Section 4.3.2. However, the inclusion of alternate code for all loop and a half code would distract from other information in the text. If you feel that the loop-and-a-half pattern is bad programming practice, please do not let that get in the way of anything else you might find positive. The author leaves you the responsibility of labeling him an idiot in all cases of the loop and a half and you must provide them with alternatives. Students can learn that it is OK to disagree.

Course Schedules

I believe a book should be written for both the instructor and the student. Java is a new language; patterns is a new idea. One of the things that makes Java exciting is the use of patterns in some of the class libraries. Students may not be ready for some of these ideas during the first semester, but instructors are. If there is not enough time to cover the material on patterns, read these sections anyway for your own benefit. They will help us better understand Java and thus better teach it. In addition, some students will be ready. They may benefit from exploring chapters not covered in the course.

There is nothing magic in Java. It sits firmly on the shoulders of all the languages that have been taught for years. It has ideas from Smalltalk, C++, Ada, Pascal, and many others. James Gosling, Java's chief architect, said that only 1% of its ideas are new. So, why all the fuss? Much of it has to do with how well it works on the web, and much has to do with its packaging of ideas. Like all languages, many of the decisions by its designers are good and others are terrible.

Because Java borrows so much from other languages it can be taught like other languages are taught. We can teach it the same way we taught Pascal, the same way we taught C++, the same way we taught Smalltalk, or the same way we taught Ada. However, each language has a personality that cries out for its own approach. The author has organized this book to reflect what Java is saying to him. Thus, the theme on patterns.

Several sample course schedules follow. Two for majors, one for non-majors, and another for a second language course. Use these schedules with the chapter summaries in the next section, and the map on page iv to fit this text into your program.

Using the Text for Majors

The schedule for majors includes a heavy dose of objects and a moderate dose of analysis intertwined within the Java. It introduces students to using objects early. There are chapters on building classes using interfaces, inner classes, and inheritance. The ideas of polymorphism, dynamic binding, persistent stores, or object patterns may be within reach. Analysis of algorithms using Big-O notation is integrated into the discussion of algorithms.

Option II, shown in Table 0.3, outlines a more traditional coverage of computer science material. Appendix A material can be covered in the lab.

Using the Text for Nonmajors

The schedule for nonmajors is more leisurely. More time is spent on selection and iteration in the beginning. Much of the analysis material is skipped. There is a choice of topics for the last two weeks.

Using the Text in a Second Language Course

The schedule in Table 0.5 is an accelerated schedule for a second course. This schedule assumes students have had a course in C, C++, or Pascal. It will need to be adjusted somewhat based on student experience. For example, a C++ student should have some experience with objects. A C student should be familiar with much of the Java syntax but need more time with objects. To a Pascal student, Java may appear very new..

Table 0.2 Schedule for Majors - Option I

week	chapter	topic
Week 1	Chapter 1	Objects
Week 2	Chapter 2	Elements of Control
Week 3	Chapter 3	Inheriting Applets
Week 4	Chapter 4	User Interfaces
Week 5	Chapter 5	Numeric Computing
Week 6	Chapter 6	Methods Abstraction
Week 7	Chapter 7	Class Abstraction
Week 8	Chapter 14	Event Handling
	Chapter 15	Graphical User Interfaces
Week 9	"	" " "
Week 10	Chapter 8	Selection Algorithms
Week 11	Chapter 9	Iteration Algorithms
Week 12	Chapter 10	Text Processing
Week 13	Chapter 11 or	List Algorithms
	Chapter 12 or	Input/Output
	Chapter 13	Arrays

Table 0.3 Schedule for Majors - Option II

week	chapter	topic
Week 1	Chapter 1	Objects
Week 2	Chapter 2	Elements of Control
Week 3	Chapter 3	Inheriting Applets
Week 4	Chapter 4	User Interfaces
Week5	Chapter 5	Numeric Computing
Week 6	Chapter 6	Method Abstraction
Week 7	Chapter 7	Class Abstraction
Week 8	Chapter 8	Selection Algorithms
Week 9	Chapter 9	Iteration Algorithms
Week 10	Chapter 10	Text Processing
Week 11	Chapter 11	List Algorithms

Table 0.3 Schedule for Majors - Option II

week	chapter	topic
Week 12	Chapter 12	Input/Output
Week 13	Chapter 13	Arrays

Table 0.4 Schedule for Nonmajors

week	chapter	topic
Week 1	Appendix A	HTML
Week 2	Chapter 1	Objects
Week 3	Chapter 2	Elements of Control
Week 4	"	" "
Week 5	Chapter 3	Inheriting Applets
Week 6	Chapter 4	User Interfaces
Week 7	Chapter 5	Numeric Computing
Week 8	Chapter 6	Method Abstraction
Week 9	Chapter 7	Class Abstraction
Week 10	"	" "
Week 11	Chapter 8	Selection Algorithms (may skip testing and analysis.)
Week 12	Chapter 9	Iteration Algorithms (may skip testing)
Week 13	Chapter 10	Character & Strings (may skip analysis)

Table 0.5 Schedule for People Who Know C++

week	chapter	topic
Week 1	Chapter 1	Objects
	Chapter 2	Elements of Control
Week 2	Chapter 3	Applets & Graphics
	Chapter 4	User Interfaces
Week 3	Chapter 5	Numeric Computing
Week 4	Chapter 6	Method Abstraction
Week 5	Chapter 7	Class Abstraction

Table 0.5 Schedule for People Who Know C++

week	chapter	topic
Week 6	Chapter 14	Event Handling
	Chapter 15	Graphical User Interfaces
Week 7	"	" " "
Week 8	Chapter 8	Selection Algorithms
	Chapter 9	Iteration Algorithms
Week 9	Chapter 10	Text Processing
Week 10	Chapter 11	List Algorithms
Week 11	Chapter 12	Input/Output
Week 12	Chapter 15	Arrays
Week 13	Chapter 16	Inheritance

Chapter Objectives

Early on as the author was thinking about this text, it occurred to him that there are at least two goals in the courses he teach. One is to teach the fundamental concepts that underlie computer science and software engineering. The second goal is to teach students the skills they need to become productive employees. In a presentation by Ed Lazowska from the University of Washington computer science department, a third goal was outlined. This goal involves student abilities. Thus, chapter objectives are partitioned into three components: concepts, skills, and abilities.

This is how Ed Lazowska describes each kind of objective:

- Concept: General notions or ideas—"A programmable digital computer."
- Skill: Focused capacity to do something—"Write Java programs."
- Abilities: Capacity to do something—"Write 100 line computer programs."

Chapter Snapshots

An outline of the chapters follows.

1. Concept: Objects. This chapter builds the basic object vocabulary needed to talk about Java programs. A robot butler is chosen as an example object because it is an example of a physical object. A physical object makes it easy to connect code with real world experiences.

1. A butler robot class is used to demonstrate the power of abstraction. All the details about implementing a butler simulation have been hidden.

   <u>Pattern</u>: Sequential pattern.

   <u>Java skills</u>: Creating objects, applying methods to objects, and assignment statements.

   Prerequisites—none.

   Prerequisites for—foundation for the rest of the text.

2. <u>Concept</u>: Elements of Control. This chapter describes how to use selection and loop statements to more fully control the behavior of the robot butler that was introduced in Chapter 1.

   <u>Patterns</u>: Flow of control patterns: guarded command, alternative action, sentinel loop, counter loop.

   <u>Java skills</u>: Booleans, `null` statement, block statement, `if` statement, and `while` statement.

   Prerequisites—Chapter 1

   Prerequisites for—Later chapters.

3. <u>Concept</u>: Inheriting from Applets. This chapter describes how to use inheritance to tap into and expand the functionality provided within the Applet class. By extending the Applet class students can create a program with a pop-up window that runs over the web.

   <u>Pattern</u>: Applet.

   <u>Java skills</u>: Applet, Graphics, Polygon, and Color classes.

   This chapter provides additional practice using classes and manipulating objects. It helps students think about abstract objects. Working with graphics objects is a lot of fun and appeals to the visual side of us. Given that new computer systems have graphical displays, graphics is as fundamental as text.

   Prerequisites—Chapter 2

   Prerequisites for—the Applet and Graphics classes are used often throughout this text.

4. <u>Concept</u>: Interfaces. Human-computer interaction.

   <u>Pattern</u>: Input-process-output (IPO), loop and a half.

   <u>Java skills</u>: Custom GUI and text based frameworks.

   This chapter focuses on two strategies for human-computer interaction. One is the event-driven model utilized by GUIs. The second is the programmer-driven model utilized by text-io.

   Prerequisites—Chapter 3.

   Prerequisites for—Whereever human-computer interaction is required.

5. <u>Concept</u>: Numeric Computing. The study of chaos provides an introduction to computer modeling and numerical computing.

   <u>Pattern</u>: Step-wise refinement (divide / remainder.)

   <u>Java skills</u>: `int`, `double`, type casting, `Math` class library, and custom GUI.

   This chapter describes basic numerical operations and the ramifications of finite precision, precedence, round-off, and overflow.

   Prerequisite—Chapter 4.

   Prerequisites for—Numbers are used everywhere.

6. <u>Concept</u>: Method Abstraction. Abstraction is a key idea in this chapter and in this text. Methods are used to hide the details necessary to draw images and to reuse repeated code.

   A supplementary section describes how to animate graphics using a thread. Double buffering is also described as a means for removing flicker.

   <u>Pattern</u>: composite action pattern.

   <u>Java skills</u>: Declaring methods, passing parameters, local variables, instance variables, returning values, and scope.

   This chapter is presented early because the author feels that abstraction should be introduced early and then reinforced throughout the rest of the text. This chapter could be taught after Chapter 3. It would require skipping some of the examples. Another option is to wait until after Chapter 8 on selection statements.

   Prerequisite—Chapter 3.

   Prerequisite for—Chapter 7.

7. <u>Concept</u>: Class Abstraction. This chapter continues the abstraction theme from the previous chapter. A supplementary section introduces rudimentary systems analysis. Another supplementary section looks at performance and maintenance trade-offs of two implementation choices. An experiment is done to compute how much time method calls take.

   <u>Pattern</u>: Composite patterns and object design issues.

   <u>Java skills</u>: Java class declarations, public, private, and static modifiers.

   Prerequisite—Chapter 6.

   Prerequisite for—All the chapters that follow.

8. <u>Concept</u>: Selection Algorithms. This chapter introduces algorithms. Displaying a 3D mesh provides an example for finding minimums and maximums. A supplementary section introduces algorithmic analysis. Another supplementary section describes software testing using statement, branch, and path coverage for test data selection.

   <u>Pattern</u>: Finding extremes and command alternative action pattern.

Java skill: Switch statement.

Parts of this chapter can be taught after Chapter 2.

Prerequisites—Chapter 2 and Chapter 4.

Prerequisite for—All the chapters that follow.

9. Concept: Iteration Algorithms. Loops are used to read and graph Intel stock prices during the Pentium crisis. Algorithms are used to smooth graphs and find maximums, minimums, and averages. A supplementary section expands the coverage of software testing.

    Patterns: Finding averages, maximum, and minimum.

    Java skills: `For` and `do` loops, `break` statement, exception handling.

    Parts of this chapter can be moved earlier.

    Prerequisites—Chapter 2 and Chapter 8.

    Prerequisite for—All the chapters that follow.

10. Concept: Text Processing. Strings are used to customize a story.

    Pattern: One loop for linear structures.

    Java skills: Characters, String class, and String GUI components (TextArea and Text-Field) are used to represent the story elements.

    Prerequisites—Chapter 2 and Chapter 7.

    Prerequisites for—All chapters that follow.

11. Concept: List Algorithms. The application in this chapter is the movie reviews by Siskel and Ebert. We write an application to sort and search their movie lists. A supplementary section expands on a previous introduction to algorithmic analysis.

    Pattern: Visiting every element in a list, and divide and conquer.

    Java skills: The `Vector` class. The vector class is easier to use and more flexible than arrays.

    Prerequisite—Chapter 10.

    Prerequisite for—Vectors are used often.

12. Concept: Input/Output. This chapter describes how to read the stock price files from Chapter 9 and Siskel and Ebert movie reviews from Chapter 11. We discuss how file buffering can increase the efficiency of a program. We look at files as stores for binary and text information.

    Pattern: Buffers

    Java skills: `BufferedReader`, `BufferedWriter`, `BufferedInputStream`, `bufferedOutputStream`, and several other io classes. `StringTokenizer` and `DecimalFormat` classes are discussed.

Prerequisite—Chapter 11 (Can teach parts of it much earlier.)

Prerequisite for—IO is used often.

13. <u>Concept</u>: Arrays. Computer simulation of automobile traffic.

    <u>Patterns</u>: One loop for linear structures.

    <u>Java skills</u>: Inserting elements into and deleting elements from arrays. One and two-dimensional arrays.

    Prerequisite—Chapter 11. However, for those who want to teach arrays early, the vector content can be skipped and ignored, allowing this chapter to be taught earlier.

    Prerequisites for—Arrays are used often.

14. <u>Concept</u>: Event Handling. A doodle program provides an opportunity to talk about events.

    <u>Patterns</u>: Callback methods.

    <u>Java skills</u>: Implementing interfaces. Using the `MouseListener` and `MouseMotionListener` interfaces.

    This chapter could be introduced after Chapter 2. This would allow students to get involved in event handling early.

    Prerequisite—Chapter 3.

    Prerequisite for—Chapter 15.

15. <u>Concept</u>: Graphical User Interfaces. Creating graphical user interfaces.

    <u>Patterns</u>: Model-View-Controller (MVC) and strategy pattern.

    <u>Java skills</u>: `Frame`, `Button`, `Menu`, and `Keyboard` classes. Various listeners and layout managers

    This chapter covers Java 2 where appropriate. The supplementary section covers this information but in Java 1.1.

    Prerequisite—Chapter 14.

    Prerequisites for—A lot of the example programs in this text use GUIs, but this material is not required.

16. <u>Concept</u>: Inheritance. Java has a persistent store class that preserves type information. In this chapter we use inheritance, polymorphism, and dynamic binding to take advantage of persistent stores to save the image components to disk.

    <u>Pattern</u>: Composite and MVC patterns (full-blown versions.)

    <u>Java skills</u>: `ObjectOutputStream` and `ObjectInputStream` classes.

    Prerequisite—Chapter 12.

    Prerequisite for—None.

A. Concept: Web and HTML. An introduction to mark-up languages. Topics include hypertext documents and word processors (WYSIWYG).

HTML skills: Basic HTML and text representation. Students will learn how to access resources on the net and create a rudimentary web page.

This chapter is an effective way to start people on the computer. Building a web document is conceptually easier than writing even a trivial Java applet. This chapter may be skipped or delegated to a lab. However, do not underestimate the importance of the text representation material in the reference section. An understanding of text representation, regardless of how dry, can get students out of trouble when working with files. It helps them differentiate between Java source and binary files.

Prerequisites—None.

Prerequisites for—None.

B. Java class library reference.

C. Vista class library reference.

Instructor's Material

An instructor's CD is available for those who adopt the book for their course. Supplemental material is also available at a link off the publisher's website: www.fbeedle.com/55-4.html.

Acknowledgments

A special thanks needs to go to Eugene Wallingford at the University of Northern Iowa for getting many of us excited about teaching patterns through SIGCSE presentations and ChiliPLOP. Many of the ideas in this book came from a ChiliPLOP workshop organized by Eugene and attended by Owen Astrachan at Duke University, Joe Bergin at Pace University, Robert Duvall at Duke University, Rick Mercer at University of Arizona, and myself. The contributions that this group of individuals made to my understanding of teaching computer science are substantial.

There are many others that have contributed to this venture. My wife Marilyn Johnson read many of the early drafts. Robert Noonan at College of William and Mary, Christopher Riesbeck at Northwestern University, Ann Ford at University of Michigan, Louis Steinberg at Rutgers University, Stuart Reges at University of Arizona, Brian Malloy at Clemson University, Joanne Houlahan at Johns Hopkins University, Ted Pawlicki at University of Rochester, Carl Sturtivant at University of Minnesota, Wayne Dyksen at Purdue University, Benjoe Juliano at California State University—Chico, and others provided many useful comments.

1 Objects

Controlling a Robot Butler

1.1 Objectives

Concepts Section 1.2, page 3

This chapter describes what it means for a programming language to be object-oriented. As a part of this process, basic computer language and object terms are defined. These terms will become the basis for communicating ideas throughout this text.

Object concepts are illustrated using robot butler simulation. This particular example is chosen because there are obvious mappings between physical objects and software objects.

Patterns Section 1.3, page 13

Patterns are independent of a particular programming language and are useful throughout our programming life. In this chapter patterns will be defined and example patterns will be described. We begin with elementary control patterns. The first pattern we encounter specifies how the order in which we write program statements determines the order in which they are executed. The sequential pattern is one of the most underrated.

Java Skills

Next this chapter addresses how Java can be used to express the above concepts and patterns.

- Identifying tokens, identifiers, and keywords   Section 1.4, page 16
- Creating objects   Section 1.5.1, page 20
- Declaring object identifiers   Section 1.5.2, page 21
- Assigning objects to identifiers   Section 1.5.3, page 22
- Applying operations to objects   Section 1.6, page 23
- Writing comments   Section 1.7, page 24

Abilities

By the end of this chapter we should be able to do the following:

Modify an existing program by adding objects and applying operations to them.

Use software tools (provided by the local institution) to edit, compile, link, and execute a Java applet.

CONCEPTS

1.2   A Robot for a Butler

On July 4, 1997, a spacecraft named Pathfinder bounced to a halt on the surface of Mars. After deflating the air bags that cushioned its fall, a small rover named Sojourner began its odyssey. Mars is a long way from Earth. It takes 11 minutes for commands to reach Pathfinder and then they are relayed to Sojourner, which acknowledges them to Pathfinder. Next it takes another 11 minutes for their impact to be seen on Earth. This 22 minute plus delay creates problems for scientists on Earth; a problem made more difficult because communication can be broken by events on Earth or the passage of Sojourner behind a rock. The Sojourner design team solved these problems by making Sojourner work autonomously.

> *Robots* are machines that link stimulus to actions. They use devices called *sensors* to check their surroundings and *actuators* to manipulate the world.

Sojourner is an interesting collaboration of humans and machines. Scientists in Pasadena, California, plot a day's journey for Sojourner and send it up. Sojourner executes the plan several hours later. These plans tell Sojourner to move from point A to point B, but not how to get there. It is Sojourner's job to use an internal set of rules to pick a path around small obstacles while eventually heading toward its goal. Sojourner's design is an example of the current status of robotics. Robots can create plans for simple goals, but managing an overall exploration plan is not yet practical.

Robots have applications on Earth as well. They are used in manufacturing and for handling hazardous waste. All of us can anticipate the benefits of a robot servant designed to make our life easier. It would be great if each of us had a robot assistant to manage some of the mundane tasks in our life, such as doing the laundry, cleaning up our rooms, fixing meals, and running errands. In this chapter we will program a machine to pick up the laundry in our room. Unlike Sojourner, which can plan how to solve a simple task, we will program explicitly every move of our robot assistant.

1.2.1   Objects and Classes

Computers can keep track of medical records, play games, and guide airliners. In some cases software may be life-critical. Object-oriented (OO) software development is one of many methodologies that have been developed to help us write high-quality and cost-effective software.

Suppose we are given the task of creating a robot butler that will pick up the dirty clothes in our room. We will need to instruct our butler to move forward, turn, and pick up clothes. There are several references to objects and operations in this task. For example, butler is a class of objects that has specific physical characteristics and a set of behaviors shared by all objects of the butler class. All butlers have arms for carrying objects, legs for moving, and sensors for detecting objects; and all respond to a set of commands.

Objects have an identity, a state, and operations. Objects have an *identity* because we must have a means to refer to them. In many cases we refer to an object through its name. For example, the name James may identify a particular butler. Some objects do not have names but we can still refer to them indirectly. For example, we may refer to a pencil as the one in our backpack or we may refer to a coat as the one on the third hook.

Objects have a *state*. The state of an object indicates its current condition. For example, the state of a butler includes its location, the direction it is facing, and whether it is carrying anything. We may refer to the state of our car as being "out of gas" or the state of our little sister as being cranky. When we design software objects, we choose items of state that are important for the problem at hand. In the case of a butler robot in this chapter's program, a butler's location is important, so location is made part of its state. Its color and temperature are not important to our simulation, so they are not included as part of the state. (In other applications—for example, a model of heat dissipation in robots—color and temperature are important and would be part of a butler's state.) One of the tasks of a program designer is to choose the critical state attributes of an object.

Objects have *operations*. Operations change the state or report on the state of an object. Operations on a butler robot include move forward, turn, and pick up an object. For example, moving forward changes the state of our robot by giving it a new location. Turning changes the state of our robot by giving it a new direction.

Objects have an identity, a state, and operations. We refer to an object by its identity. An object's *state* describes its current conditions. *Operations* are actions that change or report on an object's state.

Objects are instances of classes. For example, if we create a butler named James, James is an instance of the butler class. A class describes a range of behaviors and states an object may have. For example, robot butlers are not good for assembling cars or diving under water because they do not have the correct sensors and manipulators or because they will short out or rust under water.

Pencil is another example of a class. The pencil class is a class of objects that is used for writing. We must be careful to distinguish between class and object. The pencil we have in our hand is a particular instance of the pencil class. The phrase "the pencil in my hand is dull" refers to a particular pencil object. The phrase "bring a pencil to lab" refers to a class of pencil objects.

> The behavior and possible states of an object are specified by the *class* to which it belongs. Behavior is defined by the operations a class provides. A class defines the type or kind of an object.

Objects are easy to identify in the physical world because we can see them. They also make their presence known in day-to-day speech as nouns, e.g., James. Operations are usually verbs: move forward, turn , pick up the laundry, etc. Nouns and verbs also give us clues when we look for software objects and their operations.

Software objects are not physical. They cannot be seen, touched, held, or manipulated physically. They are ideas, scratches we make on sheets of paper, the flow of electricity in a computer, or the alignment of magnetic particles on a sheet of plastic. They are conceptual objects that we invent and manipulate in the imaginary world of the computer. Objects may represent boxes on the computer screen, a mailing address, a simulated city, or a way of organizing computer programs in RAM. Similar to James, these software objects have an identity, a state, and operations. Software objects can often be recognized because they are nouns, and the operations on these objects are often recognized as verbs.

For example, in an airline reservation system a software object may be a particular flight. It may include operations that allow a travel agent to determine the availability of the flight and add names to and remove names from the reservation list. It may include additional operations that allow an airline to assign a particular plane and crew to the flight. Thus, the state of a flight may include the passenger list, departure and arrival times, destination, airplane, and so on.

Financial planning software may include a stock object. Its state may include the name and number of shares, the current value per share, and the return over the last six months and ten years. Operations may include a method to update a share's current value, to compute expected earnings, and to assign a desirability index to the stock.

A university registrar's office may have software to maintain student records. There may be objects that store a record for each student. A student record's state may include a student number, name, and a list of courses with associated grades. There may be operations to add a course record, change a grade, and compute grade point averages.

1.2.2   Project Requirements

Suppose we are in charge of creating a room-cleaning simulation to help engineers test their robot butler designs and train butler programmers. We are given the following requirements for this project: .

Figure 1.1 Initial State of a Room with One Pile of Clothes

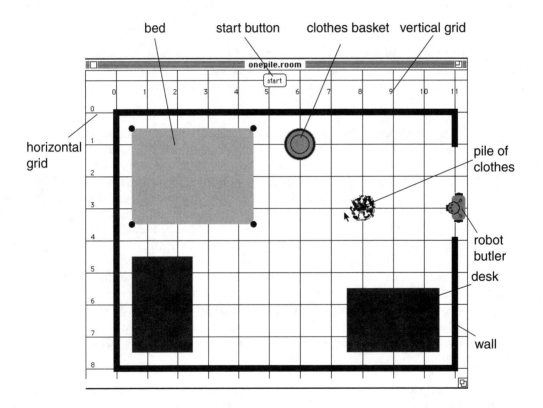

> A robot butler will start at grid location (11,3) facing the left (Figure 1.1). It must move forward until it reaches a pile of clothes at grid (8,3), pick them up, turn around, and leave the room (reach horizontal grid location 11)

Figure 1.1 is the layout of our room. To make things easier for our robot butler, we have laid down a grid on the floor with green tape. We will use this grid to direct how far our butler will move. The butler has special sensors that will allow it to move along grid lines and count how many lines it crosses.

1.2.3   Project Design

An important aspect of software development is the ability to partition a project into objects. We can partition the room-cleaning simulation into three objects (Figure 1.2.) The first is the room-cleaning simulation program. A room-cleaning simulation object will be created by a web browser. As a result, we do not have to think about it.

Figure 1.2 Room-Cleaning Simulation Objects

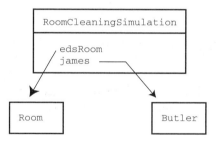

Once started, a room-cleaning simulation object creates two objects of its own: a room and butler. The room object is responsible for determining the size of the simulated window and contains objects that define the locations of the room's walls and furnishings. The only operations that can be applied to a room are to create a room and start the room-cleaning simulation.

A butler object is more interesting. Butler objects must move, turn, and handle laundry (Figure 1.3). A butler's state includes its location (myX, myY), the direction it is facing (myDeltaX, myDeltaY), and what it is carrying (myLoad). The Unified Modeling Language (UML) is a graphical notation for describing object-oriented designs. In UML a class is illustrated with a rectangle partitioned into three components. The top partition contains the name of the class, the middle partition lists the items of state for instances of

Figure 1.3 The `Butler` class

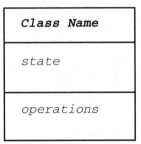

Butler
myX myY myDeltaX myDeltaY myLoad
forward() backward() turnRight() turnLeft() pickUp() putDown() putIn() takeOut()

Class Name
state
operations

this class, and the bottom partition lists the operations that can be applied to the class's objects.

The room-cleaning simulation contains many other objects, but they are hidden from us. For example, Room objects contain walls, beds, desks, baskets, and piles of clothes.

1.2.4 Program Implementation

Our goal is to command our butler to fetch the pile of dirty clothes at grid (8,3) and leave the room. To accomplish this task our butler must move two squares forward, pick up the clothes, make two right-angle turns, and move forward through the door. The program in Listing 1.1 accomplishes this task.

> *Note:* The line numbers in Listing 1.1 are not part of the Java program. They are used throughout the text to make easy reference to the code. Including them within a program will make it fail.

On first viewing, Listing 1.1 appears complex. It is not yet possible to explain the function of every word and character in the program; however, their functions will become clear as we learn more about Java. We will begin by saying that after a web browser creates a RoomCleaningSimulation object it applies the init (initialize) operation to it.

Listing 1.1 Pick Up One Pile of Clothes

```
1  //*************************************************************
2  //
3  // title:   RoomCleaningSimulation
4  // author:  © Ed C. Epp - all rights reserved
5  // date:    4-20-99
6  //
7  // Pick up the laundry and leave the room.
8  //
9  //*************************************************************
10
11 import java.applet.Applet;
12
13 public class RoomCleaningSimulation extends Applet
14 {
15   public void init()
16   {
17     Room    edsRoom = new Room("onepile.room", this);
18     Butler james    = new Butler (11, 3, edsRoom);
19     edsRoom.waitForStart();
20     james.forward();
21     james.forward();
22     james.pickUp();
23     james.turnRight();
24     james.turnRight();
25     james.forward();
26     james.forward();
27   }
28 }
```

Thus, program execution begins in the init method (Line 15). More details are forth-coming in Chapter 3.

In this chapter we will focus on creating and manipulating objects. We will begin our investigation of Java by focusing on the code that manipulates the room and butler objects. Line 17 creates a room called edsRoom. The code on the right side of the equal sign creates an object of the class Room. The string "onepile.room" is the name of a file that describes the makeup of the room. Once we have created the object we assign it the name edsRoom, which appears on the left side of the equal sign. Thus, the name edsRoom identifies a specific room object.

Once the room is created, we create our butler, named james, in the next line. It is placed at grid location (11,3) in edsRoom. Recall that objects belong to a class and have three properties: identity, operations, and state. The identity of the butler object in Line 18 is `james`. It belongs to the `Butler` class. As we mentioned in the previous section, the state of the `james` object is includes its location, direction, and what it is carrying.

In Line 19 we wait for the start button to be pressed, shown in the upper middle of the display. Once the start button is pressed, the subsequent lines instruct `james` on how to pick up the dirty clothes.

The operations on a butler are demonstrated in the subsequent lines. First we move forward twice, Lines 20 and 21, by applying the `forward` operation to `james` (Figure 1.4). Then our butler picks up our clothes with the `pickUp` operation (Figure 1.5 A). Next he rotates to the right 90 degrees (Figure 1.5 B). This is followed by another 90 degree rotation (Figure 1.5 C). Finally, our butler moves through the door by moving forward twice.

Figure 1.4 Move Forward Twice

Figure 1.5 A) Pick Up Clothes, B) Turn Right, and C) Turn Right Again

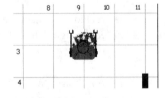
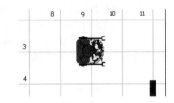

If a programmer attempts to do an illegal operation, such as instruct the butler to walk through a wall, the simulation stops and displays an error message. Possible errors include walking into another object, trying to put an object down when the butler is not carrying anything, trying to pick up a bed, etc.

This program is a testimony to abstraction. (Abstraction is defined in Chapter 6.) Without abstraction, a butler program would be well beyond our reach. The lines of code within the applet `init` method are made simple because of abstraction. Hidden beneath them are roughly 1,000 lines of Java code. All the complexities, including computing the butler's location and drawing the room, are hidden. But the abstraction does not stop there. The Java design team has hidden many tens of thousands of lines of code within the Java class library that was used to create the butler and room classes. These, in turn, are written on top of other abstractions which are written on top of others. Without these layers of abstraction, the application that we have created would not be possible for a beginning programmer. In the years to come we will begin to peel back these layers of abstraction and learn what each does: from the bits to the operating system, to the language compiler, to the final program.

1.2.5   Summary of Operations

Table 1.1 provides us with a summary of some the operations that our butler can perform. There are a few key ideas to keep in mind as we program our butler:

- Our butler cannot move into any location that contains an object. If it attempts to, it shuts down.
- Our butler can carry only clothes and baskets.
- Our butler can carry only one thing at a time. If it is carrying something, it must put the object down before it can carry anything else.
- A basket can hold many things. Thus, if our butler is carrying a basket, the basket can contain many piles of clothes or other baskets.
- The last item inserted into a basket is the first item removed.
- A basket is the only thing in which a butler can place objects (`putIn` and `takeOut` operations).
- A butler can place objects only on empty grid locations (`putDown` operation). It cannot place an object on a wall, bed, basket, or desk.

Table 1.1 Operations Supported by a Butler

operation	action
movement	
void forward ()	move forward one square error—if motion is blocked by any object
void forward (int steps)	move forward "steps" squares error—if motion is blocked by any object
void backward ()	move backward one square error—if motion is blocked by any object
void backward (int steps)	move backward "steps" squares error—if motion is blocked by any object
void turnRight ()	turn right 90 degrees error—if this butler is carrying something and the location to the right is occupied by anything except a basket
void turnRight (int count)	turn right 90 degrees "count" times error—repeats the error checks above for each 90-degree turn
void turnLeft ()	turn left 90 degrees error—similar to turnRight
void turnLeft (int count)	turn left 90 degrees "count" times error—similar to turnRight
manipulation	
void pickUp ()	pick up an item error—if there are no clothes or basket in front of this butler to pick up or if this butler is already holding something
void putDown ()	put down the item this butler is holding error—if this butler is not holding anything
void putIn ()	put the item this butler is holding in the basket in front of it error—if this butler is not holding anything or there is no basket in front of this butler
void takeOut ()	take out the item in the basket error—if there is no basket in front of this butler, there is no item in the basket, or this butler is already holding something

PATTERNS

1.3   Sequential Pattern

Lines 17 through 26 in Listing 1.1 use a fundamental pattern for constructing a program. They show a sequential ordering which specifies the order for executing statements. Christopher Alexander, a prominent American architect, coined the term *pattern* as a means to communicate common practices for solving building design problems. Software architecture, like building architecture, also contains common ways of doing things. Learning these patterns is of utmost importance for budding software engineers. Patterns communicate ideas that are applied repeatedly to solve problems. Patterns cross computer language boundaries and will serve us for a lifetime.

> A *pattern* describes a commonly used structure for solving a general problem. It contains four parts: a name, a problem, a solution, and a consequence.

Patterns can be large ideas that describe how several objects interact to accomplish a given task, or they can be small ideas that describe how several language statements can be organized to accomplish some task. This text will focus primarily on simple patterns—patterns that describe how a few statements can be organized.

We use patterns in our everyday lives to solve problems. We place convenience stores near residential districts to facilitate quick late-night access. We place supermarkets and hospitals on main thoroughfares to facilitate infrequent but convenient access. We place at arms reach those items we use at our desk most frequently. We place rest rooms near bedrooms to facilitate quick late-night trips. The food and dishes we use most often are placed on lower cupboard shelves. All these strategies are related by a pattern that states that those items needing quick or frequent access are located conveniently.

During the summer we run or do yard work in the morning. We paint the side of the house that is shaded. We water the lawn late in the evening and open our windows at night to let in the cool air. These strategies are related by a pattern of doing during the cool parts of the day those things that are adversely affected by heat.

1.3.1   Name

Each pattern has a name that must concisely communicate the nature of the pattern. The name of the pattern described in this section is "Sequential Pattern."

1.3.2   Problem

The value of each pattern is described by its ability to solve a problem that occurs repeatedly. For example, the sequential pattern is designed to assure that tasks are accomplished in the correct order. This problem of sequence appears in virtually every computer program.

Most computers are designed so that operations are evaluated sequentially. Each operation is followed by an operation that is executed after the previous one has finished. Most programming languages, as in Java, execute instructions sequentially by default. The order of statements in a program determines the order of execution.

1.3.3   Solution

The solution section of a pattern describes how to solve a recurring problem. We solve the problem of specifying the order in which statements are to be executed by organizing the statements in order. For example, an object must be created before an operation can be applied to it. Thus, we create the object in a statement that precedes using it. If a statement requires a specific situation to hold before it is executed, previous statements must establish that situation.

In the example below, taken from Listing 1.1, statement 1 must be executed before statement 2 because statement 2 relies on the room being created. Statement 3 follows statement 2 because we cannot clean up the room until the room and robot have been created.

```
1      Room    edsRoom = new Room("onepile.room", this);
2      Butler james  = new Butler (11, 3, edsRoom);
3      edsRoom.waitForStart();
4      james.forward();
5      james.forward();
6      james.pickUp();
7      james.turnRight();
8      james.turnRight();
9      james.forward();
10     james.forward();
```

The order of Lines 4 through 10 is important because they specify the order in which james accomplishes its task. The butler must be moved in Lines 4 and 5 before it can pick the clothes up in Line 6.

This model assumes that a previous statement has been completely executed before the next statement begins to execute. Execution progresses like a needle and thread being pulled from one statement through another. We can trace that thread back through time and unfold a history of statement execution. We say that the thread of execution proceeds from one statement to the next statement.

> A *flow of control* defines a sequence of statements. Each statement, except the first, is preceded by the execution of a single statement. A Java program may have more than one flow of control occurring at the same time. Each is called a *thread* of execution.

1.3.4   Consequences

Finally, we list the consequences of a pattern. A consequence of the sequential pattern is that we must describe "how" we want something accomplished. We must be aware of the order in which each statement is executed, and we must communicate explicitly step by step, never assuming the computer knows our intent.

Programming the step-by-step process of each object in a program is time consuming. If one step is incorrect, the entire program fails. This style of programming is different from that used in Sojourner. Scientists programmed Sojourner by telling it "what" they wanted it to do; for example, "move to the rock named 'Yogi' and take a sample." Sojourner determined "how" to do it.

JAVA

Thus far we have examined the fundamental ideas of objects, classes, and operations. The room-cleaning simulation demonstrated how Java may be used to capture these ideas. In this section we will look more closely at Java's syntax and semantics for expressing objects and operations.

Listing 1.1 has more detail than our description of Java in the following sections will explain. For example, in this chapter we will not explain what an applet is or how it operates. We will not explain the meanings of the `public`, `static`, and `void` keywords. These discussions will follow in the next several chapters.

1.4   Syntax and Semantics

In any spoken language there are rules about the construction of utterances. For example, there are rules about which verb forms go with plural nouns. The sentence "The Space Gizzbies are our intergalactic friends." is syntactically correct. On the other hand, "The Space Gizzbies is our intergalactic friends." is syntactically incorrect, though people usually understand what we mean even when our grammar is incorrect.

Computer languages also have rules for the construction of programs. But unlike spoken utterances, computer programs must be written in the correct form before a computer can decipher them. The Java compiler will generate syntax errors for programs that are not syntactically correct.

> *Syntax* describes the form that a programming language statement must take.
> *Semantics* describes what that statement means.

Semantics can be a problem in spoken and computer languages. For example, in the sentence "The girl takes this with her." it is not clear to what "this" refers and who the girl is. The statement is syntactically correct but we do not know what it means. Computer programs must not only be correctly stated, they must be semantically clear. A Java compiler cannot initiate the appropriate action by inferring a programmer's intent. Each program action must be placed in an appropriate context, stated correctly, and meticulously spelled out.

Programs with semantic errors will often be accepted by a Java compiler. However, when run, they will probably produce unexpected results. For example, a program may compute the incorrect insurance premium, cause airplanes to fly upside down, or cause databases to lose critical information. Even though a program compiles and executes, it is not necessarily correct.

The next several sections will describe some of Java's syntax and semantics. We will start by looking at some basic syntax building blocks and then move on to elementary statements.

1.4.1   Tokens

The smallest unit of a program that has meaning is a token.

> A *token* is a sequence of characters that have a collective meaning (Aho et al).

For example, the following Java statement

```
Location kansas = redShoes.tap(3);
```

can be partitioned into the following list of tokens.

```
Location
kansas
=
redShoes
.
tap
(
3
)
;
```

Spaces, tabs, and new lines, which collectively are called *white space*, act as token delimiters. *Delimiters* separate tokens. Without the space between `Location` and `kansas` the Java compiler would interpret `Locationkansas` as one token. Some tokens do not need white space to delimit them. For example, `kansas=redShoes` would be interpreted as three tokens. The rules for token delimination may not be clear at first. For example, `hike123` would be interpreted as one token while `123hike` would represent two tokens. The rules will become clear with time. If you are not sure, extra white space between tokens has no impact. For example, the following line is equivalent to the one above.

```
Location kansas      = redShoes    .tap(
           2    )
    ;
```

Careful and consistent use of white space makes a program easier to understand. Observe how various lines in example programs are indented. Indention provides clues about how a program is organized, and also makes a program attractive. We will describe the rules used as we move through this text. For now, follow the form of the example code or the rules provided by your instructor.

Spaces within a token are usually not permitted. For example, in the following, `red` and `Shoes` are interpreted as two tokens when the intent is to have only one.

```
Location kansas = red Shoes.tap(3);   // error
```

Each token has an important semantic meaning that, when combined with other tokens, performs a useful action. One may guess from the previous Java statement that its intent is to take us back to Kansas by tapping three times with our red shoes. "Kansas" and "red shoes" identify key objects of our action. Tap identifies an operation.

1.4.2   Identifiers

Identifiers, such as `redShoes`, `kansas`, `forward`, `tap`, and `RoomCleaningSimulation`, are arbitrary. They could be replaced everywhere with v, w, x, y, and z with no ill effects, except that it would make the intent of a program more difficult to understand. Identifiers should make a program's intent easy to infer.

> An *identifier* is a name given to an object, class, or method (operation). Identifiers may contain upper- and lowercase letters, the digits 0 through 9, the underscore character (_), and the dollar sign ($). An identifier may not begin with a digit.

Valid identifiers include `R2D2` and `Plea$eSendMoney`. Invalid identifiers include `3PO` and `%Done`. Java reserves some keywords, for example `public`, `class`, and `extends`, that cannot be used as identifiers (see Section 1.4.3).

The naming convention used in this book is that class names begin with an uppercase letter. Object and method names begin with a lowercase letter. Instance variables that define the state of an object begin with the prefix "my." These conventions are not enforced by the compiler but rather chosen by the author to make programs easier to read. Your instructor or employer may have a different coding standard that you are expected to follow.

Java is case sensitive. It makes a difference how identifiers and keywords are capitalized. For example, it is necessary that `import` is in all lowercase letters—the Java compiler will generate a syntax error if any letter in `import` is capitalized. Some capitalization errors will allow the program to compile but it will not execute correctly. For example, replacing the following line with Line 15 in Listing 1.1 will result in a valid program.

```
public void Init ()        // program will not run
```

Typing `Init` instead of `init` will not generate a syntax error. However, the program will not do anything when executed. A capitalization error can be frustrating because the program looks correct but doesn't perform.

1.4.3   Keywords

Keywords are special words that look like identifiers. Java gives special meaning to each keyword. Attempting to use it as an identifier will confuse the compiler; do not attempt to use keywords in this way. The list of Java keywords is shown in Table 1.2.

Table 1.2 Java Keywords

abstract	do	implements	package	throw
boolean	double	import	private	throws
break	else	inner	protected	transient
byte	extends	instanceof	public	try
case	final	int	rest	var
cast	finally	interface	return	void
catch	float	long	short	volatile
char	for	native	static	while
class	future	new	super	
const	generic	null	switch	
continue	goto	operator	synchoronized	
default	if	outer	this	

1.5 Creating Objects

1.5.1 Declaration Statements with Constructors

Tokens are combined into statements that express a complete action. Statements are typically terminated with a semicolon token.

> Instructions are communicated to the computer through *statements*. A statement is a sequence of tokens that collectively express an action.

The first statement we will investigate is a declaration statement. We must be able to create and name objects. The form of a statement that will accomplish this is shown below.

```
ClassIdentifier ObjectIdentifier = new Constructor ;
```

For example:

```
Butler       james     = new Butler (11, 3, edsRoom);
LunarLander  eagle     = new LunarLander (tranquility);
Shoes        redShoes  = new Shoes (Color.red);
Rectangle    box       = new Rectangle (100, 200, 13, 39);
```

The class identifier indicates the class to which an object identifier may refer. For example, the second statement above specifies that the object identifier `eagle` may refer only to objects that belong the class `LunarLander`.

The part of the example code in the above statements after the equal token creates a new object. The first statement creates a butler named `james` at grid location (11,3) in `edsRoom`. The second statement creates a lunar lander on the moon at the Sea of Tranquility. The third statement creates a red shoe. The fourth statement creates a rectangle which is 13 units wide, 39 units high, at location (100,200).

An object identifier may be declared only once. For example, in the following code fragment, an attempt is made to create two objects with the name `james`. The second attempt will generate an error message.

```
Butler       james     = new Butler (11, 3, edsRoom); // ok
Butler       james     = new Butler (4, 7, edsRoom);  // not ok
Butler       franz     = new Butler (8, 2, edsRoom);  // ok
```

The part of the above statements after the `new` keyword is called the constructor. For example, a constructor for a butler looks like `Butler (11, 3, edsRoom)`.

A *constructor* is a special operation (method) that creates an object when the new operator is applied to it. This process is called *instantiating* an object.

The new operator is an example of an operation that is applied to a class rather than an object. It invokes a constructor method that describes how the object is to be created. Constructors always have the same name as the name of the class they are creating.

Each constructor may have zero or more parameters. A parameter is a mechanism for sending special information to the constructor that customizes the creation of an object. For example, the parameter tranquility in the LunarLander constructor specifies that the lander is to be created on the moon at the Sea of Tranquility. The Color.red parameter in the Shoes constructor specifies that a red shoe is to be created. Finally, the 39 in the Rectangle constructor specifies that a 39-unit-wide face is to be created.

A *parameter* is a mechanism for passing data (information) from the current method to another method.

Finally, the equal sign specifies that the identifier on its left side is to refer to the object on the right side of the equal sign. The equal sign represents assignment, not equality. For example, the lunar lander created by the constructor LunarLander (tranquility-Base) is assigned to the identifier eagle. (See Figure 1.6 for a summary of the parts of a declaration statement.)

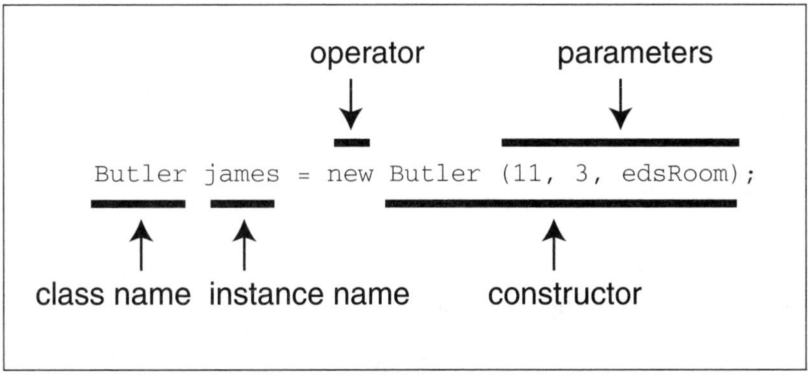

Figure 1.6 Declaring and Creating Objects

1.5.2   Declaration Statement without a Constructor

The declarations described in the previous section can be partitioned into two statements: a declaration without a constructor followed by an assignment statement. For example:

```
Butler james;
james = new Butler (11, 3, edsRoom);
```

The form of declarations without constructors is shown below.

```
ClassIdentifier  ObjectIdentifier ;
```

For example:

```
Butler      james;
LunarLander falcon;
Shoes       mudShoes;
Rectangle   wall;
```

Because only names are introduced and there are no constructors, no objects are created. For example, the above states that the identifier `falcon` can be used to refer to a lunar lander, but that it currently refers to no object. When an object identifier does not refer to an object, we say that its value is *null*.

A declaration statement merely declares that a particular identifier can be associated with specific classes of objects. A common error is to declare an object identifier without associating an object with it. Applying an operation to such a identifier will result in an error. A good rule of thumb is to assign an object to an identifier whenever one is declared.

1.5.3   Assignment Statement

An *assignment* statement is used to give an object an identity.

```
identifier  =  object  ;
```

For example:

```
darkWing = new SpaceCruiser();
falcon   = darkWing;
```

The above statements create a single object that belongs to the space cruiser class. This single object has two identities. It can be referred to as `darkWing` or `falcon`. The clue that there is only one object is that the new operator is applied to a constructor one time. Thus, a single object may have more than one identifier that refers to it. This is called *aliasing*. Thus, `falcon` and `darkWing` are aliases for the same object.

Giving a single object more than one name is called *aliasing*.

An object identifier can be assigned objects many times. However, an identifier can reference only one object at a time. Only the last assignment is retained. For example:

```
LunarLander eagle    = new LunarLander (tranquility);
eagle                = new LunarLander (storms);
LunarLander falcon   = new LunarLander (descartes);
eagle                = falcon;
eagle                = new LunarLander (apennine);
```

Four objects are created. Each is assigned to the identifier `eagle`. Only the last reference is retained. The identifier, `eagle`, refers only to the lander at Apennine. The first two objects are lost to us since we have no way of referring to them. Eventually a garbage collector will come along and recycle them.

Objects require space resources in RAM (random-access memory—computer memory). The more objects we create, the more space is used. A *garbage collector* is an action taken automatically by a program to return the resources required to maintain an object. It allows these resources to be reused. A garbage collector is typically invoked when resources become low.

1.6   Applying Operations to Objects

1.6.1   Invoking Methods

Once an object is created, we must apply operations to it. Recall that objects have three important properties: identity, state, and operations. *Methods* are the mechanisms for doing operations. A method is often used to access or modify an object's state. One form for invoking a method on an object is as follows:

ObjectIdentifier.MethodIdentifier (parameter₁, parameter₂, ...) ;

The following examples show how a method can be used to change the state of an object.

```
james.forward();
james.turnRight();
franz.forward(3);
```

In the first example, the method `forward` requests that our butler `james` move forward (Figure 1.7.) This changes the state of the object `james` by changing its location. In the next example, the butler named `james` is requested to turn 90 degrees to the right. In the final example, the butler named `franz` moves forward three grid locations. Additional operations that can be applied to butlers are shown in Table 1.1 on page 12.

The classic means for expressing the first example above is to say, "the message `forward` is sent to the `james` object." Another way of saying this is that the `james` object is commanded to move `forward`.

A *method* is an operation. Methods may change or access the state of an object.

Figure 1.7 Applying the `forward` Operation to `james`

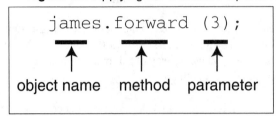

1.6.2 A Common Null Pointer Error

A common error is to try to manipulate an object that has not been created. For example:

```
Butler james;
james. forward();    // error - null pointer exception
```

In the example above `james` is supposed to reference an object, but it does not. The identifier, `james`, is said to be *null*. An error occurs when we try to apply the `forward` operation to an object called `james`. No object was created, so there is no object on which to apply an operation, and the Java program will fail with a null pointer exception.

An identifier that does not refer to an object is said to be *null*. A null pointer exception occurs when we try to manipulate an object that does not exist.

The problem is fixed by creating an object.

```
Butler james  = new Butler (11, 3, edsRoom);
james.forward();
```

1.7   Comments

Comments are meant for human consumption and are ignored by a Java compiler. They may be used to indicate who wrote a program, why it was written, and how it functions. Even though comments are not necessary for a program to function, their importance cannot be overemphasized. A program will go through many revisions. Comments furnish critical information to other programmers who must maintain a program.

A comment begins with a double forward slash (//) and extends to the end of the line.

Comments are one tool in a strategy to make programs easier to read. Several guidelines for making a program easier to read include:

- Use comments and white space to partition code into blocks of code that accomplish some purpose.
  ```
  // move james to the first pile of laundry
  james.forward ();
  james.forward ();
  james.turnRight ();
  james.forward ();

  // james puts the laundry into the basket
  james.pickUp ();
  james.turnRight ();
  james.forward ();
  james.forward ();
  james.forward ();
  james.putIn ();
  ```

- Comments should give insight that looking at the code does not reveal. Comments that repeat what the code says are not useful.
  ```
  // a comment that helps explain the code
  x = a * b;    // find the area of the display window

  // an example of a distracting comment
  x = a * b;    // x gets a multiplied by b
  ```

- Try to write code that does not need comments to understand. Using the previous example, we can make the code easy to understand by using identifier names that help make the code self-documenting. For example, the identifier names below help communicate the code's intent:
  ```
  displayWindowArea = width * height;
  ```

1.8   Compiling and Running Applets

An *applet* is a Java program that can be run from a Java-aware web browser or applet viewer. We will look at applets more carefully in Chapter 3. In this section we will learn how to set up an applet so that we can execute it.

1.8.1   Compiling an Applet

The complete source code for a robot program is in Listing 1.1. When this program is executed, the window in Figure 1.1 is displayed. The simulation is started with a press of the "Start" button.

Listing 1.1 is stored in a file named `RoomCleaningSimulation.java`. The name of the file must match the name of the class (see Line 13) followed by the `java` extension. Once the cleaning program is entered in the `RoomCleaningSimulation.java` file, it is compiled. Compiling checks the Java listing for syntax errors. If no syntax errors are found, a byte-code representation of the program is created. Java byte-codes allow the efficient execution of a Java program on many different kinds of computers.

The method used for compiling a Java applet varies by computer platform and software package. Compilation often takes place with the click of a button. The process of compiling a Java applet will create a new file. In this example, the new file will be called `Room-CleaningSimulation.class`. (See Figure 1.8.) This file has the platform-independent byte-codes that can be interpreted by a web browser or applet viewer.

> A *translator* is a computer program that converts one computer language to another. A *Java compiler* is a translator that converts Java programs to byte-code instructions. Java programs are designed to be written, read, and modified by humans. They must conform to the Java syntax exactly before they can be translated into byte-code. *Byte-code* is designed to be easy to interpret by computers. However, just because a program has correct syntax and is translated into byte-codes does not make the program correct. The Java compiler does not check for correct semantics. That must be done through program testing.

Figure 1.8 Compiling Java Programs

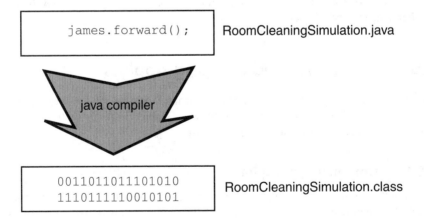

1.8.2   Including an Applet on a Web Page

Once a program is compiled it can be executed by viewing it through a Java-aware web browser or by using an applet viewer. The browser or applet viewer requires an HTML file with a link to the compiled program. For example, opening the `RoomCleaningSimu-lation.html` file in Listing 1.2 with a Java-aware web browser or with an applet viewer will run the lander simulation. This process is illustrated in Figure 1.9.

When a Java-aware web browser accesses a page that references the cleaning simulation class, the browser will first create a lander simulation object and then apply the `init` operation to it. Most Java software development environments bring up an applet viewer with a click of a button. Applet viewers allow us to execute a Java program without a web browser.

Figure 1.9 Accessing an Applet with a Web Browser

RoomCleaningSimulation.class   RoomCleaningSimulation.html

```
0011011011101010
1110111110010101
```

```
<applet
    code=RoomCleaningSimulation.class >
```

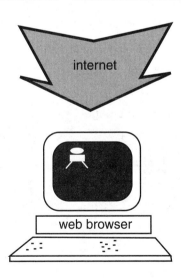

internet

web browser

An *applet viewer* is a stripped-down web browser. Its purpose is for viewing local Java applets.

Byte-code is the key to running Java programs over the network. No matter whether one has a Solaris, a Macintosh, or a Windows computer, byte-code will run on the computer if it has an appropriate byte-code interpreter.

> An *interpreter* is a program that executes a program that has not been converted into the native language of a computer. The native languages of Solaris, Macintosh, and Windows 98 computers are not byte-codes. Since each of these machines has a different native language, a new language (byte-code) was created and implemented on each machine.

The mechanism that allows cross-platform execution is an agreed-upon intermediate language, such as byte-code, that is interpreted on each machine. Interpreted code generally runs about 20 times slower than code that is translated into the native computer's machine code, but this is the price for cross-platform execution. However, there are byte-code compilers that translate byte-code into native machine code. Of course, a program compiled to machine code on a Sparc will only run on other Sparcs. The same constraints apply to PCs and Macs.

The room cleaning simulation can be run from a Java-aware browser using the web page shown in Listing 1.2 on page 28. The key line is:

```
<applet code=RoomCleaningSimulation.class width=100
height=50>
</applet>
```

The above tag states that the applet byte-code can be found in the file `RoomCleaning-Simulation.class`. In addition, the web page reserves a space 100 pixels wide and 50 pixels high for the applet.

Listing 1.2   Room Cleaning Simulation Web page

```
1 <title>Room Cleaning</title>
1 <hr>
1 <applet code=RoomCleaningSimulation.class width=100 height=50>
1 </applet>
1 <hr>
1 <a href="RoomCleaningSimulation.java">The source.</a>
```

REFERENCE

1.9　Summary

An object has identity, state, and operations. Its identity is a name we use to reference an object. Its state indicates something about an object's condition, mode, status, or situation. An operation is a command that when applied to an object will change its state or report its state. An object is an instance of a class. Classes specify the behavior of a type of object.

Patterns describe common ways of doing things. They are commonly used structures for solving general problems. Patterns communicate ideas that are applied repeatedly to solve problems. Patterns cross computer language boundaries and will serve us for a lifetime.

When the sequential pattern is used, program statement are executed in the order in which they are listed.

The smallest elements of a computer program are tokens. They are combined to create statements. Syntax describes the form that a computer language statement must take. Semantics indicate what it means.

In Java we create objects using the following syntax:

```
ObjectClass objectIdentifier = new ObjectClass (parameters) ;
```

Operations are applied to an object using the following syntax:

```
objectIdentifier.method(parameters);
```

Applets are Java classes. A Java-aware web browser can use applet classes to create objects that can run within the web browser. Applets have operations. For example, the `init` operation executes when a web browser creates an applet.

1.10　Bibliography

* Aho, Alfred V., Ravi Sethi, and Jeffrey D. Ullman. 1986. *Compiler: Principles, Techniques, and Tools*. Reading, MA: Addison Wesley.

  Often referred to as the "Dragon Book," this was used as a starting point for many of the definitions for syntactic elements.

- Booch, Grady. 1994. *Object-Oriented Analysis and Design with Applications.* Redwood City, CA: Benjamin/Cummings.

  A good intermediate introduction to object-oriented methodology. It was used as a starting point for object definitions.

- Pattis, Richard. 1981. *Karel the Robot.* New York: John Wiley & Sons.

  The `Butler` class has its roots here.

PROBLEM SETS

1.11   Exercises

Objects and Classes—Section 1.2

1   For each of these classes, identify a specific object that belongs to that class, and list operations on it.

   a.   CD player

   b.   sweatshirt

   c.   pencil

   d.   mystery novel

   e.   garden

   f.   hammer

   g.   oxygen

   h.   French door

2   For each of these objects, name a class to which it belongs.

   a.   Empire State Building

   b.   Washington Monument

   c.   Grand Canyon

   d.   Madonna

   e.   Spirit of St. Louis

   f.   ET

   g.   Sol

   h.   Oregon

3   It is your job to assist in designing a university registration system. It needs to contain the object classes listed below. For each class, list the items that make up its state and describe available operations.

   a.   student record

   b.   course record

   c.   instructor record

   d.   classroom

4   It is your job to assist in designing a personal finance system. It needs to contain the object classes listed below. For each class, list the items that comprise its state and describe available operations.

   a.   bank statement

   b.   car loan

   c.   saving statement

5   How would you change the program in Listing 1.1 on page 9 if `james` began at (11,2)?

6   How would you change the program in Listing 1.1 on page 9 if the pile of clothes were initially located at (8,2)?

7   Invent an additional operation on the `Butler` class. Describe what it should do.

Sequential Pattern—Section 1.3

8   Write down a sequence of steps you commonly perform that must be completed sequentially. For example, the following can be completed only within the following order:

   a.   Take the cap off the toothpaste tube.

   b.   Put toothpaste on the toothbrush.

   c.   Brush teeth.

Syntax—Section 1.4

9   Which of the following are valid identifiers:

   a.   `fFarPoint`

   b.   `farPoint`

   c.   `FarPoint`

   d.   `far_point`

   e.   `_far_point_`

   f.   `far-point`

   g.   `Boeing747`

   h.   `switch`

   i.   `3Corners`

   j.   `$$$`

   k.   `star*`

10 Partition the statements in Exercise 12 into tokens.

11 Identify the tokens, identifiers, and keywords in the statements in Exercise 12 Some items may have more than one designation, for example, token and identifier.

Creating Objects—Section 1.5 / Applying Operations, Section 1.6

12 For each of the following, name the class, the object, the constructor, the name of the operation in the second line, and any parameters.

   a.   `Moon europa = new Moon();`
            `europa.shine();`

   b.   `Graphics g;`
            `g.drawLine(2,3,7,1);`

   c.   `Stack plates = new Stack(100);`
            `plates.pop(5);`

   d.   `Door front = new Door(oak, 36);`
            `front.lock();`

   e.   `Account mine = new Account("Elmer Snid", 1845.12);`
            `mine.deposit(351.49);`

   f.   `w x = new w();`
            `x.y(z);`

13 Making sure your syntax is correct, create Java code fragments that will do the following:

   a.   Create a dog and assign it to the identifier `"duke"`. Apply the "roll over" operation to it.

   b.   Create a super hero and assign it to the identifier `"flashGordon"`. Apply the "fly" operation to it.

   c.   Create a cake for Ema Lou's birthday. Apply the "bake" operation to it with a parameter of 350 degrees.

14 Identify the syntax error in each of the following statements.

   a.   `CDPlayer my Player = new CDPlayer();`

   b.   `Car theWreck = new Car()`

   c.   `Point p = New Point (40, 50);`

   d.   `Box small = new Box (50 25 50 100);`

   e.   `Color new = new Color (255, 255, 255);`

```
f.      Thing mine = new Thing;
g.      Robot 3PO = new Robot();
h.      piano.play()
i.      myCar.move forward (30);
j.      computer number2.shutDown();
```

1.12   Projects

Compiling and Executing Java Applets—Section 1.8

15   Practice using your Java development system by compiling and running the butler program in Listing 1.1.

Robot Control—Section 1.2

16   Program `james`, our butler, to move through the maze stored in the file `chap1a.room` (Figure 1.10). Begin `james` at grid (6,3) and move him to grid (1,0). The beginning of a program to accomplish this task is shown in Listing 1.3.

Figure 1.10 The Maze in the File `chap1a.room`

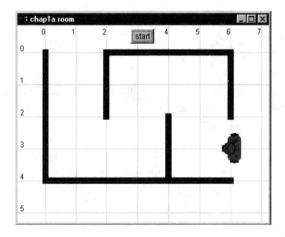

Listing 1.3 The Start for Exercise 16

```
1   import java.applet.Applet;
2
3   public class RoomCleaningSimulation extends Applet
4   {
5     public void start()
6     {
7        Room    edsRoom = new Room("chap1a.room", this);
8        Butler james  = new Butler (6, 3, edsRoom);
9
10       // add our code to control james here
11    }
12 }
```

17   Our parents just called from the front desk telling us they are on the way up. We need to hide our laundry behind the bed. Have `james` move our laundry from (6,1) to (1,4) and then have him leave the room. Change Line 8 in Listing 1.3 to start `james` at (11,3) and Line 7 to open the room file in `chap1b.room` (Figure 1.11).

Figure 1.11 The Room in the File `chap1b.room`

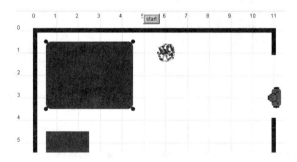

18 Our parents are on their way up again. This time we have laundry all over the room. Have james move all of our laundry at (1,3), (5,2), (6,1), (7,2), and (10,7) into the laundry basket that is at (1,1). Next, have james disappear out the door with our basket of dirty clothes. Since we are in a hurry, have james do this in the fewest possible steps. It may expedite james to have him move the laundry basket to several intermediate locations. james must put down the laundry basket before he can pick up clothes and put them in the basket. Start james at (11,3) and use the room in file chap1d.room (Figure 1.12).

Figure 1.12 The Room in the File chap1d.room

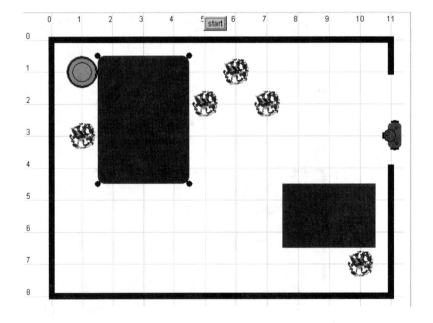

2 Elements of Control
Controlling a Robot Butler

2.1   Objectives

Concepts   Section 2.2, page 39

The programs we have written thus far depend on sequential flow. Sequential flow is clearly not enough for us to write all the programs we can imagine. Most programs have statements that should be executed only under special conditions and other statements that must be executed multiple times. Adding conditional execution and looping lets us write any program we choose. We will take advantage of conditional execution and looping to control the movements of a robot butler whose purpose is to keep our room neat. We will need to program our butler in such a way that it responds to its environment and repeatedly executes simple tasks to accomplish some greater duty.

Patterns   Section 2.4, page 53

The first pattern we encountered was the sequential pattern in Chapter 1. It specified that the order statements are written in determines the order of execution. In this chapter we extend our choice of patterns. One of these patterns assures execution of statements only if special conditions hold; another pattern provides a choice of which statements are executed; another pattern repeatedly executes statements until a particular situation occurs; and a final pattern executes statements a set number of times.

Java Skills

Next we address how we can use Java to express the above concepts and patterns.

- Boolean expressions   Section 2.6, page 60
- Null and block statements   Section 2.7, page 64
- `if` statement   Section 2.7.3, page 65
- `while` statement   Section 2.7.4, page 68

Abilities

By the end of this chapter we should be able to do the following:

- Manipulate booleans.
- Write programs with `if` statements.
- Write programs with `while` loops.
- Write and debug programs with nested control structures.

CONCEPTS

2.2 Controlling the Flow

In Chapter 1 we learned that *flow of control* defines the order in which statements are executed. We looked at sequential flow of control, in which the order statements are written determines the order in which they are executed. For example, execution begins with the first statement in an `init` method and progresses statement by statement until the last statement is executed.

Using sequential flow of control exclusively works for only a handful of problems. Many times we need statements executed only if particular conditions hold and we need to repeat steps. For example, suppose we are sorting our laundry into three piles: whites, darks, and delicates. We may proceed as follows.

```
1 while there is laundry in our basket
2    take an item out of our basket
3    if the item is white
4       put it into pile 1
5    otherwise if the item is dark
6       put it into pile 2
7    otherwise
8       put it into pile 3
```

The program above contains three kinds of flow of control: repetition, selection, and sequential.

Line 1 specifies repetition. It says that Lines 2 through 8 must be executed repeatedly until there are no more items in the basket. We take an item out of the basket, look at it, and throw it into one of our three piles. We repeat these steps until the basket is empty.

> *Loops* are flow-of-control constructs that execute statements repeatedly. The process of repetitive execution is called *iteration*. See Figure 2.1.

Line 3 is an example of the second kind of control construct, selective execution. Line 4 is executed only if the condition in Line 3 is true. If the item we have in our hand is white, we place it in pile 1. If the item is not white, Lines 5 through 8 are executed.

Figure 2.1 Repetition Control Structure

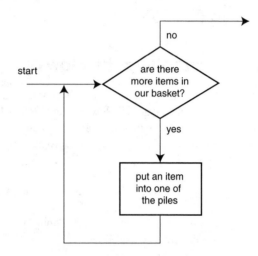

Conditionals are flow-of-control constructs that execute other statements if special conditions hold. The process of conditional execution is called *selection*. See Figure 2.2.

Figure 2.2 Selection Control Structure

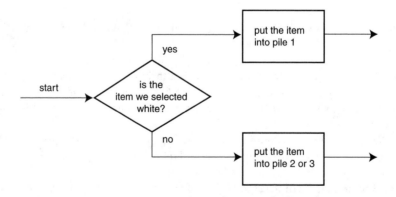

The third kind of flow of control is sequential. It is illustrated by Lines 2 and 3. When the flow of execution reaches Line 2, it is completely executed. Line 2's execution is always followed by the complete execution of Line 3. In other words, whenever we take an item out of our basket, we always check to see if it is white.

Sequential flow of control constructs execute statements in the order they are written. See Figure 2.3.

Figure 2.3 Sequence Control Structure

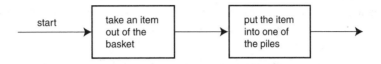

Figure 2.4 shows how our laundry-sorting program can be decomposed using the three flow-of-control constructs.

Figure 2.4 Complete Control Flow Diagram

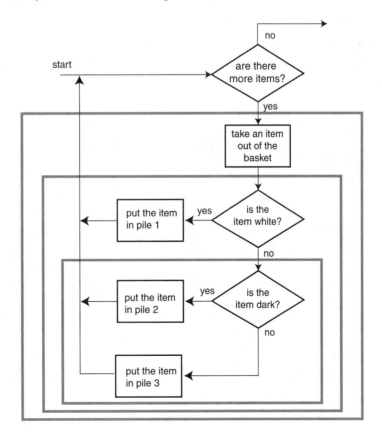

These three kinds of flow of control are all we need to write any program we choose. If that is the case, then why not stop with this chapter? Why should we go on and learn additional ways of organizing programs? These questions can be compared to questions about spoken languages. Why should we learn new ways of saying the same thing? It has to do with economy of expression. Much of what we will learn in future chapters is how to write programs that express our ideas consistently and clearly. We will also learn strategies for organizing programs and how to use the Java class library.

2.3   Conditional and Repeated Execution

In the previous chapter we needed to tell our butler exactly how many forward steps it required to locate the laundry. If our pile of laundry were in a different place, we would have to reprogram the butler the next time it picked up after us. For example, if we wanted the butler to pick up the laundry and our room looked like the one in Figure 2.5, we would write the program in Listing 2.1.

Listing 2.1 Get the Laundry

```
1 //***********************************************************
2 //
3 // title:    RoomCleaningSimulation
4 //
5 // Get the laundry.
6 //
7 //***********************************************************
8
9 import java.applet.Applet;
10
11 public class RoomCleaningSimulation extends Applet
12 {
13   public void init ()
14   {
15     // create the simulation objects
16     Room    edsRoom = new Room("small.room", this);
17     Butler james   = new Butler (11, 2, edsRoom);
18     edsRoom.waitForStart();
19
20     // get the clothes
21     james.forward();
22     james.pickUp();
23   }
24 }
```

Figure 2.5 An Example Room

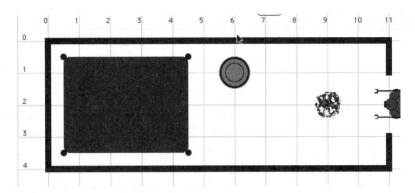

If the laundry were placed at location (8,2), we would need to rewrite Lines 21 through 22 as follows:

```
james.forward();
james.forward();
james.pickUp();
```

If the laundry were at location (7,3), the above would become the following:

```
james.forward();
james.forward();
james.forward();
james.pickUp();
```

Rewriting the program for each small change in our room is clearly not ideal. We want to enter one set of instructions and have our butler respond appropriately to minor variations. We will solve this problem by learning how to selectively and repeatedly execute statements. To make this possible we will need additional operations that check the state of our robot butler. They are summarized in Table 2.1.

Listing 2.2 shows a more general solution to the problem in Listing 2.1. Lines 13 through 16 define a loop. The program will continually execute Lines 14 through 16 (the loop body) as long as the loop condition in Line 13 is true. Thus, if the clothes are at location (9,2) as they are in Figure 2.5, the loop body will be executed once. If at location (8,2), the loop body will be executed twice. If at location (7,2), the loop body will be executed three times. This program will work when the laundry basket is placed anywhere between locations (5,2) and (10,2) inclusive.

Table 2.1 Operations (Checks) Supported by a Butler

operation	action
int getX ()	returns the x coordinate of its location in the room
int getY ()	returns the y coordinate of its location in the room
boolean isFrontClear ()	returns true if there is no object directly in front of this butler
boolean isRightClear ()	returns true if there is no object in the location directly to the right of this butler
boolean isLeftClear ()	returns true if there is no object in the location directly to the left of this butler
boolean isFrontBasket ()	return true if there is a basket directly in front of this butler
boolean isFrontClothes ()	return true if there are clothes directly in front of this butler

Listing 2.2 Get the laundry (loop version)

```
1   import java.applet.Applet;
2
3   public class RoomCleaningSimulation extends Applet
4   {
5     public void init ()
6     {
7       // create the simulation objects
8       Room    edsRoom = new Room("small.room", this);
9       Butler james   = new Butler (11, 2, edsRoom);
10      edsRoom.waitForStart();
11
12      // get the clothes
13      while (james.isFrontClear())
14      {
15        james.forward();
16      }
17      james.pickUp();
18    }
19  }
```

Let us create another challenge by adding a random element to our room. Figure 2.6 shows a narrow room that contains a basket and a pile of laundry. The location of these two items is different for each run. We are guaranteed only that they will be placed in row 2 with a horizontal position from 1 through 7. There is also a chance that the basket may be missing altogether.

Listing 2.3 Pick Up Laundry at a Random Location

```
 1   import java.applet.Applet;
 2
 3   public class RoomCleaningSimulation extends Applet
 4   {
 5     public void start()
 6     {
 7       Room    edsRoom = new Room("random.room", this);
 8       Butler james  = new Butler (11, 2, edsRoom);
 9       edsRoom.waitForStart();
10
11       // go forward until an object blocks us
12       while (james.isFrontClear())
13       {
14         james.forward();
15       }
16
17       // if the object is dirty clothes, pick them up
18       if (james.isFrontClothes())
19       {
20         james.pickUp();
21       }
22
23       // turn around and walk out the door
24       james.turnRight();
25       james.turnRight();
26       james.forward(10);
27     }
28   }
```

Our goal is to pick up the laundry and remove it from the room. If our way is blocked by a basket, we will leave without the laundry. We will assume that our butler begins at grid (11,2).

The code for accomplishing this task is shown in Listing 2.3. It involves three steps:

1. Move forward until we reach an object (Figure 2.6).

2. If the object in front of us is clothes, pick them up.

3. Turn around and leave the room.

Figure 2.6 Random Placement of Clothes and Basket

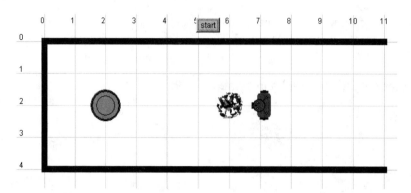

2.3.1 Repetitive Execution

Let's look at step one first. It involves the code in Lines 12 through 15 (Listing 2.3.) The while statement in Line 12 will execute the code in Lines 13 through 15 continually until the grid location directly in front of james is occupied. Once the loop condition in Line 12 no longer holds true, control will exit the loop and move to the first statement following Line 15. We will learn more about while loops in Section 2.7.4 , page 68.

A strategy that can help us understand how a loop works is to walk though the code. Table 2.2 illustrates the process. When execution reaches Line 12, james is at grid (11,2). Because there is nothing in front of james, the isFrontClear method returns true. As a result the loop body (Line 14) is executed. Line 14 moves james forward by one square. Next we evaluate the loop conditional again and find that isFrontClear returns true again. This process repeats until james reaches grid (7,2). Now when we check isFrontClear, it returns false. Control moves on to Line 18.

A code *walk-through* is a process in which a human plays the role of the computer. Each statement in the code under investigation is executed by hand and the result placed in a table. It is important to act dumb and not skip any steps. Walk-throughs are important tools for locating logical errors and for increasing our confidence in a program's correctness. They are often done by a group of software developers to increase the chance that faulty logic is found.

Table 2.2 Walk-through of Listing 2.3—Walk until an Object Found

line number	james.isFrontClear()	location of james
12	true	(11,2)
14		(10,2)
12	true	
14		(9,2)
12	true	
14		(8,2)
12	true	
14		(7,2)
12	false	
18		

2.3.2   Conditional Execution

Once we have reached grid (7,2), our second step is to pick up the object in front of us if it is clothing. Line (Listing 2.3) 18 performs this check. If the blocking item is clothing, Line 20 is executed. If it is not, Line 20 is skipped. We will learn more about if statements in Section 2.7.3 , page 65.

In the example shown in Figure 2.6, Line 20 is executed. The clothing is picked up. After turning around, Line 26 instructs james to carry the clothing away.

2.3.3   Counter Loops

A problem with the program in Listing 2.3 is that james does not return to the place where it started. Since it did not keep track of how far it moved before reaching the clothes, it does not know how far to go on the return trip. We can solve this problem by counting the number of times james moves forward. Listing 2.4 shows how this is done.

We add two statements to the code for step one. Line 12 defines an integer which we will use to count our steps. It begins with the value 0. Each time the body of the loop is executed we add 1 to the step counter (Line 16). A walk-through is shown in Table 2.3.

Next we use the number of steps in step 3, Lines 25 through 29, to move back to our previous location. Each time through the loop we decrement steps by 1. When it becomes 0, we are done. A walk-through is shown in Table 2.4.

Listing 2.4 Counting our Steps

```
1   import java.applet.Applet;
2
3   public class RoomCleaningSimulation extends Applet
4   {
5     public void start()
6     {
7       Room    edsRoom = new Room("random.room", this);
8       Butler james   = new Butler (11, 2, edsRoom);
9       edsRoom.waitForStart();
10
11      // go forward counting our steps until an object blocks us
12      int steps = 0;
13      while (james.isFrontClear())
14      {
15        james.forward();
16        steps = steps + 1;
17      }
18
19      // pick the object up and turn around
20      james.pickUp();
21      james.turnRight();
22      james.turnRight();
23
24      // retrace our steps with the object
25      while (steps > 0)
26      {
27        james.forward();
28        steps = steps - 1;
29      }
30    }
31  }
```

Table 2.3 Walk-through Listing 2.4—Counting Our Steps

line number	james.isFrontClear()	location of james	value of steps
12		(11,2)	0
13	true		0
15,16		(10,2)	1
13	true		1
15,16		(9,2)	2
13	true		2
15,16		(8,2)	3
13	true		3
15,16		(7,2)	4
13	false		4
20			4

Table 2.4 Walk-through Listing 2.4—Recounting Our Steps

line number	steps > 0	location of james	value of steps
25	true	(7,2)	4
27,28		(8,2)	3
25	true	(8,2)	3
27,28		(9,2)	2
25	true	(9,2)	2
27,28		(10,2)	1
25	true	(10,2)	1
27,28		(11,2)	0
25	false	(11,2)	0
30		(11,2)	0

2.3.4   A Maze

The selection statements in the previous section guarded against executing a statement unless special conditions held. In this section we will illustrate how to provide our butler with a choice of options as it navigates its way through a maze such as the one in Figure 2.7. Our butler begins at grid (11,3) and must make its way through the maze to grid (0,1). We will use the following maze navigation strategy. We pick a hand—for example, our left hand—and put it on a wall. We start walking, following the wall without removing our hand. If the walls are connected, eventually we make it through the maze.

Figure 2.7 An Example Maze

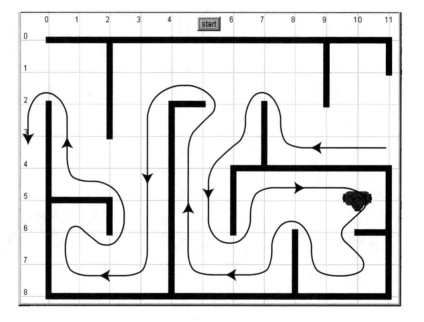

The code to accomplish maze traversal is shown in Listing 2.5. If we assume that our butler had his left shoulder against the wall at the start, there are three possible situations each time the butler moves:

1. The grid location to the left of the butler is clear. This can happen only if the butler took a step forward in the previous turn that took him past the wall to his left. It must turn to the left and step forward (Figure 2.8).

Figure 2.8 If Left Clear, Turn Left and Move Forward

2. His shoulder is against the left wall and the grid location immediately ahead is clear. The butler should follow the wall by moving one square forward (Figure 2.9).

Figure 2.9 If Left Shoulder Against Wall and Front Clear, Move Forward

3. In all other cases it should turn right. For example, if it is caught in a dead end, two such right turns will face our butler back the way it came (Figure 2.10.)

Figure 2.10 In All Other Cases, Turn Right

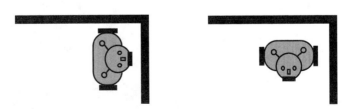

Listing 2.5 Traversing a Maze

```
1   import java.applet.Applet;
2
3   public class RoomCleaningSimulation extends Applet
4   {
5     public void start()
6     {
7       Room    edsRoom = new Room("maze.room", this);
8       Butler james  = new Butler (11, 3, edsRoom);
9       edsRoom.waitForStart();
10
11      while (james.getX() != 0)
12      {
13        if (james.isLeftClear())
14        {
15          james.turnLeft();
16          james.forward();
17        }
18        else if (james.isFrontClear())
19        {
20          james.forward();
21        }
22        else
23        {
24          james.turnRight();
25        }
26      }
27    }
28  }
```

PATTERNS

2.4   Four Flow-of-Control Patterns

In this section we will describe four control patterns that can be used to create programs. We saw examples of each in the previous sections.

2.4.1   Guarded Command Pattern

problem

We must specify that some statements are executed only when specific conditions hold. For example, we want our butler to pick up a basket only if there is one in front of it. If it attempts to pick up a basket and none is there, our butler will fail and turn himself off. In addition, we want it to go forward only when it is clear. If the way is not clear, the butler will crash into an object.

We can also find examples outside of our butler world. For example, we may want to guard against dividing by zero, we may want to apply a special discount to regular customers, we may want to allow the rear hatch of a mini van to operate only when the vehicle is in park, or we may not want to prescribe aspirin to someone who has ulcers.

name
solution

We solve these problems with the *guarded command pattern*. The basic form is shown below.

```
if some condition is true
   then perform some action
```

We have seen a Java implementation of this pattern in Listing 2.3. It is shown below.

```
1 if (james.isFrontClothes())
2 {
3   james.pickUp();
4 }
```

The condition in Line 1 serves as a guard against trying to pick up anything but clothes. Additional Java examples follow.

```
1 if (temperature > 85)
2 {
3   window.open();
4   fan.turnOn();
5 }
```

```
1 if (weather.sunny())
2 {
3   me.putOn(sunglasses);
4 }
```

```
1 if (group.size() > 5)
2 {
3   order.add (eggRoll);
4 }
```

consequences

It is awkward to use the guarded command when there is a choice among several options. The alternative action pattern solves this problem.

2.4.2   Alternative Action Pattern

problem

Often we want to choose from several possible courses of action. For example, we choose a tax rate based on one of several tax brackets, or we choose a day's events based on the weather. These alternatives are mutually exclusive. For example, we can only be in one tax bracket and we can choose to do only one event at a time.

name
solution

We solve these problems with the *alternative action pattern*. The basic form is shown below.

```
choice 1
  perform action 1
choice 2
  perform action 2
...
otherwise
  perform a default action
```

Following are some examples of how the alternative action pattern is implemented in Java.

```
1 if (age <13)
2 {
3   ticket.price(3.50);
4 }
5 else
6 {
7   ticket.price(6.75);
8 }
```

```
1 if (person.female())
1 {
1   lifeExpectancy = 80;
1 }
1 else
1 {
1   lifeExpectancy = 73;
2 }
```

Often we want more than two choices. We saw an example of a choice among three possibilities in Listing 2.5. Our butler had the choice of moving left, moving forward, or turning right. Another example follows (>= means greater than or equal to)

```
1 if (student.grade() >= 90)
2 {
3   grade = 'A';
4 }
5 else if (student.grade() >= 80)
6 {
7   grade = 'B';
8 }
9 else if (student.grade() >= 70)
10 {
11   grade = 'C';
12 }
13 else if (student.grade() >= 60)
14 {
15   grade = 'D';
16 }
17 else
18 {
19   grade = 'F';
20 }
```

2.4.3   Sentinel Loop Pattern

problem

Sometimes we want something done repeatedly until it is finished. For example, we want the ice-cream maker to turn until the ice cream becomes hard. We read a paragraph until we understand it. We polish our shoes until they shine.

name
solution

We solve these problems with the *sentinel loop pattern*. The basic form is shown below.

```
while this condition is true repeat
  commands to be repeated.
end loop
```

A *sentinel* value is a condition that governs when we are done executing a loop. We saw an example in Listing 2.3, which is repeated below. The sentinel in this example is `james.isFrontClear()`.

```
1 while (james.isFrontClear())
2 {
3   james.forward();
4 }
```

consequences   A consequence of the sentinel loop pattern is that we do not know how many times a loop will execute. A sentinel condition may hold before the loop is entered and, therefore, its body is not executed. We must be prepared for this situation. If the sentinel condition is never met, the loop will execute forever. Our program will freeze up.

Other Java examples follow.

```
1 while (file.hasMore())
2 {
3   item = file.get();
4   window.display (item);
5 }
```

```
1 while (bath.level() < 6)
2 {
3   bath.addWater();
4 }
```

2.4.4   Counter Loop Pattern

problem   The final pattern we will look at in this chapter is one in which we want to repeat the execution of code a specific number of times. For example, we print all the movie titles in a top ten list. We do 24 sit-ups every morning. We place a dozen donuts into a box.

name
solution   We solve these problems with the *counter loop pattern*. The basic form is shown below.

```
set the loop counter to zero
repeat the following while the loop counter is less than the
target
    commands to be repeated.
    increment the loop counter
end loop
```

The following prints ten movie titles.

```
1 int number = 0;
2 while (number < 10)
3 {
4   moveTitle = movieList.getTitle(number);
5   moveTitle.print();
6   number = number + 1;
7 }
```

Listing 2.4 provides us with an example which we have copied below. This example moves james a specific number of steps forward. Notice that this example counts down.

```
1 int steps = 8;              // added for completeness
2 while (steps > 0)
3 {
4   james.forward();
5   steps = steps - 1;
6 }
```

nsequences   A consequence of the counter loop is that when execution enters that loop we must know how many times that loop should execute. If something changes during the execution of the loop, we cannot respond to those changes. If we cannot determine how many times a loop must execute before we enter it, we cannot use the counter loop.

JAVA

Now let us take a closer look at the Java required to support basic flow of control. We will start by taking a look at boolean expressions because they are used to implement the conditions that govern `if` statements and `while` loops. Then we will look at `if` statements and `while` loops more closely.

2.5 A Brief Note about Numeric Computing

2.5.1 Arithmetic

Learning Java, like many other things in life, requires that we know a little about everything before we can do anything interesting. For example, in this chapter we are doing some computation that we do not explain fully until the next chapter. In Listing 2.4 we created a step counter and counted steps with the following code.

```
int step = 0;
steps = steps + 1;
```

The intent of this code fragment is fairly clear. In the first line we create an integer named `step` with the value zero. In the second line we add one to the value of `step`. The symbol for addition is "+". Other operators we discuss in the next chapter include "−" for subtraction, "*" for multiplication, "/" for division, and "%" for remainder.

2.5.2 Methods that Return Values

In Section 1.6.1, we learned how to evoke methods that do not return values. To recap, they are evoked as follows:

ObjectIdentifier . MethodIdentifier (parameter$_1$, parameter$_2$, ...);

For example:

```
james.forward(3);
sarah.forward(7);
henry.pickUp();
```

We can determine how to use a method by looking at its specification. The left column of Table 2.1 on page 44 shows the specification for the operations on butlers. Two of those specification are shown below.

```
void forward (int steps);
void pickUp ();
```

The specification for the `forward` method requires that it be passed one integer parameter. The specification for the `pickup` method takes no parameters. The keyword `void` in each indicates that a call to this method must be written as a single statement that does not return a value. The methods `forward` and `pickup` will never be used within an expression. For example, the following will never occur:

```
int somethingOrOther = james.forward(5) * 45 + anything;   // error
```

Some methods do return values—we may imagine a `getCharge` method that returns the percent charge left in our butler's batteries. Its specification is shown below. The void keyword has been replaced with `int`, which specifies that `getCharge` returns an integer.

```
public int getCharge();
```

As a result, its call is typically placed within an expression with other integers. For example:

```
int jamesCharge = james.getCharge();
int minutesLeft = 37 * (james.getCharge() - 85);
```

Figure 2.11 A Method Call

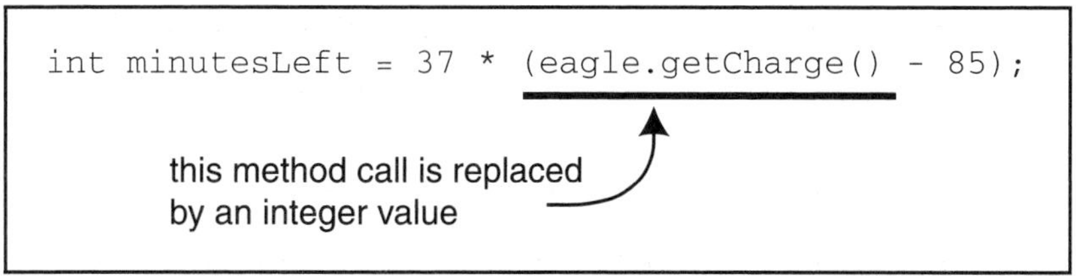

Several methods in this chapter also return values. Two example specifications are shown below. Each returns a boolean value (a true or false value), which we discuss in the next section.

```
boolean isLeftClear();
boolean isFrontClothes();
```

2.6   Booleans

2.6.1   Literal Constants

Booleans are primitive values that represent a logical quantity. Booleans have one of two possible values indicated by the literals `true` and `false`. Examples of using booleans are shown below.

```
boolean isHungry = true;
if (isHungry)
  henry.buyPizza ();

boolean isCold = temperature < 35;
if (isCold)
  furnace.setStatus(on);
```

2.6.2   Declaring Booleans

Examples of boolean values may include whether it is sunny or whether a person in a female.

```
boolean  sunny   = false;
boolean  female  = true;
```

A boolean identifier can be created and initialized with declarations of the following form:

```
boolean identifier = booleanExpression ;
```

2.6.3   Comparison Operators

Comparison operators take primitive numerical types (e.g., int, long, char, float, double) as their operands and return a boolean as a result. Table 2.5 summarizes the results of several comparison operators.

Table 2.5 Results of Comparison Operators

operator	example	x is 14	x is 15	x is 16
greater than	x > 15	false	false	true
greater than or equal	x >= 15	false	true	true
less than	x < 15	true	false	false
less than or equal	x <= 15	true	true	false

2.6.4　Relational Operators

Relational operators take primitive numerical types (e.g., int, long, char, float, double) as their operands and determine if the two values are the same. Table 2.6 summarizes the results of the two comparison operators.

Table 2.6　Results of Relational Operators

operator	example	x is 14	x is 15	x is 16
equal to	x == 15	false	true	false
not equal to	x != 15	true	false	true

It is important to be aware of the difference between applying relational operators to values and objects. When applied to values, relational operators determine whether its operands have the same value. For example:

```
int x = 15;
int y = 15;
boolean same = x == y;  // same is true
```

On the other hand, when relational operators are applied to objects, they determine whether identifiers reference the same object. For example:

```
Rectangle rect1 = new Rectangle(10, 20, 30, 40);
Rectangle rect2 = rect1;
Rectangle rect3 = new Rectangle(10, 20, 30, 40);
boolean same1   = rect1 == rect1;  // same1   is true
boolean same2   = rect1 == rect2;  // same2   is true
boolean notsame = rect1 == rect3;  // notsame is false
```

The rect1 and rect2 identifiers reference the same rectangle. However, the rect3 identifier references a different rectangle. It is not important that the rect1 and rect3 rectangle are the same size and at the same locations. They are simply different objects.

2.6.5　Logical Operators

Logical operators have boolean operands and produce boolean results. Logical operators and their Java representations are given in Table 2.7. Their semantics are summarized in Table 2.8.

For example:

```
boolean hungry    = false;
boolean lunchTime = true;
```

Table 2.7 Logical Operators

name	operator
and	&
or	|
not	!
short-circuit and	&&
short-circuit or	||

Table 2.8 Results of Logical Operations

x	y	x & y x&&y	x|y X||y	!x
true	true	true	true	false
true	false	false	true	false
false	true	false	true	true
false	false	false	false	true

```
boolean eat          = hungry || lunchTime;
boolean ARange       = grade >= 90 && grade <= 100;
boolean bikingWeather = !isRaining() && temperature > 35;
boolean goodTime     = goodMovie() || goodFriends() || goodEat-
ing();
```

The first three lines indicate that we will eat whenever we are hungry or when it is lunch time. Only one of the events needs to be true or both may be true. If both events are false, we will not eat. ARange is true when grade has the value of 90, 93, and 100. It is false when grade has the value of 89 and 119. The value bikingWeather is true when the method isRaining returns the value false and the temperature is warm. Finally, it is necessary for only one of the methods goodMovie, goodFriends, and goodEating to return true for the result goodTime to be true. If more than one of the methods is true, goodTime is still true. All the methods must return false for goodTime to be false.

The boolean results of short-circuited logical operators is the same as regular logical operators. However, a sort-circuited and will not evaluate its right operand if its left operand is false. For example:

```
if (x != 0 && 100 / x > 3)
    ...
```

Here, 100 will not be divided by zero when x is zero. If && is replaced with &, the above will generate a divide by zero error whenever x is zero.

In a similar manner, a short-circuited `or` will not evaluate its right operand if its left operand is true.

2.6.6 Operator Precedence

Operator *precedence* defines the order in which operators are evaluated. Higher precedence operators get applied before lower precedence operators.

The precedence of the boolean operators is shown Table 2.9 with some examples in Table 2.10.

Table 2.9 Precedence of boolean operators (highest to lowest)

Operators	associativity
( )	left to right
!	right to left
< <= > >=	left to right
== !=	left to right
&	left to right
		left to right
&&	left to right
||	left to right

Table 2.10 Example boolean expressions

expression	intermediate result	result
true	true & false	true	false	true
(true | true) & false	true & false	false
5 > 7 & 8 < 10	false & true	false
true && false & true	true && false	false
!true	false	false	false	false

Operator associativity refers to the order in which operators of equal precedence are evaluated. Logical operators are evaluated left to right except for the *not* operator, which is evaluated right to left. Thus, given the following expression, the leftmost *and* operator is evaluated first. Next, the result of this operation is used with the second *and* operator.

```
true & false & true & false     // leftmost and first
    false     & true & false     // second and next
          false     & false     // finally last and
                false
```

2.6.7   Boolean Class

The `Boolean` class provides an object wrapper for `booleans`. This allows booleans to be passed to methods that require objects. Notice that `Boolean` is capitalized.

```
Boolean A = new Boolean (false);
Boolean B = new Boolean (true);
boolean b = B.getValue();          // b gets true
boolean result = A.equals(B);      // result gets false
```

The `Boolean` class does not have the full complement of boolean operators. We can only test if two `Boolean` objects have the same values. As a result, the `Boolean` class is not suitable for general boolean computations. We will have little use for it in this book.

2.7   Flow of Control Statements

2.7.1   Null Statement

An empty or null statement does nothing. However, its innocent nature can cause baffling results, as we will see in the following sections. It has the following form.

```
;
```

For example, the follow code fragment does nothing:

```
;;;;;
;;
;;;;
```

2.7.2   Blocks

Blocks are compound statements. They are a composite of multiple statements that may include declaration statements. Blocks allow statements to be packaged into a single unit. Because they can be used wherever a single statement is allowed, they are often used to embed more than one statement within `if` and `while` statements. When a block is executed, the statements within the block are executed in order. They are of the form:

```
{
   statement₁ ;
   statement₂ ;
   ...
   statementₙ ;
}
```

For example:

```
{
   int width  = 13;
   int height =  5;
   int area   = width * height;
   System.out.println(area);       // prints 65
}
```

Blocks may declare their own local variables. Identifiers that are declared within a block may be used only within that block. In the example above, the identifiers `width`, `height`, and `area` can be used only in the block defined above. We say that the scope of `width` is within the block. We will talk more about scope in detail in Chapter 6.

2.7.3   If Statements

An `if` statement is an example of a *conditional* statement. The statements embedded within a conditional statement, statements within the `{}`, are called the *conditional body*. The conditional body is executed only if the condition is true.

In its simplest form, an embedded statement is executed only if its boolean expression is true.

```
if ( BooleanExpression )
   Statement ;
```

For example, in the following code fragment, everyone will enter through the double doors, but only those over 12 years of age pay full price.

```
if (age > 12)
   System.out.println("Pay full price");
System.out.println("Enter through the double doors");
```

In a second form (see below), the `if` statement contains an `else` clause. When the boolean expression is true, only statement$_1$ is executed. When the boolean expression is false, only statement$_2$ is executed. Statements 1 and 2 are mutually exclusive—one and only one will be executed.

if (*BooleanExpression*) *Statement$_1$* **else** *Statement$_2$* ;

In the following example there is a choice between paying full or half price.

```
if (age > 12)
   System.out.println("Pay full price");
else
   System.out.println("Pay half price");
```

Notice that there can only be one contained statement associated with the `if` or `else` clause. If multiple statements must be associated with an `if` or `else` clause, a block statement is required. For example:

```
if (x > 100)
{
   james.trunLeft();
   speed = speed - 2;
}
else
{
   james.turnRight();
   speed = speed + 2;
}
```

When and when not to use blocks can be the source of confusion. One school of thought states that blocks should always be used in `if` and `else` clauses. Including blocks consistently avoids errors, since we would be less apt to forget to include a block where one is needed. Furthermore, when we want to add or delete a statement from an `if` statement, placing blocks everywhere makes that process easier.

The author's personal style is minimalist; using blocks only when necessary. However, in this text we will always use blocks in an `if` statement. Hopefully, this will lead to less confusion for beginners. However, we should not be surprised if the code lapses into minimalist style on occasion.

`If` statements may be used to select one of several options. Selection from more than two items is accomplished by nesting an `if` statement in the `else` clause of another `if` statement (Section 2.7.6). Examples are shown in Listing 2.6. In the first example the `if` statement for choice two is nested within the `else` clause for choice one and the `if` statement for choice one in nested within the `else` clause for choice zero.

Listing 2.6 Two Examples of Nested if Statements

```
if (choice == 0)                        if (income >= 50000)
{                                       {
  projector.show ("Bullet");              taxRate = 0.28;
}                                         standardDeduction = 10000;
else if (choice == 1)                   }
{                                       else if (income >= 20000)
  projector.show ("Star Wars");         {
}                                         taxRate = 0.18;
else if (choice == 2)                     standardDeduction = 5000;
{                                       }
  projector.show ("Julia");             else
}                                       {
else                                      taxRate = 0.0;
{                                         standardDeduction = 0;
  projector.show ("Trailer");           }
}
```

When `if` statements are not nested, the `else` clause always matches its nearest unmatched previous `if` statement. The following illustrates this.

```
1   if (x == 1)
2   {
3     System.out.println ("one");
4   }
5   if (x == 2)
6   {
7     System.out.println ("two");
8   }
9   else
10  {
11    System.out.println ("other");
12  }
```

The `else` clause in Line 9 above is coupled with the `if` clause in Line 5 because Line 5 is closer to Line 9 than Line 1. Thus, "other" is printed whenever x is not 2.

Notice how the statements embedded within an `if` statement are indented and how the matching brackets line up vertically. Indention makes the program easier to read. It communicates to the reader that the indented statements are a part of an `if` statement.

2.7.4 while Statement

A `while` statement is an example of a loop statement. The statements embedded within a loop, statements within the {}, are called the *loop body*. The body of a loop is executed repeatedly as long as the loop condition is true. Once the conditional is false, control leaves the loop.

A `while` statement executes statements multiple times. For example, the following is a loop with one embedded statement. Normally, we will place that statement within a block for consistency.

```
int doubleIt = 1;
while (doubleIt < 100)
  doubleIt = doubleIt * 2;
System.out.println(doubleIt);
```

The output of the above loop is 128. To see how it works, we can place a print statement within the loop by using a `print` and `block` statement. A block statement is needed because a loop may have only a single statement embedded within it.

```
int doubleIt = 1;
while (doubleIt < 100)
{
  System.out.println(doubleIt);
  doubleIt = doubleIt * 2;
}
System.out.println(doubleIt);
```

The resulting output is shown below. More information about how the print statement works is found in Section 2.8.1 , page 76.

```
1
2
4
8
16
32
64
128
```

There are several items which will help us write loops.

1. The basic form of a `while` loop is shown below.

   ```
   while ( BooleanExpression )
         Statement
   ```

2. A `while` loop may contain only one embedded statement. That statement may be a `block` statement, as in this example. It may also be another `while` statement or any other legal statement. There is no limit to the depth of nesting. Always embedding a `block` statement within a `while` statement will help prevent errors and make it easier to maintain.

3. There must always be some change within the loop that makes the loop condition become false or some condition that causes an abort. If there is none, the loop is infinite. It never stops executing. In Listing 2.7 (Table 2.11), Line 7 causes the loop condition to eventually become false. It creates the change in `count` that assures that it will eventually become above 5.

Listing 2.7 Sum of First Five Integers with its Output

```
1 int sum   = 0;
2 int count = 1;
3 while (count <= 5)
4 {
5    System.out.println(count);
6    sum   = sum + count;
7    count = count + 1;
8    }
9 System.out.println(sum);
```

the output follows

```
   1
   2
   3
   4
   5
   15
```

Table 2.11 Walk-through of Listing 2.7

Line number	count	sum
1	?	0
2	1	0
3	1	0
4	1	0
5	1	1
6	2	1
3	2	1
4	2	1
5	2	3
6	3	3
3	3	3
4	3	3
5	3	6
6	4	6
3	4	6
4	4	6
5	4	10
6	5	10
3	5	10
4	5	10
5	5	15
6	6	15
3	6	15
8	6	15

4. The loop condition may be any valid boolean expression. In Listing 2.7, the loop condition is the result of a comparison expression. The loop condition may also be the result of a method call as shown below.

```
while (fred.isFrontClear())
{
    fred.forward();
}
```

5. A walk-through is one of the best ways to get a handle on how a loop works. Table 2.11 is an example.

6. Notice that the statements embedded within a `while` statement are indented. This makes them easier to read. Indentation indicates that the indented statements are the body of the loop.

2.7.5   break **Statement**

A `break` statement can be used from within a loop body to exit a loop. We will spend more time talking about using it in loops in Section 9.4.1 , page 410. An example of using it is shown below. The following is the same counter loop we encountered in Section 2.4.4.

```
1 int step = 5;
2 int count = 0;
3 while (count < steps)
4 {
5   james.forward();
6   count = count + 1;
7 }
```

We can implement it using an infinite loop and a `break` statement as follows:

```
1 int step = 5;
2 int count = 0;
3 while (true)
4 {
5   if (count >= steps)
6     break;
7   james.forward();
8   count = count + 1;
9 }
```

2.7.6   Nesting `if` and `while` **Statements**

We discovered that each `if` or `while` statement may have a single embedded statement. That embedded statement may be another `if`, `while`, or `block` statement. The result is called *nesting*. For example, the following is an example of an `if` statement nested within an `if` statement without using any blocks:

```
boolean sunny    = true;
int temperature = 75;
if (sunny)
   if (temperature > 65)
     System.out.println
          ("Go biking.");
```

The output of this program is "Go biking." It is equivalent to writing the following:

```
boolean sunny    = true;
int temperature = 75;
if (sunny && temperature > 65)
{
   System.out.println
          ("Go biking.");
}
```

Nesting can be to an arbitrary depth. For example, the following adds yet another condition to our decision to go biking:

```
boolean sunny    = true;
int temperature = 75;
if (sunny)
{
   if (temperature > 65)
   {
     if (temperature < 90)
     {
       System.out.println("Go biking.");
     }
   }
}
```

`While` loops can be nested within while loops. For example, Listing 2.8 will display a multiplication table.

Listing 2.8 Multiplication Table

```
1  int row = 0;
2  while (row < 10)
3  {
4    int column = 0;
5    while (column < 10)
6    {
7      System.out.print
8          (row * column);
9      System.out.print (" ");
10     column = column + 1;
11   }
12   System.out.println();
13   row = row + 1;
14 }
```

the output follows

```
0 0 0 0 0 0 0 0 0 0
0 1 2 3 4 5 6 7 8 9
0 2 4 6 8 10 12 14 16 18
...
0 9 18 27 36 45 54 63 72 81
```

Listing 2.9 Another Nested Loop

```
1  int row = 0;
2  while (row < 2)
3  {
4    int column = 0;
5    while (column < 3)
6    {
7      column = column + 1;
8    }
9    row = row + 1;
10 }
```

Table 2.12 Walk-through of Nested Loop (Listing 2.9)

line number	row	column
1	0	??
2	0	??
4	0	0
5	0	0
7	0	1
5	0	1
7	0	2
5	0	2
7	0	3
9	1	3
2	1	??
4	1	0
5	1	0
7	1	1
5	1	1
7	1	2
5	1	2
7	1	3
9	2	3
2	2	??
exit	2	??

A nested `while` loop, such as the one above, can look ominous. A strategy that helps tame nested statements is to walk through them. The nested loops above execute the inner block 100 times, making it impractical for a walk through. We will simplify our effort by walking through the following loop, which has smaller maximums for rows and columns. Table 2.12 shows the walk-through.

The body of the outer loop is executed two times, so the inner loop is executed two times. Each time the inner loop is executed, its embedded block statement is executed three times. Therefore, the total number of times the inner block is executed is six (2 * 3).

Another example of nesting is shown in Listing 2.10. This code will display all the positive prime numbers less than 100. We will look at this algorithm more carefully in Section 9.4.5. Note that the `while` loop has a `while` loop nested within it with an `if` statement nested within it. We can try this program out by replacing Lines 15 through 22 of Listing 2.1 on page 42 with the prime number code.

Listing 2.10 Computing primes

```
1   int number = 2;
2   while (number < 100)
3   {
4     int i = 2;
5     boolean prime = true;
6     while (i < number)
7     {
8       if (number % i == 0)
9       {
10        prime = false;
11      }
12      i = i + 1;
13    }
14    if (prime)
15    {
16      System.out.println(number);
17    }
18    number = number + 1;
19  }
```

2.7.7   Common Mistakes with If and While Statements

There are some common mistakes when using `while` and `if` statements that may create a debugging headache. The following example contains a misplaced ";". As a result, the empty statement is the only statement contained within the `if` statement.

```
double hoursWorked = 35.5;
if (hoursWorded > 40.0);        // intent error - misplaced ;
{
  double overTime = hoursWorked - 40.0;
  System.out.println("Overtime for the week is " + overTime);
}
```

Although the intent of the above code remains clear, the code within the brackets will always be executed. Thus, in the example above the value of overtime will be -4.5. The Java compiler will not realize our intent. To make this clear, we can reformat the above to show how the compiler will interpret it.

```
double hoursWorked = 35.5;
if (hoursWorded > 40.0)
  ;                              // do nothing when the if is true

{                               // always execute the block statement
  double overTime = hoursWorked - 40.0;
  System.out.println("Overtime for the week is " + overTime);
}
```

Misplaced semicolons are also problems in while statements. The misplaced semicolon in the following code creates an infinite loop (it executes forever).

```
int count = 1;
while (count <= 5);    // intent error - misplaced ;
{
  System.out.println(count);
  count = count + 1;
}
```

What this code does is easily seen when it is reformatted. The result is an infinite loop because there is no code in the loop body to change the value of count. Remove the ";" after the (x <= 5) to fix the problem.

```
int count = 1;
while (count <= 5)
  ;                              // do nothing forever
{                               // this code will not be reached
  System.out.println(count);
  count = count + 1;
}
```

The computer disregards indentations. Indenting multiple statements without using brackets communicates one thing to a human reader but another to a computer. For example:

```
double hoursWorked = 35.5;
if (hoursWorded > 40.0)             // intent error - missing {}
```

```
   System.out.println ("Overtime this month.");
   double overTimePay = (hoursWorked - 40.0) * 15.0;
```

The clear intent of the code above is to execute the last statement only when overtime has been put in. Because only one statement can be embedded within an if statement, the last statement is always executed regardless of the value for hoursWorked. As a result, the worker will get –$67.50 as overtime pay, which is clearly not what we intended. To get the result we want, we should modify the above code by adding brackets.

```
double hoursWorked = 35.5;
if (hoursWorded > 40.0)
{
   System.out.println ("Overtime this month.");
   double overTimePay = (hoursWorked - 40.0) * 15.0;
}
```

Similar problems occur in while loops. As we have stated several times, there must always be some change within the loop that causes the loop condition to become false. Missing brackets can create an infinite loop. The following loop will never exit:

```
int count = 1;
while (count <= 5)              // intent error - missing {}
   System.out.println(count);
   count = count + 1;
```

This program will print one forever.

```
   1
   1
   1
   1
   ...
```

The problem is that the last statement is not part of the loop. Thus, the value of count is not changed within the loop. The value of count will always be less than five.

Finally, misplaced else clauses can create a problem with if statements. The indention in the following code suggests that the intent is to have the else clause be coupled with the first if statement. However, else clauses match with the previous unmatched if statement. In other words, the else clause matches with the second if statement.

```
if (age > 18)
   if (sex == female)
      System.out.println("Female older than 18");
else
   Systme.out.println("Person 18 or less");
```

This situation can be fixed by using `block` statements. This is another example that illustrates how the consistent use of block statements can prevent problems.

```
if (age > 18)
{
  if (sex == female)
  {
    System.out.println("Female older than 18");
  }
}
else
{
  Systme.out.println("Person 18 or less");
}
```

2.8   Testing and Debugging

It is easy to make mistakes with selection and loop statements, particularly if they are nested. It is imperative to test our code to assure it is correct and to locate errors when we find problems. Little mistakes can have unexpected consequences. One method to help the validation and debugging process is to add print statements, such as the one in Line 11 of Listing 2.11. When this statement is executed, it will display to the standard output window a message that lets us know the `if` statement in Line 10 evaluated to `true` at the appropriate time.

2.8.1   Printing Values to Standard Output

We have been using the print statement to help us illustrate and debug loops. A print statement is used to print values to the standard output window:

```
System.out.println( expression );
```

For example:

```
double radius = 50.0;
System.out.println (radius);              // prints 50
System.out.println (radius >= 80.0);      // prints false
double pi = 3.14159.
System.out.println (2.0 * pi * radius); // prints 314.59
System.out.println("step method");        // prints step method
System.out.println("pi = " + pi);         // prints pi = 3.14159
```

The standard output window is a special window opened by a software development environment. The circumstances under which this window appears depends on the environment. Typically the window is prominently placed whenever an applet is run.

Listing 2.11 Debugging Prime Number Code

```
1   int number = 2;
2   while (number < 100)
3   {
4     int i = 2;
5     boolean prime = true;
6     while (i < number)
7     {
8       if (number / i * i == number)
9       {
10        prime = false;
11        System.out.println ("number = " + number +
12                          ", i = " + i + ",  prime = " + prime);
13      }
14      i = i + 1;
15    }
16    if (prime)
17    {
18      System.out.println(number);
19    }
20    number = number + 1;
21  }
```

The `print` method behaves similar to `println` except that `println` puts a new line marker at the end of its output. For example:

```
System.out.println ("Terminator 2: Judgement Day");
```

can be rewritten as:

```
System.out.print    ("Terminator 2:");
System.out.print    (" Judgement ");
System.out.print    ("D");
System.out.println ("ay");
```

Print statements do not start a new line after their contents have been printed. A new line is not begun until after the "ay" in the last line is printed.

The "+" operator can be used to concatenate strings together. We will learn more about this operation in Chapter 10. String concatenation is often needed within a print statement. For example, the print statement in Line 11 of Listing 2.11 will result in the following output if number = 33, i = 5, and prime = false:

```
number = 33,  i = 5,  prime = false
```

We could replace Lines 11 and 12 with the following:

```
System.out.print ("number = ");
System.out.print (number);
System.out.print (",  i = ");
System.out.print (i);
System.out.print (",  prime = ");
System.out.println (prime);
```

REFERENCE

2.9   Summary

Flow of control is a guiding theme in this chapter. Using conditional and iterative control structures makes it possible to implement the following patterns:

- Guarded commands pattern: code is executed only under special conditions.

- Alternative action pattern: one of several code choices is executed.

- Sentinel loop pattern: code is executed repeatedly until a particular condition holds.

- Counter loop pattern: code is executed a prescribed number of times.

A method we used to test our programs was to walk through them. A walk-through involves stepping through code statement by statement and recording the results of its execution. Walking through a program can also help us understand how a program works.

Another key idea of this chapter is flow of control. An `if` statement is used to selectively execute code. When an `if` conditional is true, its embedded statement is executed. When its conditional is false, its embedded statement is skipped.

Booleans are primitive values that are either `true` or `false`. Comparison operations on numbers determine the relative values of numbers. Relational operators determine whether values are the same. The logical `and`, `not`, and `or` operators combine boolean expressions.

A null statement performs no action.

Blocks and compound statements combine multiple statements into a single unit. They are used in `if` and `while` statements and other places as well.

An `if` statement implements selective execution. When its condition is true, its embedded statement is executed. When it is false, its `else` clause (if one exists) is executed.

A while statement is used to implement iteration. The statement embedded within a while loop is executed repeatedly as long as its conditional is true.

2.10   Bibliography

- Wallingford, Eugene, 1996. Toward a first course based on object-oriented patterns, pages 27–31. Paper presented at the 27th SIGCSE Technical Symposium on Computer Science Education.

- Astrachan, Owen and Eugene Wallingford. *Loop Patterns*, http://www.cs.uni.edu/~wallingf/research/patterns/chiliplop/loops/loops.html

- Bergin, Joseph. *Patterns for Selection*, http://csis.pace.edu/~bergin/patterns

PROBLEM SETS

2.11   Exercises

Flow of Control—Section 2.2

1   It's your job to create ten ham and cheese sandwiches for the school picnic. Create a flow-of-control chart patterned after the one in Figure 2.4 on page 41.

2   It's your job to create four ham and cheese sandwiches on whole wheat for family lunches. Father is the only one who wants pickles, mother does not want mayonnaise, sister will eat only white bread, and brother will eat anything. Create a flow of control chart patterned after the one in Figure 2.4 on page 41.

Robot Butler—Section 2.3

3   What would be the result if Lines 14 and 17 were removed from Listing 2.4 on page 48?

4   What would be the result if Line 25 in Listing 2.4 on page 48 were changed to the following?
```
while (steps >= 0)
```

5   What would be the result if Lines 26 and 29 were removed from Listing 2.4 on page 48?

6   Modify the maze traversal program in Listing 2.5 on page 52 so that james follows the wall on the right.

7   What happens if james does not start with its left shoulder against a wall in Listing 2.5 on page 52?

Boolean Expressions—Section 2.6

8   What is the result of each of the following expressions? Assume a == 14, b == 74, c == 39, and d == true.

   a.   d

   b.   false

   c.   ! d

   d.   d || a > 33

   e.   a > 14

   f.   a >= 14

   g.   a >= 10 || b < 100

   h.   a >= 10 && b < 100

   i.   a < 0 || b < a || d

   j.   c != 39

   k.   ! (c < 80)

if and while Statements—Section 2.7

9   What is the output of the following code fragments?

   a.

```
int x = 10;
if (x > 9)
  System.out.println("Greater");
```

b.

```
int y = 18;
if (y >= 18)
   System.out.println("young adult");
System.out.println("youth");
```

c.

```
int y = 18;
if (y >= 18)
   System.out.println("young adult");
else
   System.out.println("youth");
```

d.

```
int a = 10;
int b = 20;
if (a > 8)
   System.out.println("red");
if (a < b)
   System.out.println("blue");
if (a == b)
   System.out.println("yellow");
```

e.

```
int a = 10;
int b = 20;
if (a > 8)
   System.out.println("red");
else if (b < a)
   System.out.println("blue");
else
   System.out.println("yellow");
```

f.

```
int i = 834;
if (i > 1000)
   System.out.println("one");
else if (i > 200)
   System.out.println("two");
else if (i > 500)
   System.out.println("three");
else
   System.out.println("four");
```

g.

```
int a = 10;
int b = 20;
if (a > b)
{
  System.out.println("red");
  System.out.println("yellow");
}
if (a < b)
{
  System.out.println("blue");
  System.out.println("green");
}
```

h.

```
int i = 0;
while (i < 10)
{
  System.out.println(i);
  i = i + 1;
}
```

i.

```
int i   = 0;
int sum = 0;
while (i <= 6)
{
  sum = sum + i;
  i   = i + 1;
}
System.out.println(sum);
```

j.

```
int w = 23;
while (w < 33)
{
  System.out.println(w);
  w = w + 3;
}
```

k.

```
int i = 99;
while (i > 90)
{
  System.out.println(i);
```

```
    i = i - 2;
}
```

10 What is the output of the following code fragments? Be careful, the code may not work as the indentation indicates.

a.

```
int x = 8;
if (x > 9);
   System.out.println("Greater");
System.out.println("Always");
```

b.

```
int a = 10;
int b = 20;
if (a > b);
   System.out.println("red");
if (a < b);
   System.out.println("blue");
if (a == b);
   System.out.println("yellow");
```

c.

```
int a = 10;
int b = 20;
if (a > b)
   System.out.println("red");
   System.out.println("yellow");
if (a < b)
   System.out.println("blue");
   System.out.println("green");
```

d.

```
int i   = 0;
while (i <= 6); {
   System.out.println(i);
   i   = i + 1;
}
```

e.

```
int i   = 0;
int sum = 0;
while (i <= 6); {
  sum = sum + i;
   i   = i + 1;
```

```
  }
  System.out.println(sum);
```

f.

```
int i   = 0;
int sum = 0;
while (i <= 6)
  sum = sum + i;
  i   = i + 1;
System.out.println(sum);
```

g.

```
int i   = 0;
int sum = 0;
while (i <= 6)
  i   = i + 1;
  sum = sum + i;
System.out.println(sum);
```

Practice Writing `if` and `while` Statements—Section 2.7.3

11   Write an `if` statement that instructs a robot butler to turn around when its x location is less than or equal to 5. Use the `getX` operation from Table 2.1 on page 44.

12   Write an `if` statement that instructs a robot butler to turn around when its x location is less than or equal to 5 or its x location is greater than 8. Use the `getX` operation from Table 2.1 on page 44.

13   Write a `while` loop that instructs a robot butler go backwards until its y location is equal to 6. Use the `getY` operation from Table 2.1 on page 44.

14   Write a `while` loop that instructs a robot butler turn right until its front is clear. .

15   Write a method that returns true if a point is inside a rectangle, otherwise return false. Do not use the predefined `contains` method from the `Rectangle` class.

```
public boolean inside (int x, int y, Rectangle r)
{
   return ...
}
```

The `Rectangle` class is defined in Appendix: B on page 898. Use only a rectangle's instance variables (x, y, width, and height) to implement this method.

Testing and Debugging—Section 2.8

16 Do a walk-through of the code fragment in part f and i of Exercise 9 Create a table similar to Table 2.11 on page 69.

2.12 Projects

Robot Butler—Section 2.3 & Section 2.4

Listing 2.12 The Start for Exercises 17 through 19

```
1   import java.applet.Applet;
2
3   public class RoomCleaningSimulation extends Applet
4   {
5     public void start()
6     {
7         Room    myRoom = new Room("onepile.room", this);
8         Butler james  = new Butler (11, 2, myRoom);
9
10        // add our code to control james here
11    }
12 }
```

17 Using the program in Listing 2.12 as a beginning point and the room in Figure 1.1 on page 6, write a program that makes james pace forever between grid (11,2) and (5,2).

18 Modify the previous program so that james paces between any two objects. In other words, james goes forward until it reaches an obstacle, turns around, goes forward until it reaches an object, and turns around again. For example, if james starts at grid (5,6) in Figure 1.1 on page 6 it will pace between grid (3,6) and (7,6). Use the program in Listing 2.12 as a beginning point.

19 Using a while loop, program james to walk around the laundry two times and then leave the room without it. Use the room in Figure 1.1 on page 6 and the program in Listing 2.12 as a beginning point.

20 Modify the program in Listing 2.3 on page 45 so that when james encounters the basket, it sets it aside, picks up the laundry, and leaves the room.

21 The room in the file chap2a.room is similar to Figure 1.1 on page 6 except the laundry is at a random locations between grid (7,1) and (7,7). Program james to find it and put it in the basket.

22 The room in the file chap2b.room shown Figure 2.12. The laundry is at a random locations between grid (1,1) and (1,7). Start james at (2,1) and program him to find the laundry and take it out of the room.

Figure 2.12 Room chap2b.room

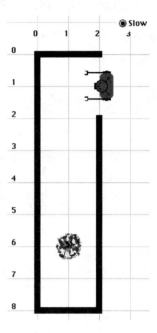

23 The room in the file chap2c.room is the same configuration as the room in Figure 1.1 on page 6, except there is no furniture in it. It contains a single basket at grid (10,1) and one pile of laundry someplace in the room. Start james at grid (11,3), have it find the clothes, place them in the basket, and leave the room.

24 Repeat the previous problem, except that there are usually five piles of clothes (there may be fewer.) Use file chap2d.room.

3 Inheriting Applets

Graphics Objects

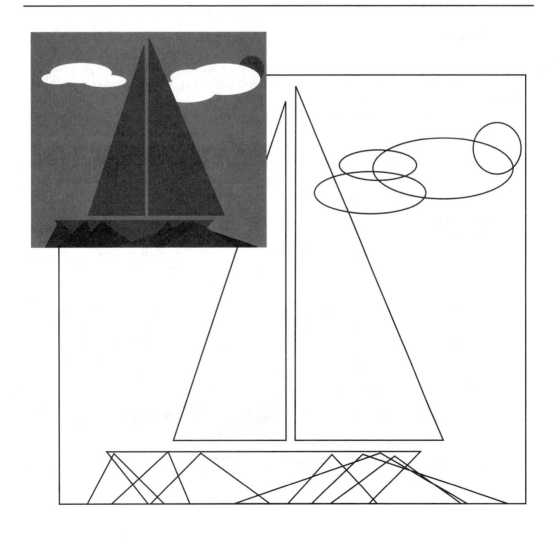

3.1 Objectives

Concepts Section 3.2, page 91

In Chapter 1 we learned how to create objects by instantiating classes. Once an object was created, we instructed it to create a useful result. However, the classes that are available to us often do not have all the functionality we need. One method to extend the functionality of a class is through inheritance. This chapter begins by using inheritance to extend the Java `Applet` class, which we use to create graphics programs.

Patterns Section 3.4, page 97

A framework is a set of interacting classes that are designed to support the construction of a particular kind of software system. A framework can be customized to solve a particular problem by creating custom subclasses. A Java applet is an example of a framework for creating programs with a window and mechanisms for running over the web.

A specific framework is not a pattern. Patterns allow us to reuse designs. Frameworks allow us to reuse code. We have included frameworks in our Patterns section because frameworks are a powerful strategy for reuse.

Java Skills

Through the process of learning about inheritance, we will learn about the Java `Applet` class. We will also get additional practice using objects by applying the Java `Graphics`, `Polygon`, and `Color` classes.

- Using the `Applet` class Section 3.5, page 99
- Using the `Graphics` class Section 3.6.1, page 104
- Using the `Polygon` class Section 3.6.4, page 107
- Using the `Color` class Section 3.6.6, page 112

Abilities

By the end of this chapter we should be able to do the following:

- Create applets.
- Create color graphics images with lines, rectangles, ovals, polygons, and images.

CONCEPTS

3.2   Using Inheritance

Often a class fulfills only a portion of our needs. For example, in the physical world the class "vehicle" is useful for talking about general objects that transport people and things. However, the class of vehicles is much too general to be useful for many of our conversations. We find it much more useful to talk about cars, trucks, campers, trains, ocean liners, canoes, rockets, and sports cars. By using these much more specialized terms in our conversations, we communicate more effectively. For example, we do not have to say, "I drove our four-wheel passenger vehicle to school today." We say instead, "I drove our car to school today."

The relationship among vehicles, trucks, and automobiles is defined by inheritance. Through inheritance one class includes all characteristics of the class it inherits, plus any additional properties it defines. For example, the properties of all vehicles include their location, speed, and cargo. A gas-powered vehicle is a vehicle that combines these properties with a gasoline engine for power. Thus, a gas-powered vehicle transports things and people, has a location, and has a speed. In addition, it contains a gas engine, a fuel tank, and fuel. Going one step further, we can say that an automobile inherits from a gas-powered vehicle. It has all the characteristics of a gas-powered vehicle plus it is designed to transport people, has four wheels, and drives on roads. Figure 3.1 depicts one possible inheritance hierarchy for a small subset of vehicles.

Figure 3.1 Hierarchy of Vehicles

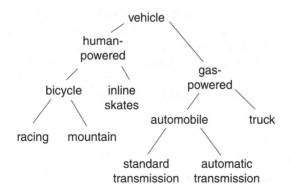

A language is said to be *object-oriented* if it supports class inheritance. *Inheritance* lets you create a new class by extending the functionality of an existing class. The original class is called the *superclass*. The class that is created from a superclass is called its *subclass*. A subclass inherits all of a superclass's operations and state.

Inheritance is an important idea in computer languages. It saves effort by allowing us to create new classes from existing ones. We do not have to write a class from scratch. We can take advantage of the features of an existing one. In addition, we can localize common features of classes in one superclass. This allows us to talk about all objects that inherit from a single superclass using a single identifier. This is the idea behind *polymorphism*, which we will discuss in Chapter 16.

The `RoomCleaningSimulation` (Listing 1.1) and `StarryNight` (Listing 3.1) classes inherit the `Applet` class. In other words, they get functionality from and add functionality to the `Applet` class. Classes that inherit from the `Applet` class are able to be run from a web browser; they contain a window and respond to paint events. As a result, it is not necessary to write code that supports the web, creates a window, or responds to events. We can simply inherit all the work done in the `Applet` class to accomplish these tasks.

In the physical world each class in a hierarchy has characteristics that are modifications or additions to the characteristics in the classes from which it inherits. For example, in the class of gas-powered vehicles it is assumed that there is a procedure that starts its engine. However, we do not know what that procedure should be for the general class of vehicles. For example, to save weight a race car may not have a starter at all. To start a race car, it is necessary to snap on a portable starter and then remove it once the engine has fired up.

Thus, by looking at Figure 3.1 we can imagine that the definition of gas-powered vehicles has an operation that starts its engine. However, the class of gas-powered vehicles is much too general for us to define what that procedure is; therefore we leave it empty. We overwrite this empty procedure in the new class that inherits it. For example, an automobile with an automatic transmission inherits the empty starting procedure from the gas-powered class. We override the empty procedure with the following:

1. Insert key.
2. Make sure the car is in park.
3. Turn the key all the way to the right.
4. After the engine has started, release the key.

We can also override the inherited procedure for starting a car with a standard transmission:

1. Insert key.

2. Make sure the emergency brake is set.

3. Throw in the clutch.

4. Turn the key all the way to the right.

5. After the engine has started, release the key.

> A method (procedure or operation) that is inherited from a superclass may be reimplemented in the subclass. This new method is said to *override* the inherited method.

Some operations are supplied by a superclass with the expectation that they will be overridden. For example, the `init` method in the `RoomCleaningSimulation` class is one such method. By overriding the `init` method we create an operation that will be executed when an applet starts up. The `StarryNight` applet described in this chapter illustrates another overridden method. By overriding the `paint` method, we create an operation that will be executed when an applet's window must be repainted.

3.3 Starry Night

The `RoomCleaningSimulation` program makes extensive use of graphics. One of our goals is to learn how to create our own graphics programs. In this section we will learn how to extend the `Applet` class and how to use the Java `Graphics` class to display graphics.

> Starry Night requirements: Display the painting of van Gogh's *The Starry Night* within a frame and on an easel. Draw an image of the painter adding some finishing touches to his painting. Figure 3.2 illustrates how the scene looks.

The code that implements these requirements is found in Listing 3.1. It begins by inheriting the `Applet` class in Line 17, which allows us to begin with all the functionality of an applet. As mentioned above, an applet will run over the web and open a window within which we can draw. More applet details are found in Section 3.5.

`StarryNight` is the new subclass that we are creating from the `Applet` superclass. One of the methods that the `Applet` class provides is the `paint` method. The code we place in the `paint` method, Lines 24 through 74, will display graphics within our win-

Figure 3.2 The StarryNight Applet Display

dow. The `paint` method was specifically created so that it could be overridden in the same way we overrode the engine-starting procedure in the previous section.

All applets have a `paint` method that displays graphics in a window on a web page. The `paint` method we inherit from the `Applet` class is empty; it does nothing because there is no code within it. It is expected that the programmer will override that method. What that `paint` method does can be different for each applet.

The `paint` method is executed whenever a web browser determines that the applet display must be redrawn. For example, if another window covers the applet's display and that window disappears, the graphics display must be redrawn.

Listing 3.1 The StarryNight Applet

```
1  //*******************************************************************
2  //
3  // title:   The Starry Night
4  //
5  // Display the painting of van Gogh's The Starry Night within a
6  // frame and on an easel.  Draw an image of the painter adding
7  // some finishing touches to his painting.
8  //
9  //*******************************************************************
10
11 import java.awt.Color;
12 import java.awt.Graphics;
13 import java.awt.Image;
14 import java.awt.Polygon;
15 import java.applet.Applet;
16
17 public class StarryNight extends Applet
18 {
19   //--------- paint ---------------------------------------------
20   //
21   // The image of van Gogh painting is drawn.
22
23   public void paint (Graphics g)
24   {
25     setBackground (Color.white);
26
27     // draw frame
28     g.setColor(Color.blue);
29     g.fillRect(  0,   0, 140, 120);
30
31     // draw the easel
32     g.setColor(Color.black);
33     g.drawLine( 30, 120,   0, 240);
34     g.drawLine(110, 120, 140, 240);
35     g.drawLine( 70, 120,  70, 240);
36
37     // draw the painting
38     Image starryNight = getImage(getDocumentBase(),
39                       "starryNight.gif");
40     g.drawImage (starryNight, 10, 10, this);
41
42     // draw van Gogh's head
43     Image vanGogh = getImage(getDocumentBase(), "head.gif");
44     g.drawImage (vanGogh, 170, 10, this);
45
```

Listing 3.1 The StarryNight Applet

```
46        // draw his torso
47        g.setColor(Color.darkGray);
48        g.fillOval(180, 60, 50, 100);
49
50        // draw arm
51        Polygon arm = new Polygon();
52        arm.addPoint(225,   80);
53        arm.addPoint(165,  130);
54        arm.addPoint(110,   90);
55        arm.addPoint(165,  110);
56        arm.addPoint(185,   80);
57        g.fillPolygon (arm);
58
59        // draw paint brush
60        g.setColor(Color.red);
61        g.drawLine(115,   80, 105, 100);
62        g.setColor(Color.yellow);
63        g.fillOval(103, 100,   5,    5);
64
65        // draw leg
66        g.setColor(Color.black);
67        Polygon leg = new Polygon();
68        leg.addPoint(230, 130);
69        leg.addPoint(210, 240);
70        leg.addPoint(170, 240);
71        leg.addPoint(200, 230);
72        leg.addPoint(180, 130);
73        g.fillPolygon (leg);
74    }
75 }
```

The paint method provides us with a "graphics context" object that we have named g in Line 23. A graphics context object is associated with the window in which we are drawing. Applying operations to a graphics context, we draw images and change its drawing state. For example, the default drawing color is black. In Line 28 we change the state of the drawing color to blue. Thus, when we draw a rectangle in Line 29, it is blue.

We use the sequential pattern from Chapter 1 within the paint method. For example, the picture frame is drawn in Line 29 before the painting is drawn in Line 40. If the drawing order were reversed, the painting would not be visible. A blue rectangle would cover it.

Other lines of code draw ovals, lines, images, and polygons. For example, Line 51 creates van Gogh's arm by creating a polygon object. A polygon can have any number of sides. They are specified by adding points to a polygon that represent the vertices of the object. We will look more carefully at these graphics objects in Section 3.6.

PATTERNS

3.4   Framework Patterns

Many software systems share a common organization. For example, the basic organization of compilers is similar. There is a component that partitions the incoming source code into tokens, another that checks for syntax errors, another that generates the target code, and yet another that maintains a list of identifiers and their meanings. Because many compilers use the same components, it is desirable to build compiler frameworks that make it easier to create compilers.

> A *framework* is a set of interacting classes that are designed to support the construction of a particular kind of software system. A framework can be customized to solve a particular problem by creating custom subclasses of the framework classes.

Frameworks can be used to create text editors, graphics editors, computer-aided design tools, financial modeling applications, and many other software systems. An applet is an example of a framework for creating programs with a window that run over the web.

Technically, frameworks are different from patterns. A pattern is language-independent and more abstract. A pattern describes general ways of organizing objects or statements to accomplish a task and allows us to share software design ideas. A framework, on the other hand, is implemented with a specific language to solve specialized problems. Frameworks allow us to share only code.

3.4.1   Name

Applet Framework.

3.4.2   Problem

Creating a program that runs over the web is a complex task. A web browser must be able to initialize the program, start the program when its page is visited, stop the program when the page is left, and return resources, such as memory needed by the applet window, back to the web browser once the program is no longer needed. In addition, the program must repaint its display when obscuring windows are removed, it must have a mechanism for responding to mouse events, and it must support graphical user interface elements, such as buttons and text fields.

Much of the code for each web program is similar to code for other web programs. We would like to ease the development process by writing this identical code only once and sharing it with all other web programs.

3.4.3   Solution

A solution to this problem is the Java applet framework described in Section 3.5. The Java applet removes much of the difficulty of creating a program that produces a display window and runs over the web. We get the full functionality of an applet by extending it. We are required only to add code specific to our particular application. As a result, we can build web programs quickly.

3.4.4   Consequences

Frameworks are designed to support the most common instances of a class of problems. They cannot anticipate each possible variation. As a result, a framework may not contain support code that is needed for some specialized applications. The framework may be organized in such a way that it is easy to use for many programs, but difficult to use for some other programs. In addition, some programs may need only a simple solution. An applet may be an overkill. It may give us functionality and code we do not need. The result may be a program that is larger or slower than a completely custom program would be.

When we run a program from someone's web page on our computer, we want to be sure that the program will not harm or access personal information in our computer. Applets must preserve the security of our local computer. As a consequence, applets have restrictions placed on the them. For example, they are not allowed to access local files.

There are many computer platforms, each with its own underlying machine language. For example, programs written for the Macintosh will not run on a Windows computer. A program written for Windows will not run on a Sparc. One solution to this problem is to create a special computer language that can be interpreted on each platform. Java has solved this problem by creating a byte-code representation of a program (Section 1.8.1). The result is a time penalty. Java byte-code interpreters typically run programs 20 times slower than native programs.

JAVA

Thus far we have learned about the benefits of using inheritance to extend a framework. In this section we will take a closer look at the Java applet framework. In addition, we will look at several other Java classes—Graphics, Color, and Polygon—which we will use to create graphics images. Learning all the details about these classes is much too ambitious. We will focus most heavily on the core functionality of two of these classes—Applet and Graphics—and only introduce a few ideas about the other classes as needed. More detail can be found in Appendix B. However, a proper reference for all the classes in Java requires thousands of pages. Appendix B documents only the most useful methods of a subset of Java classes. We will begin with a look at how Java applets are organized.

3.5   Applets

3.5.1   Creating an Applet

The basic form of an applet used in the StarryNight program is shown in Listing 3.2. Lines 6 through 9 show how the paint method is incorporated into an applet. The code that draws things in the display is placed at Line 8. The extends keyword in Line 4 specifies that StarryNight inherits from Applet.

> An *applet* is a Java program that extends the Applet class. As a result, it can be run from a web browser, contains a window, and responds to paint events. Applet is an example of a class that is designed specifically to be extended. The Applet class itself is never instantiated.

Listing 3.2 Basic Form of a Graphics Applet

```
1  import java.awt.Graphics;
2  import java.applet.Applet;
3
4  public class StarryNight extends Applet
5  {
6     public void paint (Graphics g)
7     {
8         Operations that draw on the computer display.
9     }
10 }
```

Inheritance does not stop at the `Applet` class. Applets inherit from panels that inherit from containers that inherit from components that inherit from objects (see Figure 3.3). As a result, all the operations and states associated with an `Object`, `Component`, `Container`, and `Panel` class are also associated with an `Applet` class. There are almost 200 methods in all these classes. We will cover a few of the most important ones.

Figure 3.3 Applet Inheritance Hierarchy

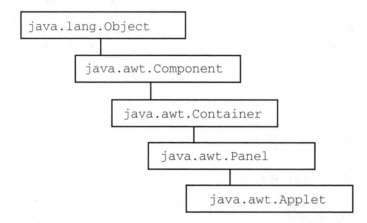

Five important methods inherited from an `Applet` class are `destroy`, `init`, `paint`, `start`, and `stop`. These methods are unique. All of them do nothing, so they must be overridden to be useful.

Each one of these five methods is called at specific times during the lifetime of an applet. The `start` method is called when an applet first starts executing. The `paint` method is called when the display window must be redrawn; for example, when the applet first begins executing, when it is deiconified (maximized), and when a window covering the applet window disappears. The events that cause each one to execute are summarized below and in Figure 3.4:

The typical sequence of events within a web browser is as follows. When a web browser encounters a page with an applet tag, the browser loads the class file (*.class) over the network from the same place that contained the HTML file. Next it creates an instance of the applet class and applies the `init` operation to it. If the `init` method has not been overridden, the browser will execute the inherited `init` method, which does nothing. When the applet is scrolled into view, the browser will apply the `start` and `paint` methods to the applet object. The code in the `paint` method will redraw the applet display. If the user

Figure 3.4 Transition States of an Applet

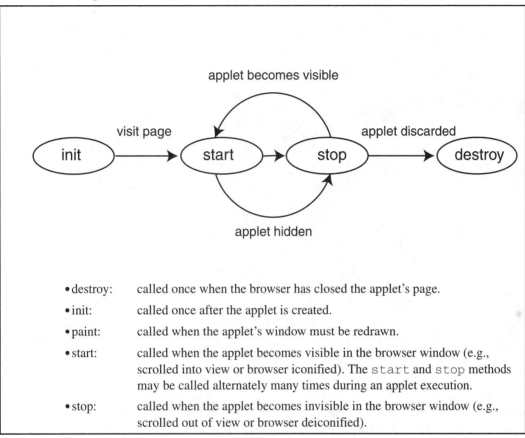

- destroy: called once when the browser has closed the applet's page.
- init: called once after the applet is created.
- paint: called when the applet's window must be redrawn.
- start: called when the applet becomes visible in the browser window (e.g., scrolled into view or browser iconified). The start and stop methods may be called alternately many times during an applet execution.
- stop: called when the applet becomes invisible in the browser window (e.g., scrolled out of view or browser deiconified).

scrolls the applet out of view, the stop method will be called. When the user scrolls the applet back into view, the start method will be called a second time. Alternate calls between start and stop can occur indefinitely. When a new web page is visited, the destroy method is called. These methods can appear within an applet class in any order. We will usually find them in alphabetic order in this text.

Figure 3.4 shows the timing relationship between the init, start, stop, and destroy methods. We know from this diagram that init is always called first and start second. We know that a call to start will always precede a call to stop. What we do not know is when paint is called. Therefore, make no assumptions—do not assume that init is called before paint or that paint is called before init.

Listing 3.3 shows an applet shell containing methods that respond to each of these five events. Since each of these methods contains no code, the methods do nothing. They are included here to demonstrate that each of them look the same except for the name of the method.

Listing 3.3 An Applet Shell

```
1  import java.awt.Graphics;
2  import java.applet.Applet;
3
4  public class Shell extends Applet
5  {
6      public void destroy ()
7      {
8      }
9      public void init ()
10     {
11     }
12     public void paint (Graphics g)
13     {
14     }
15     public void start ()
16     {
17     }
18     public void stop ()
19     {
20     }
21 }
```

Notice the inclusion of each keyword and the locations of the curly brackets. A left bracket in Line 5 indicates the beginning of the `Shell` class and the right bracket in Line 21 ends it. In a similar fashion, the left bracket in Line 13 indicates the beginning of the `paint` method and the right bracket in Line 14 ends it.

Chapter 6 and Chapter 7 will explore in greater depth how to create methods and classes. For now, we must accept the basic form of an applet and not deviate from it. For example, `paint` must be in all lowercase letters and the `Graphics` parameter must not be missing. We must be careful to spell all these names correctly and match letter case. An applet will compile and run if the method names are misspelled. However, the method will not be called by the expected event. For example, the following code will compile correctly, but the Java runtime system will not be able to find either of the `paint` methods defined. As a result, the empty inherited `paint` method will be called. A window will be displayed with no content.

```
public void Paint (Graphics g)   // capitalization error
{
  // this method will not be called by a paint event
}
public void paint ()            // parameter error
{
  // this method will not be called by a paint event
}
```

As mentioned above, there are about 200 methods provided by the `Applet` class. We have taken a look at five of these methods whose primary purpose is to be overridden. The majority of the methods provided by the Applet class implement useful functions that are not meant to be overridden. Two of these methods, `getImage` and `getDocument-Base`, are used in Line 38 of Listing 3.1 on page 95. They are used to read images from a file and are explored in Section 3.6.5. A small subset of applet methods is also documented in Appendix B on page 845.

3.5.2   Import

Lines 1 and 2 in Listing 3.2 provide access to two classes: `Graphics` and `Applet`. Without these two lines, the references to `Graphics` and `Applet` in Lines 4 and 6 would cause a syntax error.

The *import* keyword requests access to a class or class library. The identifier `java` indicates that the class is part of the standard Java libraries. The `awt` and `applet` identifiers specify particular libraries. *Libraries* are repositories of code that we can use when we program. The AWT (Abstract Windowing Toolkit) library contains graphics, window, and graphical user interface classes. One library is automatically included with all Java programs. It is the `java.lang` class library. There is no need to import it.

It is not necessary to spell out each member of a library to include it. For example, the following will import all classes in the AWT library.

```
import java.awt.*;
```

The author usually imports each class explicitly. Thus, by looking at the import statements, he can quickly determine which classes a particular program requires. The author uses this information to remind him to describe within the text each class used in a program. It's tempting to argue that importing all classes in a library may cause a program to compile slower, but this may not be true or significant depending on the way programmers have implemented the compiler. No recommendations are made.

3.6   Drawing Graphics

We will now shift our focus to using the AWT class library to draw graphics images.

3.6.1   Graphics Context

The Graphics class is used to create graphics context objects. A graphics context holds state information about the location of the drawing window, what the drawing color is, and which font should be used to write text. We will cover a few of the most useful methods in this section. Additional methods are documented in Appendix B on page 867.

The modified Cartesian coordinate system is used in Java's graphic context. The upper-left corner of the display is the origin with positive x going right and positive y going down. (See Figure 3.5.)

Figure 3.5 Coordinate System

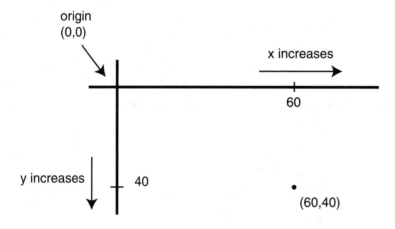

3.6.2   Drawing Rectangles

One operation that can be applied to a graphics class is to draw a rectangle. For example, the code in Listing 3.4 draws a blue box. Its output is shown in Figure 3.6.

The paint method begins in Line 7. A key component of the paint declaration is the parameter g. Since g is an instance of the Graphics class, it holds state information about the graphics window where all the drawing will take place. Within the paint method, g will be the object on which draw operations are applied. Normally single character names are not appropriate because they are not descriptive. g is used so pervasively in Java programs for graphics context objects that we allow an exception here.

Listing 3.4 The BlueBox Applet

```
1   import java.awt.Color;
2   import java.awt.Graphics;
3   import java.applet.Applet;
4
5   public class BlueBox extends Applet
6   {
7     public void paint (Graphics g)
8     {
9       setBackground(Color.white);
10      g.setColor(Color.blue);
11      g.fillRect(60, 40, 200, 100);
12    }
13  }
```

As is the case for all objects, g has a state. The state of g includes the current drawing color, the text font, and a pointer to the region of the screen buffer where it can draw things. g does not include any display pixels as part of its state. It is not possible to find out from g how the display currently looks. Thus, if the portion of the display to which g points is covered by another window, it is not possible to recover g's part of the window when the obscuring window is removed. Instead, the part of the display belonging to g must be recreated. The paint method is responsible for recreating g's image.

In Line 10 the method setColor is applied to the graphics object g. From this point on, until the setColor operation is applied again or the paint method is completed, blue will be used to draw lines, rectangles, and text.

Line 11 draws the rectangle. This is done by applying the fillRect method to the object g. The fillRect method has four parameters. Each parameter is given in pixel units where a pixel represents a single dot on the computer display. The parameters follow:

1. 60: the x location of the upper left-hand corner of the box
2. 40: the y location of the upper left-hand corner of the box
3. 200: the box width
4. 100: the box height

The order of Lines 10 and 11 is important. Recall our discussion about the sequential patterns in Section 1.3. If Line 11 were to precede Line 10, the box would have been the default graphics color, black. The order of the statements within the paint method

Figure 3.6 The BlueBox Applet Display (with Annotations)

window origin (0,0)

Applet Viewer: BlueBox.class

blue box origin (60,40)

100

200

applet started

describes the order that operations will be applied when the `paint` method is evoked. The drawing color must be set to blue before a blue box can be drawn.

The operations `fillRect` and `drawRect` do nearly the same thing. The `drawRect` operation draws only an outline of a rectangle. A `fillRect` operation fills it inside with the current drawing color. See below. These operations have counterparts for ovals and polygons as well.

drawRect   fillRect

3.6.3 Drawing Ovals and Lines

Looking at the `StarryNight` program in Listing 3.1, it is now possible to pick out the portions of the program that draw the initial starry night scene. The `fillOval` operation, Line 51, is used to draw van Gogh's torso. The `fillOval` has four parameters just as the `fillRect` operation described above. Each parameter has the same function in `fillOval` that it has in `fillRect`. The upper left-hand corner of an oval is the upper left-hand corner of the enclosing rectangle (see below).

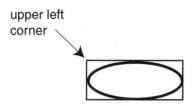

The `drawLine` operation also has four parameters, as in Line 32. They define the beginning and end points of a line as follows:

1. The x location of the start of a line

2. The y location of the start of a line

3. The x location of the end of a line

4. The y location of the end of a line

3.6.4 Painting Polygons

A polygon is used to draw van Gogh's legs and arms in Listing 3.1. Drawing a polygon is more complex because polygons have a variable number of corners. Because each method must have a set number of parameters, we cannot specify a polygon with a single operation. A different approach is taken to draw polygons than is taken to draw rectangles. First a polygon object is created, and then points are added to it. An example of drawing a star is shown in Listing 3.5 and Figure 3.7.

First a `star` object of class `Polygon` is created in Line 12. Then, by applying the `addPoint` method multiple times to the `star` object, the five points of this star are defined in Lines 13 through 18. The order the points are added to the polygon is important. The order they are added determines the order in which they are accessed to create connected lines. Finally, the `fillPolygon` method is used in Line 19 to draw the star.

The polygon was finished by adding the beginning point again as the last point. It is necessary to add the beginning point twice when `drawPolygon` is used. This will complete

Listing 3.5 Star Applet

```
1  import java.awt.Color;
2  import java.awt.Graphics;
3  import java.awt.Polygon;
4  import java.applet.Applet;
5
6  public class Star extends Applet
7  {
8     public void paint (Graphics g)
9     {
10        setBackground(Color.black);
11        g.setColor(Color.yellow);
12        Polygon star = new Polygon();
13        star.addPoint(50,10);
14        star.addPoint(74,82);
15        star.addPoint(14,38);
16        star.addPoint(86,38);
17        star.addPoint(26,82);
18        star.addPoint(50,10);
19        g.fillPolygon(star);
20     }
21 }
```

Figure 3.7 Star Display

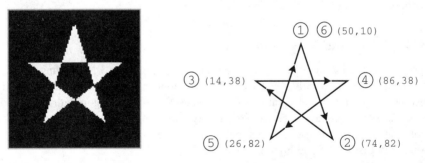

the drawing to the starting point. It is not necessary to add the beginning point at the end if `fillPolygon` is used. The `Polygon` class is summarized in Appendix B on page 895.

Java treats polygons, rectangles, and lines inconsistently. While there is a `Polygon` and `Rectangle` classes, there is no line class. When we want to draw a line in a graphics context, we use the `drawLine` method, which requires us to specify the beginning and ending points. The `drawLine` method does not have a line object parameter. When we draw a `Polygon`, we pass the `drawPoly` method a `Polygon` object. There is no method in the `Graphics` class that will draw a polygon without sending it a `Polygon` object. Just the opposite approach was taken with `Rectangle` objects. There are `Rectangle` objects, but there are no methods in the `Graphics` class that will draw a `Rectangle` object. The `drawRect` method requires that the location, width, and height of a rectangle is specified. For example:

```
g.drawRect (17, 36, 53, 28);
```

or

```
Rectangle r = new Rectangle (17, 36, 53, 28);
g.drawRect(r.x, r.y, r.width, r.height);
```

but not

```
Rectangle r = new Rectangle (17, 36, 53, 28);
g.drawRect(r);          // syntax error - no such method
```

Thus, the rectangles, ovals, and lines we see in a graphics image are not objects. They are only bits of color set by applying appropriate operations. We might prefer that the Java designers had included line objects and treated all graphics objects consistently by allowing us to draw them directly. They chose not to.

3.6.5   Painting an Image

The last element needed to understand the `StarryNight` applet in Listing 3.1 is images. An applet that will paint the single image in Figure 3.8 is shown in Listing 3.6. Line 9 reads an image from a file. Notice that there is no `new` operation in this line.

Listing 3.6 Display The Starry Night by Itself

```
1  import java.awt.Graphics;
2  import java.awt.Image;
3  import java.applet.Applet;
4
5  public class StarryNight extends Applet
6  {
7    public void paint (Graphics g)
8    {
9        Image starryNight  =
10               getImage(getDocumentBase(), "starryNight.gif");
11       g.drawImage (starryNight, 10, 20, this);
12    }
13 }
```

The `getImage` method in Line 10 is responsible for creating the image object. However, the image that has just been created is typically not in memory. Instead it may be on a local

Figure 3.8 The Starry Night Display

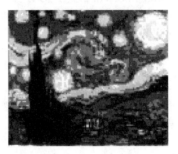

disk or at some other web site. The `getDocumentBase` method tells Java to look for the image file in the same folder that the HTML file was found.

Finally, the image is drawn in Line 11 by applying the `drawImage` method to `g` (Figure 3.9.) Because the image is not in memory, it will be read from a disk. This will cause a delay before the image is shown. Although the image is not in memory, control returns from the `drawImage` method immediately and continues on to any statements that follow.

Figure 3.9 Drawing an Image

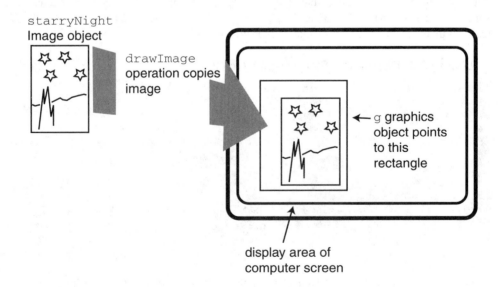

Drawing *The Starry Night* image on the display requires the interaction of several objects. The g object, as stated previously, points to the region of the display where drawing may take place. The starryNight object contains an image. The drawImage operation copies the starryNight image into the display.

The first parameter is the name of the image object to be drawn; the second and third parameters refer to the x and y locations of the upper-left corner of the image. The fourth parameter, this, is harder to explain. Let it suffice to say that the this parameter is needed because the image may not yet be in memory and some communication must be made with the this applet. All this added complication is done for the sake of efficiency and convenience. Given that the image being drawn may originate on another continent, it is not convenient to postpone execution of the rest of the applet while the remote host is being notified and the image is loaded into memory. If the image has already been loaded by some other operation, the applet can find it and display it immediately.

A Butler object requires four images to draw it. One if it is going up, one if it is going to the right, one for down, and one for going to the left. The four images are shown in Figure 3.10.

Figure 3.10 The Four Butler Images

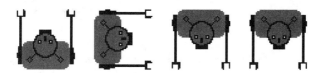

A paint method for drawing butlers is shown in Listing 3.7. The variables myDeltaX and myDeltaY specify how many squares and in what direction the butler moves every turn. myDeltaX is added to a butler's x position. If myDeltaX is negative, the butler will move left and should, therefore, be facing left. See Lines 9 and 10.

Java can read images in the GIF (Graphic Interchange Format) and JPEG (Joint Photographic Expert Group) formats. GIF images are limited to 256 colors (8 bit) and thus work well for line drawings, cartoons, text, and illustrations. JPEG images, on the other hand, use 24 bits for colors. They may contain over 16 million colors. JPEG works well for continuous-tone images such as photographs. Each of these image formats uses compression to save file space.

Listing 3.7 Paint the Butler

```
1    public void paint (Graphics g)
2    {
3      // choose the correct butler image
4      Image image = null;
5      if (myDeltaX == 1)
6        image = getImage(getDocumentBase(), "butlerRight.gif");
7      else if (myDeltaY == 1)
8        image = getImage(getDocumentBase(), "butlerDown.gif");
9      else if (myDeltaX == -1)
10       image = getImage(getDocumentBase(), "butlerLeft.gif");
11     else
12       image = getImage(getDocumentBase(), "butlerUp.gif");
13
14     // draw the butler
15     g.drawImage (image, myX, myY, myRoom);
16   }
```

3.6.6   RGB Color

Each `Color` object is composed of a red, green, and blue (RGB) component. Each component may have a value between 0 and 255. Thus, by combining these color components in various intensities, it is possible to represent 16,777,216 (256^3) unique colors. Whether the hardware will display this many colors depends on software settings as well as the amount of video memory a computer has.

The color black is created when the valuesall three RGB components are 0. White is created when all are 255. Java provides several predefined colors that can be used by specifying the `Color` class followed by the color name. For example, `Color.yellow` provides us with the yellow color. Other available colors are black, blue, cyan, dark gray, gray, green, light gray, magenta, orange, pink, red, white, and yellow. All other colors must be created by using a color constructor. An example of creating a "spicy pink" oval is shown in Listing 3.8. Table B.6 on page 855 shows the RGB values for about 100 other colors. Operations supported by the `Color` class are documented in Appendix B.

Listing 3.8 User-defined Color

```
1 public void paint (Graphics g)
2 {
3   Color spicyPink = new Color(255, 28, 174);
4   setBackground(Color.white);
5   g.setColor(spicyPink);
6   g.fillOval(50,30,150,75);
7 }
```

3.7   This

In the previous sections, we avoided explaining several lines of code such as Line 9 of Listing 3.4. Line 9 is needed to set the background color of the window to white. This makes the drawing area clearly visible against the gray color of the rest of the applet window. The `setBackgound` operation takes a color parameter, which in this case is white.

The reason we postponed the explanation of Line 9 is because its form is different from other code we have seen. In Chapter 1, we stated that the syntax for applying operations to objects requires an object followed by an operation. The `setBackground` operation appears to have broken that syntax rule:

```
object.operation(parameters);
```

There appears to be no object to which `setBackground` is being applied. In fact, the `setBackground` operation is being applied to this BlueBox applet. Line 9 could be rewritten as follows.

```
this.setBackground(Color.white);
```

If no specific object is stated, then the `this` object is assumed. What is the `this` object? Recall our discussion in Section 1.8.2 about the creation of an object when a web browser opens an applet. The web browser creates an instance of an applet. In this example the object that is created is an instance of the `BlueBox` class. It has an identity, but because we are working inside the `BlueBox` class, there is no way to determine what name the web browser has chosen for `this` object. In fact, it may not be given a name at all. Therefore, it is referred to as `this` object. In other words, the `setBackground` operation is being applied to `this` applet, which is an instance of the `BlueBox` class, which was created by the browser.

In a similar manner, Line 9 in Listing 3.6 can be rewritten as:

```
Image starryNight =
    this.getImage(this.getDocumentBase(), "starryNight.gif");
```

A example from the physical world may help us understand "this." Suppose we are in charge of writing instructions that describe how freshmen should proceed on registration day. These instructions will be handed out to each freshman upon arrival on campus, and they will be asked to carry them out. The instructions we write might look as follows:

- Fill out the enclosed registration form.
- Take it to your advisor for a signature.
- Bring it to the registrar's office.

Suppose Elmer Snid and Emma Lou are freshmen and they are given our instructions. In our object-oriented world we view Elmer and Emma as instances of the class `freshmen`. When Elmer reads the instruction: "Fill out the enclosed registration form," he understands that it means him. Similarly, when Emma reads the same instruction, she knows it refers to her. The object of the operation "Fill out the enclosed registration form" is implied. It is written to whoever is reading the instructions.

We could rewrite these instructions to be more explicit. We could write:

```
You fill out the enclosed registration form.
```

or

```
Self fill out the enclosed registration form.
```

or

```
This fill out the enclosed registration form.
```

The programming language Smalltalk uses the keyword "self" while C++ and Java use the keyword "this" to refer to the implied object. What we cannot do is write:

```
Emma Lou fill out the enclosed registration form.
```

or

```
Elmer Snid fill out the enclosed registration form.
```

If we used Emma's name explicitly and if all freshmen got the same copy of the instructions, then only Emma would follow the instructions. It just does not make sense to use someone's name explicitly because no one knows who all the freshmen will be next year or the years after that.

Let us look at how freshmen register one more time. Emma has a copy of the `register` method (the sheet with the above instructions on it). An admissions counselor then applies the `register` operation on Emma by saying:

```
Emma.register();
```

Emma than reads and carries out the `register` method. Every place it gives a command without specifying an object, she knows that she is the object of the operation. Every place it says apply an operation to "this" object, she knows that "this" refers to her.

3.8   Comments Revisited

In Section 1.7 we described how to embed comments within a program. This section describes how comments can be used to document the purpose of a program and its history. Comments are also used to make methods easy to locate and understand.

- Class header comments: Place a block of comments at the beginning of each class. The author likes to put a box around the header so it stands out. See Listing 1.1 on page 9 for an example. Class header comments often have the following fields:

```
-title: the name of the class.
-author: who created the class.
-date: when the first version was finished.
-update: date, reason, and the author of any modifications.
-The purpose of the class with additional information that
will help readers understand when this class should be used.
```

- Method header comments: Place a block of comments at the beginning of each method to describe what the operation does. Methods can be easier to find by embedding the method name in dashes. Methods should not stand out with the same intensity as the class header comments. See Listing 3.1 on page 95 for an example above the `paint` method. Method header comments have the following fields:

```
- name embedded in dashes.
- presumptions about the limits of parameters and known
  problems about this method.
```

- Embedded comments: Embedded comments are used to partition blocks of code into units that provide a particular function. Listing 3.1 on page 95 provides an example. Notice the use of blank lines to help partition the code into small chunks.

- Indentation: Notice how the code in the examples is indented. The `import` statements and class declaration are flush left. The `paint` method is indented two spaces. This indention communicates that the `paint` method is contained within the `Starry-Night` class. Finally, Line 25 in Listing 3.1 is indented another two spaces, indicating that it is contained within the `paint` method. Following a consistent indention scheme, such as the one illustrated above, makes our programs easier to read. For example, it makes it easy to see which code is part of a method because it is all indented a couple of spaces to the right.

REFERENCE

3.9   Summary

Inheritance is used to create a program by extending a framework. By extending the `Applet` class, we are able to build upon an applet's ability to work over the web, create a window, and respond to paint events. We accomplish this through inheritance and by overriding methods provided by the `Applet` class.

Inheritance allows us to create a new class of objects by extending the functionality of an existing class. The original class is called the superclass and the class that inherits from it is called the subclass.

A framework is a set of interacting classes that are designed to support the construction of a particular kind of software system. It can be customized to solve a particular problem by creating custom subclasses of the framework classes. Frameworks are not patterns because frameworks provide their benefit by sharing code and, thus, ease our development effort. They are written in a specific computer language. Patterns, on the other hand, are general-purpose design ideas that are language-independent. Their benefit is to make software design easier.

A graphic context is another example of an object. Its state includes the current drawing color, the current font, and the location of the drawing area. Operations can be applied to a graphics object to change the current drawing color and to draw rectangles, ovals, lines, polygons, and images.

The `paint` method is the standard place to put graphics code within an applet. The `paint` method is called whenever a window is resized, deiconified, or unobstructed. It has a single parameter, which defines the graphics context.

Colors are represented by three values: red, green, and blue (RGB). Specifying these colors with values between 0 and 255 can create 16,777,216 different colors.

Polygons are objects with a variable numbers of sides. They can be created and have points added to them. They can then be drawn in a graphics context.

`this` is a keyword to refer to the object to which a given operation is applied. If an operation name appears with no class or object identifier before it, `this` is assumed by default.

3.10   Bibliography

- Gamma, Erich, Richard Helm, Ralph Johnson, and John Vlissides. 1995. *Design Patterns: Elements of Reusable Object-Oriented Software*. Reading, MA: Addison-Wesley.

  Often referred to as the gang of four (GOF) book. The material on frameworks came from it.

Acknowledgments

Sonia Frojen, a CS203 student in the fall of 1997, for the basis of the graphic on page 89. It was an outcome of exercise 11 in this chapter.

REFERENCE

PROBLEM SETS

3.11   Exercises

Inheritance—Section 3.2

1   Create a hierarchy diagram, such as the one in Figure 3.1 on page 91, that captures:

a.   sporting events sponsored by your school.

b.   the student government at you school.

c.   some of your favorite foods.

d.   the clothes you typically wear.

Frameworks—Section 3.4

2   A store-bought pizza mix is an example of a framework. It contains all the basic ingredients that we inherit to create a custom pizza. We enhance the mix by adding our own toppings. Name any other frameworks, other than food, that are available in the physical world.

3   Your job is to design a document framework for writing a term paper. It should help create term papers with a title page, a table of contents, footnotes, and a bibliography. Describe the components of such a document framework.

Applets—Section 3.5

4   There are 10 errors in the code below. Find them.

```
Import java.awt.Graphics;
public class StarryNight extend applet {
  public paint (Graphics g)
     g.setColor(blue);
     g.filloval (50, 50, 75)
  }
}
```

Graphics—Section 3.6

5 Using the `drawLine` operation, write a `paint` method for drawing a box at location (10,20) that is 35 pixels wide and 15 pixels high.

6 Reorder the lines of the `paint` method in Listing 3.5 on page 108 so that a pentagon is drawn.

7 How many bytes are required to store 32-bit color images on a 640-by-480 pixel display? 32-bit color means that each pixel requires 32 bits (4 bytes). How many unique colors can be displayed if only 24 of those bits are used for color information?

8 Write a `paint` method that draws a solid gold box with a red square around it. See Table B.6 on page 855.

This—Section 3.7

9 Write a list of instructions for making a peanut butter sandwich. Number your instructions beginning at 1.

    a. Do not use any pronouns, such as "you." The pronoun "you" should be implied in each instruction.

    b. Rewrite the instructions inserting "self" everywhere that an implied "you" belongs.

    c. Rewrite the instructions inserting "this" for "self."

3.12 Projects

Figure 3.11 Concentric Squares

10 Create a Java program that displays three concentric boxes as shown in Figure 3.11.

The order in which these boxes are drawn is important. The last box drawn will cover earlier boxes.

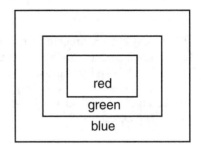

11 Create a Java program that draws one of the following using graphics operations:
 a. House
 b. Jack-o'-lantern
 c. Automobile
 d. Birthday cake
 e. Cat or some other animal
 f. City skyline
 g. Starry night
 h. Your favorite space alien
 i. Something of your own choosing

12 Create a Java program that draws a goatee and silly hat on an image. Use your image, the image of your instructor from their home page, or the image of van Gogh. The author's image is off limits.

13 Create a new color that is not in Table B.6 on page 855. Give it a name and draw a figure of your choice using it.

4 User Interfaces

Gas Mileage

4.1   Objectives

Concepts   Section 4.2, page 123

The primary focus of this chapter is human and computer interaction. We will learn how to read and display information in text-based and graphical-based environments. We will be introduced to an author-designed Java class that simplifies writing interactive programs. A supplementary section summarizes how the operations in these classes work so that interactive programming can be done without the author's classes.

Patterns   Section 4.3, page 134

We are introduced to Java applications and the IPO (input-process-output) pattern for getting information from a program user, processing that information, and displaying the results. We will also use the sentinel and counter loop patterns of the previous chapter and introduce the loop-and-a-half pattern to input data, validate it, process that information, and display results.

Java Skills

Next we address how we can use the author's interactive classes.

- VApplet, VActionButton, VField, and
  VLabel   Section 4.2.3, page 127
- VApplicationIO class.   Section 4.2.1, page 123

Abilities

By the end of this chapter we should be able to do the following:

- Create programs that use the IPO (input-process-output) pattern.
- Write programs that use counter loops to input, process, and output results.

CONCEPTS

4.2   User Interfaces

The programs we have seen thus far are atypical. Once these programs begin executing there is no interaction between the program and the program user. Their output is predetermined. For example, the butler in the programs from Chapter 1 and Chapter 2 cannot respond to human control once started. In addition, the output of the graphics programs in Chapter 3 is set once the program starts. It is important for many programs to interact with the user to get information and respond to commands.

In this section we will look at two strategies for incorporating human interaction into a program. Programs were primarily programmer-driven (text-based) through the middle 1980s. A program would display some text on a display and wait for a user to respond to it. The first strategy we will learn will be programmer-driven.

A second strategy began to develop in the 1970s at Xerox PARC (Palo Alto Research Center), where a graphical user interface (GUI) was developed. Apple popularized GUIs with the introduction of the Macintosh in 1984. GUI programs display icons, menus, text boxes, and buttons and a user selectively interacts with a program by manipulating these graphical objects. This event-driven model is controlled by a program user who determines what actions a program should take. The chief advantage of GUIs is they are easy to use. However, they are more difficult to program and need more computer resources than text-based programs.

The focus of this chapter will be on various coding techniques used to interact with programs. Writing text-based and GUI programs is not trivial in Java. We will start by using several classes defined in Vista, a class library supplied by the author. The supplementary section of this chapter will describe how this library works so that we can choose to program without it.

4.2.1   Programmer-Driven User Interactions

oblem

The programs we have seen thus far are all applets. As we may recall, applets are frameworks that contain code that allow them to be run from a web page. They include code that creates and displays information in a window. Java programs that do not inherit from applets are called applications.

An *application* is a program that does not inherit from the `Applet` class. Execution begins within a `main` method instead of an `init` method. Applications do not have a framework to automatically pop up a window, communicate over the web, or handle paint events. If we want these features we must program them explicitly in applications.

Listing 4.1 contains an example application. It computes gas mileage for an automotive trip. Notice that it does not extend `Applet` in Line 12. Furthermore, execution begins within the `main` method, Line 14, rather than an `init` method.

The program in Listing 4.1 computes gas mileage on trips that require exactly three fill-ups to get to our destination. It accomplishes this task by asking for the beginning trip odometer reading, the end trip odometer reading, and the number of gallons of gas required at each fill up. The following assumptions are made:

- The gas tank is full at the beginning of the trip and the starting odometer reading is taken.
- At each service stop the amount of gas is recorded in gallons.
- At the end of the trip the tank is filled, the amount recorded, and the ending odometer reading taken.

The following shows an example interaction with the gas mileage program. The program displays the text that is in plain font and the user types the text that is bolded. For example, the program types `Beginning trip odometer reading (miles):` and the user responds by typing `28423`. After responding to all of the program questions, the program computes that the gas mileage is 27.7 miles per gallon.

```
Beginning trip odometer reading (miles): 28423
End of trip odometer reading (miles):    29239
Amount of gas for fill 1 (gallons):      11.3
Amount of gas for fill 2 (gallons):      8.7
Amount of gas for fill 3 (gallons):      9.4

Total miles:    816.0
Total gallons:  29.4
miles / gallon: 27.7
```

Line 17 in Listing 4.1 creates a user-input object named `in`. It is responsible for getting information from the computer's keyboard. Various read operations are applied to this object to get user information. Line 18 creates an output-display object named `out`. It is responsible for displaying information on the computer's monitor. Various write operations are applied to this object to display information. The `VRead` and `VWrite` class have been written may the author to simplify the programming.

Listing 4.1 Gas Mileage Example Using Programmer-Driven Style

```
 1 //*************************************************************
 2 //
 3 // title:   Gas Mileage
 4 //
 5 // Compute trip gas mileage for three fills.  User interaction
 6 // through a text-based interface.
 7 //
 8 //*************************************************************
 9
10 import vista.VRead;
11 import vista.VWrite;
12 public class GasMileage
13 {
14   public static void main (String args[])
15   {
16     // input odometer information
17     VRead  in  = new VRead ();
18     VWrite out = new VWrite ();
19
20     out.write ("Beginning trip odometer reading (miles): ");
21     double startOdometer = in.readDouble ();
22     out.write ("End of trip odometer reading (miles):    ");
23     double endOdometer = in.readDouble ();
24
25     // input gas fills
26     out.write ("Amount of gas for fill 1 (gallons):      ");
27     double fill1 = in.readDouble ();
28     out.write ("Amount of gas for fill 2 (gallons):      ");
29     double fill2 = in.readDouble ();
30     out.write ("Amount of gas for fill 3 (gallons):      ");
31     double fill3 = in.readDouble ();
32
33     // compute mileage
34     double milesTraveled = endOdometer - startOdometer;
35     double totalGallons  = fill1 + fill2 + fill3;
36     double mileage       = milesTraveled / totalGallons;
37
38     // display results
39     out.setFractionDigits (1);
40     out.writeln ();
41     out.write   ("Total miles:   ");
42     out.writeln (milesTraveled);
43     out.write   ("Total gallons: ");
44     out.writeln (totalGallons);
45     out.write   ("miles / gallon: ");
46     out.writeln (mileage);
47     in.waitForCR (out);
48   }
49 }
```

CONCEPTS

name
solution

Listing 4.1 is partitioned into three components. Lines 20 through 31 get information from the program user, Lines 34 through 36 compute the results, and Lines 39 through 47 display the results. This is a commonly used text-based pattern called input-process-output (IPO), which is described in the Patterns section.

Lines 20 and 21 are an example of getting information from the user. Line 20 prompts the user to enter a value by displaying the message Beginning trip odometer reading (miles):. If the user types 28423, as in the example above, the double variable startOdometer is given the value 28423 in Line 21.

The gas mileage is computed by first determining the number of miles traveled (Line 34) and the total number of gallons consumed (Line 35), and then computing gas mileage (Line 36). The resulting gas mileage is displayed in Line 46. More details about reading and writing follow in the Java and supplementary sections.

Notice the waitForCR method call in Line 47. This statement is required on some computer platforms (Windows 98/NT) to keep the text output window displayed so that results can be viewed. Without it the output window will disappear as soon as results are computed. The output window will not disappear until the Enter key is pressed.

consequences

The programmer-driven style of programming has a long history in computing. It dominated before the popularization of the event-driven style. The programmer-driven style has several disadvantages. The programmer is responsible for determining how the user will interact with the program. The programmer determines the order that input will be received. The style of programming is easy to implement. However, the order chosen by the program may not be optimal for the user.

4.2.2 Interacting with Files (Optional)

The program in Listing 4.1 can be easily modified to get information from a file and put results into a different file. Listing 4.2 shows the contents of the FillData.txt file. The first line contains the beginning odometer reading, the second line contains the ending odometer reading, and the last three lines contain the amount of each fill. The resulting output is written into the MileageResults.txt file shown in Listing 4.3.

Listing 4.2 Contents of the FillData.txt File

```
28423
29239
11.3
8.7
9.4
```

Listing 4.3 Contents of the `MileageResults.txt` File

```
Total miles:     816.0
Total gallons:   29.4
miles / gallon:  27.7
```

Listing 4.4 shows the modifications to Listing 4.1 required to read from and write to a file. The important changes appear in Lines 16 and 17. The constructors that create the `in` and `out` objects are simply given file names. As a result, the `in` object reads from the `Fill-Data.txt` file and the `out` object writes to the `MileageResults.txt` file. The only other change is to remove the use prompts that appear in Lines 20, 22, 26, 28, and 30 of Listing 4.1 because there is no user with which to interact. These two styles of interaction are illustrated in Figure 4.1.

4.2.3 Event-Driven User Interactions

roblem

We learned above that in the programmer-driven style of programming the programmer determines the order that input is gathered. For example, in the gas mileage program, Listing 4.1, the program determined that first the starting odometer reading, then the ending odometer reading, and finally the three fill readings are entered (Lines 21, 23, 27, 29, and 31). The program user must follow the programmer's choice of order. If one value is entered incorrectly or if the user wants to try slight variations of the input data, the program must be rerun and all data re-entered whether it has changed or not. This is often not acceptable.

ame
olution

In an *event-driven* style of programming, the program must respond to user requests. The user controls which input fields to change and when the mileage is recomputed. The dominance of event-driven programming is recent.

Figure 4.2 Gas Mileage GUI Interface

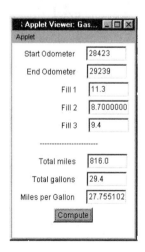

Figure 4.1 Text-based Interaction

Text-based User Interaction

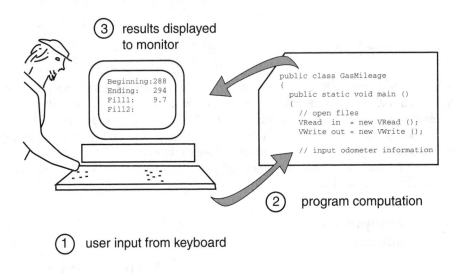

(3) results displayed to monitor

```
Beginning:288
Ending:   294
Fill1:    9.7
Fill2:
```

```
public class GasMileage
{
  public static void main ()
  {
    // open files
    VRead  in  = new VRead ();
    VWrite out = new VWrite ();

    // input odometer information
```

(2) program computation

(1) user input from keyboard

Text-based File Interaction

FillData.txt   MileageResults.txt

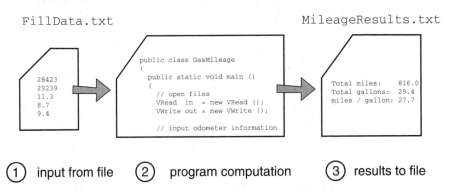

```
28423
29239
11.3
8.7
9.4
```

```
public class GasMileage
{
  public static void main ()
  {
    // open files
    VRead  in  = new VRead ();
    VWrite out = new VWrite ();

    // input odometer information
```

```
Total miles:    816.0
Total gallons:  29.4
miles / gallon: 27.7
```

(1) input from file   (2) program computation   (3) results to file

Listing 4.4   Gas Mileage Example Using Files

```
1  //****************************************************************
2  //
3  // title:    Gas Mileage
4  //
5  // Compute trip gas mileage for three fills.  File version.
6  //
7  //****************************************************************
8
9  import vista.VRead;
10 import vista.VWrite;
11 public class GasMileage
12 {
13   public static void main (String args[])
14   {
15     // open files
16     VRead  in  = new VRead ("FillData.txt");
17     VWrite out = new VWrite ("MileageResults.txt");
18
19     // input odometer information
20     double startOdometer = in.readDouble ();
21     double endOdometer = in.readDouble ();
22
23     // input gas fills
24     double fill1 = in.readDouble ();
25     double fill2 = in.readDouble ();
26     double fill3 = in.readDouble ();
27
28     // compute mileage
29     double milesTraveled = endOdometer - startOdometer;
30     double totalGallons  = fill1 + fill2 + fill3;
31     double mileage       = milesTraveled / totalGallons;
32
33     // display results
34     out.setFractionDigits (1);
35     out.write   ("Total miles:    ");
36     out.writeln (milesTraveled);
37     out.write   ("Total gallons:  ");
38     out.writeln (totalGallons);
39     out.write   ("miles / gallon: ");
40     out.writeln (mileage);
41   }
42 }
```

Figure 4.2 shows the result of incorporating a graphical user interface (GUI). We have five input text fields, labels, and a button. A user can enter new values for beginning odometer reading and fill-ups. Next, by pressing the "Compute" button or pressing the Enter key, a new mileage is computed and displayed.

We will use the *callback pattern* to implement event-driven programs. A method with a special name is written to respond to each user event of interest. Within the `callback` method we include code that carries out actions in response to the event. For example, we will write a method named `action` that responds to button press events.

> A *callback* method is a method that is called when an event occurs. It contains code written by a programmer to respond to the event that called it.

A consequence of event-driven programming is that code is distributed over multiple methods. We must be careful to place the appropriate code in the appropriate method. The incorrect placement of code can create baffling results that are difficult to associate with the line(s) of code that are responsible for the error.

In addition, adding text fields and buttons requires knowledge of Java event handling and the conversion between strings (sequence of characters) and primitive numbers. Since this is a lot to learn all at once, we have postponed these topics to later chapters. We will us a simpler approach here by using a predefined library.

In Chapter 3 we learned that frameworks are sets of classes that help support the construction of a particular kind of software system. In this chapter we will use a framework designed to make using buttons and text fields easier. As is the case with all frameworks, this ease of use comes at a price—it will not be flexible. However, we will regain that flexibility when we learn how to use GUI components in later chapters.

consequences

We stated above that using a framework will simplify our task. However, there are some complexities we cannot hide. The act of adding GUI components dictates that we must carefully partition our code across two methods. The GUI components need to be created only once in one section of code when the applet starts up. The mileage computation must occur whenever the Enter key or "Compute" button is pressed. Figure 4.3 outlines how these events and tasks are related.

The code that implements the GUI version of the gas mileage program is shown in Listing 4.5. In Line 11 we extend `VApplet` (Section 4.4.4 and page 912 in Appendix C). The `VApplet` class does everything an `Applet` class does with the addition of an `action` method. The action method is called by text fields whenever the Enter key is pressed and by buttons whenever they are pressed. We call `action` a *callback method*.

Figure 4.3 Chaos Flow of Control

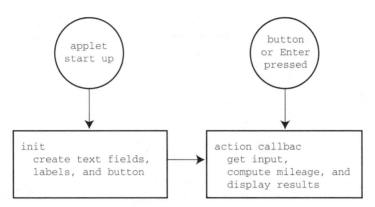

By overriding the `action` method (Line 49), we can implement code that responds to the Enter key and button presses.

The code in the `init` method creates the GUI components. The components are created in the `init` method because it is executed only once, at applet start-up time. In Lines 23, 25, 27, 29, 31, 36, 38, and 40 we create the labels for the text fields. In Lines 24, 26, 28, 30, and 32 we create the input fields. For example, in Line 24, the start odometer field is given the value 28423. Lines 37, 39, and 41 create the output text fields. Finally, we create the "Compute" button in Lines 44 and 45. Notice that the GUI components are added to the window in the same order they are created.

Finally, the `init` method calls the `action` method. The `action` method computes the gas mileage and displays the results. It is also called whenever the Enter key or "Compute" button is pressed. By and large, this code is similar to the code in Listing 4.1. The `action` method in Lines 52 through 56 inputs new values, Lines 59 through 61 compute new results, and Lines 64 through 66 output results (IPO).

There is one additional complexity in this program. The text fields must be created within `init` and they must be accessed in the `action` method. Objects can be accessed only within the method that they are declared. To make it possible to access the same objects in two different methods, we must declare these objects outside of any method. Thus, we have declared the input fields in Lines 13 through 16. Objects declared outside of a method are called *instance variables* and by the author's convention begin with the "my" prefix. Instance variables define the state of an object. We will talk more about them in Chapter 6.

Listing 4.5 Gas Mileage Example Using Event-Driven Style

```
1  //**********************************************************
2  // title:   Gas Mileage
3  //
4  // Compute trip gas mileage for three fills.  GUI version.
5  //**********************************************************
6  import vista.VActionButton;
7  import vista.VApplet;
8  import vista.VField;
9  import vista.VLabel;
10
11 public class GasMileage extends VApplet
12 {
13   VField myStartOdometerField, myEndOdometerField;
14   VField myFill1Field, myFill2Field, myFill3Field;
15   VField myTotalMilesField, myTotalGallonsField;
16   VField myMilesPerGallonField;
17
18   //------------------- init ---------------------------------
19   public void init ()
20   {
21     // Install and label input fields with default values
22     VLabel label          = null;
23     label               = new VLabel ("Start Odometer", this);
24     myStartOdometerField = new VField (28423, 6, this);
25     label               = new VLabel ("End Odometer", this);
26     myEndOdometerField   = new VField (29239, 6, this);
27     label               = new VLabel ("Fill 1", this);
28     myFill1Field         = new VField (11.3,  6, this);
29     label               = new VLabel ("Fill 2", this);
30     myFill2Field         = new VField (8.7,   6, this);
31     label               = new VLabel ("Fill 3", this);
32     myFill3Field         = new VField (9.4,   6, this);
33     label               = new VLabel ("-----------------", this);
34
35     // Install and label output fields
36     label               = new VLabel ("Total miles", this);
37     myTotalMilesField    = new VField (0, 6, this);
38     label               = new VLabel ("Total gallons", this);
39     myTotalGallonsField  = new VField (0, 6, this);
40     label               = new VLabel ("Miles per Gallon", this);
41     myMilesPerGallonField = new VField (0, 6, this);
42
43     // Install action button
44     VActionButton computeButton =
45         new VActionButton ("Compute", this);
46     action ();  // Perform default computation
47   }
```

Listing 4.5 Gas Mileage Example Using Event-Driven Style

```
48    // ----------------- action -------------------------------
49    public void action ()
50    {
51       // Get inputs
52       double startOdometer  = myStartOdometerField.getDouble ();
53       double endOdometer    = myEndOdometerField.  getDouble ();
54       double fill1          = myFill1Field.        getDouble ();
55       double fill2          = myFill2Field.        getDouble ();
56       double fill3          = myFill3Field.        getDouble ();
57
58       // compute mileage
59       double milesTraveled = endOdometer - startOdometer;
60       double totalGallons  = fill1 + fill2 + fill3;
61       double mileage       = milesTraveled / totalGallons;
62
63       // display results
64       myTotalMilesField.    setDouble (milesTraveled);
65       myTotalGallonsField.  setDouble (totalGallons);
66       myMilesPerGallonField.setDouble (mileage);
67    }
68 }
```

CONCEPTS

PATTERNS

4.3   Patterns for User Input and Output

4.3.1   Using the Counter Loop Pattern for Input

problem
solution
name

For many programs, we do not know how much input is required until we run the program. For example, a program that computes gas mileage for a cross-country trip may involve seven, ten, or any number of gas fill-ups. The solution in Listing 4.1 assumes there are exactly three fill-ups. Three will often be too few or too many fills. The new example solution in Listing 4.6 uses a *counter loop pattern* from Chapter 2 to respond to a variable number of fills.

For example, suppose we have the same trip statistic we had in Section 4.2.1. We will interact with the program as shown below. The important change is that the program now asks us for the number of fills. A walk-through is shown in Table 4.1.

```
Beginning trip odometer reading (miles): 28423
End of trip odometer reading (miles):    29239
Enter the number of fill-ups:            3
Amount of gas (gallons):    11.3
Amount of gas (gallons):    8.7
Amount of gas (gallons):    9.4

Total miles:    816.0
Total gallons:  29.4
miles / gallon: 27.7
```

consequences

A limitation of using the counter loop is that we must know the number of fill-ups when the program starts executing. Sometimes we do not know that we have seen all the input values until we have seen the last one or there are no more inputs. We can handle this situation with the loop-and-a-half pattern in the next section.

A problem will occur if a program user enters zero for the number of fills. The total number of gallons would be zero, resulting in a divide by zero in Line 36. Using a guarded command pattern, such as the one that follows, will prevent divide by zero.

```
if (totalGallons > 0.0)
   mileage = milesTraveled / totalGallons;
```

Listing 4.6   Computing Gas Mileage Using a Counting Loop

```
1  //****************************************************************
2  // title:    Gas Mileage
3  //
4  // Compute trip gas mileage.  Counter loop version
5  //****************************************************************
6
7  import vista.VRead;
8  import vista.VWrite;
9  public class GasMileage {
10
11    public static void main (String args[])
12    {
13      // create input and output objects
14      VRead  in  = new VRead();
15      VWrite out = new VWrite();
16
17      // input trip information
18      out.write ("Beginning trip odometer reading (miles): ");
19      double startOdometer = in.readDouble();
20      out.write ("End of trip odometer reading (miles):    ");
21      double endOdometer = in.readDouble();
22      out.write ("Enter the number of fill-ups:            ");
23      int numberOfFills = in.readInt();
24
25      // compute mileage
26      double totalGallons  = 0.0;
27      int counter = 0;
28      while (counter < numberOfFills)
29      {
30        out.write ("Amount of gas (gallons):               ");
31        double fill = in.readDouble();
32        totalGallons += fill;
33        counter++;
34      }
35      double milesTraveled = endOdometer - startOdometer;
36      double mileage       = milesTraveled / totalGallons;
37
38      // display results
39      out.setFractionDigits (1);
40      out.writeln ();
41      out.write   ("Total miles:    ");
42      out.writeln (milesTraveled);
43      out.write   ("Total gallons:  ");
44      out.writeln (totalGallons);
45      out.write   ("miles / gallon: ");
46      out.writeln (mileage);
47      in.waitForCR (out);
48    }
49 }
```

Table 4.1 Example Run

line Number	numberOfFills	counter	fill	totalGallons
23	3	??	??	??
26	3	??	??	0.0
27	3	0	??	0.0
31	3	0	11.3	0.0
32	3	0	11.3	11.3
33	3	1	11.3	11.3
31	3	1	8.7	11.3
32	3	1	8.7	20.0
33	3	2	8.7	20.0
31	3	2	9.4	20.0
32	3	2	9.4	29.4
33	3	3	9.4	29.4

4.3.2   Loop-and-a-Half Pattern for Input

problem
solution

We can handle an unknown number of inputs using a sentinel value to terminate input. For example, in the gas-mileage program we could ask for fill-ups until the user enters a zero or negative value. This approach is demonstrated in Listing 4.7.

name

Lines 26 through 33 demonstrate a *loop-and-a-half pattern,* which is a variation of the sentinel loop pattern. Notice that we set up an infinite input loop in Line 26. We exit in the middle using a `break` statement in Line 31. The `break` is not executed unless the input value is less than or equal to zero (Line 30).   An example interaction is shown below:

```
Beginning trip odometer reading (miles): 28423
End of trip odometer reading (miles):    29239
Enter each fill-up (exit with 0)
Amount of gas (gallons):    11.3
Amount of gas (gallons):    8.7
Amount of gas (gallons):    9.4
Amount of gas (gallons):    0

Total miles:    816.0
Total gallons:  29.4
miles / gallon: 27.7
```

Listing 4.7 Computing Gas Mileage Using a Sentinel Loop

```
1  //************************************************************
2  // title:    Gas Mileage
3  //
4  // Compute trip gas mileage.  Sentinel loop version.
5  //************************************************************
6
7  import vista.VRead;
8  import vista.VWrite;
9  public class GasMileage
10 {
11    public static void main (String args[])
12    {
13      // create input and output objects
14      VRead  in  = new VRead ();
15      VWrite out = new VWrite ();
16
17      // input trip information
18      out.write ("Beginning trip odometer reading (miles): ");
19      double startOdometer = in.readDouble();
20      out.write ("End of trip odometer reading (miles):    ");
21      double endOdometer = in.readDouble();
22      out.writeln ("Enter each fill-up (exit with 0)");
23
24      // compute mileage
25      double totalGallons  = 0.0;
26      while (true)
27      {
28        out.write ("Amount of gas (gallons):               ");
29        double fill = in.readDouble();
30        if (fill <= 0)
31          break;
32        totalGallons += fill;
33      }
34      double milesTraveled = endOdometer - startOdometer;
35      double mileage       = milesTraveled / totalGallons;
36
37      // display results
38      out.setFractionDigits (1);
39      out.writeln ();
40      out.write   ("Total miles:    ");
41      out.writeln (milesTraveled);
42      out.write   ("Total gallons:  ");
43      out.writeln (totalGallons);
44      out.write   ("miles / gallon: ");
45      out.writeln (mileage);
46      in.waitForCR (out);
47    }
48 }
```

The basic form of the loop-and-a-half pattern is shown below. It consists of an infinite loop. Pre-processing in the first half of the loop sets up an exit condition. After an exit check, additional processing is done to complete a subtask.

```
loop forever
  do some set-up preprocessing
  if set-up dictates that we are done
    exit the loop
  do some postprocessing
end loop
```

consequences One of the problems with a sentinel loop is that it may be difficult to select an appropriate sentinel value. In the gas-mileage program, natural sentinel values are any nonpositive numbers because negative and zero fill-up values do not make sense. However, some programs may require the input of the entire range of integer or real numbers. Selecting a sentinel value will restrict legal program input.

Some people object to the loop-and-a-half style of programming. They prefer using the pure sentinel loop pattern as follows:

```
1 out.write ("Amount of gas (gallons):              ");
2 fill = in.readDouble ();
3 while (fill <= 0)
4 {
5   totalGallons += fill;
6   out.write ("Amount of gas (gallons):              ");
7   fill = in.readDouble ();
8 }
```

Many argue that good structured programming dictates that a loop should only exit if the loop conditional fails. This approach is exemplified by the pure sentinel loop pattern. However, notice the duplicated code in Lines 1 and 2 and Lines 6 and 7. In addition, the order of the statements in the loop body is counter-intuitive. In the first half of the loop we are processing data that we got during the last half of its previous iteration. The author prefers the loop-and-a-half version because he feels the order of statements is more intuitive and it removes a duplicated read.

Given that both views are carefully thought through and deeply held, it is not reasonable to expect to establish agreement. Both views argue that their style produces more reliable code and each view deserves careful consideration. The author suggests that we each adapt a style that is compatible with our peers. If the instructor or project leader insists on one style over the other, follow it without hesitation. A consistent style among peers provides a code reader with consistent expectations. An individual style, even if it is arguably better, will break those expectations and result in some confusion. A hodge-podge of styles makes a program difficult to understand. Therefore, this text will consistently use the loop-and-a-half pattern. For those who are interested in pursuing this discussion further, the article by Eric Roberts in the chapter bibliography is one place to begin.

4.3.3 Validation Input

Program users often make mistakes when they are entering numbers. A good programmer will strive to make those errors less painful. For example, in the gasoline-mileage program, entering negative numbers or having a ending trip odometer reading that is less than the beginning trip reading does not make sense and should not be allowed. To prevent this problem one could add the following check after Line 21 in Listing 4.7:

```
if (startOdometer > endOdometer)
{
  io.println("End odometer must be greater than start");
  io.print("Please enter a new end odometer reading: ");
  endOdometer = io.readDouble();
}
```

However, this approach gives the user only one extra shot at entering a valid ending odometer reading. The user may make another mistake or the mistake may have been with the start reading. By using the *sentinel loop pattern* we can write code that recovers from this problem.

```
io.print("Beginning trip odometer reading (miles): ");
startOdometer = io.readDouble();
io.print("End of trip odometer reading (miles):    ");
endOdometer = io.readDouble();

while (startOdometer > endOdometer)
{
  io.println("End odometer must be greater than start");
  io.print("Beginning trip odometer reading (miles): ");
  startOdometer = io.readDouble();
  io.print("End of trip odometer reading (miles):    ");
  endOdometer = io.readDouble();
}
```

The basic strategy for input validation is shown below:

```
Prompt for a value
Read the value
Loop while value is out of range
  Prompt for a value indicating why previous attempt is wrong
  Read another value
End loop
```

consequences   The above input validation can be problematic. Users may get stuck in an input loop for-ever because they do not understand the input question. If users' input is rejected forever, they will become frustrated. It may be appropriate to give the user a way out. This can be accomplished by incorporating the counter loop pattern, which causes a loop exit after several iterations regardless of whether the user typed in a valid response.

JAVA

4.4 Implementing Human-Computer Interaction Using Vista

4.4.1 Java Applications and `System.out`

Applets are designed to be executed by a web browser. Suppose we want to create programs that are not web and browser based. To do that, we create a Java application. Applications are used for writing programs that are independent of the web. An example is the Picard application in Listing 4.8.

Listing 4.8 Picard Program

```
1  //**********************************************************
2  //
3  // title:    Picard
4  //
5  // A program that pretends to be Captain Jean-Luc Picard.
6  //
7  //**********************************************************
8
9  public class Picard
10 {
11   public static void main (String args[])
12   {
13     System.out.println("Make it so.");
14   }
15 }
```

In a sense, `main` has some of the behavior that `init` has in an applet. The big difference is that when `main` is finished executing, the program terminates. There is no facility in this program to respond to mouse or keyboard events without explicitly programming them.

Line 11 looks rather cryptic. Explaining what each keyword means now would sidetrack our current discussion. We will discuss them in Chapter 6. Just remember to type the `main` method header exactly as it appears in Listing 4.8.

In Line 13 `System.out` sends the string "Make it so." to standard output (the message window). On Unix systems, this is the command window from which the program was executed. In Windows 95, it may be the MS-DOS window. On the Macintosh, a special output window is typically opened by the Java system.

4.4.2 Using `VWrite`

As the program in the previous section illustrates, the easiest way to produce output in an application is using `System.out`. A problem with using the `System` class is that it provides little control of our output, as the first code fragment in Table 4.2 demonstrates.

Table 4.2 Formatting Output

Output Code (within `main` method)	Resulting Output (may vary with platform)

`System.out.print    (      1.0 / 3.0);`
`System.out.print    (     12.0 / 3.0);`
`System.out.println (3874928.0 / 3.0);`
	`0.33333333333333334.01291642.66666666`
	`67`

`VWrite out = new VWrite ();`
`out.setIntegerDigits (5);`
`out.setFractionDigits (3);`
`out.write    (      1.0 / 3.0);`
`out.write    (" ");`
`out.write    (     12.0 / 3.0);`
`out.write    (" ");`
`out.writeln (3874928.0 / 3.0);`
	`00000.333 00004.000 91642.666`

`VWrite out = new VWrite ();`
`out.applyPattern ("  0.0000");`
`out.write    (      1.0 / 3.0);`
`out.write    (     12.0 / 3.0);`
`out.writeln (3874928.0 / 3.0);`
	`0.3333   4.0000   1291642.6666`

`VWrite out = new VWrite ();`
`out.applyPattern (" $#,##0.00");`
`out.write    (      1.0 / 3.0);`
`out.write    (     12.0 / 3.0);`
`out.writeln (3874928.0 / 3.0);`
	`$0.33 $4.00 $1,291,642.66`

The second code fragment demonstrates how the `setIntegerDigits` and `setFractionDigits` methods from the `VWrite` class can be used to control the number of digits to the left and right of the decimal point. Notice that the first two digits of the result `1291642.666` have been truncated giving us an incorrect result. Also notice it is necessary to explicitly write a space between each output result. We could have done that in the previous example using `System.out` as well.

The third example shows how an output pattern can be used to control printed numbers. The first two spaces in the pattern `"  0.0000"` will prefix each number displayed with two spaces. The spaces serve as number deliminators. The first zero specifies that all real numbers will have a leading digit before the decimal. The default digit is zero. It prevents 0.4 from being displayed as ".4". The last four zeros specify that each number will have exactly four digits displayed in its fractional part. Thus, 0.4 is displayed as shown in Figure 4.4.

Figure 4.4 How 0.4 Is Displayed with Pattern "0.0000"

```
          | 0 | . | 4 | 0 | 0 | 0 |
```

Another common pattern is one for displaying currency. It is " $#,##0.00". The fourth example of Table 4.2 shows its impact. Notice the commas.

There are `write` and `writeln` operations for strings, characters, reals, and integers. The difference between `write` and `writeln` is that `writeln` places a carriage return at the end of its output. An example is shown in Table 4.3. The two code fragments produce the same output.

Table 4.3 `write` Vs. `writeln`

Output Code	Resulting Output

`VWrite out = new VWrite ();`
`out.write    ("Amer");`
`out.write    ("ican Be");`
`out.writeln ("auty");`
`out.write    ("The Straight");`
`out.writeln (" Story");`
	`American Beauty`
	`The Straight Story`

`VWrite out = new VWrite ();`
`out.writeln ("American Beauty");`
`out.writeln ("The Straight Story");`
	`American Beauty`
	`The Straight Story`

As we saw in Section 4.2.2 we can write to our computer display or a file by passing a file name to the `VWrite` constructor. For example, the second line below will write to the file named `movies.txt`. Keep in mind that opening this file for write will destroy all previous information in that file. Additional details about the `VWrite` class can be found in Appendix C on page 921.

```
VWrite out = new VWrite ();                // write to display
VWrite out = new VWrite ("movies.txt");   // write to file
```

4.4.3   Using VRead

The Vista `VRead` class simplifies reading information from the keyboard or a file. Listing 4.9 shows a program that reads a single price and computes an after-Christmas sale price. We begin with Lines 8 and 9, which create objects that read from the keyboard and write to the display. After Line 11 has executed, the program waits for the computer user to type a price (see Figure 4.5). Once the user types an integer and presses the Enter key, the number is returned and assigned to the `originalPrice` variable. If the input typed by the user does not represent an number, e.g., if it contains letters or punctuation characters, the value is not accepted and an error message is displayed.

Listing 4.9 Computing a Sale Price—Text-based Version

```
1   import vista.VRead;
2   import vista.VWrite;
3
4   public class SalePrice
5   {
6     public static void main(String args[])
7     {
8       VWrite out = new VWrite ();
9       VRead  in  = new VRead ();
10
11      out.write ("Enter original item price: $");
12      double originalPrice = in.readDouble ();
13
14      double salePrice = originalPrice * 0.85;
15
16      out.applyPattern ("$#,##0.00");
17      out.write ("The sale price is:            ");
18      out.writeln (salePrice);
19
20      in.waitForCR (out);
21    }
22 }
```

Resulting Output

```
Enter original item price: $14.95
The sale price is:          $12.70
```

In some software development environments, the display window will disappear before you have a chance to read it. If that is the case, add the following as we did in Line 20. The display window will stay visible until the user hits the Enter key:

```
io.waitForCR()
```

Figure 4.5 Waiting for Input

```
Enter original item price: $█
                                    ▼
                                        Cursor
```

There are additional operations for reading integers, characters, and strings. If you are reading strings, place quotes around the string to capture more than just the first word. See the following code with possible outputs. Additional details about the VRead class can be found in Appendix C on page 919.

Code
```
out.write ("Type a string  :");
String s = in.readString ();
out.write ("Entered string :");
out.writeln (s);
```

Output Example 1
```
Type a string  :"Three Kings"
Entered string :Three Kings
```

Output Example 2
```
Type a string  :Three Kings
Entered string :Three
```

A character read captures the first character of a string. The rest of the string is discarded. See below for an example:

Code
```
out.write ("Type a character  :");
char c = in.readChar ();
out.write ("Entered character :");
out.writeln (c);
```

Output Example
```
Type a character  :"Three Kings"
Entered character :T
```

We can also read from a file. To read from the file stocks.data, create an input object using the following constructor:

```
VRead  in  = new VRead ("stocks.data");
```

4.4.4 Using `VApplet`

In this section we will reimplement the sales program in Listing 4.9 using a graphical user interface. The resulting code and an example interaction is shown in Listing 4.10.

We begin by creating an applet that extends `VApplet`. `VApplet` was written by the author and adds an `action` method to the `Applet` class. Whenever the button is pressed, execution goes to the `action` callback method.

All the GUI components must be created in the `init` method. The constructor for `VLabel` creates a message string that is added to the applet display window. The first constructor parameter is the contents of message. The second parameter is the keyword `this`. All Vista GUI components have this parameter. It tells the program to put the label in "this" applet display.

```
VLabel label = new VLabel ("Original price", this);
```

A `VField` is much like a label. In addition to displaying a message to a text field, it is possible to get and set its values. The second parameter of a `VField` constructor determines how wide the filed is. The following summarizes operations of a `VField` object:

```
VField field = new VField ("123", 6, this);
int i = field.getInt ();              // i is 123
double d = field.getDouble ();        // d is 123.0
String s = field.getString ();        // s is "123"
field.setInt (456);                   // field displays "456"
field.setDouble (456.7);              // field displays "456.7"
field.setString ("456");              // field displays "456"
```

If an attempt is made to get an invalid value from a text field, its display is changed to `"***"`. For example, suppose we created the following text field with its associated read. If the program user enters the value `"yes"` into the text field, `"yes"` will be replaced by `"***"` when the `readInt` is executed, indicating that `"yes"` is not a proper integer.

```
VField sistersField = new VField ("   ", 6, this);
int numberOfSisters = sistersField.getInt ();
```

VApplets will support only one button. Additional buttons can be created and added to the display, but they all call the `action` callback method when they are pressed. There is no means to distinguish which button press involved the `action` method in Vista. An example of creating a button labeled "View" is shown below.

```
VActionButton viewButton = new VActionButton ("View", this);
```

146

Listing 4.10 Computing a Sale Price—GUI version

```
1   import vista.VActionButton;
2   import vista.VApplet;
3   import vista.VField;
4   import vista.VLabel;
5
6   public class SalesPrice extends VApplet
7   {
8     VField myOriginalPriceField;
9     VField mySalePriceField;
10
11    // -------------------- init --------------------------------
12    public void init ()
13    {
14      // Install and label input fields with default values
15      VLabel label        = null;
16      label               = new VLabel ("Original price", this);
17      myOriginalPriceField = new VField (10.0, 6, this);
18      label               = new VLabel ("       Sale price",this);
19      mySalePriceField    = new VField (29239, 6, this);
20
21      // Install action button
22      VActionButton computeButton =
23          new VActionButton ("Compute", this);
24
25      // perform default computation
26      action ();
27    }
28
29    // --------------------- action --------------------------
30    public void action ()
31    {
32      double originalPrice = myOriginalPriceField.getDouble ();
33      double salePrice     = originalPrice * 0.85;
34      mySalePriceField.setDouble (salePrice);
35    }
36 }
```

Resulting Display Window

JAVA

Notice how the application is partitioned. All the code to create the GUI components is placed in the `init` method. All the code to respond to button presses is placed in the `action` method.

Additional details about `VApplet`, `VLabel`, `VField`, and `VActionButton` can be found in Appendix C. Refer back to Section 4.2.3 for another example. The `VApplet` framework was written to make starting out easier, but with ease of use come restrictions. It is not until we get to Chapter 15 that we learn how to handle buttons and other GUI components in a flexible way. We can get a taste for how GUI components are written in Java by reading the supplementary section of this chapter.

SUPPLEMENTARY MATERIAL

4.5 Implementing Human-Computer Interaction Using Java

Section 4.4 described how to use the Vista library to create user interaction. Many of us want to know how Java handles user interaction without the help of Vista. This section will address this question. Because file IO and event handling is the topic for three later chapters in this book, we will sketch out only the basic elements of a small example here.

4.5.1 Text-based Interaction in Java

Listing 4.11 is a reimplementation of Listing 4.9 on page 144 without the benefit of Vista. This program also begins with the creation of out and in objects in Lines 15 and 16. Notice that creating the out object is a two-step process (Lines 13 and 15). Details can be found in Section 12.4, page 551.

Various errors can occur when one attempts to read from and write to a file. A file may not be found or may be corrupt. Java requires that file manipulation occur within an exception handler so that a program can respond to these errors. The try (Line 10) with its associated catch clause (Line 44) comprise an exception handler. More details may be found in Section 9.4.6, page 418.

The write in Line 19 only works with strings. If we want to write anything other than a string, we must first convert it. The valueOf method in Line 34 converts salesValue from a double to a string. See Section 10.5.8, page 455.

Out may be stuck in a buffer so that the program user cannot see it immediately. To correct this problem we must flush the output buffer before we do the read so the user can read the prompt. This is done with the flush method in Line 20. See Section 12.3, page 546.

There is no writeln method in the BufferedWriter class. Instead we must use the newLine method as we have done in Line 35 to bring the cursor to the beginning of the next line.

Listing 4.11   Computing a Sale Price—Text-based Version Revisited

```
1   import java.io.BufferedWriter;
2   import java.io.IOException;
3   import java.io.OutputStreamWriter;
4   import java.io.StreamTokenizer;
5
6   public class SalePrice
7   {
8     public static void main(String args[])
9     {
10      try
11      {
12        // create in and out objects
13        OutputStreamWriter streamOut =
14                        new OutputStreamWriter (System.out);
15        BufferedWriter out = new BufferedWriter (streamOut);
16        StreamTokenizer in  = new StreamTokenizer (System.in);
17
18        // get the original price
19        out.write ("Enter original item price: $");
20        out.flush ();
21        in.nextToken ();
22        if (in.ttype != in.TT_NUMBER)
23        {
24         System.err.println ("Error - Input must be a number.");
25          return;
26        }
27        double originalPrice = in.nval;
28
29        // compute sale price
30        double salePrice = originalPrice * 0.85;
31
32        // display new price
33        out.write ("The sale price is:          $");
34        out.write (String.valueOf(salePrice));
35        out.newLine ();
36
37        // wait for a carriage return
38        out.write ("Press 'return' to continue.");
39        out.newLine ();
40        out.flush ();
41        in.eolIsSignificant (true);
42        in.nextToken ();
43      }
44      catch (IOException e)
45      {
46        System.err.println ("IO exception raised");
47      }
48    }
49 }
```

Reading is accomplished through a stream tokenizer object. Line 21 gets the next token from the input stream tokenizer. Next, Line 22 determines whether that token is a number. If it is not, it displays an error and exits the program. If the next token is a number, it will retrieve that number in Line 27. See Section 12.6, page 569.

No attempt was made to do any number formatting in this example. See Section 12.4.4, page 562 for details.

Listing 4.12 Computing a Sale Price—GUI Version Revisited

```
1  import javax.swing.JApplet;
2  import javax.swing.JButton;
3  import javax.swing.JLabel;
4  import javax.swing.JTextField;
5  import java.awt.Container;
6  import java.awt.FlowLayout;
7  import java.awt.event.ActionEvent;
8  import java.awt.event.ActionListener;
9
10 public class SalesPrice extends JApplet
11                 implements ActionListener
12 {
13    JTextField myOriginalPriceField;
14    JTextField mySalePriceField;
15
16    // -------------------- init ----------------------------------
17    public void init ()
18    {
19       // Install and label input fields with default values
20       Container pane = getContentPane();
21       pane.setLayout (new FlowLayout ());
22       JLabel label        = null;
23       label               = new JLabel ("Original price");
24       pane.add (label);
25       myOriginalPriceField = new JTextField ("0.0", 6);
26       pane.add (myOriginalPriceField);
27       label               = new JLabel ("      Sale price");
28       pane.add (label);
29       mySalePriceField    = new JTextField ("0.0", 6);
30       pane.add (mySalePriceField);
31
32       // Install action button
33       JButton computeButton = new JButton ("Compute");
34       computeButton.addActionListener (this);
35       pane.add (computeButton);
36    }
37
```

Listing 4.12 Computing a Sale Price—GUI Version Revisited

```
38   // --------------------- action ---------------------------
39   public void actionPerformed (ActionEvent e)
40   {
41     // get the original price
42     String s = myOriginalPriceField.getText ();
43     Double d = Double.valueOf (s);
44     double originalPrice = d.doubleValue ();
45
46     // compute the sale price
47     double salePrice = originalPrice * 0.85;
48
49     // display results
50     mySalePriceField.setText (String.valueOf (salePrice));
51   }
52 }
```

4.5.2   Graphical User Interfaces in Java

Listing 4.12 is a reimplementation of Listing 4.10 on page 147. Notice that this program extends an applet and implements the `ActionListener` interface in Line 10. The `ActionListener` is required to make buttons work. See Section 14.4, page 671 and Section 15.4.4, page 702.

A label is created and added to the applet display in Lines 23 and 24. More details are found Section 10.6.1, page 458.

A text field is created in Lines 25 and 26. More details are found in Section 10.6.2, page 459. Lines 42 through 44 get a string from a text field and convert it to a double. Line 50 takes a double value and converts it to a string. Converting between strings and other values can be found in Section 10.5.8, page 455, Section 10.5.9, page 455, and Section 10.6.6, page 466.

The code in Lines 33 through 35 is responsible for creating, adding, and registering a button. Line 34 is critical. It registers the button with the Java system. Java will find the `actionPerformed` method for the `computeButton` in this applet. See Section 15.4.4, page 702.

Finally the `actionPerformed` method plays the counter part of the `action` method we used in `VApplet`. When the "compute" button is pressed execution goes to the `actionPerformed` method. See Section 15.4.4, page 702.

4.6   Summary

This chapter focused on computer and human interaction. We studied two approaches. One uses a text-based system, in which the programmer controls the interactions. We referred to it as a program-driven model. For simple text-based programming the `VRead` and `VWrite` Vista classes were used. They allow a user to read text from a keyboard or file and write text to a display or file. The program-driven model was implemented within applications. Applications are programs that do not use the applet framework to interact over the web.

The second approach uses graphical user interfaces (GUIs). This model is event-controlled. The program user controls the order in which transactions are handled. For simple GUI programming, the `VApplet`, `VLabel`, `VField`, and `VActionButton` Vista classes were used. Our programs were partitioned into two components: an initialization phase, which created the GUI components; and a `callback` method, which responded to button presses.

We were introduced to the IPO (input-process-output) pattern. It is commonly used in applications that need to input a value, do some computation on it, and display a result. We were also introduced to the loop-and-a-half pattern. It is useful for creating code that reads input values until a sentinel value is reached. The counter loop pattern can also be used for input if we know the number of inputs at the beginning of a run. In addition, we used sentinel loops for input validation.

4.7   Bibliography

- Roberts, Eric. 1995. Loop exits and structured programming: reopening the debate. *SIGCSE Bulletin* 27, no. 1 (March): 268–272.

SUPPLEMENTARY MATERIAL

PROBLEM SETS

4.8   Exercises

Patterns—Section 4.3

1   Use nested while loops to create the following output, printing only one number per iteration of the inner loop:

```
1
1 2
1 2 3
1 2 3 4
1 2 3 4 5
```

Text-based Output—Section 4.4.2

2   What is the output of the following? Assume the following out object has been created:

```
VWrite out = new VWrite ();
```

a.
```
out.writeln ("one");
out.writeln ("two");
out.writeln ("three");
```

b.
```
out.write    ("one");
out.write    ("two");
out.writeln ("three");
```

c.
```
double d = 123.45678;
out.write    ("*");
out.write    (d)
out.writeln ("*");
```

d.
```
double d = 123.45678;
out.setIntegerDigits (4);
out.setFractionDigits (2);
out.write    ("*");
out.write    (d)
```

```
    out.writeln ("*");
```
e.
```
  double d = 123.45678;
  out.setIntegerDigits (2);
  out.setFractionDigits (7);
  out.write    ("*");
  out.write    (d)
  out.writeln ("*");
```
f.
```
  double d = 123.45678;
  out.applyPattern (" 0.000");
  out.write    ("*");
  out.write    (d)
  out.writeln ("*");
```
g.
```
  double d = 123.45678;
  out.applyPattern (" $#,##0.00");
  out.write    ("*");
  out.write    (d)
  out.writeln ("*");
```

Text-based Output—Section 4.4.3

3   Write a program to read the following from a file named `"stocks.data"`. It should compute and display the value of the shares owned. Use `VWrite` for output. The first line contains the company name. The second line contains today's stock value. The third line contains how many shares we own. For example, `stock.data` may contain the following:

```
"Intel Corp."
85.7
250
```

4.9   Projects

User Interaction—Section 4.4

4   Write a complete application using the IPO architecture to compute the following. For each program select appropriate test data to try out your program:

a.   convert degrees Fahrenheit temperature to degrees Celsius
```
  celsius = (fahrenheit - 32) * 5 / 9
```
b.   the circumference of a circle

```
                    circumference = 1/4 * diameter
```
c.   the area of a triangle
```
           area = 1/2 base * width
```
d.   the area of a circle
```
           area = 1/4 radius²
```
$$area = 1/4\ radius^2$$
e.   the current going through a resistor with a given voltage drop
```
        I = V / R
```
f.   the retail cost of an item with a 35% mark-up and a 7.5% tax

g.   convert miles to kilometers (1 mile = 1.609344 kilometers)

h.   convert yards, feet, and inches to total inches

Patterns—Section 4.3

5   Write a program that reads test scores and reports on the number of tests in each grade range. The program user should be prompted for the number of test scores. Use a text-based interface.

```
A: 90 to 100
B: 80 to  89
C: 70 to  79
D: 60 to  69
F:  0 to  59
```

6   Write an application that finds the average of quiz scores. The number of quiz scores is specified by the user; thus, use a counter-controlled loop. Implement the following interaction between application and user. Information that is entered by a program's user is in bold. It should not be part of the program:

```
            Test Score Average

Number of quizzes:          5
Quiz 1:                     85
Quiz 2:                     73
Quiz 3:                     91
Quiz 4:                     96
Quiz 5:                     87

Quiz average:               86
```

7   Repeat exercise 6 with a sentinel loop. Any value less than 0 should signal the end of scores. The program should implement the following interaction between application and user. Information that is entered by a program's user is in bold. It should not be part of the program:

```
        Test Score Average

  Quiz 1:                    85
  Quiz 2:                    73
  Quiz 3:                    91
  Quiz 4:                    96
  Quiz 5:                    87
  Quiz 6:                    -1

  Quiz average:              86
```

8 Implement exercise 6 using an event-based program. This program should have three text fields and a button. One text field is a test score input, one is the number of scores handled thus far, and the third is the running average. When the program begins, all fields contain zero. The user enters the first score in the score field, and then presses Average. Because there has only been one score entered thus far, the average and score are the same with the number of scores displaying 1. When the second score has been entered and the average button is pressed, the average field displays the average of the first two scores and the number field displays 2. The process continues until all scores have been entered. *Hint:* Make the running total and count values instance variables.

9 Add input error-checking to the average program from exercise 6 or 7.

   a. Use loops to assure that all readings are positive and within an appropriate range. For example, a score of greater than 100 or less than 0 is not allowed.

   b. Use loop counters to get the program user out of the input loop after five iterations.

   c. The program should display "No computations are possible" and quit if the first score is entered as a negative.

5 Numeric Computing

Chaos

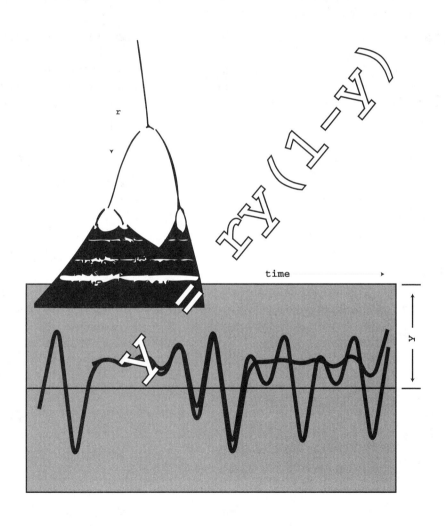

5.1 Objectives

Concepts   **Section 5.2, page 161**

The primary focus of this chapter is numerical computing. We are introduced to precedence, precision, round-off errors, overflow, and type casting.

The journey begins with an example chaotic system that computes animal populations. Equations are often used to model real-world systems. We will learn what makes some of those systems chaotic.

Patterns   **Section 5.3, page 171**

Thus far we have looked at coding patterns. In this chapter we will introduce a process pattern. The stepwise refinement pattern is a process used to implement a program using a top-down approach.

Java Skills

Next we address how we can use Java to express the above concepts and patterns.

- Java primitive type: `int`   Section 5.4, page 176
- Java operator precedence   Section 5.4.5, page 179
- Type coercion   Section 5.4.8, page 185
- Java primitive type: `double`   Section 5.5, page 186
- Java `Math` class   Section 5.5.7, page 194

Abilities

By the end of this chapter we should be able to do the following:

- Write programs that perform numeric computations.
- Understand the stepwise refinement process.

CONCEPTS

5.2   Chaos

In 1960 Edward Lorenz was working at the Massachusetts Institute of Technology (MIT) with a program he had written to model weather. Every minute this program printed out a row of numbers that represented prevailing winds and temperatures around the globe. The weather in this imaginary world was governed by 12 rules expressed as mathematical equations that he had developed.

> A *simulation* is the use of a computer program to model a dynamic system. Sometimes this process is referred to as *modeling*.

One day Lorenz decided to take a closer look at a sequence of weather events. Instead of starting the simulation from the beginning, he typed in the weather's initial conditions at the beginning of the sequence he was interested in. The initial conditions were found on the printout of an earlier run. After the simulation started, he left for a cup of coffee. When he returned, he was surprised to discover that the resulting weather was completely different from the initial run. At first he thought there was something wrong with the simulation program or his computer. After careful investigation, he realized that the conditions he typed in were slightly different than the original values. For example, one of the variables was typed in as .506, which was the number displayed on the printout. However, the number stored within the computer was actually .506127. The printer was rounding numbers to three decimal places and Lorenz assumed that this small deviation would be inconsequential. However, this small change in initial conditions caused a completely different end result. Out of this chance discovery grew the science of chaos.

> *Chaotic* systems are systems that have a sensitive dependence on initial conditions.

In chaotic systems, small deviations in initial conditions have a large impact on the final outcome. This is often called the Butterfly Effect, sometimes stated this way: "A butterfly stirring the air in Peking can cause a storm the next month in New York."

 Modeling animal populations is a typical application for a computer program. Computers are used to forecast economic development, weather, the outcome of war, wildlife ecology, and the results of chemical reactions. It is important to fully understand the system dynamics before one makes premature conclusions. If the model is chaotic, the accuracy of the initial conditions may not be sufficient to predict long-term effects. If the equations are wrong, the predictions will be wrong.

Many physical systems other than weather behave in chaotic ways. Mario Markus of the Max Planck Institute for Nutrition found additional examples while he was investigating how enzymes break down carbohydrates during digestion. The model developed by Markus is based on a variation of the following equation: $y_1 = r\ y_0\ (1 - y_0)$. This is the simplest known formula that models chaotic behavior in a dynamic system. This formula is known as a logistics formula, which gets its name from the logistics of animal populations. The next generation of an animal population y_1 is based on r, which signifies the reproductive fertility of the animals. It represents the ability of an animal population to respond to disaster. The higher the r value the quicker the animal recovers from low populations. y_0 represents the current population. The more animals there are, the more will be born. However, the food supply is also important. As the number of animals grow, the food supplies dwindle, which is represented in the equation by $(1 - y_0)$.

Suppose that r has the value 3.69 and y_0 has the value 0.5 (the current population.) This will give us the value of 0.9225 for y_1 (population of the next generation—see Figure 5.1). A population value of 0.5 or 0.9225 looks strange. This does not mean a population of half an animal. It means one half of the maximum possible population. So it could mean half of a million or half of a thousand animals.

Figure 5.1 Computing the Next Generation of Animals

$$
\begin{aligned}
y_1 &= r * y_0 * (1.0 - y_0) \\
&= 3.69 * 0.5 * (1.0 - 0.5) \\
&= 3.69 * 0.5 * \quad 0.5 \\
&= \quad 1.845 \quad * \quad 0.5 \\
y_1 &= \quad\quad 0.9225
\end{aligned}
$$

We can continue to compute populations of future generations by using y_1 for the next value of y_0 and recomputing the new result for y_1. Doing this, the population of the next generation becomes 0.263812 (Figure 5.2). The results for the first 14 generations of ani-

Figure 5.2 Computing the Next Three Generations of Animals

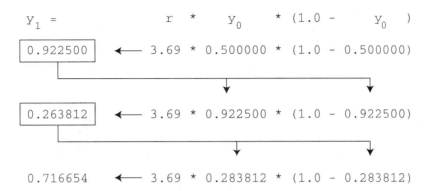

Table 5.1   The First 15 Generations of Animals with Two Different Starting Populations

Generation	Population 1	Population 2
0	0.500000	0.510000
1	0.922500	0.922131
2	0.263812	0.264962
3	0.716654	0.718654
4	0.749295	0.746083
5	0.693174	0.699045
6	0.784804	0.776306
7	0.623193	0.640788
8	0.866499	0.849360
9	0.426853	0.472127
10	0.902757	0.919633
11	0.323934	0.272721
12	0.808113	0.731890
13	0.572196	0.724078
14	0.572196	0.737221

Figure 5.3 Animal Populations in Table 5.1 Represented as a Graph

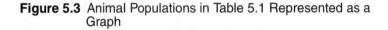

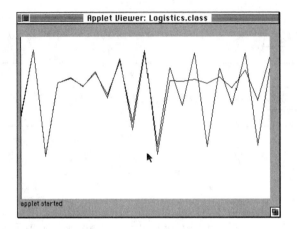

Figure 5.4 Single Attractor of 0.642857 When r = 2.8

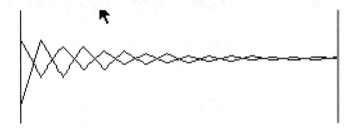

Figure 5.5 Double Attractor When r = 3.2

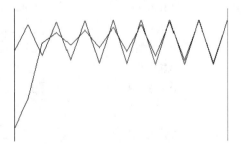

mals are shown in Table 5.1 for two different animal populations starting with slightly different initial values: one starting at 0.50 and the other at 0.51. The resulting population fluctuations are dramatized by the graph shown in Figure 5.3. Notice how the animal populations slowly diverge for the first several generations, then become radically different.

This logistics equation is also sensitive to the value of r. When r is 2.8, populations converge to a single stable value, 0.642857, which is called an *attractor*. Once the population reaches this value, it does not change. Figure 5.4 shows the result when one population begins at 0.5 and the other at 0.7. Even though the population curves start out very differently, they converge to a single value. This, of course, is not chaotic behavior.

For values of r equal to 3.2, there is a double attractor (0.513045 and 0.799455). In Figure 5.5 the populations begin at 0.1 and 0.6. After a few generations they oscillate between the same two points.

When r has the value of 3.5 there is a four-point attractor. Greater values of r result in an eight point attractor, a 16-point attractor, and so on for different values of r. Finally, when r is around 3.57, the behavior becomes chaotic.

Figure 5.6 illustrates how the number of attractors is related to r by plotting r against the possible values for y (population). A single attractor is illustrated when r has the value of 2.8 and a double attractor when r is 3.2. When r is above 3.5, there are many values for the population—the behavior has become chaotic.

5.2.1   Chaos Program Requirements

We will use the logistics formula $y_1 = r\ y_0\ (1 - y_0)$ to predict animal populations. We will follow two animal populations with r values of 3.69. Let the first start with a population of 0.50 and the second with a population of 0.51. We will then compute populations for 20 generations. The results are displayed in a graph as shown in Figure 5.3.

Figure 5.6 Bifurcation: r Versus Possible Populations

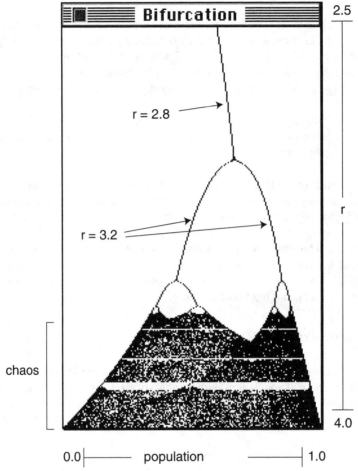

5.2.2   Chaos Program Design

Several steps are required to implement this program:

- Initialization—responsible for creating an empty graph
- Plotting generation 1—responsible for calculating sets of populations that begin at 0.50 for 20 generations
- Plotting generation 2—responsible for calculating sets of populations that begin at 0.51 for 20 generations
- Painting—responsible for drawing the two plots

This design description is missing a lot of detail. We will show how to add detail using a process called stepwise refinement in Section 5.3.1.

5.2.3   Chaos Implementation

The implementation is found in Listing 5.1. Line 19 defines one of four important program constants: the number of generations. Writing the identifier GENERATIONS is equivalent to writing the number 20.

Instead of defining a constant named GENERATIONS, we could simply write the number 20 each time it appears. As we will see in Section 5.5.8 there are two important reasons to use a constant named GENERATIONS. The name GENERATIONS communicates better than 20 to a program reader.

The second reason to use constants is because it makes a program easier to modify. For example, if we want to compute the animal populations over 35 generations, it is only necessary to modify the definition of GENERATIONS at the beginning of the program. This is much easier and more reliable than scanning through all of the code looking for all instances of the value 20 and changing only the appropriate ones.

Lines 20 through 22 define the other three constants: the reproductivity rate (r) and the initial values of the blue and red populations.

Program execution begins in paint with the creation of a graphing window in Line 33. VGraph is a Vista class that displays line graphs. Each graph can hold multiple lines with an unlimited number of points. VGraph provides a constructor that specifies minX, maxX, minY, maxY, and a reference to the applet that instantiates it. For example, in the constructor VGraph (0.0, generations, 0.0, 1.0, this), the first two parameters specify that the x-axis has values from 0.0 to 20.0 (Figure 5.7). Genera-

Listing 5.1 Logistics Class Code

```
1  //*************************************************************
2  //
3  // title:   Chaos
4  //
5  // Plot two lines for the graph of y1 = r * y0 * (1 - y0).  r
6  // is constant for each plot while the initial value of y0 is
7  // typically different for each plot.
8  //
9  //*************************************************************
10
11 import java.awt.Color;
12 import java.awt.Graphics;
13 import java.applet.Applet;
14 import vista.VGraph;
15
16 public class Chaos extends Applet {
17
18   // define the initial conditions for this run
19   final int    GENERATIONS          = 20;
20   final double R                    =  3.69;
21   final double INIT_BLUE_POPULATION =  0.50;
22   final double INIT_RED_POPULATION  =  0.51;
23
24   //---------- paint ---------------------------------------------
25   //
26   // Draw the graph.
27
28   public void paint (Graphics g)
29   {
30     // define the graph on which to plot
31     //   the x axis starts at 0.0 and ends at GENERATIONS
32     //   the y axis starts at 0.0 and ends at 1.0
33     VGraph plot = new VGraph (0.0, GENERATIONS, 0.0, 1.0, this);
34
35     // plot a blue line starting at INIT_BLUE_POPULATION
36     double population = INIT_BLUE_POPULATION;
37     plot.addLine(Color.blue);
38     plot.addPoint(0,population);
39     int time = 1;
40     while (time<=GENERATIONS)
41     {
42       population = R * population * (1.0 - population);
43       plot.addPoint(time,population);
44       time++;
45     }
46
```

Listing 5.1 Logistics Class Code

```
47      // plot a red line starting at INIT_RED_POPULATION
48      population = INIT_RED_POPULATION;
49      plot.addLine(Color.red);
50      plot.addPoint(0,population);
51      time = 1;
52      while (time<=GENERATIONS)
53      {
54        population = R * population * (1.0 - population);
55        plot.addPoint(time,population);
56        time++;
57      }
58
59      // draw the plot
60      plot.paint();
61    }
62 }
```

tions, which is plotted horizontally, has the value 20. The second two parameters specify that the y-axis has values between 0.0 and 1.0, which is the range of population values. Once the graph is created, it is assigned the name `plot`.

The fifth parameter in the constructor is `this`. This parameter informs the VGraph object that the graph is to be plotted in the window associated with this `Chaos` object. The `VGraph` class is documented in Appendix C on page 914.

Plots will be made for two different starting populations: a blue one and a red one. Line 36 assigns the initial value of the animal population for the blue plot. The `INIT_BLUE_POPULATION` has the value 0.50.

Line 37 adds a blue plot line to the `plot` graph. The first point added to the line is at time=0, population=0.5 (Line 38).

The loop defined in Lines 40 through 45 is responsible for adding the next 20 points to the blue plot line. It uses the counter loop pattern.

The statements in Lines 42 through 44 will be executed 20 times. The first time through the loop, `time` will have the value of 1 and `population` will have the value of 0.9225. This will be followed by `time` with a value of 2 and `population` with a value of 0.263812. Table 5.1 shows the next 12 iterations.

The above process is repeated a second time with `population` given an initial value 0.51. This time the plot is done in red. This completes the graphic initialization. The remaining activity is to draw the plot. This is done in Line 60.

Figure 5.7 `myPlot`

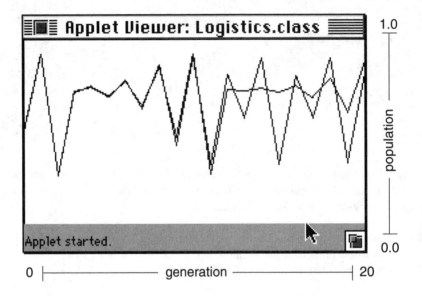

PATTERNS

5.3   A Couple of Patterns

5.3.1   Stepwise Refinement

blem

In many of the programs we have written so far it is possible to sit at the computer with lit-tle preplanning and write the solution from start to finish. Typically, it is not possible to write a program without planning and designing. In many projects the coding phase may account for only about 5% of the overall cost. Two-thirds of the cost may go to program maintenance such as bug fixes and enhancements. The rest of the cost is partitioned between planning, designing, and testing.

Several software engineering processes have been invented to make creating software sys-tems more methodical. We will cover one of those design methodologies in this section. It is call stepwise refinement.

ne
ution

Thus far we have looked at coding patterns. They described how snippets of code can be used to accomplish a task. The stepwise refinement pattern is a different kind of pattern. It describes a human process for accomplishing a task. Stepwise refinement is a process in which we take a look at the major tasks we need to do and then break those into smaller and smaller tasks until we have completely described what needs to be done. It is also called top-down because the major tasks are often called the high-level or top-level view of a system, and the details are called the low-level or bottom-level view.

> *Stepwise refinement* is a *top-down* design methodology that begins by taking
> a problem and partitioning it into smaller subproblems. Each of these smaller
> pieces can be further partitioned. This process is repeated until it becomes
> obvious how to translate a design step into code.

Stepwise refinement takes advantage of an often-used process for solving tough problems. The process of dividing a large problem into smaller subproblems is called "divide and conquer." Many tasks look formidable when first viewed. However, partitioning some-thing large into smaller tasks makes this large thing look manageable. If each of the small tasks can be accomplished, the entire task can be done.

Divide and conquer is a problem-solving strategy in which a problem is partitioned into components. Each component can be solved independently.

consequences   The ideas behind stepwise refinement and divide and conquer sound simple on the surface. Designers and programmers apply these principles without giving them a second thought. However, they require a great deal of skill that only comes through experience. For example, how do we know what the components are to partition a problem? Choosing the wrong partitioning can make a problem more difficult to solve.

Let us begin by using the chaos program as an example. In Section 5.2.2 we partition our design into four components which are executed sequentially. They are summarized below. These partitions are reflected in the code in Listing 5.1 on page 168.

- Initialization   Line 33
- Plotting generation 1   Lines 36–45
- Plotting generation 2   Lines 48–57
- Painting   Line 60

Once we have partitioned the problem we are free to think about one part of it without being distracted by the other parts. Each of these components can be further refined to provide the detail needed to program the solution.

Fortunately, the initialization and painting steps have been implemented within the VGraph class. The author took the responsibility to define a class to create plotting objects. We will not need to refine those steps here. The steps required to display information are hidden from us so that we do not have to deal with them.

The two steps that plot the populations are almost identical. We need only refine one of them as below. These steps are reflected in the code in Listing 5.1.

```
Plotting generation 1                              Line #
   Initialize the population                         36
   Add the population to the plot                    37,38
   Repeat 20 times:                                  39-45
   Compute the population of the next generation     42
   Add the population to the plot                    43
```

We have been using stepwise refinement in previous chapters without giving it much notice. For example, in Listing 3.1 on page 95 we partitioned the `StarryNight` applet into components. Each component represents one step. Each step represents implementing a single idea. Imagine how difficult it would be to understand this program if the code for drawing van Gogh's art were scattered throughout the program.

- Draw the frame   Lines 28–29
- Draw the easel   Lines 33–35
- Draw The Starry Night painting Lines 38–40
- Draw van Gogh's head   Lines 43–44
- Draw his torso   Lines 47–48
- Draw his arm   Lines 51–57
- Draw his paint brush   Lines 60–63
- Draw his leg   Lines 66–73

The butler problems in Chapter 1 and Chapter 2 are another place to apply stepwise refinement. The problem in exercise 22 on page 88 is a good example. We can break it into two parts:

1. Get the laundry if it is directly in front of our butler.
2. Get the laundry if it is further down the hall.

Next, we can break each of these steps further as follows:

1. If the laundry is directly in front of our butler:
   - Pick up the laundry
   - Turn around
   - Leave
2. Otherwise:
   - Move into the hall
   - Move forward until the butler finds the laundry
   - Pick it up
   - Leave

Some of these steps correspond directly to lines of code and cannot be further partitioned. An example is "pick up the laundry." Other steps can be partitioned. The following from step 2 are examples of steps that can be partitioned:

- Move into the hall
  - Step forward
  - Turn left

or

- Leave
  - Turn around
  - Move forward until the butler finds the wall
  - Turn right
  - Move forward

It is clear that we need to refine steps only until each step corresponds to a single line of code. However, often we stop refining when it is clear how to implement a step into a few lines of code. The point at which that occurs will vary individually and with the difficulty of a problem. A good rule of thumb for a beginner is to refine code until a step can be implemented with between one and seven lines of code. There are many exceptions.

5.3.2   Divide and Remainder Pattern

The divide and remainder pattern is a numeric pattern used to partition small units into coarser units. For example, we may be given the number of minutes an event takes and need to convert it to hours and minutes. This pattern is included here because it is a natural companion of the example in the previous section and relates to the chapter topic.

problem

Suppose we want to go from the total value of money to the least amount of change required to represent that money. This kind of operation is done by clerks and automatic change machines in supermarkets and department stores. A code fragment from an automatic change program is shown in Listing 5.2. If `value` gets the integer 118 in Line 1, quarters will get 4, dimes 1, nickels 1, and pennies 3.

Listing 5.2 Code Fragment for Minimum Change for an Amount of Money

```
1       value    = io.readInt();
2       quarters = value /  25;
3       value    = value %  25;
4       dimes    = value /  10;
5       value    = value %  10;
6       nickels  = value /   5;
7       pennies  = value %   5;
```

A *code fragment* is a subset of a program.

me
lution

The change program takes advantage of the characteristics of integer *divide and remainder* computations adapted for Java. Integer division works somewhat differently than many first-time programmers expect. When the expression `13.0 / 5.0` is evaluated, the result is 2.6. Just what we would expect. The divide operator when applied to two reals gives a real. This same principle must hold when the expression `13 / 5` is evaluated. Because both operands are ints, the result must be an int, which in this case is 2. The fractional part (the remainder) is lost. If the remainder is required, the modulus operator (%) is provided to extract the remainder of division. For example, `13 % 5` evaluates to 3.

The use of divide and remainder operators is a common pattern for partitioning small units of measure into coarser units. The divide operator computes how many whole units are in the value, and the remainder operator computes what is left over. It can be used to determine the number of days, hours, minutes, and seconds associated with the time given in seconds or to determine the number of miles, feet, and inches in a length given in inches.

JAVA

In the following sections we will take a deeper look at how Java handles numbers. The early focus of computers was on computation. Charles Babbage worked on his Difference Engine in 1823 so he could compute accurate mathematics tables. Modern day computers owe their ancestry to the work of John Mauchly and J. Presper Eckert, Jr. who were contracted by the military to create a computer that calculated firing tables for artillery. Only a few of the early visionaries saw other purposes for computers besides calculations. One of those persons was Alan Turing, who in the 1940s envisioned the computer as a potential intelligent agent. In this section we will take a look at the computer's early roots in numeric computation.

5.4　Discrete Numbers

We begin with integers. Integers are called *discrete* because there are no values between successive integers. For example, there is no integer between the integers 6 and 7. In contrast, real numbers have an unlimited number of real values between each number. For example, 5.1285 and 5.1286 have the value 5.12855 and many more between them.

> *Integers* are numbers without a fractional part. Java has four primitive types of integers: `byte`, `short`, `int`, and `long` (Table 5.2). In addition, Java has two integer classes: `Integer` and `Long`.

It is appropriate to use `int`s for almost all of our work in this book. Use them unless there is some compelling reason to use the other integer types.

5.4.1　Range

Programming languages and their implementation place limits on the range of numbers. Table 5.2 documents the sizes of various primitive types in Java. Many languages, such as Pascal, C, C++, and Ada, do not specify the range and precision of numbers. This is left to the compiler implementor. The result may be programs that run differently on different platforms. Because Java is designed to run over the web on many different platforms, the Java developers decided to impose a standard so that a program's behavior would be consistent across machines.

Java gives a programmer choices for the range and precision of integers. For example, if only small integers are needed, then using the `byte` type (-128 to 127) will save space. If larger numbers are needed, then the `long` type can be chosen (-9,223,372,036,854,775,808 to 9,223,372,036,854,775,807).

Table 5.2 Range of Integer Values

Type	Size	Range
byte	1 byte	-128 to 127
short	2 bytes	-32,768 to 32,767
int	4 bytes	-2,147,483,648 to 2,147,483,647
long	8 bytes	-9,223,372,036,854,775,808 to 9,223,372,036,854,775,807

5.4.2   Literal Constants

Literal constants are the character representations of numbers. For example, `10` is the literal constant for the value ten. Integer literal constants can be expressed in hexadecimal (base 16) and octal (base 8) in addition to decimal (base 10). The `0x` (the digit 0 followed by the letter x) prefix is used for hexadecimal and the `0` (the digit 0) prefix is used for octal literal constants. The following shows three ways to assign the integer 1522 to the identifier i:

```
int i = 1522;    // decimal       - base 10
int i = 0x5F2;   // hexadecimal - base 16
int i = 02762;   // octal         - base  8
```

Literals are the text representations of numbers.

One needs to be careful about using the appropriate literal constants in the appropriate integer expressions:

```
byte b = 127;    // ok
byte b = 128;    // error - will not compile
```

A `byte`'s largest positive value is 127.

An integer literal constant can be forced to be long by adding the "L" or "l" suffix. "5L" is a `long`.

```
int  i = 5L;     // error - cannot assign a long to an int
long i = 5L;     // ok
```

5.4.3 Declaring the Type of a Number

In Chapter 1 we used a declaration to introduce a reference to an object. In this chapter we are using declarations to introduce a primitive value into a program.

> Primitive values are implemented using the underlying computer hardware. As a result, they behave different from objects. They may not be aliased as objects may be (Section 1.5.3 , page 22 and Section 5.6 , page 196). We use special operators, such as +, -, *, /, etc., to manipulate them instead of the `object.operation` notations. Finally, we cannot inherit them.

An `int` is an example of a primitive value. They are declared as follows in Java:

```
int   days      =      7;
int   population = 10847;
```

Java is strongly typed. It is not possible to assign a character, boolean, or double to `days` or `population`. They have been declared as `ints`. Once a numeric identifier is declared and given a value it can be used within an expression. For example:

```
int totalHours = days * 24;
```

The result is that `totalHours` gets the value 168. The form for declaring and initializing a numeric value is as follows:

```
type numericIdentifier  =  numericExpression  ;
```

It is not necessary to initialize a number when it is declared. Another form of a numeric declaration is as follows:

```
type NumericIdentifier  ;
```

For example:

```
int    shoes;
```

The value of `shoes` is undefined, which may cause a problem. The value is called undefined because we have not assigned it a specific value, and therefore it cannot not be determined what value it contains. A good rule of thumb is always to initialize a number in its declaration, even if it is only to zero. As a result, its value will always be known.

5.4.4 Assignment Statements

Assignment statements are used to give an identifier a new value. For example:

```
height  = 480;
area    = width * height;
grade = (test1 + test2 + test3) / 3;
```

Its basic form is as follows:

```
identifier  =  numericExpression  ;
```

An identifier must be declared before it is used, it can only be declared once, and it should be initialized before it is used. For example, suppose a program contains the following sequence of statements:

```
int days = 5;
int hours;                 // not recommended but ok
int days = 6;              // error - days already declared
days    = 7;               // ok
int totalHours = days * hours; // error - hours has no value
```

5.4.5   Numeric Expressions

Numeric expressions compute values. They can be as simple as writing a numeric literal such as 42 or numeric identifier such as age. The following are examples of expressions:

```
42
age
24 * 7
base * height / 2
base * (height / 2)
```

Numeric expressions are of the form:

```
numericIdentifier
numericLiteral
numericExpression numericOperator numericExpression
( numericExpression )
```

We learned in Chapter 1 that Java provides a method call mechanism for applying operations to objects. The mechanism used for primitive numeric values is somewhat different. Java provides special symbols, such as +, −, and *, for applying operations to numbers. Thus, Java's arithmetic expressions look much like those we see every day.

 Applying arithmetic operators (multiplying, dividing, or adding) to two integers results in an integer. This may not seem like a significant fact, but it is essential to know. The division of one integer by another must always give an integer. Thus, 23 / 5 is 4. It does *not* give the real value 4.6.

Table 5.3 defines the operator precedence and meaning of Java's basic numeric operators. Table 5.4 contains some example expressions.

Table 5.3 Numeric Operators: Precedence, Meaning, and Associativity

precedence	Description	Symbol	Associativity
highest	parenthesis	( )	left to right
high	unary plus	+	right to left
high	unary minus	–	right to left
high	increment	++	right to left
high	decrement	– –	right to left
medium	multiplication	*	left to right
medium	division	/	left to right
medium	remainder	%	left to right
low	addition	+	left to right
low	subtraction	–	left to right

Table 5.4 Example Numeric Expressions

Expression	Result
3 * 5	15
12 / 3 * 2	8
7 + 4 * 5	27
(7 + 4) * 5	55
19 % 4	3
6 / 11	0
6 % 11	6
27 % 5 * 4 / (5 - 2)	2

All numeric operators are left associative (evaluated left to right) except for unary plus, unary minus, increment, and decrement. For example, "40 / 4 / 2" yields 5 because "40 / 4" is evaluated first. The leftmost division is done first. However, unary minus and plus are right associative. The rightmost operator is evaluated first. For example, given the expression "- + 5", we first evaluate "+ 5".

Associativity determines the order in which operators with the same precedence are evaluated.

Table 5.5 Precedence of Numeric and Boolean Operators (Highest to Lowest)

operators	associativity
( )	left to right
! ++ -- + - (unary)	right to left
* / %	left to right
+ -	left to right
< <= > >=	left to right
== !=	left to right
&	left to right
|	left to right
&&	left to right
||	left to right
= += -= *= /= %= &= |=	

Table 5.6 Example Boolean Expressions

expression	intermediate result	result
true | true & false	true | false	true
(true | true) & false	true & false	false
5 > 7 & 8 < 10	false & true	false
3 * 8 == 6 * 4	24 == 24	true
!true | false	false | false	false

The remainder operator evaluates the remainder returned with integer division. The sign of the result is the sign of the dividend. Thus, "-13 % 5" yields -3 but "13 % -5" yields 3.

Numeric operators also find themselves in boolean expressions. A more complete precedence listing is shown in Table 5.5 with some examples in Table 5.6.

5.4.6   Special Operators

The assignment operator can be used in conjunction with multiplicative and additive operators to create the shortcut expressions in Table 5.7. Table 5.8 contains some examples.

Table 5.7 Special Assignment Operators

expression	equivalent expression
x += y	x = x + y
x -= y	x = x - y
x *= y	x = x * y
x /= y	x = x / y
x %= y	x = x % y

Table 5.8 Example Assignment Operations

expression	result
x = 7; x += 5;	x is 12
a = 23; a %= 5;	a is 3
n = 11; n *= 3 + 2;	n is 55
n = 11; n = n * (3 + 2);	n is 55

There are prefix and postfix increment and decrement operators. Prefix operators appear before an operand and postfix operators appear after an operand. They may only be applied to identifiers (not to expressions) and are summarized in Table 5.9.

Table 5.9 does not capture the differences between the prefix and postfix operators. The prefix increment operator retrieves the value of the identifier, increments it, and stores its

Table 5.9 Special Increment and Decrement Operators

description	expression	equivalent expression
prefix increment	++x	x = x + 1
prefix decrement	--x	x = x - 1
postfix increment	x++	x = x + 1
postfix decrement	x--	x = x - 1

value back in the identifier. The value of the expression is the new value stored in the identifier.

```
a = 5;
b = ++a;
```

The above gives a and b the value of 6. It is the same as:

```
a = 5;
a = a + 1;
b = a;
```

The postfix increment operator behaves differently. Again the value of the identifier is retrieved, it is incremented, and the result is stored back into the identifier. However, this time the value of the expression is the value of the identifier *before* the new value is stored in the identifier.

```
a = 5;
b = a++;
```

The above gives a the value of 6, and b the value of 5. It is the same as:

```
a = 5;
b = a;
a = a + 1;
```

In many situations it makes no difference whether prefix or postfix versions of the increment or decrement operator are used. In other situations, the difference is critical. For example:

```
a = 25;
Math.sqrt(a++)yields 5.000
a = 25;
Math.sqrt(++a) yields 5.099

b = 14;
System.out.println(b++);displays 14
```

```
b = 14;
System.out.println(++b);displays 15
```

The increment and decrement operators can be used in expressions, but it is not recommended.

```
a = 5;
b = - a ++;    // too confusing
```

The above sets a to 6 and b to –5.

```
a = 5;
b = - ++ a;
```

The above sets a to 6, and b to -6. Although it is not too difficult to explain these results, expressions like the above are error-prone and easily misunderstood. If you are not sure what effect operator precedence or associativity will have on an expression, rewrite it. Use multiple statements or add parentheses to make the computation easy to understand.

The increment and decrement operators in conjunction with an identifier can be used as stand-alone statements. For example:

```
int x = 5;
x++;
```

The purpose of the above statement is to increment the value of x. The expression x++ also returns a value that is thrown away.

5.4.7   Overflow

Programmers must also be careful about numeric *overflow*. Computations may cause results that are larger than a value can hold. For example, when x and y are added in the code that follows, there is a numeric overflow. The maximum permitted integer value is roughly 2.2 billion, but the sum of x and y is 2.5 billion. Java does not give any warning about a problem. It computes an unexpected result. In this case, it computes -1794967296 for z. The result appears random; however, it is a direct result of two's complement arithmetic. Two's complement arithmetic is a topic for another course.

```
int   x = 1500000000;
int   y = 1000000000;
int   z =           0;
z = x + y;
System.out.println(z);
```

5.4.8 Type Coercion

A programmer must be careful when mixing number types. When numeric types are mixed, some values must be coerced into other types. The results may be unexpected. It is appropriate to assign numbers of low precision to identifiers of high precision because no information will be lost. As a result, it is permissible to assign a `short` to an `int` because a short uses only two bytes while an integer uses four bytes (see Table 5.2 on page 177). However, it is not permissible to assign an `int` to a `short` because information in two of the four bytes of the `int` value will be lost. See Figure 5.8. A rule of thumb is that the values of different types should not be mixed. Listing 5.3 show some examples.

> *Type coercion* is the process of converting a value of one type into a value of another type.

Figure 5.8 Not All Assignments Are Appropriate

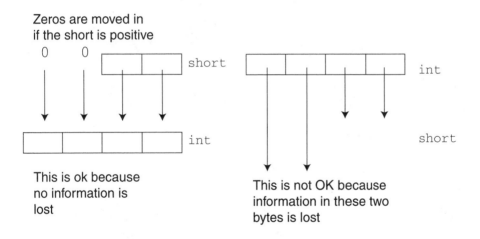

The conversion of one type to another is called a type *cast*. It is possible to do a type cast implicitly as is done above. It is also possible to do explicit type casts. There are times when it is important to assign ints to bytes. Java allows this to be done with an explicit type cast. By requiring explicit type casts, the Java compiler is assured that the programmer is aware of the possible loss of information.

> An *implicit* type cast is a type conversion done automatically by the Java compiler without the programmer giving instructions to do so. An *explicit* type cast is a type conversion requested by a programmer.

Listing 5.3   Type Coercion

```
1    {
2        byte    b = 1;
3        short   s = 2;
4        int     i = 3;
5        long    l = 4;
6
7        // implicit type coercion
8        b = s;  // error
9        b = i;  // error
10       b = l;  // error
11       s = b;
12       s = i;  // error
13       s = l;  // error
14       i = b;
15       i = s;
16       i = l;  // error
17       l = b;
18       l = s;
19       l = i;
20
21       // explicit type coercion
22       b = (byte)s;
23       s = (short)i;
24       i = (int)l;
25   }
```

5.5   Real Numbers

There are many instances when discrete numbers do not meet our needs. We often need numbers that have a fractional part, e.g., to represent money, distances, etc.

> *Reals* are numbers with a fractional part. Java has two primitive types of reals: `float` and `double`. In addition, Java has two real classes: `Float` and `Double`.

It is appropriate to use `double`s for almost all of our work in this book. They are a little more convenient to use. We will use them unless there is some compelling reason to use `float`s.

5.5.1   Real Declarations and Assignments

Real numbers are declared and assigned to identifiers in a similar manner to integers (Section 5.4.3). For example:

```
double windSpeed     = 13.7;
double pi            = Math.PI;
double radius        = 5.5;
double circumference = 2.0 * pi * radius;
double celsius       = (fahrenheit - 32.0) * 5.0 / 9.0;
```

5.5.2   Precision and Range

Reals come in several sizes, as illustrated in Table 5.10. A number's size indicates how much storage it requires and thus how many bits of information it can represent. Doubles have a greater size than floats and thus can represent numbers with a greater precision and magnitude.

The precision for reals indicates how many significant digits the *mantissa* holds (Figure 5.9). For example, a `double` can represent the value of pi with 15 digits as 3.14159265358979, while the best a `float` can do is 7 digits as 3.141592 (Figure 5.10).

Figure 5.9 Scientific Notation

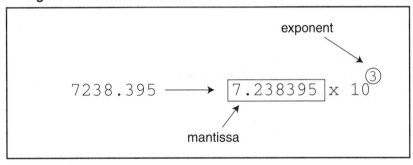

Figure 5.10 Precision

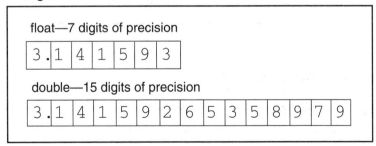

The *precision* of a real number determines with what accuracy a real number can represent a value. Precision is determined by the number of significant digits a number contains.

Do not confuse the magnitude of a number with its precision. For example, the double number 12300000000000000000.0D and the float number 12300000000000000000.0F may appear to be identical. They have the same magnitude. However, the precision of the double is 15 digits. Thus, we know that it is not 12300000000000123456.0D. However it may be 12300000000000012345.0D.

Precision has an impact when we do arithmetic. In the following example, adding one to a does not change it. We could add 1 to a forever without a changing. See Figure 5.11.

```
double a = 10000000000000000000.0;
double b = 1.0;
double c = a + b;   // c is 10000000000000000000.0
```

In addition to precision, doubles also have a greater range (magnitude) than floats: 10^{308} versus 10^{38} (Table 5.10).

Figure 5.11 Addition without Change

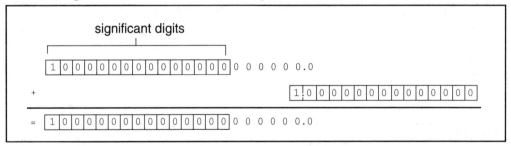

Table 5.10 Range of Real Types

type	size	range and precision
float	4 bytes	roughly ±3.4 E38 7 significant digits
double	8 bytes	roughly ±1.8 E308 15 significant digits

The value of floats is that they are smaller and faster than doubles. This performance comes at the cost of precision and range. Most of the problems we solve will not be influenced by our choice of `float` or `double`. Doubles are slightly easier to use and are generally fast enough. On the other hand, floats generally give us sufficient range and precision. A good rule of thumb is to use doubles unless space and time concerns are critical. If the program behaves too slowly or if data take up too much space, do some analysis and create experiments to determine the impact of using doubles versus floats.

Choosing the correct numeric representation is not the only issue. We must also be careful about how numbers are computed. For example, Listing 5.4 computes the two series in Figure 5.12.

Figure 5.12 Equivalent Series

$$\sum_{i=1}^{10000} \frac{1}{i^2} \qquad\qquad \sum_{i=10000}^{1} \frac{1}{i^2}$$

Listing 5.4   Computing a Series of Numbers

```
1  {
2      int  maxCount = 10000;
3      long i         =      0;
4
5      float  floatResult   = 0.0F;
6      int i = 1;
7      while (i<=maxCount)
8      {
9        floatResult   += 1.0F / (i * i);
10        i++;
11      }
12      System.out.println(floatResult);
13
14      floatResult   = 0.0F;
15      i = maxCount;
16      while i>0)
17      {
18        floatResult   += 1.0F / (i * i);
19        i--;
20      }
21      System.out.println(floatResult);
22  }
```

The two series are mathematically equivalent. The order in which the first 10,000 integers are added does not make a difference mathematically, but it does make a difference when they are executed by a computer. The two loops in Listing 5.4 produce different results. The first loop computes 1.64473, and the second loop computes 1.64483. The problem is in the first loop. The larger numbers are computed first and successive smaller number are added to the result. Adding small numbers to large numbers causes a higher loss of information because the least significant digits of the smaller numbers are thrown away. However, in the second loop the small numbers are added first. By adding enough of the small numbers first, the small parts of them have time to accumulate and create an impact. Notice that we used floats in Listing 5.4. They have small precision and thus it was easier to demonstrate the round-off error.

To illustrate a problem adding numbers with different magnitudes we will look at the task of adding 4.832178 to 1023.267. If floating point values have seven significant digits, then adding the two numbers will cause a loss of information (Figure 5.13). A loss of information is inevitable because reals cannot be represented with arbitrary precision.

Figure 5.13 Computing a Series of Numbers

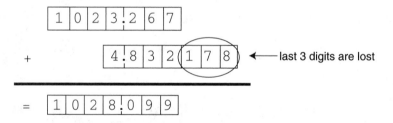

It is important, however, to control how much information is lost. We should get the same result if we add 0.4832178 to 1023.267 10 times. However, it makes a difference in which order we do the addition, as illustrated in Figure 5.14. In the left column we added the small numbers to the large number and ended up with a result slightly smaller than the result in the right column, where we added the small numbers to themselves first. We can see that fewer digits were lost in the right column. An error of less than 0.0002% appears hardly enough to quibble about. However, some computations require billions of computations. Small errors add up quickly.

Be careful when using relational operators with real numbers. For example, the result of the following may be false:

```
1.1F + 1.1F + 1.1F + 1.1F + 1.1F + 1.1F + 1.1F + 1.1F + 1.1F + 1.1F
== 11.0F
```

Figure 5.14 Adding 10 Small Numbers to a Large Number

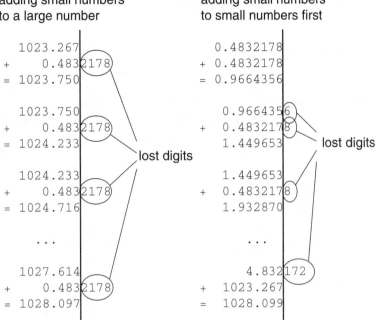

The precision of real numbers is limited. Round-off errors may cause repeated additions and multiplications to be slightly different. If there is a need to compare real numbers, check to see if they are within a specific range. An example follows. (Math.abs returns the absolute value of a number. More math methods are described in Appendix B on page 885.)

```
double x = 8.837465932;
double y = 8.837465938;
if (Math.abs(x - y) < 0.0000001)
   ...
```

5.5.3   Literal Constants

By default all real literal constants are doubles. Alternately, real literals can be designated as float by using the "F" or "f" suffix. A double can be explicitly specified by using the "D" or "d" suffix. Reals can be written in decimal format (for example, 3.14159) or in floating point format using an "E" or "e" (for example, 0.314159e1, which is the equivalent of 0.314158 x 10^1.) The following are `float` literals for the value 12.34:

```
12.34f        12.34e0f.       1234e2f        1234.e-2f+
.1234e+2F
```

The following are double literals for the value 12.34:

```
12.34d        12.34           .1234e2D
```

Because reals default to double, one should be careful when mixing floats and literal constants. This is why the author prefers to use doubles. Float literals must have a "f" suffix.

```
float  e = 2.71828;    // error
float  e = 2.71828f;   // ok
double d = 1.71828;    // ok
```

5.5.4   Operators

Operators for real values work much as they do for integers. Any arithmetic operator that has a real value on its left or right side will produce a real result. Arithmetic operators produce integer results only if both operands are integers. For example:

```
int i = 3;
int x = 13.8;
4 * x - 1                  => int result of 11
4.0 * x - 1                => double result of 11.0
4 / x - 1                  => int result of 0
4.0 / x - 1                => double result of 0.3333...
```

5.5.5   Overflow

Overflow with real numbers behaves differently from overflow with integers. For example, the range of floats is roughly 10^{38}. Thus, a times b in the code below results in an overflow. The value `"Inf"`, which stands for infinity, is the value printed for c.

```
float  a = 4.0E20F;
float  b = 6.0E25F;
float  c = 0.0F;
c = a * b;
System.out.println(c);    // "Inf" is printed
```

Underflows can also occur with real numbers. For example, 4.0E-30 multiplied by 6.0E-30 results in a value of 0.0. The result is 0.0 because the smallest float is about 1.4E-45. The result of the above computation is 2.4E-59, which is smaller than the smallest float. No error is given.

5.5.6   Type Coercion

Assigning integers to real identifiers is always permissible. There may be a loss of information, but that loss will occur in the least significant digits. However, assigning a real to an integer is not permissible because it will result in the loss of the real's fractional part. Listing 5.5 illustrates permissible assignments.

Listing 5.5   Implicit Type Coercion

```
1   {
2       byte    b = 1;
3       short   s = 2;
4       int     i = 3;
5       long    l = 4;
6
7       float  f = 5.5F;
8       double d = 6.6;
9
10      // implicit type casts
11      f = d;  // error
12      f = b;
13      f = s;
14      f = i;
15      f = l;
16
17      d = f;
18      l = f; // error
19
20      // explicit type casts
21      f = (float)d;
22      f = (float)1.23;
23      i = (int)f;
24  }
```

The result of an expression with only integers within it is an integer, and the result of an expression with only reals within it is a real. For example:

```
int width            = 25;
int height           = width * 2;
int depth            = width * 1.5;   // error
double pi            = Math.PI;
double markup        = 0.25;
double list          = 15.78;
double price         = list + list * markup;
double circumference = 4 * width;    // not recommended but ok
double length        = 4.0 * width;  // better than above
```

Mixing integers and reals within an expression is permissible. When any subexpression is mixed, the result is a real because that results in the least information lost. For example, the following is not a problem. The subexpression d * 2 gives the result 246.912:

```
double d = 123.456;
double result = d * 2 + 1.5;
```

However, mixed arithmetic expressions should be avoided. In some cases they create problems. For example, using the following to convert from Fahrenheit to Celsius will cause incorrect results

```
celsius = 5 / 9 * (fahrenheit - 32)
```

The first computation is 5 / 9. Because 5 and 9 are both integers, integer division is used, giving the result 0. Thus, celsius will always be 0. However, replacing 5 with 5.0, 9 with 9.0, and 32 with 32.0 will assure that incorrect results do not occur.

It is not necessary to be overzealous. For example, Listing 5.4 on page 189 contains the following statement (i is an integer).

```
floatResult += 1.0F / (i * i);
```

Insisting that i is explicitly cast to a float is not necessary. However, we should feel uncomfortable enough with that statement that we look at it carefully and make sure that it will not cause us any problems.

5.5.7 Java Math Class and Static Methods

The Java Math class contains methods needed to perform such mathematical operations as computing the sine, power, absolute value, and random functions. The Math class is different from other classes we have seen thus far. All of its methods are static. As a result, we never create a Math object, but rather apply operations to the class instead. For example, if we need to compute $23.97^{3.45}$ we write it as Math.pow(23.97, 3.45). The signature for the power function is shown below:

```
public static double pow(double a, double b)
```

Notice that it requires two double parameters and returns a double result. The clue that pow is a static method is the static keyword.

A particularly useful Math method is random. It returns a pseudo-random double between 0.0 and 1.0. To generate an integer between 1 and 6 we can write the following code:

```
int number = (int)(Math.random() * 0.5999) + 1;
```

We multiply the random number by a number slightly smaller than 6.0 because there is a slight chance that the random number that is generated is 1.0. In that case our random integer is 7, which is out of our range.

Pseudo-random numbers are numbers that are actually computed. If we know one of the random numbers returned by `Math.random` and the equation used, we can predict what the following number is. However, the equation for computing random numbers is written such that the generated numbers are well distributed between 0.0 and 1.0. Without knowing the random number equation, it is impossible to predict what the next number will be. As a result, the numbers appear random.

Other `Math` methods are outlined in Appendix B on page 885. In addition, we will learn more about the static modifier in Section 7.6.6.

5.5.8   Constants

Constants are values that do not change. They are specified by using the `final` keyword. They are of the form:

```
final type constantIdentifier = expression ;
```

For example,

```
final double  PI       = Math.PI;
final double  WIDTH    = 27;
final boolean DEBUG    = false;
final int     AREA     = WIDTH * WIDTH / 2;
final double  GRAVITY  = 9.8;
```

Their values may not be changed. For example,

```
private final int MINIMUM_AGE = 18;
private       int MAXIMUM_AGE = 29;

public void foo ()
{
  MINIMUM_AGE = 16; // syntax error: cannot change constant.
  MAXIMUM_AGE = 32; // ok
}
```

Constants are values that do not change.

We stated earlier that there are two important reasons to use a constant rather than a value such as 20. The first is that constant identifiers help communicate the intent of a value to a program reader. Thus, the identifiers AREA and MINIMUM_AGE carry a meaning. The values 79.3 and 18 by themselves do not suggest any meaning.

The second reason to use constants is because they make a program easier to modify. For example, if we want to change the minimum age in a program, we only have to change its value in one location. We do not have to search the program for every location that 18 appears and decide if we should change its value or whether 18 has a meaning other than minimum age. For example, in Listing 5.1 on page 168 GENERATIONS is used in Lines 33, 40, and 52. However, when we want to change the number of generations we need only change it once in Line 19.

By convention, constant identifiers are all capitals. This makes them easy to spot in a program.

5.6   Object and Value Models for Numerical Representation

Thus far we have introduced the declaration of two kinds of values: reference and primitive. The declarations for primitive values are not consistent with the declarations we have seen for objects in previous chapters. Declaring a double with the value of 0.0 appears as follows:

```
double y = 0.0;
```

There is no new operator or constructor because int and double are not classes; thus, y is not an object. If double were a class, what we should expect to see is:

```
double y = new double(0.0); // error
```

As we saw in Chapter 1, Butler is a class; thus, it is declared as follows.

```
Butler james = new Butler (11, 3, edsRoom);
```

As is discussed in Chapter 1, Butler is a class that provides a constructor for creating objects. In this case, the new object's name is james. When objects are created, they have a set of methods that belong to them and can be used to access and modify their state.

The Java design team faced many decisions that traded off ease of use with ease of implementation. One of those trade-offs concerned the efficient execution of integer and real arithmetic. They chose to make Java a hybrid language to improve the efficient translation of numbers. Thus, Java is not purely object-oriented. Integers and reals can be represented as objects or as primitive values. They are usually represented as primitives when they appear in expressions or are used as parameters to methods. They can be represented as objects when it is important to view them in a consistent way with other objects. Primitives have many of the characteristics of objects, but also have some striking differences.

An object may have more than one name. For example, your parents may call you "Samantha," your friends may call you "Sammie," your boyfriend "kid," and the computer science instructor "Ms. Torez." We all recognize that these names refer to the same person (object). We call these names aliases for the same object. When "Ms. Torez" is happy because she got an A on her last project, so is "Samantha" and "Sammie" because they are the same person.

The same principle holds true for objects in Java. Figure 5.15 illustrates how Java objects can also be aliased. An assignment attaches a new name to an existing object. Because james and jimmy identify the same object, the forward operation is applied twice to that single object.

Figure 5.15 Two Names, One Object

```
Butler james =
        new Butler (11, 3, edsRoom);
Butler jimmy = james;
james.forward ();
jimmy.forward ();
```

To create a new object, one must use the new operation in conjunction with a constructor. Figure 5.16 illustrates this. Because james and jimmy identify different objects, the forward operation is applied once to each object.

Ints are not classes, and they are not instantiated into objects. Instead they are used to introduce primitive values.

Figure 5.16 Two Names, Two Objects

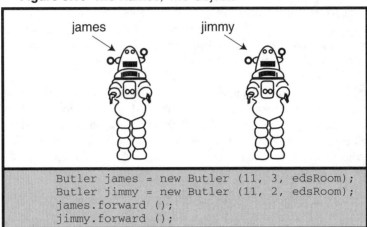

```
Butler james = new Butler (11, 3, edsRoom);
Butler jimmy = new Butler (11, 2, edsRoom);
james.forward ();
jimmy.forward ();
```

```
int age    = 19;
int years  = age;
age        = age + 5;
years      = years -3;
```

The value of `age` in the code above is 24. The value of `years` is 16. Notice that `years` and `age` do not refer to the same entity.

age   years

```
24              16
```

The preceding discussion focuses on the differences between objects and values. It is more useful to focus on their similarities. `Int` and `float` values have an identity, have a state, and can be operated upon. Even though primitives are technically not objects, it is useful to thing of them as objects.

REFERENCE

5.7   Summary

Java integers come in four sizes: `byte`, `short`, `int`, and `long`. They are discrete values that are manipulated with the special symbols `+`, `-`, `*`, `/`, and `%`. Numeric overflow is not checked and can cause unexpected results.

Java reals come in two sizes: `float` and `double`. They contain a fractional component and can be manipulated with the special symbols `+`, `-`, `*`, and `/`. Numeric overflow results in a special infinite value. Underflow results in a zero value. Reals have limited precision, so care must be taken in constructing mathematical systems.

Operator precedence and associativity are consistent with our expectations. Addition and subtraction have the lowest precedence of the arithmetic operators with multiplication, division, and modular operations higher and unary operators at the top. Parentheses are used to change precedence. The associativity of most operators is left to right. The major exceptions are the unary operators.

Conversion between numbers of different types is possible with implicit and explicit type casts. Implicit type casts are done automatically when the danger of losing precision is low. Explicit type casts are necessary when the danger is high.

Integers and reals are values. They have a lot in common with objects, but also some important differences. Objects can be aliased—referenced by more than one name. Values, on the other hand, have only one name associated with each value. In addition, it is possible to extend objects but not primitive values.

Chaotic systems are numeric models that are susceptible to small changes in initial conditions. Small differences can cause vastly different results. An example of a chaotic system is one governed by the equation $y_1 = r\ y_0\ (1 - y_0)$.

5.8   Bibliography

- Dewdney, A.K. 1990. The strange attractions of chaos. Chap. 4 in *The Magic Machine: A Handbook of Computer Sorcery.* New York: W. H. Freeman and Company, 1990.

    ———. 1993. A portrait of chaos. Chap. 10 in *The Tinkertoy Computer.* New York: W. H. Freeman and Company

————. 1993. Weather in a jar. Chap. 9 in *The Tinkertoy Computer*. New York: W. H. Freeman and Company.

Dewdney is good at using computers to illustrate fundamental ideas in a way that is fun and educational.

- Gleick, James. 1987. *Chaos: Making a New Science*. New York: Viking.

An easy-to-read popular introduction to chaos.

- Wirth, Niklaus. 1971. Program development by stepwise refinement. *Communications of the ACM* 14, no. 4 (April): 221–227.

The original and readable paper that describes the process of design by incrementally adding detail.

5.9   Acknowledgments

The authors of previous CS1 textbooks, such as Doug Cooper, Michael Clancy, and Rick Mercer, for problem ideas.

David Kroon of the University of Portland for the series example.

PROBLEM SETS

5.10 Exercises

Chaos—Section 5.2

1   You will find a variation of the program in Listing 5.1 on the web page for this chapter. Run it to answer the following question: Given an r of 3.7 and initial populations of 0.5 and 0.50001, roughly how many generations does it take for the two populations to diverge significantly?

2   Read the book *Chaos: Making a New Science* by James Gleick and write a book report.

Stepwise Refinement Pattern—Section 5.2

3   Apply the stepwise refinement technique and design a solution for the following tasks:

    a.   brushing your teeth

    b.   washing a car

    c.   baking a cake

    d.   getting ready for school

    e.   planning a birthday party

4   Use stepwise refinement to decompose the following exercises:

    a.   exercise 25

    b.   exercise 27

5   Read the article by Niklaus Wirth called "Program Development by Stepwise Refinement" in *Communications of the ACM,* vol. 14, no. 4 (April 1971), pp. 221–227. Write a report.

Computation—Section 5.4 and Section 5.5

6   Express the following scientific notation with a value between 1.0 and 9.999 for each number mantissa (the number on the left side of the "E").

    a.   1.0

    b.   0.00000003815

    c.   123456789.0

    d.   -45.2

7   Express the following as ordinary decimal fractions:

    a.   8.34E0

    b.   -1.1111E11

    c.   5.2E-2

    d.   0.0E0

8   What is the result of each of the following expressions?

    a.   5 * 3 - 2

    b.   (5 * 3) - 2

    c.   5 * (3 - 2)

    d.   36 / 3

    e.   36 / 7

    f.   36 % 3

    g.   36 % 11 - 1

    h.   63 % 10 * 10

    i.   Math.min (23, 14)

    j.   Math.max (-84, -37)

    k.   Math.max (Math.abs(-84), -37)

    l.   Math.max (18, Math.abs(18))

    m.   Math.power(2,8);

    n.   Math.power(25.0, 0.5);

    o.   Math.power(Math.sqrt(18.3),2)

    p.   Math.ceil(Math.random())

9 What is the result of each of the following expressions?

   a.   3.8 * 2.1 / 7.1

   b.   18.2 - 9.8 / 3.7 - 1.0

   c.   Math.max (11.3, 1.13E2)

   d.   Math.round (12.67)

   e.   Math.floor (12.67)

   f.   Math.ceil (12.67)

   g.   Math.cos (0.0)

   h.   Math.pow (2.3, 4.6)

   i.   Math.sqrt (Math.ceil (25.8) - 1.0)

   j.   Math.random()

   k.   Math.pow (27.0, -3.0)

   l.   Math.log (Math.E)

   m.   180 / Math.PI

   n.   Math.exp (Math.log (14.1))

10 Syntax errors will result if the following are compiled. What is wrong with each?

   a.   double d = 5.0 (3.0 + 1.0);

   b.   float f = 6.8 + 1.1;

   c.   double d = sqrt(25.0);

   d.   double d = 6.0 ** 2.0;

   e.   int i = 4.3;

   f.   double d = Math.pow(2.3);

   g.   double d = Math.round(11.1, 5.0);

   h.   double d = Math.Sin(0.123);

11 Why will the following two consecutive lines result in a syntax error?

```
int x = 3;
int x = 2 * x;
```

12 What is the result of each of the following expressions? Is the result an `int` or `double`?

   a.   36.0 / 5 - 5 / 3

   b.   36 / 5 - 5 / 3.0

   c.   Math.round (36.0) / 5 - 5 / 3

d.   36 / Math.sqrt(25)

e.   Math.pow (2, 3)

13   Write Java expressions for the following mathematical expressions:

a. 2^8

b.   Pythagorean theorem

c.   a random number between zero and four inclusive.

14   Suppose there is a type small float with four decimal digits of precision. As a result, all intermediate computations and all final computations are rounded off to four digits. What is the result of the following computations?

a.   24.8 + 0.6439 + 0.5

b.   2.0 / 6.0

c.   1.0 + 0.0001 + 0.0001 + 0.0001 + 0.0001 + 0.0001 + 0.0001

d.   1.0 + (0.0001 + 0.0001 + 0.0001 + 0.0001 + 0.0001 + 0.0001)

15   What is the output of the following?

a.
```
int x = 1;
while (x < 3)
{
  System.out.println(x);
  int y = 5;
  while (y < 8)
  {
    System.out.println(y);
    y++;
  }
  x++;
}
```

b.
```
int x = 1;
while (x < 5)
{
  int y = 1;
  while (y < x)
  {
    System.out.println(y);
    y++;
  }
  x++;
}
```

c.
```
int a = 0
int x = 4;
while (x < 6)
{
   int y = 11;
   while (y > 8)
   {
     a += x + y;
     y--;
   }
   x++;
}
System.out.println(a);
```

d.
```
int sum = 0;
int i = 1;
while (i < 4)
{
   int j = 1;
   while (j < 4)
   {
     if (i < j)
       sum += i;
     j++;
   }
   i++;
}
System.out.println(sum);
```

e.
```
int x = 1;
while (x < 3)
{
   int y = 1;
   while (y < 4)
   {
     int z = 1;
     while (z < 4) {
       System.out.println(x + " " + y + " " + z);
       z++;
     }
     y++;
   }
   x++;
}
```

16 Create a walk-through table that shows the change of values for a walk-though for parts c and d in Exercise 15

5.11 Projects

Chaos—Section 5.2

17 Listing 5.1 does not allow user input. The program must be modified and recompiled for each initial population value.

    a.   Create a GUI interface. There should be input text fields for the initial population, reproductive rate r, and number of generations.

    b.   Create a text-based interface.

18 Write a program that reads in an integer and computes its factorial using a loop. The program should prompt the application user for n and then display the value of n factorial ($n!$).

$$n! = 1 * 2 * 3 * \ldots * n$$

19 Write a program that computes the sum of the integer from 1 to n. The program should request an n and print the sum.

20 Write a program the computes the value of the following series given an x and n supplied by the program user:

$$1 + x + \frac{x^2}{2!} + \frac{x^3}{3!} + \ldots + \frac{x^n}{n!}$$

Computations—Section 5.4 and Section 5.5

21 Completely implement the code fragment in Listing 5.2 on page 174 using the IPO or callback pattern.

22 Write a complete application using the IPO or callback pattern to compute the following. For each program select appropriate test data to try out your program.

    a.   the hypotenuse of a right triangle

$$hypotenuse = (a^2 + b^2)^{1/2}$$

    b.   the day, hours, minutes, and seconds represented by a time given in seconds

    c. $\log_2 x$ where:

$$\log_2 x = \frac{\log_e x}{\log_e 2}$$

d.   a program that computes 1 if a number is odd, and 0 if a number is even.

23   Write a program using the IPO or callback pattern that computes income tax at 0% for income less than $20,000, 20% for income from $20,000 to less than $35,000, and 28% for income greater than $35,000.

24   Suppose you have gotten tired of your professors' insistence on correctness and precision and choose to fire them out of a circus cannon. You know the missile velocity and angle that the cannon is above the horizon. You want to figure how high and how far they have gone after a given number of seconds. Input will be: velocity (miles/hour), angle(degrees), and time (seconds). Output will be: height (feet) and distance (feet). Remember to convert degrees to radians and miles to feet. Use meaningful identifier names (not x,v,s, etc.)

$$x = v\ cos(\alpha)\ s$$

$$y = \frac{1}{2}g\ s^2 + v\ sin(\alpha)\ s$$

```
x:   distance
y:   height
s:   time
v:   velocity
α:   angle
g:   acceleration of gravity (32 feet / sec²)
```

25   Suppose you are interested in a car loan and want to determine if you can afford the monthly payments. Write a program to compute monthly payments. Monthly loan payments are computed using the following formula (remember to use meaningful identifier names—not P,A,R, or M):

$$P = AR\frac{(R+1)^M}{(R+1)^M - 1}$$

```
P:   monthly Payment
A:   loan Amount
R:   monthly Rate - interest rate paid each month as a fraction.
For example, a rate of 12% would translate into 0.12 for a
yearly rate and 0.01 for a monthly rate
M:   number of Months over which the loan is to be paid
```

a.   Use the IPO pattern.

b.   Use the VApplet framework with text fields and buttons.

26   This problem is an extension of problem 25 Create an amortization table shown below. Information that is entered by a program's user is in bold. It should not be part of the program.

```
Enter loan amount:       3600
Enter term in months:    36
Enter percentage rate:   12


       ------------------------------------------------

loan amount:        $3600.00
term:               36 months
interest:           12%
monthly payment:    $119.57

    month    interest       principal       principal
             this month     this month         left
    ------------------------------------------------------
      1        36.00           83.57          3516.40
      2        35.17           84.40          2432.00
      .
      .
      .
     36        ...             ...               0.00

total principal = 3600.00
total interest  =  704.52
grand total     = 5304.52
```

You need to create a class whose methods support the following:

```
// take out a car loan for $3,600 at 12.0% for 36
// months.
Loan carLoan = new Loan(3600.0, 12.0, 36);
... carLoan.getMonthlyPayment();

// compute monthly status
loop for 36 times
   ... carLoan.getInterestPayment();
   ... carLoan.getPrincipalPayment();
   ... carLoan.getPrincipalLeft();
   carLoan.monthlyPaymentReceived();
```

27   Acme has created the next generation of computer applications which they want to
     protect with serial numbers. Each shipped package will contain a unique serial num-
     ber, which the application user must enter when installing the program. Acme does
     not want the program to accept just any number, so you have been assigned the task
     of creating a serial number encryption code. Each serial number is five digits long.
     The fifth digit is the sum of the previous four digits with the tens digit removed. For
     example, 23544 is a valid serial number because 2 + 3 + 5 + 4 yields 14. Remove the
     1 and add the 4 as the fifth digit. Write a program that reads a four-digit number and
     displays its valid five-digit serial number.

6 Method Abstraction

Abstraction
Computer Animation

6.1　Objectives

Concepts　　　　　　　　　　　　　　　　**Section 6.2, page 211**

The primary focus of this chapter is creating abstractions. We will look at operation abstractions, parameter passing techniques, and scope. This chapter begins by describing why abstraction is important. This is followed by a section that describes how to partition a drawing program using method abstraction.

Section 6.7, page 249

For those of us who are more adventurous there is an optional supplementary section about making computer animation. This will require some knowledge of multi-threading. In addition, we will look at strategies for eliminating motion flicker.

Patterns　　　　　　　　　　　　　　　　**Section 6.4, page 218**

This chapter will introduce the delegation action pattern. Decomposing a problem into subproblems is a common strategy to help manage complexity. We will organize our problems into small chunks, each of which can be solved independently. This problem-solving strategy is called "divide and conquer." It is the basis for stepwise refinement, which we introduced in Chapter 5.

Java Skills

Next we address how we can use Java to express behavioral abstractions.

- Declaring Java methods　　　　　　　　　Section 6.6.1, page 223
- Passing parameters　　　　　　　　　　　Section 6.6.2, page 225
- Scope, local variables, and instance variables　　Section 6.6.3, page 227
- Returning values　　　　　　　　　　　　Section 6.6.5, page 236

Abilities

By the end of this chapter we should be able to do the following:

- Write methods that require parameters and return values.
- Some of us should be able to create a multithreaded applet.

CONCEPTS

6.2   Abstraction

Abstraction helps us manage our complex lives. For example, when we start our cars, we are not concerned about the firing order of the pistons, the formula used by the fuel injection system, or the metal alloy contained in the exhaust manifold. Mechanical engineers have kindly encapsulated (hidden) these details, and most internal details have become nonessential information for the typical driver. This allows us to focus on important details such as is engaging the clutch and turning the steering wheel in order to avoid traffic (Figure 6.1).

> *Abstraction* is the process of focusing on the essential details of a system. *Encapsulation* is the process of hiding information that is not useful to a system user.

We give object characteristics to software systems because they give us a metaphor for thinking about and organizing software items in a manner with which we are familiar. After all, we have been interacting with physical objects since we were born. Without some kind of organization, it would be impossible to create a program such as Myst. The CD-ROM for Myst contains 520 MB, or over 4 billion bits of information. A sequence of 4 billion bits is impossible to comprehend without using abstraction. Thus, the program for Myst has abstractions for images, sounds, and code. In this chapter and the next we will learn about the mechanisms that Java provides for creating abstractions. We will learn how we can create classes. This chapter starts that process by illustrating how method abstractions are used to define operations. Methods are one of the building blocks of classes. In the next chapter, we will look at how methods together with instance variables are used to create classes.

6.3   Defining Our Own Operations

When we think about a day's events, we think of them in abstract terms. For example, if we say we had dinner and then went out to the movies, we communicate clearly to everyone what our evening was about. We do not have to say that we went to the theater box office, purchased a ticket, bought popcorn, found a seat, and watched a motion picture. All those ideas are already encapsulated in the idea of going to a movie.

Figure 6.1 Abstraction: A Simple Interface for a Complex Task

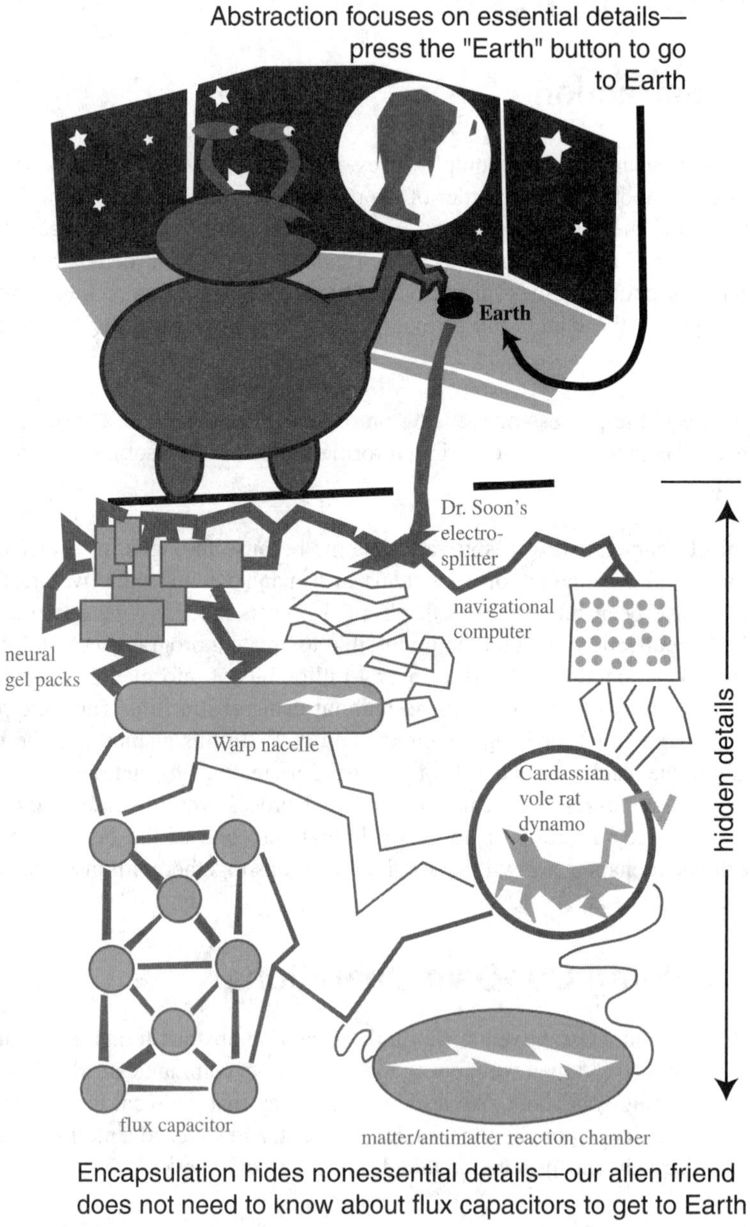

Abstraction focuses on essential details—
press the "Earth" button to go
to Earth

Earth

Dr. Soon's
electro-
splitter

navigational
computer

neural
gel packs

Warp nacelle

Cardassian
vole rat
dynamo

hidden details

flux capacitor

matter/antimatter reaction chamber

Encapsulation hides nonessential details—our alien friend
does not need to know about flux capacitors to get to Earth

It is useful to do a similar kind of abstraction when we write programs. Suppose we want to create a program that draws our butler robot doing yard work (Figure 6.2). By creating method abstractions, we can more clearly communicate our ideas. We start by partitioning our problem into two action items: draw a background and draw a butler. In this section, we will see how to implement each of these actions with a method. Making our butler move as it does in the `RoomCleaningSimulation` applet from Chapter 1 requires an understanding of Java threads. A description of that process is optional (Section 6.7).

Figure 6.2 Our Butler against a Background

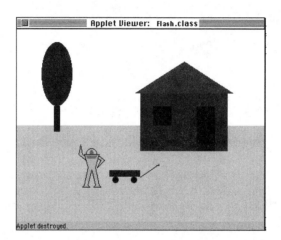

6.3.1 Simple Methods

Methods are the Java mechanism that allows programmers to create operation abstractions. An example of using a method is shown in Listing 6.1. It contains a subset of the code required to draw the background in Figure 6.2. Because the complete code is rather lengthy—but not difficult—it has been placed in the reference section (Listing 6.26 on page 263).

The `Butler` applet contains two methods. We are familiar with the `paint` method at Line 18. It is called whenever the display must be repainted. The only responsibility the `paint` method has in this applet is to call the `paintBackground` method, which draws the background.

If the only thing we are going to do is draw a background, we gain little by placing the code that draws a background in a separate method. All the code in the `paintBack-ground` method could be placed within the `paint` method. We have placed it in a sepa-

Listing 6.1 Draw a Background for Our Butler

```
1  //*********************************************************
2  //
3  // title:   Butler
4  //
5  // Draw a butler against a background.
6  // Phase 1: draw the background.
7  //
8  //*********************************************************
9
10 import java.awt.Color;
11 import java.awt.Graphics;
12 import java.awt.Polygon;
13 import java.applet.Applet;
14
15 public class Butler extends Applet
16 {
17    // Called automatically by Java to paint the window.
18    public void paint(Graphics g)
19    {
20      paintBackground();
21    }
22
23    // pre:  none
24    // post: The background is painted
25    public void paintBackground()
26    {
27      // Get the graphics context.
28      Graphics g = getGraphics();
29
30      // Create the sky and ground
31      g.setColor(Color.blue);
32      g.fillRect(0,0,400,150);
33      Color springGreen = new Color(0, 255, 127);
34      g.setColor(springGreen);
35      g.fillRect(0,150,400,150);
36
37      ... additional code to draw a tree, house, and wagon ...
38    }
39 }
```

rate method in anticipation of adding a second method that draws a butler. Partitioning code into methods makes the program easier to manage. If there is a problem with the background, we know to look in the paintBackground method. If the problem is with our butler, we look in the paintButler method. We could further partition the paintBackground into methods that draw the house, tree, and wagon. We have left that as an exercise.

Details about the syntax of Java methods are left for a later section. Let us first concentrate on the mechanics of methods. We begin by walking through the code, which will help us understand how it executes.

We know that when a web browser captures a `paint` event, an applet's `paint` method is executed. Table 6.1 documents the sequence of events after the `paint` method is called for the program in Listing 6.1. The flow of control is also shown pictorially in Figure 6.3.

Table 6.1 Flow of Control for Listing 6.1

line	action
18	enter `paint`
20	call `paintBackground`
25	enter `paintBackground`
28	get graphics context
31	set drawing color
32–37	compete execution of the `paintBackground` body
38	exit `paintBackground`
21	exit `paint`

6.3.2   Methods with Parameters

In Listing 6.1, a graphics context is automatically made available to the `paint` method through its parameter named `g` (Line 18). There is no need to get the graphics context again in Line 28. We could pass it from the `paint` method to the `paintBackground` method as shown in Listing 6.2.

Recall that a parameter is a mechanism for passing information from one method to another. Once we have passed the graphics context from the `paint` method in Line 3 to the `paintBackground` method in Line 6, we can use it throughout the `paintBackground` method.

6.3.3   Adding the Butler

A butler is added to the code shown in Listing 6.3. The `paintButler` method has two parameters that specify its upper-left corner. By changing the values passed to the `paintButler` method we can place the butler anywhere in the window. In addition, we can add more butlers by making multiple calls to `paintButler` (Figure 6.4).

Figure 6.3 Flow of Control

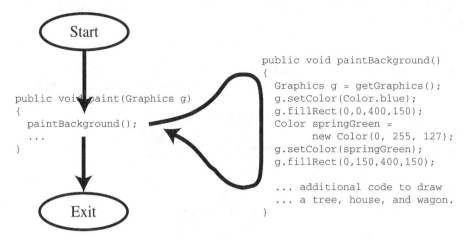

Listing 6.2 Using a Parameter to Pass the Graphics Context

```
1    public void paint(Graphics g)
2    {
3      paintBackground(g);
4    }
5
6    public void paintBackground(Graphics g)
7    {
8    // Create the sky and ground
9    g.setColor(Color.blue);
10   g.fillRect(0,0,400,150);
11
12   ...
13 }
```

The paintButler method illustrates two important motivations for using methods. The first is abstraction. The paint method is simplified and communicates our intent more clearly by allowing us to state our intent in a single line of code. In addition, we are able to draw multiple butlers by calling a single butler method multiple times. Code reuse makes code maintenance easier by providing a single location to correct coding problems. Method parameters provide a mechanism for customization. We need to change only the value of a method's parameters to change the location of our butler.

Recall our sequential pattern from Chapter 1. The order in which statements appear is important. Thus, the order of the method calls in Lines 3 through 6 of Listing 6.3 is impor-

Listing 6.3 Adding a Butler

```
1    public void paint(Graphics g)
2    {
3       paintBackground(g);
4       paintButler(50, 170, g);
5       paintButler(90, 190, g);
6       paintButler(75, 210, g);
7    }
8
9    // pre:  graphicsContext is valid
10   //       (x,y) is this butler's upper left corner
11   //       0 < x < window width
12   //       0 < y < window height
13   // post: this butler is drawn at location (x,y)
14   public void paintButler (int x, int y, Graphics g)
15   {
16      // Draw head
17      Color flesh = new Color(188, 143, 143);
18      g.setColor(flesh);
19      g.fillOval(x+18, y+8, 6, 14);
20
21      // Draw helmet
22      g.setColor(Color.black);
23      g.drawOval(x+12, y+6, 18, 18);
24
25      ... additional code to draw the rest of this butler ...
26   }
```

Figure 6.4 Three Butlers

tant. The background should be painted first. If it were painted after a butler were painted, the background would be painted over our butler. In addition, if a butler overlaps another butler, it should be drawn lower than the previous butler. Otherwise it will appear to be floating in air.

PATTERNS

6.4   Delegation Action Pattern

6.4.1   Problem / Name

The *delegation action pattern* is designed to address the problems we have introduced above. One problem is that large software systems are difficult to manage. Placing all the code in one monolithic method places all detail at the same level. The result is information overload. We are faced with the struggle of separating essential information from nonessential detail.

Another problem arises when we write identical or nearly identical code several times. Repeated code adds to the size of a program, making it difficult to navigate. When bugs are found or the code needs to be updated, we may have to apply corrections in many places.

6.4.2   Solution

To address these problems we introduced a mechanism that partitions code and delegates the responsibility for executing each section of code to a method. The examples in the previous sections illustrate that doing something often involves doing several smaller things. In other words, a task is the sum of its subtasks. For example, making a peanut butter sandwich is composed of a whole series of subtasks. Everything from fetching a jar of peanut butter from the cupboard to opening a jar of jam can be seen as subtasks. Subtasks can often be broken down further into smaller tasks. For example, fetching the peanut butter involves walking to the cupboard, opening its door, reaching out for the jar, grasping it, lifting it out, and closing the cupboard door. Each of these subtasks can also be broken down into still smaller tasks.

6.4.3   Consequences

The consequence of using methods is less time efficiency (see Section 7.7, page 315). Each method call has an execution penalty. However, unless the method call is part of a time-critical task, the execution penalty is worth the cost. The potential benefits are programs that are easier to understand, modify, and reuse.

6.5 Design

The question often arises, when do we stop the process of decomposition? How many sub-tasks are there? It stops when we reach agreed-upon primitive operations. In the case of a programming problem, those agreed-upon primitives are language statements and pre-defined method calls.

Partitioning a task into subtasks makes a problem easier to manage. It helps us organize problems into small chunks, each of which can be solved independently. This problem-solving strategy is called "divide and conquer." It is the basis for stepwise refinement (Section 5.2.2, page 167).

The divide-and-conquer design methodology works hand in hand with the delegation action pattern. Each subtask is a candidate for delegation and may be encapsulated within a method. For example, in Exercise 19 on page 87 we want to program our butler, james, so that he walks around the laundry two times and then leaves the room. We can use step-wise refinement to partition that problem into subtasks as shown in Listing 6.4.

Listing 6.4 Chapter 2, Exercise 19

```
1 moveToLaundry(james);
2 james.turnLeft();
3 walkAroundLaundry(james);
4 walkAroundLaundry(james);
5 leaveRoom(james);
```

The subtask, moveToLaundry, may be implemented as follows:

```
public void moveToLaundry (Butler aButler)
{
  aButler.forward();
  aButler.forward();
}
```

This looks like a lot of effort to move forward two steps, particularly when we realize we could replace moveToLaundry() with james.forward(2). However, a more general solution for moveToLaundry is the following code, which does not assume that the laundry is two steps in front of us. We can use this method in many situations, saving effort when we have similar problems to solve:

```
public void moveToLaundry (Butler aButler) {
  while (aButler.isFrontClear()) {
    aButler.forward();
  }
}
```

The `walkAroundLaundry` code is more complex, making a method welcome. An example implementation follows:

```
public void walkAroundLaundry(Butler aButler)
{
  aButler.forward();
  int count = 3;
  while (count > 0)
  {
    aButler.turnRight();
    aButler.forward(2);
    count--;
  }
  aButler.turnRight();
  aButler.forward();
}
```

The `moveToLaundry` and `walkAroundLaundry` methods raise an important issue. How does one determine that a group of statements should be encapsulated into a method?

This question is hard to answer. It requires skill and judgement. People often disagree. However, there are some guidelines we can apply.

1. People can keep about seven things (plus or minus 2) in their head at one time. If a method contains around seven steps or more, we should consider partitioning it.

2. Replacing a single step with a method call that does not simplify how we think about a problem may be ill-advised. For example, replacing `james.forward(2)` with `moveToLaundry(james)` is not useful on the surface. It is useful only if `moveToLaundry` gives use a more general and flexible solution today, or perhaps makes our code easier to extend tomorrow.

3. If we see the same sequence of steps or similar steps done over and over again in various parts of our program, we should consider a method that generalizes the repeated actions. Writing a sequence of actions once makes code easier to write because we have to implement an idea only once. In addition, if we make a mistake expressing an idea or we want to expand on an idea, we have to modify code in only one place. This makes program maintenance easier.

4. A method should contain a single coherent idea. For example, the `walkAround-Laundry` method does one thing, and its action is easy to describe. This is called cohesion. An example of a method with lower cohesion is `walkAroundLaun-dryAndLeaveRoom`. The "And" is a give-away of a potential problem. However, the action of walking around the laundry and leaving the room has some cohesion because

these actions relate to the same object. An example of a method with lower cohesion is a method that moves our butler around the laundry and changes the background color of the room.

A method is *cohesive* if all the actions in the method are highly related. The method actions cooperate to perform a single action. Strong cohesion often signifies good design.

5. A method should be weakly coupled. Weakly coupled methods are independent of each other. For example, a Butler's `forward` method is independent of its `pickUp` method. There are no requirements about the order these methods are executed or how they share information. On the other hand, methods such as `moveLeftFootForward` and `moveRightFootForward` are coupled. If we were to issue two consecutive commands to move a left foot `forward`, the butler may fall. It is better to have a simple `step` method. Another example of coupled methods is an initialization method. If we must assume that an initialization method is executed before any other method is called, it is easier for a programmer to make mistakes by forgetting to initialize. This is one of the benefits of constructors. They combine the actions of object creation and initialization, reducing the chances of out-of-order mistakes.

Coupling indicates the interconnectedness of methods. Low coupling often indicates a good design.

We are ready to take a look at a more difficult example. In Exercise 23 on page 88 we want our butler to find a pile of laundry someplace in the room, carry it to our basket, and leave. One possible solution is the following:

Listing 6.5 Chapter 2, Exercise 23

```
1  findLaundry(james);
2  james.pickUp();
3  findBasket(james);
4  james.putIn();
5  leaveRoom(james);
```

Now let us spend some time assessing the abstraction, encapsulation, cohesion, and coupling characteristics of Listing 6.5. Do the operations represent abstractions? The method `findLaundry` does focus on a key component to solving our problem. In addition, it hides (encapsulates) unnecessary detail. We do not care how it finds the laundry. It could search row by row or column by column, or take advantage of a vision system. The key characteristic is that we are able to focus on important ideas.

The methods in Listing 6.5 are also cohesive. What they do is easy to describe in a short phrase. In addition, their coupling is low. We could have james find the basket first and then find the laundry with no ill effects. In addition, james will not malfunction if it leaves the room before finding the basket. We may not accomplish our desired task, but james will not be placed in some unpredictable or fatal state.

The findLaundry method may be further partitioned into subtasks as we have done in Listing 6.6. (Notice how we are using stepwise refinement.) The findBasket method is decomposed into five methods: goToStartCorner, huntInCurrentRow, basketFound, noMoreRows, and moveToNextRow.

Listing 6.6 Finding a Basket

```
1   public void findBasket (Butler aButler)
2   {
3     goToStartCorner (aButler);
4     while (true)
5     {
6       huntInCurrentRow (aButler);
7       if (basketFound (aButler) | noMoreRows (aButler))
8         break;
9       moveToNextRow (aButler);
10    }
11  }
```

JAVA

6.6 Implementing Methods

In this section we will review and expand upon the mechanisms provided by Java to support method abstractions. Operations are created in Java by writing methods. We will start by demonstrating how to write methods with no parameters and then move to methods with parameters and methods that return values.

6.6.1 Simple Methods

The `paintBox` method declared in Lines 31 through 36 of Listing 6.7 has no parameters. When the Web browser calls the `paint` method, execution begins in Line 20 and progresses as demonstrated to the right of the listing.

Another example of a simple method comes from our butler world. We can write a simple method that moves our butler until it runs into something. It can be called by `moveToObject (james)`.

```
1 public void moveToObject (Butler theButler)
2 {

3   while (theButler.isFrontClear ())

4     theButler.forward ();

5 }
```

The basic form for declaring a parameterless method is shown below:

```
public void methodIdentifier ()
{
  list of statements
}
```

We invoke these methods with a statement of the following form. An example is shown in Line 23 of Listing 6.7. This statement will cause execution to transfer from Line 23 to 31. Once Lines 31 through 36 have been executed, control returns to Line 24.

```
methodIdentifier ();
```

Listing 6.7 A Box Painting Method with No Parameters

Code

Sequence of Actions

Line	Action
20	enter `paint`
22	call `setBackground`
23	call `paintBox`
31	enter `paintBox`
33	get graphics context
34	set drawing color
35	draw rectangle
36	exit `paintBox`
24	exit `paint`

```
1  //********************************
2  //
3  // title:    Box
4  //
5  // Draw a box.
6  //
7  //********************************
8
9  import java.awt.Color;
10 import java.awt.Graphics;
11 import java.applet.Applet;
12
13 public class Box extends Applet
14 {
15   //---------- paint --------------
16   //
17   // pre:  Called automatically
18   // post: Program output displayed.
19
20   public void paint(Graphics g)
21   {
22     setBackground(Color.white);
23     paintBox();
24   }
25
26   //---------- paintBox -----------
27   //
28   // pre:  none
29   // post: A single box is drawn.
30
31   public void paintBox()
32   {
33     Graphics g = getGraphics();
34     g.setColor(Color.blue);
35     g.fillRect(50, 20, 100, 67);
36   }
37 }
```

or

```
this.methodIdentifier ();
```

In Section 2.5.2, page 58, we learned that `void` indicates that we have a method that does not return a value. A call to this method will not be part of an arithmetic expression, but rather a stand-alone statement like the one we see in Line 23. We will learn what `public` means in Chapter 7.

6.6.2 Methods with Parameters

In Chapter 1 we learned that a parameter is a mechanism for sending information from one method to another. For example, in Listing 6.8 the graphics context object is passed from the `paint` method to the `paintBackground` method.

Listing 6.8 A Box Painting Method with a Parameter

```
1    public void paint (Graphics g)
2    {
3       paintBackground(g);
4    }
5
6    public void paintBackground(Graphics graphicsContext)
7    {
8       graphicsContext.setColor(Color.blue);
9       graphicsContext.fillRect(0, 0, 400, 150);
10   }
```

The identifiers `g` in `paint` and `graphicsContext` in `paintBackground` are used to refer to the same graphics context (see Figure 6.5). Both names could be the same. Different names are used only for the sake of illustration. When we need to refer to this graphics context, we use `g` between Lines 2 and 4 because it was named `g` in Line 1. When we need to refer to it between Lines 7 and 10 we use the name `graphicsContext` because it was named `graphicsContext` in Line 6. We say that the scope of `g` is the method `paint`. In a similar manner, the scope of the identifier `graphicsContext` is the `paintBackground` method. More details about scope appear in Section 6.6.3.

When parameters appear in a method call, they are called *actual parameters*. When parameters appear in a method definition, they are called *formal parameters*. See Figure 6.6.

The `paintBackground` method declares a single parameter of class `Graphics`. Whenever `paintBackground` is called, a `Graphics` object must be passed to it. In other words, when calling a method, the actual parameter list must match the formal parameter list with respect to its type, order, and number of parameters. Parameter names do not have to match. For example, the following code shows legal and illegal calls to the `paintBackground` method declared in Listing 6.8.

Figure 6.5 Passing Parameters in Listing 6.8

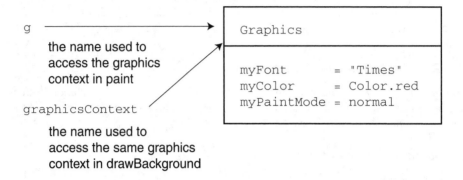

Figure 6.6 Formal and Actual Parameters

```
public void paint(Graphics g)                    formal parameters
{
  paintBackground(g);
}                                    actual parameter

public void paintBackground(Graphics graphicsContext)
{
  // Create the sky and ground
  graphicsContext.setColor(Color.blue);
  graphicsContext.fillRect(0,0,400,150);
  ...
}
```

```
public paint (Graphics thingy)
{
  Polygon triangle = new Polygon();
  paintBackground(thingy);          // ok: name need not be "g"
  paintBackground(thingy, thingy);  // error: too many parameters
  paintBackground();                // error - too few parameters
  paintBackground(triangle);        // error - parameter wrong type
}
```

In a sense, parameter passing acts as an assignment statement. The formal parameter is the left side and the actual parameter is the right side of an assignment. Java applies the same type coercion rules we discussed in Chapter 5. For example, the following code fragment is legal. It is permissible to pass an int to a double but not the other way around:

```
public void init()
{
  addOne (14);
}
public void addOne (double x)
{
  x = x + 1.0;
}
```

A method's *signature* is defined by the order, number, and kind of parameters a method has in addition to the method's name and return type and to the class to which it belongs. The ability of a programming language to distinguish methods by their signature is called *overloading*.

Another example of using a method with parameters is shown in Listing 6.9. The paint-Box method has more than one parameter. Notice that the parameters in Line 26 match those in Line 36. The first parameter belongs to the Graphics class, the second to the Color class, and the last two are integers.

Actual parameters may be any valid expression that returns an object or value of the appropriate type. Lines 26 through 28 demonstrate that actual parameters can be identifiers, literal constants, and numeric expressions.

6.6.3   Scope

Recall our first encounter with scope in Section 2.7.2, page 65. We discovered that the scope of an identifier declared within a block is the block in which it is declared.

Scope defines the locations within a program where a particular identifier is bound to a particular object or primitive storage area for a value.

Listing 6.9 Method with Multiple Parameters

```
1  //****************************************************************
2  //
3  // title:    Box
4  //
5  // Draw boxes using a method with parameters.
6  //
7  //****************************************************************
8
9  import java.awt.Color;
10 import java.awt.Graphics;
11 import java.applet.Applet;
12
13 public class Box extends Applet
14 {
15   //---------- paint ------------------------------------------
16   //
17   // pre:  Called automatically
18   // post: Box is drawn.
19
20   public void paint(Graphics g)
21   {
22     setBackground(Color.white);
23     Color lightGray = new Color (168, 168, 168);
24     int x = 50;
25     int y = 20;
26     paintBox(g,               lightGray,   x,   y);
27     paintBox(g,               Color.red,   75, y*2);
28     paintBox(getGraphics(), Color.blue, 40, 50);
29   }
30
31   //---------- paintBox ---------------------------------------
32   //
33   // pre:  none
34   // post: Draw the box.
35
36   public void paintBox(Graphics graphicsContext,
37                         Color color, int x, int y)
38   {
39     graphicsContext.setColor(color);
40     graphicsContext.fillRect(x, y, 100, 67);
41   }
42 }
```

For example, in the code fragment below the identifier b refers to a particular storage area that may be accessed only in method foo. The identifier c refers to another storage area that may be accessed only in the method bar. The same identifier may be bound to multiple storage areas. For example, a refers to one storage location in foo and to a different storage location in bar. The values of the two a's are not related. They have no impact on each other. They could be different types.

```java
public void foo()
{
  int a = 10;
  int b = 20;
  System.out.println(a);      // 10 is printed
  System.out.println(b);      // 20 is printed
  System.out.println(c);      // syntax error
}
public void bar()
{
  int a = 30;
  int c = 40;
  System.out.println(a);      // 30 is printed
  System.out.println(b);      // syntax error
  System.out.println(c);      // 40 is printed
}
```

The storage for a value or reference to an object is said to be local to the block (or method) in which it is declared. Local variables cannot be used for sharing information among methods.

> A *local variable* is an object or value declared within a block. It must be declared before it can be used.

The values or references of local variables are lost when the block in which they are declared is exited. Look at the example in Listing 6.10. We can refer to henry in Lines 6 and 11 because it has scope until Line 15. On the other hand, sam can be referenced only in Lines 7 through 9. Its scope ends at Line 10.

It is important to realize that when we leave sam's scope in Line 10, the sam reference value is destroyed, but not the object that sam references. We lose only our ability to reference it with the identifier sam. Also note that the changes we make to sam impact henry because they refer to the same object. When we leave henry's scope in Line 15, the butler object that henry references is again not destroyed. However, we can no longer reference it with the identifier henry. In fact, there is no identifier with which we can reference it. In Section 1.5.3, page 22, we learned that objects that cannot be referenced

Listing 6.10 Henry and Sam

```
1  public void init ()
2  {
3    Butler henry    = new Butler (...);
4    int henrysAge   = 3;
5    {
6      Butler sam    = henry;  // henry is in this nested scope
7      sam.forward();
8      int samsAge   = henrysAge;
9      samsAge       = samsAge + 1;
10   }
11   henry.forward();     // ok, henry is in this scope
12   sam.forward();       // syntax error, sam not in this scope
13   display(henrysAge);  // ok, henrysAge is in this scope
14   display(samsAge);    // syntax error, samsAge not in this scope
15 }
```

are subject to the garbage collector. As a result, the garbage collector will eventually recycle our butler.

The semantics for the values `henrysAge` and `samsAge` are different. Changing `samsAge` in Line 9 has no impact on `henrysAge`. They are different primitive values. In addition, the values associated with these two identifiers are lost when we leave their scope. There is no need for garbage collecting values because their storage is automatically reclaimed when we leave their scope. Only objects are garbage collected.

Sometimes we want to be able to share information among methods. There are two ways of doing this: 1) through parameters and 2) through instance variables.

We discussed the first way, passing parameters, in Section 6.6.2. For example, in the code fragment below the value for `a` in the method `foo` is passed to `bar`. The scope of a formal parameter is the method in which it is declared. The scope of `b` is the method `bar`.

```
public void foo()
{
  int a = 10;
  bar(a);
  System.out.println(a);     // 10 is printed
}
public void bar(int b)
{
  System.out.println(b);     // 10 is printed
}
```

Figure 6.7 Locals, Formal Parameters, and Instance Variables

```
public class Butler
{
    int myX;  ←————————— instance variable

    public paintButler (int x)
    {                     — ←—— formal parameter
        Color flesh = new ...;
        ...          ←———————— local variable
    }
}
```

The second way of getting information to a method is shown in Figure 6.7. The instance variable myX may represent part of the state of a Butler object. Instance variables are shared by all methods in a class.

> *Instance variables* are used to implement an object's state. They are declared outside of a method and have references and values that persist between method calls.

This figure illustrates an important difference between parameters, instance variables, and local variables. Their scope is different. This difference is further illustrated in Listing 6.11.

Careful thought must be given to whether information is shared among methods by using instance variables or parameters. A rule of thumb is to ask whether the information describes the state of an object. If it does, use an instance variable. If it does not, using parameters is probably better. We will talk more about what should be an instance variable and what should be a parameter in the next chapter.

It is tempting to overuse instance variables. Too many instance variables make a program hard to understand. Before defining something as an instance variable, ask yourself whether it defines an object's state. Is it a value that needs to persist? If you can get by with local variables, use them instead.

The author's convention is to begin all instance variables with "my." This makes them easy to spot in a program. This convention is not enforced by a compiler. Instance variables may have any legal name.

Listing 6.11 A Scope Example

```
1   public class Thingies extends Applet
2   {
3     private int something = 10;
4
5     public void doSomething (int a, int b)
6     {
7       int w = 300;
8       System.out.println(something);    // ok - 10
9       System.out.println(a);            // ok - 77
10      System.out.println(b);            // ok - 35
11      System.out.println(w);            // ok - 300
12      System.out.println(c);            // scope error
13      System.out.println(z);            // scope error
14    }
15
16    public void doNothing (int a, int c)
17    {
18      int z = 123;
19      System.out.println(something);    // ok - 10
20      System.out.println(a);            // ok - 82
21      System.out.println(c);            // ok - 65
22      System.out.println(z);            // ok - 123
23      System.out.println(b);            // scope error
24      System.out.println(w);            // scope error
25    }
26
27    public void init ()
28    {
29      doSomething (77, 35);
30      doNothing   (82,65);
31    }
32  }
```

We must be careful how we name things. Reusing identifiers in different scopes can confuse a program reader. For example, in Listing 6.12, the scope of the a declared in Line 3 is the foo method. A new a is declared in Line 8. Its scope is within bar. We can still access the object named a in the foo method by using the name b in the bar method because it was passed to bar as a parameter. To further complicate things, another object named a is declared within the if block in Line 12. This declaration masks the declaration of a in Line 8 but does not destroy it. We again have access to the a declared in Line 8 when we reach Line 14.

Listing 6.12 Creating Confusion

```
1 public void foo()
2 {
3    Color a = new Color (255, 0, 0);        // a is red in foo
4    bar (a);
5 }
6 public void bar(Color b)                   // b is red in bar
7 {
8    Color a = new Color (0, 255, 0);
9    ...                                      // a is green here
10   if (true)
11   {
12      Color a = new Color (0, 0, 255);     // a is blue in if
13   }
14   ...                                      // a is green here
15 }
```

Listing 6.13 Methods Calling Methods

```
1  public class Clouds extends Applet
2  {
3     private int myX = 200;
4     private int myY = 250;
5
6     public void paint (Graphics g)
7     {
8        int x = 100;
9        int y =  50;
10       paintClouds (x, y, g);
11    }
12    public void paintClouds (int x, int y, Graphics g)
13    {
14       int count = 0;
15       while (count < 5)
16       {
17          int deltaX = (int)(Math.random() * 50.0);
18          int deltaY = (int)(Math.random() * 25.0);
19          paintOneCloud (x + deltaX, y + deltaY, g);
20          count++;
21       }
22    }
23    public void paintOneCloud (int cloudX, int cloudY, Graphics g)
24    {
25       g.setColor (Color.white);
26       g.fillOval (cloudX, cloudY, 25, 10);
27    }
28 }
```

6.6.4   Methods That Call Methods

A quick look at Listing 6.1 on page 214 will show that methods can call other methods. In this case the `paint` method called the `paintBackground` method. Each time a method calls a method we create a whole new set of local variables and temporarily lose access to the current set. We will illustrate this with the `paint` method in Listing 6.13.

When `paint` is called by a web browser, a frame is created that holds all the variables local to `paint`. In addition to being able to access the local variables g, x, and y, `paint` can also access the instance variables myX and myY. This is illustrated in Figure 6.8.

Figure 6.8 The Situation after the Call to `paint`

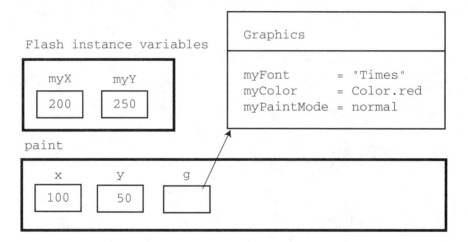

A *frame* is a structure designed to hold all the local variables associated with a method. (Do not confuse the use of the term *frame* here with the `Frame` class, which is used to create windows in Java.)

Once `paint` calls `paintClouds` in Line 10, a second frame is created. This frame contains all the local variables associated with the `paintClouds` method. See Figure 6.9. `paintClouds` cannot access the local variables in `paint`, but those instance variables still persist. They will be available at some time in the future when we return from `paintClouds`.

Next `paintClouds` calls `paintOneCloud` in Line 19. Again a new frame is created, as illustrated in Figure 6.10. The previous two frames persist but their local variables cannot currently be accessed.

Figure 6.9 The Situation after the Call to `paintClouds`

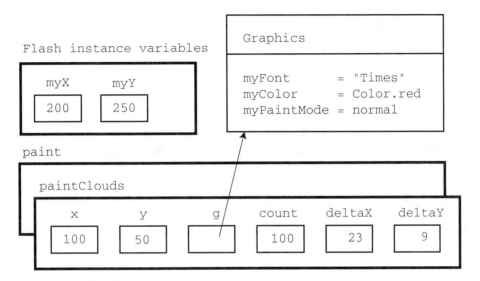

Figure 6.10 The Situation after the Call to `paintOneCloud`

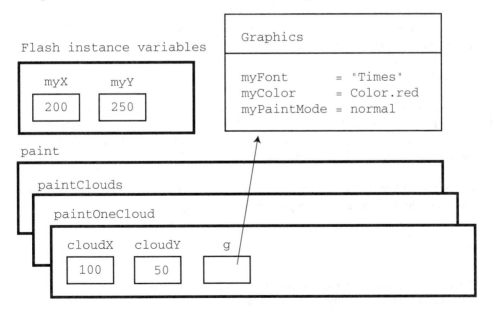

Once we leave the `paintOneCloud` method in Line 27, the frame associated with `paintOneCloud` is discarded. The result is that we are back to the situation we had in Figure 6.9. We can again access the frame associated with `paintClouds`.

Next we leave the `paintClouds` method in Line 22. The frame for `paintClouds` is destroyed, leaving us with the situation in Figure 6.8. We can again access the frame associated with `paint`.

Finally we leave the `paint` method in Line 11. The only values that persist are the instance variables `myX` and `myY`. Recall that instance variables persist between method calls. They discard only when their associated object is discarded through garbage collection.

6.6.5 Methods That Return Values

All the methods we have investigated thus far have taken information through their parameters and done something with it. Often, we want a method to return the result of some kind of computation or creation process. For example, temperature can be computed by counting the chirps of a cricket. This is done by counting the number of chirps over the period of one minute, adding 40, and dividing by 4. Listing 6.14 shows a program that computes temperature based on a cricket thermometer.

The body of the `getTemperature` method contains a single line of code, Line 21. It carries out the temperature computation based on the number of chirps per minute. This computed value is returned as the value of the `getTemperature` call in Line 36 (Figure 6.11).

The cricket program illustrates one more item we must attend to when writing applications. Notice the keyword `static` in Line 19. `static` methods can only call `static` methods. Because `main` is static, `getTemperature` must be static as well. We'll talk more about `static` in Section 7.6.6, page 310.

This is not the first time we have worked with operations that return something. For example, the methods in the `Math` library returned values.

```
x = Math.floor(5.5)  - Math.floor(3.8);
  =        5.0       -        3.0
  =                2.0
```

A quick look at the `Math` class reference on page 885 will reveal that the `floor` method returns a double. Because the method call `Math.floor(5.5)` returns the value 5.0, 5.0 replaces the expression. Similarly, 3.0 replaces the `Math.floor(3.8)` expression.

Listing 6.14 The `Cricket` Application

```
1  //****************************************************************
2  //
3  // title:    Cricket
4  //
5  // Cricket chirps are based on the temperature.
6  //
7  //****************************************************************
8
9   import vista.VRead;
10 import vista.VWrite;
11
12 public class Cricket
13 {
14    //---------- getTemperature --------------------------------
15    //
16    // pre:  none
17    // post: The current temperature is returned.
18
19    public static int getTemperature (int chirps)
20    {
21       return (chirps + 40) / 4;
22    }
23
24    //---------- main ------------------------------------------
25    // execution begins here
26
27    public static void main (String args[])
28    {
29       // Input chirps
30       VRead  in  = new VRead ();
31       VWrite out = new VWrite ();
32      out.write("Please enter number of cricket chirps per minute:
");
33       int chirps = in.readInt();
34
35       // Compute temperature
36       int temperature = getTemperature(chirps);
37
38       // Output temperature
39      out.write("The current temperature is:                    ");
40       out.writeln(temperature);
41    }
42 }
```

The return type in the declaration must match the type in the return statement (see Figure 6.12). The value computed by `(chirps + 40) / 4` is an int. It must match the type of the value returned by the `getTemperature` function in the first line.

Another way to implement the `getTemperature` method is shown below. A return statement returns an expression. That expression may be an identifier, a literal constant, or a numeric expression. Notice again how the types match:

```
public int getTemperature (int chirps)
{
  int i = (chirps + 40) / 4;
  return i;
}
```

Figure 6.11 The Returned Value

```
int temperature = getTemperature();
                  _____
                          ↑
                  ┌───────┴───────┐
                  (chirps + 40) / 4
```

Figure 6.12 Return Type and Returned Value Must Match in Type

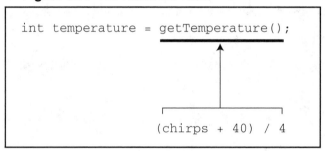

```
public int getTemperature(int chirps)
{
  return (chirps + 40) / 4;
}

public void init()
{
  int t = getTemperature();
}
```

must match in type
(`int` in this case)

An example of a method that returns a value in the butler world is one that counts the number of steps that our butler must take before it reaches an object. It is shown below and invoked with the `call below`:

```
public void init ()
{
  ...
  Butler james = ...;
  int numberOfSteps = countSteps (james).
}
public int countSteps (Butler aButler)
{
  int count = 0;
  while (aButler.isFrontClear ())
  {
    aButler.forward ();
    count ++
  }
  return count;
}
```

In the previous examples we returned a primitive integer. We can return other primitive types and objects as well. For example, the `clear` method below returns a boolean:

```
public boolean clear (Butler aButler)
{
  return aButler.isRightClear() & aButler.isFrontClear() &
        aButler.isLeftClear();
}
```

Although it is possible to use parameters to send as many things to a method as one wants, only one thing may be returned. This can be a problem in some cases. For example, there is an applet method that returns the size of the display window. Size requires two pieces of information: width and height. Java provides a `Dimension` class, which has two fields: a width and height. Once a dimension object is returned, it is possible to access each of its components as shown in Listing 6.15.

When more than one piece of information needs to be returned from a method, it must be done through using an object.

6.6.6   Return Statement

A `return` statement returns control from the current method to the method that called it.

```
return ;
return expression ;
```

Listing 6.15 Returning an Object

```
1  public void init ()
2  {
3     Dimension d = getSize();
4     System.out.println(d.width);    // prints 25
5     System.out.println(d.height);   // prints 14
6  }
7  public Dimension getSize()
8  {
9     return new Dimension (25, 14);
10 }
```

The Java compiler will perform analysis to determine whether statements are unreachable. For example, the following code will generate a syntax error because Line 4 cannot be reached. The `return` in Line 3 causes an exit from the `average` method before Line 4 is executed.

```
1 public int average(int x, int y)
2 {
3    return (x + y) / 2;
4    int z = 20;              // error - unreachable code
5 }
```

6.6.7   Pass by Value

All parameters in Java are passed by value. That means that the called method gets a copy of what we are passing it. In the case of primitive values, the called method gets a copy of the value itself. In the case of objects, the called method gets a copy of a reference to the object. In other words, it gets an alias for that object.

> *Pass by value* refers to a parameter-passing technique in which the value of the actual parameter is copied to the method and initializes a new value for the formal parameter. In Java all objects have their reference and all primitives have their primitive values passed by value.

Let us first see what that means for primitive values. Suppose we want to write a method that swaps the values of two integers. We cannot easily do it. For example, the code in Listing 6.16 does not result in a change in values for x and y in Line 5. Our intent is to give the value of x to y and the value of y to x. However, the act of changing the values a and b in the swap method has no impact on the values for x and y. Thus, x and y remain with their original values. The same is true if we attempt to swap two objects (Listing 6.17).

Listing 6.16 Swapping Two Integers (Does Not Work)

```
1   public void init ()
2   {
3      int x = 10;
4      int y = 20;
5      swap (x, y);          // x and y are unchanged
6   }
7   public void swap (int a, int b)
8   {
9      int temp = a;
10     a        = b;
11     b        = temp;
12  }
```

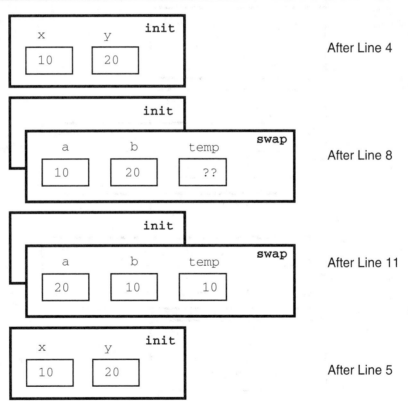

After Line 4

After Line 8

After Line 11

After Line 5

Listing 6.17 Swapping Two Objects (Does Not Work)

```
1   public void init ()
2   {
3     Butler james = new Butler (10, 3, myRoom);
4     Butler fred  = new Butler ( 8, 5, myRoom);
5     swap (james, fred);          // x and y are unchanged
6   }
7   public void swap (Butler a, Butler b)
8   {
9     Butler temp = a;
10    a            = b;
11    b            = temp;
12  }
```

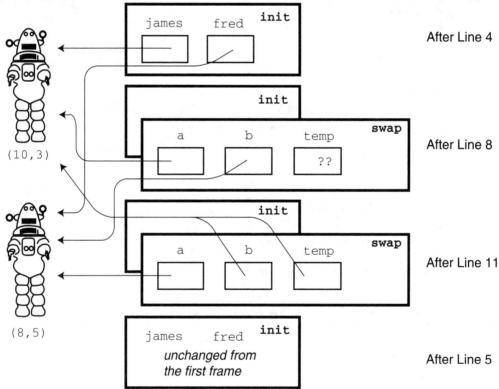

After Line 4

After Line 8

After Line 11

After Line 5

However, the impacts of passing object references and primitive values are different. Remember that an object identifier is a reference to an object and not the object itself. When an object reference is passed to a method, only a copy of the reference is passed to the formal parameter. For example, `james` and `aButler` are aliases for the same object in Listing 6.19. Changing the state of the object `aButler` in Line 8 has the impact of changing the state of `james`. The references `james` and `aButler` refer to the same object. There is no counterpart to aliasing for primitive values. Primitive values cannot be aliased.

`Butler` objects are examples of objects we can change the state of. For example, we can change the location of a butler. Sometimes changing the state of an object can be problematic. For example, changing the state of a color would be confusing. For that reason Java has made objects created from the `Color` class immutable, they cannot be changed.

Immutable objects have no operations that will change their state.

For example, in Line 12 of Listing 6.18 `red` and `c` are aliases for the same `Color` object. Suppose we had an operation that allowed us to add 255 units of green to `c`. This would have the impact of making `c` yellow in Line 12. However, this action would have a side effect totally unexpected to the person reading the code in Line 7. The `Color` object referenced by the name `red` was the color red in Line 4 but was really the color yellow in Line 7. To prevent this kind of confusion, `Color` objects are immutable.

Listing 6.18 Why Colors Are Immutable

```
1   public void paint (Graphics g)
2   {
3       Color red = new Color (255,0,0);
4       g.setColor (red);
5       g.fillrect (25, 50, 100, 50);
6       paintCircle (g, red);
7       g.setColor (red);
8       g.fillrect (150, 50, 100, 50);
9   }
10  public void paintCircle (Graphics g, Color c)
11  {
12      c.setGreen (255);   // illegal operation - syntax error
13      g.fillOval (25, 200, 25, 25);
14  }
```

Listing 6.19 Changing the State of an Object

```
1  public void init ()
2  {
3    Butler james = new Butler (10, 3, myRoom);
4    moveToLaundry (james);
5  }
6  public void moveToLaundry (Butler aButler)
7  {
8    aButler.forward ();
9  }
```

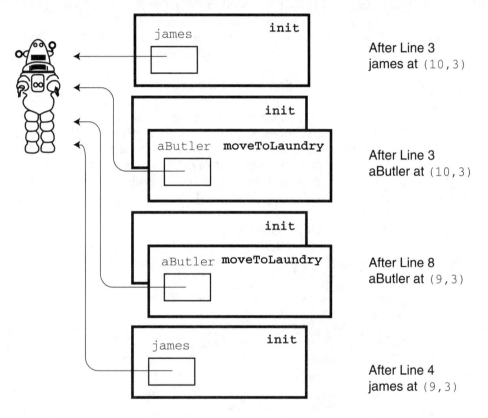

After Line 3
james at (10,3)

After Line 3
aButler at (10,3)

After Line 8
aButler at (9,3)

After Line 4
james at (9,3)

6.6.8   Pre and Post Conditions

You may have noticed the pre and post conditions that are part of the comments for many methods in this text. An example is the `paintButler` method in Listing 6.3 on page 217.

```
// pre:  graphicsContext is valid
//       (x,y) this butler's upper left corner
//       0 < x < window width
//       0 < y < window height
// post: this butler is drawn at location (x,y)
```

The preconditions describe legal values for the parameters when the `paintButler` method is called. In this example, x is expected to have a value between 0 and the window width. If x is out of this range, the method does not guarantee appropriate action.

We can view pre and post conditions as a contract. The contract states that if the pre conditions are met, the method guarantees the post conditions. If the pre conditions are not met, all bets are off. We may not know what will happen if the pre conditions are violated.

Post conditions describe what the method does, but not how it does it. For example, the code in Listing 6.20 shows two methods for moving a butler from grid location $(11,3)$ to grid location $(7,1)$.

Listing 6.20 Move a Butler to the Basket

```
1   public int moveToBasket (Butler aButler)
2   {
3       aButler.forward(2);
4       aButler.turnRight();
5       aButler.forward(2);
6       aButler.turnLeft();
7       aButler.forward(2);
8   }
9
10  public int moveToBasket (Butler aButler)
11  {
12      aButler.forward();
13      aButler.turnRight();
14      aButler.forward();
15      aButler.turnLeft();
16      aButler.forward();
17      aButler.turnRight();
18      aButler.forward();
19      aButler.turnLeft();
20      aButler.forward(2);
21  }
```

Appropriate pre and post conditions are as follows:

```
// pre:    aButler is at (11,3)
// post:   aButler is at (7,1)
```

However, the following post condition may not be appropriate because it describes implementation details, which should be hidden. It is only appropriate if the route that the butler takes is an essential detail.

```
// not an appropriate post condition
// post:  Butler moves forward 2, turns right, moves forward 2
//              turns left, moves forward 2
```

When we use a method, we should not rely on knowing any internal details. For example, the pre and post conditions for the method in Listing 6.21 do not specify what will happen if x is 3. If you assume that 0 will be returned, our program will fail if the programmer later decides to return max integer or removes the if statement altogether and lets the method try to divide by zero.

Listing 6.21   Rely on Only the Knowledge Stated in Pre Conditions

```
1 // pre:    x is not equal to 3
2 // post:   x / (x - 3) is returned
3 public int foo (int x)
4 {
5    if (x == 3)
6       return 0;
7    else
8       return x / (x - 3);
9 }
```

We have stated that the pre and post conditions act as a contract. What should happen if that contract is broken? There are two ways the contract can be broken. The first is if the pre conditions are met but the post conditions are not met. This case signifies a program bug that must be fixed. When we write a method, we should rigorously test it by exercising its pre conditions and checking whether its post conditions hold.

A second way that the contract may be broken is if the pre conditions are not met. What should we do with precondition violations? There are several things we could do:

1. Do nothing special in the method—there is a bug in the program and our efforts should be placed on finding and removing that bug.

2. Modify the method to respond to illegal pre conditions. A method may return a message indicating whether pre conditions have been met. For example, a method may return `true` if it succeeded or `false` otherwise. The program may choose to write code that responds to this violation.

```java
// pre:  x >= 0
// post: moves the butler to x if x is not negative and returns
true
//       otherwise it does not move the butler and returns false
public boolean moveButler (int x)
{
  if (x < 0)
  {
    return false;
  }
  else
  {
    myX = x;
    return true;
  }
}

...

public void run ()
{
  int x = 100;
  while (move(x))
  {
    x = x - 2;
  }
}
```

3. A method may raise an exception if its pre conditions are not met. An exception is an error-handling technique in which code in a `catch` clause is executed when an exception is raised. We will wait until Chapter 8 to talk about this option.

4. A method may display error messages if pre conditions are not met. This can be a problem for a program user. What is a user to do if an unexpected message appears such as "List index out of range in `get` method—operation aborted." A travel agent may not know how to respond to such an error. It may even cause some panic if the agent interprets it to mean that a flight was aborted at take-off.

```java
// pre:  x >= 0
public void moveButler (int x)
{
  if (x < 0)
  {
```

```
      System.out.println ("Butler attempted to move off the dis-
   play");
      }
   else
   {
      myX = ,x;
   }
}
```

5. A programmer may check if the pre conditions are met before every method call. For user input, this may be necessary. In other cases, the extra checking may result in too much overhead. The programmer may be able to write code in such a manner that pre-conditions cannot be violated. However, this approach may mask a serious programming error and just delay a program failure.

```
if (x < 0.0)
   x = 0.0;
return Math.sqrt(x);
```

or

```
if (x < 0.0)
   return 0.0;
else
   return Math.sqrt(x);
```

6. Finally, a method may alter its inputs to meet the pre conditions. For example, if a parameter must be greater than 0, a method may change negative inputs to 0. Again, this approach may mask a serious programming error and just delay a program failure.

```
// pre:  x >= 0
public void moveButler (int x)
{
   if (x < 0)
   {
      myX = 0;
   }
   else
   {
      myX = x;
   }
}
```

Various approaches are used in Java. For example, the square root method in the Math class will raise an ArithmeticException if it gets a negative number. If the programmer didn't anticipate a problem with a negative number, the program will abort.

SUPPLEMENTARY MATERIAL

6.7   Animation—Making Our Butler Move

Now we can take advantage of the `paintButler` parameters to move our butler across the screen. Animation is accomplished by drawing a figure, such as a butler, in one location, displaying it for an instant, moving it to a new location, and repeating the previous steps.

There are several factors that control the quality of an animation. One is how often the object is moved. An object needs to be moved at least 10 times a second for its motion to appear smooth. Another factor is how far an object is moved. If it is moved too far in each move, it may be difficult for our eyes to follow it (Figure 6.13).

Figure 6.13 Animation

One temptation is to use the following as an applet's `init`, `start`, or `paint` methods:

```
while ( ... )
{
  move the butler
  paint him
  wait a little while
}
```

Although the above may work on one platform, it may not work on another. On some platforms the butler is moved but it is not drawn until the `init`, `start`, or `paint` method completes. As a result, the butler moves completely across the screen before being painted. We see it only in its final position.

An applet begins with a single thread of execution that is managed by a web browser. Our applet program may make multiple calls to a `paint` method, but the web browser is really in control. It determines when `paint` methods get executed. In many systems, a web browser will not execute `paint` methods until the `start` or `paint` methods have finished. The web browser will not support simultaneous calls to its methods. Thus, the above code fragment does not have the desired effect.

> Recall that we defined a *thread* in Chapter 1 as a single flow of control. The programs we have written thus far have had only one thread.

To solve the problem of calling `paint` multiple times, we will add a second thread of execution that we can control. The new thread will be in charge of moving our butler and requesting repaints. Threads make it appear that two activities are occurring simultaneously, when in fact they are taking turns. Figure 6.14 shows how the two threads execute. Listing 6.22 shows how threads are implemented.

Managing an animation thread requires adding code that will create and manage that new thread. This code can be broken into two parts:

1. Code for the new thread
   - Promise to implement the `Runnable` interface.
   - Implement a `run` method.
2. Code for the original thread
   - The original thread must create a new thread object.
   - The new thread must be started when our applet is active.
   - The new thread must be stopped when our applet is idle.

These components of code can be identified in Listing 6.22. In step one we write the code for the new thread. First, we promise to implement the `Runnable` interface in Line 14. We fulfill our promise by implementing a `run` method. Implementing the `Runnable` interface allows us to add another thread of execution. We will talk more about interfaces in a later chapter.

The next part of step one is the implementation of the new thread. Execution of a new thread begins in a `run` method, Lines 117 through 125. The `run` method is called when we start a thread. In this example, the `run` method contains an infinite loop that will loop 20 times per second. The effect will be moving our butler 20 times a second. It accom-

Figure 6.14 The Two Threads

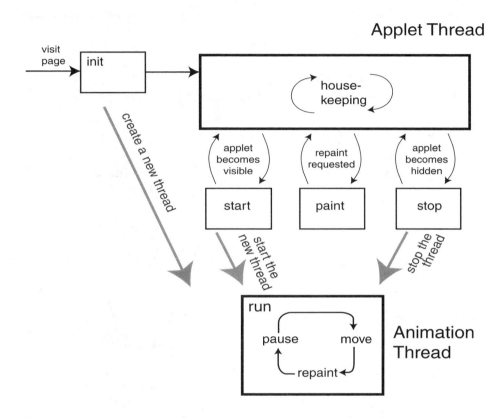

plishes this with the following three steps during each iteration of the loop. First, the animation thread sleeps (does nothing) for 50 milliseconds. It then moves our butler by a small amount and requests a display repaint.

The move method, Lines 89 through 96, changes our butler's horizontal location by a small amount. The amount of change is determined by the value of the myDeltaX instance variable declared in Line 18. The larger its value, the faster our butler moves. Positive values move our butler to the right and negative values to the left. If our butler attempts to move offscreen, its direction of movement is reversed.

Listing 6.22 Making Butler Move

```
1  //************************************************************
2  //
3  // title:   Butler
4  //
5  // Animate Butler.  Make him move across a background.
6  //
7  //************************************************************
8
9  import java.awt.Color;
10 import java.awt.Graphics;
11 import java.awt.Polygon;
12 import java.applet.Applet;
13
14 public class Butler extends Applet implements Runnable
15 {
16   private int myX;
17   private int myY;
18   private int myDeltaX;
19   private int myDeltaY;
20
21   private final int WIDTH  = 400;
22   private final int HEIGHT = 300;
23   private final int SPEED  =   3;
24
25   private Thread myAnimation;
26
27   //********** Original Thread *************************
28
29   //---------- init ------------------------------------------
30   // called automatically - execution begins here
31   // post: Initialize this butler's location and create the
32   //       animation thread.
33   public void init()
34   {
35     myX      =   0;
36     myY      = 200;
37     myDeltaX =   3;
38     myDeltaY =   0;
39
40     myAnimation = new Thread(this);
41   }
42
```

Listing 6.22 Making Butler Move

```
43   //---------- paint -----------------------------------------
44   // pre:  g is valid
45   // post: Butler and background are drawn.
46   public synchronized void paint(Graphics g)
47   {
48     paintBackground(g);
49     paintButler (myX, myY, g);
50   }
51
52   //---------- paintBackground -----------------------------
53   // pre:  g is valid
54   // post: ground, house, and tree are drawn.
55   public void paintBackground(Graphics g)
56   {
57     ...
58   }
59
60   //---------- paintButler --------------------------------
61   // pre:  g is valid
62   // post: Butler is drawn with upper left corner at (x,y).
63   public void paintButler (int x, int y, Graphics g)
64   {
65     ...
66   }
67
68   //---------- start --------------------------------------
69   // called automatically
70   // post: start the animation thread.
71   public void start()
72   {
73     myAnimation.start();
74   }
75
76   //---------- stop ---------------------------------------
77   // called automatically - execution ends here
78   // post: Stop the animation
79   public void stop()
80   {
81     myAnimation.stop();
82   }
83
```

Listing 6.22 Making Butler Move

```
84    //********** Animation Thread ***************************
85
86    //---------- move ------------------------------------------
87    // pre:  myX > 0 & myX < WIDTH
88    // post: Butler's position is changed by delta X.
89    public synchronized void move()
90    {
91      if (myX > WIDTH - 50)
92        myDeltaX = -SPEED;
93      if (myX < 0)
94        myDeltaX =  SPEED;
95      myX += myDeltaX;
96    }
97
98    //---------- pause ------------------------------------------
99    // pre:  milliseconds >= 0
100   // post: This thread of control sleeps for "milliseconds".
101   public void pause (int milliseconds)
102   {
103     try
104     {
105       Thread.sleep(milliseconds);
106     }
107     catch (InterruptedException e)
108     {
109       System.out.println
110         ("*** InterruptedException thrown in sleep ***");
111     }
112   }
113
114   //---------- run ------------------------------------------
115   // Called automatically by starting the animation thread
116   // post: Butler is moved back & forth across the background.
117   public void run()
118   {
119     while(true)
120     {
121       move();
122       repaint();
123       pause(50);
124     }
125   }
126 }
```

Notice that the butler's location and velocity are instance variables. They are part of the applet's state. As a result, the butler's location and velocity are preserved between method calls and can be shared between methods. For example, the butler's location is initialized in `init`, modified by the `move` method, and used by the `paint` method to draw our butler at its current location.

The `pause` method, Lines 101 through 112, hides the complexity of using the `sleep` method. Whenever the `pause` method is called by a thread, the thread stops doing anything for the period of time specified by its parameter. The parameter determines for how many milliseconds the thread is to sleep. The smaller the pause, the faster our butler moves.

The second step is to create and manage the animation thread. The new thread is created in the `init` method in Line 40. It is declared as an instance variable in Line 25. As a result, the thread will be preserved after the `init` method finishes executing.

The new thread is started in the `start` method (Line 73) and stopped in the stop method (Line 81). The `start` method is called when the applet is visible and the `stop` method is called when the applet is invisible (Section 3.5.1, page 99). Our butler program demonstrates the utility of the `init`, `start`, and `stop` methods in an applet. We want to create a thread only once. However, it may be started and stopped many times.

Notice the `synchronized` keyword in the declaration of the `paint` and `move` methods in Lines 46 and 89. There are potential problems with multithreaded programs. One thread may attempt to access a value at the same time another method is changing it. For example, the `paint` method could be accessing the location of our butler in Line 49 at the same time the `move` method is changing the location in Line 95. As a result, the `paint` method could be accessing corrupted information. By introducing the `synchronized` keyword we are informing Java of the two threads' shared state. Only one thread is allowed in a synchronized method at any given time. Since `paint` and `move` are both synchronized, a thread will not attempt to access `myX` and `myY` in `paint` at the same time another thread is trying to change them in `move`.

6.8   Removing Flicker

You may have noticed that the butler and the background flicker while the butler is moving. The flicker is caused by the process of redrawing the display. Line 122 in Listing 6.22 is executed 20 times per second. The `repaint` method calls `update`. The `update` method first clears the screen. This is accomplished by drawing a rectangle over the entire

Figure 6.15 Sometimes the Screen Is Blank

Suppose the hardware redraws the display between these two statements. ──────→ The result is a blank screen.

```
public void update (Graphics g)
{
  g.setColor(getBackground());
  g.fillRect(0,0,width,height);
  g.setColor(getForeground());
  paint(g);
}

public void paint (Graphics g)
{
  paintBackground(g);
  paintButler(myX, myY, g);
}
```

g

display output buffer

display that is the background color (Figure 6.15). Thus, when `paint` is called, it starts with a clear drawing surface.

Associated with g is some memory that holds the display image. We will call it the display buffer. Typically between 50 and 100 times a second the hardware grabs a copy of the display buffer and shows it on the screen. The Java program and hardware are not synchronized. The hardware may grab the display buffer at any time. If the hardware grabs the display buffer after `update` clears the screen but before `update` calls `paint`, a blank display will be shown (Figure 6.15).

If the hardware grabs the display buffer after `update`'s call to `paint` is complete, the display will contain the complete image (Figure 6.16). In addition to displaying a blank or completely drawn screen, the hardware may grab the display buffer in many partially complete states. The result is a flicker pattern that appears to dance around the screen. The result is anything but pleasing.

There are several strategies to reduce and remove flicker. We will demonstrate a couple in the following subsection.

Figure 6.16 Sometimes the Screen Is Complete

Suppose the hardware redraws the display after paint has completed. → The result is a complete screen.

```
public void update (Graphics g)
{
  g.setColor(getBackground());
  g.fillRect(0,0,width,height);
  g.setColor(getForeground());
  paint(g);
}

public void paint (Graphics g)
{
  paintBackground(g);
  paintButler(myX, myY, g);
}
```

g
display output buffer

6.8.1   Localizing Flicker

The first step in all of our strategies will be to remove any code that erases the display buffer. The culprit is the `update` method we inherit through `Applet`. It erases the display before calling `paint`. We override `update` to remove the erasure and only call `paint`. Listing 6.23 shows the resulting additional code.

Listing 6.23 Reducing the Motion Flicker—1

```
1   public void update (Graphics g)
2   {
3     paint(g);
4   }
```

Flickering is reduced but remains prominent. The hardware continues to grab the display buffer in various intermediate states. For example, the hardware may grab the buffer after the sky and ground have been drawn but before any of the other objects have been drawn.

The result is that the sky and ground are drawn but no other objects are. Although the sky and ground no longer flicker, the house, tree, wagon, and our butler flicker.

Given that the butler is over a solid green background, we can draw a green rectangle over it and redraw our butler in a new place. This technique is implemented in Listing 6.24. This time the call to `repaint` is removed from the `run` method and replaced by Lines 18 and 19. Line 19 makes a direct call to `paintButler`, which draws a green rectangle over the butler before redrawing it.

Listing 6.24 Reducing the Motion Flicker—2

```
1    public void paintButler (int x, int y, Graphics g)
2    {
3      // Erase this butler
4      Color springGreen = new Color(0, 255, 127);
5      g.setColor(springGreen);
6      g.fillRect(x-3, y, 49, 67);
7
8      // the code that draws this butler
9      ...
10   }
11
12   public void run()
13   {
14     while(true)
15     {
16       pause(50);
17       move();
18       Graphics g = getGraphics();
19       paintButler (myX, myY, g);
20     }
21   }
```

There are several problems with this approach. First, it works only if the background is a solid color. Second, it does not remove all the flicker. Our butler still flickers because the hardware often grabs the display buffer before the butler is completely drawn.

6.8.2   Reducing Flicker with Double Buffering

The most pleasing technique to solve the flicker problem is to use double buffering. This technique is called double buffering because we use two image buffers. We will draw the scene in a hidden buffer. When the scene is complete, we will copy the scene from the hidden buffer to the display buffer in one step. By drawing a completed scene in one operation, it is not possible to draw it before components have a chance to be added to it.

Listing 6.25 Reducing Flicker with Double Buffering

```
1   public class Butler extends Applet implements Runnable
2   {
3     private Image  myHiddenBuffer;
4     ...
5
6     public void init()
7     {
8       ...
9       myHiddenBuffer = createImage(WIDTH, HEIGHT);
10      ...
11    }
12
13    public void update (Graphics g)
14    {
15      paint(g);
16    }
17
18    public void paint(Graphics g)
19    {
20      Graphics hiddenG = myHiddenBuffer.getGraphics();
21      paintBackground(hiddenG);
22      paintButler (myX, myY, hiddenG);
23      g.drawImage(myHiddenBuffer, 0, 0, this);
24    }
25  }
```

Our first step is again to eliminate the screen erasure in the update method (Line 13 of Listing 6.25).

Next we must implement the double buffering. First we create our hidden buffer. This is done in Lines 3 and 9. Next we change the paint method so that it draws into our hidden buffer. We begin by getting its graphics context in Line 20. Next we call paintBackground and paintButler, sending it the graphics context for the hidden buffer rather than the graphics context for the display buffer. As a result paintBackground and paintButler draw the scene in our hidden buffer. Finally, we copy our hidden buffer into the display buffer by drawing the hidden buffer's image in the display buffer (Line 23 of Figure 6.17). The result is smooth animation.

There remain some imaging artifacts. For example, the hidden buffer may not be completely copied to the display buffer when the hardware grabs the output display buffer. The result may be a jagged object, as illustrated in Figure 6.18. The top of the butler has moved but its bottom part was not copied over in time. Fortunately, this artifact is not distracting.

Figure 6.17 Double Buffering

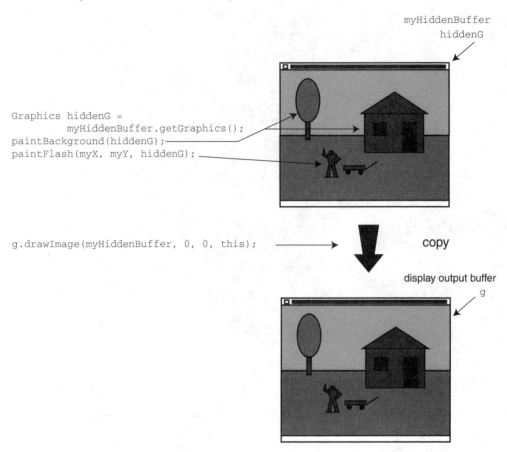

Double buffering can be made more efficient by copying only the part of the image that has changed. It requires keeping track of a change bounding rectangle and using clipping regions. We will not show this technique.

One final note. We have made myHiddenBuffer an instance variable (Section 4.2.3, page 127). We declared it in Line 3 and created it in Line 9 (Listing 6.25). We could define it locally within the paint method. If we were to do that, the hidden buffer would be created 20 times per second. Because images require large amounts of memory, the program would slow down. Once it ran out of memory, it would have to invoke the garbage collector to recover spent images, slowing down the animation even further. The result would be jerky movement and a sluggish computer.

Figure 6.18 Animation Artifact

REFERENCE

6.9   Summary

Abstraction focuses on essential detail. Limiting the detail a programming needs to remember makes programming more manageable. We do not have to think about how these chunks of code are implemented; we can concentrate on how to use them. Encapsulation is the flip side of abstraction. It hides nonessential detail.

"Divide and conquer" (stepwise refinement) is a problem-solving technique that often takes advantage of operational abstraction. Each operation can be decomposed into sub-operations. Operational decomposition is the basis for the delegation action pattern, which states that an operation is the sum of its components.

Java uses a class construct for abstraction. Methods are one component of a class definition. A method's signature is defined by its name, parameters, and return type and the class in which it is defined. A method call must match the signature of the method declaration.

Scope defines the locations within a program where a particular identifier can be used. Instance variables define the state of an object and have scope throughout the entire class in which they are defined. The scope of parameters is limited to the method in which they are defined. Local variables have scope from the point of declaration to the end of the block in which they are defined.

Pre and post conditions are an important part of a method's definition. They tell the programmer what condition must be met before the method is called, and they tell the result of executing the method.

We implement animation by using threads. Each thread represents a flow of control. One thread is controlled by a web browser and is responsible for maintaining the display and other applet bookkeeping tasks. A second thread is added by the programmer to control the animation.

Animation screen flicker is the result of display images that have not been completely generated. We can effectively control it by using double buffering. The program constructs an image in a hidden buffer. Once the image is complete, it is copied into the display buffer.

PROGRAM LISTINGS

6.10 Butler

The complete implementation of the Butler program is found in Listing 6.26.

Listing 6.26 Butler

```
1  //*************************************************************
2  //
3  // title:   Butler
4  //
5  // Draw a robot against a background.  The exercises will ask
6  // us to partition the paintBackground method into smaller
7  // methods.
8  //
9  //*************************************************************
10
11 import java.awt.Color;
12 import java.awt.Graphics;
13 import java.awt.Polygon;
14 import java.applet.Applet;
15
16
17 public class Butler extends Applet
18 {
19    //---------- paint ----------------------------------------
20    //
21    // pre:  graphicsContext is valid
22    // post: 3 Butlers and background are drawn.
23
24    public void paint(Graphics g)
25    {
26       paintBackground(g);
27       paintButler(50, 170, g);
28       paintButler(90, 190, g);
29       paintButler(75, 210, g);
30    }
31
```

Listing 6.26 Butler

```
32   //---------- paintBackground -------------------------------
33   //
34   // pre:  graphicsContext is valid
35   // post: ground, house, and tree are drawn.
36
37   public void paintBackground(Graphics graphicsContext)
38   {
39     // Create the sky and ground
40     graphicsContext.setColor(Color.blue);
41     graphicsContext.fillRect(0,0,400,150);
42     Color springGreen = new Color(0, 255, 127);
43     graphicsContext.setColor(springGreen);
44     graphicsContext.fillRect(0,150,400,150);
45
46     // Draw a tree
47     graphicsContext.fillOval(40, 20, 50, 100);
48     Color brown = new Color(166, 42, 42);
49     graphicsContext.setColor(brown);
50     graphicsContext.fillRect(60, 120, 10, 40);
51
52     // Draw a house
53     Color brick = new Color(230, 35, 35);
54     graphicsContext.setColor(brick);
55     graphicsContext.fillRect(200,100, 140, 90);
56     Polygon roof = new Polygon();
57     roof.addPoint(190,100);
58     roof.addPoint(350,100);
59     roof.addPoint(270, 50);
60     roof.addPoint(190,100);
61     Color forestGreen = new Color(35,142,35);
62     graphicsContext.setColor(forestGreen);
63     graphicsContext.fillPolygon(roof);
64     graphicsContext.setColor(Color.black);
65     graphicsContext.fillRect(220, 120, 30, 30);
66     graphicsContext.fillRect(290, 120, 30, 70);
67
68     // Draw a wagon
69     graphicsContext.setColor(Color.red);
70     graphicsContext.fillRect(150, 220,  50,  10);
71     graphicsContext.setColor(Color.black);
72     graphicsContext.fillOval(155, 230,  10,  10);
73     graphicsContext.fillOval(185, 230,  10,  10);
74     graphicsContext.drawLine(200, 230, 230, 210);
75     graphicsContext.drawLine(226, 212, 230, 212);
76   }
77
```

Listing 6.26 Butler

```
78   //---------- paintButler -----------------------------------
79   //
80   // pre:  graphicsContext is valid
81   // post: Butler is drawn with upper left corner at (x,y).
82
83   public void paintButler(int x,int y,Graphics graphicsContext)
84   {
85      // Draw head
86      Color flesh = new Color(188, 143, 143);
87      graphicsContext.setColor(flesh);
88      graphicsContext.fillOval(x+18, y+8, 6, 14);
89
90      // Draw helmet
91      graphicsContext.setColor(Color.black);
92      graphicsContext.drawOval(x+12, y+6, 18, 18);
93
94      // Draw left arm
95      Polygon leftArm = new Polygon();
96      leftArm.addPoint(x+ 3, y);
97      leftArm.addPoint(x+ 6, y+15);
98      leftArm.addPoint(x+12, y+18);
99      leftArm.addPoint(x+12, y+24);
100     leftArm.addPoint(x   , y+15);
101     leftArm.addPoint(x+ 3, y);
102     Color silver = new Color(202, 204, 222);
103     graphicsContext.setColor(silver);
104     graphicsContext.fillPolygon(leftArm);
105     graphicsContext.setColor(Color.black);
106     graphicsContext.drawPolygon(leftArm);
107
108     // Draw right arm
109     Polygon rightArm = new Polygon();
110     rightArm.addPoint(x+30, y+36);
111     rightArm.addPoint(x+36, y+24);
112     rightArm.addPoint(x+30, y+21);
113     rightArm.addPoint(x+30, y+15);
114     rightArm.addPoint(x+42, y+24);
115     rightArm.addPoint(x+30, y+36);
116     graphicsContext.setColor(silver);
117     graphicsContext.fillPolygon(rightArm);
118     graphicsContext.setColor(Color.black);
119     graphicsContext.drawPolygon(rightArm);
120
```

Listing 6.26   Butler

```
121        // Draw body
122        Polygon body = new Polygon();
123        body.addPoint(x+ 9, y+15);
124        body.addPoint(x+33, y+15);
125        body.addPoint(x+27, y+36);
126        body.addPoint(x+33, y+63);
127        body.addPoint(x+36, y+66);
128        body.addPoint(x+24, y+66);
129        body.addPoint(x+27, y+63);
130        body.addPoint(x+21, y+39);
131        body.addPoint(x+15, y+63);
132        body.addPoint(x+18, y+66);
133        body.addPoint(x+ 6, y+66);
134        body.addPoint(x+ 9, y+63);
135        body.addPoint(x+15, y+36);
136        body.addPoint(x+ 9, y+15);
137        graphicsContext.setColor(silver);
138        graphicsContext.fillPolygon(body);
139        graphicsContext.setColor(Color.black);
140        graphicsContext.drawPolygon(body);
141
142        // Draw breast plate
143        Polygon breastPlate = new Polygon();
144        breastPlate.addPoint(x+11, y+17);
145        breastPlate.addPoint(x+31, y+17);
146        breastPlate.addPoint(x+27, y+22);
147        breastPlate.addPoint(x+14, y+22);
148        breastPlate.addPoint(x+11, y+17);
149        Color limeGreen = new Color (50, 205, 50);
150        graphicsContext.setColor(limeGreen);
151        graphicsContext.fillPolygon(breastPlate);
152    }
153 }
```

PROBLEM SETS

6.11   Exercises

Abstraction—Section 6.2

1   Which of the following interactions and properties of a word processor demonstrate abstraction and which demonstrate encapsulation?

    a.   The Times font is represented in a file as the integer value 59.

    b.   To change to the Times font, a user selects "Times" from the Font menu.

    c.   To set the text insertion location, a user moves the mouse pointer to the desired location and presses the left mouse button.

    d.   To compute the insertion location, the program computes the y location of the mouse, divides it by the font size, and . . ..

Delegation Action Pattern—Section 6.4

2   Using Listing 6.4 on page 219 and Listing 6.5 on page 221 as models, write the method calls necessary to solve the following exercises in Chapter 2. Assess the abstraction, encapsulation, cohesion, and coupling characteristics of the solution.

    a.   Exercise 21

    b.   Exercise 24

Declaring methods—Section 6.6.1 and Section 6.6.2

3   Find the three syntax errors in the following code fragment:

```
public void factorial (n)
  int count = 1;
  int fact  = 1;
  while (count <= n)
  {
    fact = fact * count;
    count++;
  }
  return fact;
}
```

4   Find the syntax error in the following code fragment:

```
public void init ()
{
  double x = 3.5;
  square (x);
}
public void square (int y)
{
  int result = y * y;
}
```

5   Find the syntax error in the following code fragment:

```
public void init ()
{
  sum (11.0, 12.4, 19.8);
}
public void sum (double x, double y)
{
  double result = x + y;
}
```

Scope—Section 6.6.3

6   Name an example of each of the following from Listing 6.27 on page 269:

    a.   instance variable

    b.   local variable

    c.   parameter

7   What is the scope of each of the following in Listing 6.27? Give a range of line numbers, for example, Lines 6 through 9.

    a.   a

    b.   b

    c.   c

    d.   d

    e.   e

    f.   f

8   Indicate if the following code when placed within the `init` method of Listing 6.27, is legal or illegal. If it is legal, indicate what is printed. If it is illegal, state why.

Listing 6.27 Exercises 6 through 8 —Refer to the Following Applet

```
1  public class Gizmo extends applet
2  {
3    private int    a;
4    private double b;
5
6    public void init ()
7    {
8      // exercise code is inserted here
9    }
10
11   public void set(int c)
12   {
13     a = c;
14     b = 17.3;
15   }
16
17   public void set(int d, double e)
18   {
19     a = d;
20     b = e;
21   }
22
23   public double add()
24   {
25     double f = a + b;
26     return f;
27   }
28
29   public void print()
30   {
31     System.out.println(a + " " + b);
32   }
33 }
```

```
a. a = 15;
   b = 12.34;
   print();

b. set(23, 12.12);
   print();

c. set(77.66, 11);
   print();

d. b = 9.87;
   set(39);
   print();
```

```
e. a = 48;
   set(13.1);
   print();

f. a = 11;
   b = 33.3;
   set (22, 44.4);
   print();

g. set (22, 44.4);
   a = 11;
   b = 33.3
   print();

h. a = 9;
   b = 9.0;
   print(17);

i. set (1, 22.2, 3);
   print();
```

9   Which of the assignment statements in Listing 6.28 are legal?

Returning Values—Section 6.6.5

10   Write a method that returns the average of two integers. It should have two parameters, one for each integer.

11   Write a method for one of the problems in Exercise 22 of Chapter 5.

Use the following information for Exercises 12–14

The Rectangle class is defined in Appendix B on page 898. Use only a rectangle's instance variables (x, y, width, and height) to implement each of the methods in Exercises 12–14.

12   Write a method that returns true if a point is inside a rectangle, and otherwise returns false. Do not use the predefined `contains` method from the `Rectangle` class.

```
public boolean inside (int x, int y, Rectangle r)
{
    return ...
}
```

13   Write a method that returns true if a circle is completely within a rectangle, other-

Listing 6.28 Exercise 9—Refer to the Following Classes

```
1   public class Seven
2   {
3     private int a;
4
5     public void ObjectInt (int b)
6     {
7       int c;
8       a = 7;         // assignment 1
9       b = 7;         // assignment 2
10       c = 7;         // assignment 3
11      d = 7;         // assignment 4
12      e = 7;         // assignment 5
13    }
14
15    public void set (int d)
16    {
17      int e;
18      a = 7;         // assignment 6
19      b = 7;         // assignment 7
20      c = 7;         // assignment 8
21      d = 7;         // assignment 9
22      e = 7;         // assignment 10
23    }
24  }
```

wise it returns false.

```
public boolean inside (int x, int y, int size, Rectangle r)
{
   return ...
}
```

14   Write a method that returns true if one rectangle overlaps another, otherwise it returns false. (Two rectangles overlap if there is at least one point on a rectangle boarder or in its interior that is shared.)

```
public boolean overlap (Rectangle a, Rectangle b)
{
   return ...
}
```

Pre and Post Conditions—Section 6.6.8

15 Write pre and post conditions for the following methods:

a.

```
public void setRoomTemperature (int setting)
```

b.

```
public double computeIncomeTax
        (double grossIncome, int dependents)
```

c.

```
public int daysSinceJanuary1
        (int month, int day)
```

6.12   Projects

Butler—Section 6.3

16 Add the following to the program in Listing 6.26 on page 263:

a.   A ball in the wagon

b.   An image of a puppy in the wagon

c.   A person pulling the wagon

17 Partition the `paintBackground` method in Listing 6.26 on page 263 into `paintSky`, `paintEarth`, `paintTree`, `paintHouse`, and `paint-Wagon` methods.

18 Repeat Exercise 17 with location parameters for `paintTree`, `paintHouse`, and `paintWagon`. Draw a forest of trees around a small village of houses with wagons in their front yards.

19 Include a size parameter for the `drawTree` method in Exercise 18. Create a forest of different sized trees around the house and wagon.

20 Make each tree randomly a slightly different color of green. For help with random numbers see Section 5.5.7, page 194.

Our Butler—Section 6.4

21 Listing 6.4 on page 219 uses the delegation action pattern to outline an approach for solving Exercise 19 in Chapter 2. Finish the implementation.

22 Listing 6.5 on page 221 uses the delegation action pattern to outline an approach for solving Exercise 23 in Chapter 2. Finish the implementation.

23 Using Listing 6.4 on page 219 and Listing 6.5 on page 221 as models, use the delegation action pattern to completely implement the following exercises in Chapter 2.

a. Exercise 21

b. Exercise 24

Writing Methods—Section 6.6

24 Replace the computation of the next generation on Lines 46 and 55 in Listing 5.1 on page 168 with a method. So instead of writing:

```
population = r * population * (1.0 - population);
```

you can write:

```
population = nextGeneration(population, r);
```

25 In Listing 5.1 on page 168 Lines 48 through 57 repeat Lines 36 through 45. Replace the repeated code with a method that plots a line. The method signature should be:

```
// pre:  0.0 <= initial population <= 1.0
//       0.0 < rate of growth <= 4.0
// post: A single line of the given color is added to graph
//       for the given population
public void plotPopulation (double population, double rate,
                            VGraph graph, Color color);
```

26 Modify the code in the `plotPopulation` method of Exercise 25 to check its pre conditions and display an error message if its pre conditions are not met.

27 Many would argue that a method should report violations to its pre conditions. This allows a programmer to write code that responds to errors and avoids unexpected program behavior. Modify the code to the `plotPopulation` method of Exercise 25 so that it returns `true` if computation can be trusted and `false` if the pre conditions have been violated. Modify the `paint` method so that it checks for errors and reports any problems to the user.

28 Write a method that rounds doubles to the nearest hundredth; for example, 136.3578 to 136.36.

Animating the Butler—Section 6.7

29   Modify the program in Listing 6.26 on page 263 using the animation code in Listing 6.22 on page 252. Add instance variables for the butler's x and y locations. Make the butler move up and down in addition to left and right.

30   Make our butler jump over the wagon. Do this by adding a `fly` method to exercise 29

31   Make our butler appear to walk by repeatedly drawing four side views with its legs in different positions.

32   Animate a child pulling the wagon. Use methods with parameters for both the child and wagon.

33   Create an animation using three or more images. For example, create a person walking across the screen, a teddy bear doing jumping jacks, or a person doing cartwheels. Each image is a different snapshot of the action. Then by displaying the icons in sequence, you can create an illusion of motion.

7 Class Abstraction

Object Animation

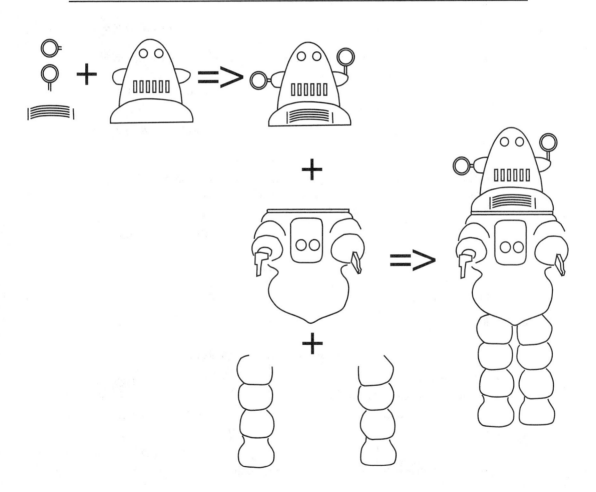

7.1   Objectives

Concepts

Section 7.2, page 277

Section 7.3, page 279

This chapter continues the focus on abstractions and encapsulation. We will build on our experience with method abstractions from the last chapter to create object abstractions. This chapter begins by partitioning the `Butler` applet into classes. We begin with a simple background class without state or constructor. We then move on to a `Butler` class that has a state and a constructor.

Section 7.7, page 315

Finally, we begin the long process of determining when and when not to be concerned about program efficiency. An experiment is performed to compare direct and indirect access speeds of instance variables. We use these results to help us weigh the impact of our coding decisions.

Patterns

Section 7.4, page 293

An object pattern describes a commonly used structure for organizing objects and classes to help solve a general design problem. The first object pattern we will investigate is the delegation object pattern. This pattern builds a new object from subobjects.

Section 7.5, page 295

Object patterns are one of the tools we can use to guide us through an objected-oriented design. We look at several design issues raised when we partition a problem into objects.

Java Skills

Next we address how we can use Java to express object abstractions.

- Class declarations   Section 7.6.1, page 305
- Using private and public modifiers   Section 7.6.3, page 308
- Using static modifier   Section 7.6.6, page 310

Abilities

By the end of this chapter we should be able to do the following:

- Create classes that we can instantiate.
- Create experiments that test the efficiency of implementation strategies.

CONCEPTS

7.2   Creating Classes

We have been building and using classes since Chapter 1. The first Java program we investigated is one that simulates a robot butler. Within it we used the `Butler` class. That program took advantage of encapsulation by hiding all the details about displaying a room, determining when collisions occurred, and moving the butler. The `Butler` class contained `turnRight` and `forward` methods, hiding many lines of Java code that manipulate a butler's state. In this chapter we will see how to create a simple `butler` class.

In Chapter 3 we were introduced to the `Graphics` class, which hides the machine-specific details of drawing graphics on a display. This is just one example of the hundreds of classes that comprise the standard Java class library. The Java development team has created a library that can be used to create simple windowed applications, interact with the Internet, and play sounds. All of these classes are examples of abstractions. They provide us essential operations to manipulate the computing environment while hiding all those details that do not help us solve problems.

The classes provided by the Java programming environment and with those provided in this text represent only a handful of the possible classes that are useful to a programmer. Each nontrivial problem for which we must write a program requires abstraction. Banking applications require abstractions that capture financial and management organizations, industry requires abstractions that control machines, and science requires abstractions that represent the physical world. It is not possible for a language designer to foresee all possible abstractions. Thus, languages provide features that allow programmers to implement their own abstractions. In OO (object-oriented) languages, such as Java, the abstraction mechanism is the class.

The first class that we built extended the `Applet` class. We defined `init` and `paint` methods, which are used by the browser to control the behavior of an applet. In Chapter 6, we learned how to add operations to a class by defining new methods and add state to a class by adding instance variables. Because we have been creating classes for a long time, this chapter contains little new technical detail. We will focus on understanding the ramifications of the decisions we make when we define classes.

A software design specifies how a project will be partitioned into objects and the operations that are available on those objects. Defining module interfaces is key to partitioning a software project. Interfaces determine how modules are used by other programmers.

> An *interface* is composed of all the signatures that define the operations on an object. Recall that a signature is defined by the order, number, and kind of parameters a method has in addition to the method's name, return type, and the class to which it belongs.

The interface for the `Butler` class is shown in Listing 7.1. Other examples include the interfaces we have seen for the `Graphics` and `Math` classes in Appendix: B.

Listing 7.1 Butler Interface

```
1   public class Butler
2   {
3      public          Butler (int x, int y, Room room);
4      public void     backward ();
5      public void     backward (int count);
6      public void     forward ();
7      public void     forward (int count);
8      public boolean  isBackClear ();
9      public boolean  isFrontBasket ();
10     public boolean  isFrontClear ();
11     public boolean  isFrontClothes ();
12     public boolean  isLeftClear ();
13     public boolean  isRightClear ();
14     public void     paint (Graphics g);
15     public void     pickUp ();
16     public void     putDown ();
17     public void     putIn ();
18     public void     takeOut ();
19     public void     turnLeft ();
20     public void     turnLeft (int count);
21     public void     turnRight ();
22     public void     turnRight (int count);
23  }
```

In addition to making it easier for people to use code developed by other programmers, classes also make it easier to partition a project into smaller components. Project partitioning allows groups of programmers to work independently on each module. For example, the group working on the `Graphics` class can work on its implementation details with little fear that their actions will interfere with groups writing classes that depend on their work. Each group must make sure it does not violate the interface. For example, the `Graphics` group is not allowed to change the name of any of its methods, what those methods accomplish, and the type, number, or order of the method parameters. Thus, any program that uses the `Graphics` class should still work after it has been changed.

The interface is visible for all to see; its implementation is hidden. Thus, when programs are moved from one computer architecture to another, it does not matter that the underlying hardware and software are different. It only matters that the interface does not change.

Modularity makes a complex project easier to comprehend. We do not have to understand all the details. We can begin to learn how a system works by looking at its major components and how they interact.

The underlying motivation for abstraction is the need to create reliable systems. A beginning programmer may easily wonder what all the fuss is about because the programs we have seen thus far are simple, and it is easy to show that they are correct. However, these programs appear simple only because they are resting on top of tens of thousands of lines of other people's work.

Programs for many systems are many millions of lines long. Subtle coding errors have caused long distance telephone lines to go down, delayed the launch of a space shuttle, and delayed the opening of the Denver Airport. As programs become larger, it is difficult to show their correctness through inspection. An error in a single byte resulted in the destruction of Mariner 1, the first U.S. interplanetary spacecraft. This error cost between 18 and 20 million dollars (1962 dollars).

Building abstractions will require extra effort on our part because we will need to think about how other people may use our code. This will require understanding and coding. By spending extra time up front, we can save time later. Anything we can do to make a program easier to understand and easier to test is usually worth the up-front cost needed to rethink the design and follow prescribed software practices.

7.3   Butler as an Object

In Chapter 6, we created an applet with several methods that drew a background with trees, a house, a wagon, and a butler. None of those images were objects. They were drawn by creating methods in the `Butler` applet class. In this chapter, we will rewrite that applet using background and butler objects.

7.3.1 A Background Object

We will start with two objects, the applet and the background (Figure 7.1), and add additional ones later. The applet object is just like the ones we have created since Chapter 1. It will be instantiated by a web browser (Listing 7.2).

Figure 7.1 Scene Objects

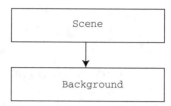

Listing 7.2 Scene Class

```
1  //************************************************************
2  //
3  // title:    Scene
4  //
5  // Draw only the background.
6  //
7  //************************************************************
8
9  import java.awt.Graphics;
10 import java.applet.Applet;
11
12 public class Scene extends Applet {
13
14   //---------- paint ------------------------------------------
15   //
16   // Called automatically
17   // post: Background are drawn.
18
19   public void paint(Graphics g)
20   {
21     Background earth = new Background();
22     earth.paint(g);
23   }
24 }
```

The Scene applet is simple. All it does is create a background object in Line 21 and paint it in Line 22. Thus, whenever the Scene applet is repainted, a new background is created and painted. We do not need to import the Background class as long as it is in the same directory that the Scene class resides within.

The Background class shown in Listing 7.3 is rather peculiar. It has no constructor and no state. When the Scene class creates a Background object, a default constructor provided by Java is called, which does nothing. It has no parameters and no code body.

Listing 7.3 Background Class

```
1  //*******************************************************************
2  //
3  // title:    Background
4  //
5  // Background object. Draws the sky and ground.
6  //
7  //*******************************************************************
8
9  import java.awt.Color;
10 import java.awt.Graphics;
11
12 public class Background
13 {
14    private final int WIDTH  = 400;
15    private final int HEIGHT = 300;
16
17    //---------- paint -------------------------------------------
18    //
19    // pre:  g is valid
20    // post: Background is drawn.
21
22    public void paint(Graphics g)
23    {
24       g.setColor(Color.blue);
25       g.fillRect(0, 0, WIDTH, HEIGHT/2);
26       Color springGreen = new Color(0, 255, 127);
27       g.setColor(springGreen);
28       g.fillRect(0, HEIGHT/2, WIDTH, HEIGHT/2);
29    }
30 }
```

Background objects have only the paint method. It draws two filled rectangles—a blue one for the sky and a green one for the earth. Figure 7.2 shows the order in which statements are executed when a Scene applet is repainted.

Figure 7.2 Flow of Control

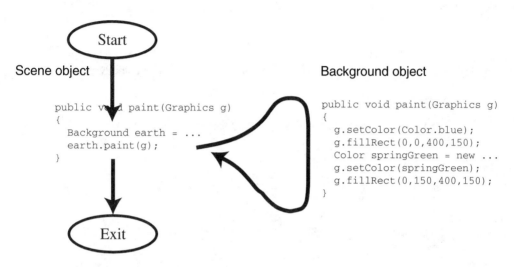

In the following sections, we will add to and modify the Scene project. When it becomes difficult to see how the modifications fit into the entire project, refer to Section 7.10 , page 324 for the final listing of the classes.

Figure 7.3 The Butler Class

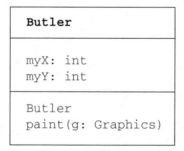

7.3.2   A Butler Object

Let us add a `Butler` object to our drawing. Our butlers have state: their location. See Figure 7.3 and Listing 7.4. The two instance variables declared in Lines 15 and 16 define the butler's state. The constructor in Lines 27 through 31 sets a butler's location to a ran-

Listing 7.4 The Butler Class

```
1  //************************************************************
2  //
3  // title:   Butler
4  //
5  // Class for creating butlers.
6  //
7  //************************************************************
8
9  import java.awt.Color;
10 import java.awt.Graphics;
11 import java.awt.Polygon;
12
13 public class Butler
14 {
15    private int myX;
16    private int myY;
17
18    // Size of the window that holds the butler.
19    private final int WIDTH  = 400;
20    private final int HEIGHT = 300;
21
22    //---------- Butler ----------------------------------
23    //
24    // pre:  none
25    // post: a butler is created at a random location.
26
27    public Butler ()
28    {
29       myX = (int)(Math.random() * (WIDTH  - 40));
30       myY = (int)(Math.random() * (HEIGHT - 50));
31    }
32
33    //---------- paint -----------------------------------
34    //
35    // pre:  g is a valid graphics context
36    // post: a butler is drawn.
37
38    public void paint(Graphics g)
39    {
40       // Draw head
41       Color flesh = new Color(188, 143, 143);
42       g.setColor(flesh);
43       g.fillOval(myX+18, myY+8, 6, 14);
44
45       ...
46    }
47 }
```

dom position. The possible x locations are between 0 and 360, and the y locations are between 0 and 250. The primary function of a constructor is to initialize an object's state. The `paint` method is shown in Lines 38 through 46.

Listing 7.5 shows how the `paint` method in the `Scene` class is modified to create and draw a butler. `Butler` is a class. When we create `Butler` objects we will need to give them names. Line 5 creates a Butler named `albert` by calling the `Butler` constructor. Line 6 then draws `albert`. The flow of control for the applet `paint` is shown with the sequence diagram in Figure 7.4.

Listing 7.5 Scene `paint` method

```
1    public void paint(Graphics g)
2    {
3       Background earth = new Background();
4       earth.paint(g);
5       Butler albert = new Butler();
6       albert.paint(g);
7    }
```

A *sequence diagram* shows how groups of objects collaborate to get a task done. Typically, a sequence diagram captures a scenario, a particular sequence of events. Time is shown by reading the sequence diagram from top to the bottom. The horizontal dimension shows different objects. The example in Figure 7.4 shows that the `earth` object is first created by executing the `Background` constructor, the `paint` operation is applied to `earth`, `albert` is created using the `Butler` constructor, and finally the scene is painted. See Appendix: B for more details about sequence diagrams.

We have just made the `Butler` program we wrote in Chapter 6 more complicated. It is common practice to place only one class within a single file. Thus, what used to be in one file is now in several. We have to deal with the declaration of two new classes: one for the butler and one for the background. We now have to instantiate butler and background objects before we can paint them. We should be asking ourselves, why?

The answer to that question is that the `Scene` class in Listing 7.2 and Listing 7.5 is much simpler than the applet in Listing 6.26 on page 263. Once the `Butler` class is created, all of its details are encapsulated in a single file. The details of how a butler is drawn are hidden. We don't have to look at them again. To use a butler in any program, we just have to import it. We can use `Butler` in an arcade game where it saves the Space Gizzbies from the tyrannical Zoltarians. We can use it in a public safety program that shows children how

Figure 7.4 Flow of control of the `Scene` applet

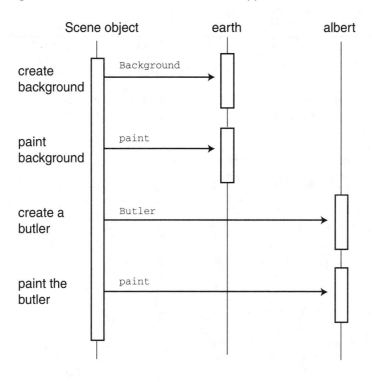

to find the fire exit from their classroom. We can use it in a learning program where a butler bounces over the words of a song.

There is a cost in planning and coding to make a `Butler` class. The benefit is that it makes reusing it simple. Our life has been made much simpler by the hundreds of classes designed and created by the Java design team. There are thousands of details about Macintoshes, Windows 95, and Sparcs that we do not have to learn because they have been hidden from us. To make ourselves valuable programmers we cannot get by only using classes, we must also learn how to write classes.

7.3.3   Adding Another Constructor to Our Butler

Constructors can be overloaded just as other methods can. Listing 7.6 shows a second constructor that can be added to the `Butler` class in Listing 7.4. It is distinguished from the first constructor by its parameters. The original constructor puts our butler at random locations. The new constructor puts butlers at a specific location.

Listing 7.6 Second Butler constructor (insert in Listing 7.4 at Line 33)

```
1   public Butler (int x, int y)
2   {
3     myX = x;
4     myY = y;
5   }
```

Listing 7.7 is a modification to the Scene class. It creates four butlers in a row and a fifth butler, named eddie, which is placed at a random location. See Figure 7.5.

Listing 7.7 Four butlers in a row plus a random one

```
1    public void paint(Graphics g)
2    {
3      Background earth    = new Background();
4      earth.paint(g);
5      Butler albert       = new Butler(110,200);
6      albert.paint(g);
7      Butler betty        = new Butler( 90,200);
8      betty.paint(g);
9      Butler clarence     = new Butler( 70,200);
10     clarence.paint(g);
11     Butler doris        = new Butler( 50,200);
12     doris.paint(g);
13     Butler eddie        = new Butler();
14     eddie.paint(g);
15   }
```

Figure 7.5 Four butlers in a row plus a random one

7.3.4 Adding State to the Scene Class

Each time the Scene applet is repainted, all five butlers must be recreated and the five previous butlers are lost. This is a waste of resources and it can become a problem during animation. When the paint method is called 20 times a second, memory space will be used and the garbage collector will be required to return unused butlers. Not only does allocating new butlers from memory take time but the garbage collector will cause a temporary halt in animation. Listing 7.8 shows how to create the five butlers only once when the applet is started. Each of the butlers is declared as an instance variable in Lines 14 through 18. They are created at applet start up in Lines 27 through 32. Finally, they are painted when required in Lines 42 through 47.

Figure 7.6 is an object diagram that shows the seven objects that comprise this applet. The top compartment of each object shows the object name and class. The bottom compartment shows its state.

A problem with the butlers being part of the Scene state is that the complexity of the program goes up. Code for drawing a butler is distributed in three parts of the program. In one location an instance variable is defined (Line 14), in a second location a butler is created (Line 28), and in a third location butler is drawn (Line 43). Placing all the code close together within the paint method makes it easier to find and modify. We used this approach early in the book because of its simplicity.

The trade-off between efficiency and clarity is a choice that a programmer is constantly making. Programmers must not only make programs work well; they must also make programs that can be easily understood. The lifetime of commercial programs may be 5 to 20 years. Sixty to 70 percent of the expense of developing that program often goes into program maintenance: correcting errors and adding enhancements. If the program is easily understand, it is cheaper to maintain. The cost of the extra execution time may be justified. A good rule of thumb is to make the program easy to understand and only optimize it if absolutely necessary.

> *Optimization* is the process of making a system more efficient. In a computer program, that may entail making it run faster or run with less memory. A problem with optimizing computer programs is that it is easy to focus on the wrong elements and optimization can make a program more complex.

Listing 7.8 Scene Class with State

```
1   //*****************************************************************
2   // title:    Scene
3   //
4   // Draw four butlers in a row plus one at a random location.
5   // Make the background and the butlers part of this state.
6   //*****************************************************************
7
8   import java.awt.Graphics;
9   import java.applet.Applet;
10
11  public class Scene extends Applet
12  {
13     private Background  myEarth;
14     private Butler      myAlbert;
15     private Butler      myBetty;
16     private Butler      myClarence;
17     private Butler      myDoris;
18     private Butler      myEddie;
19
20     //--------- init -------------------------------------------
21     //
22     // called automatically
23     // post: Butler and background are created.
24
25     public void init()
26     {
27        myEarth    = new Background();
28        myAlbert   = new Butler(110,200);
29        myBetty    = new Butler( 90,200);
30        myClarence = new Butler( 70,200);
31        myDoris    = new Butler( 50,200);
32        myEddie    = new Butler();
33     }
34
35     //--------- paint ------------------------------------------
36     //
37     // called automatically
38     // post: Butler and background are drawn.
39
40     public void paint(Graphics g)
41     {
42        myEarth.paint(g);
43        myAlbert.paint(g);
44        myBetty.paint(g);
45        myClarence.paint(g);
46        myDoris.paint(g);
47        myEddie.paint(g);
48     }
49  }
```

Figure 7.6 Object Diagram

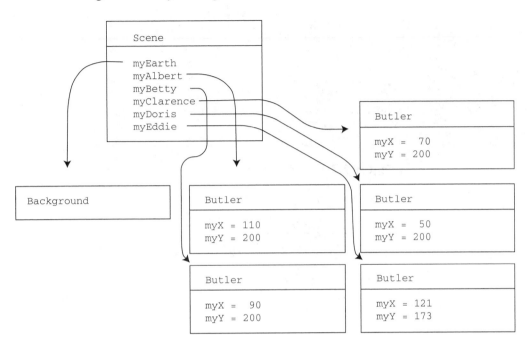

7.3.5 Adding a `setLocation` Method to Butler

The Butler class in Listing 7.4 is not flexible. Once a butler is created, we cannot move him. The `setLocation` method in Listing 7.9 can be added to the Butler class. It allows us to move a butler by changing its state. Recall that one of the functions of a method is to change an object's state.

Listing 7.9 Adding a `setLocation` Method to Listing 7.4

```
1    public void setLocation (int x, int y)
2    {
3       myX = x;
4       myY = y;
5    }
```

The code in Listing 7.10 shows how we can modify Scene to put all five butlers in a row. See Figure 7.7. Eddie was created at a random location in Line 8 and moved to a specific location in Line 9. We could have simply created Eddie at a specific location. We did it in two steps to illustrate how to use the `setLocation` method.

Listing 7.10 Modification to the `start` Method in Listing 7.8

```
1    public void init()
2    {
3        myEarth     = new Background();
4        myAlbert    = new Butler(110,200);
5        myBetty     = new Butler( 90,200);
6        myClarence  = new Butler( 70,200);
7        myDoris     = new Butler( 50,200);
8        myEddie     = new Butler();
9        myEddie.setLocation(30,200);
10   }
```

Figure 7.7 Five in a Row

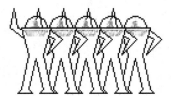

7.3.6   Partitioning `paint` into Private Methods

The `paint` method in Listing 7.4 is long. We can make it more manageable by partition-ing it into smaller methods as shown in Listing 7.11. Notice that the `paint` method is `public` (Line 2). It can be called by an object from any class. All the other `paint` meth-ods are `private` (Lines 12, 18, 24, 37, and 43). They can only be called from within the `Butler` class. The following shows what can be done within the `Scene` class:

```
myEddie.paint(g);        // ok because paint is public
myEddie.paintHead(g);    // error because paintHead is private
```

Let us conclude this section with another look at `this`. We first talked about `this` in Section 3.7 , page 113. The `This` keyword is used when a method refers to the object on which that method was involved. For example, in the `Butler` `paint` method the object to which the various paint methods are applied is `this` object (Lines 4 through 8). Those lines could be rewritten as follows.

```
this.paintHead(g);
this.paintLeftArm(g);
this.paintRightArm(g);
```

Listing 7.11 Partitioning Butler's `paint` into Additional Methods

```
1    //---------- paint -----------------------------------------
2    public void paint(Graphics g)
3    {
4      paintHead(g);
5      paintLeftArm(g);
6      paintRightArm(g);
7      paintBody(g);
8      paintBreastPlate(g);
9    }
10
11   //---------- paintBody -------------------------------------
12   private void paintBody(Graphics g)
13   {
14     ...
15   }
16
17   //---------- paintBreastPlate ------------------------------
18   private void paintBreastPlate(Graphics g)
19   {
20     ...
21   }
22
23   //---------- paintHead -------------------------------------
24   private void paintHead(Graphics g)
25   {
26     // Draw head
27     Color flesh = new Color(188, 143, 143);
28     g.setColor(flesh);
29     g.fillOval(myX+18, myY+8, 6, 14);
30
31     // Draw helmet
32     g.setColor(Color.black);
33     g.drawOval(myX+12, myY+6, 18, 18);
34   }
35
36   //---------- paintLeftArm ----------------------------------
37   private void paintLeftArm(Graphics g)
38   {
39     ...
40   }
41
42   //---------- paintRightArm ---------------------------------
43   private void paintRightArm(Graphics g)
44   {
45     ...
46   }
```

```
this.paintBody(g);
this.paintBreastPlate(g);
```

When the `paint` method is applied to Albert, `this` object is `myAlbert`. When the `paint` method is applied to Doris, `this` object is `myDoris`. Within the `Butler` class, we will never know the identity of the object that the `paintHead` method is to be applied.

Figure 7.8 This

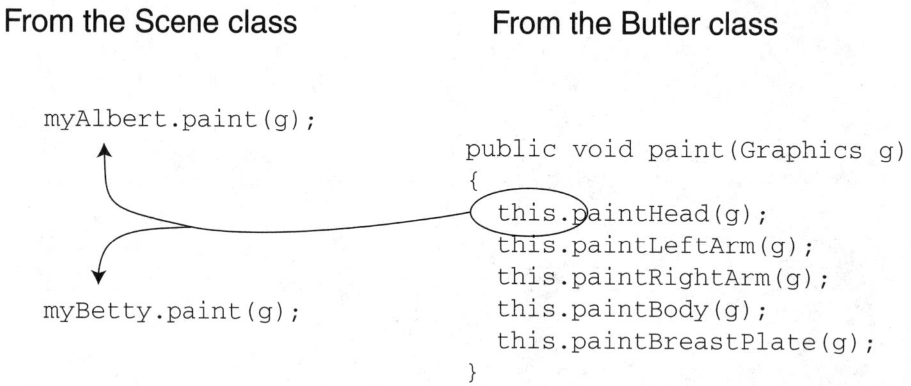

From the Scene class

```
myAlbert.paint(g);



myBetty.paint(g);
```

From the Butler class

```
public void paint(Graphics g)
{
    this.paintHead(g);
    this.paintLeftArm(g);
    this.paintRightArm(g);
    this.paintBody(g);
    this.paintBreastPlate(g);
}
```

PATTERNS

7.4   Delegation Object Pattern

7.4.1   Problem

In the previous chapter we introduced the delegation action pattern. We discovered that a task is the sum of its subtasks. By decomposing a problem into subtasks, we are better able to manage programs. In this chapter we are adding more "teeth" to our delegation pattern. We are discovering that an object is the sum of its subobjects. We are again using a metaphor with the real world to help us manage complexity. For example, in the real world dinner is a composite of soup, salad, sandwich, and something to drink. An automobile is a composite of an engine, transmission, wheels, and a frame. We decompose large systems into objects because it marks modifications to the system predictable. For example, adding mustard to our sandwich does not change the flavor of the soup and changing the carburetor on our engine does not make the wheels fall off. In programming we delegate behavior to each class so that we can better predict and manage the whole system.

For example, suppose that we have a system that monitors and manages a telephone network. One of its components is a customer database. We maintain telephone numbers, client names and addresses, and long-distance usage. Now suppose our telephone company purchases an electronic network provider with the goal of integrating telephone, email, and web services. As part of the new systems support staff, we are left with a question. How do we integrate the software systems that maintain our client records? We may have to reorganize our data to accommodate email addresses for each member of a family or every employee in a company. In addition, we must maintain web access statistics. We must be careful about how we change our data representation because it is not clear which old telephone methods depend on how the data is organized. A seemingly insignificant change in how we organize data may have an unforeseen and significant impact on seemingly unrelated actions. By carefully delegating state and operations to particular classes we can make change easier to manage.

As our software world becomes more complex we cannot think about all the operations and all the data at once. We need to group operations and data. We must be able to decompose a system into subcomponents. We must have some expectations about the impact of change in one area on the rest of the system. The decomposition must give us choices about the level of detail we wish to engage at a particular time. For example, are we interested in working with the software components that control a family's web access? Are we interested in the components that control access to the Internet backbone? Are we interested in the components that monitor security or the components that do the monthly accounting?

7.4.2 Solution

Decomposing a system into objects is one means we can use to manage the complexity of a system. Classes allow use to group-related data and operations. It allows us to manage change by hiding data representation. We can control how programmers access and manipulate data by writing appropriate methods.

Software systems are as varied as the problems they seek to address. There are many ways we can organize objects and classes. In this chapter we are looking at one such object pattern. We are investigating the delegation object pattern. .

An *object pattern* describes a commonly used structure for organizing objects and classes to help solve a general design problem.

The delegation object pattern builds a new object by grouping and delegating work to sub-objects. For example, in the beginning of this chapter we discovered that our scene is a composite of a butler, wagon, house, and tree objects (Figure 7.9). Thus, we can view the `Scene` class as a *container* class. The code for implementing this example can be patterned after the code in Listing 7.8 on page 288.

Figure 7.9 Delegation Object Pattern

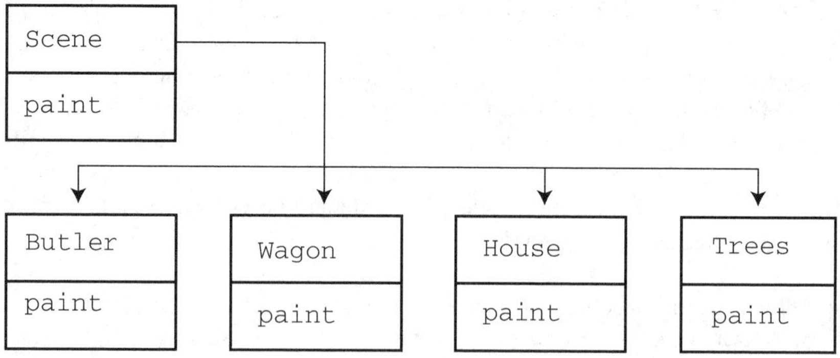

We may also view the client data for our expanded telephone system as a container for address, email, web, and voice mail objects. A student record may be a container for address, accounting, aid, and transcript objects. An airline reservation system may be a container for flights.

Containers are often more than one layer deep. We may view a software window as a container for scroll bars, a header area, and a text field. A window header may be a container for an icon, checkboxes, and a title. A software development environment may be a container for source code, an output, a debug, and a project status window.

7.4.3   Consequences

The delegation pattern makes a software system easier to manage. We can define an interface for a new class and delegate implementation to a different programming team. This approach follows a key strategy for developing many complex systems. We must carefully define the responsibilities of key components and delegate the work.

Object delegation does not come free. It means that the software designer and implementor have more to think about. The designer must carefully decompose a system into the appropriate system of classes. Choosing the wrong classes can make a hard problem worse. In addition, a programmer must understand the language syntax of classes. The program is distributed across many files. If the code is distributed poorly, it may be difficult to remember where critical code lies. Until one masters object-oriented design and implementation, objects make the problem harder. We will begin the long processes of mastering object-oriented design in the next section.

7.5   Design—Picking Classes

We all know something about design. We talk about the design of a new car or building. We argue endlessly about what makes a design good and what makes it bad. In the end we come to believe that design is as much science as it is art. So it is with software design as well. Good design is both science and art. We can admire, learn, and debate software design. In addition, there are underlying principles that hold for all good designs. We will begin to learn what those principles are in this section.

We cannot learn to ride a bike from a book. We must feel our feet against the peddles, the weight of our bodies as we turn, and the ground against our knees when we fall. It is the same for design. Although reading about design is critical, we cannot learn it from one chapter, from one book, or from a dozen books. It has been said that "good design comes from experience and experience comes from bad design."

Our focus in this book will be to study pre-existing designs. The programs we have seen thus far incorporate elements of design. We have gotten some experience with design because we have been asked to modify and enhance several of them. However, creating a design of even a few classes is surprisingly difficult for a first-time programmer. It is only through the process of creating our own designs and having these designs critiqued that we will learn good design. That is something no book can provide. We must begin by creating a small system composed of a few objects and find a good mentor or teacher to evaluate those designs. In this chapter we begin modestly. We will use the designs we have seen thus far as a backdrop for learning a few design issues.

> *Software design* is the process of decomposing a system into components and determining how those components interact with each other. When the components are classes, we call it *object-oriented design*.

Design is more than a quest for elegance. Good products come from good designs. The following are several characteristics of good design described by Priya Marsonia of NORTEL (Northern Telecom):

- Functionality—A design, no matter how elegant, that does not support a program's requirements is an obstacle. We must always begin with what we want our product to do. Next we look for a design that supports those requirements.

- Maintainability—Programming is expensive. Thus, our efforts must last a long time. We must be able to fix programs when they go wrong, adapt them to new situations, and make them work when the world around them grows in size.

- Modularity—A software system is decomposed into components. We must be able to partition it into tasks that can be attacked by small teams of programmers. When the world changes, we want to isolate those changes in a small set of components.

- Extensibility—A design is not conceived on one day and a product created on the next. A design often grows incrementally. We begin with a design. As we implement that design our understanding of the world increases. We continue through a process of design enhancement and implementation. A good design supports incremental development.

7.5.1   Patterns

When we are faced with a new problem it is helpful to look for things that are familiar. Identifying patterns is one technique used to develop good designs. We use the experience of past projects to help us with the design of current project.

We have seen several example programs that have been partitioned into classes. One of those systems is the chaos program from Chapter 5. The program was partitioned into two components, the Chaos class (Listing 5.1) and the VGraph class (Appendix: C on page 914). From this example, we see the benefits of partitioning a program into a display and a computing component. We will eventually develop this snippet of a design into the Model View Controller (MVC) object design pattern.

In Chapter 6 we discussed some of the design guidelines required when using the delegation action pattern (Section 6.4). We talked about appropriate ways to partition an action into subtasks. We used coupling and cohesion to measure our success. We learned about the divide and conquer (stepwise refinement) strategy for design. We will apply those ideas to objects within this chapter.

This chapter introduces the delegation object pattern. Recall that a pattern is a snippet of design that can be used to help solve a problem. For example, in this chapter we took the butler program from the previous chapter and partitioned it into classes. A question we must ask ourselves is how do we know that background, house, tree, and a butler make good objects? Where to we stop the delegation process? Do we further decompose a house into window, door, and roof class? Do we decompose a window into glass and window frame objects? Do we continue this process until we get to the subatomic level? Surely, this is taking the problem too far. Thus, the first rule of design is to learn and use familiar design patterns. We know that using the object delegation pattern is good. The rest of this section will help us decide when and how to use it.

7.5.2   Building User Expectations

Notice that the Background class and Butler class have paint methods that look identical. Applying similar operations using the same syntax helps users build expectations. If we use a paint operation to draw a butler and a draw operation to draw a house, a programmer will often forget which class uses paint and which class uses draw. For example, when we write a method to move a wagon, use a setLocation method that looks like the one in the Butler class.

One of the differences between Java JDK 1.0 and JDK 1.1 is that the class method names were made more consistent. For example, some classes used setLocation and others used move, some used setSize and others reSize, and some used append and others appendText. These inconsistencies caused programmers to make errors. The author is not immune to making these same mistakes. An effort has been made to remove inconsistencies within the classes used in this text, but there are sure to be inconsistencies in any system.

We must be consistent with parameters. Do not put y before x in some methods and x before y in others. If there is a commonly held convention, such as placing x before y, follow it. Building user expectations and fitting into the expectations of the world around us will make our classes more valuable. They become easier to use and to maintain.

7.5.3   A Minimal Set

Adding `setLocation` to `Butler` in Section 7.3.5 brings up an important question: What operations should a class support? Answering that question relies heavily on experience. A rule of thumb is to provide the minimum set of methods that all classes understand.

It is usually better to provide a few general-purpose methods that in combination provide a great deal of flexibility rather than to provide dozens of special-purpose methods for all conceivable actions. For example, three operations such as move forward, turn right, and turn left are better than specialized operations such as "turn right then move forward," "turn left then move forward," "move forward then turn right," and so on. We do not need both an `isFrontClear` and `isFrontBlocked` methods. We can easily get the functionality of `isFrontBlocked` by typing `!isFrontClear`.

We should not be rigid in our enforcement of this guideline. It is always important to see how an object is used. In some situations, providing special-purpose methods or redundant methods that differ only by parameters may provide sufficient flexibility to warrant their inclusion.

When we added the `setLocation` method to `Butler` we provide two means for creating and locating a butler to a specific location. For example,

```
Butler albert = new Butler (100, 50);
```

or

```
Butler albert = new Butler ();
albert.setLocation (100, 50);
```

It is tempting to say that the first approach is better because it requires only one line of code. However, suppose that there are 20 items that describe the state of an object. Do we really want a constructor with 20 parameters? Maybe some state has reasonable defaults that need to be changed only in special situation. We would not want to specify these items of state with a constructor parameter. There are no general rules that indicate when it is better to initialize all of an object's state through a constructor's parameters and when it is better to use explicit set operations.

Providing many special-purpose methods will make a class difficult to learn and maintain. The best way to determine if a class interface works well is to write several client programs. Look for methods that are seldom used or for clumsy code. Also look for code sequences that are pervasive. If the special code sequence appears in only one application, a specialized method should be made part of the client. If the special code sequences appears in many clients, consider adding a new method to the class.

7.5.4 Cohesion

Just as we did with methods, we will look at cohesion to help us evaluate our decisions. Cohesion helps us partition our design into components. Each component has a single well-defined function. Our definition of a cohesive class is slightly different than that for a cohesive method.

> A class is *cohesive* if all the methods and instance variables that comprise it are related. In a strongly cohesive class all instance variables and methods are necessary for the support of a single idea. Strong cohesion often indicates a good design.

Each of the classes in the Scene program is cohesive. A house, a tree, and butler all communicate a single idea. An example of something that is not cohesive is a butler and sky. Again, the conjunction "and " is a tip-off.

Another example of a system that benefits from the delegation pattern is a system to maintain university records. A student represents a cohesive idea. It captures the idea of student addresses, finances, and transcripts. Other examples are a course class, department class, or room class.

A class with lower cohesion is a course-offering class that combines a course description, number of desks, and instructor's schedule. It may be better to think of a course offering as a composite of a course object, room object, list of students object, and an instructor object. The number of chairs may be part of the room object, which also contains its location and multimedia features. The instructor object contains the instructor's schedule, telephone number, location, and department.

7.5.5 Coupling

Coupling is an indication of how interconnected objects are. The fewer components that are coupled, the better they are partitioned. Examples include the Room and Butler classes from Chapter 1. Notice in Listing 1.1 on page 9 we create a room first and pass it to the constructor for a butler. Thus the Butler and Room class are coupled. Coupling is acceptable and unavoidable. A butler needs to know which room it is in. However, too much coupling is not good. The more interconnection between objects, the more difficult it is to work with them.

> *Coupling* is an indication of how interconnected objects are. Low coupling often indicates a good design.

The coupling between the butler and the room is explicit. We can see that a `butler` object is coupled to `room` by looking at its constructor. Some objects are coupled implicitly. For example, we must draw the background in the Scene program before we draw a house, a butler, or tree. If we draw the background last, it will cover all the other objects in our scene. In addition, we must be careful about objects that overlap. For example, notice that the placement of `eddie` on top of and above `doris` in Figure 7.5 makes `eddie` appear to float.

High coupling is bad because it requires a programmer to resolve more issues than with low coupling. When we have to think about the order in which we must do things, we are more apt to make mistakes.

7.5.6   When to Use Instance Variables

In Listing 7.7, we declared five `Butler` objects as local variables and in Listing 7.8 we declared them as instance variables. In Listing 7.3, the `Background` class has no state, and in Listing 7.4 the `Butler` class defines its locations as its state.

A rule of thumb is to make something a part of an object's state if it distinguishes one object of the class from another. For example, the `Butler` objects named Albert, Betty, Clarence, Doris, and Eddie are distinguished by their location (Figure 7.6). They are not distinguished by the color of their breastplate or their height. Therefore, color and height are not part of their state. However, we could envision modifying the `Butler` class so that color and height were part of the state. Then we could have different sized and different colored butlers.

Another reason for making something part of an object's state is to preserve state between method calls. For example, in Listing 7.8 we made all the butlers part of `Scene`'s state so that they would be preserved between calls to `Scene`'s `paint`.

7.5.7   Class Granularity

When applying the divide and conquer principle, we must ask ourselves when to stop. For example, recall the question we asked earlier. Why not partition our house class into door, window, and other classes? Why not partition Butler into left arm, right arm, right leg, and other classes?

We state above that we make variables instance variables if they are needed to distinguish the state of an object. Taking this rule of thumb, reversing, and expanding it, we can state the following rule. : We will make something a class if it has state or behavior that distinguishes it from another class.

We have made `Butler` a class because it allows us to have multiple butlers. Each is distinguished by its state (its current location). The same is true of trees and houses. In addition, the behavior of butlers is different from a tree. In particular, when we paint different butlers, they look different. In addition, butlers move but houses do not.

In our representation of a butler, we do not distinguish the state of its arms, legs, or torso. We draw a butler's left arm and right arm as a simple constant offset from a butler's location. However, if we chose to animate a butler's arms and legs, it may make sense to make them unique classes.

Let us take another look at university records. Clearly, `student` is a class. We distinguish students from each other by name, address, and transcript. Furthermore, a `student` object has different behavior from a `course` object. We ask `student` objects for a grade point average. On the other hand, we ask a `course`'s for its current enrollment.

One component of a student may be the name. Each student name is different; thus, a `name` is also a class. A name has behavior—we may ask if one name comes before another when we alphabetize student lists. We may view each course in a student transcript as an object. We may ask a course if it fulfills a major requirement, who is its instructor, or what are its prerequisites.

Are address zip codes or grade point averages objects? In Java, technically they are not. They are primitive types. However, they have state and behavior. Thus, we can view them as objects. But integers are primitive in yet another way. Integers are examples of types (classes) that are provided by the standard Java definition. There is no need to further partition them into subcomponents. We naturally stop our decomposition when we reach language types and classes that can not be further decomposed.

7.5.8   The Rule of Seven

Programmers should be able to keep the components of a class in short-term memory. If programmers cannot keep the components of a class in short-term memory, they are more apt to omit critical interactions between components, and thus introducing bugs.

A favorite number is six or seven items. More than that number and we begin to forget some of them. The number of items we can work with may be determined by how related they are. For example, in a student transcript it may not be difficult to maintain eight fields that comprise a core course curriculum. In the scene program it may not be difficult to work with ten trees, three houses, and one butler, even though we have a composite of 14 objects. However, if the relationship between those objects becomes complex, we may need to partition that class. If the number of components in a class grows larger than six or seven, we can partition components into related groups. For example, we can partition scene classes into forests, neighborhoods, or other groupings.

Student records may be grouped into components associated with their addresses, fields associated with their finances, and grades into transcript components.

Use the rule of seven as a warning when classes may become too complex. Do not enforce it rigidly.

7.5.9   Nouns and Verbs

Classes are typically nouns; for example, tree, house, room, butler, student record, course, transcript, and lunar lander. Methods are typically verbs; for example, paint, move forward, turn right, get a transcript, print an instructor's schedule.

Avoid the temptation of turning an operation into a class. Bad choices for classes are compute "grade point average," "display the class roster," "find a basket," and "paint a picture. ." These are all operations that belong to a class. They should not be a class. If it is not obvious to which class an operation belongs, it may be necessary to reorganize the program.

7.5.10   Private vs. Public

Make all methods public that are part of an object's interface. Make all methods private that are used only within the class in which they are defined. Internal methods are useful for partitioning methods into more manageable units, as we did in Listing 7.11. Private methods are also useful for collecting code that is common to other methods. It is easier to maintain one copy of common functionality.

7.5.11   Make Instance Variable Private

At first glance, using public instance variables makes the code easy to write. It bypasses the necessity of writing public methods that modify only modify private instance variables. Also, the code is faster because method calls are avoided. However, there is a hidden danger to direct access. If the instance variables are reorganized, all the programs that access these instance variables directly will break. For example, suppose a programmer initially writes an Oval class in which the location of an oval is represented by two integers (Listing 7.13). Later, the programmer may decide to represent a location as a Point within the Oval class, as we have done in Listing 7.12. By making the instance variable private, we are able to make this change without changing any of Oval's clients. If the Oval class were used hundreds of times within a large program or used by many programs, this simple modification may have a profound maintenance effect. By making instance variables private, the impact was limited to one class. Make instance variables private and access them through methods.

On occasion, this rule is broken if the nature of the class clearly limits the instance variables it should contain. For example, it may be argued that the Point class should clearly contain an x and y component. These instance variables are public in Java's implementation. However, we could think of a point in polar coordinates, which would be represented as a radius and angle. There may be implementation advantages to one representation in some cases and another in different cases. A class designer should be careful about limiting future options, yet mindful of computer performance.

A prevailing reason for direct access to instance variables is efficiency. Section 7.7 describes an experiment that focuses on instance variable access. Method calls take more time than a direct access. When making arguments about efficiency, it is always important to carry out some analysis. Intuition is often wrong. Knowing when to optimize is an important skill. Optimization requires a large effort and can make a program more difficult to maintain. It does not make sense to spend a day shaving a second of execution time off a program that is run automatically at night when the computer is primarily idle. It does not make sense to spend a lot of time making a menu pop up 1/1000 of a second faster. However, it does make sense to optimize code that executes thousands of times a second in a time-critical system, such as an aviation navigation system. It also makes sense to highly optimize code that will be a part of a language library used in millions of programs. For example, the Java Dimension and Point classes make their instance variables visible because they are used so extensively within the graphics code.

Listing 7.12 Oval Class Using a Point Object for Location

```
1 import java.awt.Color;
2 import java.awt.Graphics;
3 import java.awt.Point;
4
5 public class Oval {
6
7   private Point myLocation;
8   private Color myColor;
9
10   public Point getLocation()
11   {
12     return myLocation;
13   }
14
15   public Oval()
16   {
17     myLocation = new Point (35, 25);
18     myColor  = Color.blue;
19   }
20
21   public Oval(int x, int y, Color color)
22   {
23     myLocation = new Point (x,y);
24     myColor  = color;
25   }
26
27   public void paint(Graphics g)
28   {
29     g.setColor(myColor);
30     g.fillOval(myLocation.x, myLocation.y, 20, 30);
31   }
32
33   public void setColor(Color color)
34   {
35     myColor = color;
36   }
37
38   public void setLocation(int x, int y)
39   {
40     myLocation = new Point(x,y);
41   }
42 }
```

JAVA

7.6 Classes

Within this section we will take a look at the Java syntax that supports classes. The Oval class in Listing 7.13 and the OvalTester class Listing 7.14 will serve as examples. Comments have been removed for brevity. Removing comments allowed the author to display the entire class on one page.

A *client* is someone or something that makes use of services of something else. In this case the OvalTester class is the client because it uses the Oval class.

Although it takes time and skill to create a class, in the long term time is often saved. For example, the code for creating and drawing a butler need be written only once (Listing 7.4). If it needs to be changed, enhanced, or corrected, those changes need to be done in only one place. For example, if you want to add an apron to butlers, only the paint method needs to be modified. It is not necessary to change any of the client code that creates the butler objects.

7.6.1 Defining a Class

The Oval class in Listing 7.13 is used by the client program to create and draw ovals. Granted, this can be done much more easily by using the fillOval method in the Graphics class. It may not be a good candidate for a class. We are using it as an example in this section because is simple. Looking at the Oval class, you will see that it differs only slightly from applet classes we have constructed in previous chapters. The basic form of all classes is shown below:

```
public class ClassIdentifier
{
  // state
  instance variable and constant declarations

  // operations
  method declarations
}
```

It does not make any difference in what order instance variables and methods are declared within a class. They do not need to be declared ahead of where they are used. Within this

Listing 7.13 Oval Class

```
1  import java.awt.Color;
2  import java.awt.Graphics;
3  import java.awt.Point;
4
5  public class Oval {
6
7     private int   myX;
8     private int   myY;
9     private Color myColor;
10
11    public Point getLocation()
12    {
13       return new Point(myX, myY);
14    }
15
16    public Oval()
17    {
18       myX      = 35;
19       myY      = 25;
20       myColor  = Color.blue;
21    }
22
23    public Oval(int x, int y, Color color)
24    {
25       myX      = x;
26       myY      = y;
27       myColor  = color;
28    }
29
30    public void paint(Graphics g)
31    {
32       g.setColor(myColor);
33       g.fillOval(myX, myY, 20, 30);
34    }
35
36    public void setColor(Color color)
37    {
38       myColor = color;
39    }
40
41    public void setLocation(int x, int y)
42    {
43       myX = x;
44       myY = y;
45    }
```

Listing 7.14 `OvalTester` class - the client

```
1  import java.awt.Color;
2  import java.awt.Graphics;
3  import java.awt.Point;
4  import java.applet.Applet;
5
6  public class OvalTester extends Applet {
7
8    public void paint(Graphics g)
9    {
10       setBackground(Color.white);
11
12       Oval blueOval = new Oval();
13       blueOval.paint(g);
14       Point location = blueOval.getLocation();
15       System.out.println (location.x + " " + location.y);
16
17       Oval redOval  = new Oval(10,10,Color.red);
18       redOval.setColor(Color.green);
19       redOval.paint(g);
20    }
21 }
```

text, instance variables are placed first, followed by constructors. All the methods are listed in alphabetical order. This convention is not followed religiously. Sometime other ordering is more clear. Other programmers have different conventions. For example, Sun Microsystems orders the constructors, instance variables, and methods alphabetically.

7.6.2   Instance Variables

Instance variables are declared within a class and outside of all the methods. They are accessible by any method within the class.

Instance variables store the internal state of an object and act as its memory.

Examples of instance variables are `myX`, `myY`, and `myColor` in Lines 7 through 9 of Listing 7.13. They define the state of an `Oval` object. Thus, ovals can be distinguished by their location and color, but not their size. For example, the following code creates the objects shown in Figure 7.10:

```
Oval redOval  = new Oval (50, 25, Color.red);
Oval blueOval = new Oval (73, 18, Color.blue);
```

Figure 7.10 State of Two Ovals

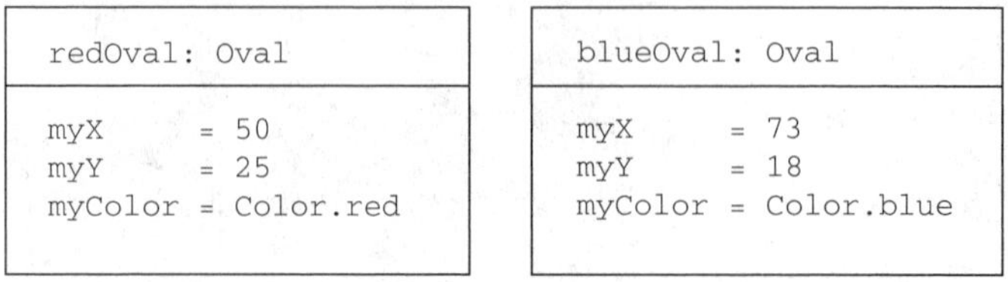

redOval: Oval
myX   = 50
myY   = 25
myColor = Color.red

blueOval: Oval
myX   = 73
myY   = 18
myColor = Color.blue

7.6.3   Public and Private Instance Variables and Methods

There are strict rules about accessing private information. Private instance variables and methods can be accessed only within the class in which they are defined. (See the definition and use of "i" in Lines 3, 9, and 19 in Listing 7.15.)

Listing 7.15 Accessing Private Class Members

```
1 public class one
2 {
3    private int i;
4    ...
5    private void foo()
6    {
7      one x = new one();
8      x.foo();                 // ok within the class "one"
9      int j = x.i;             // ok within the class "one"
10   }
11 }
12 public class two
13 {
14   ...
15   public void bar()
16   {
17     one z = new one();
18     z.foo();                 // error - foo is private
19     int k = z.i;             // error - i is private
20   }
21 }
```

We learned how to write methods in the previous chapter. Methods are used to change an object state, query an object about its state, or do something, such as paint. Instance variables and methods have the same access rules. Private methods can be accessed only from within the class they are defined. Listing 7.15 demonstrates the rules for accessing private methods. The private method `foo` defined in Line 5 may be accessed in Line 8 because the access is within the class in which it is declared. It may not be accessed in Line 18 because that access is within a different class than the class `foo` is defined.

Methods that define an object interface should be public. All others should be private. Good candidates for private methods are those that partition a large method into smaller components or ones that implement code that is shared among other methods.

7.6.4 Constructor

Constructors are called when an object is instantiated. Their primary function is to initialize an object's state. The `Oval` constructors are found in Lines 16 through 28 of Listing 7.13.

The basic form for a constructor follows:

```
public ClassIdentifier(parameter1, ...)
{
    constructor body - initialize state
}
```

A constructor is not required. An object will be created if one is not supplied. However, the state of that object may not be known after the object is created. An important function of a constructor is to initialize the state of an object. Subtle bugs can be traced to uninitialized objects.

The constructor must have the same name as the class and it has no return type (Figure 7.11). Otherwise it looks and behaves much like other methods. The `public` modifier allows the constructor to be accessed anywhere that the class is accessible.

7.6.5 File Names and Compilation

Typically code for the class named `OvalTester` is entered in a file named `OvalTester.java` and the code for the class named `Oval` is entered in a file named `Oval.java`. Many Java implementations insist that the file name be the same as the class name with the `java` suffix added. Adhering to this convention, even though not enforced by all compilers, will make your programs more portable.

Some Java compilers allow more than one class to be in a single file. Others allow this only in restricted cases. If more than one class is placed in a file, many compilers insist that there be only one class that has the `public` modifier. Placing only one class in a file will typically make life easier.

Figure 7.11 Class Name and Constructor Name Must Match

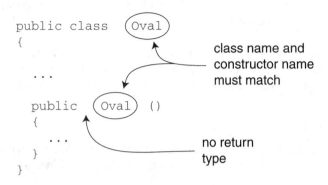

Java also enforces rules about the placement of files within directories. Until we learn what those rules are, we will place all project files. If we are using any Vista classes, there should be a `vista` directory within our project directory that contains the Vista `*.class` files. See Figure 7.12. Some of the most prevalent errors in novice programs occur with project files spanning several directories. Be aware that some software development environments place files in unexpected places. Double check to make sure that files are not misplaced.

7.6.6 Static

We have seen the keyword `static` used in a couple of contexts. One place we used it was in the introduction of applications (Section 4.4.1 , page 141). The `main` method used static. Another place that we saw it was the `Math` class library (Section 5.5.7 , page 194.)

The `Math` class has two static constants: e and pi. Recall that static constants are accessed through a class name rather than an object's name. For example, to get the value for pi we can write the following. There is no need to instantiate an object.:

```
double pi = Math.PI;
```

The `Math` class also has static methods. They are accessed through the class name as well. For example:

```
double number = Math.random();
```

In this section we will see how to use static instance variables and methods by creating a `Salary` class modeled after the `Math` class. The `Salary` class computes monthly take-

Figure 7.12 Directory Structure for Projects

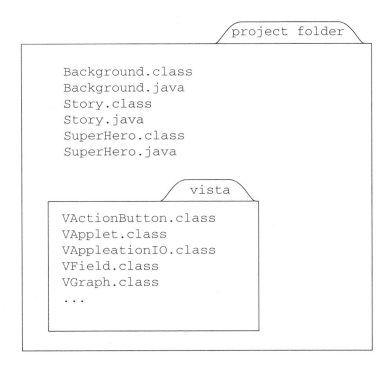

Listing 7.16 The `Salary` Class Using Static

```
1  public class Salary
2  {
3     public static final double FICA    = 0.0765;
4     public static final double FEDERAL = 0.15;
5     public static final double STATE   = 0.07;
6
7     public static double takeHome (double yearlyGross)
8     {
9        double monthlyGross = yearlyGross / 12.0;
10       return monthlyGross -
11              monthlyGross * (FICA + FEDERAL + STATE);
12    }
13 }
```

home pay based on a yearly gross. It is shown in Listing 7.16. Notice the use of the `static` modifier in Lines 3, 4, 5, and 7.

We use the `Salary` class just as we used the `Math` class.:

```
double thePayCheck = Salary.takeHome(15000);
System.out.println (thePayCheck);
double federalTax  = Salary.FEDERAL;
System.out.println (federalTax);
```

We use the `Salary` class name to access the `takeHome` method and `FEDERAL` constant. Contrast this with the nonstatic version in Listing 7.17. Notice it has a constructor and we access the `takeHome` method and `FEDERAL` constant through an object, as shown below

Listing 7.17 The `Salary` class without static

```
1 public class Salary
2 {
3    public final double FICA    = 0.0765;
4    public final double FEDERAL = 0.15;
5    public final double STATE   = 0.07;
6
7    private double myYearlyGross;
8
9    public Salary (double yearlyGross)
10   {
11      myYearlyGross = yearlyGross;
12   }
13
14   public double takeHome ()
15   {
16      double monthlyGross = myYearlyGross / 12.0;
17      return monthlyGross -
18             monthlyGross * (FICA + FEDERAL + STATE);
19   }
20 }
```

```
Salary payForSally = new Salary (15000);
double thePayCheck = payForSally.takeHome();
System.out.println (thePayCheck);
double federalTax = payForSally.FEDERAL;
System.out.println(federalTax);
```

There are three uses for static instance variables and methods. The first is to collect non-class-based utilities (`Math` and `Salary` classes are examples. We talked about the first reason at the beginning of this section.)

The second reason, singleton instances, occurs when it only makes sense to create one object of a particular class. An example is the System class. There is only one display, one keyboard, or one CPU in our computer. Another example is an application. The main method is static because we create one instance of an application when we execute it.

There is one important rule that must be obeyed when writing static methods such as main. Static methods may access only static instance variables and static methods. See Listing 7.18 and Listing 6.14 on page 237. On the other hand, any method can access a static instance variable.

Listing 7.18 Accessing Instance Variables from `main`

```
 1 public class Example
 2 {
 3    private static int myX = 100;
 4    private         int myY =  50;
 5
 6    public static void main (String args[])
 7    {
 8       System.out.println(myX);
 9       System.out.println(myY);  // error - myY not static
10 }
```

A third reason for using static variables is when we need to do bookkeeping between object instances. By adding the static keyword to an instance variable declaration, we make it a class variable. Its value is shared by all objects that are members of that class. Class variables are useful for keeping track of information that is common to all instances of a class; for example, keeping a count of how many objects have been instantiated by a class or how many times a particular operation has been performed.

> *Class variables* store the internal state of an object that is shared with all instances of its class.

Although it is trivial to create example classes that use static instance variables, it is more difficult to find examples that are compelling. The static modifier should be used carefully. It is only discussed here because of its use in the Math class and main method. We will not attempt to master its usage within this text.

Listing 7.19 shows an example of how a class variable may be used. The class variable defined in Line 5 is shared by all Ball objects. The "our" prefix is a programming convention used to inform us that the variable is shared. Each time a new ball is created, this single shared value is incremented in Line 11. Thus, after creating three balls by Line 28 the value ourNumberOfBalls is 3. Therefore, the output of Lines 28, 29, and 30 is 3.

Listing 7.19 A Class Variable

```
1   public class Ball
2   {
3     private int myX;
4     private int myY;
5     private static int ourNumberOfBalls = 0;
6
7     public Ball (int x, int y)
8     {
9       myX = x;
10      myY = y;
11      ourNumberOfBalls++;
12    }
13
14    public int getNumberOfBalls ()
15    {
16      return ourNumberOfBalls;
17    }
18    ...
19  }
20
21  public class BallClient
22  {
23    public static void main (String args[])
24    {
25      Ball emmasBall  = new Ball (25, 39);
26      Ball elmersBall = new Ball (73, 82);
27      Ball jamesBall  = new Ball (48, 19);
28      System.out.println (emmasBall.getNumberOfBalls());
29      System.out.println (elmersBall.getNumberOfBalls());
30      System.out.println (jamesBall.getNumberOfBalls());
31    }
32  }
```

SUPPLEMENTARY MATERIAL

7.7   Optimizing Java Code—An Experiment

In Section 7.6.3, we stated that direct access to instance variables is faster than access through a method call. We are thus tempted to use direct access rather than a method to get instance variables. However, good software practice dictates using a method call because it provides abstraction and more flexibility. It is important not to accept statements like these at face value. Intuition is often wrong, particularly when it comes program optimization. In this section, we will test this hypothesis by performing an experiment.

Based on experiments such as the one we perform here it is tempting to look at every line of code and twist it in some way to make it run a little faster. In a few cases this may be critical, but typically it is more harmful than beneficial. In addition, a good compiler will optimize code better than many seasoned programmers. The advice to beginning programmers is to not to optimize programs at the statement level. This is not an invitation to be sloppy. Be watchful of wasted or repeated code. In addition, we will find in later chapters that some program organizations will run significantly faster than others.

The procedure for carrying out an experiment follows:

1. An experiment begins by stating a hypothesis for what we hope to prove.
2. The next step is to devise an experimental procedure for testing the hypothesis.
3. This is followed by gathering the experimental results, which involves creating and documenting the software needed for the test and taking test measurements.
4. Finally, conclusions are drawn from the results.

7.7.1   Hypothesis

It is faster to access instance variables directly than through method calls.

7.7.2   Experimental Procedure

The experiment is carried out on the class in Listing 7.20. The instance variable myV is accessed using two different techniques. In one technique, instance variable myV is accessed directly. In the second technique, instance variable myV is accessed through method m. Times are recorded for both access techniques. The program in Listing 7.21 provides an outline for the program used in the tests.

Listing 7.20   The class under Test

```
1 public class Thingie
2 {
3    public int myV;
4
5    public Thingie()
6    {
7       myV = 123;
8    }
9
10   public int m()
11   {
12      return myV;
13   }
14 }
```

In any experiment, it is important to think hard about what is being measured. In this case, we are measuring elapsed time between two occurrences in the program (see Lines 33 and 44). Elapsed time can be skewed by events that the computer is managing that do not relate to the execution of our test code. While the program is being tested, make sure that it is not printing in the background, no other programs are running, and that the keyboard and mouse are not touched. Each one of these activities will require a computer response that will affect our measurements. As a result, this experiment will not give accurate results on a time sharing system because other users and the operating systems will interrupt this program periodically.

In Line 25 the testing program enters a busy loop. The purpose of this loop is to let the computer system settle down after the program is started. There is much more going on in most computers than running our program. Memory must be allocated, disks must be updated, and networks accessed. On some stand-alone computers, this initial loop will allow the computer to complete tasks that do not focus directly on the code we are measuring.

Once the computer settles down, we get the current time in milliseconds in Line 33. (The System.currentTimeMillis() returns the number of milliseconds since January

Listing 7.21   The Class under Test

```
1  //*****************************************************************
2  //
3  // title:    instance variables
4  //
5  // Test access times for instance variables
6  //
7  //*****************************************************************
8
9  import java.applet.Applet;
10
11 public class Fields extends Applet {
12
13   final int iterations = 10000000;
14
15   public void init ()
16   {
17     Thingie t = new Thingie();
18     int i;
19     int j;
20     int k;
21
22     // give the system time to settle down
23     System.out.println("getting ready");
24     i = 0;
25     while (i<10000000)
26     {
27       k = i;
28       i++;
29     }
30
31     // basic timing loop
32     System.out.println("Start");
33     long startTime = System.currentTimeMillis();
34     i = 0;
35     while (i<iterations)
36     {
37       k = i;
38       // j = i;          // case 2 test
39       // j = t.myV;      // case 3 test
40       // j = t.m();      // case 4 test
41       i++;
42     }
43
44     long endTime = System.currentTimeMillis();
45     System.out.print("Elapsed time is (milliseconds): ");
46     System.out.println(endTime - startTime);
47   }
48 }
```

1, 1970). We will be able to determine how long it takes to execute the code by getting the time again in Line 44 and taking the difference between the two times. No printing should be done within the timed code because methods such as `System.out.println()` require disproportionate system resources.

The code we wish to test will be executed 10,000,000 times to provide times that can be easily measured. There are four timing test cases. Each is run three times with all times averaged. Tests are performed by commenting and uncommenting several lines in the timing loop.

- Test case 1: The loop looks as follows:
  ```
  i = 0;
  while (i<iterations)
  {
     k = i;
     i++;
  }
  ```
  This loop provides us with a control (base) case. We can subtract the timing results of this test from tests that follow. The dummy assignment statement is added to the control so that the compiler will not remove the loop when it discovers that it is empty.

- Test case 2: The following line is added to the loop by uncommenting Line 38.
  ```
  j = i;
  ```
  We will use the timing result from this case to help us determine how long it takes to assign a number to j.

- Test case 3: Line 38 is commented and Line 39 is uncommented. Thus, the following is added to the control loop:
  ```
  j = t.myV;
  ```
  We can use this test to determine how long direct access takes.

- Test case 4: Line 39 is commented and Line 40 is uncommented. Thus, the following is added to the control loop:
  ```
  j = t.m();
  ```
  We can use this to determine how long access takes through a method call.

It is easy to make mistakes when writing programs that measure execution times. For example, in the following loop:

```
1    i = 0;
2    while (i<iterations)
3    {
4       k = i;
5       int j = t.myV;
6       i++
7    }
```

The compiler can determine that Line 5 has no impact on anything outside the loop and remove it. Be careful when making measurements. Look at the data. If it does not make sense, it may mean that the loop has been optimized away and must be rewritten. For example, a compiler may change the following (from Listing 7.21):

```
int iterations = 10000000;
int k;
int i = 0;
while (i<iterations)
{
  k = i;
  i++;
}
```

to:

```
int k = 9999999;
```

Be warned—some compiler programmers are clever. Their compilers may recognize that the loop is not doing anything useful and eliminate it.

Table 7.1 shows a summary of what each case will test.

Table 7.1 Timing results

case	the test	code added to the basic timing loop body
1	no accesses	
	no assignments	
2	access a simple integer	j = i;
	assignment to a simple integer	
3	directly access an integer instance variable	j = t.myV;
	assignment to a simple integer	
4	access an integer using a method	j = t.m();
	assignment to a simple integer	

7.7.3   Results

The experimental results are shown in Table 7.2.

Table 7.2 Results

case	time in milliseconds for 10,000,000 iterations (3 runs and an average)	times in microseconds for each iteration
1	14897	1.490
	14898	
	14895	
	14897 average	
2	18434	1.842
	18434	
	18403	
	18424 average	
3	21805	2.182
	21832	
	21831	
	21823 average	
4	38062	3.805
	38060	
	38054	
	38054 average	

Table 7.3 Equipment

Computer - Macintosh 6100/60

Java Compiler - Metrowerks Academic Pro 11

7.7.4   Conclusions

- Test case 1: Time for each iteration of the loop:
  ```
  Control loop = 1.490 microseconds    // from table - case 1
  ```

- Test case 2: For each iteration:
  ```
  Control loop = 1.490 microseconds    // from table - case 1
  j = i;       = ????? microseconds    // what we want to compute
  total        = 1.842 microseconds    // from table - case 2
  ```
  Therefore j = i; requires 0.352 microseconds. If we assume that accessing the value for i takes the same time as storing the value in j, then the time to store a value in j should take roughly 0.176 microseconds. (Note: this is an assumption which may not be correct.)
  ```
  j =          = 0.176 microseconds
  ```

- Test case 3: For each iteration:
  ```
  Control loop = 1.490 microseconds    // from table - case 1
  t.myV;       = ????? microseconds    // what we want to compute
  j =          = 0.176 microseconds    // conclusion from case 2
  total        = 2.182 microseconds    // from table - case 3
  ```
  Therefore t.myV requires **0.516** microseconds.

- Test case 4: For each iteration:
  ```
  Control loop = 1.490 microseconds    // from table - case 1
  t.m();       = ????? microseconds    // what we want to compute
  j =          = 0.176 microseconds    // conclusion from case 2
  total        = 3.805 microseconds    // from table - case 4
  ```
  Therefore t.m() requires **2.139** microseconds.

From Test case 3 we learned that t.myV took 0.516 microseconds and from Test case 4 that t.m() took 2.139 microseconds. Thus, it takes about four times longer to access an instance variable through a method call than through a direct access. The hypothesis is true at least for the software and hardware configuration in this test. Is this an argument for always using direct access? Definitely not. To answer that question, one needs to run a program profiler and determine how many times instance variable accesses are performed. A program would need to do roughly 62,000 integer accesses per second before saving a tenth of a second. This savings will not be noticed in many programs.

> A *profiler* is a program that counts the number of times each unit, for example a statement or method, is executed. If we want to optimize a program for speed, the best place to start is with the code that is executed most often.

Note that these times are for integer accesses. Accessing objects, bytes, doubles, and other things will have different times. Also note that these measurements were done on a Macintosh 6100/60. The 6100/60 was the least expensive Power PC in 1994. Timing on other machines will be vastly different. There are many improvements made to Java compilers and interpreters. Some interpreters compile Java byte-codes to machine code on the fly. One expects code compiled to native machine code to be much faster. For example, students at the University of Portland ran these tests under Symantec Cafe 1.0 and Symantec Cafe 1.5. They found over a 10 times speed increase between versions because 1.5 had a "just-in-time" (compile on the fly) compiler.

REFERENCE

7.8   Summary

Classes are Java's mechanism for object abstraction. They make managing large software systems easier by hiding unimportant details and allowing a client to focus on key ideas.

A class is comprised of instance variables which define an object's state and methods that are used to access and modify that state. Class constructors are special methods with the same name as the class and with no return type. They are executed when an object is created. Their primary function is to initialize an object's state.

Public and private modifiers control outside access to methods and instance variables. Instance variables are generally made private and accessed only through methods. This allows instance variables to be reorganized without breaking a client's code. Accessing instance variables directly saves time but will not be noticeable in most programs. Methods should be made private if their function is to help implement other methods.

Static methods can be accessed without instantiating an object. They are class methods that are applied to a class and not an object. Class variables are also declared with the `static` modifier. They are shared by all instances of a class.

7.9   Reference

- Astrachan, Owen. *Object Design in the First Year: An Oxymoron*, http://www.bk.psu.edu/faculty/mercer/design/Owen_Astrachan.htm. (Document has moved.)
- Gamma, Erich, with Richard Helm, Ralph Johnson, and John Vlissides. 1995. *Design Patterns: Elements of Reusable Object-Oriented Software*. Reading, MA: Addison Wesley.
  An influential book on object design patterns.
- Marsonia, Priya, and Steven Fraser. 1998. Evaluating OO Design, Evaluating Object-Oriented Design, OOPSLA'98 Workshop, Vancover, BC.
- Riel, Arthur J. 1996. *Object-Oriented Design Heuristics*. Reading, MA: Addison Wesley.
  An excellent source of design heuristics.

PROGRAM LISTINGS

7.10   Scene Applet

Listing 7.22 Scene Class

```
 1 //*************************************************************
 2 //
 3 // title:   Scene
 4 //
 5 // Draw five butlers in a row using setLocation.
 6 // Make the background and butlers part of this state.
 7 //
 8 //*************************************************************
 9
10 import java.awt.Graphics;
11 import java.applet.Applet;
12
13 public class Scene extends Applet
14 {
15   private Background  myEarth;
16   private Butler      myAlbert;
17   private Butler      myBetty;
18   private Butler      myClarence;
19   private Butler      myDoris;
20   private Butler      myEddie;
21
22   //---------- init ---------------------------------------
23   //
24   // called automatically
25   // post: Butler and background are created.
26
27   public void init()
28   {
29     myEarth     = new Background();
30     myAlbert    = new Butler(110,200);
31     myBetty     = new Butler( 90,200);
32     myClarence  = new Butler( 70,200);
33     myDoris     = new Butler( 50,200);
34     myEddie     = new Butler();
35     myEddie.setLocation(30,200);
36   }
37
```

Listing 7.22 Scene Class

```
38   //---------- paint ------------------------------------------
39   //
40   // called automatically
41   // post: Butler and background are drawn.
42   public void paint(Graphics g)
43   {
44     myEarth.paint(g);
45     myAlbert.paint(g);
46     myBetty.paint(g);
47     myClarence.paint(g);
48     myDoris.paint(g);
49     myEddie.paint(g);
50   }
51 }
```

Listing 7.23 Background Class

```
1 //****************************************************************
2 //
3 // title:    Background
4 //
5 // Background object.  Draws the sky and ground.
6 //
7 //****************************************************************
8
9 import java.awt.Color;
10 import java.awt.Graphics;
11
12 public class Background
13 {
14   private final int WIDTH  = 400;
15   private final int HEIGHT = 300;
16
17   //---------- paint ------------------------------------------
18   //
19   // pre:  graphicsContext is valid
20   // post: Backgroun is drawn.
21
22   public void paint(Graphics g)
23   {
24     g.setColor(Color.blue);
25     g.fillRect(0, 0, WIDTH, HEIGHT/2);
26     Color springGreen = new Color(0, 255, 127);
27     g.setColor(springGreen);
28     g.fillRect(0, HEIGHT/2, WIDTH, HEIGHT/2);
29   }
30 }
```

Listing 7.24 `Butler` class

```
1  //************************************************************
2  //
3  // title:   Butler
4  //
5  // Class for creating Butlers.  Split paint.
6  //
7  //************************************************************
8
9  import java.awt.Color;
10 import java.awt.Graphics;
11 import java.awt.Polygon;
12
13 public class Butler
14 {
15   private int myX;
16   private int myY;
17
18   // Size of the window that holds Butler.
19   private final int WIDTH  = 400;
20   private final int HEIGHT = 300;
21
22   //---------- Butler --------------------------------------
23   //
24   // pre:  none
25   // post: Butler is created at a random location.
26
27   public Butler ()
28   {
29     myX = (int)(Math.random() * (WIDTH  - 40));
30     myY = (int)(Math.random() * (HEIGHT - 50));
31   }
32
33   //---------- Butler --------------------------------------
34   //
35   // pre:  none
36   // post: Butler is created (x,y).
37
38   public Butler (int x, int y)
39   {
40     myX = x;
41     myY = y;
42   }
43
```

Listing 7.24 Butler class

```
44   //---------- paint ------------------------------------------
45   //
46   // pre:  g is a valid graphics context
47   // post: Butler is drawn.
48
49   public void paint(Graphics g)
50   {
51     paintHead(g);
52     paintLeftArm(g);
53     paintRightArm(g);
54     paintBody(g);
55     paintBreastPlate(g);
56   }
57
58   //---------- paintBody -------------------------------------
59
60   private void paintBody(Graphics g)
61   {
62     Polygon body = new Polygon();
63     body.addPoint(myX+ 9, myY+15);
64     body.addPoint(myX+33, myY+15);
65     body.addPoint(myX+27, myY+36);
66     body.addPoint(myX+33, myY+63);
67     body.addPoint(myX+36, myY+66);
68     body.addPoint(myX+24, myY+66);
69     body.addPoint(myX+27, myY+63);
70     body.addPoint(myX+21, myY+39);
71     body.addPoint(myX+15, myY+63);
72     body.addPoint(myX+18, myY+66);
73     body.addPoint(myX+ 6, myY+66);
74     body.addPoint(myX+ 9, myY+63);
75     body.addPoint(myX+15, myY+36);
76     body.addPoint(myX+ 9, myY+15);
77     Color silver = new Color(202, 204, 222);
78     g.setColor(silver);
79     g.fillPolygon(body);
80     g.setColor(Color.black);
81     g.drawPolygon(body);
82   }
83
```

Listing 7.24 `Butler` class

```
84    //---------- paintBreastPlate -------------------------------
85
86    private void paintBreastPlate(Graphics g)
87    {
88      Polygon breastPlate = new Polygon();
89      breastPlate.addPoint(myX+11, myY+17);
90      breastPlate.addPoint(myX+31, myY+17);
91      breastPlate.addPoint(myX+27, myY+22);
92      breastPlate.addPoint(myX+14, myY+22);
93      breastPlate.addPoint(myX+11, myY+17);
94      Color limeGreen = new Color (50, 205, 50);
95      g.setColor(limeGreen);
96      g.fillPolygon(breastPlate);
97    }
98
99    //---------- paintHead ------------------------------------
100
101    private void paintHead(Graphics g)
102    {
103      // Draw head
104      Color flesh = new Color(188, 143, 143);
105      g.setColor(flesh);
106      g.fillOval(myX+18, myY+8, 6, 14);
107
108      // Draw helmet
109      g.setColor(Color.black);
110      g.drawOval(myX+12, myY+6, 18, 18);
111    }
112
```

Listing 7.24 `Butler` class

```
113    //---------- paintLeftArm -------------------------------------
114
115    private void paintLeftArm(Graphics g)
116    {
117       Polygon leftArm = new Polygon();
118       leftArm.addPoint(myX+ 3, myY);
119       leftArm.addPoint(myX+ 6, myY+15);
120       leftArm.addPoint(myX+12, myY+18);
121       leftArm.addPoint(myX+12, myY+24);
122       leftArm.addPoint(myX   , myY+15);
123       leftArm.addPoint(myX+ 3, myY);
124       Color silver = new Color(202, 204, 222);
125       g.setColor(silver);
126       g.fillPolygon(leftArm);
127       g.setColor(Color.black);
128       g.drawPolygon(leftArm);
129    }
130
131    //---------- paintRightArm ------------------------------------
132
133    private void paintRightArm(Graphics g)
134    {
135       Polygon rightArm = new Polygon();
136       rightArm.addPoint(myX+30, myY+36);
137       rightArm.addPoint(myX+36, myY+24);
138       rightArm.addPoint(myX+30, myY+21);
139       rightArm.addPoint(myX+30, myY+15);
140       rightArm.addPoint(myX+42, myY+24);
141       rightArm.addPoint(myX+30, myY+36);
142       Color silver = new Color(202, 204, 222);
143       g.setColor(silver);
144       g.fillPolygon(rightArm);
145       g.setColor(Color.black);
146       g.drawPolygon(rightArm);
147    }
148
149    //---------- setLocation --------------------------------------
150    //
151    // pre:  none
152    // post: Butler is moved to (x,y).
153
154    public void setLocation (int x, int y)
155    {
156       myX = x;
157       myY = y;
158    }
159 }
```

PROBLEM SETS

7.11   Exercises

Delegation Object Pattern and Design—Section 7.4 and Section 7.5

1   You are in charge of creating a program maintains the status of each customer of a video store. A customer record should contain a name, account number, and fields for a maximum of three checked out movies. It should have operation to determine if any movies are past due and keep track of unpaid balance. Include operations for checking movies out, determining if they are delinquent, and if the have checked out the movie quota. Comment on why you feel each component is a good class.

2   Use the delegation object pattern to decompose a university student record into components. Those components should include student name, id number, address, financial aid, housing, and transcript. Partition each component into subcomponents. For each component, list its operations and all of its subcomponents. Comment on why you feel each component is a good class.

Creating Classes—Section 7.6.1 through Section 7.6.4

3   Create a class called `Time` that contains seconds and minutes. It should have the following methods:

    a.   A constructor with second and minute parameters that initializes a `Time` object.

    b.   A constructor with no parameters that initializes the time to zero.

    c.   A method to determine the total number of seconds.

    d.   Methods to set and get the number of minutes.

    e.   A method to add two `Time` objects and return a new `Time` object which is their sum.

4   Create a rectangle class which contains an x and y that defines its upper left corner, a width, and a height. Use ints to represent all items of state. It should have the following methods:

    a.   A constructor with four parameters to initialize a rectangle.

    b.   A method to return the area of the rectangle.

c.   A method to return true if two rectangles intersect. (Two rectangles overlap if there is at least one point on a rectangle boarder or in its interior that is shared.)

5   Using the Gizmo class defined in Listing 7.25, indicate if the following code is legal or illegal. If it is legal, indicate what is printed. If it is illegal, state why.

```
a. Gizmo thing = new Gizmo();
   thing.print();
b. Gizmo thing = new Gizmo(91);
   thing.print();
c. Gizmo thing = new Gizmo(81.33);
   thing.print();
d. Gizmo thing = new Gizmo(17.11);
   thing.print();
e. Gizmo thing = new Gizmo(123, 456.78, 90);
   thing.print();
f. Gizmo thing = new Gizmo(39, 77.54);
   thing.print();
g. Gizmo thing = new Gizmo(18.18, 98);
   thing.print();
h. Gizmo thing = new Gizmo();
   thing.set();
   thing.print();
i. Gizmo thing = new Gizmo();
   thing.Set(45);
   thing.print();
j. Gizmo thing = new Gizmo();
   thing.set(35);
   thing.print();
k. Gizmo thing = new Gizmo();
   thing.set(6.5, 7.3);
   thing.print();
l. Gizmo thing = new Gizmo();
   thing.set(4.55);
   thing.print(11);
m. Gizmo thing = new Gizmo();
   thing.change(43, 54.32);
   thing.print();
```

6   Add a method to Listing 7.25 called printSum that prints the sum of the i and d instance variables. The result printed by the following code should be 33.731.

```
Gizmo thing = new Gizmo();
thing.printSum();
```

Listing 7.25 Exercises 5 and 6 Refer to the Following Class

```
1 public class Gizmo
1 {
2   private int    i;
3   private double d;
4
5   public Gizmo ()
6   {
7     i = 25;
8     d = 8.731;
9   }
10
11  public Gizmo (int j)
12  {
13    i = j;
14    d = 5.421;
15  }
16
17  public Gizmo (int j, double g)
18  {
19    i = j;
20    d = g;
21  }
22
23  public void set(int j)
24  {
25    i = j;
26  }
27
28  public void set(double g)
29  {
30    d = g;
31  }
32
33  public void set(int j, double g)
34  {
35    i = j;
36    d = g;
37  }
38
39  public void print()
40  {
41    System.out.print(i);
42    System.out.print(" ");
43    System.out.println(d);
44  }
45 }
```

Private and Public Modifier—Section 7.6.3

7   Using the `WhatsIt` class defined in Listing 7.26, indicate if the following code is legal or illegal:

Listing 7.26   Exercise 7 Refer to the Following Class

```
1  public class WhatsIt
1  {
2     private int   MyI;
3     public  int   myJ;
4
5     public WhatsIt ()
6     {
7        setI (14);
8        setJ (39);
9     }
10    public void setI(int i)
11    {
12       myI = i;
13    }
14    private void setJ (int j)
15    {
16       myJ = j;
17    }
18 }
```

```
a. WhatsIt w = WhatsIt ();
   System.out.println (w.myI);
b. WhatsIt w = WhatsIt ();
   System.out.println (w.myJ);
c. WhatsIt w = WhatsIt ();
   w.setI(54);
d. WhatsIt w = WhatsIt ();
   w.setJ(22);
```

Static Methods—Section 7.6.6

8   Create a class named `Utility` with a method that finds the average of two integers. The following code should display 15 as the result:

```
System.out.println(Utility.average(10,20));
```

9   Create a class named `Utility` with a method that finds the area of a circle given its radius as a double. The following code should display roughly 184.6 as the result:

```
System.out.println(Utility.area(18.7));
```

Primitive Values vs. References to Objects (see Listing 7.27)

Listing 7.27   Exercises 11 through 12 Refer to the Following Classes

```
1 public class ObjectInt {
2
3    private int i;
4
5    public ObjectInt (int j)
6    {
7      i = j;
8    }
9
10   public void set (int j)
11   {
12     i = j;
13   }
14
15   public int get ()
16   {
17     return i;
18   }
19 }
```

10   What is printed by the following:

```
int firstInt  = 17;
int secondInt = firstInt;
firstInt      = 23;

System.out.print(firstInt);
System.out.print(" ");
System.out.println(secondInt);
```

11   What is printed by the following (Listing 7.27):

```
ObjectInt firstObjectInt  = new ObjectInt (31);
ObjectInt secondObjectInt = firstObjectInt;
firstObjectInt.set(44);
System.out.print(firstObjectInt.get());
System.out.print(" ");
System.out.println(secondObjectInt.get());
```

12   What is printed by the following (Listing 7.27):

```
ObjectInt firstObjectInt  = new ObjectInt (31);
ObjectInt secondObjectInt = new ObjectInt (31);
firstObjectInt.set(44);

System.out.print(firstObjectInt.get());
System.out.print(" ");
System.out.println(secondObjectInt.get());
```

7.12   Projects

Objects—Section 7.3

13   Create the following classes. Each should have a constructor and paint method. The constructor should take no parameters and place the object at the same position it is found in Listing 6.26 on page 263. Thus, each of these object's locations is part of its state. Modify the `Scene` class in Listing 7.2 on page 280 to create and paint each one.

    a.   Tree class.

    b.   House class.

    c.   Wagon class.

14   Add one constructor to each of the classes in exercise 13 to create an object at a specific position. The constructor should take two parameters: its x and y location. For example, the following should create a tree at (100, 40).:

```
Tree oak = new Tree(100,40);
```

Modify the `Scene` class to draw forest of trees with a small village of houses that have wagons in their front yards.

15   Add a method to the `Wagon` class that changes the location of a wagon. The following code should create a wagon at (50, 150) and move it to (100, 150).

```
Wagon redRider = new Wagon (50, 150);
redRider.setLocation(100,150);
redRider.paint(g);
```

16   Make color part of a tree's state. Create a constructor that requires a tree's locations and color. Add a method that allows the client to change the color of a tree.

Creating Classes—Section 7.6

17 Create a class called `Change` that manipulates the money found in your pocket. It should respond to the following operations.

```
// left pocket has 3 quarters, 5 dimes, 1 nickel, and
// 3 pennies.
Change leftPocket  = new Change (3, 5, 1, 3);

// right pocket has 3 dimes and 1 pennies.
Change rightPocket = new Change (0, 3, 0 , 1);

// total change should be 3 quarters, 8 dimes, 1 nickel,
// and 4 pennies
Change totalChange = leftPocket.sum(rightPocket);
totalChange.println();

// the total value should be 166 cents
int amount = totalChange.value();
System.out.print(amount);
System.out.println(" cents");
```

The output of the above program should be:

```
3 quarters, 8 dimes, 1 nickel, 4 pennies
166 cents
```

18 Create a class called `Time` that computes time. Implement it with three instance variables: seconds, which is an integer less than 60; minutes, which is an integer less than 60; and hours, which is an integer. It should respond to the following operations:

```
// The time is set to at 9 hours, 25 minutes, and 14 seconds.
Time classStarts  = new Time ( 9, 25, 14);
Time classEnds    = new Time (10, 20, 53);

Time elapsed = classEnds.subtract(classStarts);
elapsed.println();

int secondsElapsed = elapsed.seconds();
println(secondsElapsed);
```

Expand and make it look nice with input and output.

19 Create a class called `Temperature` that provides temperature operations. It should have static methods that convert between Fahrenheit and Celsius. It should respond to the following method calls:
```
System.out.println(Temperature.Fahrenheit2Celsius(96.8));
System.out.println(Temperature.Celsius2Fahrenheit(21.3));
```

Experiments—Section 7.7

20 Repeat the instance variable access experiment. Write a full report which includes your hypothesis, procedure, results, and conclusions. Do the experiment to show one of the following:

a.   Different computer hardware.

b.   Different Java interpreters.

c.   Difference between interpreter and native code.

d.   Differences between access of bytes, shorts, ints, longs, floats, and/or doubles.

Email your results to the publisher so they can be posted on the text's web page.

8 Selection Algorithms

Meshes

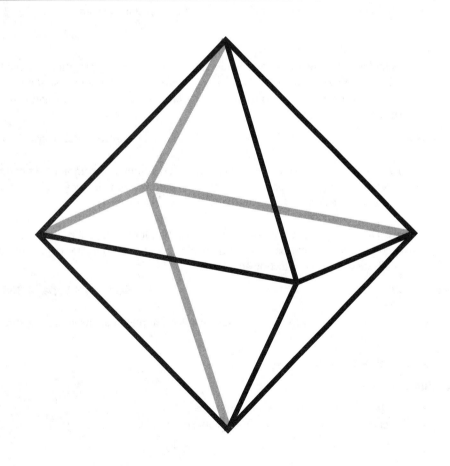

8.1   Objectives

Concepts   **Section 8.2, page 341**

We begin with a look a 3D graphics. After a glimpse at ray tracing we are introduced to a program that displays a tetrahedron using a mesh. This example provides an opportunity to talk about algorithms and specifically algorithmic patterns for finding minimums and maximums.

Section 8.6, page 361

There are often several algorithms that accomplish the same task. The question becomes how do we choose? In a supplementary section we are introduced to elementary complexity analysis which can help us answer this question.

Section 8.7, page 369

Other supplementary sections describe the importance of testing programs and methodologies for choosing good test data for code with selection statements. Statement, branch, and path coverage are introduced. In addition, boundary testing and debugging strategies are covered.

Patterns   **Section 8.3, page 350**

Finding extreme values such as minimums and maximums is a common computing task. It is required in our graphics application to determine which faces are in front of other faces. Patterns for finding extreme values are discussed.

Next we shift away from our graphics application and look at a pattern that responds to user commands in a text-based system. Its placement in this chapter reinforces our general discussion about selection statements.

Java Skills   **Section 8.5, page 358**

Chapter 2 introduced us to the `if` statement. We complete our discussion of selection statements.

- `Switch` statement

Abilities

- Use the pattern for finding extreme values.
- Select data sets for testing programs with selection statements.

CONCEPTS

8.2   3D Graphics

One thing that a computers do well is take us to places that do not exist, that are too expensive to travel to, or too dangerous to visit. In the movie *Toy Story*, for example, we are taken to an imaginary world of toys. Each toy has a personality and a role in a fantasy world created with the computer. This world is created by representing each toy with geometry. The computer builds the movie by taking geometric descriptions and generating each scene. The intensity and color of each pixel in every movie frame must be computed.

Figure 8.1 Ray Tracing

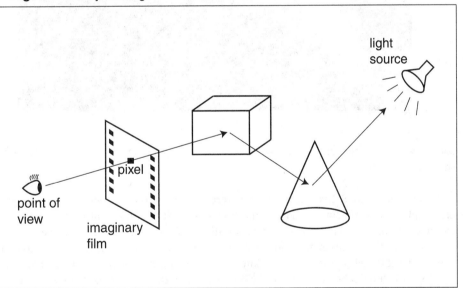

Ray tracing is one of the methods that can be used to generate a scene from a geometric description. First a point of view and a direction of sight are chosen. Next, a line, called a ray, is calculated from the point of view through a pixel on an imagined frame of film (Figure 8.1). That ray is extended until it hits an object within the scene. If the ray hits a reflective object, the laws of physics are used to compute its new trajectory and to create any new rays that result from scattering. These new rays travel on to reflect off other objects. Color changes are computed as the ray encounters various surfaces. If a ray eventually hits a light source, the pixel on the imagined film will get a computed intensity and

Figure 8.2 Ray Traced Image of a Space Shuttle

color based on its encounters with objects in the scene and the light it struck. Figure 8.2 shows an example image.

The image in Figure 8.2 is comprised of several geometric objects. They include a cylinder, a sphere, clipped cones, and prisms (Figure 8.3). Substantial computational effort is required to compute each point. Surfaces will absorb, scatter, and change the color of light. The six simple geometric forms illustrated in these figures took 55 seconds to compute with a 250 MHz computer. The addition of more objects, complex textures, and irregular forms will quickly add hours to the compute time. Ray tracing is so time-consuming that the creators of *Toy Story* used clever shortcuts that eliminated the need for computing reflections and limited the interaction with surrounding objects. However, even with these simplifications and the use of fast computers, each frame in *Toy Story* still took hours to compute.

Spending hours rendering each frame in a movie is acceptable. Once each frame is created, it can be assembled and shown at 30 frames per second. However, long rendering times are not acceptable in virtual reality, simulations, or games where the user expects the computer to respond in real time. For example, people using a computer to walk through a

Figure 8.3 Space Shuttle Components

building that exists only on a drawing board expect the screen to change as their heads turn. Several 3D images must be computed each second.

Compromises must be made. Computing how much reflected light each pixel receives is prohibitive. One compromise is to break each figure into triangles and treat each triangle as a single unit. For example, Figure 8.4 shows how a clipped cone can be represented with 64 triangles. The light value for each triangle is computed without regard to shadows and reflection. Thus, a much simpler computation returns the light value of every pixel in a triangle. As the number of triangles increases and their size decreases, the rendering of a scene become more accurate. This improvement comes at the expense of computation time.

> A *mesh* is a decomposition of a geometric form into polygons. This decomposition may also be called a *polygonal mesh*.

Once a scene has been decomposed into triangles, substantial effort is still required to render it. For example, each three-dimensional (3D) representation of a triangle must be converted into a two-dimension representation based on a given point of view. Its color value

Figure 8.4 Representing a Clipped Cone with a Mesh Composed of Triangles

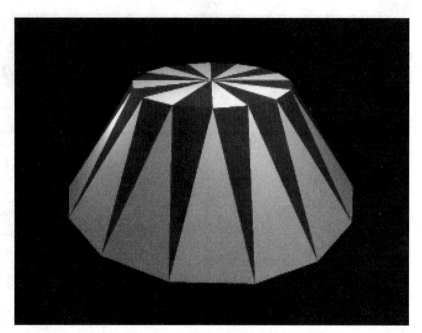

must be computed based on lighting, and its visibility must be determined based on the location of other triangles.

For example, Figure 8.5 shows a tetrahedron. Tetrahedrons are composed of four triangular faces. Not all these faces are visible at one time. A near face hides the faces behind it. When representing a three-dimensional tetrahedron in two-dimensional space, we want to draw only the visible faces. Although this may sound simple, there are many issues that make determining invisible faces difficult.

We will take a simplified approach. We will order the faces by distance from our point of view and then draw them in order from farthest to nearest. Thus, the faces in the back of an object will be covered by faces in the front. The result will be a somewhat flawed 3D representation that will, on occasion, show a hidden triangle. A spurious line will appear from time to time, making the drawing look rather odd. The program in Listing 8.1 draws the 3D representation of the tetrahedron in Figure 8.5. The program is partitioned into the following steps.

Figure 8.5 A Tetrahedron

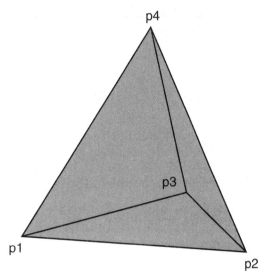

- init (Lines 42–65): create the 3D representation of a tetrahedron.
- paint (Lines 108–120):
  - minimum (Lines 90–103): Find the distance to the closest triangle.
  - maximum (Lines 71–84): Find the distance to the farthest triangle.
  - paint (Lines 126–143): Draw the triangles farthest away.
  - paint (Lines 126–143): Draw the triangles from mid-distance to the nearest.
  - paint (Lines 126–143): Draw the closest triangle(s).

The code for creating the tetrahedron begins by creating the four points that define its vertices. For example, Line 47 creates a point named p1 where x=-90, y=51, and z=51. After the four points are created, each of the triangles is created. For example, Line 51 creates the triangle [p1, p2, p3]. The points should be entered in a clockwise manner when a triangle is viewed from the outside of an object. The fourth parameter in the triangle constructor gives it an identity. It is not used in this program. Finally, the tetrahedron is rotated on the y and x axes to give it a more interesting perspective. See Section 8.12 for the interface to the 3D library.

Listing 8.1   The tetrahedron code

```
1 //
**********************************************************************
2 //
3 // title:    Tetrahedron
4 //
5 // This applet displays a 3D rendition of a tetrahedron.
6 //
7 //
**********************************************************************
8
9 import java.awt.Color;
10 import java.awt.Graphics;
11 import java.applet.Applet;
12 import ThreeD.*;
13
14 public class Tetrahedron  extends Applet
15 {
16    // the four faces of a tetrahedron
17    private TDTriangle3D myFace1;
18    private TDTriangle3D myFace2;
19    private TDTriangle3D myFace3;
20    private TDTriangle3D myFace4;
21
22    // perspective of the viewer - don't change
23    private final  TDPoint3D EYE =
24                   new TDPoint3D (0.0, 0.0, -1000.0);
25
26    // window size
27    private final int WIDTH  = 400;
28    private final int HEIGHT = 300;
29
30    //---------- distance -------------------------------------
31    // pre:  none
32    // post: Distance from "p" to triangle "t" is returned from
33    //       the triangle's centroid.
34    public double distance (TDTriangle3D t, TDPoint3D p)
35    {
36      return p.distance (t.centroid());
37    }
38
```

Listing 8.1 The tetrahedron code

```
39   //---------- init -----------------------------------
40   // Execution begins here.  Create the tetrahedron,
41   // hidden second display buffer, and animation thread.
42   public void init()
43   {
44     setBackground (Color.white);
45
46     // create the four faces on the tetrahedron
47     TDPoint3D p1 = new TDPoint3D (-90,  51,  51);
48     TDPoint3D p2 = new TDPoint3D ( 90,  51,  51);
49     TDPoint3D p3 = new TDPoint3D (  0,  51,-105);
50     TDPoint3D p4 = new TDPoint3D (  0,-105,   0);
51     myFace1 = new TDTriangle3D (p3, p2, p1, 1);
52     myFace2 = new TDTriangle3D (p4, p3, p1, 2);
53     myFace3 = new TDTriangle3D (p2, p3, p4, 3);
54     myFace4 = new TDTriangle3D (p1, p2, p4, 4);
55
56     // rotate to provide a more interesting perspective
57     myFace1.rotateY(5);
58     myFace2.rotateY(5);
59     myFace3.rotateY(5);
60     myFace4.rotateY(5);
61     myFace1.rotateX(-5);
62     myFace2.rotateX(-5);
63     myFace3.rotateX(-5);
64     myFace4.rotateX(-5);
65   }
66
```

Listing 8.1 The tetrahedron code

```
67    //---------- maximum -------------------------------------
68    //  The distance to the furthest triangle in the tetrahedron
69    //  is returned.  The "distance" method defines how the
70    //  distance is computed.
71    public double maximum()
72    {
73      double max = distance(myFace1, EYE);
74      double d   = distance(myFace2, EYE);
75      if (d > max)
76        max = d;
77      d   = distance(myFace3, EYE);
78      if (d > max)
79        max = d;
80      d   = distance(myFace4, EYE);
81      if (d > max)
82        max = d;
83      return max;
84    }
85
86    //---------- minimum -------------------------------------
87    //  The distance to the closest triangle in the tetrahedron
88    //  is returned.  The "distance" method defines how the
89    //  distance is computed.
90    public double minimum()
91    {
92      double min = distance(myFace1, EYE);
93      double d   = distance(myFace2, EYE);
94      if (d < min)
95        min = d;
96      d   = distance(myFace3, EYE);
97      if (d < min)
98        min = d;
99      d   = distance(myFace4, EYE);
100     if (d < min)
101       min = d;
102     return min;
103   }
104
```

Listing 8.1   The tetrahedron code

```
105   //---------- paint -----------------------------------
106   //  The tetrahedron is drawn from the vantage point of
107   //  the z axis.
108   public void paint (Graphics g)
109   {
110      // center the x/y axis
111      g.translate(WIDTH/2,HEIGHT/2);
112
113      // draw the triangles
114      double min = minimum();
115      double max = maximum();
116      double mid = (min + max) / 2.0;
117      paint (mid, max, g);  // draw far
118      paint (min, mid, g);  // draw near
119      paint (min, min, g);  // draw nearest
120   }
121
122   //---------- paint -----------------------------------
123   //  pre:  none.
124   //  post: All triangles between the "low" and "high"
125   //        distances are painted.
126   public void paint (double low, double high, Graphics g)
127   {
128      double d = distance(myFace1, EYE);
129      if (low <= d && d <= high)
130         myFace1.paint(g);
131
132      d = distance(myFace2, EYE);
133      if (low <= d && d <= high)
134         myFace2.paint(g);
135
136      d = distance(myFace3, EYE);
137      if (low <= d && d <= high)
138         myFace3.paint(g);
139
140      d = distance(myFace4, EYE);
141      if (low <= d && d <= high)
142         myFace4.paint(g);
143   }
144 }
```

PATTERNS

8.3   Patterns for Finding Extreme Values

The process described above requires finding the relative distances of faces. This is accomplished by finding minimum and maximum distances. Coding patterns that find minimums and maximums are used repeatedly in computer applications. Understanding these patterns can help us write code that performs efficiently and is easy to understand.

Each pattern has its own trade-offs. In 3D applications, we are often faced with the trade-off between reality and speed. The more real a scene looks, the more time is required to create it. Before we can make these trade-offs, we must be able to analyze our coding decisions. In this section, we will look at some simple algorithms for finding extremes. This is followed by Section 8.6, where we begin our journey into the study of the complexity of algorithms. Algorithmic complexity is a mathematical tool used to evaluate the relative performance of algorithms.

> *Algorithms* describe a step-by-step procedure to accomplish a particular task. These steps must be carried out in a finite amount of time and must give identical answers given identical initial conditions.

We focused on several algorithmic patterns in previous chapters. In Chapter 3 we used the sequential pattern to write code that displays graphics within a window. Each step followed another step in order. In Chapter 2 we used counter and sentinel loop patterns to control the action of a robot butler. Each time we ran these programs, we got the same results. Furthermore, they completed their tasks within a finite amount of time. Thus, we know they are algorithms.

We should not confuse algorithmic patterns with object patterns introduced in Chapter 7. Object patterns describes ways that we can organize objects and classes. Algorithmic patterns describe commonly used steps to accomplish a particular task. In this section we will investigate an algorithmic pattern for finding maximums. Finding minimums is similar to finding maximums. It is a simple task to adapt finding maximums to finding minimums or other extreme values.

8.3.1   Maximum of Two Items

Finding the maximum of several numbers sounds rather mundane, but it turns out to be an important process to do well. We might choose a stock based on its maximum expected earnings. An automobile ignition system may select a fuel mixture for maximum performance. An aircraft navigation system may choose a landing path by computing maximum safety. A computer game may select winners by determining the maximum score, the greatest distance traveled, or some other maximizing scheme.

Listing 8.2 shows a fragment of code to determine the maximum of two numbers. It begins by assuming that x has the largest value. That assumption is checked in Line2. If our assumption is incorrect, we correct our assumption in Line3.

Listing 8.2   Maximum of Two Numbers

```
1 int max = x;
2 if (y > max)
3   max = y;
```

8.3.2   Maximum of Three Items

Finding the maximum of three numbers is a minor modification of finding the maximum of two numbers. In Listing 8.3 we again assume that x is the largest number (Line 1). Next, in Line 2 we challenge our assumption. If y is greater than our current maximum, we correct our assumption in Line 3. We do this one more time by checking if z is larger than our current maximum. If it is, we reset our maximum in Line 5. Lines 71 through 84 in our tetrahedron program in Listing 8.1 expand this process to four numbers.

Listing 8.3   Maximum of Three Numbers

```
1   int max = x;
2   if (y > max)
3     max = y;
4   if (z > max)
5     max = z;
```

8.3.3   Maximum of n Items

Now that we have found the maximum for two through four numbers, it is a simple extension to find the maximum for any number of numbers. However, the prospect of creating n variables and writing two lines of code to test each variable is not attractive. For example, if a 3D object is composed of 300 triangles, 300 variables plus 600 lines of code would be needed to find the maximum. In addition, we would need to modify this code for each mesh. We can do much better by using a loop.

The algorithm begins by assuming that the first data value is the maximum. It then looks at each number after that. If a new number violates our current assumption, we readjust the maximum (Listing 8.4). An example implementation is in Listing 8.5. We will take advantage of this pattern in Chapter 9 when we find minimum and maximum stock prices. However, it will not be until we get to the chapter on lists (Chapter 11) and arrays (Chapter 13) that we can fully take advantage of its potential.

Listing 8.4 Pattern for finding the Maximum of n Items, n >= 1

```
get the first data item and call it the current maximum
while more numbers
  get a data item from the file
  if it is greater than the current maximum
    make the current maximum the new data item
end loop
```

Listing 8.5 Finding the Maximum of n Positive Integers

```
1   int number = io.readInt();
2   int max    = number;
3   while (true)                    // a number <= 0 is loop sentinel
4   {
5     number = io.readInt();
6     if (number <= 0)
7     {
8        break;
9     }
10    if (number > max)
11    {
12       max = number;
13    }
14 }
```

The code in Listing 8.5 reads numbers from a file looking for the maximum value. For simplicity we used a non-positive number as a sentinel value. The code fragment reads values until it reads a zero or negative integer. In addition, this fragment has an important limitation. It works only with files that begin with at least one non-negative number. If the file is empty, then Line 1 will fail. If the file contains only a sentinel value, the readInt in Line 1 will return the sentinel value. The next readInt, Line 5, will fail. This problem is a consequence of how we have determined the initial maximum values. We have elected to select the first item in a list as the maximum. One way around this problem is to put a guard around this code. A second solution is to choose zero or a negative number as the initial maximum value. If negative numbers and zero are also possible candidates for maximums, we will need to find a different strategy for finding a sentinel value. One such strategy, detecting the end-of-file, is discussed in Chapter 12. Currently, it is sufficient to know the basic strategy for finding the maximum of n numbers.

There are many ways of accomplishing the same task. Even the simple task of finding the maximum of several numbers has different solutions. We are left wondering how do we choose? For those of us interested in pursuing that question, the material in Section 8.6 will get us started.

8.4 Command Alternative Action Pattern

Many of the programs today use graphical user interfaces. However, there are many applications that rely of text-based interactions. Text-based applications are characterized by interactions in which the program prints text to a display and waits for a user response. The introduction of the IPO pattern (Section 4.2.1 , page 123) was our first introduction to text-based processing. The text-based programs we have developed thus far are limited. They ask the user for input and then compute and produce output. However, there are many times when a user needs some control of what processing is done.

The user can gain control of a program if we implement the command alternative action pattern. This pattern is related to the alternative action pattern introduced in Section 2.4.2. The user enters a command and the program selects from several alternatives based on that entry. The pattern that accomplishes this task is outlined in Listing 8.6.

Listing 8.6 Command Alternative Action Pattern

```
1 loop forever
2    get a user command
3    based on the command do one of the following
4       if command 1 do action 1
5       if command 2 do action 2
6       ...
7       if command n do action n
8       if command not recognized display error
9 end loop
```

We will use this pattern to implement a checkbook balancing program. We can us it to enter the withdrawals and deposits we have had on our account and display our new balance. It will have the following commands.

- Deposit: enter a deposit into our checking account.

- Inquiry: display our current balance.
- Quit: exit the program.
- Set: set our checking account balance to some initial value.
- Withdraw: withdraw money from our checking account.

An example interaction with the check balancing program in show in Listing 8.7. Information entered by the user is displayed in bold. For example, the first command entered by the user is s to set the initial balance to \$1,353.76. Subsequent commands withdraw, deposit, and display the current balance.

Listing 8.7 Example Run of the Checkbook Balance Program

```
Checkbook balance program.
Please enter one of the following commands.
  d: deposit money
  i: balance inquiry
  q: quit
  s: set balance
  w: withdraw money

> s
Enter a new balance:   1353.76

> w
Enter the withdrawal: 14.95

> d
Enter the deposit:     318.45

> w
Enter the withdrawal: 259.99

> i
Your balance is:       $1,397.27

> q
```

An example implementation on the checkbook balancing program using the command alternative pattern is shown in Listing 8.8. The command loop begins in Line 16. The command prompt is displayed in Line 18. Line 19 gets the single character command from the user. Lines 21 through 47 execute an action based on the command received. For example, if the command entered by the user is the character s for set initial balance, the method setBalance in called in Line 37. The setBalance method is implemented in Lines 80 through 85.

Listing 8.8 Checkbook balancing program

```
1  import vista.VRead;
2  import vista.VWrite;
3  public class BankBalance
4  {
5    private static double myBalance = 0.0;
6
7    //---------- main --------------------------------------------
8    public static void main(String args[])
9    {
10     VRead   in  = new VRead ();
11     VWrite  out = new VWrite ();
12     out.applyPattern("$#,##0.00;($#,##0.00)");
13     out.setFractionDigits(2);
14
15     printInstructions(out);
16     while (true)
17     {
18       out.write("> ");
19       char command = in.readChar();
20
21       switch (command)
22       {
23         case 'd':            // deposit
24         case 'D':
25           deposit(in, out);
26           break;
27         case 'i':            // inquiry
28         case 'I':
29           inquiry(out);
30           break;
31         case 'q':            // quit
32         case 'Q':
33           System.exit(0);
34           break;
35         case 's':            // set balance
36         case 'S':
37           setBalance(in, out);
38           break;
39         case 'w':            // withdraw
40         case 'W':
41           withdraw(in, out);
42           break;
43         default:             // error
44           out.write   ("i: inquiry;   d: deposit;  ");
45           out.writeln ("w: withdraw;  s: set; q: quit");
46           break;
47       }
48     }
49   }
```

Listing 8.8 Checkbook balancing program

```
50    //---------- printInstructions ----------------------------
51    private static void printInstructions (VWrite out)
52    {
53      out.writeln ("Checkbook balance program.");
54     out.writeln ("Please enter one of the following commands.");
55      out.writeln ("  d: deposit money");
56      out.writeln ("  i: balance inquiry");
57      out.writeln ("  q: quit");
58      out.writeln ("  s: set balance");
59      out.writeln ("  w: withdraw money");
60      out.writeln ();
61    }
62
63    //---------- deposit ----------------------------------------
64    private static void deposit (VRead in, VWrite out)
65    {
66      out.write ("Enter the deposit:     ");
67      myBalance += in.readDouble();
68      out.writeln ();
69    }
70
71    //---------- inquiry ----------------------------------------
72    private static void inquiry (VWrite out)
73    {
74      out.write ("Your balance is:      ");
75      out.writeln (myBalance);
76      out.writeln ();
77    }
78
79    //---------- setBalance -------------------------------------
80    private static void setBalance (VRead in, VWrite out)
81    {
82      out.write ("Enter a new balance:  ");
83      myBalance = in.readDouble();
84      out.writeln ();
85    }
86
87    //---------- withdraw ---------------------------------------
88    private static void withdraw (VRead in, VWrite out)
89    {
90      out.write ("Enter the withdrawal: ");
91      myBalance -= in.readDouble();
92      out.writeln ();
93    }
94 }
```

We could also implement the command alternative pattern with if statements as follows:

```
if (command == 'd' || command == 'D')
  deposit (io);
else if (command == 'i' || command == 'I')
  inquiry (io);
...
else
  io.printing ("error");
```

Patterns that select one of several alternatives are used often. As a result, many computer languages have special statements to facilitate their implementation. Java provides the switch statement, which is discussed in Section 8.5.1. The switch statement is a natural for implementing the command alternative action pattern.

JAVA

8.5   Selection

We were introduced to selection statements, which can be used to implement any selection pattern we need, in Chapter 2. However, some patterns appear so often that many languages provide special statements to make these patterns easier and more efficient to implement. The `switch` statement is an example.

8.5.1   `Switch` **Statement**

The alternative action pattern introduced in Section 2.4.2 , page 54 is a prime candidate for a special statement. Often it can be implemented with the `switch` statement. It transfers control to one of several statements depending on the value of an expression.

```
switch ( Expression ) {
  case ConstantExpression : Statements
    . . .
  case ConstantExpression : Statements
  default : Statements
}
```

For example, in the following `switch` statement, the color blue is selected when `count` `mod` 4 is 0; green when 1, red when 2, and yellow when 3.

```
switch (count % 4) {
  case 0:
    color = Color.blue;
    break;
  case 1:
    color = Color.green;
    break;
  case 2:
    color = Color.red;
    break;
  case 3:
    color = Color.yellow;
}
```

The `switch` statement must adhere to the following constraints:

- The type of the switch expression must be a discrete value such as char, byte, short, or int. For example, you *cannot* use a double of string value in the switch expression.

- The semantics of the switch statement dictate that once execution is transferred to a case label, execution continues until the end of the switch statement or until a break is encountered. Thus the following code would set the color to green for counts with remainders of 0 and 1. The color would never be blue because it would be reset to green immediately:

```
switch (count % 4) {
  case 0:
    color = Color.blue;
    // this break was removed
  case 1:
    color = Color.green;
    break;
  case 2:
    color = Color.red;
    break;
  case 3:
    color = Color.yellow;
}
```

- The case labels must be unique and must all be constant expressions. Constant expressions can be computed at compile-time. Examples of constant expressions are shown below.:

```
25
'A'
11*3-2
K           // given: final int K = 14;
K * 39      // given the above
```

The following code is not allowed:

```
switch (aNumber) {
  case 73:
    System.out.println(73);
    break;
  case 0:
    System.out.println(0);
    break;
  case 73:                       // syntax error - duplicate label
    System.out.println(73);
  case aNumber < 50:         // syntax error - not a constant
    system.out.println("small");
}
```

- If the value of the switch expression does not match any of the case labels, execution is transferred to the default clause if one exists. The default clause is optional. An example follows:

```
char c = 'F';
boolean pass;
switch (c) {
   case 'A':
   case 'B':
   case 'C':
   case 'D': pass = true; break;
   default:  pass = false;
}
```

In the above, `pass` gets the value false. If none of the case labels match and there is no default statement, execution is transferred to the statement following the `switch`.

Because `switch` statements are special cases of the if statement, it may be argued that they are not necessary. They are *syntactic sugar*. However, the restrictions placed on their expressions and case labels make it possible to execute them efficiently. A nested `if` statement often requires the evaluation of several conditional expressions before the appropriate statements are executed. For example, the movie selection code in Listing 2.6 on page 67 requires the evaluation of three conditional tests if the remainder of count divided by 4 is 3. On the other hand, the Java compiler can create byte code that immediately branches to the appropriate statement once the value of the `switch` expression is computed. The color code at the beginning of this section requires only one comparison regardless of the value of `count % 4`. The result is faster program execution.

8.5.2   Common Mistakes with Switch Statements

Missing a `break` statement within a `switch` statement can cause problems. In the following example, the color is set to blue for color values of 0 and 1:

```
switch(color)
{
   case 0: g.setColor(Color.red);
   case 1: g.setColor(Color.blue);    // this statement always
}                                      // undoes the previous
```

SUPPLEMENTARY MATERIAL

8.6 Algorithmic Analysis

There is often more than one way to accomplish the same task. The question we have been asking in this chapter is how do we choose. We will begin by looking at several algorithms that find the maximum of three numbers. We will find that by carefully analyzing these algorithms we can improve their efficiency by almost 200%. However, we must question what benefits are produced. Increasing the execution speed of a small part of program may have negligible impact on the entire program.

A more effective means to improve a program's performance is to select algorithms that have good established performance characteristics. *Algorithmic analysis* classifies algorithms by placing them into broad categories. Algorithms in one category are more efficient than algorithms in another category. Computer science is rich with algorithms. These include algorithms for sorting lists of addresses, maintaining network tables, performing 3D graphics, and many others. Each has a set of characteristics that determine to which efficiency category it belongs.

8.6.1 Constant Factor Improvements

In some cases it is important how fast we can find a maximum. For example, if we are landing a jumbo jet or rendering 3D graphics, we will be computing maximums thousands of times per second. It is important to do it quickly. If, on the other hand, we are computing the winner of a computer game, it will make little difference if we accomplish that task in 10 or 100 microseconds. We are only computing the maximum once and a player will not notice a 90 microsecond savings in speed.

We will begin by looking at what is required to improve an algorithm by a constant factor. Listing 8.9 through Listing 8.11 show three options for finding the maximum of three numbers. The algorithm in Listing 8.9 contains three `if` statements. Each `if` statement uses two comparisons to determine whether one of three numbers is the maximum. As a result, it will take us six comparisons to find the maximum of three numbers.

Notice that we are checking each of `x > y`, `x > z`, and `y > z` twice. To make this algorithm more efficient, we need to remove this duplicative effort. In addition, we are

Listing 8.9 Maximum of Three Numbers - Option 1

```
1  int x   = ...;
2  int y   = ...;
3  int z   = ...;
4  int max = 0;
5
6  if (x > y & x > z)
7     max = x;
8  if (y > x & y > z)
9     max = y;
10 if (z > x & z > y)
11    max = z;
```

doing unnecessary checks. If we know that x is not the maximum and y is not the maximum, we do not need to check if z is the maximum. In Listing 8.10 we have removed the duplication. In the first if statement, we determine if x is the greatest. If it is, there is no need for any addition testing. We have accomplished our task with two comparisons. If x is not the largest, we need to do another comparison to determine whether y or z is the largest. We can accomplish this task with an additional comparison. Thus, finding that x is the largest requires two comparisons, and finding that y or z is the largest requires three comparisons. If the chance that x, y, or z is the greatest is equal, we expect to do 2.7 comparisons on average.

Listing 8.10 Maximum of Three Numbers—Option 2

```
1  int x   = ...;
2  int y   = ...;
3  int z   = ...;
4  int max = 0;
5
6  if (x > y & x > z)
7     max = x;
8  else if (y > z)
9     max = y;
10 else
11    max = z;
```

If one number has a greater chance of being the largest, we can rearrange the comparisons so that the number that is probably the largest is checked first. This will increase performance. For example, Listing 8.10 performs the best when x has the highest chance of being the greatest.

In Listing 8.11 the number of comparisons has been reduced to two for all cases. This has been done at the expense of extra assignment statements. In option 2 an assignment statement is executed only once. In option 3 assignment is executed twice if x is not the largest. Thus, a comparison has been traded for an assignment.

Listing 8.11 Maximum of Three Numbers—Option 3

```
1    int x   = ...;
2    int y   = ...;
3    int z   = ...;
4    int max = 0;
5
6    if (x > y)
7       max = x;
8    else
9       max = y;
10   if (z > max)
11      max = z;
```

Table 8.1 summarizes the number of comparisons required by the three options. The results assume that x, y, and z are equally probable to be the maximum. It is clear that option 1 is a poor choice because of repeated comparisons. It is more difficult to argue whether option 2 or 3 or is faster. How do we determine which is better? Is a comparison faster or slower than an assignment statement?

Table 8.1 Number of Comparisons for Finding the Maximum of Three Numbers

situation	option 1	option 2	option 3
x > y > z	6	2	2
x > z > y	6	2	2
y > x > z	6	3	2
y > z > x	6	3	2
z > x > y	6	3	2
z > y > x	6	3	2
average	6	2.7	2

Timing runs were done on the three options using a Macintosh 6100/60 running Metrowerks Java release 11. The results are summarized in Table 8.2. These timing runs reinforce our conclusion that option 1 is a poor choice. Option 2 is about 90% faster.

The choice between option 2 and 3 is less clear. By trading a comparison for an assignment statement we increased the code's speed by about 40%. However, the results may be

Table 8.2 Timing Runs on Finding the Maximum of Three Numbers

option	1	2	3
time (microseconds)	8.87	4.60	3.24

different on a different computer or with a different compiler. For example, some computers may be optimized for evaluating conditional expressions. As a result, option 2 may be faster. No generalities should be drawn. We can choose either option 2 or 3. If the code appears in a time-critical section, we must do tests to determine an appropriate choice.

When we compare the algorithms above, our time comparisons are of the form:

```
Algorithm a is c times faster than algorithm b.
```

where c is a constant. Thus, the comparison we did above resulted in constant time differences. Another example of a constant time difference is the experiment we did in Section 7.7. We found that it took about four times longer to access instance variables through method call than by using direct access.

Be careful about picking one algorithm over another because of constant time differences. The code that we are optimizing may be so insignificant that the optimizations we do are futile. For example, spending hours making six lines of code 90% faster may has no impact on a 10,000 line program. In addition, optimization efforts often backfire. For example, making one part of the program run faster may make another part run slower, may require excessive memory, may make the program difficult to maintain, may cause incorrect results, or may provide result that are insignificantly better.

A good rule of thumb about optimizing code is "Don't do it." Code optimization is a final endeavor and must only be done if necessary. In the situations where code optimization is required, it is important to do careful analysis:

- Determine the required performance.
- Measure the current program performance.
- If performance benchmarks are not met, profile the code to determine where the program spends most of its time. This place is often not obvious.
- Concentrate improvements on the code executed most often.
- Measure the impact of any optimizations.

A common mistake, which we introduced in Chapter 7, is to optimize the wrong code early in a project. The result is a poorly designed program that is difficult to test, maintain, and does not perform well. Deferring optimization to the end does not mean writing sloppy code. There are many straightforward algorithms that give good performance. We should select these algorithms first. We will look at this topic in the next section. In addition, we should partition our code into classes that hide optimization decisions. This will allow us to limit the impact of modifications to small sections of code.

A good example of this point is Microsoft Excel. During its development there were three competing platforms: Windows, OS/2, and the Macintosh OS. It was not clear to the development team which of these platforms would dominate. To hedge their bets, they created a *virtual machine*. A virtual machine is a computer that exists only in software. The Java interpreter is an example of a virtual machine. In Microsoft's case, a virtual machine provided the operations required by Excel to open files, get memory, and manipulate windows. This virtual machine was then implemented on each of the three platforms. Once the virtual machine was implemented on each platform, each platform looked the same to the programmer. As a result, it was not necessary to rewrite any of the Excel code to work on any of the three platforms.

There is a cost to Microsoft's approach. Extra operation calls are required to go through the layers of abstraction required to get system resources. However, as we discovered in our experiment in Section 7.7, these are constant time costs. The Excel team found that this cost was insignificant. Instead, they concentrated on writing algorithms that gave better than constant time improvements.

There are several things we need to remember from this section.:

- Constant factor improvements often buy us little. The first rule of optimization is "don't."

- Counting the number of comparisons an algorithm performs can be a useful method for comparing algorithms.

- If we can reasonably avoid making an algorithm do the same thing more than once, do so.

8.6.2   Order of Complexity

Now let's take a look at improving algorithms using other than constant time factors. Two ways of finding the sum of the first n integers are shown in Listing 8.12. The one on the left executes in constant time. In other words, the value n does not make a difference in how long it takes to compute the result. The algorithm on the right is proportional to n. For example, if we double n from 8 to 16, the algorithm will loop twice as many times.

Listing 8.12 Finding the Sum of the First n Integers

```
                                     1 int count = 1;
                                     2 int sum    = 0;
                                     3 while (count <= n)
int sum = (1 + n) * n / 2;           4 {
                                     5    sum =+ count;
                                     6    count ++;
                                     7 }
```

Let us take a closer look at how we arrive at the idea that the algorithm on the right is proportional to n. To make our analysis easier, we suppose that each statement takes the same amount of time to execute. Table 8.3 summarizes how many statements must be executed for values of 1, 2, 3 and n. The last line gives us a general equation for computing the number of statements executed. As n becomes large, adding the constant 3 has insignificant impact. Thus we can say that the polynomial term 2n dominates for large n. For all practical purposes the time required for this algorithm is proportional to n. Thus, we say its *order of complexity* is n. This is written in Big-O notation as O(n). O(n) defines one category of algorithm.

Table 8.3 Finding the Sum Using a Loop

n	number of statements executed
1	5
2	7
3	9
...	...
n	2 * n + 3

An algorithm's order of complexity defines the efficiency category to which an algorithm belongs. It is described by a polynomial term that dominates the function that computes the time required to execute the algorithm.

The algorithm on the left is on the order of a constant, O(1). The size of n makes no difference. It does not matter if n is 5 or 10,000. Only one statement is executed. O(1) defines another category of algorithm. O(1) algorithms are more efficient than O(n) algorithms.

Our computations of the time required to compute the sum of n numbers was not done accurately. The time required to execute one statement may be substantially different than another statements. However, no matter how carefully we count the work being done by our computer, we will still arrive at a value of O(n) for this algorithm. The advantage for using the order of complexity notation is that it is not influenced by the computer hardware or programming language used.

Sometimes many algorithms that do the same thing belong to the same complexity category. Algorithmic analysis does not help us distinguish between them. For example, if 2n+5 is the time it takes to find the sum of the first n integers for one algorithm and 5n+7 for another, they both belong to the same complexity category. It is not important if one algorithm is some constant times faster than another. These multiplicative constants are unreliable. They will differ based on how we choose to count the work an algorithm is doing. By ignoring the multiplicative constants we make our analysis machine- and language-independent.

Another example of an O(n) algorithm is finding the maximum of n numbers (Listing 8.5 on page 352). A typical procedure for finding the order of complexity of an algorithm is to pick a critical operation and compute the number of times that operation is executed on average. Experience dictates that a good candidate is a comparison operation such as the one in Line 6 or Line 10. This is consistent with our experience in the previous section, when we found that the cost of comparisons higher than an assignment.

In addition to analyzing an algorithm for time efficiency, we can also analyze its space efficiency. Space efficiency refers to how much memory or disk space an algorithm requires. In this book we will focus primarily on time efficiency.

8.6.3   Why Do We Care?

The advantage of placing algorithms into categories is that their order of complexity is not influenced by computer languages or by hardware. We can say that constant order algorithms are better than order n algorithms. No matter how much time a constant order algorithm takes we can find an n for which an order n algorithm takes more time.

There are other categories than O(1) and O(n). $O(n^3)$ algorithms are less efficient that $O(n^2)$ algorithms, which are less efficient than O(n) algorithms. For example, suppose we are managing a computer system in which our user base is growing 12% per month. After 10 months the number of users has tripled. For an O(n) algorithm, what used to take one hour now takes 3. For an $O(n^2)$ algorithm it now takes nine hours. For an $O(n^3)$ algorithm, it now takes 27 hours.

There are some algorithms which are $O(2^n)$. One example is an algorithm for finding the optimal course schedules for n students. If we add one student, it takes twice as long because there are twice as many combinations. If we add 20 students, it takes a million times as long.

Other algorithms are O($\log_2$ n); for example, finding our name in alphabetized phone directory. Doubling the list size from one million to two million may cost only an additional 5% in time. Multiplying the list size by 1000 may cost only an addition 50% in time.

Writing an algorithm well on a slow computer is often better than writing it poorly on a fast computer. For example, suppose the time required to do something poorly on a fast Super Z4000 computer is given by Equation 8.1.

$$10n^3 + 15 microseconds$$ **Equation 8.1**

Suppose somebody on a slow Turtle B4 computer finds a better way of doing the same thing. The time is given by Equation 8.2.

$$10000n + 20000 microseconds$$ **Equation 8.2**

Table 8.4 shows how long each of these algorithms would take on these computers for four values on n. For n=1, the Super Z4000 computer is over one thousand times faster. For n=10, the Super Z4000 computer is about 12 times faster. For n=100, the Turtle B4 computer is about 10 times faster. For n=10,000, the task is impractical on the fast computer.

Table 8.4 A Comparison of Algorithms and Computers

	time	
n	$10n^3$ + 15 μ sec.	10000n + 20000 μ sec.
1	25 μ sec.	30,000 μ sec.
10	10,015 μ sec.	120,000 μ sec.
100	10 sec.	1 second
1000	17 minutes	10 seconds
10,000	115 days	2 minutes

 We may not be able to save a poor design by buying a faster computer. The complexity category to which an algorithm belongs says a lot about how it will perform compared to algorithms in other complexity categories.

These comparisons assume that n is reasonably large. For example, if we compare how long it takes to find the maximum of four versus two numbers, we will probably find that the time required for four numbers is nearly the same as for two numbers. There are time performance hits for setting things up, such as initializing loops. When n is small, these initialization details dominate.

For example, the time required for finding the sum of the first n number using a loop on a Super Z4000 computer may be governed by the following equation:

$$5\,n + 300 \text{ microseconds} \qquad\qquad \text{Equation 8.3}$$

When n doubles from 5 to 10, the time goes from 325 to 350 microseconds. For small n, the additive constant 300 dominates. However, once n is larger than 60, the n part begins to dominate. When n doubles from 5,000 to 10,000, the time nearly doubles from 25,300 to 50,300 microseconds. As n grows, the influence of the constant part continues to decline until, for all practical purposes, the constant part is unimportant. Thus, when n is small, complexity analysis does not help us.

So why do we care? When we work with information, n is often large. We will find that if we have a choice of algorithms from different categories, the one we choose can have a significant impact on program execution. This approach is consistent with Microsoft's experience with Excel. They found that working hard at selecting the best algorithm gave them a much better payoff than constant time optimizations.

8.7 Software Testing

The software for the Space Shuttle is life and mission critical. It must be carefully tested. In 1962 a missing hyphen resulted in the destruction of an $18.5 million Atlas-Agena rocket. It was carrying a spacecraft that was to make the first Venus flyby. The rocket went berserk 90 miles up and was blown up by ground control.

On March 21, 1986, a man in Tyler, Texas received a massive overdose of radiation while undergoing medical treatment. He lost the use of his left arm and died five months later from complications. In all there were six instances of massive overdoses by the Therac-25, a computer-controlled radiation therapy system. Three resulted in deaths. The accidents were a result of poor interface design, inadequate safety checks, and the lack of hardware safety interlocks.

A woman from Vancouver, British Columbia, attempted to withdraw $1100 from an ATM in Honolulu. A satellite delay between Honolulu and New Jersey and problems in the communications software resulted in her account being debited without dispensing any money. After seeing her monthly bill when she arrived home, she thought her fiancé used her ATM card without permission. She had him arrested for theft .

These examples of software errors caused loss of life, property, and credibility. Software errors in some systems are important to avoid at great cost. Errors in other systems are tolerated because we realize that error-free code is often too expensive to make a system marketable. So we tolerate occasional computer crashes and computer games that fail. Popular practices dictate that spending extra effort on finding glitches in the next release of an operating system or in a computer game may result in a delay to market and a loss in market share. This attitude creates an atmosphere of complacency. Regardless of the system, careful attention to testing in the beginning can save embarrassment and substantial effort to fix problems later. In the next section we look at some minimal methodologies that can be used to uncover problems.

8.8   Test Coverage

When we cook, we test each dish to make sure it tastes good. If we add a little salt to the sauce, we test it again. If it needs a little pepper, we add it and taste again. So should it be with software systems. Each statement of code must be tested. If it is faulty, corrections must be made and the statement tested again. We must make certain that every statement has been executed at least once and that its execution produces correct results. This is called statement coverage.

8.8.1   Statement Coverage

Listing 8.13 illustrates a contrived situation in which the absence of testing can be disastrous. The code governs ground-based control of a rocket for the first 600 seconds of its flight. After 600 seconds control is turned over to the rocket's internal navigation system. However, there is a contingency plan if radar contact is lost with the rocket before the 600-second time period. If radar contact is lost prematurely, ground control should be turned off and the internal navigation system of the rocket take over.

There is a flaw in the code. The on/off status for the rocket auto-pilot and ground control have been reversed in the case when radar contact is lost. As a result, when radar contact is lost, ground control continues to control the rocket.

This program may work correctly for many launches because typically the 600-second time limit is reached before radar contact is lost. But some day situations may arise that cause the faulty code to execute. For example, weather conditions or operator error may cause the radar to fail before the 600 second time limit. In that event ground control computers will continue to control the rocket. Since ground control computers do not know the location of the rocket (recall radar contact was lost), the rocket will be guided aimlessly. The rocket's behavior will appear erratic, resulting in its destruction by a launch supervisor.

Listing 8.13 Rocket Control

```
1   GroundControl.setStatus(on);
2   RocketAutoPilot.setStatus(off);
3   GroundControl.executeCountDown();
4   Rocket.ignite();
5       .
6       .
7       .
8   if (GroundControl.isRadarOutOfRange()) {
9     RocketAutoPilot.setStatus(off);      // error
10    GroundControl.setStatus(on);         // error
11    }
12  if (time > 600) {
13    RocketAutoPilot.setStatus(on);
14    GroundControl.setStatus(off);
15    }
```

Statement coverage: Test cases must be provided until every statement has been executed at least once.

The scenario described above indicates that at the very minimum each statement in a program should be tested at least once. Table 8.5 contains three numbered statements (an `if` statement with two embedded assignment statements). Statement 1 is always executed. Statements 2 and 3, on the other hand, are executed only for specific values of x. Thus, statement coverage requires a minimum of two test cases, for example: `x == 33` and `x == 19`. When x is 33, statements 1 and 2 are tested. When x is 19, statements 1 and 3 are tested

Table 8.5 Statement Coverage

code	value of x	statements executed
1. if (x > 25)	33	1,2
2. y = 40;	19	1,3
else		
3. y = 17;		

Statement coverage may not be enough. In Table 8.6 statement coverage can be satisfied with a single test case, for example x `== 33`. This is clearly inadequate. Our intuition says that the `if` statement should be tested for both true and false branches. Branch coverage will provide a more rigorous test.

Table 8.6 Statement Coverage

code	value of x	statements executed
1. y = 17; 2. if (x > 25) 3. y = 40;	33	1,2,3

8.8.2   Branch Coverage

Branch coverage is designed to more rigorously test `if` statements.

> *Branch coverage*: Test cases must be provided until the conditional in every `if` statement evaluates to true and to false at least once.

In Table 8.6 branch coverage requires a minimum of two test cases, for example `x == 33` and `x == 19`. When `x` is 33, the `if` conditional is true. When `x` is 19, the `if` conditional is false.

Table 8.7 Branch Coverage for Table 8.6

value of x	if statement 2
33	true
19	false

A little reflection will convince us that branch coverage also satisfies statement coverage. In other words, if we select test cases that test all possible branches, they will also test all statements. We say that branch coverage *subsumes* statement coverage.

Table 8.8 illustrates a slightly more complicated case. Branch coverage can be satisfied with the two cases presented in the table. Both `if` conditionals are true at least once and both are false at least once. However, we will find that branch coverage is also inadequate.

8.8.3   Path Coverage

Branch coverage may not be enough. Listing 8.14 contains a contrived code fragment designed to control a medical instrument for radiation treatment. The instrument is typically operated in standard mode where a burst of 200 units of radiation is applied for 100 milliseconds. However, on occasion the machine is operated in burst mode where a higher

Table 8.8 Branch Coverage

code	data values		if Statement	
	w	**y**	**1**	**4**
1. if (w > 25) 2. x = 40; else 3. x = 17;	42	83	true	true
4. if (y == 83) 5. z = 74; else 6. z = 51;	18	90	false	false

intensity burst of radiation (2000 units) is applied for a shorter period of time (10 micro-seconds). In both the standard and burst mode the dosage is the same (`200 * 100 == 2000 * 10`)

The machine is supplied with a reset button that resets it to standard mode. However, there is a fatal flaw in this code. Notice that the reset button returns the radiation time to 100 milliseconds but fails to reset the radiation intensity to 200 units. If the operator has selected burst mode and then pressed the reset button, the dosage will be 2000 units for 100 seconds. This is 10 times the intended dosage. This error may not be found through branch coverage. For example, the tests in Table 8.9 satisfy branch coverage but will not detects this error. We will need a stronger test criterion, such as path coverage, to detect this error.

Listing 8.14 Radiation Treatment

```
1.   if (standardMode())
     {
        radiation = 200;
        time      = 100;
     }
     else
     {
        radiation = 2000;
        time      =   10;
     }
        .
        .
        .
2.   if (resetButtonPressed())
        time = 100;
```

Table 8.9 Branch Coverage for Listing 8.14

data values		if statement	
StandardMode()	resetButtonPressed()	1	2
true	true	true	true
false	false	false	false

Path coverage: A *path* is defined by a unique sequence of statements. Test cases must be provided until every executable path is executed at least once.

An example of an execution path for the code in Table 8.8 is [1, 2, 4, 5]. This means that statement 1 is executed first, followed by statement 2 then 4 and finally 5. This path is executed when w has the value 42 and y the value 83. Table 8.10 shows three additional paths and their corresponding test values.

Table 8.10 Path Coverage for Table 8.8

path	w	y
[1, 2, 4, 5]	42	83
[1, 3, 4, 5]	18	83
[1, 2, 4, 6]	42	90
[1, 3, 4, 6]	18	90

Not all program paths may be executable. For example, the path [1, 2, 4, 5] in Listing 8.15 is not executable because w cannot be greater than 25 and equal to 25 at the same time.

Listing 8.15 Unexecutable Path - 1 2 4 5

```
1.   if (w > 25)
2.      x = 40;
     else
3.      x = 17;
4.   if (w == 25)
5.      z = 74;
     else
6.      z = 51;
```

Unfortunately, path coverage may be impractical for software testing. There are often too many possible paths to test. It is important to look at the work of Nancy Leveson. One of the questions she asks when evaluating a system is what bad things can happen and how does the software prevent them from occurring. This approach is called *software safety*.

8.8.4   Boundary Conditions

The last testing criterion we will look at in the chapter is boundary conditions. *Boundary conditions* arise when the change in a value by one unit causes a conditional to switch between true and false. It is important to test on both sides of a boundary because off-by-one errors are common. For example, the following code fragment may be used to book an airline flight.

```
if (passengers > 275)
   flightFull = true;
```

Suppose the maximum capacity of the airplane is 275. This example will trigger a flight full message when the number of passengers in 276. Thus, each flight will be overbooked by one person. This problem may not be found with any of the coverage techniques discussed earlier. To find this error, test the program with the number of passengers equal to 275 and 276. Other examples of boundary testing are shown in Table 8.11

Table 8.11   Boundary Testing

expression	x boundary values
x > 23	23, 24
x >= 23	22, 23
x == 23	22, 23, 24
x > 5 & x < 23	4, 5, 22, 23

8.8.5   Troublesome Values

There are some additional troublesome values that should be a part of many tests. They include −1, 0, 1, maximum positive number, and maximum negative number. For example, the code below finds the average of n items.

```
sumOfItems / n
```

If n is 0, the program will fail. This situation may occur rarely but when it does it will cause problems. Some programs fail on empty files because they cannot handle the zero case. If zero is an inappropriate value, there should be a check that prevents that possibility.

8.9   Debugging Selection Statements

A *bug* is an error of logic in a computer program.

Programs that do not execute appropriately are called buggy. There is some disagreement about the origin of the term. A common story involves Navy Captain Grace Hopper who during the summer of 1945 was helping to finish the Mark II, the first American large-scale computer.

The Mark II was constructed with relays, mechanical switches activated by a small electrical current. Captain Hopper reports in the *Annals of the History of Computing*:

> It was a hot summer with no air conditioning, so all the windows were open. Mark II stopped, and we were trying to get her going. We finally found the relay that had failed. Inside the relay—and these were large relays—was a moth that had been beaten to death by the relay. We got a pair of tweezers. Very carefully we took the moth out of the relay, put it in the logbook, and put scotch tape over it.

> Now Commander Howard Aiken had a habit of coming into the room and saying, "Are you making any numbers?" From then on if we weren't making any numbers, we told him that we were debugging the computer.

It is common to discover a bug with a program and then look at the code and it looks fine. For example, the following may look OK at first:

```
public boolean mouseDown (Event e, int x, int y)
{
  if (x > y);
    iBlueSprite.move(x, y);
}
```

However, the code does not execute as the code indention suggests. This code will always cause the blue sprite to move to location (x,y) regardless of the values of x and y. Close inspection reveals that there is a misplaced semicolon at the end of the if conditional.

The misplaced semicolon causes the empty statement to be executed when x is greater than y. It is easy to miss the presence of a spurious semicolon when one is trying to track a bug across dozens of lines of code. Adding some print statements will help us focus on the problem area. For example:

```
public boolean mouseDown (Event e, int x, int y)
{
   if (x > y); {
     iBlueSprite.move(x, y);
     System.out.println
        ("mouseDown: x > y when x = " + x + " y = " + y);
     }
   System.out.println
        ("mouseDown: all values when x = " + x + " y = " + y);
}
```

When this program is executed, it will be easy to notice that the first print statement is executed every time the second print statement is executed regardless of the value of x and y. This will help us narrow down the error to this part of the program.

Sometimes the processes of inserting print statements will make us take a closer look at the code, and the bug will be discovered without a need for a test run. Once the bug is corrected, the print statements can be removed or commented out so they can be used at some later time.

Notice that the name of the method is included in addition to the important values in the print statement. This convention helps keep track of which print statements caused the output.

REFERENCE

8.10   Summary

We finished our discussion about selection, which we started in Chapter 2. Algorithms for finding maximum and minimums are used to determine the order in which faces of a mesh are drawn. A mesh is a 3D representation of an object using polygons.

We were introduced to the `switch` statement as a specialized selection statement that can replace and improve on the `if` statement is some situations. In particular, we used the `switch` statement to implement the command alternative action pattern. This pattern is used to respond to user commands in a text-based system.

`switch` statements can be used only under special conditions. Case labels must be discrete constants: integers or characters. Control is transferred to a unique case label. Execution continues until a `break` statement is reached.

We also learned that the wise selection of known algorithms can help us create programs that are easy to understand and typically work effectively. Complexity analysis is used to measure efficiency. We looked at algorithms that fall into one of two categories, $O(1)$ and $O(n)$. Algorithms that are order of complexity of a constant, $O(1)$, take the same amount of time regardless of the input. They are typically better than algorithms that do the same thing but are $O(n)$. $O(n)$ algorithms take time proportional to the size of the data set.

We also learned that constant time optimization are often of little benefit. Optimization is a process that is applied only as a last resort.

Test data section criteria are an important component of this chapter. We learned how to assure statement, branch, and path coverage and how each helps us to find subtle errors. In addition, we looked at boundary testing. It is useful for detecting off-by-one errors.

8.11   Bibliography

- Gibbs, W. Wayt. 1994 Software's Chronic Crisis, . *Scientific American*, September, 86–95.
- Gosling, James with Bill Joy and Guy Steele. *The Java Language Specification*. Reading, MA: Addison Wesley, 1996.

- Leverson, Nancy G. *Safeware: System Safety and Computers*. Reading, MA: Addison Wesley, 1995.

- Littlewood, Bev and Lorenzo Strigini, *The Risks of Software*, Scientific American, November 1992, pp. 62-75.

- Neumann, Peter G. *Computer Related Risks*. Reading, MA: Addision Wesley, 1995.

  The examples from Section 8.7 come from this book.

- Oz, Effy. 1994. When Professional Standards are Lax: The CONFIRM Failure and its Lessons. *Communications of the ACM* 37 (October): 29–36

8.12   3D Library

Listing 8.16 `TDTriangle3D` **Class**

```
1  //*****************************************************************
2  // title:   TDTriangle3D
3  //
4  // A class to create, rotate, and paint 3D triangles.
5  //*****************************************************************
6
7  public class TDTriangle3D
8  {
9    //---------- TDTriangle3D ----------------------------------
10   // pre:  v0, v1, and v2 are valid 3D points and in a
11   //          clockwise order (viewing the font of a triangle)
12   // post: a 3D triangle is created with vertices (v0, v1, v2)
13   public TDTriangle3D (TDPoint3D v0, TDPoint3D v1,
14                       TDPoint3D v2, int id);
15
16   //---------- paint ----------------------------------------
17   // pre:  g is a valid graphics context
18   // post: this 3D triangle is drawn in g
19   public void paint (Graphics g);
20
```

REFERENCE

Listing 8.16 `TDTriangle3D` Class

```
21   //--------- rotateX -------------------------------------
22   // pre:  none
23   // post: rotate this triangle about the X axis
24     public void rotateX (double angle);
25
26   //--------- rotateY -------------------------------------
27   // pre:  none
28   // post: rotate this triangle about the Y axis
29     public void rotateY (double angle);
30
31   //--------- rotateZ -------------------------------------
32   // pre:  none
33   // post: rotate this triangle about the Z axis
34     public void rotateZ (double angle);
35
36   //--------- centroid ------------------------------------
37   // pre:  none
38   // post: the centroid point of this triangle is returned
39     public TDPoint3D centroid ();
40 }
```

Listing 8.17 `TDPoint3D` Class

```
1  //*************************************************************
2  // title:   TDPoint3D
3  //
4  // A class to create, manipulate, and paint 3D points.
5  //*************************************************************
6
7  public class TDPoint3D
8  {
9    //--------- TDPoint3D ------------------------------------
10   // pre:  none
11   // post: a 3D point is created at (x,y,z)
12   public TDPoint3D (double x, double y, double z)
13
14   //--------- TDPoint3D ------------------------------------
15   // pre:  none
16   // post: a 3D point is created at (0,0,0)
17   public TDPoint3D ()
18
19   //--------- distance ------------------------------------
20   // pre:  none
21   // post: distance of this point from p is returned
22   public double distance(TDPoint3D p)
23
```

Listing 8.17 `TDPoint3D` Class

```
24   //---------- equal ------------------------------------------
25   // pre:  none
26   // post: return true if the location of this point and p
27   //       are the same
28   public boolean equals(TDPoint3D p)
29
30   //---------- getX ------------------------------------------
31   // pre:  none
32   // post: the x component of this point is returned
33   public double getX ()
34
35   //---------- getY ------------------------------------------
36   // pre:  none
37   // post: the y component of this point is returned
38   public double getY ()
39
40   //---------- getZ ------------------------------------------
41   // pre:  none
42   // post: the z component of this point is returned
43   public double getZ ()
44
45   //---------- length ------------------------------------------
46   // pre:  none
47   // post: distance of the point from the axis origin is returned
48   public double length ()
49
50   //---------- minus ------------------------------------------
51   // pre:  none
52   // post: the difference of this point and p is returned
53   public TDPoint3D minus (TDPoint3D p)
54
55   //---------- plus ------------------------------------------
56   // pre:  none
57   // post: the sum of this point and p is returned
58   public TDPoint3D plus (TDPoint3D p)
59
```

Listing 8.17 TDPoint3D Class

```
60   //---------- rotateX ----------------------------------------
61   // pre:  none
62   // post: rotate this line about the X axis
63   public void rotateX (double angle)
64
65   //---------- rotateY ----------------------------------------
66   // pre:  none
67   // post: rotate this line about the Y axis
68   public void rotateY (double angle)
69
70   //---------- rotateZ ----------------------------------------
71   // pre:  none
72   // post: rotate this line about the Z axis
73   public void rotateZ (double angle)
74 }
```

PROBLEM SETS

8.13   Exercises

Algorithms—Section 8.3

1   Write an algorithm for

    a.   making a sandwich.

    b.   playing a tape in a VCR.

    c.   changing your automotive oil.

    d.   brushing your teeth each morning.

    e.   baking a cake.

2   Write an algorithm for computing the absolute value of an integer. The absolute value is a number without regard to its sign. For example, the absolute value of –23 is 23 and the absolute value of 45 is 45.

3   Rewrite the program in Listing 8.3 on page 351 to find the minimum value.

4   Which of the algorithms for finding the maximum of three numbers (Listing 8.9 through Listing 8.11) do you find easiest to understand and easiest to extend to more numbers? Why?

5   Rewrite Listing 8.10 so that it performs better when y has the greatest chance of being the largest.

6   Write a code fragment in Java for determining the minimum of three numbers. Use Listing 8.3 on page 351 as a guide.

7   Can you create an algorithm with fewer comparisons than the one in Listing 8.3 on page 351? If you can, show it.

8   Write a code fragment in Java to find the maximum of four numbers using the least number of comparisons. Indicate the number of comparisons required on average. Create a table similar to Table 8.1.

9   Does the following code find the maximum of three numbers? Test your hypothesis by walking though the code for each of the six possible orders of x, y, and z. What is the average number of comparisons required to find the maximum assuming all orders are equally likely? Does it make a difference if x==y or x==z or y==z?

```
int x   = ...;
int y   = ...;
int z   = ...;
int max = 0;

if (x > y)
  if (y > z)
    max = x;
  else
    if (x > z)
      max = x;
    else
      max = z;
  else
    if (x > z)
      max = y;
    else
      if (y > z)
        max = y;
      else
        max = z;
```

10   Rewrite the maximum code in Listing 8.5 so that it works with an empty file.

11   Rewrite the maximum code in Listing 8.5 so that it works with all integers, positive and negative.

    a.   Use the largest negative number as the sentinel.

    b.   The first number in the file is the number of numbers in the file. It may be zero but not negative.

    c.   If the number of numbers is zero, the maximum should be set to the largest negative number.

`Switch` **Statements—Section 8.5**

12 What is printed by the following statements:

a.
```
int m = 25;
switch (m)
{
  case 24: System.out.println("Portland");    break;
  case 17: System.out.println("Austin");      break;
  case 25: System.out.println("Lincoln");     break;
  case  8: System.out.println("Springfield"); break;
  default: System.out.println("Chicago");     break;
}
```

b.
```
int z = 16;
switch (z*2)
{
  case 4*8:    System.out.println("Computer Science"); break;
  case 33:     System.out.println("Software Engineering");
break;
  case 17 / 3: System.out.println("History"); break;
}
```

c.
```
int k = 33;
switch (k)
{
  case 100/4:  System.out.println("glass"); break;
  case 33:     System.out.println("paper");
  case 17*2:   System.out.println("steel");
  default:     System.out.println("water");
}
```

Computational Complexity—Section 8.6

13 What is the order of complexity of the following method?

```
public int square(int n)
{
  return n * n;
}
```

14 What is the order of complexity of the following method?

```
public int square(int n)
{
  int sum = 0;
  int i   = 0;
  while (i < n)
  {
    sum += n;
    i++;
  }
  return sum;
}
```

Software Safety—Section 8.7

15 Pick a mishap from chapter 2 of Neumann's *Computer Related Risks* (see bibliography in this chapter), write a summary, and describe how you would prevent the problem from recurring.

16 Go to the library and find additional information on the Therac-25 incident. Write a report on the causes of the its problems and how they might be prevented.

Test—Section 8.8

17 Create a test set that performs a minimum number of tests that will satisfy each of the following test coverage criteria. For example, the test set a == 40 and a == 50 will satisfy statement coverage.

a. statement coverage

b. branch coverage

c. path coverage

d. boundary coverage

```
if (a < 45)
  System.out.println("yes");
else
  System.out.println("no");
```

18 Repeat problem 17 for the following:
```
if (a > 73 & b == 10)
  System.out.println("east");
else
  System.out.println("west");
```

19   Repeat problem 17 for the following:

```
if (a != 18 | b >= 47)
   System.out.println("red");
else
   System.out.println("blue");
if (c < 5 | c > 11)
   System.out.println("green");
else
   System.out.println("yellow");
```

20   Find unexecutable paths (if any) in the following:

```
if (a > 73 | a <= 90)                // statement 1
   System.out.println("up");         // statement 2
else
   System.out.println("down");       // statement 3
```

21   Find unexecutable paths (if any) in the following.

```
if (a > 73 & a <= 90)                // statement 1
   System.out.println("up");         // statement 2
else
   System.out.println("down");       // statement 3
```

22   Find unexecutable paths (if any) in the following:

```
if (a == 100)                        // statement 1
   System.out.println("zip");        // statement 2
else
   System.out.println("zap");        // statement 3
if (a != 50)                         // statement 4
   System.out.println("flip");       // statement 5
else
   System.out.println("flap");       // statement 6
```

8.14 Projects

23   Modify the program in Listing 8.1 to display an octahecron (see figure at right). An octahedron is composed of eight equilateral triangles with vertices at: (60, 0, 60), (60, 0, –60), (–60, 0, 60), (–60, 0, –60), (0, 85, 0), and (0, –85, 0). See Section 8.12 for the 3D library interface.

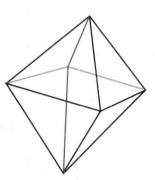

24   Modify the program in Listing 8.1 to display a cube. Each face requires two triangles. Thus, 12 triangles will be needed in all. See Section 8.12 for the 3D library interface.

25   Add a help command to the program in Listing 8.8. When a user types an "H" or "h," it should execute the `printInstructions` method.

26   Use the command action pattern to create a simple text-based calculator. It should support the following user interface (user responses are in bold). The program uses the ">" character as a prompt for a new user command.

```
Calculator commands.
  +: add
  -: subtract
  *: multiply
  /: divide
  h: help
  q: quit

> -
left operand:   24.53
right operand:  19.37
result:         5.16

> q
```

27   Write a program that displays 1000 random colored balls in the display window. Use a `switch` statement to map a random number to a color.

Computational Complexity—Section 8.6

28   Create a timing experiment to determine which of the algorithms in Listing 8.9 through Listing 8.11 (finding the maximum of three numbers) is the fastest. Write a full report that includes your hypothesis, procedure, results, and conclusions. Use the example in Section 7.7 , page 315 as a guide.

29 Create a timing experiment to compute the time required to execute the code in Listing 8.12 for various values of n. Write a full report that includes your hypothesis, procedure, results, and conclusions. Use the example in Section 7.7 , page 315 as a guide.

9 Iteration Algorithms

Graphing Stock Trends

SYMBOL	LAST	CHG	VOLUME	HIGH	LOW	%CHG	LINKS
COMS	26 7/8	-11/16	4,531,100	28 3/8	26 1/2	-2.50	H N O Q S
ADPT	11	-1 1/16	2,987,600	12	10 1/2	-8.81	H N O Q S
ADCT	34	+1/4	681,900	34 7/8	33 5/8	+0.74	H N O Q S
ADBE	37 9/16	-1 5/16	675,500	39 3/16	37 3/8	-3.37	H N O Q S
ADTN	25	+1/8	167,000	25 1/4	24 7/8	+0.50	H N O Q S
ALTR	37 1/4	+13/16	1,553,000	37 5/8	36 3/8	+2.23	H N O Q S
APCC	28 15/16	-1/16	348,300	29 1/4	28 1/4	-0.21	H N O Q S

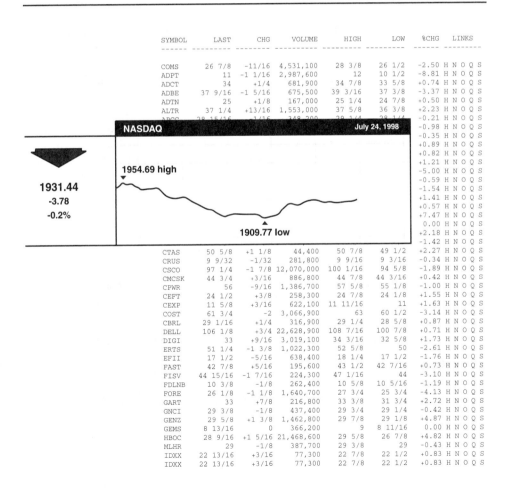

NASDAQ July 24, 1998

1954.69 high

1931.44
-3.78
-0.2%

1909.77 low

						-0.98	H N O Q S
						-0.35	H N O Q S
						+0.89	H N O Q S
						+0.82	H N O Q S
						+1.21	H N O Q S
						-5.00	H N O Q S
						-0.59	H N O Q S
						-1.54	H N O Q S
						+1.41	H N O Q S
						+0.57	H N O Q S
						+7.47	H N O Q S
						0.00	H N O Q S
						+2.18	H N O Q S
						-1.42	H N O Q S
CTAS	50 5/8	+1 1/8	44,400	50 7/8	49 1/2	+2.27	H N O Q S
CRUS	9 9/32	-1/32	281,800	9 9/16	9 3/16	-0.34	H N O Q S
CSCO	97 1/4	-1 7/8	12,070,000	100 1/16	94 5/8	-1.89	H N O Q S
CMCSK	44 3/4	+3/16	886,800	44 7/8	44 3/16	+0.42	H N O Q S
CPWR	56	-9/16	1,386,700	57 5/8	55 1/8	-1.00	H N O Q S
CEFT	24 1/2	+3/8	258,300	24 7/8	24 1/8	+1.55	H N O Q S
CEXP	11 5/8	+3/16	622,100	11 11/16	11	+1.63	H N O Q S
COST	61 3/4	-2	3,066,900	63	60 1/2	-3.14	H N O Q S
CBRL	29 1/16	+1/4	316,900	29 1/4	28 5/8	+0.87	H N O Q S
DELL	106 1/8	+3/4	22,628,900	108 7/16	100 7/8	+0.71	H N O Q S
DIGI	33	+9/16	3,019,100	34 3/16	32 5/8	+1.73	H N O Q S
ERTS	51 1/4	-1 3/8	1,022,300	52 5/8	50	-2.61	H N O Q S
EFII	17 1/2	-5/16	638,400	18 1/4	17 1/2	-1.76	H N O Q S
FAST	42 7/8	+5/16	195,600	43 1/2	42 7/16	+0.73	H N O Q S
FISV	44 15/16	-1 7/16	224,300	47 1/16	44	-3.10	H N O Q S
FDLNB	10 3/8	-1/8	262,400	10 5/8	10 5/16	-1.19	H N O Q S
FORE	26 1/8	-1 1/8	1,640,700	27 3/4	25 3/4	-4.13	H N O Q S
GART	33	+7/8	216,800	33 3/8	31 3/4	+2.72	H N O Q S
GNCI	29 3/8	-1/8	437,400	29 3/4	29 1/4	-0.42	H N O Q S
GENZ	29 5/8	+1 3/8	1,462,800	29 7/8	29 1/8	+4.87	H N O Q S
GEMS	8 13/16	0	366,200	9	8 11/16	0.00	H N O Q S
HBOC	28 9/16	+1 5/16	21,468,600	29 5/8	26 7/8	+4.82	H N O Q S
MLHR	29	-1/8	387,700	29 3/8	29	-0.43	H N O Q S
IDXX	22 13/16	+3/16	77,300	22 7/8	22 1/2	+0.83	H N O Q S
IDXX	22 13/16	+3/16	77,300	22 7/8	22 1/2	+0.83	H N O Q S

9.1   Objectives

Concepts   Section 9.2, page 393

We begin by using various looping patterns to take a rudimentary look at stock trends.

Section 9.5, page 422

The supplementary section in this chapter builds on our work in the previous chapter by creating test data sets that exercise loops. Statement, branch, and path coverage are used as techniques to evaluate test data selection.

Patterns   Section 9.3, page 399

The primary benefit of the stock graphing program is to provide a backdrop for revisiting and introducing looping patterns. We begin by looking at several sentinel and counter loop patterns that we have used before. We also use the pattern for finding extreme values from the previous chapter. To these we add patterns that find averages and smooth graphs.

Finally, we take a look at a couple of loop patterns that are related to the stock analysis example. In one pattern we assume some property is true and then look at all possible cases until our assumption is shown true or until we find a counter example that proves our assumption false. We also look at a pattern that visits all the pixels in an image or display.

Java Skills

We follow this by exploring several special Java statements that support the various algorithmic patterns.

- `break` statement   Section 9.4.1, page 410
- `for` statement   Section 9.4.2, page 413
- `do` statement   Section 9.4.3, page 416
- `try` statement   Section 9.4.6, page 418

Abilities

- Write loops using any of the Java syntax forms.
- Create test data sets that provide test coverage for looping statements.

CONCEPTS

9.2   A Hardware Glitch

9.2.1   Sequence of Events

On November 7, 1994, a mathematics professor published a report that a computer processor contained a floating-point flaw. During the next six weeks, the manufacturer was faced with the problem of how to respond to its customers and stock holders. Table 9.1 is an abbreviated summary of how these events played out.

Table 9.1 Major Events Responding to a Hardware Glitch

date	event
November 7, 1994	Professor publishes problem about computer processor.
November 25, 1994	Reports surface that many scientists are angered by a slow response to the problem.
November 29, 1994	The manufacturer's CEO defends a conditional replacement policy for heavy users only. He explains that errors occur infrequently.
December 12, 1994	Announcements surface that errors could occur more frequently than had been projected. Some vendors halt shipments of computers based on the new processor.
December 20, 1994	The manufacturer establishes a "no questions asked" return policy at an expected cost of $200 million.

All products have flaws. Flaws arise from mistakes in design, the incorrect implementation of a design, and problems during manufacturing. When a new product is released, each company has made a critical decision. It has determined that the product is reliable enough to serve its clients. It is hoped that the flaws that remain will not distract significantly from its value. A company may have concluded that performing additional quality assurances will make the product less attractive by raising its cost and that a delay in release may cost market share.

Sometimes an error slips through that is not minor. A company's reputation is built on how it responds to these situations. A response typically depends on the severity of the problem and the cost of a solution. For example, if a word processor infrequently displays a menu item in the wrong color, a fix can wait until the next release. However, if a word processor corrupts its documents in one out of ten saves, a product recall is in order.

The product recall described above was expected to cost $200 million and the manufacturer felt that the error would result in infrequent floating-point errors. It is not surprising that they hesitated to initially provide a "no-questions-asked" refund policy. However, public perception of the problem was different than expected. Thus, the manufacturer changed its policy. It decided to recall its processors and eventually absorbed a $475 million write-off.

Public perception is important to a company. It needed to know how its response to the processor flaw affected its short- and long-term profitability. One indicator that measures a company's public perception is its stock prices. In this section we will see what clues we can gather about the public's perception of a manufacturer by taking a cursory look at its stock prices before and after the problem became public.

The stock market is difficult to analyze. Stock prices are governed by world events, national monetary policies, and a corporation's day-to-day decisions. In this section. we will use primitive techniques to take a look at stock prices and the NASDAQ composite index to see if we can make any conclusions. Because the techniques that we are using are primitive, we must be careful about any conclusions we draw.

Figure 9.1 graphs our manufacturer's stock prices from October 3, 1994, to January 31, 1995. Five vertical lines that correspond to the five dates given in Table 9.1 have been added to the graph. The announcement of a problem with the processor does not appear to have affected the stock market. However, bad publicity of how the company was handling the problem, Lines 2 and 4, coincides with a downturn. When the manufacturer announced their unconditional replacement policy, its stock returned to an upward trend. This appears to support the idea that how a company handles a problem is important to stock holders. The fact that a solution was expected to cost $200 million does not appear to be an issue.

The top graph in Figure 9.2 shows the change in the manufacturer's stock prices during the same period described above. Points above the zero axis indicate a rise in prices. Those points below the axis indicate a drop in prices. Some of the noise was removed from the graph by averaging each point over a seven day period. Thus, each point represents the change is stock prices for a given day averaged with the previous three and next three days. We can see that the change in stock prices between the November 25 and December 12 events was negative.

CONCEPTS

Figure 9.1 The company's stocks 10-3-94 to 1-31-95

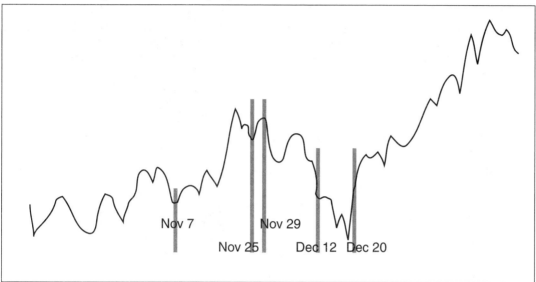

Figure 9.2 Averaged company and NASDAQ stock change

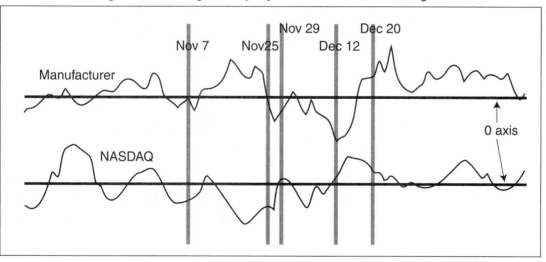

Before we become too satisfied with our analysis and go on to take a look at loops, let us take a another look at this problem. How do we know that other events in the world are not the cause of the fluctuation in the manufacturer's stocks? We can take a look at some indicator of how other stocks are doing. One such indicator is the NASDAQ index, which is based on the performance of 100 selected stocks. Figure 9.2 shows the change in the NASDAQ index in the same period. It shows a general negative trend in the stock market from November 7 through December 7. This raises some interesting questions.

- Are the trends in the manufacturer's stocks and the NASDAQ index related?
- Did the performance of the general market play a more important role than the hardware problems?
- Did the hardware problem have a market-wide impact?

Thomas Bundt and Todd Shank of the University of Portland analyzed the affects the processor flaw had on the manufacturer's stock prices. Using the events surrounding the crisis, they applied the event study methodology to determine stock risk. They uncovered no change in the manufacturer's long-term stock risk. They also suggested the following:

- Investors care about a firm's willingness to unconditionally guarantee a product.
- Investors care more about how a problem is handled than the problem.

9.2.2   Graphing Stocks

Listing 9.1 contains the code for displaying the graph shown in Figure 9.1. It depends on several classes that hide details about reading from files and creating graphs. For reference, the details of the `StockPriceFile` can be found in Section 12.10 on page 588 and `StockPrice` classes can be found in this chapter's reference section (Listing 9.20 on page 429). These classes are responsible for reading stock prices from a file and for storing the manufacturer, NASDAQ, and Standard and Poor's 500 prices for a given day. The `VGraphFrame` class works similar to the `VGraph` class described in Appendix: C on page 914.

Our strategy for graphing stocks will be to implement the loop and a half pattern from Chapter 5. We will read information from a stock file until a `null StockPrice` object is returned. Null signifies the end of file. The basic form of the loop is shown below.

```
loop                // loop and a half with null sentinel
  get a data item from the file
  exit if a data item could not be retrieved because
    of an end-of-file condition
  process the data item
end loop
```

Listing 9.1 Stock code

```
1  //****************************************************************
2  //
3  // title:   Stocks
4  //
5  // Plot stock prices starting 10-3-94 and ending 1-31-95.
6  //
7  //****************************************************************
8
9  import java.awt.Color;
10 import java.io.FileNotFoundException;
11 import java.io.IOException;
12 import vista.VGraphFrame;
13
14 public class Stocks
15 {
16   //---------- main ------------------------------------------
17   public static void main(String[] args)
18   {
19     try
20     {
21       // Open the stock file and create a graph
22       StockPriceFile priceFile = new
23                 StockPriceFile("Stock.prices");
24       VGraphFrame plot = new VGraphFrame(0, 84, 50, 90);
25       plot.addLine(Color.blue);
26
27       // Add stock prices to graph
28       int day = 0;
29       while (true)
30       {
31         StockPrice dailyReport = priceFile.read();
32         if (dailyReport == null)
33           break;
34       plot.addPoint(day++,dailyReport.getManufacturePrice());
35       }
36       plot.repaint();
37     }
38     // Handle IO errors
39     catch (FileNotFoundException e)
40     {
41       System.out.println("File not found");
42     }
43     catch (IOException e)
44     {
45       System.out.println("IO Error");
46     }
47   }
48 }
```

In Listing 9.1 we open a stock price file by creating a `stockPriceFile` object in Lines 22 and 23. Next we read items from this file by implementing the above loop (Lines 29 through 35). Most of the details about working with files have been hidden in `stock-PriceFile` to simplify our discussion.

Notice that all the code for reading from a file is placed within an *exception handler*. Exception handlers respond to events that should not occur. Our exception handler is implemented with the `try` statement, which begins in Line 19. If a file-not-found or IO exception occurs between Lines 20 and 35, one of the `catch` clauses in Lines 39 and 43 will be executed. For example, if we try to open a file but give it an incorrect file name, a `FileNotFoundException` occurs. A message specified in Line 41 will be printed, indicating the file could not be opened. Exception handlers are designed to prevent a program from crashing if something bad happens. More details about exception handlers is given in Section 9.4.6.

PATTERNS

9.3   Looping Patterns

In the previous section we took advantage of the loop and a half pattern to read from a file. We will explore a couple of other strategies for reading from a file within this section. We will also use the pattern for finding extreme values to help us locate minimum and maximum stock price values. Finally we will introduce several new patterns. One will help us find the average stock price and the second will help us smooth graphs. The final two patterns are not associated with the stock price program. They find prime numbers and scan all the pixels in a display.

Listing 9.2   Using Sentinel Values to Terminate Input

```
1   // Throw everything away through 9-30-94
2   StockPrice dailyReport;
3   do
4      dailyReport = priceFile.read();
5   while (!dailyReport.getDate().equals("9/30/94"));
6
7   // Add stock prices to graph through 1-31-95
8   int day = 0;
9   while (true)
10  {
11     dailyReport = priceFile.read();
12     if (dailyReport.getDate().equals("2/1/95"))
13        break;
14     plot.addPoint(day++, dailyReport.getManufacturePrice());
15  }
```

9.3.1   Variant Forms of the Input Loop

We used an end-of-file sentinel to end our loop and a half input statement in Listing 9.1. We could also use a specific data value for the sentinel. This approach is shown in Listing 9.2. In this example, a stock price input file that contains stock values from April 11, 1994, through April 20, 1995, is used. To narrow the graph to the same four-month period used in the previous program we use two loops terminated with sentinel values. Data is thrown away in the first loop until the October 3 record is ready to be read. (The do loop is covered in Section 9.4.3.) Then a second loop that plots the data is entered. This loop terminates when the February 1 record is read. The major change in the loops is the exit condition.

Another method for terminating an input loop is to use the counter loop pattern. It is outlined below:

```
// counter input loop
loop a given number of times
  get a data item from the file
  process the data item
end loop
```

Listing 9.3 implements a counter loop for input. The first loop throws away the first 121 records. (The `for` loop is covered in Section 9.4.2.) The second loop plots the next 84 records. The result is the same as those in Listing 9.1 and Listing 9.2.

Listing 9.3 Using a Counter-controlled Loop to Terminate Input

```
1   // Throw everything away through 9-30-94
2   for (int day=0; day<121; day++)
3   {
4     StockPrice dailyReport = priceFile.read();
5   }
6
7   // Add stock prices to graph through 1-31-95
8   for (int day=0; day<84; day++)
9   {
10    StockPrice dailyReport = priceFile.read();
11    plot.addPoint(day, dailyReport.getManufacturePrice());
12  }
```

The counter loop pattern is used so often in programs that many languages provide a special counter loop statement to make their implementation easier. Java has a `for` loop, which is designed for this purpose. The `for` loop in Line 2 of Listing 9.3 executes its body 121 times. The `for` loop is discussed in more detail in Section 9.4.2.

Notice that the code fragments in Listing 9.2 and Listing 9.3 will behave in an unknown manner if sentinel values are not found or if record counts are wrong. There are two viewpoints for dealing with this issue. One is that if sentinel or count values are incorrect, it is reasonable that the program will not behave as expected. Therefore, it is OK if the program aborts. In general this is not a good approach. None of us likes a program that aborts. A better view is that a program should behave in a well-defined manner regardless of file problems or user misuse. Exception handlers are ideal for this use. They can be incorporated to handle any unexpected problems. Modifying the program so it responds to these file problems is left as an exercise.

9.3.2   Minimums and Maximums

Now let us move on to another application of a pattern we were introduced to in Chapter 8. Programs that automatically scale graphs need to determine minimum and maximum values. In addition, it may also be instructive to know when a stock has reached its minimum or maximum value. Listing 9.4 implements finding both the minimum and maximum stock price.

Listing 9.4   Minimum and Maximum

```
1    // Open the stock file and create a graph
2    StockPriceFile priceFile = new
3             StockPriceFile("Stock.prices");
4    StockPrice dailyReport = priceFile.read();
5    if (dailyReport == null)
6      System.out.println ("Empty file");
7    else
8    {
9     // Assume first price is the max and min
10    double min = dailyReport.getManufacturePrice();
11    double max = dailyReport.getManufacturePrice();
12    // Look at all remaining prices and reset min and max as
13    // required

14    while (true)
15    {
16      dailyReport = priceFile.read();
17      if (dailyReport == null)
18        break;
19      double price = dailyReport.getManufacturePrice();
20      if (price < min)
21        min = price;
22      if (price > max)
23        max = price;
24    }

25
26    // Display results
27    System.out.println("Min is: " + min + "      Max is: " + max);
28 }
```

Notice the empty file check. Many programs behave unexpectedly with empty files. This program begins by assuming the first item in a file is its minimum and maximum value. If the file were empty, we are not sure what value it would return. An empty file should not report a maximum or minimum.

9.3.3 Averages

Finding the average of a list of items is another well used pattern. The basic strategy is to find the total of all the items and divide by the number of items. First, we initialize a running sum and set count to zero. Then we add each data value to the sum. Finally, we divide the sum by the number of records. This pattern is outlined below and shown in Listing 9.5.

Listing 9.5 Average Stock Price

```
1   // Initialize variables for computing average
2   StockPriceFile priceFile = new
3               StockPriceFile("Stock.prices");
4   double total = 0.0;
5   int     day   = 0;
6
7   // Compute total and number of stock prices
8   while (true)
9   {
10    StockPrice dailyReport = priceFile.read();
11    if (dailyReport == null)
12      break;
13    total += dailyReport.getManufacturePrice();
14    day++;
15  }
16
17  // Display results
18  if (day == 0)
19    System.out.println("Empty file");
20  else
21  {
22    double average = total / (double)day;
23    System.out.println("Average is: " + average);
24  }
```

```
// finding average
initialize sum to zero
initialize the count to zero
loop
  get a data item from the file
  add it to the sum
  add one to the count
end loop
compute average by dividing sum by the count
```

Notice the empty file check. If not checked, an empty file will cause a divide by zero exception.

9.3.4 Smoothing a Graph

The daily fluctuations in the stock market can make trends hard to see. For example, the top graph in Figure 9.3 shows the daily change in stocks without averaging. One method of filtering out daily fluctuations is to apply a smoothing operation to data. The smoothing technique used in the bottom graph in Figure 9.3 averages each point in the data stream with the three data points before and after it. Thus, wild daily swings are moderated. It corresponds to the top graph in Figure 9.2. A pattern for smoothing a graph is shown below. In this example, each point is averaged with one point before and after it.

Figure 9.3 Change in stock prices

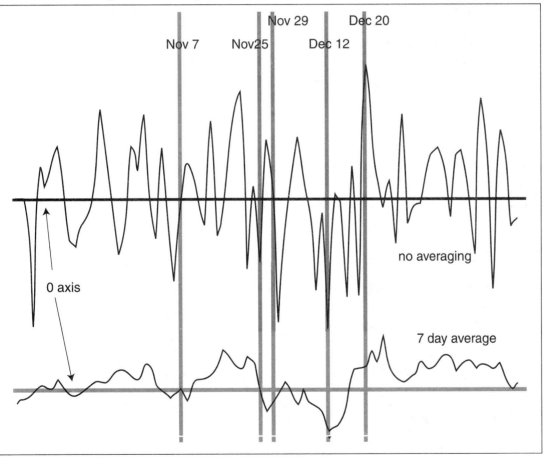

```
// smoothing a graph
get first data item and plot it
get next data item
loop
  get next data item from the file
  average this data item with the previous two
  plot the average as the previous point
end loop
plot last data point
```

This technique is implemented in Listing 9.6. It smooths the current stock price with the stock price before and after it. Notice the code necessary to maintain the three points needed for averaging.

Listing 9.6 Plotting Smooth Graphs

```
1    // Before loop set up.
2    double leftPoint    = 0.0;
3    double middlePoint  = 0.0;
4    double rightPoint   = 0.0;
5    double averagePoint = 0.0;
6    int day = 0;
7
8    // Plot first point
9    StockPrice dailyReport = priceFile.read();
10   middlePoint = dailyReport.getManufacturePrice();
11   plot.addPoint(day++, middlePoint);
12
13   // Set up for averaging
14   dailyReport = priceFile.read();
15   leftPoint    = dailyReport.getManufacturePrice();
16
17   // Add stock prices to graph
18   while (true)
19   {
20     dailyReport  = priceFile.read();
21     if (dailyReport == null)
22        break;
23     rightPoint   = middlePoint;
24     middlePoint  = leftPoint;
25     leftPoint    = dailyReport.getManufacturePrice();
26    averagePoint = (leftPoint + middlePoint + rightPoint) / 3.0;
27     plot.addPoint(day++, averagePoint);
28   }
29
30   // Plot last point
31   plot.addPoint(day++, leftPoint);
```

Algorithms that use a previous or future data point to compute a current value often contain special cases. They must handle beginning data values that have no predecessor values and ending data values that have no successor values. This is accomplished in Listing 9.6 by including pre- and post-loop code to handle the special cases. However, the code does not behave correctly if there are fewer than three data records in a file. Correcting this problem is left as an exercise.

9.3.5   Assume and Find a Negative Case

Computers are good at tedious tasks. For example, if we want to find all the prime numbers between 2 and 100, we need to look at each one and decide whether it has any divisors other than 1 and itself.

The process for finding a prime number is related to that for finding an extreme value. When we find an extreme value we begin by assuming the first number we look at is the extreme value. Next we look at each number in turn. If our next number is a new extreme we adjust our assumption.

We will solve the prime number problem by looking at each number in turn. We will assume that the current number is prime and hunt for its factors. If we find one, we know our assumption is false and discard the number. The prime number program is an example of a pattern in which we assume something is true and then look at all cases for a negative. If nothing disproves our initial assumption, the assumption of truth stands. This pattern is shown below.

```
// disprove a true assumption
assume something is true
while there are new cases
  generate a new case
  if it violates our assumption
    our assumption is false
    exit
end loop
```

A program for finding the positive prime numbers less than 100 is in Listing 9.7. Table 9.2 shows a walkthrough for one iteration of the outer loop. The block in Lines 7 through 10 is executed only if a `number` is not prime. For example, 15 is not prime because `15 % 3 == 0`. Eleven, on the other hand, is prime. It is prime because we cannot find a number from 2 through 3 that is its factor. The number 2 is not a factor because `11 % 2` is 1. In addition `11 % 3` is 2 not 0. Thus, we assumed that 11 was prime and our assumption held.

Listing 9.7 Prime Numbers

```
1  for (int number = 2; number < 100; number++)
2  {
3    boolean prime = true;
4    for (int i=2; i <= (int)Math.sqrt(number); i++)
5    {
6      if (number % i == 0)
7      {
8        prime = false;
9        break;
10     }
11   }
12   if (prime)
13     System.out.println(number);
14 }
```

Table 9.2 Walk-through of Inner Loop for Number = 15

	Values of		
Line number	number	i	prime
3	15	?	true
4	15	2	true
5	15	2	true
6	15	2	true
11	15	3	true
5	15	3	true
6	15	3	true
7	15	3	true
8	15	3	false
9	15	3	false
12	15	3	false
13	15	3	false

9.3.6   Raster Scan Pattern

The pattern in the previous section has a nested loop. We may also use a nested loop when we scan all the pixels in a display. Image filters for programs such as Adobe Photoshop use this basic pattern. For example, a filter that converts a color image to a grayscale image visits each pixel in the image, averages the red, green, and blue values of that pixel, and resets each color component to that average. In our raster scan pattern the inner loop visits each pixel in a row and the outer loop visits each row.

```
// Raster scan pattern
loop by rows
  loop by columns
    manipulate a pixel
  end loop
end loop
```

We will use this pattern to create a program that blends color across a window. It begins by placing a black pixel in the upper left corner of the window. It scans the window from left to right, slowly adding blue until the upper right corner is completely blue. With each subsequent row we add a little red until the last row contains the maximum red value. Figure 9.4 shows a black and white rendition of what occurs .

Figure 9.4 Color Blend Image

Figure 9.5 shows how a display four pixels wide by three pixels high would be colored. Notice how the blue values change from left to right and the red values change from top to bottom. We can imagine that as the number of pixels in a display grows that each color's

Figure 9.5 Color Distribution

Y \ X	0	1	2	3
0	(0,0,0) black	(0,0,85)	(0,0,170)	(255,0,255) blue
1	(127,0,0)	(127,0,85)	(127,0,170)	(127,0,85)
2	(255,0,0) red	(255,0,85)	(255,0,170)	(255,0,255) magenta

Table 9.3 Example Run: Width = 4, Height = 3

location		color		
x	y	red	green	blue
0	0	0	0	0
1	0	0	0	85
2	0	0	0	170
3	0	0	0	255
0	1	127	0	0
1	1	127	0	85
2	1	127	0	170
3	1	127	0	255
0	2	255	0	0
1	2	255	0	85
2	2	255	0	170
3	2	255	0	255

value would change more slowly between pixels. Table 9.3 puts these numbers in a linear table format. It steps through the colors in the same order our program will scan.

Listing 9.8 shows the code necessary to create any sized display. The inner loop, Lines 21 through 27, scans a single row pixel by pixel. It uses a counter loop to iterate through a pixel's x location. The outer loop, Lines 18 through 28, scans the display row by row. It uses a counter loop to iterate through a row's y location.

Listing 9.8 Scanning All the Pixels in a Display

```
1   //*********************************************************
2   //
3   // title:   ColorBlend
4   //
5   // Assign each pixel in an applet window a unique color.
6   //
7   //*********************************************************
8   import java.awt.Color;
9   import java.awt.Dimension;
10  import java.awt.Graphics;
11  import java.applet.Applet;
12
13  public class ColorBlend extends Applet {
14
15    public void paint (Graphics g)
16    {
17      Dimension d = getSize();
18      for (int y = 0; y < d.height; y++)
19      {
20        int red = (y * 255) / (d.height - 1);
21        for (int x = 0; x < d.width; x++)
22        {
23          int blue = (x * 255) / (d.width - 1);
24          Color c = new Color(red, 0, blue);
25          g.setColor(c);
26          g.fillRect(x, y, 1, 1);
27        }
28      }
29    }
30  }
```

JAVA

9.4   Iteration

We have been using loops since their introduction in Section 2.7.4. We can write any loop we choose using the `while` statement introduced there. However, there are loop patterns that occur so frequently that special Java loop structures have been created to make implementing these patterns easier. An example is the counter loop pattern, which is easily implemented with the Java `for` statement.

Within this section, we will expand our knowledge of the `break` statement, introduce the `for` and `do` loop statements, and look at how Java handles exceptions.

9.4.1   Break Statement

There are two ways to get out of a loop. One method is to make the loop condition false. The second method is abort a loop with a `break` statement. We were introduced to the `break` statement method with the introduction of the loop and a half pattern in Chapter 5. For example, Listing 9.9 shows how a break statement can be used to exit a loop that sums integers until a negative sentinel is encountered.

Listing 9.9   Sum Inputs until Negative Sentinel—Version 1

```
1 int sum = 0;
2 while (true)
3 {
4    int value = io.readInt();
5    if (value < 0)
6       break;
7    sum += value;
8 }
```

In Section 8.5.1 we also saw a `break` statement used to transfer control out of a `switch` statement. A `break` statement causes an abrupt statement completion of the statement in which it is embedded. The rules are rather complicated but follow common sense. For the sake of brevity, we will simply say that a `break` statement transfers control out of the innermost enclosing `switch`, `while`, `for`, or `do` statement.

As mentioned in Section 4.3.2 on page 136 there is an ongoing controversy about the wisdom of using breaks to abort loops. For example, some people prefer to rewrite the loop in

Listing 9.9 as the one in Listing 9.10. The advantage of this form is that the conditions for loop exit can be specified in only one location, the loop conditional, and the body of the loop can be viewed as a single unit. Other people feel that the loop and a half pattern is more natural for many applications. In particular, the repeated code in Lines 2 and 6 is objectionable to some.

Listing 9.10 Sum Inputs until Negative Sentinel—Version 2

```
1 int sum = 0;
2 int value = io.readInt();
3 while (value >= 0)
4 {
5    sum += value;
6    int value = io.readInt();
7 }
```

One fear of introducing breaks is that it may be abused. A loop with too many breaks can be difficult to understand and formally analyze. The following are some rules of thumb that may be helpful when using breaks.

1. Giving a loop two or more ways of exiting is confusing. Try to avoid that situation. One should be able to look at the loop conditional and determine under what circumstances a loop is exited. A loop with a true loop condition, such as the one in Listing 9.9, communicates that the loop must have another method of exit. Otherwise, the loop conditional communicates under what conditions a loop is executed.

2. A `for` loop normally already has an exit condition. Therefore, placing a break within a `for` loop violates the previous rule and should be avoided. An obvious exception is the loop forever form of the `for` loop: `for(;;)`. We violated this rule in Listing 9.7 on page 406. The author felt that converting an inner `for` loop to a single exit loop would make the code confusing.

3. Responding to exceptions may be one reason for breaking the above rules. For example, the `for` loop in Listing 9.3 may have a break that responds to an unexpected end-of-file situation. We may also use a `break` statement to exit a search loop after finding an item of interest.

4. On the other hand, if a `break` statement makes a loop simpler and easier to understand, use it.

Sometimes poor placement of a `break` statement will result in code that cannot be executed. Java compilers will carry out analysis to determine whether statements are reachable. For example, the following is not allowed:

```
{
   int x = 10;
   break;
   int y = 22;    // unreachable
}
```

Because the declaration of y is not reachable, the compiler will flag the above as an error. However, the compiler may not discover the following declaration of y as unreachable.

```
{
   int x = 10;
   if (x == 10)
      break;
   int y = 22;
}
```

A break aborts the inner most loop that contains it. For example, the loops below contain three nested loops:

```
1   // Avoid code like this
2   int x = 0;
3   while (true)
4   {
5     int y = 0;
6     while (true)
7     {
8       int z = 0;
9       while (true)
10      {
11        if (z > 10)
12          break;
13        z++;
14      }
15      if (y > 10)
16        break;
17      y++;
18    }
19    if (x > 5)
20      break;
21    x++;
22  }
```

The break in Line 12 will cause the loop at Line 9 to abort. Control will jump to Line 15. The break in Line 16 will cause the loop at Line 6 to abort. Control will jump to Line 19. The above code fragment demonstrates how breaks can make code confusing. It is easy to lose track of where we are. Avoid writing code like this. The following equivalent code is easier to understand.

```
1  int x = 0;
2  while (x <= 5)
3  {
4    int y = 0;
5    while (y <= 10)
6    {
7      int z = 0;
8      while (z <= 10)
9      {
10       z++;
11     }
12     y++;
13   }
14   x++;
15 }
```

Breaks can be labeled such as in the example below. A label is placed in front of a statement. It is an identifier followed by a colon such as the one seen in Line 2. A corresponding labeled `break` statement must be enclosed within this loop. In this code the break at Line 8 drops out of two loops to resume execution after Line 12.

```
1  int x = 0;
2  leave: while (true)
3  {
4    int y = 0;
5    while (true)
6    {
7      if (x > 5 && y > 8)
8        break leave;
9      y++;
10   }
11   x++;
12 }
```

One common convention is to label all `break` statements. Others, such as the author, do not use labeled breaks.

9.4.2   For Statement

Counter loops, such as the ones in Listing 9.3, appear so often that there is a special loop statement for them. Listing 9.11 shows an example in which a counter loop is used to sum the first 10 integers.

The `for` statement is a specialized loop that is useful for counting.

```
for ( InitStatement ; BooleanExpression ; UpdateStatement )
    BodyStatement
```

Listing 9.11 Computing the Sum of the First 10 Integers—Using a `for` Loop

```
1 int     n   = 10;
2 double sum  = 0.0;
3 for (int i = 0; i < n; i++)
4 {
5    sum += n;
6 }
```

1. The `InitStatement` is executed once when the `for` loop is first started. The typical role of the `InitStatement` is to initialize a loop counter. It may be a list of statements separated with commas.

2. Next `BooleanExpression` is executed. If it is true, we go to step 3. Otherwise we are done. The typical role of `BooleanExpression` is to test `for` loop exit.

3. The `BodyStatement`, the loop body, is executed.

4. The `UpdateStatement` is executed after the loop body. The typical role of the `UpdateStatement` is to eventually cause a change which will make the `BooleanExpression` become false so the loop can terminate. The `UpdateStatement` may be a list of statements separated with commas.

5. The process repeats at step 2.

A `for` loop can be replaced with a `while` loop using the following template.:

```
InitStatement ;
while ( BooleanExpression )
{
  BodyStatement ;
  UpdateStatement ;
}
```

As a result, every `for` loop can be easily transformed into an equivalent `while` loop. The `for` loop is called "syntactic sugar" because it adds little expressive power to a programming language. Its primary benefit is convenience.

Placing `break` statements and extra incrementers in a `for` loop can make a loop hard to understand. Avoid doing the following.

```
1 // a confusing loop - bad style
2 int    n   = 50;
3 for (int 1 = 1; i <= n; i+=3)
4 {
5   i++;                        // bad idea
6   System.out.println (i);
7   if (i > 20)
8     break;
9   i++;                        // bad idea
10 }
```

The loop above is syntactically correct . It will execute with the following output: 2, 7, 12, 17, 22. However, the loop takes a moment more to understand than it should because i is incremented in three places: Lines 3, 5, and 9.

Any of the `for` loop expressions and statements can be null. If they are all null, the loop is infinite. The following loop will print "Again" forever.

```
for (;;)
  System.out.println("Again");
```

The result is the same as the following `while` loop:

```
while (true)
  System.out.println("Again");
```

The potential problems we listed with `while` loops in Section 2.7.7 can also appear in `for` loops. For example, the `println` statement is not part of the loop in the following code because of a badly placed semicolon. The only value printed is 10 when the intent is to print the values 0 through 9:

```
int i;
for (i=0; i<10; i++);
  System.out.println(i);
```

The following code contains a syntax error that may at first appear mysterious. The scope of the identifier i is the `for` statement. The semicolon in the first line ends the `for` statement. Because the `print` statement is not within the `for` statement, i cannot be used within the `print` statement.

```
for (int i=0; i<10; i++);
  System.out.println(i);
```

9.4.3 Do Statements

There is another form of the loop called the do statement. It is similar to the while statement but has the loop condition check at the end of the loop. It is useful in those situations where a loop must execute at least one time. An example can be found in Listing 9.2 on page 399. Its form is shown below:

```
do
  Statement
while ( BooleanExpression )
```

A do loop is equivalent to the following while loop:

```
Statement
while ( BooleanExpression )
  Statement      // same statement as above
```

Using a do statement avoids repeated code in those cases where a statement must be executed one or more times. In the following example the user is prompted for data at least once. If the program user types inappropriate information, the prompt and read are repeated.

```
double tripStart = 0.0;
double tripEnd   = 0.0;
do
  io.print ("Enter beginning trip odometer reading: ");
  tripStart = io.readDouble();
while (tripStart < 0.0);
do
  io.print ("Enter ending trip odometer reading:    ");
  tripEnd = io.readDouble();
while (tripEnd < tripStart);
```

9.4.4 Choosing a Loop statement

Given that a while loop can be used to implement all loops, we may wonder when we should use a for or do loop.

- A for loop is a good candidate to implement counter loops.

- A do loop is a good candidate if a statement must be executed one or more times.

- A while loop is a good candidate for all other situations.

9.4.5 Nested Loops

The raster scan patterns we described in Section 9.3.6 contain a nested loop. Nested loops appear frequently in programs. We saw a couple of examples of nested loops in Section 2.7.6. Let us quickly review how they work and then look at a strategy for avoiding them.

Listing 9.12 Fill Rectangle with Walkthrough

code	Line number	Values of x	y
	1	1	?
	3	?	1
`1  public void fillARect ()`	5	1	1
`2  {`	7	1	1
`3    for (int y = 1; y <= 3; y++)`	5	2	1
`4    {`	7	2	1
`5      for (int x = 1; x <= 4; x++)`	5	3	1
`6      {`	7	3	1
`7        g.fillRect(x, y, 1, 1);`	5	4	1
`8      }`	7	4	1
`9    }`	5	5	1
`10 }`	3	?	2
	5	1	2
	7	1	2
	5	2	2
	7	2	2
	5	3	2
	7	3	2
	5	4	2
	7	4	2
	5	5	2
	3	?	3
	5	1	3
	7	1	3
	5	2	3
	7	2	3
	5	3	3
	7	3	3
	5	4	3
	7	4	3
	5	5	3
	3	?	4
	exit	?	?

Listing 9.12 is an example of a nested loop that implements the raster scan pattern. It creates a rectangle by drawing three rows of four pixels. Each pixel is drawn with a rectangle that is one pixel by one pixel wide. The walkthrough of this code is shown to its right and provides us with a good review of how nested loops work.

Now that we understand how nested loops work, let us see how to get rid of them. Nested loops can be confusing. They present us with too much detail at one time. Some people suggest getting rid of nested loops by replacing the inner loop with a method call. For example, the nested loop in Listing 9.12 can be replace with the `fillARow` call in Listing 9.13. Some people argue that the `fillARow` method communicates intent better than the innermost nested loop and hides detail. By hiding the detail of the inner loop we have fewer things to think about at any given time. It localizes all information about a loop in one location, making it harder to make mistakes.

Listing 9.13 Fill a Rectangle—Version 2

```
1   public void fillARect ()
2   {
3     for (int y = 1; y <= 3; y++)
4     {
5       fillARow (y);
6     }
7   }
8   public void fillARow (int y)
9   {
10    for (int x = 1; x <= 4; x++)
11    {
12      g.fillRect(x, y, 1, 1);
13    }
14  }
```

9.4.6   Exception Handling

When we write programs, we make assumptions about the computer and software that support that program. For example, each class has an associated `*.class` file. We assume that each of these files is available for our program to load. When we open a file, we assume that the file is available. When we apply an operation to an object, we assume the object has been created. When we divide by a number, we assume that that number is not zero. However, sometimes our assumptions fail. It is in these circumstances that Java raises an exception, and if our program does not respond to that exception our program will fail.

We introduced a new Java statement in Listing 9.1, an exception handler. An exception handler is a control statement which responds to exceptions. If something may go wrong with one of our assumptions, we write code that tells Java what to do.

> *Exceptions* are occurrences that violate a constraint. A constraint is a condition that the Java designers assumed must be true for a program to execute properly. When a constraint is violated, an exception is *raised*. An *exception handler* responds to an exception.

There are many causes of exceptions. For example, a program may attempt to divide a number by zero. A program may attempt to load a class file (`*.class`), but the file cannot be found or the network connection between the client and host may be broken. A data file may not be found or it is corrupted. A program may run out of memory. A programmer may have written code that explicitly raises an exception.

Java has divided exceptions into two categories: checked and unchecked. A *checked exception* is one in which the compiler insists that the programmer provide an exception handler. An example is the `FileNotFoundException` in Listing 9.1. (We will show more examples of file exceptions in Chapter 12.) If that exception is not handled, a syntax error will occur. If we try to convert a string of characters into a number but the string does not represent a legal number, for example, `"23@A9"` (Chapter 10), an exception is raised. Many of the checked exceptions result from file and network interactions.

The Java language designers felt that to require a programmer to handle all exceptions would be irritating and add little to the quality of a program. For example, the following two examples raise unchecked exceptions:

```
Polygon p;
p.add (10, 20);      // null pointer exception
int x = 0;
int y = 25 / x;      // divide by zero exception
```

The Java designers decided to allow the programmer to choose whether unchecked exceptions are checked. An *unchecked exception* does not have to be handled. A few examples follow:

- `ArithmeticException`: divide by zero error.

- `ClassCastException`: raised when we try to cast objects to things that are not appropriate.

- `IndexOutOfBoundsException`: attempting to access array elements that do not exist (Chapter 13).

- `NegativeArraySizeException`: trying to create an array with a negative size (Chapter 13).

- `NullPointerException`: attempting to manipulate an object when none has been created.

- `SecurityException`: an attempt by a remote applet to access inappropriate information on a local machine.

Any statement that can raise a checked exception must be placed within a `try` statement. A `try` statement handles exceptions. If an exception occurs, one of the `catch` clauses associated with a `try` statement is executed. In other words, we will "try" to execute some code that may fail. If the code raises an exception, we "catch" the exception. The basic form of an exception handler is shown below with an example in Listing 9.14. In this code we try to create a `StockPriceFile` object. If we fail, we print out the message "File not found."

```
try
{
    statements
}
catch ( exceptionClass exceptionObject )
{
    statements
}
```

Listing 9.14 Catching an Exception

```
1    try
2    {
3        StockPriceFile priceFile = new
4                StockPriceFile("Stock.prices");
5    }
6    catch (FileNotFoundException e)
7    {
8        System.out.println("File not found");
9    }
10   ... additional catch clauses ...
```

A method is not required to handle an exception. It can pass that responsibility on to its calling method. For example, in Listing 9.15 the constructor in the `StockPriceFile` class is implemented so that it throws an exception. Notice the `throws` clause in Line 2. It informs the compiler that the constructor may throw a `FileNotFoundException`. It is this line that forces us to handle the exception in Listing 9.14. Even though an exception may be raised in Line 4 or 5 of Listing 9.15, it does not need to be caught here. We will describe how Lines 4 and 5 open a file in Chapter 12. It is sufficient for the present to understand that the constructor for the `FileReader` class throws the `FileNotFoundException`.

Listing 9.15 Catching an Exception and Rethrowing It

```
1    public StockPriceFile (String fileName)
2                    throws FileNotFoundException
3    {
4        FileReader in = new FileReader(fileName);
5        myInputFile  = new BufferedReader(in);
6    }
```

Similarly, the `read` method in the `StockPriceFile` class throws an `IOException`. As a result, we must catch `IOExceptions` in Line 43 of Listing 9.1. We can also create our own exceptions by extending existing exception classes. However, we do not have time for that discussion.

The author could have made our lives easier by rewriting Listing 9.15 as shown in Listing 9.16. If he had done this, the code in Listing 9.14 would have been reduced to Lines 3 and 4. First, exceptions are used so pervasively in Java that we will have to learn how to use them eventually. Second, a client should decide how to handle an exception. A client may wish to display a message in a dialog box, ignore the exception, abort the program, or give the program user a chance to recover from the exception. That decision should not be left to a service class.

Listing 9.16 Catching an Exception and Not Rethrowing It

```
1    public StockPriceFile (String fileName)
2    {
3        try
4        {
5            FileReader in = new FileReader(fileName);
6            myInputFile  = new BufferedReader(in);
7        }
8        catch (FileNotFoundException e)
9        {
10            System.out.println("File not found");
11        }
12    }
```

Exceptions are designed to handle unexpected occurrences. They should not be used for general flow of control. For example, do not use an exception handler to differentiate between male and female insurance applicants. It is expected that some insurance applicants will be male and some will be female. Use a selection statement instead.

SUPPLEMENTARY MATERIAL

9.5   Test Coverage

The discrete nature of computer programs make them much more difficult to test than ana-
log devices. For example, if a metal support beam is tested and can hold 5,000, 10,000,
and 15,000 pounds, we can infer that it will hold 9,000 pounds. This is not the case for
computer programs. If a program works with the values 100, 150, and 200, it may not
work with the value 160. In this section, we will explore some of the methodologies
required to better test our programs.

9.5.1   Off-by-one Errors

Off-by-one errors create a category of errors in which a value is too large or
too small by single unit. These errors manifest themselves in loops that iterate once too often or once too few. They are also found in selection statements where a boundary between true and false is off by one. Common
culprits are using the wrong comparison operators; for example, using >
when >= is required. Another culprit is forgetting that many items in Java are
counted by beginning at 0.

Off-by-one errors are easy to make in loops. Two such possible errors are demonstrated
using the color blend program in Listing 9.8 on page 409. The first is to reason that
because there are 256 colors, the equations for computing red and blue should look like
the following.

```
int red  = (y * 256) / (d.height - 1);
int blue = (x * 256) / (d.width  - 1);
```

A problem occurs when y is its maximum value. It will equal d.height - 1. As a
result, red will get the value 256. However, the allowable range of red is from 0 to 255.
Setting it to 256 has the effect of setting it to zero. The same is true for blue. The result is
a strip, one pixel wide, along the right and bottom border with the wrong color. The bottom right corner pixel will now be black (0, 0, 0) instead of magenta (255, 0, 255). (See
Figure 9.6.)

Figure 9.6 Off-by-one Error

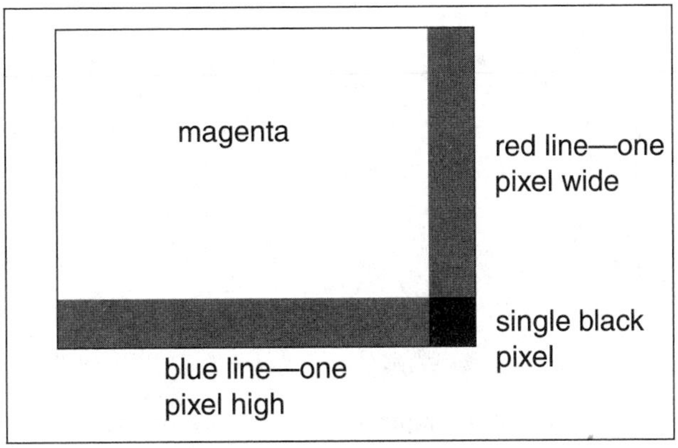

Another possible off-by-one error is to compute red and blue using the following code fragment.

```
int red  = (y * 255) / (d.height);
int blue = (x * 255) / (d.width );
```

This equation looks correct until we realize that we count starting at zero. Thus, if the window width is 8, y goes from 0 to 7. Red on the right edge would be incorrectly computed as:

```
red = (7 * 255) / 8 = 233
```

Red will never become completely saturated. This will not be noticed for normal screen widths of few hundred pixels. Our eyes will not be able to pick up the small difference in color. The error will probably go unnoticed. In other contexts, a similar off-by-one error can cause devastating results.

The best way to uncover these errors is to step through a program using a debugger or add print statements to verify results. For example, the following print statement can be placed within the inner loop of Listing 9.8. If it contains the off-by-one error described above, it provides the output in Listing 9.17 for a 4 by 3 window. A quick scan through the values indicates that something is wrong because the component colors never reach saturation.

```
System.out.println(x + " " + y + " " + red + " " + blue);
```

However, the code embedded within an inner loop may be executed so often that we may be overwhelmed with output. For example, looking through over 300,000 lines of debugging information for a 640 by 480 window is not practical. There are several ways to manage debugging information in large and nested loops. One is to make the number of

Listing 9.17 Debugging Output (Width = 4, Height = 3)

```
0 0    0    0
1 0    0   63
2 0    0  127
3 0    0  191
0 1   85    0
1 1   85   63
2 1   85  127
3 1   85  191
0 2  170    0
1 2  170   63
2 2  170  127
3 2  170  191
```

iterations for a loop smaller (for example 4 by 3). If that is not possible, another possibility is to print only selected information. For example, the values computed for red can be tested by placing a print statement in the outer loop. The number of blue values can also be restricted with the following `if` statements.

```
if (y == 0)
    System.out.println(x + " " + blue);
```

or

```
if (x % 20 == 0 | x == d.width - 1)
    System.out.println(x + " " + blue);
```

Notice that we made sure to print out the extremes, i.e., when x is 0 or `d.width - 1`.

9.5.2   Statement Coverage

In Section 8.8 we took a look at testing selection statements using statement, branch, and path coverage. We will continue that discussion here on loop statements. Let us begin with the program in Listing 9.18.

We will first investigate how to assure that all statements are executed at least once. Regardless of the value of n, statements 1, 2, 3, 4, 7, and 8 get executed once. To satisfy statement coverage we only need to assure that statements 5 and 6 are executed. If n>0, statements 5 and 6 get executed n times. If n<=0, then statements 5 and 6 are never executed. Thus, providing a value of n > 0 assures statement coverage.

Listing 9.18 Finding the Average of n Integers Using a While Loop

```
1.      int n        = getInt();
2.      int sum      = 0;
3.      int count    = 1;

4.      while (count <= n)
        {
5.        sum += count;
6.        count++;
        }
7.      count--;
8.      int average = sum / count;
```

9.5.3 Branch Coverage

Branch coverage is satisfied when the conditional (count <= n) in statement 4 is true at least once and false at least once. This occurs for any n>0. For example, if n is 1, the first time (count <= n) evaluates to true. Statement 5 and 6 will be executed, at which point count will be larger than n. The next time (count <= n) evaluates to false.

9.5.4 Path Coverage

We discovered in the previous chapter that statement and branch coverage may not be enough. For example, the program in Listing 9.5 on page 402 computed the average of n stock prices. It contains a check for day == 0. This is the special case when the number of stocks is zero. Attempting to compute the average of zero stocks will cause a divide by zero exception. The programmer may have thought that the number of stocks will never be zero. However, the zero case may appear naturally in a program. For example, an auto-mated program may pick a range of days to analyze. During the holiday season the stock market may be closed for an extended period, resulting in a range of zero days. Another common problem is an empty file. Statement or branch coverage will not necessary uncover these problems, but path coverage will.

Figure 9.7 Possible Paths of Listing 9.18

```
n <= 0:      1 3 4 7 8
n == 1:      1 3 4 5 6 4 7 8
n == 2:      1 3 4 5 6 4 5 6 4 7 8
...
n == 2147483647: 1 2 3 4 5 6 4 5 6 4 5 6 4 5 6 ...
```

However, path coverage is impractical with loops. Recall that a path is a unique sequence of statements. Figure 9.7 shows that the number of paths in Listing 9.18 is equal to n+1 for n greater than zero. Because n is an int, there are over 2 billion possible paths. That is too many to test.

Given that we cannot realistically test all paths and statement and branch coverage are unsatisfactory, we must find a middle ground. One possible set of guidelines for selecting test data for loops is shown below. Each loop should be tested for:

- Zero iterations—this possibility is often overlooked and can result in unexpected errors.

- One iteration—this possibility is also often overlooked and can result in unexpected errors.

- Typical number of iterations—normal case.

- Maximum reasonable iterations—test an extreme case.

Nested selection and iteration statements make test data selection difficult. The number and characteristics of possible paths through the program can confound a tester. Listing 9.19 provides such an example. For example, if m==n **and** and the if statement in Line 3 is true, there is a divide by zero exception. This can happen only if the method returns a value less than zero when n == m. The combinations of m, n, and z that result in this situation may be rare. If test cases are not set up carefully, this situation can be easily missed.

Listing 9.19 Cryptic Example - Divide by Zero Possible

```
1.    for (int i=0; i<n; i++)
2.      for (int j=0; j<m; j++)
3.        if (Math.sqrt(Math.abs(n-m)) > foo(z))
4.          result = 1.0 / (n*n - m*m);
        else
5.          result = ...;
```

Code can be written in such a way that unnoticed time bombs exist when certain combinations of programs are run during special times of the year. The best defense against these time bombs is to write code where all interactions are clearly and simply stated. Clearly written code will reduce the number of obscure test cases.

Some software houses test their code with test harnesses that generate random test cases. They may generate millions of random test cases by running automated testers for days. If an error is uncovered, the code is corrected and the testing process is repeated. The test, locate error, and error fix process may require a week of work. Each week that delays the release of a product is costly. Errors caught early can save substantial testing later.

A *test harness* is a program that executes a piece of code under test.

REFERENCE

9.6 Summary

The key idea covered in this chapter is iteration. By the end of this chapter we should be able to use iterative statements to write effective algorithms and test them for correctness.

The `while` statement is the most general form of a loop statement. The statement embedded within a `while` loop executes repeatedly until the loop condition becomes false. A `for` statement is a specialized form of the loop used primarily for counting. A `do` statement is another specialized form of a loop in which its body is executed at least once. A `break` statement can be used to abort a loop.

We reviewed patterns for terminating input loops: end-of-file, sentinel, and counter. We were introduced to another example for using the pattern form finding extreme values. Common algorithms were introduced for smoothing lines and for averaging sets of numbers. We also looked at a nested loop pattern that found prime numbers by assuming a number was prime and looking for a counter case. Our final pattern used a nested loop to scan through all the pixels in a display.

We learned how to assure statement, branch, and path coverage and how each helps us to find subtle errors. In particular, we looked at off-by-one errors. Path coverage requires too many test cases to be practical in many iterative algorithms. We relaxed the path coverage requirements of loops by specifying that each should be tested for zero, one, and more iterations.

9.7 Bibliography

- Bundt, Thomas and Todd Shank, University of Portland, stock information.

- Wise, Eric. 1982. Self-Assessment Procedure IX—Ethics in Computing. *Communications of the ACM* 25 (March): 181–195.

- Wise, Eric. 1990. Self-Assessment Procedure XXII- Ethics in Computing. *Communications of the ACM* 33 (November): 110–132.

- Astrachan, Owen and Eugene Wallingford, *Loop Patterns*, http://www.cs.uni.edu/~wallingf/research/patterns/chiliplop/loops/loops.html

PROGRAM LISTINGS

9.8   Support Classes for Stock Program

The stock program contains four important classes. The `Stocks` class contains the `main` method. It is implemented in Listing 9.1 on page 397. When its main method is invoked, three objects are created: a stock price file, a stock price for a given day, and a graph. The code for the stock price file is shown in Listing 12.28 on page 588. It is responsible for managing the process of reading information from a file. The daily record class is responsible for maintaining information about a single day's stock prices. Its code is in Listing 9.20. The `VGraphFrame` class works similar to the `VGraph` class described in Appendix: C on page 914. `VGraphFrame` creates a new window in which to display results while `VGraph` uses an existing applet window.

Figure 9.8 Stock program design

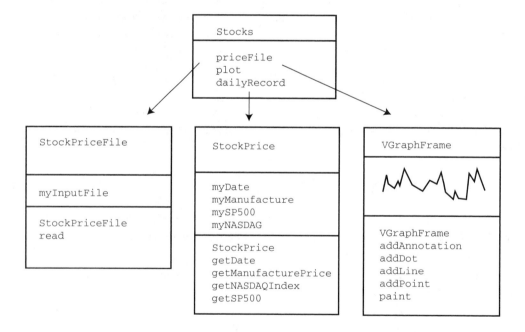

Listing 9.20 StockPrice Class

```
1  //*********************************************************************
2  //
3  // title:   StockPrice
4  //
5  // Stock price and indices for a processor manufacture,
6  // NASDAQ, and Standard, and Poors for one day.
7  //
8  //*********************************************************************
9
10 import java.io.IOException;
11
12 public class StockPrice {
13
14    private String  myDate;        // Date
15    private double  myManufacture; // Manufacture's price
16    private double  mySP500;       // Standard & Poors 500
17    private double  myNASDAQ;      // NASDAQ
18
19    //---------- getDate ------------------------------------------
20    // pre:  this file is open & a stock day has been read
21    // post: the date of the last stock day read is returned.
22    public String getDate()
23    {
24       return myDate;
25    }
26
27    //---------- getManufacturePrice ------------------------------
28    // pre:  this file is open & a stock day has been read
29    // post: the price of the manufacturer's stock is returned.
30    public double getManufacturePrice()
31    {
32       return myManufacture;
33    }
34    //---------- getNASDAQIntex ------------------------------------
35    // pre:  this file is open & a stock day has been read
36    // post: the NASDAQ price index is returned.
37    public double getNASDAQIndex()
38    {
39       return myNASDAQ;
40    }
41
```

Listing 9.20 StockPrice Class

```
42   //---------- getSP500 ------------------------------------
43   // pre:  this file is open & a stock day has been read
44   // post: the Standard and Poor price index is returned.
45   public double geSP500Intex()
46   {
47     return mySP500;
48   }
49
50   //---------- StockPrice ----------------------------------
51   // pre:       "input" is a valid open stock price file
52   // post:      If more prices in the file, this stock price is
53   //            the next stock price in the file.
54   //            If no more prices in the file, the date of this
55   //            price is null.
56   // exception: "IOException" raised for read errors
57
58   public StockPrice
                 (String date, double manufacture, double nASDAQ,
59                  double sP500)
60   {
61     myDate      = date;
62     myManufacture = manufacture;
63     myNASDAQ     = nASDAQ;
64     mySP500      = sP500;
65   }
66
67   //---------- toString ------------------------------------
68   // pre:  none
69   // post: String representation of this object is returned.
70   public String toString()
71   {
72     return new String  (myDate +
73                  ":   Manufacture at " + myManufacture +
74                  ",   NASDAQ at " + myNASDAQ +
75                  ",   Standard & Poors at " + mySP500);
76   }
77 }
```

PROBLEM SETS

9.9   Exercises

Ethics—Section 9.2

1   The Association for Computing Machinery (ACM) produced a series of self assess-ments for computing professionals. Two of those are related to ethics. Find the No-vember 1990 issue of the *Communications of the ACM* (see bibliography). Read scenarios II.6, II.11, and V.7, which relate to products with software or hardware bugs. Write a one half to one page paper detailing whether you feel professional eth-ics was violated by individuals in these scenarios.

2   It can be argued that the processor manufacturer with the defective product acted in an ethical manner because it responded in a way that was in the best interest of its customers, share holders, and its own well being. It may also be argued that their ac-tions are suspect because they did not respond to user concerns until they were forced to. Write a one half to one page essay stating your position clearly and sup-porting it.

Patterns—Section 9.3

3   Do a walkthrough for the prime numbers code in Listing 9.7 on page 406 for number = 16 and 17.

4   Implement the prime numbers code in Listing 9.7 on page 406 with a `for` loop.

5   Go to the library and track down other prime number algorithms. Write a report on the techniques they use to compute prime numbers efficiently.

6   Use nested `for` loops to create the following square. Print only one "*" during each iteration of the inner loop.

```
* * * * *
* * * * *
* * * * *
```

7. Use nested for loops to create the following triangle. Print only one "*" during each iteration of the inner loop.

```
   *
  **
 ***
****
```

Loops—Section 9.4

8 Convert each of the `while` loops in exercise 9 h through k from Chapter 2 to a `for` loop.

9 Repeat exercise 8 using a `do` loop.

10 Write a `for` loop that sums the number from 1 to 10. and print the result.

11 Suppose you get a 3.5% cost of living raise every year. Write a loop that will compute how long it will take your salary to double.

12 Write a `for` loop that creates the following output printing only one number per iteration:

```
9  7  5  3  1  -1  -3  -5  -7  -9
```

13 Write a method with an embedded `for` loop that computes N!. It should have the following signature:

```
public int factorial(int n)
```

Implement it and determine for what value of n the computation overflows.

14 Write a method with an embedded `for` loop that computes n^{th} number in the Fibonacci sequence. In the Fibonacci sequence each number is the sum of the previous two. We will start with 1 for the first two numbers. Thus, the first eight numbers in the sequence are:

```
1   1   2   3   5   8   13  21
```

It should have the following signature:

```
public int fibonacci(int n)
```

Implement it and determine for what value of n the computation overflows.

Exception Handling—Section 9.4

15　Modify the code fragment in Listing 9.5 so that it uses an exception handler to respond to a divide by zero rather than an explicit check for (day == 0).

Test Coverage—Section 9.5

16　Using the guidelines for test data selection in Section 9.5.4 on page 425, pick test data for the loops in exercise 9 h through k from Chapter 2.

17　Using the guidelines for test data selection in Section 9.5.4 on page 425, pick values for x that will test the following loop:

```
int x = ...;
int i = 0;
int sumSquares = 0;
while (i < x) {
  sum += i * i;
  i++;
  }
```

18　Using the guidelines for test data selection in Section 9.5.4 on page 425, pick values for x that will test the following loop:

```
int x = ...;
for (int i=-6; i<x; i++)
  doSomething(i);
```

19　Replace <= with < in Line 6 of the prime number program in Listing 9.7. What kind of error does this cause? Which numbers pass through as prime which should not?

Algorithmic Complexity—Section 8.6

20　What is the order of complexity of the code for finding stock price averages in Listing 9.5 on page 402?

21　What is the order of complexity of the following method?

```
public void times9Table(int n)
{
  for (int i=0; i<n; i++)
  {
    int result = 9 * i;
    System.out.println("9 x " + i + " = " + result);
  }
}
```

9.10   Projects

Stocks—Section 9.2

22   If the sentinel values are not found in Listing 9.2 on page 399, the program will reach the end of the file. Make the program exit the sentinel loops if end of file is encountered.

23   End of file may be reached in Listing 9.3 on page 400 before the expected number of reports are read. Make the program exit the counter loops if end of file is encountered.

24   Modify smooth plotting for Listing 9.6 on page 404 so that it behaves properly on empty files and files with only one record.

25   Modify Listing 9.6 on page 404 so that smoothing is accomplished by averaging five data points.

26   In Section 9.4.1 there are two styles of loops presented. Convert the loop and a half version in each of the listings below to version 2 illustrated in Listing 9.10.
  a.   Listing 9.1
  b.   Listing 9.2
  c.   Listing 9.6

Patterns—Section 9.3

27   Modify the program in Listing 9.8 on page 409 to display random colored pixels.

28   Modify the program in Listing 9.8 on page 409 to create an interesting new pattern.

29   Write a program that creates an 8 by 8 checkerboard pattern in the display.

30   Write a method that creates a checkerboard of any size. It should adhere to the following signature:
```
public void paint (int squaresWide, int squaresHigh,
                   int pixelsPerSquare, Graphics g);
```

10 Text Processing

Customizing a Story

e conductor ca

kets please" a

m all the comp

then went to tl

d knocked on t

10.1 Objectives

Concepts **Section 10.2, page 437**

This chapter provides an introduction to text manipulation. It begins by demonstrating how a story can be created and modified. A story template is created in which key players are represented with special character patterns. A custom story is created by substituting user-supplied names for these string patterns.

Patterns **Section 10.3, page 444**

Initially the pattern-matching method provided by the Java `String` class is used to find target strings. We investigate how pattern-matching methods work by writing and analyzing a simple method to accomplish the same task. We will implement matching with a loop for the linear structures pattern.

Java skills:

Next, a description of the primitive `char` type and the `String` class is presented. In addition, we introduce the GUI components necessary to get text input and display text output. These structures are required to implement the story creation application.

- Characters Section 10.4, page 448
- Java `String` class Section 10.5, page 449
- `Label` class. Section 10.6.1, page 458
- `TextField` class. Section 10.6.2, page 459
- `TextArea` class. Section 10.6.3, page 460
- `TextComponent` class Section 10.6.4, page 462
- `Font` class Section 10.6.5, page 465

Abilities

By the end of this chapter we should be able to do the following:

- Manipulate strings.
- Capture strings from user input through GUI components.
- Display strings within scrollable windows.

CONCEPTS

10.2   Computer-Generated Stories

10.2.1   Insults on Demand

The following story was mailed to the author by his niece, who is a civil engineer.

On a train to a large computer convention there were a bunch of computer programmers and a bunch of computer engineers. Each of the programmers had a train ticket. The group of engineers had only *one* ticket for all of them. The programmers started laughing, figuring the engineers were going to get caught and thrown off the train.

When one of the engineers, the lookout, said "Here comes the conductor," all of the engineers went into the bathroom. The programmers were puzzled.

The conductor came aboard, said "tickets please" and got tickets from all the computer programmers. He then went to the bathroom and knocked on the door and said "ticket please." The engineers stuck the ticket under the door. The conductor took it and moved on. A few minutes later the engineers came out of the bathroom.

The computer programmers felt really stupid.

On the way back from the convention, the group of programmers decided that they would try that method, too. They bought one ticket for the whole group. They met up with the engineers in the same car.

Again, the programmers started snickering at the engineers. This time *none* of the engineers had tickets. When the lookout said "Conductor coming!" all the engineers went to one bathroom and all the computer programmers went to the other bathroom.

Before the conductor came on board, one of the engineers left their bathroom, knocked on the programmer's bathroom, and said "ticket please."

Stories such as the one above circulate endlessly through the Internet. The players and locations change to suit the intended audience. In this case, the author did not want to be shown up by his hardware-oriented niece. He converted the email message into an applet that allows the program's user to easily customize the story players.

The players in the story can be changed with two input text fields: one for the clever group, which defaults to computer scientists, and another for the dull group, which defaults to civil engineers. After the fields are set by the program user, a click of the button rewrites the story (see Figure 10.1). In addition to this GUI-style implementation, we can find a text-based version in Section 10.7.

Figure 10.1 StoryManager Display

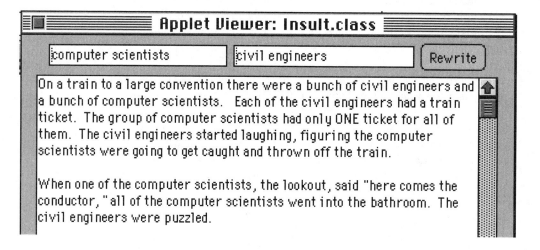

Two classes are used to implement the story generator:

- `StoryManager` class: This class extends `Applet` and handles the input text fields, the rewrite button, and the story display field.
- `Story` class: This class is responsible for creating a template for the story and creating various instantiations of it.

Figure 10.2 `StoryManager` Applet Design

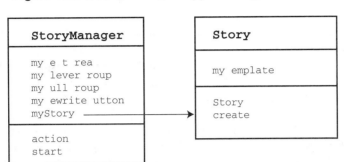

10.2.2 String Manipulation

Strings are sequences of characters. They can represent arbitrary text. The story program depends heavily on strings to represent a template for our story, for representing the players within the story, and for operations that build each story. Strings are discussed in detail in Section 10.5.

We will start by seeing how strings are used in the `Story` class. The `Story` class has two operations (Figure 10.2). The first is its constructor, which creates the story template. The template is the text of the story in which the main characters have been replaced by special character sequences. The name of the clever group is replaced by the string `$clever` and the dull group with `$dull`. For example, the beginning of the template looks like the following:

```
"On a train to a large convention there were a bunch of $dull
and a bunch of $clever."
```

Once a client has instantiated a story template, it builds a new story with the `create` method. For example, suppose we want to build the following story:

```
"On a train to a large convention there were a bunch of civil
engineers and a bunch of computer scientists."
```

To create this story we write the following two lines of code. The first line constructs the story template. The second line creates the story by substituting "computer scientist" for the string `$clever` and substituting "civil engineers" for `$dull` everywhere in the template. This code appears in the `StoryManager` class, which can be found in Listing 10.13 on page 475 (Lines 65 through 67).

```
myStory = new Story (DEFAULT_TEMPLATE, this);
myTextArea.setText
       (myStory.create (DEFAULT_CLEVER, DEFAULT_DULL));
```

The `string` class is used to create the story template and store the names of the players (Listing 10.1). The `Story` constructor, Lines 18 through 23, is responsible for creating the story template. It reads a template string from a text file. The `TemplateFile` class that accomplishes the task can be found in Listing 10.14 on page 477.

The `create` method is responsible for constructing a new story from the story template. It has two string parameters: one for the clever group's name and the other for the dull group's name. Most of its work is done within the `replace` method (Lines 41 through 55), one call for each group. In the first call to `replace` (Line 32), all the instances of the substring `$clever` are replaced by the name of the clever group. In the second call (Line 33) all the instances of the substring `$dull` are replaces by the name of the dull group.

The `replace` method has three string parameters: the first is the template, which is the target of the replacement. The second parameter is for the pattern string that is to be replaced in the template. The last parameter is the name of the group that is to be substituted for the pattern in the template. For example, the `replace` method can be used as follows:

```
String target = new String ("The $clever had one ticket.");
String story = replace (target, "$clever", "computer scientists");
```

After the above call to `replace`, the `$clever` substring in `target` gets replaced with `computer scientists`. The `story` string becomes `The computer scientists had one ticket.`

The `replace` method starts by finding the length of the pattern string. This is done with the string `length` method. The length will be used to remove the appropriate number of characters from the target once the pattern is found.

The pattern string is located by using the `indexOf` method. For example:

```
String target   = new String ("The $clever had one ticket.");
String pattern  = new String ("$clever");
int index       = target.indexOf(pattern, 0);
```

The `indexOf` method will search for the pattern string beginning at character index zero in `target`. Index zero is the first character in a string. If the pattern is found, it will return the index of its starting location. In the example above, it will return four. Zero is the index

Listing 10.1 The Story Class

```
1  //****************************************************************
2  //
3  // title:    Story
4  //
5  // Objects of this class create a story about adventures of two
6  // groups of people on the way to a conference.  The name of the
7  // groups of people can be changed.
8  //
9  //****************************************************************
10
11 public class Story
12 {
13   String myTemplate;
14
15   //---------- Story ------------------------------------------
16   // pre:  none
17   // post: A message template is created
18   public Story (String templateFileName, Applet applet)
19   {
20     TemplateFile templateFile =
21         new TemplateFile (templateFileName, applet);
22     myTemplate = templateFile.get ();
23   }
24
25   //---------- create -----------------------------------------
26   // pre:  none
27   // post: The clever and dull strings are substituted into
28   //        template story.
29   public String create (String clever, String dull)
30   {
31     String message = new String(myTemplate);
32     message = replace (message, "$clever", clever);
33     message = replace (message, "$dull"  , dull);
34     return message;
35   }
36
```

Listing 10.1 The Story Class

```
37   //---------- replace ------------------------------------------
38   // Substitute the string "source" for the string "pattern" in
39   // the string "target".
40   // For internal use only.
41   private String replace
42          (String target, String pattern, String source)
43   {
44     int length = pattern.length();
45     int index  = 0;
46     while (true)
47     {
48       index = target.indexOf(pattern, index);
49       if (index == -1)
50          break;
51       target = target.substring(0, index) + source +
52              target.substring(index + length, target.length());
53     }
54     return target;
55   }
56 }
```

of the first character. If the pattern is not found, −1 is returned, which results in the search loop exit. We will describe the indexOf method in greater detail in the next section.

In Lines 51 and 52 the target string is disassembled, the pattern discarded, and the string components reassembled with the name of the new group. Strings are disassembled with the substring method and reassembled using the concatenation command + (Figure 10.3). For example:

```
String target   = new String ("The $clever had one ticket.");
String frontPart = target.substring(0, 4);
String endPart   = target.substring(11, 27);
String story     = frontPart + "scientist" + endPart;

// result is "The CS students had one ticket."
```

We continue to replace the pattern with source string until the pattern is no longer found. This completes the description of the replace method and the Story class.

Figure 10.3 Reconstructing a String

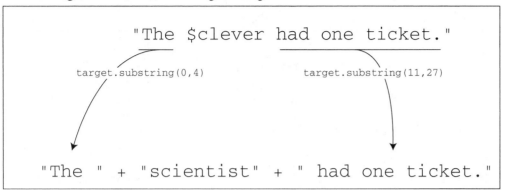

PATTERNS

10.3   One Loop for Linear Structures

The Story class in Listing 10.1 takes advantage of the indexOf method to find the pattern $dull in the target string The $dull started laughing. In this section, we will investigate one algorithm for implementing the indexOf method.

A straightforward strategy for finding a match string is to look at the first character in the pattern and find a match in the target. When a match is found, look at the next character in the pattern and the next character in the target. If there is a match, go on to the third character. Continue until all characters in the pattern have been matched or there is no more target string. This process is illustrated in Figure 10.4 for the target "babassu" and the pattern "bass." A match is found at index 2.

Figure 10.4 Matching the Pattern "bass" in "babassu"

```
target:    babassu        babassu        babassu
           ↑ match        ↑ match        ↑ mismatch
pattern:   bass           bass           bass
            (1)            (2)            (3)


           babassu
           ▲ mismatch
           bass
            (4)


           babassu        babassu        babassu        babassu
           ▲ match        ▲ match        ▲ match        ▲ match
           bass           bass           bass           bass
            (5)            (6)            (7)            (8)
```

```
// pattern matching
set our focus to the first characters of the target and pat-
tern
while there are more target characters to look at and
            a complete match has not been found
  if our focus characters match
    move our focus ahead one in the target and pattern
  else
      reset our focus in the target to the previous starting
                  point plus one
      reset our focus in the pattern to the first character
end loop
```

The technique is implemented in Listing 10.2. Finding the match for the pattern "bass" in the target "babassu" requires eight iterations of the while loop. Each loop iteration has a corresponding number displayed in Figure 10.4. Table 10.1 shows how the values of the indices change during each loop iteration.

oblem

Owen Astrachan has observed that novice programmers often implement an algorithm, such as our search method, with two loops. One loop is used to find the match with the first character of the pattern and the target. The second loop is used to iterate through the pattern. The result invariably leads to off-by-one bugs, problems running off the end of the string, and problems with boundary cases (e.g., partial matches at the end of the target). A single loop results in concise and easy-to-understand code. We call this pattern "one loop for linear structures."

me
lution

Astrachan (see his paper in the references) describes the problem as follows. "Algorithmically, a problem may seem to call for multiple loops to match intuition on how control structures are used to program a solution to a problem, but the data is stored sequentially ... Programming based on control leads to more problems than programming based on structure. Therefore, use the structure of the data to guide the programming solution: one loop for sequential data."

sequences

Although using the one loop for sequential data patterns will create code that is easier to understand and help us prevent several coding problems, it is not trivial to implement. Notice the `if-else` statement in the pattern-matching algorithm above. The code in each of the `if-else` clauses must be carefully implemented. Match them with Line 25 to 39 in Listing 10.2.

Now that we know how the algorithm works, let us take a look at how well it works. To analyze our algorithm, we will count the number of character comparisons required to detect a match. The number of character comparisons is the same as the number of iterations through the `while` loop.

Listing 10.2 Straightforward string matching algorithm

```
1   //---------- match ------------------------------------------
2   // pre:  none
3   // post: If found the index of the first occurrence of string
4   //         "pattern" in string "target" is returned.
5   //         Otherwise, -1 is returned.
6   // from: Computer Algorithms
7   //         Sara Baase
8   //         Addison Wesley, 1988, p211/
9   public static int match (String target, String pattern)
10  {
11     // Initialize the string indices
12     int matchIndex   = 0;
13     int targetIndex  = 0;
14     int patternIndex = 0;
15
16
17     // Check for a match until
18     //   1. there are no more characters to check in the target or
19     //   2. all the characters in the pattern matched
20     while (targetIndex  < target.length() &
21             patternIndex < pattern.length())
22     {
23        // if there is a character match, move to the next
24        // characters in the target and pattern
25        if (target.charAt(targetIndex) ==
26                               pattern.charAt(patternIndex))
27        {
28           targetIndex++;
29           patternIndex++;
30        }
31
32      // if there is not a character match, reset the pattern and
33      // move to the next spot in target
34      else
35      {
36         matchIndex++;
37         targetIndex = matchIndex;
38         patternIndex = 0;
39      }
40     }
41
42    // if the complete pattern was matched then a match was found
43    if (patternIndex >= pattern.length())
44       return matchIndex;
45    else
46       return -1;
47  }
```

Suppose the pattern string cannot be found in the target. In the best case the first character of the pattern does not match any of the characters in the target. The number of comparisons is n where n is the length of the target. An example is the search for the pattern # `dull` in the target `The $dull started laughing.`

In the worst case every character in the pattern would need to be compared at each match location in the target. An example is the search for the pattern "iiiix" in the target "iiiiiiiiii". If the length of the target is n and the pattern is m, the number of character comparisons is mn.

The worst case is unlikely to occur in a natural language text. Sara Baase, in her book *Computer Algorithms: Introduction to Design and Analysis*, reports that empirical studies of this algorithm reveal that in natural language text there are typically 1.1 character comparisons for every character in the target. Now we can see the advantage of creating our templates in Listing 10.1 with a beginning dollar sign ($). Dollar signs do not appear often in natural language text. As a result, most attempts at matching the pattern with the target result in a mismatch on the first try. Thus the expected number of comparisons is close to the length of the target string.

Timothy Budd, in his book *Classic Data Structures in C++*, gives an example of pattern-matching situations in which our straightforward algorithm would not fair as well. The example he gives is matching patterns in DNA sequences. Patterns are more repetitive, resulting in close matches. Budd states that the Knuth-Morris-Pratt and the Boyer-Moore pattern-matching techniques are more appropriate in these cases. These algorithms are saved for a future course.

Table 10.1 Stepping Through Listing 10.2—Finding "bass" in "babassu"

iteration	matchIndex	targetIndex	patternIndex
1	0	0	0
2	0	1	1
3	0	2	2
4	1	1	0
5	2	2	0
6	2	3	1
7	2	4	2
8	2	5	3

JAVA

10.4   Char

Characters are symbols we use to write programs and represent data. They can be letters such a "A," "e," or "m" or digits such as "3" and "7" or special symbols such as "%," "@," and "~". Characters are another example of a primitive type in Java. Like ints and doubles, they are values.

> *Numeric* characters are defined as those from "0" through "9." In English *alphabetic* characters are defined as those from "A" through "Z" and "a" through "z." *Alphanumeric* characters are defined as alphabetic and numeric characters.

Characters in Java require two bytes of storage and follow the Unicode standard. They include the 128 ASCII characters listed in Table A.5 on page 836 plus some 65,000 other possibilities. Using two bytes allows the representation of alphabets from around the world.

Characters in many text files use only one byte of storage. They are represented using the type `byte` and limited primarily to the 128 ASCII characters. It is important not to get bytes and characters confused.

In the example below the ASCII character "A" is assigned to c and d.:

```
char c = 'A';
char d = '\u0041'    // d also gets 'A'
```

The assignment in the first line is clear. The second line assigns the Unicode character represented by the hexadecimal number `0041` (65 decimal) to `d`. A quick look at Table A.5 will confirm that 65 is the encoding for the character "A."

The most common operations on characters are to cast them to integers or increment them. For example, the ASCII character A is assigned to c below. It is then cast to an integer and back to a character.

```
char c = 'A';
int  i = (int)c;    // i has the value 65
c = (char)i;        // c has the value 'A'
c++;                // c has the value 'B'
c--;                // c has the value 'A'
```

A common operation is to convert a sequence of character digits into a number. Part of this process is to convert each digit into its corresponding number. We can accomplish this conversion by taking advantage of the sequential ordering of digits in the ASCII encoding scheme. The digit "5," for example, has the value 5 greater than the digit "0." A common technique for converting ASCII digits to numbers is shown below.

```
char digit  = '5';    // digit holds the character '5'
int  number = (int)digit - (int)'0'; // number holds the in-
teger 5
```

The following loop will convert a sequence of character digits into its corresponding integers. Digits must be retrieved from left to right. We will begin by converting the leftmost character (most significant digit) to an integer.

```
// convert sequence of digits to an integer
int number = (int)mostSignificantDigit - (int)'0'
loop
   get next digit
   exit if no more digits
   number = number * 10 + (int)digit - (int)'0'
end loop
```

Fortunately, Java has implemented this conversion for us. We will see how to use it in Section 10.6.6.

Some characters have special meaning in Java. They must be represented with two character sequences, using the backslash (\) escape character followed by another character (see below).

```
'\b'    backspace
'\t'    tab
'\n'    linefeed
'\f'    formfeed
'\r'    carriage return
'\"'    double quote
'\''    single quote
'\\'    backslash
```

10.5   Strings

Strings are critical for communication with people. They are used to represent people's names, ideas, and history. Within this section, we will look at several of the key operations on strings. Appendix: B on page 902 shows additional examples and covers a few methods not demonstrated in this section.

A *string* is a fixed-length sequence of characters. Once created, they are immutable. They cannot be changed. Each character within a string has a character that precedes it, except the first character; and a character that succeeds it, except the last character. A *string literal* is a sequence of characters between double quotes, for example, "R2D2". The first double quote signals the beginning of a string literal and the second signals the end.

10.5.1   String Construction

There are several constructors for creating strings. The following shows some of them:

```
String r = new String();          // creates an empty string
String t = new String("");        // creates an empty string
String u = new String("Shine");   // creates the string "Shine"
String w = new String(u);         // string w is a copy of u
```

Strings are also created by using string literals. The following shows how to create a string using string literals with and without a constructor:

```
String HAL1 = "My mind is going.";
String HAL2 = new String ("I can feel it.");
```

We stated that string literals are sequences of characters enclosed in double quote marks. If a double quote needs to be part of the string, it is necessary to place the escape character "\" before it. For example,

```
System.out.println ("The conductor said \"ticket please.\"");
```

prints as

```
The conductor said "ticket please."
```

An empty string is different from a null string (Section 1.6.2). A null string indicates that an identifier does not reference an object. Empty strings are string objects without any characters. They have zero length. Empty and null strings can be created as follows:

```
String anEmptyString      = String();   // empty string
String anotherEmptyString = "";         // empty string
System.out.println (anEmptyString);     // nothing is printed
String aNullString        = null;       // null string
System.out.println (aNullString);       // run-time error
```

10.5.2 String Length

The `length` method returns the number of characters within a string. The length of three of the strings defined above is determined as follows:

```
int i = HAL1.length();         // i is 17
int j = anEmptyString.length();  // j is 0
int k = aNullString.length();    // run-time error
```

10.5.3 String Concatenate

A string is a special object in Java. In addition to the typical methods associated with an object, the operator + can be used with strings. The `String` class is the only class that uses this special symbol as an operator. New strings can be created by concatenating strings together.

> Concatenation is the process of combining several strings to create a new string.

Concatenation is accomplished with two different operations. The first uses the + operator. For example,

```
"Fast, Ch" + "eap" + " and Out of Control"
```

creates a new string `Fast, Cheap and Out of Control`. The `concat` method can also be used to create the same effect.

```
String s = new String ("Fast, Ch");
s = s.concat ("eap");
s = s.concat (" and Out of Control");
```

Concatenation does not change the original string. Recall that strings are immutable. Thus, in the following code the string `r` is not changed. A new string that is a combination of `r` and `s` is created and returned.

```
String r = new String ("Cookie's ");
String s = new String ("Fortune");
String t = r.concat (s);
```

There is a mutable string class called `StringBuffer`. It is efficient for creating strings within a loop and contains operations to convert it to a `String` object. We will not cover it in this text.

10.5.4   Substrings

We stated that once created a string cannot be changed. For example, it is not possible to change a character, delete characters, or insert characters into a string. However, it is possible to get copies of parts of a string using the `substring` method. When a `substring` method has two parameters, the first parameter is the index of the beginning of the substring. The second parameter is the index of the character one beyond the last character of the substring. Thus, the substring includes all those characters from start index through the end index minus 1 (see Figure 10.5) Each character within a string has an index which specifies its location. The index of the first character in a string is 0.

Using substrings and concatenation is a good tool for reconstructing strings:

```
String question  = "Is Ralph going to the movies?";
String statement = question.substring(3, 9) +
                   question.substring(0, 3) +
                   question.substring(9, 28) + ".";
```

The result is "Ralph Is going to the movies."

Figure 10.5 Substring

```
String s = new String("Fried Green Tomatoes");
String t = s.substring(6, 11);
// t is "Green"
```

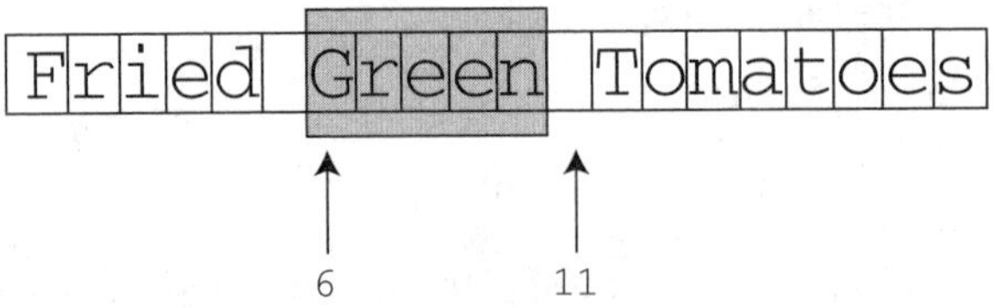

10.5.5   Strings to Characters

We can convert strings to characters by using the `charAt` method. We supply it with an index into a string, and `charAt` returns a character. For example, we can extract all the characters from a string with the following loop:

```
String title = "The Green Mile";
for (int i=0; i < title.length(); i++)
{
  char c = title.charAt (i);
}
```

10.5.6 String Search

Another important operation on strings is search. For example, a word processor needs to find words within a document. An automated indexing tool looks for keywords within articles. The search method for Java strings is `indexOf`. The first parameter is the string for which we are looking. Some examples follow (See Figure 10.6).

```
String s  = "Night Falls on Manhattan";
int index = s.indexOf("hat");  // index gets 18
index     = s.indexOf("N");    // index gets 0
```

Figure 10.6 `indexOf`

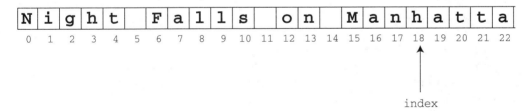

```
String s  = "Night Falls on Manhattan";
int index = s.indexOf("hat");
// index is 18
```

If a matching string is not found in the target, indexOf returns minus 1. An example follows:

```
index     = s.indexOf("Day");  // index gets -1
```

There may be a second parameter that specifies the start offset of the hunt. For example, the string s we defined above has three 't's. By starting the search for t at offset 7, the first t in the string is bypassed.

```
index     = s.indexOf("t", 7); // index gets 20
```

10.5.7 Comparing Strings

Strings have an alphabet ordering. We use alphabetic ordering to make word searches faster. For example, a phone directory consists of a sequence of names and phone numbers in alphabetic order. String comparisons are required to create such an ordering or efficiently find a string with such a list. The string method that supports this ordering is the `compareTo` method. It returns a:

- negative integer if this string object alphabetically precedes the argument string.
- zero if they are equal.
- positive number if this string object alphabetically follows the argument string.

Some examples follow:

```
String aPlace = "Everglades";
String aTree  = "Evergreen";
int result;
result = aPlace.compareTo (aTree);      // result is negative
result = aTree.compareTo (aPlace);      // result is positive
result = aTree.compareTo (aTree);        // result is 0
```

If one string is a prefix of another string, the longer string is considered alphabetically after the shorter string.

```
result = aTree.compareTo ("Ever");      // result is positive
```

A string's order is determined by the ASCII order of characters in the string. See Table A.5 on page 836. Thus, alphabetic ordering in Java is different than alphabetic ordering in a dictionary. Java's ordering is case-sensitive. The lower case letters come after the upper case letters.

```
result = aTree.compareTo ("evergreen"); // result is negative
result = aTree.compareTo ("birch");     // result is negative
result = aTree.compareTo ("EverGreen"); // result is positive
```

Recall that the `compareTo` method returns a "0" if two string are equal. The `equals` method can also be used to determine if two string are equal. For example:

```
boolean b = aTree.equals ("EverGreen"); // b is false
        b = aTree.equals ("Evergreen"); // b is true
```

Do not use the equal operator, ==, when comparing strings or any other object. The equal operator determines whether two identifiers reference the same object. For example,

```
String car1 = new String ("VW");
String car2 = new String ("VW");
String car3 = car2;
if (car1 == car2) ...               // result is false
if (car2 == car3) ...               // result is true
```

10.5.8   Converting Strings

The `String` class contains several static methods that convert primitive values to strings. An example follows:

```
int     i = 123;
String  s = String.valueOf(i);    // s holds the string "123"
boolean b = true;
String  t = String.valueOf(b);    // t holds the string "true"
```

The `valueOf` method is overloaded. It can convert `int`, `long`, `double`, `float`, `char`, and `boolean` values to strings.

10.5.9   `toString` method

Every class inherits the `toString` method from the `Object` class. When an object appears in a location where a string is expected, the compiler automatically invokes the `toString` method. This can be particularly handy during debugging. It is a good idea to define `toString` for all our classes so that they can be printed out easily in debugging messages. For example, Listing 10.3 shows a `LoanRecord` class that contains a `toString` method. The following code can be used to test its implementation:

```
LoanRecord myNewCar =
        new LoanRecord ("Elmer Snid", "Nova", 2349.96);
System.out.println (myNewCar);
myNewCar.deposit (56.34);
System.out.println (myNewCar);
```

It will produce the following output:

```
  name Elmer Snid: car Nova: balance 2349.96: monthly payment in
false
  name Elmer Snid: car Nova: balance 2293.62: monthly payment in true
```

Notice that the `toString` method was called automatically. It can be called explicitly as follows:

```
System.out.println (myNewCar.toString());
```

Listing 10.3 Address Class with `toString` Method

```
1  public class LoanRecord
2  {
3     private String  myName;
4     private String  myCar;
5     private double  myBalance;
6     private boolean myMonthlyPaymentIsIn;
7
8     public LoanRecord (String name, String car, double balance)
9     {
10       myName              = name;
11       myCar               = car;
12       myBalance           = balance;
13       myMonthlyPaymentIsIn = false;
14    }
15
16    public void deposit (double payment)
17    {
18       myBalance -= payment;
19       myMonthlyPaymentIsIn = true;
20    }
21
22    public String toString ()
23    {
24       return "name " + myName +
25              ": car " + myCar +
26              ": balance " + myBalance +
27              ": monthly payment in " + myMonthlyPaymentIsIn;
28    }
29 }
```

10.6   Text Display Classes

The `Graphics` class provides us with one method for placing text in an applet window. The `drawString` method will display a string at a specific location within a window. For example, displaying the movie title "The Full Monty" at location (50, 25) is accomplished with the following command:

```
g.drawString ("The Full Monty", 50, 25);
```

There are a couple of disadvantages to using `drawString`. First, we have to know the placement of every string we are going to display. As a result, it is not easy to append one string to the end of another in the display or insert another string in the middle of another. Because the display characteristics for various computers are different, any effort we make will be platform-dependent. Second, it is not possible for a program user to modify a displayed string. It cannot be used for user input. We would need to write code that maintains a copy of the strings we are displaying, write operations to modify them, and then redraw them. It is much easier to use the various classes in Java that do all this for us.

The `Label`, `TextField`, and `TextArea` classes solve these problems. (Each of these classes was part of the Java 1.1 definition. Java 2.0 supplies corresponding Swing classes that have a `J` prefix. See Chapter 15.) All these classes inherit from the `Component` class, Figure 10.7, which provides such common operations as setting color, fonts, layout, and handling events.

Figure 10.7 Inheritance Structure for Text Components

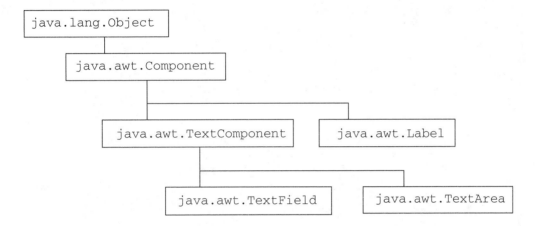

- `Label` class: Label objects are used for displaying a single line of text in a display. The displayed text can be modified under program control but never directly by a program's user.

- `TextField` class: Text field objects are also used for displaying a single line of text in a display. A text field is editable. It can be modified by a program user and those changes can be retrieved under program control.

- `TextArea` class: Text area objects are similar to text field objects. Text area objects are used for displaying multiple lines of text. They contain vertical and horizontal scrollbars.

The following three steps are required whenever we use any of these text components:

1. Create the component.
2. Add the component to the display window.
3. Manipulate the component.

10.6.1 Label

A label is used for displaying a single line of uneditable text. The term "uneditable" is used in the sense that the program user may not change a label. A label is useful for identifying various elements within a window. It can be changed only under program control. In this section, we will take a quick look at using the `Label` class (Listing 10.4). A summary of its methods can be found in Appendix: B on page 883.

Listing 10.4 A Label Demo

```
1   import java.awt.Color;
2   import java.awt.Label;
3   import java.applet.Applet;
4
5   public class LabelDemo extends Applet{
6
7     public void init()
8     {
9       setBackground(Color.white);
10
11      Label nebraska = new Label ("");
12      add (nebraska);
13      nebraska.setText("Nebraska");
14
15      Label massachusetts = new Label ("Massachusetts");
16      add (massachusetts);
17
18      Label oregon = new Label ("Oregon");
19      add (oregon);
20
21      Label kansas = new Label ("Kansas");
22      add (kansas);
23    }
24  }
```

Listing 10.4 demonstrates the three steps required to use a label:

1. A label is created in Line 11.

2. It is added to the display window in Line 12.

3. Line 13 changes the text string associated with the label. Often, a label is not changed once it is created. This third step can be skipped, as demonstrated in Lines 15 and 16.

Figure 10.8 shows the result of the display using the default flow layout manager. Notice that the labels are added to the display until we run out of room. Then they start filling up the next row, centering as we go. Layout managers are discussed briefly in Section 15.4.4 and Section 15.4.13.

Figure 10.8 Output of Listing 10.4

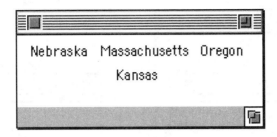

10.6.2 TextField

A text field contains a single line of editable text. It is often used for text input. Listing 10.5 shows how to copy the contents of one text field into another. Initially the string "Emma Lou" is displayed only in the upper text field. Figure 10.9 shows the resulting window before and after the "Copy" button has been pressed. Once the button is pressed, the string in the upper field is copied into the bottom field.

Listing 10.5 Text field demonstration

```
1   import java.awt.TextField;
2   import vista.VActionButton;
3   import vista.VApplet;
4
5   public class Name extends VApplet
6   {
7     TextField myInputName;
8     TextField myOutputName;
9
10    public void init ()
11    {
12     VActionButton copyButton = new VActionButton ("Copy", this);
13      myInputName = new TextField ("Emma Lou", 10);
14      add(myInputName);
15      myOutputName = new TextField("", 10);
16      add(myOutputName);
17    }
18
19    public void action ()
20    {
21      String aName = myInputName.getText();
22      myOutputName.setText(aName);
23    }
24 }
```

Figure 10.9 Output of Listing 10.5 before and after button press

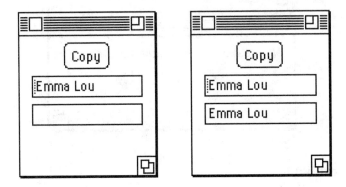

A strategy for dealing with text fields is to create and add them to an applet within the init method. Next, a callback method, such as the `action` method in Line 19, is written to respond to button clicks or some other event.

The three steps for using the text fields are outlined below:

1. Lines 13 and 15 create the text fields.
2. Lines 14 and 16 add them to the display.
3. Lines 21 and 22 manipulate the two text fields. Line 21 extracts a copy of the string in one text field and Line 22 copies the string into the second text field.

The second parameter in the text field constructor in Line 13 specifies that the field will be about 10 characters wide.

10.6.3   TextArea

A text area contains multiple lines of text with vertical and horizontal scroll bars. It looks and behaves much like a text editor window. It can be used for displaying the text output of programs or for entering messages. Listing 10.6 demonstrates how they work.

1. Line 10 creates a text area.
2. Line 11 adds it to the applet display.
3. Lines 12 through 14 manipulate it.

The parameters to the text area constructor in Line 10 indicate that it will be 5 lines of about 16 characters per line. A summary of the `TextArea` class can be found in Appendix: B on page 905.

JAVA

Listing 10.6 Text Area Demonstration

```
1   public class ToDo extends Applet
2   {
3     public void init ()
4     {
5       setBackground (Color.white);
6
7       Label listLabel = new Label ("To Do List");
8       add (listLabel);
9
10      TextArea toDoList = new TextArea(5,16);
11      add(toDoList);
12      toDoList.setText("Run\n");
13      toDoList.append("Shower\n");
14      toDoList.append("CS study group\n");
15    }
16  }
```

Figure 10.10 Output of Listing 10.6

10.6.4 TextComponent

The primary purpose of the `TextComponent` class is to encapsulate the functionality that is common to the `TextArea` and `TextField` classes. It is the base class for these two classes (Figure 10.7). As a result, the methods described in this section are available to `TextArea` and `TextField` objects. `TextComponent` objects are not created directly.

Text components display text that can be modified by the user or the program. They have an editable property that determines whether the text component can be modified by the program user.

Listing 10.7 TextComponent—Computer Text Selection

```
1 TextArea story = new TextArea(5,20);
2 story.setEditable(false);
3 add(story);
4 story.append("When one of the");
5 story.append(" computer ");
6 story.append("scientists, a look out");
7 story.select(16, 35);
8 String group = story.getSelectedText();
9 // group has the value "computer scientists"
```

Figure 10.11 Result of Code in Listing 10.8

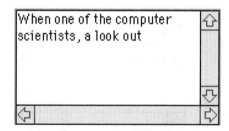

The first example, Listing 10.7 with its corresponding display captured in Figure 10.11, demonstrates a text area that is uneditable by a program user (Line 2). Line 7 selects the text starting at character 16 and ending with character 34. Recall that we start counting at zero.

Listing 10.8, with its corresponding display captured in Figure 10.12, demonstrates how text selection works. This applet contains a text area and two text fields. The user can modify and select text within the text area. When the "show selection" button is pressed,

Listing 10.8 Text Selection Demonstration

```
1  import java.awt.Color;
2  import java.awt.TextArea;
3  import java.awt.TextField;
4  import vista.VActionButton;
5  import vista.VApplet;
6
7  public class Logical extends VApplet
8  {
9     TextArea  mySomeWords;
10    TextField mySelectedText;
11    TextField myBounds;
12
13    //---------- init ----------------------------------------
14    public void init ()
15    {
16       // create the "show" button
17       VActionButton showButton =
18                   new VActionButton ("show selection", this);
19       showButton.setBackground (Color.white);
20
21       // create the text area
22       mySomeWords = new TextArea(5,16);
23       add (mySomeWords);
24       mySomeWords.setEditable (true);
25       mySomeWords.setBackground (Color.white);
26       mySomeWords.append ("Someone who thinks\nlogically");
27       mySomeWords.append (" is a ");
28       mySomeWords.append ("nice\ncontrast to the real\n");
29       mySomeWords.append ("world.\n");
30       mySomeWords.select (12, 18);
31
32       // create the two text fields
33       mySelectedText = new TextField(20);
34       mySelectedText.setBackground (Color.white);
35       add (mySelectedText);
36       myBounds = new TextField (20);
37       myBounds.setBackground (Color.white);
38       add (myBounds);
39    }
```

Listing 10.8 Text Selection Demonstration

```
40
41   //---------- action -----------------------------------------
42   public void action ()
43   {
44     // get the selected text and its location from the text area
45     String aWord = mySomeWords.getSelectedText();
46     int begin = mySomeWords.getSelectionStart();
47     int end   = mySomeWords.getSelectionEnd();
48
49     // display results in the text fields
50     String theSelection = "The selection  is \"" + aWord + "\"";
51     mySelectedText.setText (theSelection);
52     String theBounds    =
53               "It starts at " + begin + " and ends at " + end;
54     myBounds.setText (theBounds);
55   }
56 }
```

Figure 10.12 Output of Listing 10.8

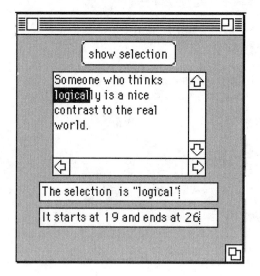

text is displayed within one text field and its starting and ending index are displayed in a second text field. For example, in Figure 10.12 the text "logical" was highlighted by the user and the "show selection" button pressed. Notice that the following text box displayed the string "logical" and said that it started at location 19 and ended at 26.

When the program starts up, Lines 22 through 29 in Listing 10.8 create and displays the text area. The word "thinks" is initially selected in Line 30. When the button is pressed, the word "thinks" is displayed in one text field and the starting index 12 and ending index 18 are displayed in the second text field. The ending index is one greater than the end of the text.

A summary of the `TextComponent` class can be found in Appendix: B on page 906.

Listing 10.9 Font Demonstration

```
1  import java.awt.Color;
2  import java.awt.Font;
3  import java.awt.TextArea;
4  import java.applet.Applet;
5
6  public class FontDemo extends Applet{
7
8    public void init()
9    {
10       TextArea errorMessage = new TextArea(3, 24);
11       errorMessage.setBackground(Color.white);
12       errorMessage.setEditable(false);
13     Font boldSansSerif18 = new Font("SansSerif",Font.BOLD, 18);
14       errorMessage.setFont(boldSansSerif18);
15       add(errorMessage);
16
17       errorMessage.append("Chaos reigns within.\n");
18       errorMessage.append("Reflect, repent, and reboot.\n");
19       errorMessage.append("Order shall return.\n");
20    }
21 }
```

10.6.5 Fonts

The font of a `Component` object can be set with the `setFont` method. Because `Label`, `TextField`, and `TextArea` inherit the `Component` class, they all share the same `setFont` method. Listing 10.9 and Figure 10.13 show an example of changing the font of a text area. Notice that the text for the entire text area is changed to the same font.

Figure 10.13 Output of Listing 10.9

The font is created in Line 13. The text area font is set in Line 14. In addition to "Sans-Serif," there is "Serif," "Monospaced," and "Dialog." They may be PLAIN, ITALIC, or BOLD. A description of the Font class is in Appendix: B on page 865.

10.6.6 Text fields and Numbers

It is often desirable to use text fields for numeric input and output. However, text fields work only with strings. Thus, we must be able to convert between strings and numbers. Listing 10.10 demonstrates this process by extracting strings from two text fields, converting them to integers, adding them, converting the result back to a string, and placing it in a third text field. See Figure 10.14 and Figure 10.15.

Figure 10.14 Output of Listing 10.10

The stringToInteger method in Lines 46 through 51 is used to convert a string to an integer. Lines 49 and 50 demonstrate how to convert a string to an int. Notice that this code is placed within an exception handler. If integerString cannot be converted into an int, an exception is thrown. For example, "24#A" cannot be converted into an integer.

JAVA

Figure 10.15 Error Output of Listing 10.10

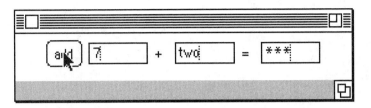

Listing 10.10 Reading and Writing Numbers to Text Fields

```
1  import java.awt.Color;
2  import java.awt.Label;
3  import java.awt.TextField;
4  import vista.VActionButton;
5  import vista.VApplet;
6
7  public class Adder extends VApplet
8  {
9
10   TextField myOperand1;
11   TextField myOperand2;
12   TextField myResult;
13
14   public void init()
15   {
16     setBackground(Color.white);
17     VActionButton addButton = new VActionButton ("add", this);
18     myOperand1 = new TextField ("39", 4);
19     add(myOperand1);
20     Label plusLabel = new Label ("+");
21     add (plusLabel);
22     myOperand2 = new TextField ("23", 4);
23     add(myOperand2);
24     Label equalsLabel = new Label ("=");
25     add (equalsLabel);
26     myResult = new TextField ("", 4);
27     myResult.setEditable (false);
28     add (myResult);
29   }
30
```

Listing 10.10 Reading and Writing Numbers to Text Fields

```
31   public void action()
32   {
33     try
34     {
35       int operand1 = stringToInteger (myOperand1.getText());
36       int operand2 = stringToInteger (myOperand2.getText());
37       int result = operand1 + operand2;
38       myResult.setText(String.valueOf(result));
39     }
40     catch (NumberFormatException exception)
41     {
42       myResult.setText("***");
43     }
44   }
45
46   public int stringToInteger (String integerString)
47          throws NumberFormatException
48   {
49     Integer value  = Integer.valueOf(integerString);
50     return value.intValue();
51   }
52 }
```

The `stringToInteger` method passes the exception on up to its calling method (Line 47). This method does not determine how the exception is handled.

The `stringToInteger` method is called in Line 35 to convert the first string into an integer and in Line 36 to convert the second string. These calls are placed within an exception handler. The `NumberFormatException` is appropriately handled by the `action` method because it contains the logic for adding the numbers. If an invalid integer is entered, asterisks are placed in the result text field. If they are valid integers, they are added and the result displayed. Line 38 uses the string `valueOf` method to convert an integer to a string.

Strings can be converted to doubles in a similar manner. It is only necessary to rename the method in Line 46 and to replace Lines 49 and 50 with the following:

```
Double doubleValueObject = Double.valueOf(doubleString);
double doubleValue       = doubleValueObject.doubleValue();
```

All this is a lot of work to do every time we want to use an integer input field. An appropriate approach is to create a `IntField` class that allows only integer input and a `DoubleField` class that allows only double input. Another approach is to use the

`VTextFieldUtilities` class defined in Appendix: C on page 921. It contains two static methods. For example, if we pass a `TextField` object to the `getInt` method, it returns an integer number.

JAVA

SUPPLEMENTARY MATERIAL

10.7 Programmer-driven (Text-based) Story Version

Listing 10.11 reimplements the Story program in Listing 10.1 by using a programmer-driven technique described in Section 4.5.1. Lines 13 and 14 open the template file. Lines 16 though 25 get the names of the story characters. Lines 28 to 36 convert the story template to it final form and print in. Notice that Lines 33 and 34 make the same calls to the `replace` routine we used in Listing 10.1. An example output is shown in Listing 10.12. The bolded characters are what the user typed in.

The `train.txt` file contains story template. You can create your own stories by making your own files. The first four lines of the template file are shown below:

```
On a train to a large convention there were a bunch of
$dull and a bunch of $clever. Each
of the $dull had a train ticket.  The group of
$clever had only ONE ticket for all of them.  The
```

Listing 10.11 Text-based Story Application

```
1 import java.io.BufferedReader;
2 import java.io.FileReader;
3 import java.io.IOException;
4 import java.io.StreamTokenizer;
5
6 public class Story
7 {
8   public static void main(String args[])
9   {
10     try
11     {
12       // create in and out objects
13       FileReader    reader      = new FileReader ("train.txt");
14       BufferedReader templateIn = new BufferedReader (reader);
15
16       // get the players
17       StreamTokenizer keyboard  = new StreamTokenizer (System.in);
```

Listing 10.11 Text-based Story Application

```
18        System.out.print ("Name of clever group: ");
19        System.out.flush ();
20        keyboard.nextToken ();
21        String clever = keyboard.sval;

22        System.out.print ("Name of dull group:    ");
23        System.out.flush ();
24        keyboard.nextToken ();
25        String dull = keyboard.sval;
26
27        // do the conversion
28        while (true)
29        {
30          String originalLine = templateIn.readLine ();
31          if (originalLine == null)
32            break;
33        String newLine = replace (originalLine, "$clever", clev-
er);
34          String finalLine   = replace (newLine, "$dull", dull);
35          System.out.println (finalLine);
36        }
37        // wait for carriage return
38        keyboard.eolIsSignificant (true);
39        keyboard.nextToken ();
40      }
41    catch (IOException e)
42    {
43        System.err.println ("IO exception raised");
44    }
45  }
```

Listing 10.11   Text-based Story Application

```
46    //---------- replace -------------------------------------
-
47    private static String replace
48          (String target, String pattern, String source)
49    {
50      int length = pattern.length();
51      int index  = 0;
52      while (true)
53      {
54        index = target.indexOf(pattern, index);
55        if (index == -1)
56          break;
57        target = target.substring(0, index) + source +
58              target.substring(index + length, target.length());
59      }
60      return target;
61    }
62 }
```

Listing 10.12 Output of Listing 10.11

```
Name of clever group: "women"
Name of dull group:    "men"
On a train to a large convention there were a bunch of
men and a bunch of women.  Each
of the men had a train ticket.  The group of
women had only ONE ticket for all of them.  The
men started laughing, figuring the
women were going to get caught and thrown
off the train.

When one of the women, the lookout, said
"Here comes the conductor," all of the women
went into the bathroom.  The men were puzzled.

The conductor came aboard, said "tickets please" and
got tickets from all the men.  He then went to
the bathroom and knocked on the door and said "ticket
please".  The women stuck the ticket under
the door.  The conductor took it and moved on. A few
minutes later the women came out of the
bathroom.

The men felt really stupid.

On the way back from the convention, the group of
men decided that they would try that method,
too.  They bought one ticket for the whole group.  They
met up with the women in the same car.

Again, the men started snickering at the
women.  This time NONE of the
women had tickets.  When the lookout
said  "Conductor coming!",  all the women
went to one bathroom and all the men went
to the other bathroom.

Before the conductor came on board, one of the
women left their bathroom, knocked on the
men bathroom, and said "ticket please."
```

REFERENCE

10.8 Summary

The key topic covered in this chapter is strings. By the end of this chapter, we should be able to create and manipulate strings. Strings are created with the string constructor. The `concat` method and "+" operator concatenates strings. We can use the `indexOf` method to search strings and the `substring` method to extract strings from another string.

We learned about a string search algorithm. We found that in the typical case, string search is O(n) where n is the length of the target string. String search can be implemented using the "one loop for linear structures" pattern. We used a single loop to move the pattern through the target and to check each character in the pattern with its corresponding character in the target.

We were also introduced to the `Label`, `TextField`, and `TextArea` classes. These classes allow us to get strings from user input and display strings in scrollable text areas. When numeric input is needed, we learned how to use operations in the numeric classes to convert from strings to numbers.

10.9 Bibliography

- Astrachan, Owen with Geoffrey Berry, Landon Cox, and Garrett Mitchener. 1998 Design patterns: an essential component of CS curricula. *The Proceedings of the Twenty-ninth SIGCSE Technical Symposium on Computer Science Education.* (February): 153.

- Baase, Sara. 1988. String matching. In *Computer Algorithms: Introduction to Design and Analysis.* Reading, MA: Addison-Wesley, 1988.

- Budd, Timothy A. 1994. Strings—an example ADT. In *Classic Data Structures in C++.* Reading, MA: Addison-Wesley.

PROGRAM LISTINGS

10.10 StoryManager **Class**

The StoryManager class is responsible for interacting with the applet user. The names of the two player groups need to be read in and the story displayed. The code for the StoryManager class appears in Listing 10.13. It uses a button to fire an event, which will invoke the action callback method. The code for extracting the clever and dull groups from the text fields and creating a new story are located within this method.

Listing 10.13 The StoryManager **Class**

```
 1 //****************************************************************
 2 //
 3 // title:    StoryManager
 4 //
 5 //   An applet that allows any one group of people to insult
 6 //   another by telling a story.
 7 //
 8 //****************************************************************
 9
10 import java.awt.Button;
11 import java.awt.Color;
12 import java.awt.Graphics;
13 import java.awt.TextArea;
14 import java.awt.TextField;
15 import vista.VApplet;
16 import vista.VActionButton;
17
18 public class StoryManager extends VApplet
19 {
20    private TextArea       myTextArea;
21    private TextField      myCleverGroup;
22    private TextField      myDullGroup;
23    private VActionButton  myRewriteButton;
24    private Story          myStory;
25
26    private final String DEFAULT_TEMPLATE = "train.txt";
27    private final String DEFAULT_CLEVER = "computer scientists";
28    private final String DEFAULT_DULL   = "civil engineers";
29
```

Listing 10.13 The `StoryManager` Class

```
30    //---------- action -------------------------------------------
31    // Called automatically when the button is pressed
32
33    public void action ()
34    {
35        String clever  = myCleverGroup.getText ();
36        String dull     = myDullGroup.getText ();
37        myTextArea.setText(myStory.create (clever, dull));
38    }
39
40    //---------- init ---------------------------------------------
41    // Initialize and create the first story.
42    // Called automatically
43
44    public void init()
45    {
46      // create the text input fields
47      myCleverGroup = new TextField (DEFAULT_CLEVER, 18);
48      myCleverGroup.setBackground (Color.white);
49      add (myCleverGroup);
50      myDullGroup   = new TextField (DEFAULT_DULL, 18);
51      myDullGroup.setBackground (Color.white);
52      add (myDullGroup);
53
54      // create the rewrite button
55      myRewriteButton = new VActionButton ("Rewrite", this);
56      myRewriteButton.setBackground (Color.green);
57
58      // create the text display area
59      myTextArea = new TextArea (24, 50);
60      myTextArea.setBackground (Color.white);
61      myTextArea.setEditable (false);
62      add (myTextArea);
63
64      // create the default message
65      myStory = new Story (DEFAULT_TEMPLATE, this);
66      myTextArea.setText
67          (myStory.create (DEFAULT_CLEVER, DEFAULT_DULL));
68    }
69 }
```

String input is accomplished with the `TextField` class. The text field for the clever group is declared in Line 21 and the dull group in Line 22. They need to be instance variables so that they can be accessed by the `init` and `action` methods.

The clever text field object is created within the `init` method in Line 47 and added to the display window in Line 49. The code for the dull group is similar.

The new story is displayed in a scrollable text area. The text area is defined as an instance variable in Line 20, created in Line 59, its background color set to white in Line 60, set to not editable in Line 61, and added to the display window in Line 62.

The default story is created and displayed in Line 65 and 66 on program start up. New stories are created and displayed in Line 37 when the "rewrite" button is pressed.

The `TemplateFile` class is found in Listing 10.14. It is responsible for reading a template file from a text file. An explanation of its code can be found in Section 12.4.5 on page 564.

Listing 10.14 `TemplateFile` Class

```
1  //*************************************************************
2  //
3  // title:     TemplateFile
4  //
5  //   Read a template file.
6  //
7  //*************************************************************
8
9  import java.applet.Applet;
10 import java.io.InputStreamReader;
11 import java.io.BufferedReader;
12 import java.io.IOException;
13 import java.net.MalformedURLException;
14 import java.net.URL;
15
16 public class TemplateFile
17 {
18    String myTemplate;
19
```

Listing 10.14 `TemplateFile` Class

```
20    //---------- TemplateFile ------------------------------------
21    // pre:  none
22    // post: read the template file
23    public TemplateFile (String templateFileName, Applet applet)
24    {
25      myTemplate = "";
26
27      try
28      {
29        URL fileURL = new URL (applet.getDocumentBase(),
30                               templateFileName);
31        InputStreamReader reader =
32            new InputStreamReader (fileURL.openStream());
33        BufferedReader templateFile  =
                             new BufferedReader (reader);
34
35        while (true)
36        {
37          String aLine = templateFile.readLine();
38          if (aLine == null)
39            break;
40          myTemplate = myTemplate + aLine + "\n";
41        }
42      }
43      catch (MalformedURLException e)
44      {
45        System.out.println ("File could not be opened.");
46      }
47      catch (IOException e)
48      {
49        System.out.println ("File read error.");
50      }
51    }
52
53    //---------- get ------------------------------------------
54    // pre:  none
55    // post: get the template string
56    public String get ()
57    {
58      return myTemplate;
59    }
60 }
```

PROBLEM SETS

10.11 Exercises

Pattern Matching—Section 10.3

1   Using Table 10.1 on page 447 as a guide, build an execution history of the matching algorithm in Listing 10.2 on page 446 for the following situations:

a.   `target = "Pong" and pattern = "on"`

b.   `target = "Pong" and pattern = "Song"`

c.   `target = "Pong" and pattern = "n"`

d.   `target = "Checkbox" and pattern = "Check"`

String—Section 10.5

2   Given the following string definition, what is the result of the following operation:

`String title = new String("Das Boot");`

a.   `title.charAt(0)`

b.   `title.charAt(7)`

c.   `title.charAt(8)`

d.   `title.charAt(3)`

e.   `title.charAt(4)`

f.   `title.compareTo("The Boat")`

g.   `title.compareTo("das Boot")`

h.   `title.equals("das Boot")`

i.   `title.equals("das Boot")`

j.   `title.equalsIgnoreCase("das booT")`

k.   `title.length()`

l.   `title.indexOf("Boot")`

m.   `title.indexOf("boot")`

n.   `title.indexOf("o")`

o.   `title.indexOf("o", 5)`

p.   `title.indexOf("o", 6)`

q.   `title.compareTo("There is a boat")`

r.   `title.compareTo("A Boat")`

s.   `title.toUpperCase()`

t.   `title.toLowerCase()`

u.   `title.substring(0,2) + " " + title.substring(0,2)`

v.   `title.substring(4,7) + title.substring(3,7)`

w.   `title.substring(0, 3).length()`

3   Given the following string definition, what is the result of the following operation:

```
String title = new String("The English Patient");
```

a.   `title.substring( 4, 11)`

b.   `title.substring(12, 15)`

c.   `title.substring( 3,  4)`

d.   `title.substring( 6,  6)`

e.   `title.substring(0,3) + title.substring(11, 19) +`
       `title.substring(2, 11)`

f.   `title.substring(4, 11).substring(4, 6)`

4   Suppose the second parameter is removed from the String `indexOf` method in the `create` method of the `Story` class in Listing 10.1 on page 441. See below. What are the ramifications to the execution efficiency of the `create` method?
```
index = target.indexOf(pattern);
```

5   Write a method that converts a string to an integer using the algorithm in Section 10.4. Assume the string is a non-empty valid integer. It should respond to the following call:
```
int i = StringUtilities.toInt ("3289");
```

10.12 Projects

Stories—Section 10.2

6   Find a story or joke and make it customizable like the one in Section 10.2.

Characters—Section 10.4 and Section 10.6

7   Write a program that codes and decodes secret messages in a text area. The encoding process is accomplished by shifting each character of the message by a given increment. For example, suppose the shifting increment is five. Then each character in the a word is changed to the character that is five positions greater than it in the ASCII table. For example, string "secrets" becomes "xjhwjyx." Only shift characters with ASCII values between 32 and 127 inclusive. Characters encoding should wrap around. For example, shifting the ASCII character 127 by 1 should result in the ASCII character 32.

```
...  >  ?  @  A  B  C  D  ...      original character
...  C  D  E  F  G  H  I  ...      new character

...  >  ?  @  A  B  C  D  ...      original character
...  C  D  E  F  G  H  I  ...      new character
```

Coding and then decoding a message with the same shift constant should reproduce the original message.

A GUI implementation may have the following components (Section 4.2.3 on page 127):

a.   editable text area for the secret text

b.   text field for entering the shift constant

c.   coded text

d.   code button

A text-based implementation may have the following user interaction (Section 4.2.1 on page 123). Using the command pattern describe in Section 8.4 on page 353 will provide extract program flexibility.:

e.   ask user to enter secret text

f.   ask user for shift constant

g.   display coded text

String—Section 10.5 and Section 10.6

8   Write a program that tests whether a string is a palindrome, i.e., a string that reads the same forward and backwards. Example palindromes:

```
radar, toot, kayak, civic, I, racecar
```

a.   Use a text-based interface.
- enter text
- display "passed" or "not passed"

b.   Use a GUI interface.
- text field for the string under test
- a test button
- a label that displays "passed" or "failed"

Make sure your program returns false on the empty string.

9   Extend exercise 8 to ignore case, spaces, and punctuation so that it will accept

```
A man, a plan, a canal, Panama!
A Toyota
Dammit, I'm Mad.
Dogma? I am God.
Ed, I saw Harpo Marx ram Oprah W. aside.
Ma is as selfless as I am.
Never odd or even.
Now, Ned, I am a maiden nun. Ned, I am a maiden won.
Step on no pets.
Too hot to hoot.
Was it a car or a cat I saw?
```

10   Write a program that counts the number of words in a text area. For simplicity, assume that all words contain letters only (upper and lower case). Word delimiters are spaces, periods, commas, and question marks. No other characters will be found in the text.

The program should contain the following GUI components:

a.   text field for the text to be counted

b.   button to initiate the count

c.   a label to display the number of words counted

An alternative is to build a text-based application that reads a story from a file. Find a story on the internet. See `http://eserver.org/fiction`

11 List Algorithms

Locating Movie Reviews

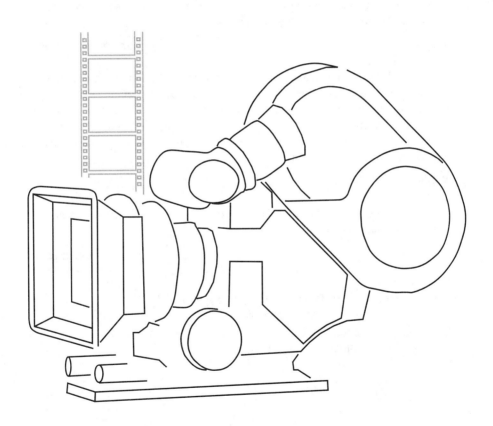

11.1　Objectives

Concepts　　　　　　　　　　　　　　　　　　**Section 11.2, page 485**

Lists play a dominant role in computer programs. We begin our introduction with a program that manipulates a list of movie reviews. We learn how to implement sequential and binary search algorithms and use them to find movie titles. We learn how to sort reviews into alphabetic order.

Section 11.5, page 513

Supplementary material continues our analysis of these algorithms. We analyze the sequential search and selection sorting algorithms. In addition, we informally classify the algorithmic complexity of binary search.

Patterns　　　　　　　　　　　　　　　　　　**Section 11.3, page 491**

We introduce two new patterns to facilitate search. The sequential search algorithm uses a pattern that visits every element in a list and a variation that exits once an item is found. This pattern is used again in the selection sort algorithm. It visits every element in a list and then uses the finding extreme values pattern to place the appropriate list element in the appropriate position. Finally, we use the binary search algorithm to make searches faster.

Java Skills

Lists are implemented with the Java vector class. We learn how to access, append, insert, and delete items from a vector.

- `Vector` class.　　　　　　　　　　　　　Section 11.4, page 504

Abilities

- Use the `Vector` class to implement a list class.
- Implement search and sort operations.
- Analyze sequential search algorithms.
- Analyze selection sort algorithms.

CONCEPTS

11.2 Movie Reviews

Watching a good movie with friends on a Friday night after a hard week at school or work can be a welcome break. With popcorn and soda in hand, we can find our fun spoiled by a bad movie. Video guides, such as the ones produced by Leonard Maltin, can help, but its 20,000 entries make it unwieldy and it soon goes out of date. It would be nice to go into a video store with a few sheets of paper that list the best recent movies.

One source of current reviews were those by Gene Siskel and Roger Ebert. Until Siskel's death, they had a syndicated television show with the results of their reviews recorded in a web site at `http://www.Siskel-Ebert.com`. A search of their web site would uncover a list of their recommendations starting in 1996.

Their list has a problem. It is organized by the date their reviews were aired on television. A typical video store organizes their videos alphabetically. This makes their list difficult to use. This chapter explores an application that allows us to sort movie reviews alphabetically and list only those movies that are recommended. .

Figure 11.1 Movie Guide Screen

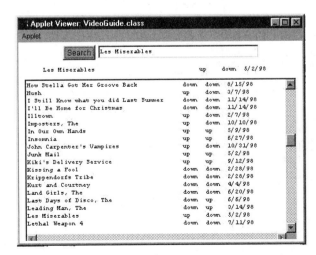

11.2.1 Movie Guide Utility

When the Movie Guide application starts up, it displays a list of movie reviews and gives the user an opportunity to search for one. See Figure 11.1

11.2.2 Movie Guide Design

The Video Guide application is partitioned into five classes (see Figure 11.2). In this chapter we will focus on two: the `MovieReviewList` and `Vector` classes. The other classes are summarized below to provide us with a context. Their complete listings can be found in Section 11.8 on page 518 .

Figure 11.2 Video Guide Program Design

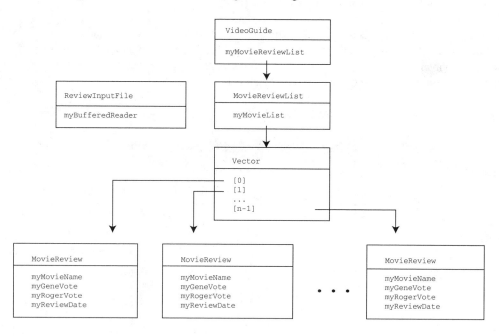

- `VideoGuide`: An object of this class is responsible for displaying and providing a means to search for movie reviews. It is responsible for creating the window shown in Figure 11.1. Its implementation can be found in Listing 11.12 on page 518.

- `MovieReviewList`: An object of this class contains a list of movie reviews. Operations include list creation, sorting, searching, and review access. Its implementation can be found in Listing 11.13 on page 521.

- `Vector`: The `Vector` class is a standard Java class. It is used to implement our list of movies. We will learn how to use this class. Operations include creating, adding, inserting, and deleting from a vector. We will also look at a strategy for implementing a vector class in Chapter 13.

- `MovieReview`: Objects of this class are a single movie review. Operations include creation, retrieving movie names, retrieving review dates, retrieving reviewer votes, and storing in a file. Its implementation can be found in Listing 11.14 on page 525.

- `ReviewInputFile`: An object of this class is responsible for opening and reading reviews from files. Its implementation can be found in Listing 12.27 on page 586. We will describe how it works when we get into Chapter 12.

11.2.3 `MovieReview` Class

The `MovieReviewList` class is a list of reviews. Each review is an object of the `MovieReview` class. The MovieReview class is responsible for maintaining information about a single review. Its interface is shown in Listing 11.1, and its complete implementation is shown in Listing 11.14 on page 525.

Listing 11.1 MovieReview Class

```
1  public class MovieReview
2  {
3    public MovieReview (String name, boolean gene, boolean roger,
4                String date);
5    public boolean equals(String other);
6    public String  getDate();
7    public boolean getGeneThumb();
8    public String  getName();
9    public boolean getRogerThumb();
10   public boolean greaterThan (MovieReview other);
11   public boolean greaterThan(String other);
12   public boolean lessThan(String other);
13   public String  toString();
14 }
```

Using the constructor in Line 3, we can create a review. A thumbs up is true and a thumbs down is false. For example, to create a two "thumbs up" for Emma, which was reviewed on August 3, 1996, we write the following:

```
MovieReview aReview =
        new MovieReview ("Emma", true, true, "08/03/96");
```

Once we have created a movie review we can later get a movie's name or Roger Ebert's vote using the following 'get' operations.

```
String title = aReview.getName();
Boolean vote = aReview.getRogerThumb();
```

In addition, we can compare reviews for their alphabetic ordering of titles.

```
aReview.equals ("Emma")            // result is true
aReview.greaterThan("Fargo")       // result is false
```

The last comparison is false because "Emma" does not come later in an alphabetic listing than "Fargo." Notice that there are four comparison methods. Three of them take strings as parameters (Lines 5, 11, and 12). These methods are used by the review search methods. When we do a search we start with a movie title, which is a string, and hunt for the movie review whose title matches that string.

The comparison method in Line 10 is a little different. It takes a movie review as a parameter. This method is used when sorting because the sort method needs to compare entire reviews, including the review's votes and date in addition to the movie's name.

Finally, the `toString` method allows us to print movie reviews.

```
System.out.println(aReview.toString());
```

This can be simplified to the following:

```
System.out.println(aReview);
```

11.2.4 Lists

A list of movie reviews forms the backbone of the Video Guide application. Lists are used extensively in everyday life. We maintain lists of addresses and phone numbers, grocery lists, and lists of things to do. It is not surprising that computers must also maintain lists. They maintain lists of magazine subscriptions, client billings, grades, courses, movie reviews, and many other things. Listing 11.13 on page 521 shows the entire code for the `MovieReviewList` class. We will look as some of its highlights here.

A *list* is a sequential ordering of items. Each element in a list, except for the first, has a predecessor and each element has a successor, except for the last.

There are many operations typically performed on lists. The most common are listed below:

- Create a new list.
- Determine the number of elements in a list.
- Retrieve the ith element in a list.
- Replace the ith element in a list.
- Remove the ith element in a list.
- Insert a new element into a list.
- Find an element in a list.
- Sort a list.

11.2.5 Basic List Operations

We will use the Java `Vector` class to implement lists. It supports several of the list operations described above. This section takes a brief look at a handful of these operations. A more detailed examination is found in Section 11.4.

The following code demonstrates how to create a list of three movies. Each time the `addElement` method is applied to `movieList`, a new movie review is added to the end of the list.

```
Vector movieList = new Vector();
MovieReview aReview;
aReview = new MovieReview("Emma", true, true, "08/03/96");
movieList.addElement(aReview);
aReview = new MovieReview("Lone Star", true, true, "06/22/96");
movieList.addElement(aReview);
aReview = new MovieReview("Fargo", true, true, "03/02/96");
movieList.addElement(aReview);
```

Movie reviews can be inserted into the middle of a list with the `insertElementAt` method. The following inserts the movie review for "Big Night" between the reviews for "Emma" and "Lone Star." (Notice that items in a vector are counted beginning with zero.)

```
aReview = new MovieReview("Big Night", true, true, "09/21/96");
movieList.insertElementAt(aReview, 1);
```

The resulting list is shown below. "Emma" is index location 0, "Big Night" at 1, and "Fargo" at 3.

```
Emma                        up      up      08/03/96
Big Night                   up      up      09/21/96
Lone Star                   up      up      06/22/96
Fargo                       up      up      03/02/96
```

Once a list is created, members can be accessed with the `elementAt` method. The following retrieves the third review. In our list it is the review for the movie "Lone Star." Notice the cast to a `MovieReview` object. Regardless of what kind of object we put into a vector, it returns a generic object. We must cast it to the object of interest. See Section 11.4.5 for more detail.

```
MovieReview loneStar = (MovieReview)(list.elementAt(2));
```

PATTERNS

11.3 Lists Patterns

11.3.1 Visit All Elements in a List Pattern

Search is a common operation applied to lists. *Leonard Maltin's Movie & Video Guide* has almost 20,000 entries. When lists become large, we need tools to help us find target listings. Simply scrolling through a long list is too time-consuming.

The `Vector` class has an `indexOf` method that returns the index of an object within a vector. For example, the following searches the list above for the movie review for "Lone Star." It will return the index value of two.

```
aReview = new MovieReview("Lone Star", true, true, "06/22/96");
int index = movieList.indexOf(aReview);  // index gets 2
```

Using the `indexOf` method is highly restrictive. It looks for an exact match. We must know the exact movie title, the reviewer votes, and the review date. In other words, by using the `indexOf` method we cannot find the answer to our question without knowing the answer. If we want to find the review "Fargo" but do not know how Siskel and Ebert evaluated it, we are out of luck. However, the reason for doing a search is to find information that we do not know.

In this section we will implement a searching method that allows us to search by movie title alone. We will start by assuming we have an unsorted list. Our strategy will be to start at the beginning of the list, check for a match, and continue to the next item if a match is not found.

Search is an application of the Visit All Elements in a List pattern shown below:

```
// visit all elements in a list pattern
while more elements in a list
  get the next data item from the list
  do something with that item
end loop
```

Adapting the "visit all elements in a list" pattern to the search problem, we get code that looks like the following:

```
create an empty foundReview list
```

491

```
while more elements in our movie review list
  get the next data item from the list
  if item is a match
    add it to our foundReview list
end loop
```

The above algorithm is appropriate when we want to find all movies that have the word "Friday" in it. Thus, we would get Jodie Foster's 1977 film *Freaky Friday*, Cary Grant's 1940 film *His Girl Friday*, *Friday the 13th* and sequels, plus many others. Implementing keyword searches is left as an exercise. We will implement searches for exact title matches in this section (Listing 11.2).

Listing 11.2 Sequential Search of Movie Reviews

```
1   //---------- search ------------------------------------
2   // pre:  none
3   // post: The review with a name that matches "targetName"
4   //       is returned.
5   //       If no match is found, null is returned
6   public MovieReview sequentialSearch (String targetName)
7   {
8     int i = 0;
9     MovieReview review = null;
10    while (i<size() && review == null)
11    {
12      if (elementAt(i).equals (targetName))
13        review = elementAt(i);
14      i++;
15    }
16    return review;
17 }
```

Table 11.1 Example Search for "Big Night"

iteration	statement number	i	comment
1	12	0	no match
2	12	1	no match
3	12	2	match
	16	2	exit search

Suppose we know there is only one match or that finding a single match is sufficient. Once we find a matching item there is no need to continue our hunt. Thus, we will modify the "visit all elements" pattern to exit early. Listing 11.2 shows an implementation in which we leave the loop once a match has been found. As a result, we return the first matching item. Table 11.1 shows an example walk-through for finding "Big Night" in the list of reviews shown in Listing 11.3.

Listing 11.3 Unsorted Movie List

```
0   Bound
1   Evita
2   Big Night
3   Beavis & Butthead
4   English Patient, The
```

sequences

The `while` condition in Line 10 (Listing 11.2) can be a challenge to create. An alternative is to use a `for` loop as shown in Listing 11.4. Notice that the `for` loop is exited prematurely if the movie title is found. If the target title is not found, the `for` loop exits normally and `null` is returned. Table 11.2 shows an example walk-through for finding "Big Night" in the list of reviews shown in Listing 11.3.

Listing 11.4 Sequential Search that Violates Loop Exit Guidelines

```
1    //---------- search -------------------------------
2    // pre:  none
3    // post: The review with a name that matches "targetName"
4    //       is returned.
5    //       If no match is found, null is returned
6    public MovieReview sequentialSearch (String targetName)
7    {
8      for (int i=0; i<size(); i++)
9      {
10       MovieReview review = elementAt(i);
11       if (review.equals(targetName))
12         return review;
13     }
14     return null;
15   }
```

The `return` statement in Line 12 violates the break guidelines we stated in Section 9.4.1. Many people argue that it is confusing if a `for` loop exits prematurely. The author prefers this code because it is short and clean.

Table 11.2 Example Search for "Big Night"

iteration	statement number	i	comment
1	11	0	no match
2	11	1	no match
3	11	2	match
3 continued	12	2	exit search

Listing 11.5 A Confusing Sequential Search Using a Flag

```
1    //---------- sequentialSearch ---------------------------
2    // pre:  none
3    // post: The review with the movie name that match "targetName"
4    //       is returned.
5    //       If it is not found, null is returned
6    public MovieReview sequentialSearch (String targetName)
7    {
8        int i = 0;
9        boolean found = false;
10       MovieReview review = null;
11       while (i<size() & !found)
12       {
13          review = elementAt(i);
14          if (review.equals(targetName))
15             found = true;
16          i++;
17       }
18       if (found)
19          return review;
20       else
21          return null;
22   }
```

The version in Listing 11.5 uses a found flag to signal the end of the loop. The flag is set true when the review is found in Line 15. It allows us to specify the conditions for leaving the loop in one location. We can express those condition solely within the single loop conditional expression in Line 11.

> A *flag* is a special boolean value used to control the flow of a program. It is set in one location and checked in another.

Many find the use of flags confusing because they add complexity to our code. It requires the maintenance of a flag and a special check at the end of the loop. With a little thought, we can eliminate flags and create solutions such as the one in Listing 11.2.

When testing these algorithms, be certain to test for targets that are at the beginning and end of the list in addition to those in the middle. Data elements at extreme locations are often not dealt with appropriately. Also test for titles not found within the list. Finally, test special cases; for example, when the list size is 0 and 1.

The implementations in this section depend on an exact title match. There can be no differences in spelling, capitalization, or spacing. Finding exact title matches is prohibitive. It is easy to forget if the name of a movie is Terminator *II* or *Terminator 2*. It is also hard to remember that *Frisco Kid* starred James Cagney and Margaret Lindsay in 1935 and *The Frisco Kid* starred Gene Wilder and Harrison Ford in 1979. We would like to search for keywords that we remember from the title, such as "Frisco" or "Kid." As mentioned above, this task is left as an exercise.

11.3.2   Selection Sort

blem

In the next section we will use a "divide-and-conquer" strategy to implement a binary search. "Divide and conquer" speeds up a search dramatically. However, it assumes that our list is ordered. In this section we will look at an algorithm for sorting lists in ascending order.

me
ution

One strategy, called the *selection sort*, for sorting a list is to visit each location in our list and determine which element belongs in that spot. For example, we can begin at the end of the list and place the largest element there. (The element that comes last in alphabetic order is referred to as the largest element.) Next, we can look at the second location from the end of the list and place the second highest item there. We continue until all locations in the list have been visited.

While running, this algorithm partitions a list into two components. The first part of the list is unsorted and the second part is sorted. At the beginning of the sort process, the entire list is unsorted. As sorting progresses, the sorted part grows until the entire list is sorted. An algorithm that sorts using this strategy is shown below:

```
// selection sort
assume the entire list is unsorted
while there are items in the unsorted part of the list
   find the largest item in the unsorted part of the list
   swap it with the current item (the highest index of the
        unsorted part)
   subtract one from the current index (decrease the size of
        the unsorted part)
end loop
```

We use two familiar patterns. We use the pattern described in the previous section to visit every element in a list (starting at the end of the list). Then we use the "finding extremes" pattern to find the largest element in the unsorted part of the list.

Listing 11.6 Sort Method

```
1    //---------- sort ----------------------------------------------
2    // pre:  this list is not null
3    // post: this list is sorted by movie name
4    public void sort()
5    {
6      int n = myMovieList.size();
7      for (int current=n-1; current>0; current--)
8      {
9        int largestPosition = 0;
10       for (int j=1; j<=current; j++)
11       {
12         MovieReview largeReview = elementAt(largestPosition);
13         MovieReview jReview     = elementAt(j);
14         if (jReview.greaterThan(largeReview))
15           largestPosition = j;
16       }
17       swap(largestPosition, current);
18     }
19   }
20
21   //---------- swap ----------------------------------------------
22   // Swap two reviews in this list.
23   // For internal use only
24   private void swap (int a, int b)
25   {
26     MovieReview temp = elementAt(a);
27     myMovieList.setElementAt(myMovieList.elementAt(b), a);
28     myMovieList.setElementAt(temp,b);
29   }
```

Listing 11.6 shows an implementation of the selection sort. It begins by setting the last element as the current location of interest (Line 7). It looks at the item at this current location plus the items in all locations before it for the largest item (Lines 9 through 16). It swaps the largest item with the item at its current location (Line 17). The current location now contains the item that belongs there. As a result, all items from the current position to the end of the list are sorted.

Figure 11.3 Sort Animation

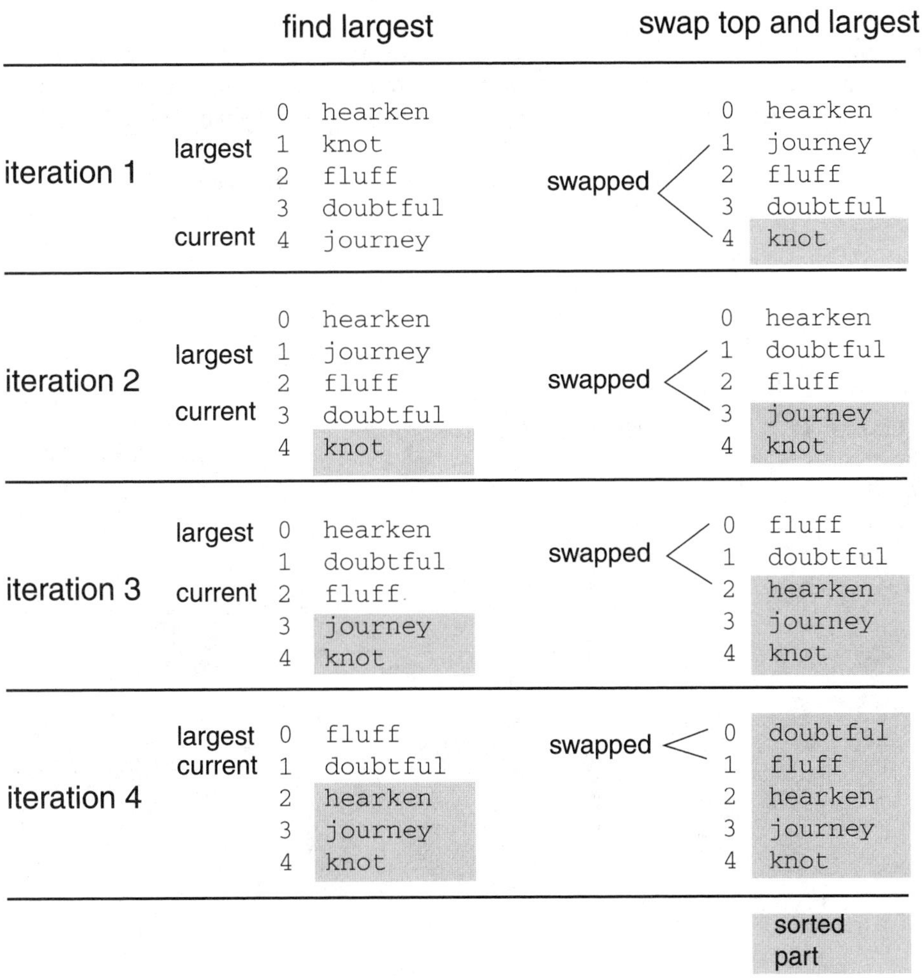

		find largest		swap top and largest	
iteration 1	largest	0 hearken 1 knot 2 fluff 3 doubtful	swapped	0 hearken 1 journey 2 fluff 3 doubtful	
	current	4 journey		4 knot	
iteration 2	largest	0 hearken 1 journey 2 fluff	swapped	0 hearken 1 doubtful 2 fluff	
	current	3 doubtful 4 knot		3 journey 4 knot	
iteration 3	largest	0 hearken	swapped	0 fluff	
	current	1 doubtful 2 fluff		1 doubtful 2 hearken	
		3 journey 4 knot		3 journey 4 knot	
iteration 4	largest current	0 fluff 1 doubtful	swapped	0 doubtful 1 fluff	
		2 hearken 3 journey 4 knot		2 hearken 3 journey 4 knot	
				sorted part	

The sort algorithm now visits the item at the previous location by subtracting one from the current position (Line 7). It looks at this item and all items before it to again find the largest. After a swap, the two locations at the end of the list have items in the appropriate locations. The process continues until there is only one location left, which will have the appropriate item assigned to it

The inner loop is responsible for finding the maximum value. It is similar to the maximum algorithms we have seen before. In Line 9 we assume that the element in the first position of the list is the largest. Then we loop through the remaining items and adjust our assumptions each time they are disproved.

Notice how `current` is decremented by one each time through the outer loop. Thus, the size of the inner loop becomes smaller with each iteration of the outer loop. With each iteration of the outer loop, there is one less element that the inner loop must check.

Table 11.3 and Figure 11.3 demonstrate how this technique works when sorting the list of words shown below:

```
hearken          index 0
knot             index 1
fluff            index 2
doubtful         index 3
journey          index 4  . .
```

Listing 11.7 Sorting with Nested Loop Removal

```
1    public void sort()
2    {
3      int n = myMovieList.size();
4      for (int top=n-1; top>0; top--)
5        swap (top, findMax (0, top));
6    }
7
8    private int findMax (int lowerBound, int upperBound)
9    {
10     int largestPosition = lowerBound;
11     for (int j=lowerBound+1; j<=upperBound; j++)
12     {
13       MovieReview largeReview = elementAt(largestPosition);
14       MovieReview jReview     = elementAt(j);
15       if (jReview.greaterThan(largeReview))
16         largestPosition = j;
17     }
18     return largestPosition;
19   }
```

Table 11.3 Walk-through of the Selection Sort

statement number	top	j	largest-Position	comments
9	4	1	0	assume "hearken" is max
15	4	1	1	"knot" is new max
15	4	2	1	
15	4	3	1	
15	4	4	1	
17	4	-	1	swap "knot" and "journey"
9	3	1	0	assume "hearken" is max
15	3	1	1	"journey" is new max
15	3	2	1	
15	3	3	1	
17	3	-	1	swap "journey" and "doubtful"
9	2	1	0	assume "hearken" is max
15	2	1	0	
15	2	2	0	
17	2	-	0	swap "hearken" and "fluff"
9	1	1	0	assume "fluff" is max
15	1	1	0	
17	1	-	0	swap "fluff" and "doubtful"
20	-	-	-	done

In Section 9.4.5 we described an approach to getting rid of nested loops. Many people find their removal makes code easier to understand. Listing 11.7 shows the result when applied to our selection sort. Notice how the resulting sort algorithm is simplified. We have a call to a `findMax` method, which we learned how to write in Chapter 8. The resulting sort method is only a few lines long

11.3.3   Binary Search Pattern

When looking for a friend's number in a phone directory, no one starts at the beginning of the list and looks at each name until a match is found. We do something far more clever. We guess about where the name should appear in the directory, open to that location, and flip pages left or right depending on whether our guesses are too high or too low. This approach is called binary search. We continually divide our work roughly in half.

```
// binary search pattern
while there are items of interest to investigate
  split the items into two groups
     those items that may be of interest
     those item that are not of interest
end loop
```

solution

For the binary search pattern to work the process of splitting items into two groups must be efficient. For example, when we apply the "divide and conquer" pattern to movie searches, the list must be sorted alphabetically. By looking at a single element in the middle of a list we can narrow our search to one half of the list. If the list were not sorted, we would need to look at all items in the list to determine which are greater and which are smaller. We would do just as well using a sequential search.

Listing 11.8 Binary Search of Movie Reviews

```
1   //---------- binarySearch ------------------------------
2   // pre:  none
3   // post: The review with the movie name that matches "name"
4   //       is returned.
5   //       If it is not found, null is returned
6   public MovieReview binarySearch (String targetName)
7   {
8      int bottom = 0;
9      int top    = size() - 1;
10
11     // do binary search
12     while (top >= bottom)
13     {
14        int middle = (bottom + top) / 2;
15        MovieReview middleReview  = elementAt(middle);
16        if (middleReview.greaterThan(targetName))
17           top = middle - 1;
18        else if (middleReview.lessThan(targetName))
19           bottom = middle + 1;
20        else
21           return middleReview;
22     }
23
24     return null;
25  }
```

We begin by first looking at the movie in the middle of the list. If the target movie title matches the middle movie title, we have found the movie review. If the target movie is alphabetically greater, we know the target movie is in the top half of the list. Otherwise it is in the bottom half. We then repeat this process on the appropriate half list until the target is found or the remaining list is empty. This strategy is called *binary search* because the list is continually divided in half. An implementation of this algorithm is shown in Listing 11.8.

Table 11.4 Search for Infinity

title	index	Iteration 1	2	3	4
Vertigo	19	top			
Star Trek: First Contact	18				
Space Jam	17				
Sling Blade	16				
Shine	15				
Secrets and Lies	14				
Ransom	13				
Preacher's Wife, The	12				
Microcosmos	11				
Michael Collins	10				
Michael	9	middle			
Jerry Maguire	8		top	top	top
Infinity	7				bottom middle
Hamlet	6			middle	
Extreme Measures	5			bottom	
Evita	4		middle		
English Patient, The	3				
Bound	2				
Big Night	1				
Beavis & Butthead	0	bottom	bottom		

```
// binary search in an ordered list
while there are items in the list
   get the middle data item from the list
   if the data item is less than the target
     narrow the list to the bottom half
   else if the data item is greater than the target
     narrow the list to the top half
   else
     return the data item
end loop
return not found
```

The integers bottom, middle, and top are indices into the list. The top and bottom indices specify the current boundaries of the part of the list we are searching. The middle index is halfway between them. Table 11.4 shows an example run for the target movie "Infinity." (Note: The items in the table are listed backwards. The item at index zero is placed at the bottom and the highest index at top.)

The integers bottom, middle, and top begin with the values of 0, 9, and 19 respectively. After the first iteration it has been determined that "Infinity" comes before the middle movie "Michael." As a result, the search is narrowed to movies in locations 0 through 8. In the next iteration, it is determined that "Infinity" comes after "Evita." As a result, the search is narrowed to movies in locations 5 through 8. This process continues until "Infinity" is located at index seven.

Table 11.5 outlines an unsuccessful search for the title "Phenomenon." Notice that the loop is exited when the top index is less than the bottom index. Null is returned to indicate that the movie title is not found.

consequences   The binary search strategy does not support keyword searches. For example, if we want to find all the movie titles that have the keyword "English" in them we will have to look through all the movie titles. We will need to apply a sequential search.

Table 11.5 Example Search for "Phenomenon"

iteration	bottom	middle	top
1	0	9	19
2	10	14	19
3	10	11	13
4	12	12	13
final values	12	11	11

It is easy to make off-by-one mistakes when implementing a binary search. Choosing test cases is not trivial. The combination of `if` statements within the loop generates many possible paths. We know that testing all possible list sizes is not practical. Without a clear criteria for test data selection, we may miss key test cases. An exhaustive test of one list size, say 20, is reasonable. For example, make sure that each movie title in a list of 20 can be found and that movie titles lying between existing ones are not found. Forty-one test cases is clearly overkill. We could get by with much fewer. However, cutting these few test cases in half will not save use much time. Again, we should also test the list sizes 0 and 1.

JAVA

As we mentioned in Section 11.2, lists can be implemented with the Java `Vector` class. We will take a closer look at the `Vector` class now. A summary of Vector class operations is found in Appendix: B on page 908.

11.4   The Java Vector Class

A vector is an indexed collection of objects. They are indexed beginning at zero and ending at n minus 1, where n in the number of objects. For example, the elements in a 10-item list are indexed from 0 through 9. Starting with the index 0 is consistent with other numbering schemes in Java. For example, numbering the characters in a string also begins with 0.

Vectors automatically grow and shrink. As elements are added to a vector, its size grows. When elements are removed from a vector, it shrinks in size. Growing and shrinking vectors takes time. Because we do not know which event will cause a vector to grow or shrink, the time performance of vector operations is unpredictable. Sometimes, an insert will make a vector grow, but usually not.

11.4.1   Constructor

There are several `Vector` constructors. We will use the one with no parameters to create an empty vector. An empty vector has a size of 0 and, thus contains no elements.

```
Vector gradeList = new Vector();
```

11.4.2   addElement

The `addElement` method is used to append new items to the end of a vector. For example, the following will append three grade reports to the grade list created above. (Listing 11.9 shows the example `GradeReport` class, which we will use to illustrate vectors.)

```
GradeReport aReport = new GradeReport ("Bart", 89);
gradeList.addElement(aReport);
aReport = new GradeReport ("Lisa", 73);
gradeList.addElement(aReport);
aReport = new GradeReport ("Maggie", 94);
gradeList.addElement(aReport);
```

Listing 11.9 `GradeReport` Class

```
1   public class GradeReport
2   {
3      private String iName;
4      private int    iScore;
5
6      public int getScore ()
7      {
8         return iScore;
9      }
10
11     public GradeReport (String name, int score)
12     {
13        iName = name;
14        iScore = score;
15     }
16
17     public String toString()
18     {
19        return iName + " " + iScore;
20     }
21  }
```

As a result the list will contain the following items:

```
Bart    89
Lisa    73
Maggie  94
```

Any object can be added to a vector. It does not need to make sense. For example, the following adds a triangle and a color object to our grade report list:

```
Polygon triangle = new Polygon();
triangle.addPoint( 50,  50);
triangle.addPoint(100, 100);
triangle.addPoint( 50, 100);
gradeList.addElement(triangle);
Color neonBlue = new Color (77, 77, 255);
gradeList.addElement(neonBlue);
```

However, we may not add primitive values to a vector. Recall our discussion in Section 5.6. Technically, primitive values are not objects. Vectors work only with objects. For example, the following are illegal:

```
gradeList.addElement (23);    // syntax error
gradeList.addElement (false); // syntax error
```

To get around this problem, the Java developers include wrapper classes for primitive values. We can use the Integer, Boolean, and Double wrappers if we need to store single numbers.

> A *wrapper* is a class with the purpose of providing a new interface for an existing set of classes or primitive values.

For example, by providing a wrapper for ints, we can use them places where objects are required. A simplified integer wrapper is shown in Listing 11.10. We can use this wrapper class to record daily temperatures in a vector (Listing 11.11).

Listing 11.10   Integer Wrapper Class

```
1  public class Integer
2  {
3    private int iValue;
4
5    public Integer (int i)
6    {
7      iValue = i;
8    }
9    public int intValue()
10   {
11      return iValue;
12   }
13 }
```

Listing 11.11   Using an Integer Wrapper Class in a Vector

```
1  public void init ()
2  {
3    Vector temperatures = new Vector ();
4    temperatures.addElement (new Integer (69));
5    temperatures.addElement (new Integer (73));
6    temperatures.addElement (new Integer (65));
7    temperatures.addElement (new Integer (63));
8    Integer temp = (Integer)(temperatures.elementAt (2));
9    int seccondTemperature = temp.intValue ();   // 65
10 }
```

11.4.3   size

The `size` method returns how many elements are in a vector. For example:

```
Vector gradeList = new Vector();
GradeReport aReport = new GradeReport ("Bart", 89);
gradeList.addElement(aReport);
aReport = new GradeReport ("Lisa", 73);
gradeList.addElement(aReport);
aReport = new GradeReport ("Maggie", 94);
gradeList.addElement(aReport);
int size = gradeList.size();   // size get the value 3
```

11.4.4   elementAt

When we retrieve an element from a vector, it returns an item of class `Object`. For example, given the list we created in Section 11.4.3, the following code can be used to retrieve elements:

```
Object item = gradeList.elementAt(2);
```

We have retrieved the grade report for "Maggie." It is illegal to access an item at a location where none exists. The following causes index-out-of-range errors when the program is run.

```
Object item = gradeList.elementAt(-1);            // run-time error
Object item = gradeList.elementAt(gradeList.size());  // ditto
Object item = gradeList.elementAt(150);           // run-time error
```

11.4.5   Typecast on Retrieval

We have stated that Java vectors hold objects. This statement may seem rather innocent, but it has a far reaching impact. All classes inherit from the `Object` class by default. Thus, we can store a `GradeReport` object in a vector because `GradeReport` inherits from `Object`. All vector retrieval methods return objects. However, a vector does not know or care what kind of object it returns.

In Chapter 3 we learned that when one class inherits another, the subclass gets all the characteristics of the superclass plus additional ones. The superclass is more generalized. For example, *flower* is a more general term than *rose*. Thus, when we say we are sending flowers to our sister, they may or may not be roses. We could be even more vague. We could say we are sending objects to our sister. That would include flowers, candy, and ball-peen hammers. Again, in a similar manner, when we say vectors hold objects, they can be any object. (We will revisit inheritance in more depth in Chapter 16.)

Let us start with a human analogy to build a little intuition about the role of a vector. In one sense we can view a vector as a peanut butter jar. A peanut butter jar can hold many kinds of objects: paper clips, marbles, grasshoppers, etc. Suppose our mother has given us a peanut butter jar full of jelly beans. It does not matter that the jar says peanut butter on the outside, we know that it contains jelly beans because our mother said it does. Since our mother has no sense of humor we believe her without question. Thus, when we open the jar and take an object out we pop it into our mouth without looking at it. We know it will not be a grasshopper.

Now, suppose that our roommate, who has a twisted sense of humor, puts a marble into the peanut butter jar. Later we take the marble out of the jar, pop it in our mouth, and break a tooth. It is exactly this situation that Java is trying to prevent through type checking.

Notice that `item` in the previous section belong to the `Object` class. The programmer knows that `item` is a `GradeReport` object but the Java compiler knows only that it could be any kind of object, thus, the following statements are not allowed:

```
Object item = gradeList.elementAt (2);        // ok
int score = item.getScore ();                 // compile error
```

The Java compiler determines that the `Object` class does not support the `getScore` operation. Thus, applying the `getScore` method to `item` is not allowed.

The following line is no better. The Java compiler will not allow it because it does not know that `item` at index two is a `GradeReport`. This may seem rather fantastic because we, the programmer, remember explicitly placing a `GradeReport` at index two. However, compilers are not very smart.

```
GradeReport item = gradeList.elementAt(2);   // compile error
```

Now we may appear to be stymied. How do we get a `GradeReport` object out of a vector and apply the `getScore` method to it? We tell the compiler that we know that the item we are retrieving is a `GradeReport` by using a type cast. The following will store Maggie's grade in `score`:

```
Object item = gradeList.elementAt(2);
GradeReport aReport = (GradeReport)item;
int score = aReport.getScore();              // score gets 94
```

or

```
GradeReport aReport = (GradeReport)(gradeList.elementAt(2));
int score = aReport.getScore();              // score gets 94
```

What we are telling the compiler is "trust me." We know that `item` is a `GradeReport`. However, in doing so we take a risk. If code that we did not write or if we by accident placed a different object in our vector, the program will abort (much like breaking our tooth on a marble). The following illustrates:

```
Vector gradeList = new Vector ();
gradeList.addElement (new GradeReport ("Elmer", 77);
gradeList.addElement (new Polygon ());
Object item = gradeList.elementAt(0);
GradeReport aReport = (GradeReport)item;   // OK at run-time
int score = aReport.getScore();
item = gradeList.elementAt(1);
Polygon aPolygon = (Polygon)item;          // OK at run-time
g.fillPolygon(aReport);
item = gradeList.elementAt(1);
aReport = (GradeReport)item;               // run-time error
score = aReport.getScore();
```

We must know our vector before we do a cast. If we are not sure what kind of objects we have in our peanut butter jar, we can always inspect each one as we take them out. For example, if we want to print only the grades, we look at each item in the vector first as follows:

```
for (int i=0; i<movieList.size(); i++)
{
  Object item = gradeList.elementAt(i);
  if (item instanceof GradeReport)
  {
    GradeReport aReport = (GradeReport)item;
    System.out.println(item.getScore());
  }
}
```

The `instanceof` operator checks whether an object belongs to a particular class. An example follows:

```
GradeReport aReport = new GradeReport ("Henry", 83);
boolean b = aReport instanceof GradeReport;   // b is true
boolean c = aReport instanceof MovieReview;   // c is false
```

One means to avoid all this confusion is to only place one kind of object in a vector. By making our vector homogeneous, we do not have to check what kind of object is stored in each location. This is what we did with the movie reviews. All the items in our vector belong to the class `MovieReview`.

11.4.6   setElementAt

The `setElementAt` operation is used to replace an item in a vector. For example, suppose our list contains the following three items:

```
Bart     89
Lisa     73
Maggie   94
```

The following code can be used to replace Lisa's grade report with Homer's:

```
aReport = new GradeReport ("Homer", 61);
gradeList.setElementAt(aReport, 1);
```

The result of the above is shown below:

```
Bart     89
Homer    61
Maggie   94
```

Index values must be within the range of valid elements within a vector. It is illegal to set an item at a location where none exists. See the `elementAt` method for examples of indices that are out of range.

It is not necessary to replace an object with an object of the same class. We could have replaced Lisa's report with a `Polygon`, `Color`, or any other object. For example:

```
Color red = new Color (255, 0, 0);
gradeList.setElementAt(red, 1);
```

11.4.7   insertElementAt

In addition to appending items to the end of a vector, we can insert them in the middle. This is accomplished with the `insertElementAt` operation. For example, suppose our list contains the following three items:

```
Bart     89
Lisa     73
Maggie   94
```

The following code can be used to insert Marge's grade report between Bart's and Lisa's:

```
aReport = new GradeReport ("Marge", 99);
gradeList.insertElementAt(aReport, 1);
```

The result of the above is shown below:

```
Bart    89
Marge   99
Lisa    73
Maggie  94
```

Notice that the new record is placed at the specified index. All the records from this location and higher are moved one index higher. Lisa's record was at index 1. Now it is at index 2. Maggie's record was at index 2. Now it is at index 3.

Again, the index must be within the range of the vector. Inserting an item at index 0 appends that item to the beginning of a vector. Inserting an item at the index for the size of a vector appends an item to the end of a vector. It does the same thing `addElement` does. Thus, the following appends Homer's record to the end of the list:

```
aReport = new GradeReport ("Homer", 61);
gradeList.insertElementAt(aReport, gradeList.size());
```

11.4.8   removeElementAt

A parallel operation to `insertElementAt` is `removeElementAt`. It allows us to remove any item within a list. For example, suppose our list contains the following five items:

```
Bart    89
Marge   99
Lisa    73
Maggie  94
Homer   61
```

The following code can be used to remove Lisa's grade report from the vector:

```
gradeList.removeElementAt(2);
```

The result of the above is shown below:

```
Bart    89
Marge   99
Maggie  94
Homer   61
```

Notice that all records above the deleted record are moved to fill in the gap. All the records from the location above the deleted record are moved one index down. Maggie's record changes from index 3 to 2. Marggie's record changes from index 4 to 3.

The following removes an item at the beginning of a vector:

```
gradeList.removeElementAt(0);
```

The following removes an item at the end of a vector:

```
gradeList.removeElementAt(gradeList.size() - 1);
```

It is illegal to remove an item from a location where none exists. The following causes index-out-of-range errors when the program is run.:

```
gradeList.removeElementAt(-1);                    // run-time error
gradeList.removeElementAt(gradeList.size());  // run-time error
```

SUPPLEMENTARY MATERIAL

11.5 Analyzing List Algorithms

11.5.1 Sequential Search

The sequential search algorithm contains a single loop in which the number of iterations depends on the number of movies in the list. One expects that the order of complexity of this algorithm is O(n). (See Section 8.6 on page 361.) On average we expect to have to look through half the list. However, sometimes our intuition can fool us. Let us take closer look.

We will assume that the number of movies in the list is n and that the target movie is in the list. We will also assume that the probability of finding the target movie at any location in the list is equal. For example, the probability that the target movie is at index 2342 is the same that it is at index 1593 or index 0 or index n minus1.

To find the average work required to find the target movie, we compute the work required to find the movie at each possible location, sum the results, and divide by n.

$$A(n) = \frac{work1 + work2 + \dots + workn}{n} \qquad \textbf{Equation 11.1}$$

One option for computing the work done to find a movie at each index is to count how much work each statement in the program contributes to the task. Although this method would give us an exact value, it will vary from computer to computer and compiler to compiler. Instead we will pick one key operation and count the number of times it is executed. This will not give us the exact amount of work being done, but it will provide us with a means to determine the order of complexity.

Experience has taught us that a good operation to count is a comparison such as the one in Line 11 of Listing 11.4. If the target movie is in the first location, the comparison in Line 11 is executed once; thus, the measure of work done is 1. If the target movie is in the second location, the work is 2. If the target movie is in the ith location, the work done is i. Thus, the average work done is:

$$A(n) = \frac{1 + 2 + 3 + \ldots + n}{n}$$ **Equation 11.2**

The equation $1 + 2 + 3 + \ldots + n$ can be simplified by pairing elements on opposite ends of the equation (see Figure 11.4).

Figure 11.4 Summing a Series

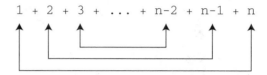

Each pair contributes n + 1 and there are n / 2 pairs; thus:

$$1 + 2 + 3 + \ldots + n = \frac{1}{2} \cdot n \cdot (n + 1)$$ **Equation 11.3**

Substituting Equation 11.3 into Equation 11.2, we get:

$$A(n) = \frac{1}{2} \cdot (n + 1) = \frac{1}{2} \cdot n + \frac{1}{2}$$ **Equation 11.4**

The polynomial term that dominates is $\frac{1}{2} \cdot n$. Our intuition is correct. Equation 11.4 is O(n).

We have gone through a lot of work to make an obvious conclusion. We make the effort here to help us understand the analysis process. As we encounter more complex algorithms in later courses, the basic analysis tools we learn here will become important.

11.5.2　Selection Sort

The clue to the order of complexity of the selection sort is the nested loop. We may expect it to be $O(n^2)$. We can confirm this with a little analysis.

Again, we will count the number of times a comparison is done as a basis for work. The target comparison is in Line 14 of Listing 11.6. During the first iteration of the outer loop, there will be n – 1 comparisons to find the largest item. During the second iteration, there will be n – 2 comparisons to find the second largest number. The next pass will require n –

3 comparisons and so on until the number of comparisons is 1. Thus, the average work done is:

$$A(n) = 1 + 2 + 3 + \ldots + (n - 1)$$

Equation 11.1

Using the same pairing strategy in Figure 11.4 we can simplify this to:

$$a(n) = \frac{n}{2} \cdot n$$

Equation 11.2

This is $O(n^2)$.

Algorithms that are $O(n^2)$ are typified by nested loops. There are a couple of examples of a nested loop in Section 9.3.6 and Section 9.4.5. One of these algorithms creates a multiplication table and the other computes a unique color for each pixel in a window. The outer loops iterates through each row. The inner loop iterates though each element in a row. These algorithms are O(rows * columns). If the number of rows and columns must always be equal, they are $O(n^2)$ where n == rows == columns. For example, if the dimensions of the paint window double, the number of pixels increases by four times.

Computer science is rich with algorithms that sort lists. To illustrate the variety of performance characteristics that these algorithms exhibit, Table 11.6 shows a summary of the performance for four sorting algorithms. Only the selection sort is described in this text. Each algorithm has characteristics that gives it an advantage in a given circumstance.

Table 11.6 Order of Complexity of Sorts

sort	order of complexity		
	best	average	worst
selection sort	$O(n^2)$	$O(n^2)$	$O(n^2)$
insertion sort	$O(n)$	$O(n^2)$	$O(n^2)$
bubble sort	$O(n^2)$	$O(n^2)$	$O(n^2)$
Quicksort	$O(n \log_2 n)$	$O(n \log_2 n)$	$O(n^2)$
Heap sort	$O(n \log_2 n)$	$O(n \log_2 n)$	$O(n \log_2 n)$

11.5.3   Binary Search

We will now informally classify the binary search algorithm. A formal derivation will wait for a later course. We will begin with an observation. If we double the size of our list, the number of comparisons required for a binary search goes up by only one. For example, if our list size is 1000 and we double it to 2000, the first comparison on the 2000-element list cuts our list in half. Thus, after the first comparison, our search has been reduced to the problem of finding an element in a 1000-item list. This is clearly better than the $O(n)$ for sequential search.

The order of complexity for a binary search is $O(\log_2 n)$. We can easily justify this by arguing that the average work done is proportional to $\log_2 n$. To make our argument, we will define x to be $\log_2 n$.

$$x = \log_2 n$$ **Equation 11.1**

Using the definition of log, this means that

$$n = 2^x$$ **Equation 11.2**

Table 11.7 shows several solutions to Equation 11.2. Notice that when n doubles, x goes up by one. This is the same behavior we expect from a binary search.

Table 11.7 $n = 2^x$

x	n
0	1
1	2
2	4
3	8
4	16
5	32
20	~10^6
40	~10^{12}

Look at the last two rows in the table. When we increase the number of movie titles from one million to one trillion, the number of times through the loop only doubles. If we used the sequential search, the number of times through the loop would be a million times more.

REFERENCE

11.6   Summary

The focus of this chapter is lists. We learned the basic operations on lists which include determining how many elements are in a list, retrieving an element from a list, replacing an element, removing an element, and inserting an element.

We introduced the "visit all elements" pattern and used it to implement a sequential search algorithm. We started our search at the beginning of the list and looked at each item until our target was found. We showed that the sequential search is O(n) for time.

We used the "visit all elements" and "find extreme values" patterns to implement a selection sort. It sorts by looking for the largest element in the unsorted partition of a list and swapping. We showed that the selection sort is $O(n^2)$ for time.

We introduced the "divide and conquer" pattern to quickly find items in a sorted list. We started by determining which half of a list our item is in. A binary search continues to cut our list in half until the item of interest in found. We argued that a binary search is $O(\log_2 n)$ for time.

We used the `Vector` class to implement a list. The vector class is dynamic. It grows and shrinks as items are added and deleted. Vector operations include ones to create a list, retrieve items, replace items, insert items, delete items, find items, plus others.

11.7   Bibliography

- Baase, Sara. 1988. *Computer Algorithms: Introduction to Design and Analysis*. Reading, MA: Addison Wesley.
- Budd, Timothy A. 1994 *Classic Data Structures in C++, Reading*, MA: Addison Wesley.

PROGRAM LISTINGS

11.8   Video Guide Program

The design of the VideoGuide application is found in Section 11.2.2 on page 486. The explanation of the `ReviewInputFile` is found and discussed in Chapter 12.

- `VideoGuide` class - Listing 11.12 on page 518
- `MovieReviewList` class - Listing 11.13 on page 521
- `MovieReview` class - Listing 11.14 on page 525
- `ReviewInputFile` class - Listing 12.27 on page 586

Listing 11.12 `VideoGuide` Class

```
1 //
*********************************************************************
2 //
3 // title:    VideoGuide
4 //
5 // Display and sort movie reviews.
6 //
7 //
*********************************************************************
8
9 import java.awt.Color;
10 import java.awt.Font;
11 import java.awt.Graphics;
12 import java.awt.Label;
13 import java.awt.TextArea;
14 import java.awt.TextField;
15 import vista.VApplet;
16 import vista.VActionButton;
17 import java.io.IOException;
18 import java.net.MalformedURLException;
19
```

Listing 11.12 VideoGuide Class

```
20 public class VideoGuide extends VApplet
21 {
22    private MovieReviewList myMovieReviewList;
23
24    private VActionButton    mySearchButton;
25    private TextField        mySearchTextField;
26    private Label            myFoundMovieReview;
27    private TextArea         myMovieDisplayArea;
28
29    private Label            myErrorLabel;
30
31    //---------- action --------------------------------
32    // pre:  none - called automatically on button press
33    // post: movie list is sorted
34    public void action ()
35    {
36       String target = mySearchTextField.getText ();
37       target = target.trim ();
38       MovieReview review =
39              myMovieReviewList.binarySearch(target);
40       if (review == null)
41          myFoundMovieReview.setText ("*** not found ***");
42       else
43          myFoundMovieReview.setText (review.toString());
44    }
45
46    //---------- ErrorMessage ---------------------------
47    // private method used to put the movie list into the
48    // display text area
49    private void ErrorMessage (String message)
50    {
51       Graphics g = getGraphics ();
52       g.setColor (Color.red);
53       Font big = new Font ("Serif", Font.PLAIN, 24);
54       g.setFont (big);
55       g.drawString (message, 20, 70);
56    }
57
```

Listing 11.12 `VideoGuide` Class

```
58    //---------- init ------------------------------------
59    // pre:  none - called automatically
60    // post: movie review list and display created
61    public void init ()
62    {
63      setBackground(Color.white);
64      Font monoSpaced = new Font ("Monospaced", Font.PLAIN, 10);
65
66      // create the "search" interface
67      mySearchButton = new VActionButton ("Search", this);
68      mySearchTextField = new TextField
69        ("put movie title here                    ");
70      mySearchTextField.setFont (monoSpaced);
71      add (mySearchTextField);
72      myFoundMovieReview = new Label
73        ("                                                      ");
74      myFoundMovieReview.setFont (monoSpaced);
75      add (myFoundMovieReview);
76
77      // create the movie review text area
78      myMovieDisplayArea = new TextArea (20, 70);
79      myMovieDisplayArea.setFont (monoSpaced);
80      add (myMovieDisplayArea);
81
82      // create the movie review list
83      try
84      {
85        myMovieReviewList =
86          new MovieReviewList("MovieReviews98.txt", this);
87      }
88      // Catch file problems
89      catch (MalformedURLException e)
90      {
91        ErrorMessage ("*** Bad file name ***");
92      }
93      catch (IOException e)
94      {
95        ErrorMessage ("*** File error ***");
96      }
97    }
98
```

Listing 11.12 VideoGuide **Class**

```
99    //---------- start ---------------------------------
100   // pre:  none - called automatically
101   // post: the display is updated with the list
102   // note: this method may take a little time.  If it is
103   //        placed in "init" the display may be blank for
104   //        long enough to cause user concern.
105   public void start ()
106   {
107     myMovieReviewList.sort();
108     updateMovieDisplayArea ();
109   }
110
111   //---------- updateMovieDisplayArea --------------------
112   // private method used to put the movie list into the
113   // display text area
114   private void updateMovieDisplayArea ()
115   {
116     myMovieDisplayArea.setText("");
117
118     for (int i=0; i<myMovieReviewList.size(); i++)
119     {
120       MovieReview  aReview = myMovieReviewList.elementAt(i);
121       myMovieDisplayArea.append(aReview.toString());
122       myMovieDisplayArea.append("\n");
123     }
124   }
125 }
```

Listing 11.13 MovieReviewList **class**

```
1 //***********************************************************
2 //
3 // title:   MovieReviewList
4 //
5 // Objects of this class are lists of movie reviews.
6 //
7 //***********************************************************
8
9 import java.applet.Applet;
10 import java.util.Vector;
11 import java.io.IOException;
12 import java.net.MalformedURLException;
13
```

Listing 11.13 `MovieReviewList` class

```
14 public class MovieReviewList
15 {
16   private Vector          myMovieList;
17
18   public static final int GENE  = 0;
19   public static final int ROGER = 1;
20
21   //---------- MovieReviewList -------------------------------
22   // pre:  "in" is a valid open movie review file
23   // post: this list contains all the movie reviews in the "in"
24   //       file
25   public MovieReviewList(String movieReviewListName,
                    Applet applet)
26             throws MalformedURLException, IOException
27   {
28     // create an empty list
29     myMovieList = new Vector();
30
31     // open the file
32     ReviewInputFile inputFile =
33           new ReviewInputFile (movieReviewListName, applet);
34
35     // read the file into the list
36     while (true)
37     {
38       MovieReview aReview = inputFile.read();
39       if (aReview == null)
40         break;
41       myMovieList.addElement(aReview);
42     }
43   }
44
45   //---------- addElement ------------------------------------
46
47   private void addElement (MovieReview t)
48   {
49     myMovieList.addElement(t);
50   }
51
```

Listing 11.13 `MovieReviewList` class

```
52    //---------- binarySearch ----------------------------------
53    // pre:  none
54    // post: The review with the movie name that matches
55    //        "targetName" is returned.
56    //        If it is not found, null is returned
57    public MovieReview binarySearch (String targetName)
58    {
59      int bottom = 0;
60      int top    = size() - 1;
61
62      // do binary search
63      while (top >= bottom)
64      {
65        int middle = (bottom + top) / 2;
66        MovieReview middleReview = elementAt(middle);
67        if (middleReview.greaterThan(targetName))
68          top = middle - 1;
69        else if (middleReview.lessThan(targetName))
70          bottom = middle + 1;
71        else
72          return middleReview;
73      }
74
75      return null;
76    }
77
78    //---------- elementAt ----------------------------------
79    // pre:  index >= 0 & index < size()
80    // post: The review at "index" is returned.
81    //        This method removes the need for type casts.
82    public MovieReview elementAt(int index)
83    {
84      return (MovieReview)(myMovieList.elementAt(index));
85    }
86
```

Listing 11.13 `MovieReviewList` class

```
87    //---------- sequentialSearch -----------------------------
88    // pre:  none
89    // post: The review with a name that matches "targetName"
90    //       is returned.
91    //       If no match is found, null is returned
92    public MovieReview sequentialSearch (String targetName)
93    {
94      for (int i=0; i<size(); i++)
95      {
96        MovieReview review = elementAt(i);
97        if (review.equals(targetName))
98          return review;
99      }
100     return null;
101   }
102
103   //---------- size -----------------------------------------
104   // pre:  none
105   // post: The number of reviews is returned.
106   public int size()
107   {
108     return myMovieList.size();
109   }
110
```

Listing 11.13 `MovieReviewList` class

```
111   //---------- sort -------------------------------------
112   // pre:  this list is not null
113   // post: this list is sorted by movie name
114   // from: Classic Data Structures in C++
115   //         Timothy A. Budd
116   //         Addison Wesley, 1994, p169/
117   public void sort()
118   {
119     int n = myMovieList.size();
120     for (int top=n-1; top>0; top--)
121     {
122       int largestPosition = 0;
123       for (int j=1; j<=top; j++)
124       {
125         MovieReview largeThumb = elementAt(largestPosition);
126         MovieReview jThumb     = elementAt(j);
127         if (jThumb.greaterThan(largeThumb))
128           largestPosition = j;
129       }
130       swap(largestPosition, top);
131     }
132   }
133
134   //---------- swap -------------------------------------
135   // Swap two reviews in this list.
136   // For internal use only
137   private void swap (int a, int b)
138   {
139     MovieReview temp = elementAt(a);
140     myMovieList.setElementAt(myMovieList.elementAt(b), a);
141     myMovieList.setElementAt(temp,b);
142   }
143 }
```

Listing 11.14 `MovieReview` class

```
1  //************************************************************
2  //
3  // title:   MovieReview
4  //
5  // This object is a container for the components of a movie
6  // review.  It contains the movie name, Gene Siskel's and Roger
7  // Ebert's votes, and the date of each movie review.
8  //
9  //************************************************************
10
```

Listing 11.14 `MovieReview` class

```
11  import java.io.IOException;
12
13  public class MovieReview
14  {
15    private String  myName;
16    private boolean myGene;
17    private boolean myRoger;
18    private String  myDate;
19
20    private static String myCurrentDate;
21
22    //---------- MovieReview -------------------------------
23    // pre:  none
24    // post: This object contains a review based on the values of
25    //       "name", "gene", "roger", and "date".
26    public MovieReview (String name, boolean gene, boolean roger,
27                        String date)
28    {
29      myName  = fixBeginningArticle(name);
30      myGene  = gene;
31      myRoger = roger;
32      myDate  = date;
33    }
34
35    //---------- equal -------------------------------------
36    // pre:  none
37    // post: If this movie is the same as the
38    //       "other" movie, true is returned
39    //       otherwise false is returned
40
41    public boolean equals(String other)
42    {
43      return myName.equals(other);
44    }
45
```

Listing 11.14 `MovieReview` class

```
46   //---------- fixBeginningArticle -------------------------
47   // Put beginning "The" and "A" articles at the end of a string
48   // For internal use only
49   private String fixBeginningArticle (String name)
50   {
51     int length = name.length();
52     if (name.startsWith("The "))
53       return name.substring(4, length) + ", The";
54     else if (name.startsWith("A "))
55       return name.substring(2, length) + ", A";
56     else
57       return name;
58   }
59
60   //---------- getDate -------------------------------------
61   // pre:  none
62   // post: the date of this review is returned
63   public String getDate()
64   {
65     return myDate;
66   }
67
68   //---------- getGeneThumb --------------------------------
69   // pre:  none
70   // post: Gene Siskle's vote is returned
71   public boolean getGeneThumb()
72   {
73     return myGene;
74   }
75
76   //---------- getName -------------------------------------
77   // pre:  none
78   // post: the name of the movie reviewed is returned
79   public String getName()
80   {
81     return myName;
82   }
83
```

Listing 11.14 `MovieReview` class

```
84    //---------- getRogerThumb ----------------------------------
85    // pre:  none
86    // post: Roger Ebert's vote is returned
87    public boolean getRogerThumb()
88    {
89      return myRoger;
90    }
91
92    //---------- greaterThan -----------------------------------
93    // pre:  none
94    // post: If this movie should come alphabetically after the
95    //          "other" movie, true is returned
96    //          otherwise false is returned
97
98    public boolean greaterThan (MovieReview other)
99    {
100       return myName.compareTo(other.myName) > 0;
101   }
102
103   //---------- greaterThan -----------------------------------
104   // pre:  none
105   // post: If this movie should come alphabetically after the
106   //          "other" movie, true is returned
107   //          otherwise false is returned
108
109   public boolean greaterThan(String other)
110   {
111     return myName.compareTo(other) > 0;
112   }
113
114   //---------- lessThan ---------------------------------------
115   // pre:  none
116   // post: If this movie should come alphabetically before the
117   //          "other" movie, true is returned
118   //          otherwise false is returned
119
120   public boolean lessThan(String other)
121   {
122     return myName.compareTo(other) < 0;
123   }
124
```

Listing 11.14 `MovieReview` class

```
125    //---------- namePadding -----------------------------------
126    // Add spaces to the end of the name to give them all the same
127    // length.
128    // For internal use only
129    private String namePadding ()
130    {
131      String s = "";
132      int spaces = 42 - myName.length();
133      for (int i=0; i < spaces; i++)
134        s += " ";
135      return s;
136    }
137
138    //---------- thumbToString -----------------------------------
139    // convert true to the string "up   " and false to "down"
140    // For internal use only
141    private String thumbToString(boolean vote)
142    {
143      if (vote)
144        return new String("up  ");
145      else
146        return new String("down");
147    }
148
149    //---------- toString -----------------------------------
150    // pre:  none
151    // post: a string representation of this review is returned
152    public String toString()
153    {
154      return myName + namePadding() +
155             thumbToString (getGeneThumb())  + "   " +
156             thumbToString (getRogerThumb()) + "   " +
157             getDate();
158    }
159  }
```

PROBLEM SETS

11.9   Exercises

Lists—Section 11.2

1   List four places you used a list in the last two days. What kind of operations did you apply to these lists?

2   Imagine the kinds of things a computer must keep track of. List those cases where you think a list may be used.

Patterns—Section 11.3

3   What will happen if Line 8 of Listing 11.4 is changed to the following?

```
for (int i=0; i<=size(); i++)
```

4   Which implementation of the sequential search (Listing 11.2, Listing 11.4, or Listing 11.5) do you find easiest to understand? Why?

5   What is the impact of the following change to Line 7 of the selection sort in Listing 11.6?

```
for (int current=n; current>0; current--)
```

6   What is the impact of the following change to Line 7 of the selection sort in Listing 11.6?

```
for (int current=n-1; current>=0; current--)
```

7   What is the impact of the following change to Line 10 of the selection sort in Listing 11.6?

```
for (int j=0; j<=current; j++)
```

8   What is the impact of the following change to Line 10 of the selection sort in Listing 11.6?

```
for (int j=1; j<current; j++)
```

9   Rewrite the sequential sort algorithm in Listing 11.6 so that it starts placing elements at the front of the list rather than at the back.

10   The binary search algorithm is notorious for off-by-one errors. Study the algorithm's behavior in Listing 11.8 on page 500 when:

a.   ">=" is replaced with ">" in line 13

b.   lines 17 and 19 are replaced with:

```
top = middle;
bottom = middle;
```

Vectors—Section 11.4

11   Given the following list:

```
Vector list = new Vector();
list.addElement(Color.blue);
list.addElement(Color.yellow);
list.addElement(Color.red);
list.addElement(Color.green);
```

a.   What color is `list.elementAt(1)`?

b.   What color is `list.elementAt(3)`?

12   Using the list created in exercise 11, write the contents of the list in order after:

```
list.insertElementAt(Color.black, 2);
```

13   Using the list created in exercise 11, write the contents of the list in order after:

```
list.deleteElementAt(1);
```

14   Write a code fragment that finds the average temperature of values stored in the `temperatures` vector in Listing 11.11 on page 506.

15   Use a vector to create a list of strings that contain your favorite foods.

Complexity—Section 11.5

16   What is the order of complexity of the following method?

```
public void timesTable (int n)
{
  for (int i=0; i<n; i++)
    for (int j=0; j<10; j++) {
      int result = i * j;
      System.out.print(i + " x " + j + " = " + result);
    }
    System.out.println();
}
```

17   What is the order of complexity of the following method?

```
public void timesTable (int n)
{
  for (int i=0; i<n; i++)
    for (int j=0; j<n; j++) {
      int result = i * j;
      System.out.print(i + " x " + j + " = " + result);
    }
    System.out.println();
}
```

18   What is the order of complexity of the prime number program in Listing 9.7 on page 406?

Sequential Search—Section 11.5.1

19   Compute the best-case performance of the sequential search. We say that a situation that requires the least amount of work is the best case. In a sequential search, the best case is when the target movie is always located in the first location.

20   Compute the worst-case performance of the sequential search. We say that a situation that requires the most amount of work is the worst case. In a sequential search, the worst case is when the target movie is always located in the last location.

21   Redo the analysis in Section 11.5.1 on page 513 assuming that one half of the time the target movie is not found.

22   Redo the analysis in Section 11.5.1 on page 513 assuming that we search through the entire list for each search. (There is no loop break when an item matches.)

11.9.1   Sorting—Section 11.5.2

23   Modify the sort algorithm in Listing 11.6 to sort list in descending order.

24   Is either of the following two strategies is more time efficient? Justify your answer based on the order of complexity of each of these processes.

    a.   make a list smaller by constraining it to thumbs up reviews and then sort it.

    b.   first sort a list and then constrain it to thumbs up reviews.

11.10   Projects

Lists and Patterns—Section 11.2, Section 11.3

25   The goal of a keyword search is to find all titles that contain a particular word. Do a keyword search through movie titles. Display all movie matches. The following strategy will be helpful:

    a.   Use a string search method, such as `indexOf`, to locate substrings in a title.

    b.   Each time a match is found, add the review to a match list.

    c.   When the entire list of movies has been searched, return the match list.

    d.   Display the match list in a text area.

26   Rewrite the movie review program using text-based input and output (i.e. use VRead and VWrite).

27   Combine problems 25 and 26

28   Write a program that maintains a list of all your CDs. It should contain a CD class that contains a field for the name of the CD, the name of the performers, and a rating from one to five stars (five stars is the highest rating).

A second class should maintain a list of CDs. It should support the operations of sort and search.

Create an interface that asks for each CD's name, performer, and rating. Based on your instructors wishes, use a text-based or GUI based interface. Otherwise create a text-based application.

29. In the selection in Listing 11.6 on page 496, Line 17 swaps list items in cases where the item at the top of the unsorted part is already the maximum. Swapping the largest item with itself is a waste of time. One can prevent such a swap with the following check:

```
if (largestPosition != top)
   swap(largestPosition, top);
```

However, this presents an extra check that must be performed for each iteration of the outer loop. Devise an experiment to determine whether the above check saves or costs more time. In addition to doing timing runs, keep a count of how many times the above if statement is encountered and how many times it is true. Follow the guidelines outlined in Section 7.7 on page 315.

12 Input /Output

Reading Movie Reviews and Stock Prices

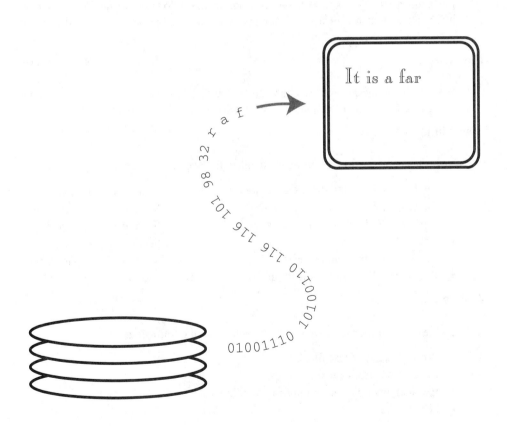

12.1 Objectives

Concepts   **Section 12.2, page 537**

This chapter begins by looking at why we need files. We also describe the difference between text and binary files. We then investigate the file manipulation code that is used in the movie guide application in Chapter 11 and used to read stock prices in Chapter 9. Both examples use text files.

Section 12.7, page 572

An optional section looks at binary manipulation of files. We create a simple copy file application. We explore a snoop program that allows us to investigate a how information is stored in a file. We look at command line arguments and random access files.

Patterns   **Section 12.3, page 546**

We investigate the Java classes that support buffered file access. Next we show how using a buffer can make displaying information in a text area faster.

Java skills

Next the chapter addresses how Java handles file access.

- FileReader & BufferedReader classes   Section 12.4.1, page 554
- StringTokenizer class   Section 12.4.2, page 558
- FileWriter & BufferedWriter classes   Section 12.4.3, page 560
- DecimalFormat class   Section 12.4.4, page 562
- Reading files from an applet   Section 12.4.5, page 564
- Binary, file dialogs, command line, random files   Section 12.7, page 572

Abilities

By the end of this chapter we should be able to do the following:

- Write strings to a text file.
- Read strings from a text file.
- Extract numeric information from text input.
- Format output.

CONCEPTS

12.2   Text Input and Output

Most useful programs depend on access to stored information. Writers retrieve and store stories, financial planners retrieve and store spreadsheets, astronomers retrieve data about the heavens, movie critics retrieve information about movies, accountants retrieve information about income and expenses, artists retrieve and store images, and universities retrieve and store information about students, faculty, and parents.

> *IO* is an abbreviation for input/output. It can refer to input from a user's keyboard and output to a CRT display, and it can refer to input from and output to a file.

We store information in files because we want information to persist when our computer is turned off and we want to share information with other people. The amount of information stored in a file may vary from a few bytes used by an application to store a user's preferred display font to the colossal databases required by the Internal Revenue Service to maintain records of millions of American workers.

All files share some key properties:

- They are nonvolatile.
- They have an identity.
- They have an internal format.
- They support operations for access and manipulation.

The data elements we have looked at thus far; for example, ints, Integers, Strings, booleans, lunar landers, etc., are all *volatile*. When the program terminates, this volatile information is lost. In contrast, the information stored within files is *nonvolatile*. Its lifetime is longer than the lifetime of a running program, or for that matter, the computer on which it is created.

We depend on the nonvolatile nature of files. When we write a term paper we save our efforts in a file. We can work on that paper over a period of days. Each time we turn off our computer the term paper file persists. The same is true of the Java programs and the web pages we create. We save them in files so they will persist beyond our current editing sections. The email messages we send to our friends and teachers are files that are copied from one location to another. Files can be stored on local hard disks, tape, zip disks, floppies, CDs, or on remote sites and accessed at a later time.

A second property of files is that they have an identity, some means of locating a file. In many cases all we need is a file name and the floppy disk to uniquely identify a file. In other cases a file is within several nested folders on a hard drive. We must know the name of the disk drive on which the file is stored and the name of each directory that embeds it. Files can also be stored on remote machines. A university campus or a corporate office may have its files stored in a central file server. A file server's job is to maintain the files for an organization in a central location so that they can be easily accessed by other computers. In this case the identity of a file includes the computer on which it resides. Networking requires us to think about files more globally. The HTML documents and Java applets that we attach to our web pages can be uniquely identified and accessed anywhere in the world.

A *file path* is the name of a file that uniquely identifies it. It includes its name, the directories that embed it, and the disk on which it can be found.

At the lowest level, a file is no more than a sequence of ones and zeros. They may be represented by the orientation of small magnetic particles on a thin metal platter, they may be represented by the positioning of small pits on a plastic disk, and by many other means. This low-level view makes working with files difficult.

In this chapter we will focus on files as lines of text. Each byte in a *text file* corresponds to an ASCII character. Although this view is primitive, it is universally understood. These files are called human readable because they can be displayed with simple text editors. Our Java source files (`*.java`) and HTML documents are stored in text format.

Special-purpose files are typically stored in a binary format. They are called *binary files*. Each word processor has a unique format for representing character fonts and page layouts. Image files have representations for color palettes and individual pixels. Spreadsheets represent the data and formulas stored in each cell using special byte sequences. Java uses a special format to store the compiled versions of programs in its `*.class` files. Binary files are not human readable. If we open a binary file with a simple text editor, the editor would not know how to display the characters for which there are no ASCII encodings. This would include all characters with values above 127. Section A.5.3 contains more detail on text and binary files.

The final property of files is a set of operations that access and manipulate it. File access is accomplished by creating a file object using a process which is said to "open" a file. When we open a file we must uniquely identify it.

Just because we know a file's name and location does not mean we can open it. Many file systems restrict access to information by including information about who owns the file, who may open it, and what can be done to the file once opened. If we do not have appropriate access privileges to a file, file open will fail. File opens may also fail if the file is corrupted or if connections to a remote site are unavailable.

Once a file is opened, each file class provides a plethora of methods to read, write, and skip data. Methods are available to read and write bytes, characters, strings, and numbers. When we are finished with a file we apply the close operation. The close operation is important because it writes information to the file that may still be in the computer's main memory. In addition, some files are accessible by only one user at a time. By closing a file we release that file resource so that others can use it.

We have used files in two previous examples. In the stock price program in Chapter 9 we read a file of stock prices, NASDAQ indexes, and dates. In the movie guide program in Chapter 11 we read a file of movie reviews and created a file of sorted reviews for our reference. In this chapter we will look at how these examples accomplished IO (input/output).

12.2.1 Reading Movie Reviews

The video guide program in Chapter 11 works with text files. Each line contains a movie title, votes, and a date. Listing 12.1 shows a snippet of one of the movie files. Since this is a text file, Listing 12.1 shows how that file looks in a simple text editor.

Listing 12.1 Movie Review File

```
Mulholland Falls                        down up    04/27/96
Sunset Park                             up   down  04/27/96
The Truth About Cats and Dogs           up   up    04/27/96
I Shot Andy Warhol                      up   up    04/27/96
Wings of Courage                        down up    04/27/96
```

The class that is used to read these files is in Listing 12.27 on page 586. This version of the `ReviewInputFile` class is designed to work with applets. Opening a file from an applet is a slightly different process from opening a file from an application. We will begin

Listing 12.2 Opening a Buffered Reader

```
1   public ReviewInputFile (String fileName)
2            throws IOException
3   {
4     FileReader reader = new FileReader(fileName);
5     myBufferedReader  = new BufferedReader(reader);
6   }
```

by showing how to open files in applications and postpone opening files in applets until Section 12.4.5.

A constructor for opening a file in an application is shown in Listing 12.2. It takes a single string parameter, which uniquely identifies the review file. Line 4 opens a text file with the name of the file stored in the `fileName` string. Line 5 uses the `reader` object created in Line 4 to create a new input file object named `myBufferedReader`. It is an instance variable so that it can be accessed by other methods, for example, `read`. We will talk about buffering in Section 12.3.

Listing 12.3 `read` Method

```
1    public MovieReview read() throws IOException
2    {
3      String line = myBufferedReader.readLine();
4      if (line == null)
5      {
6        return null;
7      }
8      else if (line.length() <
9          NAME_WIDTH + THUMBS_WIDTH + THUMBS_WIDTH +  DATE_WIDTH)
10     {
11       throw new IOException();
12     }
13     else
14     {
15       String  name  = line.substring(0, NAME_WIDTH).trim();
16       boolean gene  = line.charAt (NAME_WIDTH) == 'u';
17       boolean roger = line.charAt(NAME_WIDTH +
                                      THUMBS_WIDTH)=='u';
18      String  date  = line.substring(NAME_WIDTH + THUMBS_WIDTH +
19              THUMBS_WIDTH, NAME_WIDTH + THUMBS_WIDTH +
20              THUMBS_WIDTH + DATE_WIDTH);
21       return new MovieReview (name, gene, roger, date);
22     }
23   }
```

Many Java IO operations throw exceptions. Opening a file is one of those. For example, a file open may fail because the file name is incorrect or remote computers are not available. Thus, files must be opened in an exception handler. We could have simply printed an error message indicating that an error had occurred, but that is not very elegant. Let us repeat a point made in Section 9.4.6. In general it is better for a service class to rethrow an exception and let the client decide what to do. Thus, the client can decide whether to display an error message in window, display an error message to system out, ask the user to enter a new file name, ignore the error, or abort the program.

Once a buffered reader object is created, lines can be read by using the readLine method. The readLine method returns a string that holds the next line from the file, minus the end-of-line character(s). Section A.5.3 describes end-of-line characters.

Listing 12.3 shows the method used in the video guide program to get a single line of text and respond to errors. If there are no more reviews in the file we say we are at end-of-file. The readLine method returns null at end-of-file and we return a null review to reflect end-of-file as well (Line 6). Lines 8 through 12 throw an exception if the retrieved line is not long enough to contain a movie name, votes, and date.

Listing 12.4 Using the ThumbsInputFile Class

```
1   try
2   {
3     ReviewInputFile reviewFile =
4                   new ReviewInputFile ("Thumbs96.up");
5     while (true)
6     {
7       MovieReview aReview = reviewFile.read();
8       if (aReview == null)
9         break;
10      // do something with this information
11    }
12    reviewFile.close();
13  }
14
15  catch (IOException e)
16  {
17    // respond to the error
18  }
```

The constants, NAME_WIDTH, THUMBS_WIDTH, and DATE_WIDTH, are used to define the locations of each movie review field. The movie name starts at column 0, Siskel's vote starts at column NAME_WIDTH (40), Ebert's vote starts at NAME_WIDTH + THUMB_WIDTH (45), and the date field starts in column NAME_WIDTH +

THUMB_WIDTH + THUMB_WIDTH (50). We use these values to extract the appropriate information from the input line, create a review object, and return it in Line 21.

Listing 12.4 outlines how we can use the ThumbsInputFile class to read a file. Similar code appears in the constructor for the ThumbsList class in Listing 11.13 on page 521. It uses the loop and a half pattern to completely read a file.

12.2.2 Writing Movie Reviews

Writing to a file is similar to reading. Listing 12.5 shows a class that can be used to create a file and write reviews to it. The constructor in Lines 9 through 13 creates a new file. Opening a file for writing is similar to opening a file for reading. Line 11 opens a file named by the fileName string. Line 12 takes the file object created in Line 11 to create a new output file objected named myDataOut. It is an instance variable, so it can be referenced by the close method in Line 17 and the println method in Lines 22 and 23. .

Listing 12.5 Opening a Buffered Writer

```
1  import java.io.BufferedWriter;
2  import java.io.FileWriter;
3  import java.io.IOException;
4
5  public class ReviewOutputFile
6  {
7      private BufferedWriter myDataOut;
8
9      public ReviewOutputFile (String fileName) throws IOException
10     {
11         FileWriter fileOut = new FileWriter(fileName);
12         myDataOut = new BufferedWriter(fileOut);
13     }
14
15     public void close() throws IOException
16     {
17        myDataOut.close();
18     }
19
20      public void println (MovieReview review) throws IOException
21      {
22         myDataOut.write(review.toString());
23         myDataOut.newLine();
24      }
25  }
```

Lines 20 through 24 write a single review to this file. Line 22 writes the string representation of a review to a file, and Line 23 places a platform-specific end-of-line character at the end of the review string.

Listing 12.6 shows how to use the `ReviewOutputFile` class to write a single movie review.

Listing 12.6 Using the `ThumbsOutputFile` Class

```
1  try
2  {
3      ReviewOutputFile reviewFile =
4                      new ReviewOutputFile ("Reviews.txt");
5      MovieReview aReview = new MovieREview
6              ("Gingerbread Man", TRUE, TRUE, "1-24-98");
7      reviewFile.println(aReview);
8      aReview =
9          new MovieReview ("Deep Rising", FALSE, FALSE, "1-24-98");
10     reviewFile.println(aReview);
11     reviewFile.close();
12 }
13
14 catch (IOException e)
15 {
16     // respond to any errors
17 }
```

12.2.3 Extracting Stock Price Numbers from Text Files

Recall that a text file contains only the ASCII encoded characters found in Table A.5 on page 836. For example, representing the word "Pez" in a files is done with the sequence of bytes with values 80, 101, and 122. Numbers in text files are also represented by individual ASCII characters for each digit. For example, "96" is represented by the byte 57 for the ASCII digit "9" followed by the number 54 for the ASCII digit "6." This is what makes text files different from binary files. In a binary file, the integer 96 would be represented by the number 96. Another example appears in Figure 12.1. It shows how the line "R2D2" is stored in a file. (<eol> stands for end-of-line character(s). This example shows the eol characters for DOS/Windows.)

The stock market program in Chapter 9 needs to read numbers from a text file such as the one shown in Listing 12.7. As a result, we must devise a scheme to convert the ASCII representation of numbers to binary. The `read` method, shown in Listing 12.8, reads a single

Figure 12.1 ASCII Characters Stored as Bytes

82	50	68	50	13	10	bytes
R	2	D	2	\<eol>		characters

Listing 12.7 Stocks File

```
10/3/94,60.25,461.74,760.88
10/4/94,58.00,454.59,747.30
10/5/94,58.75,453.52,746.28
10/6/94,58.94,452.36,744.19
10/7/94,59.44,455.10,749.96
10/10/94,60.44,459.04,756.81
10/11/94,60.50,465.79,765.57
```

Listing 12.8 read Method from the Stock Program

```
1    public StockPrice read() throws IOException
2    {
3      // read the data for the next star
4      try
5      {
6        String buffer = iInputFile.readLine();
7        if (buffer == null)
8          return null;
9
10       StringTokenizer tokens = new StringTokenizer(buffer, ",");
11       String date      = tokens.nextToken();
12       Double d         = Double.valueOf(tokens.nextToken());
13       double stock     = d.doubleValue();
14       d                = Double.valueOf(tokens.nextToken());
15       double sP500     = d.doubleValue();
16       d                = Double.valueOf(tokens.nextToken());
17       double nASDAQ    = d.doubleValue();
18
19       return new StockPrice (date, stock, sP500, nASDAQ);
20     }
21
22     // catch IO read errors
23     catch (IOException e)
24     {
25       throw new IOException();
26     }
27   }
```

line of data from the stock file and extracts the stock prices. The stock file shown in Listing 12.7 contains a date and three real numbers separated with commas.

Lines 6 through 8 are familiar. They read a single line from the file and check for the end of file. However, something new is occurring in Line 10. A string tokenizer object is created from the line we read. When we create the tokenizer, we specify the string to be tokenized and the delimiter that separates them, commas in this case. Recall that we introduced the terms *token* and *delimiter* in Section 1.4.1. We repeat their definitions below.

> A *token* is the smallest unit of a string that is of interest; for example, a number, word, or punctuation mark. A *delimiter* is a character that separates tokens.

Figure 12.2 Tokenizing

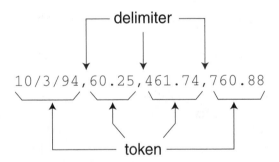

Once we have created the tokenizer in Line 10, the `nextToken` method extracts a token from the tokenizer object in Lines 11, 12, 14, and 16. These strings are converted to doubles in Lines 13, 15, and 17.

A delimiter in one situation may be a token in another. For example, commas are important to compilers. Thus a comma to a compiler is a token rather than delimiter. When we use the `StringTokenizer` class we decide which characters are delimiters. For example, in Line 10 of Listing 12.8 we decided that a comma is a delimiter and everything else is part of a token (see Figure 12.2). We could add "/" to our delimiter list so that each of the numbers in the date field is a token. Because we do not need to manipulate the date, we treat the date as a single string field. More information can be found about the `String-Tokenizer` class in Section 12.4.2.

PATTERNS

12.3   The Buffer Pattern

So far in this text we have utilized several patterns for manipulating files. We have used the loop and a half pattern for file input and the counter loop for file output. In this section we will introduce another pattern often used with files: buffering.

name

> *Buffering* is a mechanism that improves communication efficiency by working with large chunks of information.

problem

Suppose we are at a movie with our date. Our date keeps bothering us for a few kernels of popcorn. If the movie is more interesting than our date, we can get our date off our back by dumping a bunch of popcorn in his or her lap and then paying attention to the movie. When the lap is empty, we can dump some more popcorn. This is buffering.

We take advantage of buffering often. Something as simple as a box of cereal is a buffer. It contains more than a single serving. Our cereal bowl is also a buffer. It contains more than a single bite. Another buffer is the neighborhood store. No one would consider walking to the factory to pick up ten flakes of cereal and to a dairy farm for a half teaspoon of milk, walking home with them, mixing the two together, taking a byte, and repeating the process until we are full. This is a waste of a producer's and our time. We would spend hours eating and paying heavily for administrative costs.

Similarly, we must be careful that we do not make the computer process information in chunks that are so small that it spends most of its time with system administration and little time manipulating information. Just as in the cereal example there may be more than one layer of buffer. For example, the disk controller often has a buffer, the operating system has a buffer, and a program has a buffer.

12.3.1   File Buffering

A computer can also be affected with fragmented attention. Each request to a computer's IO services may entail substantial overhead. The amount of overhead depends on the platform. On some systems the request for IO services involves a shift in context from user mode where the current application has control to a supervisor mode where the operating system has control. This involves juggling programs and allocating resources. On other systems the request for IO services involves a simple method call which may be handled quickly. If a program asks for only one character at a time, substantial effort may be devoted to program management on some computers. .

Figure 12.3 Buffer Example

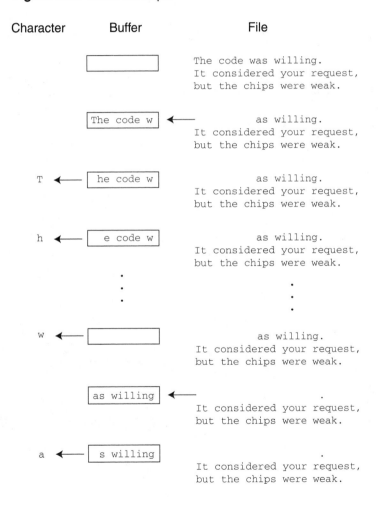

solution

Buffering can substantially improve the performance of a computer program. Information from a file is obtained in blocks of 512, 1048, or more bytes and placed in a buffer. These buffers are maintained in the user's corner of a computer's memory. When the user has exhausted all the information in a buffer, a request is made to the computer's runtime system to refill the buffer.

consequences

This sounds a little overwhelming. Programming is required to test for empty buffers, to transfer a blocks of data to a buffer, and to access the appropriate bytes. Fortunately, this code comes prewritten. All we need to do is select the appropriate IO classes. Listing 12.2 shows an example of using buffering. In Line 5 we create a buffered input object.

Read requests are accomplished by applying the read method on the buffered file, as in Line 3 of Listing 12.3. The read method may get a few characters from the buffer if the line is short, or many characters if the line is long. If all the characters from the buffer have been read, the read operation will request that the buffer be refilled. But, as mentioned above, we do not have to worry about how it is done. Figure 12.3 illustrate this hidden process of repeatedly requesting a character from a buffer 10 characters long.   .

Listing 12.9 Sending Many One-character Strings to a Text Area

```
1    public static void timeNotBuffered ()
2    {
3      int i = 0;
4      long startTime = System.currentTimeMillis();
5
6      for (i=0; i<NUMBER_CHARACTERS; i++)
7      {
8        if (i%LINE_SIZE < LINE_SIZE-1)
9        {
10         myTextArea.append ("A");
11       }
12       else
13       {
14         myTextArea.append ("\n");
15       }
16     }
17
18     long endTime = System.currentTimeMillis ();
19     System.out.print ("Not buffered time is (milliseconds): ");
20     System.out.println (endTime - startTime);
21   }
```

12.3.2 Text Area Buffering

Next we look at an example of buffering that does not use files. Updating a GUI display can take a lot of time. Each time a text area is updated the computer must recompute the layout of the text, the location of the scroll bars, and redisplay the results. For example, the timeNotBuffered method in Listing 12.9 appends a single character string to a text area repeatedly. When ITERATIONS has the value of 2000, it takes a 250 MHz computer 3 minutes and 34 seconds to display the 2000 characters.

We can speed up the process of displaying to a text area through buffering. However, we will not have the good fortune we had when implementing file buffering. We will have to implement our buffer.

Listing 12.10 shows how we can group characters into longer strings before updating a text area. When this program is run on a 250 MHz computer, it takes three seconds to display the 2000 characters in 80 character chunks. That is about 70 times faster.

Thus, it takes roughly 10 hundredths of a second to send each character to a text area. It takes roughly 13 hundredths of a second to group 80 characters together and send them to a text area. We can see that the dominate operation is updating the text area. Thus, we should try to do so infrequently.

Listing 12.10 will not be completely explained. Lines 3, 13, and 17 manipulate arrays which we talk about in Chapter 13. In a nutshell, Line 3 creates a buffer of 80 characters (LINE_SIZE has the value 80). Line 13 places a character into this buffer. When the buffer contains 80 characters, the buffer is sent to the text area in Line 18. The process starts over.

Listing 12.10 Sending a Few Strings to a Text Area

```
1    public static void timeBuffered ()
2    {
3      char outputBuffer[] = new char[LINE_SIZE];
4
5      char c = 'A';
6      int i = 0;
7      long startTime = System.currentTimeMillis();
8
9      for (i=0; i<NUMBER_CHARACTERS; i++)
10     {
11       if (i%LINE_SIZE < LINE_SIZE-1)
12       {
13         outputBuffer[i%LINE_SIZE] = c;
14       }
15       else
16       {
17         outputBuffer[i%LINE_SIZE] = '\n';
18         myTextArea.append (new String (outputBuffer));
19       }
20     }
21     String theRest = new String (outputBuffer);
22     myTextArea.appendText (theRest.substring(0, i%LINE_SIZE));
23
24     long endTime = System.currentTimeMillis ();
25   System.out.print ("Buffered elapsed time is (milliseconds):
");
26     System.out.println (endTime - startTime);
27   }
```

JAVA

Given the diversity of the applications that require file access, Java provides nearly four dozen classes to give programmers choice. File classes may be chosen based on their ease of use, quick access to information, or space requirements. We will focus on a few of the file classes that illustrate some key ideas. The main focus of this chapter are the four reader and writer classes. The other classes appear in the supplementary section of this chapter or in Chapter 16.

A summary of a few of the key IO classes is provided in Table 12.1. These classes are illustrated in this chapter and Chapter 16. Additional details are also found in Appendix: B. The accompanying diagram in Figure 12.4 shows how these classes are related through inheritance. Several classes that are not illustrated in this text are included in the diagram because of their position in the inheritance hierarchy. Several of the classes are abstract. They are classes that cannot be instantiated. We will talk about abstract classes in Chapter 16.

One of the reasons for the large set of file classes is that we can view files as text files or as binary files. Text files are a stream (sequence) of bytes in which each byte is an ASCII character. See Section A.5 on page 834 for more details. Binary files are a stream of bytes. Those bytes may be parts of numbers, pixels in an image, formatting information in a word-processing document, or part of a cell in a spreadsheet. In this section we will focus on text files. They are shaded in Table 12.1.

Most web browsers place restrictions on file IO. The restrictions are provided to protect the unwary applet user. Without these restrictions it would be possible for a programmer to create an applet that can access and destroy critical information on the user's computer. Thus, we must be careful when opening files from an applet. Depending on security settings, it is generally possible to open a file from an applet at the same URL in which the applet is found. We will see how to do that at the end of the next section. Most of the examples in this chapter will use applications. Because applications do not run over the web, there are no web security issues for us to face.

12.4   Text Input and Output: A Closer Look

We will begin with a look at text files. This section provides more detail about the file-access procedures we were introduced to in Section 12.2.

Table 12.1   IO Classes and Their Use
(highlighted classes are key to this chapter)

class	application	examples
BufferedInputStream	Use together with FileInputStream for buffered byte input of binary data.	Section 12.7.1
BufferedOutputStream	Use together with FileOutputStream for buffered byte output of binary data.	Section 12.7.1
BufferedReader	Use together with FileReader for buffered character and line input of text information.	Section 12.2.1 Section 12.4.1
BufferedWriter	Use together with FileWriter for buffered character and string output of text information.	Section 12.2.2 Section 12.4.1
DataInputStream	Use together with DataOutput stream for reading primitive data values.	Section 12.7.5
DataOutputStream	Use together with DataInput stream for writing primitive data values.	Section 12.7.5
FileInputStream	Use for byte input of binary data.	Section 12.7.1 Section 12.7.2
FileOutputStream	Use for byte output of binary data.	Section 12.7.1 Section 12.7.2
FileReader	Needed by a BufferedReader constructor	Section 12.2.1 Section 12.4.1
FileWriter	Needed by a BufferedWriter constructor	Section 12.2.2 Section 12.4.1
ObjectInputStream	Use together with FileInputStream for reading persistent storage of serialized objects. File must be constructed with an ObjectOutputStream.	Section 16.2.3
ObjectOutputStream	Use together with FileOutputStream for writing persistent storage of serializable objects. File must be constructed with an ObjectOutputStream.	Section 16.2.3
RandomAccessFile	Use to read and write primitive values (e.g., boolean, byte, characters, ints, doubles, and floats) at arbitrary locations within a file. Information is stored in binary format.	Section 12.7.6

Figure 12.4 File Inheritance Diagram (subset)

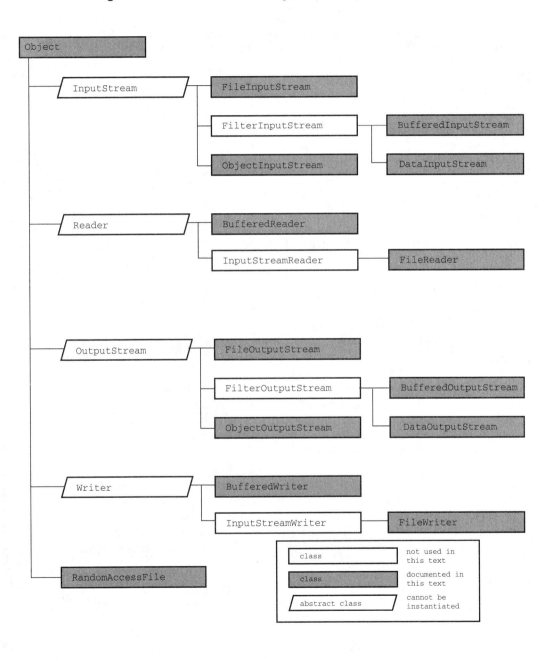

12.4.1   Buffered Reader

A common technique for reading from a file is outlined below. The key operations we will use are to create a text file object (open a file), read from that file, and close it.

```
// reading from a text file
get a file name
open the file
loop
  get the first/next item from the file
  if end-of-file
    break
  do something with the data
end loop
close the file
```

The `BufferedReader` class is designed to work with ASCII bytes. An example of a text file is shown in Listing 12.11. It contains four lines of text. Each byte in the file encodes a single character.

Listing 12.11 Contents of the File `"Solo.txt"`

```
Traveling through hyperspace
ain't like dusting crops, boy.

Han Solo in "Star Wars"
```

In addition to letters, the file also encodes end-of-line characters. Each platform has its own encoding scheme. Unix uses a byte with the value 10, Macintosh a 13, and Windows uses two bytes: 13 10. (See Section A.5.3 on page 835 for more detail.) A good programmer does not depend on knowing these values but rather uses the appropriate methods to handle end-of-line in a platform-independent way.

Before we can manipulate a file it must be opened. Opening a file consists of instantiating a file object. A file object maintains important state information about the location of the file, any errors that have occurred while accessing it, a buffer of characters (Listing 12.3), and a pointer to the next character to be read. For example, when a file is first opened, the file pointer points to the first character in the file (Figure 12.5). We open a buffered reader as follows:

```
FileReader     reader    = new FileReader("Solo.txt");
BufferedReader soloFile  = new BufferedReader(reader);
```

The first line opens the Solo.txt file for reading. The second line passes the file through a buffer to increase read efficiency and provides us with a readLine method.

Figure 12.5 Initial State of soloFile

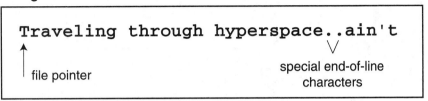

These operations can raise exceptions. As a result, they must be placed within an exception handler.

```
try
{
   FileReader     reader   = new FileReader("Solo.txt");
   BufferedReader soloFile = new BufferedReader(reader);
}
catch (FileNotFoundException e)
{
   System.out.println ("File could not be opened");
}
```

The counterpart to opening a file is closing a file. It returns resources required to manage a file. A file is closed as follows:

```
soloFile.close();
```

Once a file is open, we can read from it. Reading from a closed file will generate an exception. The following will read the first line from our file:

```
String aLine = soloFile.readLine();
```

The first time readLine is applied to soloFile, aLine will be the string "Traveling through hyperspace". The special characters that specify end-of-line will not be included. In addition, the file pointer will be moved to the beginning of the next line in anticipation of the next readLine (Figure 12.6)..

A file read can throw an IOException and must be placed within an exception handler.

Figure 12.6 Next State of `soloFile`

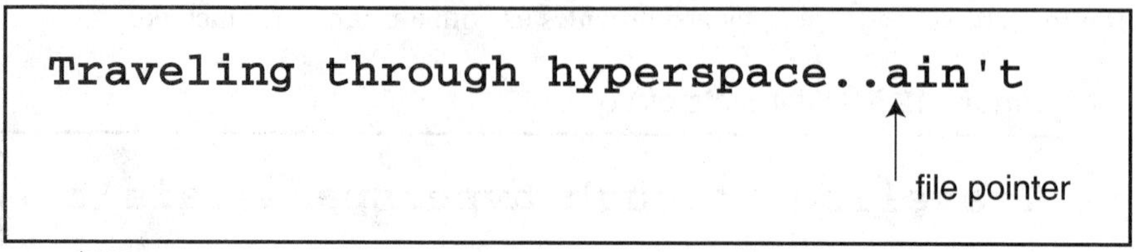

```
Traveling through hyperspace..ain't
                                    ↑
                                    |
                                    | file pointer
```

```
try
{
   String aLine = soloFile.readLine();
}
catch (IOException e)
{
   System.out.println ("File read error.");
}
```

When end-of-file is reached, `readLine` returns a null object. This will occur on the fifth application of the `readLine` method. Notice that this is different from the third call, which will return an empty string. An application that reads and displays the entire Solo.txt file is shown in Listing 12.12.

When we run this program, the interaction with the computer will look as follows. The characters in bold are what we type in:

```
Enter a file name to read: Solo.txt
Traveling through hyperspace
ain't like dusting crops boy.

Han Solo in "Star Wars"
```

In addition to reading information one line at a time, we can read in one character at a time. This is accomplished with the `read` method. See Listing 12.13.

The `read` method returns an integer, which is the ASCII encoding of the character. We know we have reached the end-of-file when `read` returns a –1 (Line 4). Line 6 converts that ASCII integer value into a character. All characters are read. Even the special end-of-line characters.

Another useful method is `skip`. It will skip the specified number of characters in a file. Adding the following line after Line 6 will make our loop display every fourth character:

```
long skipped = soloFile.skip(3);
```

The skip method returns how many characters were actually skipped. In the example above, the only time it would not return three is when it reaches the end of the file.

Listing 12.12   Read Any Text File

```
1  import java.io.FileReader;
2  import java.io.BufferedReader;
3  import java.io.FileNotFoundException;
4  import java.io.IOException;
5  import vista.VRead;
6  import vista.VWrite;
7
8  public class TextReader
9  {
10    public static void main(String args[])
11    {
12      VRead  in  = new VRead ();
13      VWrite out = new VWrite ();
14      out.write ("Enter a file name to read: ");
15      String fileName = in.readString();
16
17      try
18      {
19        FileReader     reader   = new FileReader (fileName);
20        BufferedReader soloFile = new BufferedReader (reader);
21
22        while (true)
23        {
24          String aLine = soloFile.readLine();
25          if (aLine == null)
26            break;
27          out.writeln (aLine);
28        }
29      }
30      catch (FileNotFoundException e)
31      {
32        out.writeln ("File could not be opened.");
33      }
34      catch (IOException e)
35      {
36        out.writeln ("File read error.");
37      }
38    }
39  }
```

Listing 12.13 Reading characters

```
1 while (true)
2 {
3   int i = soloFile.read();
4   if (i == -1)
5     break;
6   char c = (char)i;
7   out.write (String.valueOf(c));
8 }
```

12.4.2   String Tokenizer

In Section 1.4.1 we learned that a program is decomposed into tokens. Each token represents the smallest sequence of characters that have a collective meaning. The `String-Tokenizer` class is used to decompose a string into tokens. One place we have used it is to extract stock prices from a text file (Section 12.2.3).

A string tokenizer is created by specifying the string to be tokenized and its delimiters. For example, the following tokenizer can be used to extract words from a movie title:

```
String movieTitle = "While You Were Sleeping";
String delimiter  = " ";
StringTokenizer wordTokenizer =
        new StringTokenizer (movieTitle, delimiter);
```

Once we have created the tokenizer, we can extract tokens from it one by one. For example, the following will print the tokens in the movie title on separate lines:

```
while (wordTokenizer.hasMoreTokens())
{
   String word = wordTokenizer.nextToken();
   System.out.println (word);
}
```

Notice the use of the `hasMoreTokens` method in the first line to check for move tokens in the string and the `nextToken` method in the second line to extract each token. The output of this code fragment is shown below:

```
While
You
Were
Sleeping
```

More than one character can be placed in a delimiter string:

```
String sentence = "Stop!!!  Pi is not 3.51.  Understand?";
StringTokenizer wordTokenizer = new
        StringTokenizer (sentence, " .!");
```

Notice there a three delimiters. They are a space, period, and exclamation point. Since the question mark is not included in the token characters, it becomes part of the last word. The tokens extracted from this string are listed below:

```
Stop
Pie
is
not
3
51
Understand?
```

We can use tokenizers to extract numeric literals from an input line and convert them into numbers. A technique that can be used is outlined in the following steps:

- Extract a numeric substring from an input line using a string tokenizer.

- Convert the numeric string into a numeric object using the static `valueOf` method provided with numeric classes.

- Convert the numeric object into a primitive value.

For example, Listing 12.14 demonstrate how information can be extracted from a table delimited with a "|" character in an HTML document.

Listing 12.14 StringTokenizer Example

```
1      String buffer = "|Disney      | 37|294 57|  105|  2.25|";
2      StringTokenizer line  = new StringTokenizer(buffer, " |");
3      String iName          = line.nextToken();
4      String token;
5      token                 = line.nextToken();
6      Integer i             = Integer.valueOf(token);
7      int priceToEarnings   = i.intValue();
8      token                 = line.nextToken();
9      Long l                = Long.valueOf(token);
10     long volume           = l.longValue();
11     token                 = line.nextToken();
12     Integer j             = Integer.valueOf(token);
13     int latestPrice       = j.intValue();
14     token                 = line.nextToken();
15     Double d              = Double.valueOf(token);
16     double change         = d.doubleValue();
```

This whole process appears unnecessarily convoluted. In languages such as Pascal, C++, and Ada, there are operations that make this process easier. In Pascal and C these 16 lines can be replaced with a single line of code if the numbers are delimited with spaces.

Java provides a shortcut that allows us to combine two of the steps outlined above. For example, Lines 6 through 13 can be replaced with the following three lines. This shortcut does not work with doubles and floats:

```
int priceToEarnings = Integer.parseInt(line.nextToken());
long volumn         = Long.parseLong(line.nextToken());
int latestPrice     = Integer.parseInt(line.nextToken());
```

12.4.3   Buffered Writer

The technique for writing to a file is similar to reading a file. These steps are outlined below:

```
// writing to a text file
get a file name
open the file
while there is data to write
  assemble the data
  write it to the file
end loop
close the file
```

Creating a buffered writer is similar to creating a buffer reader. It is a two-step process and must be placed in an exception handler. There are several reasons a file cannot be opened. There may be no room on the output disk, or the user may not have permission to write in a specified location.

```
try
{
  FileWriter fw = new FileWriter("Student.data");
  BufferedWriter studentData = new BufferedWriter(fw);
}
catch (IOException e)
{
  System.out.println ("File could not be opened");
}
```

It is possible to open a new file or one that already exists. Opening an existing file will destroy all the information currently in the file and start writing at the file beginning.

A file is closed with the `close` method. In addition to returning resources to the system it empties all buffers. The output buffer does not write its contents to its file until it is full. On average, the buffer will be half full when we are done writing. If we do not close a file, this information may be lost.

```
studentData.close();
```

There are times when it is desirable to empty buffers without closing a file. This is done with the `flush` method. It will send the contents of its buffer to disk.

```
studentData.flush();
```

Once a file is opened we can write to it. An exception will occur if we attempt to write to a closed file. Listing 12.15 shows how to write strings, characters, integers, and doubles to a file. Notice that numeric types must be converted to a string first. This code will add the single line of information shown below to the Student.data file:

```
Elmer Snid 19 75.3 S
```

Listing 12.15 Writing to a File

```
1   String name              = "Elmer Snid";
2   int    age               = 19;
3   double gradePointAverage = 75.3;
4   char   maritalStatus     = 'S';
5
6   studentData.write(name);
7   studentData.write(" ");
8   studentData.write(String.valueOf(age));
9   studentData.write(" ");
10  studentData.write(String.valueOf(gradePointAverage));
11  studentData.write(" ");
12  studentData.write(String.valueOf(maritalStatus));
13  studentData.newLine();
```

We can replace Lines 6 through 12 with the single statement shown below:

```
studentData.write(name + " " + age + " " + gradePointAverage +
   " " + maritalStatus);
```

The `newLine` method in Line 13 starts a new output line. It appends the end-of-line characters that are specified by a particular computer platform. Calling the `newLine` method makes our code platform-independent and thus is preferable to explicitly writing the platform-dependent characters to a file.

```
StudentData.write(10);        // bad style
```

We can also write characters and integers to buffered writers. Writing a character sends a single ASCII-encoded character to a file. Writing an integer writes the least significant byte of the integer to the file. For example, the following three lines send three bytes to a file that represents the string "ABC":

```
studentData.write('A');
studentData.write('B');
studentData.write('C');
```

The following three lines do exactly the same thing:

```
studentData.write(65);
studentData.write(66);
studentData.write(67);
```

Writing a real number is not allowed:

```
studentData.write(3.15);    // syntax error.
```

12.4.4   Formatting Output

The `DecimalFormat` class provides us with a means to convert base-ten numbers into formatted strings. We can control the number of integer and fractional digits printed. It is used by the `VWrite` class to format its output.

The easiest way to learn how to use it is to look at some examples. First we create a decimal format template. This template will be used to take a number and return an appropriately formatted string. We specify how the numbers will appear by applying a pattern to the template. Finally, we use the `format` method to take a number and return an appropriately formatted string. For example:

```
DecimalFormat template = new DecimalFormat();
double aValue = 12345678.9012;
double aHalf   = .5;

template.applyPattern("#.#");
System.out.println(template.format( aValue) + " " +
                   template.format(-aValue));
System.out.println(template.format( aHalf) + " " +
                   template.format(-aHalf));
```

Applying the `"#.#"` pattern to a format will result in the output shown below. Notice that the single "*#*" on the right side of the period will truncate the decimal part to one digit. The left side of the number is allowed to grow to any size:

```
12345678.9 -12345678.9
.5 -.5
```

Applying the `"#,###.#"` pattern will add commas between groups of three digits:

```
template.applyPattern("#,###.#");
System.out.println(template.format( aValue) + " " +
                    template.format(-aValue));
System.out.println(template.format( aHalf) + " " +
                    template.format(-aHalf));
```

The result is shown below:

```
12,345,678.9 -12,345,678.9
.5 -.5
```

Finally, we can specify monetary amounts by using the following pattern. Notice the single zero on the left side of the decimal. It specifies that when the integer part is zero, include a zero. The two zeros on the right side specify that two digits are always to be included on the right side of the decimal even when they are zero:

```
template.applyPattern("$#,##0.00;($#,##0.00)");
System.out.println(template.format( aValue) + " " +
                    template.format(-aValue));
System.out.println(template.format( aHalf) + " " +
                    template.format(-aHalf));
```

The portion on the format on the right side of the ";" specifies how a negative number is to appear. We have chosen to put negative number in parentheses. Enclosing numbers in parenthesis to represent negative values is common in accounting circles. The result is shown below:

```
$12,345,678.90 ($12,345,678.90)
$0.50 ($0.50)
```

We can also control the maximum and minimum number of digits that appear to the right and left side of a decimal. The following demonstrates this feature on integers:

```
int anInt = 123000;
for (int i=0; i<8; i++)
{
  template.setMinimumIntegerDigits(5);
  template.setMaximumIntegerDigits(5);
  String s = template.format(anInt);
  System.out.println (s);
  anInt /= 10;
}
```

The resulting output follows:

```
23,000
12,300
01,230
00,123
00,012
00,001
00,000
00,000
```

The following demonstrates this feature for reals:

```
double aReal = 123000.0;
template.setMinimumIntegerDigits(4);
template.setMaximumIntegerDigits(4);
template.setMinimumFractionDigits(3);
template.setMaximumFractionDigits(3);
for (int i=0; i<10; i++)
{
   String s = template.format(aReal);
   System.out.println (s);
   aReal /= 10.0;
}
```

The resulting output follows:

```
3,000.000
2,300.000
1,230.000
0,123.000
0,012.300
0,001.230
0,000.123
0,000.012
0,000.001
0,000.000
```

12.4.5   Opening a File from an Applet

We need to be careful when doing IO with applets. Because applets run over the web, we must avoid situations in which an innocent click on someone's web page will make our files vulnerable to attack or inspection by third parties. Thus, a remote applet is not allowed to open a file on a local host. However, a remote applet may open a file on the applet's host. In other words, it is possible for an applet to open a file in the same directory in which the applet is found. An example is shown in Listing 12.16.

Listing 12.16 Opening a file in an applet.

```
1 import java.applet.Applet;
2 import java.io.InputStreamReader;
3 import java.io.BufferedReader;
4 import java.io.IOException;
5 import java.net.MalformedURLException;
6 import java.net.URL;
7
8 public class TextReader extends Applet
9 {
10   public void start()
11   {
12     try
13     {
14       URL fileURL = new URL (getDocumentBase(), "Solo.txt");
15       InputStreamReader reader =
16           new InputStreamReader (fileURL.openStream());
17       BufferedReader soloFile  = new BufferedReader (reader);
18
19       while (true)
20       {
21         String aLine = soloFile.readLine();
22         if (aLine == null)
23           break;
24         System.out.println (aLine);
25       }
26     }
27     catch (MalformedURLException e)
28     {
29       System.out.println ("File could not be opened.");
30     }
31     catch (IOException e)
32     {
33       System.out.println ("File read error.");
34     }
35   }
36 }
```

There are a few differences between Listing 12.16 and Listing 12.12 that should be high-lighted. First notice the creation of a URL object in Line 14. The call to `getDocument-Base` gets the URL for the directory where the applet was found. The `fileURL` object is used to open an `InputStreamReader` object in Line 15. Line 14 may throw a `Mal-formedURLException`, which we catch in Line 27.

SUPPLEMENTARY MATERIAL

12.5   System in, out, and err

In Section 2.8.1 we learned how to use standard output to print debugging information. Standard output is a place where Java can display messages at a platform-dependent location. For example, the following will print a message to standard output:

```
System.out.println ("It could happen to you.");
```

There is also a standard place where error messages can be written. Again, that location is platform-dependent, but it is often the same place that standard output messages go. Some platforms allow the user to capture all messages sent to standard error in a special place for later perusal. Standard err and out are based on the PrintStream class, which is not covered in this text. For the sake of simplicity we do not use standard error within this text.

```
System.err.println ("The theater is full.");
```

In addition, there is a standard input stream that can be used for user input. However, its functionality is limited, as the program in Listing 12.17 demonstrates. This program uses only standard input and output streams.

Notice the use of the flush method in Lines 21, 25, 29, and 33. Standard out guarantees that lines will be sent to a display only if its buffer is full or if an end-of-line has been encountered. If we want to print part of a line without an end-of-line character, we should flush the buffer. The call to flush does not appear to be needed on all computer platforms Platforms and development environments vary so greatly that the author chose to use flush to be safe.

The standard input stream is primitive. It is based on the InputStream class, which reads only bytes. Thus, to read an integer we need to create two methods. One, Lines 64 to 83, to read a single line into a string. Next, we create a method that converts a string into an integer (Lines 47 to 59). Now we know why the author has chosen to hide all this detail in the Read class. It is not something we want to encounter early in our experience.

Sometimes it is possible to take advantage of other input streams for standard input. For example, the follow may work:

Listing 12.17 The Pocket Money Applications Using Standard Streams

```
1  //
   ******************************************************************
2  //
3  // title:    Pocket Change
4  //
5  // Compute the value of pocket change (pennies, nickels, dimes,
6  // and quarters.
7  //
8  //
   ******************************************************************
9
10 import java.io.IOException;
11
12 public class PocketMoney
13 {
14    // ------------- main ---------------------------------
15    public static void main (String args[])
16    {
17       // get the number of pennies, nickels, dimes, and quarters
18       System.out.println("Please enter the amount of change:");
19
20       System.out.print  ("  pennies:  ");
21       System.out.flush ();
22       int pennies  = readInt();
23
24       System.out.print  ("  nickels:  ");
25       System.out.flush ();
26       int nickels  = readInt();
27
28       System.out.print  ("  dimes:    ");
29       System.out.flush ();
30       int dimes    = readInt();
31
32       System.out.print  ("  quarters: ");
33       System.out.flush ();
34       int quarters = readInt();
35
36       // Computer the value of the change
37       int value = quarters * 25 + dimes * 10 +
                         nickels * 5 + pennies;
38
39       // Display results
40       System.out.print("The value of this change is ");
41       System.out.print(value);
42       System.out.println(" cents.");
43    }
44
```

Listing 12.17 The Pocket Money Applications Using Standard Streams

```
45    // ------------- readInt ----------------------------------
46    // read a single integer from standard input
47    private static int readInt ()
48    {
49      int result = 0;
50      try
51      {
52        result = Integer.parseInt(readLine());
53      }
54      catch (Exception e)
55      {
56          System.err.println(" *** invalid integer ***");
57      }
58      return result;
59    }
60
61    // ------------- readLine ----------------------------------
62    // Read a single line from standard input.  The line terminator
63    // is not part of the returned string.
64    private static String readLine ()
65    {
66      String buffer = new String ();
67      int i;
68      try
69      {
70        while ((i = System.in.read()) != -1)
71        {
72          char c = (char)i;
73          if (c == '\n')
74            break;
75          buffer += c;
76        }
77      }
78      catch (IOException e)
79      {
80        System.err.println (e);
81      }
82      return (buffer);
83    }
84 }
```

```
InputStreamReader input = new InputStreamReader (System.in);
myReader = new BufferedReader (input);
String line = myReader.readLine();
```

The advantage of sending the standard input stream through a `BufferedReader` is that it allows us to take advantage of the `readLine` method in `BufferedReader`. This works with Symantec Cafe under Windows NT, it works with some versions of Metrowerks on a Macintosh, and it works with Sun's development system under Solaris. However, it does not work with Symantec Cafe under Windows 95. Input seems to get hung up in a buffer someplace.

Although Java is advertised to be platform-independent, its given implementation may contain hidden dependencies. IO is particularly vulnerable to them.

12.6 StreamTokenizer

The Java `StreamTokenizer` class combines some of the features of the `BufferedReader`, `StringTokenizer`, and `number` classes. It can be used to read ASCII-encoded words and numbers directly from a file or keyboard and convert them into strings or numbers. Those of us who read the supplementary material in Section 4.5.1 on page 149 have seen an example.

The `StreamTokenizer` class is best used for tokenizing computer programs. It has flexible ways of dealing with program comments, end-of-line characters, and pushing tokens back into the input stream. Listing 12.18 shows an example `StreamTokenizer` program with its associated input and output in Listing 12.19. Lines 10 and 11 show how to use a stream tokenizer to read from a file. We have also used it to read from the keyboard. Examples are in Listing 4.11 on page 150 and Listing 10.11 on page 470. See below. :

```
StreamTokenizer keyboard  = new StreamTokenizer (System.in);
```

After we have created a stream tokenizer we can get tokens from it, as we have in Line 12 of Listing 12.18. We will process tokens in the `while` loop (Lines 12 through 28) until we reach end-of-file (`TT_EOF`). By default, all ASCII characters in the integer range from 0 through 32 are delimiters (white space). This includes spaces, end-of-lines, end-of-files, tabs, etc. There is a `whitespaceChar` operation that allows this range to be modified. However, it does not allow a programmer to specify multiple ranges or multiple single character delimiters, as we can with `StringTokenizer` objects.

Listing 12.18 `StreamTokenizer` Example

```
1    import java.io.FileReader;
2    import java.io.IOException;
3    import java.io.StreamTokenizer;
4    public class Parser
5    {
6      public static void main(String args[])
7      {
8        try
9        {
10         FileReader fileReader = new FileReader ("example.txt");
11         StreamTokenizer in    = new StreamTokenizer (fileReader);
12         while (in.nextToken() != in.TT_EOF)
13         {
14           switch (in.ttype)
15           {
16             case in.TT_WORD:
17               System.out.println ("word:      " + in.sval );
18               break;
19             case in.TT_NUMBER:
20               System.out.println ("number:    " + in.nval );
21               break;
22             case '"':
23               System.out.println ("string:    " + in.sval );
24               break;
25             default:
26               System.out.println ("other:     " + (char)(in.ttype) );
27           }
28         }
29       }
30       catch (IOException e) {}
31     }
32 }
```

The `nextToken` operation returns a token type (Line 12). We can also access the token type through the `ttype` instance variable (Line 14). Token types are either `TT_WORD`, `TT_NUMBER`, `TT_EOF`, `TT_EOL`, or other. A `TT_WORD` type indicates that the current token is a properly formed identifier. Thus, the input stream `Terminator1()` is three tokens, as demonstrated in Listing 12.19. A tokenizer tries to create the longest token it can. Therefore, `Terminator1` is a single word token rather than a word and number token. The characters "( )" cannot be part of a word token, so they are not included. The string value of a word can be accessed through the `sval` instance variable, as we have done in Line 17.

Listing 12.19   Stream Tokenizer Input/Output

``
// An example file to demonstrate
// StreamTokenizer
class Terminator1
{
  public Terminator1()
  {
    String s = "I'll be back";
    double x := 23.4 + 56;
  }
}
``
	``
	word: class
	word: Terminator1
	other: {
	word: public
	word: Terminator1
	other: (
	other:)
	other: {
	word: String
	word: s
	other: =
	string: I'll be back
	other: ;
	word: double
	word: x
	other: :
	other: =
	number: 23.4
	other: +
	number: 56.0
	other: ;
	other: }
	other: }
	``

A `TT_NUMBER` `ttype` is a token that contains only properly formed numbers. Its `double` value can be accessed through the `nval` instance variable, as we have done in Line 20. If we are interested in integers, we must do a type cast.

`TT_EOL` and `TT_EOF` correspond to end-of-line and end-of-file tokens. `TT_EOF` can be used to detect end-of-file, as we have done in Line 12. However, the end-of-line characters are treated as white space and thus ignored by default. It is returned only if the `eolIs-Significant` operation has been applied (Line 41 in Listing 4.11 on page 150).

All other tokens, for example punctuation, are saved in `ttype` as the ASCII integer value of the character that it comprises. For example, the token "=" is store in `ttype` as its ASCII value 61. See Table A.5 on page 836. Line 26 of Listing 12.18 shows how to retrieve its value and cast it into a character.

Quoted strings are treated specially. Once we have determined that we have a string token (a sequence of anything between a pair of double quote marks) we can find the contents of the string in the `sval` instance variable. See Lines 22 and 23.

`StreamTokenizer` is not as well suited as the `StringTokenizer` class for tokenizing ASCII input data. It's primary fault is the semantics for delimiters. However, Listing 4.11 on page 150 and Listing 10.11 on page 470 demonstrate that in simple cases `StreamTokenizer` is easier to use.

12.7 Binary Files

12.7.1 Reading and Writing Bytes—File Copy

In this section we will see how to read and write binary files. We will begin by creating a useful utility program. It makes a copy of a file by reading an existing file byte by byte and placing its data into a new output file byte by byte. Because it copies byte by byte, this program will copy all files: text files, image files, sound files, etc. Every computer platform provides a file copy application for us. The usefulness of writing such a programs is to see how it may be done and to demonstrate how to use binary IO classes. The application is shown in Listing 12.20.

Listing 12.20 File Copy Application

```
 1 //
 **************************************************************
 2 //
 3 // title:   Copy
 4 //
 5 // This application demonstrates reading from and writing to
 6 // a file.  One file is copied into another.
 7 //
 8 //
 9 //
 **************************************************************
10
11 import java.io.FileInputStream;
12 import java.io.FileNotFoundException;
13 import java.io.FileOutputStream;
14 import java.io.IOException;
15
16 public class Copy
17 {
18   public static void main(String args[])
19   {
```

Listing 12.20 File Copy Application

```
20    try
21    {
22        // open files
23        FileInputStream  inputFile  =
24                        new FileInputStream("Solo.txt");
25        FileOutputStream outputFile =
26                        new FileOutputStream("SoloCopy.txt");
27
28        // do the copy
29        while(true)
30        {
31            int theByte = inputFile.read();
32            if (theByte == -1)
33                break;
34            outputFile.write(theByte);
35        }
36
37        // done so close up
38        inputFile.close();
39        outputFile.close();
40        System.out.println ("Copy done");
41    }
42
43    // Cannot find a file by that name
44    catch (FileNotFoundException e)
45    {
46        System.out.println ("File not found");
47    }
48
49    // File read or write exception
50    catch (IOException e)
51    {
52        System.out.println ("File exception occurred");
53    }
54  }
55 }
```

Opening the input and output files is similar to our approach with text files, except we have chosen not to send them through a buffer. Notice that the files names are part of the program code. As a result, this program is not flexible. We will show how to specify file names at run-time shortly. Each iteration of the loop reads one byte from the input file, advances the input file pointer by one byte, writes the byte to the output file, and advances the output file pointer by one. When the end of the input file is reached, a −1 value is returned from the read (see Line 31). As a result, the loop is exited when the end of the input file is reached.

We can buffer the input and output by changing Lines 23 through 26 to the following:

```
FileInputStream  in  = new FileInputStream ("Solo.txt");
BufferedInputStream inputFile = new BufferedInputStream (in);
FileOutputStream out = new FileOutputStream ("SoloCopy.txt");
BufferedOutputStream outputFile = new BufferedOutputStream
(out);
```

12.7.2 Reading Bytes—File Snoop

Let us continue our investigation of primitive file operations. As the previous section demonstrates, a file can be viewed as a stream of bytes. When a file is copied, it is only necessary to read and write bytes. We do not know whether the byte we are reading is a character, part of an integer, or a pixel in an image.

In this section we will create a file snoop program. We will look inside a file at the byte level. Snoop programs are useful for looking at the raw contents of a file, so we can determine how information is formatted or if we have written information to the file correctly.

The program in Listing 12.29 on page 590 reads each byte in a file and then displays it as a decimal. Figure 12.7 shows how the Solo.txt file from Listing 12.11 on page 554 looks when dumped in decimal format. Thus, this program serves a foundation for the program described in Section A.5 on page 834. We used it to investigate the representation of HTML files on various computer platforms.

Figure 12.7 Decimal Dump of `Solo.txt`

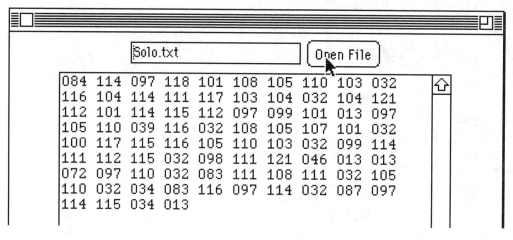

When a file is dumped in decimal format, each byte is displayed as its integer value. This format is good for investigating the underlying representation of a file. The loop that accomplishes this task is shown in Listing 12.21.

Listing 12.21 Decimal Format Loop

```
1      while(true)
2      {
3          int    theByte = inputFile.read();
4          if (theByte == -1)
5             break;
6          String s = Integer.toString (theByte);
7          if (s.length() == 1)
8             s = "00" + s;
9          else if (s.length() == 2)
10            s = "0" + s;
11          count++;
12          if (count % 10 == 0)
13             myTextArea.append (s + "\n");
14          else
15             myTextArea.append (s + " ");
16      }
```

12.7.3   File Dialog Boxes

The copy program in Listing 12.20 is rather inflexible. It allows us to copy files only of the name Solo.txt to files of the name SoloCopy.txt. If we want to copy other files, it is necessary to modify our copy program and recompile. An option is to provide a text field for file names. A user would type a name into the field and then press an Open button. Java has happily made this unnecessary by providing a FileDialog class. The bad news is that this does not work for applets for security reasons. This prevents an applet user from browsing through files on a remote computer.

The FileDialog class does not work with applets because the this in Line 5 of Listing 12.22 must be a Frame object. Thus, this code must appear in a class that extends Frame. As a result, we will not be able to use them until we cover them in Chapter 15. There is some reason to this madness.

The Java FileDialog class will allow us to open an arbitrary file. The FileDialog class is used in the open method shown in Listing 12.22. The first step is to create a file dialog object in Line 5. The last parameter in its constructor specifies dialog mode. If the mode is load (FileDialog.LOAD), the dialog expects to read an existing file. The

SAVE constant puts a dialog object in the save mode. However, save mode does not require an existing file, as load does.

Listing 12.22 Opening a File with a Dialog Box

```
1    private FileInputStream openFile ()
2    {
3      // Create the file dialog
4      String fileName;
5      FileDialog fileDialog = new FileDialog (this,
6                          "Input File Name", FileDialog.LOAD);
7      fileDialog.setDirectory(".");
8      fileDialog.show();
9      fileName = fileDialog.getFile();
10
11     // Check if we got a valid file name
12     if (fileName == null)
13       return null;
14     else
15     {
16       // We got a valid file name so get its directory
17       String fileDirectory;
18       fileDirectory = fileDialog.getDirectory();
19       try
20       {
21         // Open the file
22         return new FileInputStream (fileDirectory + fileName);
23       }
24
25       // Catch file open problems
26       catch (FileNotFoundException e)
27       {
28         e.printStackTrace();
29         myTextArea.appendText ("\nCould not open " +
30                         fileDirectory + fileName + "/n");
31         return null;
32       }
33     }
34   }
```

Once the file dialog is created, its directory property is set (Line 7). The dot specifies the current directory. What the setDirectory method does depends on the platform. This must be done before the show method is executed.

The file dialog does not become visible (see Figure 12.8 and Figure 12.9) until the show operation is applied to it (Line 8). Once the show method is evoked, control does not return to the caller method until the user exits the file dialog box by clicking Open or Cancel.

Figure 12.8 File Name Dialog—Windows 95

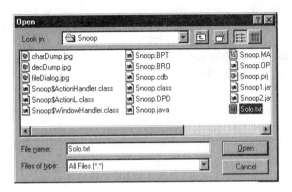

Figure 12.9 File Name Dialog—Macintosh

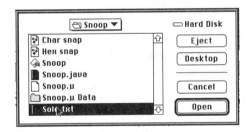

When the dialog box is exited, control returns to Line 9, where the user-selected file name is extracted. A null value indicates that the user pressed the Cancel button.

If a valid file name is extracted, the directory path can also be retrieved as is shown in Line 18. The directory path and file name are concatenated to form a complete file path, which is used to open the file in Line 22.

12.7.4   Command-line Arguments

Programs run from a Unix shell or DOS command prompt window may have parameters. Java applications can be given list of command arguments via these parameters. All the arguments are placed in an array of strings and are accessible through the `main` method. The code below shows how Lines 23 through 26 in Listing 12.20 can be modified to accommodate command line arguments. This code allows us to specify the name of the input and output files at the time we invoke the copy program. We will talk about what the square brackets do in Chapter 13:

```
FileInputStream  inputFile  = new FileInputStream(args[0]);
FileOutputStream outputFile = new FileOutputStream(args[1]);
```

In a Unix or DOS command window we could enter the following command:

```
java Copy Solo.txt SoloCopy.txt
```

The first argument goes into index 0, the second into index 1, and so on.

12.7.5   Reading and Writing Primitive Data

Java also supports reading and writing primitive values to and from binary files. This alleviates the translation step between string and binary representation. However, these files are not human-readable and cannot be modified or created by simple text editors. An example of using a data streams is shown in Listing 12.23.

The program first writes an integer, double, boolean, character, a character string, and text string to a file named `data.file`. Once the information is written, the file is closed and a new file object is created to read it. The data read from the file is finally displayed, demonstrating that the write and read occurred successfully. The output of the program is shown below:

```
123
123.456
TRUE
A
 J a v a
Java
```

The data in the `data.file` file is not human-readable. The snoop program reveals the following character dump. The only readable results are the strings. Notice the presence of the null characters between each letter of the string written in Line 20. This occurs because

Listing 12.23 Data Stream Example

```
1  import java.io.FileInputStream;
2  import java.io.FileOutputStream;
3  import java.io.DataInputStream;
4  import java.io.DataOutputStream;
5  import java.io.IOException;
6
7  public class DataFiles
8  {
9    public static void main (String args[])
10     {
11       try
12       {
13        FileOutputStream out = new FileOutputStream ("data.file");
14         DataOutputStream dataOut = new DataOutputStream (out);
15
16         dataOut.writeInt (123);
17         dataOut.writeDouble (123.456);
18         dataOut.writeBoolean (true);
19         dataOut.writeChar ('A');
20         dataOut.writeChars ("Java");
21         dataOut.write ("Java".getBytes());
22
23         dataOut.close();
24
25         FileInputStream in = new FileInputStream ("data.file");
26         DataInputStream dataIn = new DataInputStream (in);
27
28         int     i = dataIn.readInt();
29         double  d = dataIn.readDouble();
30         boolean b = dataIn.readBoolean();
31         char    c = dataIn.readChar();
32         byte[]  s = new byte[8];
33         dataIn.readFully (s);
34         byte[]  t = new byte[4];
35         dataIn.readFully (t);
36         dataIn.close();
37
38         System.out.println(String.valueOf (i));
39         System.out.println(String.valueOf (d));
40         System.out.println(String.valueOf (b));
41         System.out.println(String.valueOf (c));
42         System.out.println(new String (s));
43         System.out.println(new String (t));
44
45         System.out.println ("done");
46         System.in.read();
47       }
48
```

Listing 12.23 Data Stream Example

```
49        catch (IOException e)
50        {
51           System.out.println ("IO error");
52        }
53     }
54 }
```

characters are two bytes long. In Line 21 the string was converted to a byte stream before being written. There are nulls between characters:

```
...{@^./...w..A.J.a.v.aJava
```

A decimal representation of the `data.file` file reveals the following data. Notice that the integer takes the first four bytes of the file. The next eight bytes are the double. The boolean value true follows next. It is stored as a binary one.

```
000 000 000 123 064 094 221 047 026 159
190 119 001 000 065 000 074 000 097 000
118 000 097 074 097 118 097
```

Once something is sent to a binary file there is nothing that preserves its type. For example, Listing 12.24 show how we can write a four-character string to a file and read it back in as an integer. The result of sending the string "Java" to a file and reading it as an integer is 1247901281.

Listing 12.24 An Undetected Typing Violation

```
1        FileOutputStream out = new FileOutputStream("data.file");
2        DataOutputStream dataOut = new DataOutputStream (out);
3        dataOut.write("Java".getBytes());
4        dataOut.close();
5
6        FileInputStream in = new FileInputStream("data.file");
7        DataInputStream dataIn = new DataInputStream(in);
8        int i = dataIn.readInt();
9        dataIn.close();
10
11       System.out.println(String.valueOf(i));
```

Chapter 16 describes a set of more useful classes called `ObjectInputStream` and `ObjectOutputStream`. They preserve the type information in their files.

12.7.6 Random Access Files

To do justice to random access files would require much more time than is appropriate at this junction. To leave the subject completely out would leave us with a narrow view of file IO. This brief section is designed to provide us with an flavor of what random access files do.

All of the IO classes we have seen thus far give us two choices: we can read a file starting at its beginning or we can write a file starting from the beginning. If we are creating an airline reservation system that tracks thousands of flights with hundreds of passengers, we do not want to read a file from the beginning to find a particular flight and then write the entire file to disk after we make a small change. Instead, we want to jump to the locations of interest, read the information there, and make a small change.

> A *random access file* is one in which we can read and write to arbitrary locations within the file. It is not random in the sense that the information within it is random. On the contrary, a random access file is well organized.

The class that supports this is the `RandomAccessFile` class. Random access files support the following:

- Read and write are supported in a single file object.

- Access to an arbitrary byte in the file using a seek method.

- Read and write of primitive data values (similar to the `DataInputStream` and `DataOutputStream` classes).

The program in Listing 12.25 demonstrates the following functionality of a random access file. The output of this program is shown in Figure 12.26:

- **Creation**: Lines 22 through 46 create a random access file. They read stock prices from a file. We call each instance of a date and three stock prices as a record. A key component of this process is to assure that each record has the same length. If they are the same length, we can compute the location of any record by multiplying the record length times the record number.

- **Random read**: Lines 51 through 57 demonstrate how to read an arbitrary record. They read and displays record number 23.

- **Modify a record**: Lines 60 through 66 perform another random read. This time we read record number 65. Lines 70 through 73 modify the record and replace the original record in the file with the modified one. Lines 77 through 83 reread this record to confirm that it has been modified. Thus we update a single record in place. We do not have to read the entire file and save a complete new version.

Listing 12.25 Contrived Random Access Example

```
1  import java.awt.Color;
2  import java.io.FileNotFoundException;
3  import java.io.IOException;
4  import java.io.RandomAccessFile;
5
6  public class Random
7  {
8    //---------- main -------------------------------------------------
9
10   public static void main(String[] args) {
11     try
12     {
13       // --- open files ---
14       // Open the stock text file for read.
15       StockPriceFile inputFile = new
16               StockPriceFile("IntelStock.prices");
17       // Open the random access file for read and write
18       RandomAccessFile randomFile = new
19               RandomAccessFile("RandomAccess.file", "rw");
20
21       // --- Add stock prices to random access file ---
22       while (true)
23       {
24         // Get the record from input
25         StockPrice dailyReport = new StockPrice(inputFile);
26         if (inputFile.endOfFile())
27           break;
28
29         // Make all date strings 10 characters
30         // They are easier to read from a random file with
31         // a terminating end of line.
32         String date = dailyReport.getDate();
33         if (date.length() == 6)
34           date = "   " + date;
35         if (date.length() == 7)
36           date = " " + date;
37         date = date + " \n";
38         if (date.length() != 10)
39           System.out.println("Date length error");
40
41         // Write the date, stock prices, and NASDAQ index
42         // to random access file
43         randomFile.writeBytes (date);
44         randomFile.writeDouble(dailyReport.getIntelPrice());
45         randomFile.writeDouble(dailyReport.getNASDAQIndex());
46       }
```

Listing 12.25 Contrived Random Access Example

```
47      // Compute the length of each random access file record
48      int recordLength = 10 + 8 + 8;
49
50      // Read and display the record at location 23
51      int recordNumber = 23;
52      randomFile.seek(recordLength * (recordNumber - 1));
53      String record23Date      = randomFile.readLine();
54      double record23IntelPrice = randomFile.readDouble();
55      System.out.println ("record 23 - Intel sold at " +
56                           record23IntelPrice +
57                           " on " + record23Date);
58
59      // Read and display the record at location 66.
60      recordNumber = 66;
61      randomFile.seek(recordLength * (recordNumber - 1));
62      String record66Date      = randomFile.readLine();
63      double record66IntelPrice = randomFile.readDouble();
64      System.out.println ("record 66 - Stock sold at " +
65                           record66IntelPrice +
66                           " on " + record66Date);
67
68      // Modify the date and stock prices of the
69      // record at location 66.
70      randomFile.seek(recordLength * (recordNumber - 1));
71      randomFile.writeBytes("modified");
72      randomFile.seek(recordLength * (recordNumber - 1) + 10);
73      randomFile.writeDouble(99.99);
74
```

Listing 12.25 Contrived Random Access Example

```
75        // Reread and display the record at location 66
76        // validating the changes.
77        recordNumber = 66;
78        randomFile.seek(recordLength * (recordNumber - 1));
79        record66Date      = randomFile.readLine();
80        record66IntelPrice = randomFile.readDouble();
81        System.out.println ("record 66 - Intel sold at " +
82                            record66IntelPrice +
83                            " on " + record66Date);
84      }
85
86    // Handle IO errors
87    catch (FileNotFoundException e)
88    {
89      System.out.println("File not found");
90    }
91    catch (IOException e)
92    {
93      System.out.println("IO Error");
94    }
95  }
96 }
```

Listing 12.26 Example run of Listing 12.25

```
>java Random
record 23 - Stock sold at 62.5 on  11/2/94
record 66 - Stock sold at 64.13 on   1/5/95
record 66 - Stock sold at 99.99 on modified
```

REFERENCE

12.8   Summary

The focus of this chapter is file input and output. We should be able to open text files and use buffering to increase time efficiency. Text files are human-readable because all the information within them is represented with ASCII encoded characters. Binary files contain bytes that do not translate into ASCII characters.

`FileReader` and `BufferedReader` classes are used for text input. They contain methods for reading an entire line of text. When text input needs to be partitioned into components, the `StringTokenizer` class is valuable. `FileWriter` and `BufferedWriter` classes are used for text output. The `DecimalFormat` class is used to format numeric output. Input and output operations must be performed within an exception handler so IO errors can be handled.

The buffer pattern is useful for improving the efficiency of programs. Buffers allow a computer to work with information in large chunks.

Standard input and output can be used to interact with a user using a text-based interface. The `VRead` and `VWrite` classes hide much of this detail.

There are a wide variety of binary file classes. The `FileInputStream` and `FileOutputStream` allow use to manipulate files at the byte level. The `DataInputStream` and `DataOutputStream` allow us to read and write binary representations of primitive types. Random access files allow us to read and write arbitrary locations within a file.

PROGRAM LISTINGS

12.9   Reading and Writing Movie Reviews

Listing 12.27   ThumbsInputFile Class

```
1  //***************************************************************
2  //
3  // title:     ReviewInputFile.java
4  //
5  // Read a thumbs file.
6  //
7  //***************************************************************
8
9  import java.applet.Applet;
10 import java.io.BufferedReader;
11 import java.io.InputStreamReader;
12 import java.io.IOException;
13 import java.net.MalformedURLException;
14 import java.net.URL;
15
16 public class ReviewInputFile
17 {
18   private final int NAME_WIDTH    = 40;
19   private final int THUMBS_WIDTH  =  5;
20   private final int DATE_WIDTH    =  8;
21
22   private BufferedReader   myBufferedReader;
23
24   //---------- ReviewInputFile ----------------------------
25   // pre:       none
26   // post:      A review file is opened if possible.
27   // exception: "FileNotFoundException" raised if file cannot
28   //            be opened
29
30   public ReviewInputFile (String fileName, Applet applet)
31           throws MalformedURLException, IOException
32   {
33    URL fileURL  = new URL (applet.getDocumentBase (),fileName);
34     InputStreamReader reader =
35        new InputStreamReader(fileURL.openStream ());
36     myBufferedReader  = new BufferedReader(reader);
37   }
38
```

Listing 12.27 ThumbsInputFile Class

```
39    //---------- close ------------------------------------------
40    // pre:  none
41    // post: this file is closed
42    public void close() throws IOException
43    {
44      myBufferedReader.close();
45    }
46
47    //---------- read -------------------------------------------
48    // pre:  none
49    // post:       returns true if the next review is read
50    //             returns false if end of file
51    // exception: "IOException" raised for read errors
52    public MovieReview read() throws IOException
53    {
54      String line = myBufferedReader.readLine();
55      if (line == null)
56      {
57        return null;
58      }
59      else if (line.length() <
60          NAME_WIDTH + THUMBS_WIDTH + THUMBS_WIDTH +  DATE_WIDTH)
61      {
62        throw new IOException();
63      }
64      else
65      {
66        String  name  = line.substring(0, NAME_WIDTH).trim();
67        boolean gene  = line.charAt (NAME_WIDTH) == 'u';
68        boolean roger = line.charAt(NAME_WIDTH +
                                THUMBS_WIDTH)=='u';
69     String  date  = line.substring(NAME_WIDTH + THUMBS_WIDTH +
70             THUMBS_WIDTH, NAME_WIDTH + THUMBS_WIDTH +
71             THUMBS_WIDTH + DATE_WIDTH);
72        return new MovieReview (name, gene, roger, date);
73      }
74    }
75 }
```

12.10 Reading Stock Prices

Listing 12.28 StockPriceFile Class

```
1  //*************************************************************
2  //
3  // title:    StockPriceFile
4  //
5  // Class that reads stock price files.
6  //
7  //*************************************************************
8
9  import java.io.BufferedReader;
10 import java.io.FileReader;
11 import java.io.FileNotFoundException;
12 import java.io.IOException;
13 import java.util.StringTokenizer;
14
15 public class StockPriceFile
16 {
17    private static BufferedReader myInputFile;
18
19    //---------- StockPriceFile -------------------------------
20    // pre:        none
21    // post:       a stock file is opened if possible.
22    // exception: "FileNotFoundException" raised if file cannot be
23    //             opened "IOException" raised for read errors
24    public StockPriceFile (String fileName)
25                  throws FileNotFoundException
26    {
27       FileReader in = new FileReader(fileName);
28       myInputFile   = new BufferedReader(in);
29    }
30
```

Listing 12.28 StockPriceFile Class

```
31    //---------- read --------------------------------------------
32    // pre:        this stock file was successfully opened
33    // post:       returns the next stock record
34    // exception: "IOException" raised for read errors
35    public StockPrice read() throws IOException
36    {
37        // read the data for the next stock record
38        String buffer = myInputFile.readLine();
39        if (buffer == null)
40            return null;
41
42        StringTokenizer tokens = new StringTokenizer(buffer, ",");
43        String date      = tokens.nextToken();
44        Double d         = Double.valueOf(tokens.nextToken());
45        double stock     = d.doubleValue();
46        d                = Double.valueOf(tokens.nextToken());
47        double sP500     = d.doubleValue();
48        d                = Double.valueOf(tokens.nextToken());
49        double nASDAQ    = d.doubleValue();
50
51        return new StockPrice (date, stock, sP500, nASDAQ);
52    }
53 }
54
```

12.11 Snoop

Listing 12.29 Snoop Applet

```
1  //***************************************************************
2  //
3  // title:    Snoop
4  //
5  // This applet will dump files to a text area in
6  // decimal format.  It can be used for exploring the
7  // format of arbitrary files.
8  //
9  //***************************************************************
10
11 import java.awt.Color;
12 import java.awt.Font;
13 import java.awt.TextArea;
14 import java.io.BufferedInputStream;
15 import java.io.IOException;
16 import java.net.URL;
17 import vista.VActionButton;
18 import vista.VApplet;
19 import vista.VField;
20
21 public class Snoop extends VApplet
22 {
23   private VField   myFileName;
24   private TextArea myTextArea;
25
26   //---------- start -----------------------------------------
27   public void start()
28   {
29     // set up window
30     setBackground (Color.white);
31
32     // Set up file open text field and button
33     myFileName = new VField ("Solo.txt          ", this);
34     VActionButton openButton =
                      new VActionButton ("Open File", this);
35
36     // Set up text area
37     myTextArea = new TextArea (14, 42);
38     add(myTextArea);
39     Font courier = new Font ("Courier", Font.PLAIN, 12);
40     myTextArea.setFont (courier);
41   }
42
```

Listing 12.29 Snoop Applet

```
43   //---------- action --------------------------------------------
44   public void action ()
45   {
46     try
47     {
48       // Open the file
49       String fileName = myFileName.getString();
50       URL fileURL = new URL (getDocumentBase(), fileName);
51       BufferedInputStream inputFile =
52                 new BufferedInputStream(fileURL.openStream());
53
54       // Dump it
55       int count = 0;
56       while(true)
57       {
58         int    theByte = inputFile.read();
59         if (theByte == -1)
60           break;
61         String s = Integer.toString (theByte);
62         if (s.length() == 1)
63           s = "00" + s;
64         else if (s.length() == 2)
65           s = "0" + s;
66         count++;
67         if (count % 10 == 0)
68           myTextArea.append (s + "\n");
69         else
70           myTextArea.append (s + " ");
71       }
72     }
73
74     // Respond to IO errors
75     catch (IOException e)
76     {
77       myTextArea.append ("\nFile exception occured\n");
78       return;
79     }
80   }
81 }
```

PROBLEM SETS

12.12 Exercises

Input and Output—Section 12.2

1 Investigate three computer applications with which you are familiar. Describe how they rely on file IO. In addition to the word processing and spreadsheet documents, look at the program settings that persist between runs. For example, some programs store default fonts settings and high scores in a file or series of files.

2 Listing 12.3 returns a null in Line 6 on end-of-file. How would this code and the code in Listing 12.4 change if we raised an exception for end-of-file?

Buffering—Section 12.3

3 We use buffering every day with little thought that we are doing something special. Indicate how each of these events represents a buffered activity. Why is buffering in each case more efficient than not using a buffer? What is the buffer size for each?

　a. We are out of milk for our morning cereal so we go to the store and buy a gallon of milk.

　b. The convenience store gets its Wednesday shipment of three cases of milk.

　c. A local bottling company takes delivery of a tanker trailer filled with milk.

Input and Output Classes—Section 12.4

4 Which IO class would you use for the following projects:

　a. Java code editor.

　b. A sound file, each sound point can have a value between 0 and 255.

　c. A store inventory hooked to a cash register.

　d. A simple "to do" list.

12.13 Projects

12.13.1 Text Input and Output—Section 12.4

The following web site contains complete works of fiction that make good input for various exercises. For example, in the short fiction category we can find Lewis Carroll's *Alice's Adventures in Wonderland* and in the novels section we can find Jane Austen's *Sense and Sensibility.*

```
http://eserver.org/fiction
```

5 Rewrite the multiplication table program in Listing 2.8 on page 72 so that each number takes exactly four spaces. The result should look as follows:

```
0    0    0    0    0    0    0    0    0    0
0    1    2    3    4    5    6    7    8    9
0    2    4    6    8   10   12   14   16   18
...
0    9   18   27   36   45   54   63   72   81
```

6 Read the stock file used in Chapter 9 and display it to standard output so that it looks as follows:

```
date     Stock    Standard      NASDAQ
                  and Poor
4/11/94  69.19     449.87       748.11
4/12/94  65.75     447.57       739.22
4/13/94  63.75     446.26       727.38
...
```

7 Create an application that reads a letter template from one file and names and addresses from a second file. It should create junk mail letters by embedding names and addresses in the letter template and saving them to a third file.

8 Count the number of words and characters in a file. Use one of the novels found on the web site listed at the beginning of this section.

9 Count the number of times a particular string appears in a novel found on the web site listed at the beginning of this section.

10   Use the `StringTokenizer` class to extract works from a novel found on the web site listed at the beginning of this section. Print the first 100 words of each on an individual line. No punctuation should be printed.

For a greater challenge print contractions and single quoted phrases appropriately. For example "I can't spell 'mustard' today" should appear as follows.:

```
I
can't
spell
mustard
today
```

11   Use the `StringTokenizer` class to extract all integers from a novel found on the web site listed at the beginning of this section. For example "Raise flaps to 25 degrees for 7 seconds" should appear as follows:

```
25
7
```

12   The following web site shows several formulas for computing the readability of text. Use either the Flesch-Kincaid or Gunning readability test to compute the readability of novel found in the web site listed at the beginning of this section.

A computer does not know anything about syllables. Multiply the number of vowels by a constant to determine the relationship between vowels and syllables. Determine this constant by looking at a 100-word passage and counting the number of syllables and vowels.

```
http://www.timetabler.com/reading.html
```

a.   Flesch-Kincaid Formula—this is a U.S. Government Department of Defense standard test for writing manuals.

- Calculate L, the average sentence length (number of words ÷ number of sentences). Estimate the number of sentences to the nearest tenth, where necessary.
- Calculate N, the average number of syllables per word (number of syllables ÷ number of words).
- Then compute grade level = (L x 0.39) + (N x 11.8) – 15.59
- So the computed Reading Age = (L x 0.39) + (N x 11.8) – 10.59 years.

b.   Gunning "FOG" Readability Test—This "FOG" measure is suitable for secondary and older primary age groups.

- Select samples of 100 words, normally three such samples.
- Calculate L, the average sentence length (number of words ÷ number of sentences). Estimate the number of sentences to the nearest tenth, where necessary.

- In each sample, count the number of words with three or more syllables.
- Find N, the average number of these words per sample.
- Then compute the grade level needed to understand the material = (L + N) x 0.4
- So the calculated Reading Age = [(L + N) x 0.4] + 5 years.

13 Write a program that maintains a list of all your CDs. It should contain a CD class that contains a field for the name of the CD, the name of the performers, and a rating from one to five stars (five stars is the highest rating). It should be able to save and load your list from a file.

Create another class that is a list of CDs. It should support the operations of sort and search.

Create an interface that asks for each CD's name, performer, and rating. In addition, there should be support menus, buttons, and text fields for input, searching, and sorting.

Binary Input and Output—Section 12.7

14 Write a utility that reads two files and checks them for differences. When it finds a difference it displays the first place where the files differ.

15 Modify the copy program so that it uses buffered IO.

16 Create an experiment to determine the time saved with buffering. Use Section 7.7 on page 315 as a guide to setting up the experiment. If available, try your experiment on Unix, Windows, and Macintosh platforms. Compare the results and explain any differences.

17 Modify the snoop application Listing 12.29 on page 590 to display files in character format. Display a "." for all unprintable characters, ; e.g., those between 0 and 31 and greater than 126.

18 Modify the snoop application to display files in hexadecimal format.

19 Modify the snoop applet (Listing 12.29 on page 590) so that it displays decimal and character representations at the same time (see Listing A.3 on page 837). Include a file offset count in the leftmost column.

13 Arrays

Traffic Simulation

13.1   Objectives

Concepts   **Section 13.2, page 599**

We begin this chapter with a traffic simulation of cars driving down a highway. This example demonstrates the utility of arrays for keeping track of the cars in a simulation. In addition, arrays of integers are used to create graphs of automobile speeds.

Section 13.7 , page 633

A second thread of execution is required to animate our simulation. While one thread of execution is busy updating the display, the second thread computes the location and speed of each car ten times per second.

Patterns   **Section 13.3, page 608**

Vectors are revisited. This time we look at how arrays can be used to implement a vector class. We demonstrate how to insert elements into a vector by moving elements within an array to make room and removing elements from a vector by moving elements in an array to fill dead space. In addition, we dynamically grow and shrink our vector by creating new arrays. We will implement these operations with the one loop for sequential data pattern from Chapter 10.

Java Skills

The Java section illustrates how to define and manipulate arrays of objects and arrays of primitive values. We learn how to access elements and make copies.

- Using one-dimensional arrays   Section 13.5.1, page 615
- Using two-dimensional arrays   Section 13.5.8, page 627
- Threads   Section 13.7.2, page 635

Abilities
- Create and initialize array objects.
- Visit each element of an array.
- Insert elements into an array.
- Delete elements from an array.
- Use threads

CONCEPTS

13.2   Traffic Simulation

13.2.1   Rules of the Road

We have all experienced a comfortable drive down an interstate highway when suddenly there are brake lights ahead. Like a wave these lights speed toward us and we too are forced to brake. These sudden waves of braking can be aggravating and dangerous. Knowing how driving conditions affect traffic flow is essential for any road designer. Designers are interested in traffic phenomena because it can help them create safer and more efficient road systems. The program in this section will create a simple model of the phenomenon described above.

> *Simulation* is a methodology that employs computers to model the important features of a physical system.

The goal of a simulation is to focus only on those aspects of a model that give us insight into the world. We must select features of the physical world that are critical to the understanding of some aspect of its behavior. In our traffic model, we are interested in how road hazards create a wave of braking through a line of cars. Important features of this model are the speeds of the cars, safe following distances, and reaction time. Other features, such as a car's make, number of passengers, or engine size, will be ignored. As a result, our simulation will not mirror the real world, but it will give us important insight into some of its behavior.

> *Discrete event simulation* models the world in discrete time steps. For example, the state of a simulation may be computed every tenth of a second for quickly changing events such as traffic, or every 1000 years for slower changing events such as galaxies.

We will use a technique called discrete event simulation to model traffic. Every tenth of a second, we will compute the state (location and speed) of each car. Figure 13.1 shows a snapshot of our model roadway with cars, a road, and hazard.

In the program that creates this snapshot, hazards are initiated by clicking the mouse button beside the road. The road hazard appears as a red rectangular object. When cars encounter a hazard, they apply their brakes. A car that is braking appears red. Once a car has passed a hazard, it is free to speed up again. It will change color to green. When a car reaches cruising speed, it appears blue.

Figure 13.1 Snapshot of the Simulated Roadway

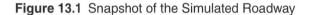
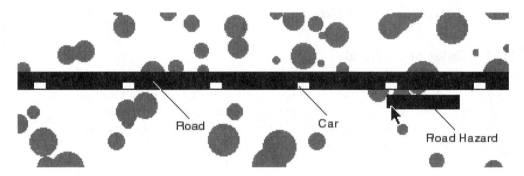

Road   Car   Road Hazard

The traffic simulation uses some simple rules that govern the behavior of each car:

- If there is sufficient space between a car and the car ahead, a car speeds up until it is traveling 5 mph over the speed limit.
- If the car ahead is too close, a car applies its brakes.
- If a car encounters a hazard, it slows down until it is traveling at one half the speed limit.

Based on this simple model, Figure 13.2 shows how the appearance of a brief hazard, such as a deer running across the road, can cause a flurry of braking. This figure shows two plots of car speeds. The car speeds are plotted from right to left with the cars in front of the pack appearing at the right side of the plot and the cars at the rear of pack at the left side of the plot. The top line shows the speed of all the cars when the hazard is first encountered. The bottom line shows the speed of the cars at some time in the future when the hazard has been gone for a few seconds. Notice how the wave of slowing cars moves quickly down the line.

This model is clearly an oversimplification. It does not show the dynamics of drivers with different personalities. For example, some people drive more aggressively and faster. Others follow at a greater or closer distance. In addition, the roadway in this simulation is a single lane with no passing. To model our world more accurately we would need to account for different passing strategies for our car drivers. However, it is astounding that a model this simple can reproduce the observed behavior of cascading brake lights. More

Figure 13.2 Slowing When a Hazard is Briefly Encountered (Graph of Car Position vs. Car Speed)

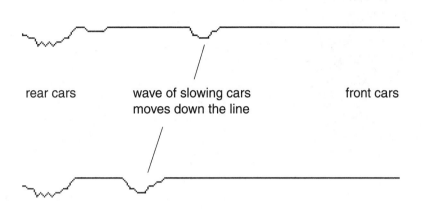

rear cars   wave of slowing cars   front cars
moves down the line

complex models, however, would be needed to help traffic engineers design new road-ways.

13.2.2 Design

The traffic simulator is partitioned into four classes (see Figure 13.3):

- `World`: The world applet is responsible for drawing the road and trees. It creates a `Traffic` object and also handles the occurrence, disappearance, and placement of a road hazard (see Listing 13.22 on page 645). Mouse handling, required to place the hazard, is discussed in Chapter 14.

- `Traffic`: This chapter will focus primarily on the `Traffic` class. It creates, updates, and draws all the cars. It also creates and updates a speed graph (See Listing 13.20 on page 640).

- `Cars`: Each car is responsible for maintaining its speed, location, and color (blue for cruising, red for slowing, and green for speeding up). Based on an internal set of rules and interactions with the world, a car will speed up, slow down, or remain constant. A car will brake if it is too near a car in front of it or encounters a road hazard. If the road is clear, it will attempt to maintain a constant or accelerate to achieve a cruise speed of 5 mph over the speed limit (see Listing 13.21 on page 642).

- VPlot: A plot object is used to display the speed of all cars (see Appendix: C, page 919).

Figure 13.3 Traffic Simulator Design

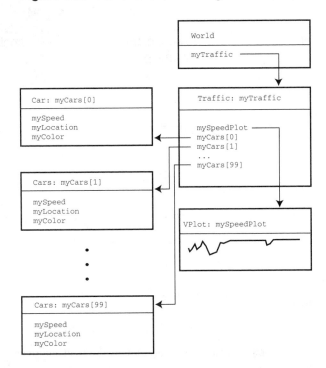

13.2.3 Discrete Time Steps

A World object creates a second thread of execution. It is needed to manage the movement of cars at one-tenth second intervals. This leaves the original thread available to do housekeeping tasks such as maintaining the display and managing various events.

Execution of the second thread begins in the World class's run method, which is dominated by an infinite loop. This loop is shown in Listing 13.1 (Lines 160 through 174 from Listing 13.22). Each time though the loop the cars are moved a small distance and drawn in their new positions, and the speed graph is updated. Next, the thread pauses for a tenth of a second before the process repeats.

Listing 13.1 Animation Loop

```
1   public void run ()
2   {
3     Graphics g = getGraphics();
4
5     while(true)
6     {
7       myTraffic.update (this);
8       myTraffic.paint (g);
9       myTraffic.graph ();
10      pause (DELTA_TIME);
11    }
12  }
```

Some sort of timing loop, like the one in the `run` method, is at the heart of discrete event simulation. It determines the order in which the state of a simulation is updated. We will save the details about the second thread for an optional discussion in Section 13.7.

13.2.4   Managing Cars

Before we take a look at how we maintain a list of cars using an array, we will take a brief look at the `Car` class. Listing 13.2 shows its interface. The constructor requires a starting location. When a car needs to update its state, it must look at the car ahead and look for road hazards to determine whether to slow down, speed up, or stay at the same speed. Thus, the `update` method has a reference to the car in front of it so that it can determine how closely it is following. In addition, it has a reference to the `World` so that it can ask about road hazards. Other methods provided by the `Car` class allow us to get a car's current speed and to draw it. Section 13.7.3 describes the `paint` method in more detail. It contains some special code to reduce flicker.

Listing 13.2 `Car` Class Interface

```
1 public class Car
2 {
3   public Car(int location)
4   public int getSpeed()
5   public void paint(Graphics g)
6   public void update (Car carAhead, World world)
7 }
```

13.2.5   Traffic Implementation

We need to maintain a list of cars. A vector is a good choice. However, we will use an array to illustrate how an array can do the same job as a vector. Later we will discuss some guidelines for determining when to choose an array and when to choose a vector.

An array has many of the same properties as a `Vector`. We can create one and refer to each item by using an index. A major difference is that when we create an array we must specify its size. The number of elements in an array does not grow or shrink. In addition, we use square brackets to retrieve or set array elements rather than the `elementAt` or `setElementAt` methods used for vectors. Arrays can hold primitive types in addition to objects. Because we specify the type of object or value an array holds when we declare it, there is no need to type cast, as we do with a vector when we retrieve elements from it.

Arrays are covered in detail in Section 13.5. This section will focus on how arrays are used in the `Traffic` class (Listing 13.20 on page 640). There are four important parts. The first part is in the constructor. It creates an array of cars. The relevant code is shown in Listing 13.3. An array named `myCars`, which can hold 100 cars, is created in Line 6. Next, 100 cars are created and added to the array (Lines 8 through 12). Each car is placed between 20 and 120 feet behind the car in front of it (Line 11).

Listing 13.3 Create an Array of Cars

```
1   private final int MAX_CARS    = 100;
2   private Car[]  myCars;      // instance variable
3
4    public Traffic()
5    {
6      myCars      = new Car[MAX_CARS];
7      int x       = 0;
8      for (int i=0; i<MAX_CARS; i++)
9      {
10        myCars[i] = new Car(x);
11        x -= (int)(Math.random() * 100 + 20);
12      }
13      ...
14  }
```

The second part draws all the cars on the roadway (Listing 13.4). We use a counter loop to iterate through all the cars in the `myCar` array. Array indices begin at 0 and run through array size minus 1. If we were to implement these first two parts with a vector, our code would look like the code in Listing 13.5.

Listing 13.4 Drawing the Cars

```
1    public void paint (Graphics g )
2    {
3      for (int i=0; i<MAX_CARS; i++)
4      {
5        myCars[i].paint(g);
6      }
7    }
```

Listing 13.5 Create and Draw Cars Using a Vector

```
1    // create list of cars - part 1
2    Vector myCars = new Vector();
3    int x        = 0;
4    for (int i=0; i<MAX_CARS; i++)
5    {
6      myCars.addElement (new Car(x));
7      x -= (int)(Math.random() * 100 + 20);
8    }
9
10   // draw the cars - part 2
11   for (int i=0; i<MAX_CARS; i++)
12   {
13     ((Car)(myCars.elementAt(i))).paint(g);
14   }
```

The third part updates the location of each car in the myCar array ten times per second (Listing 13.6). Notice that the cars are updated in reverse order. First, the last car is updated (index 99), then the second to the last (index 98), and so on. When we update each car we pass the car ahead of it through a parameter. Thus, when we update the car at index 99, the car ahead of it at index 98 is passed along (Line 6). Within this loop we process all but the first car. The counter variable i begins at 99 and ends at 1. The first car, index 0, is treated as a special case because it has no cars in front of it (Line 9).

Listing 13.6 Update the Cars

```
1    public void update (World world)
2    {
3      // update all but first car
4      for (int i=MAX_CARS-1; i>0; i--)
5      {
6        myCars[i].update(myCars[i-1], world);
7      }
8      // first car has none in front of it
9      myCars[0].update(null, world);
10   }
```

The cars are updated in reverse order to simulate reaction time. A driver does not respond immediately to the events of the car ahead. Thus, when we update the car at index 99, we are passed the state of car 98 before it is updated. The result is a one-tenth second delay between when the car ahead changes and the car behind responds.

In the fourth part we plot car speeds. It helps us visualize traffic dynamics (Figure 13.2). To create a plot, the `Traffic` constructor creates a `VPlot` object. The first two parameters set the limits of the y-axes range. For example, the constructor in Line 4 of Listing 13.7 creates a plot that has a minimum speed of 0 and a maximum speed of the speed limit plus 15. The third parameter sets the number of points in the plot, which in this case is the number of cars. Finally, the fourth parameter sets the window title.

Listing 13.7 Graphic Car Speeds

```
1    public Traffic()
2    {
3      ...
4      mySpeedPlot = new VPlot(0, Car.SPEED_LIMIT + 15, MAX_CARS,
5                              "Car Speeds");
6      mySpeedPlot.reverse();
7    }
8
9    public void graph ()
10   {
11     int[] speeds = new int[MAX_CARS];
12     for (int i=0; i<MAX_CARS; i++)
13     {
14       speeds[i] = myCars[i].getSpeed();
15     }
16     mySpeedPlot.setLine(speeds);
17   }
```

The `reverse` method (Line 6) makes the plot go from right to left. This will cause the first car to be drawn on the right side of the graph rather than the left side.

The `graph` method in Lines 9 through 17 is called ten times a second. It begins by creating an array of integers in Line 11. Each element will hold the speed of its corresponding car. Thus, the element at index 0 will hold the speed of the car at index 0 of the `myCar` array. The loop in Lines 12 through 15 initializes the `speeds` array with car speeds. Line 16 passes this array to the plotting object.

Listing 13.3 and Listing 13.7 demonstrate that we can have arrays of objects and of primitives. Vectors cannot hold primitives. Listing 13.4 and Listing 13.5 demonstrate another difference between vectors and arrays. Vectors hold items only of the class `Object`. We must cast this object to type `Car` whenever we paint it (Line 13 in Listing 13.5). Arrays can have elements of any class type. The `myCar` array can only hold `Car` objects. There is no cast required when we access its elements (Line 5 in Listing 13.4). We made this restriction when we declared and created the array. See below:

```
Car[] myCars = new Car[MAX_CARS];
```

PATTERNS

13.3 Implementing a Vector Class with Arrays

We stated in the pervious section that we could maintain a list of cars with an array or vector. In this section we will make the difference between arrays and vectors clear by implement a mini vector class with arrays. In so doing we will use the "one loop for linear structures" pattern repeatedly (Section 10.3). The algorithms required to implement these vector operations are used often. Learning how to implement them is important. In addition, studying these algorithms will give us insight into how the vector class will perform under various conditions.

Vectors have several advantages over arrays. In particular, elements can be added to the beginning or in the middle of a vector and the index of all higher elements is automatically adjusted to make room for the new elements. Elements can be removed from the middle of a vector, and again all higher elements will be automatically adjusted to fill in the empty space. Finally, a vector can grow and shrink in size as space is required or released. This functionality must be explicitly programmed when arrays are used.

When implementing a vector with an array, we must specify the size of an array when the vector is created. Thus we must know the size of the array before we know how many elements the array must hold. One option is to make the array fixed in size. It can be made large to accommodate most reasonable vector sizes. This approach typically wastes substantial space because the arrays must be made large enough to accommodate all reasonable situations. A problem will inevitably occur in special cases when vector sizes need to be larger than normal.

We will use an approach that creates an array of modest size. When its capacity is exceeded, a new larger array is created and the elements from the old array are copied to the new. We will save space, but there will be an execution penalty because of the time required to copy elements.

In this implementation we must distinguish between the size of a vector and its capacity. The size of the vector is the number of elements that are currently stored in it. This is different from its capacity, which determines the number of elements that a vector can hold before it must grow. Size and capacity are two key instance variables associated with each of our vectors. In addition, we will define a constant that specifies how much larger the new array will grow when the vector's capacity is exceeded. The value of the capacity increment is important. If it is too small, a new array will need to be created often. On the other hand, if the increment is too large, there is wasted space.

Increasing the capacity of a vector by a fixed amount each time its capacity is exceeded is one option. A better alternative is to double the increment each time the capacity is exceeded. We will use a constant increment for simplicity.

A complete implementation for a vector subset is shown in Listing 13.23 on page 649. In the following sections we will describe portions of that code.

13.3.1 Creating a Vector

A vector will contain the following state:

- `myElements`—the array that holds the vector's elements.
- `myCapacity`—the size of `myElements` array. How many elements the vector can hold without growing.
- `mySize`—the number of elements currently stored in the array. It must always be less than or equal to its capacity.

We will begin our investigation with a look at the vector constructor. Within it, an array with the size of the capacity increment is created. The capacity of a vector is how many elements it can hold without growing the size of its array. The size of a vector is how many elements are actually stored within the vector. Thus, the initial vector size is set to zero and its capacity is set to the size of the array. See below:

```
myElements = new Object[CAPACITY_INCREMENT];
mySize = 0;
myCapacity = CAPACITY_INCREMENT;
```

13.3.2 Adding an Element to a Vector

Next we will look at the `addElement` method, which appends new items to the end of a vector. In the typical case, adding an element to the end of a vector is straightforward. The next available element of the array is set to the new element and the vector size is incremented by one. See below:

```
myElements[mySize] = obj;
mySize++;
```

If adding a new element will exceed the capacity of the vector, the process becomes more difficult. Three steps are required. They are listed below and illustrated in Figure 13.4:

Figure 13.4 Adding "Windy" to the end of a vector with no more capacity

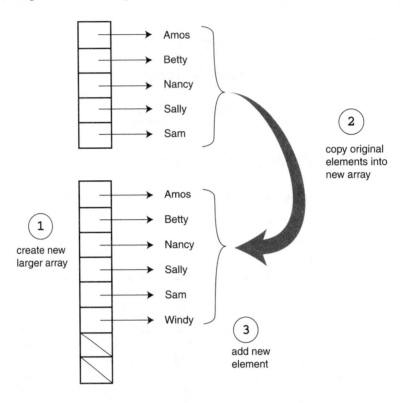

1. Create a larger array.
2. Copy all the existing elements to the new array.
3. Add the new element to the vector.

These steps are implemented in Listing 13.8. Since an array is a linear structure, we use our one loop for linear structures to iterate through all the elements of our array.

13.3.3   Inserting Into a Vector

Implementing the `insertElementAt` method is more of a challenge. First, the index of the insertion must be checked. Inserting an element at an index less than 0 or beyond the end of the vector is not appropriate, so an exception must be thrown. Next, existing elements must be moved to higher index locations to accommodate the new one.

Listing 13.8 Appending When the Array is Full

```
1 // step 1
2 Object[] newElements = new Object[myCapacity +
CAPACITY_INCREMENT];
3
4 // step 2
5 for (int i=0; i<mySize; i++)
6    newElements[i] = myElements[i];
7
8 // step 3
9 newElements[mySize] = obj;
10 mySize++;
11 myCapacity += CAPACITY_INCREMENT;
12 myElements = newElements;
```

Again, there are two cases. In the first case the vector has enough capacity. The steps involved in this process are listed below and illustrated in Figure 13.5. These steps are implemented in Listing 13.9:

1. All the vector elements at the insertion index and higher must be moved to a position one higher.

2. Then the new element is placed at the index location.

Figure 13.5 Insert "Connie" at Index 2

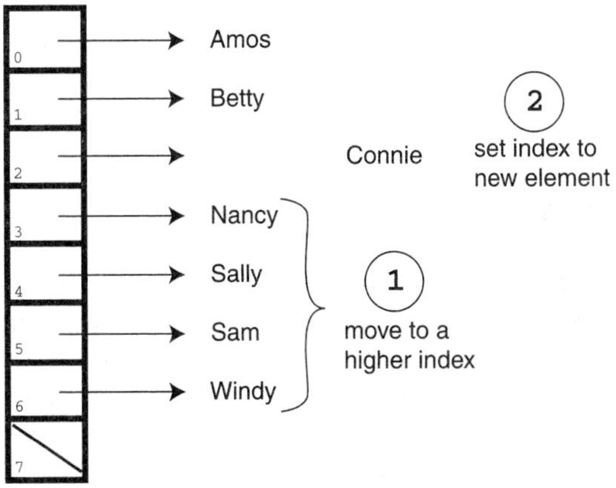

Again, we use the "one loop for linear structures" pattern to accomplish our task. Notice that the elements are moved in reverse order to their index values. If they were moved in order, the elements at the higher indices would be lost. For example, if we moved element

Listing 13.9 Insert—Sufficient Capacity

```
1 for (int i=mySize; i>index; i--)
2   myElements[i] = myElements[i-1];
3 myElements[index] = obj;
4 mySize++;
```

14 to index 15, the item at index 15 would be lost. Thus, we must move the item at index 15 before the item at index 14.

Figure 13.6 shows the steps involved in adding "Connie" to our array in more detail. We start with the array as shown at (0). The initial list size is 6. Therefore, i begins with the value of 6 (Listing 13.9). The first time we execute Line 2 the element at index 6 is assigned the same item that the element at index 5 references. The result is shown at (1). The loop is executed three more times, resulting in the situation depicted at (2), (3), and (4). The loop exits and Line 3 is executed. It places the new element into the array. The final result is shown at (5). The only remaining task is to increment the list size in Line 4.

The second case involves inserting a new element when there is not enough capacity in the vector. The steps required follow:

1. Create a larger array.
2. Copy the current elements to their appropriate places in the new array.
3. Add the new element.

The code needed to accomplish this is a variation of code we have seen. All the other operations required for a vector are straightforward or minor modification of code we have seen. See Listing 13.23 on page 649 for the complete implementation.

13.4   Mini Vector Analysis (Optional)

In Section 11.4 we stated that the performance of a vector is unpredictable. After looking at its implementation in Section 13.3, we can see why. For example, when we add an element to a vector, usually it takes constant time, $O(1)$. We just add it to the array. However, when we have reached the capacity of the vector, adding an element to a vector is $O(n)$ where n is the current size of the vector. Time is required to create a new array and copy the original elements into it. The larger the capacity increment, the less often this case will occur. This is accomplished at the cost of space. So one must decide what is more important for a given application: time or space.

Inserting an element into a vector is $O(n)$ on average. If the insertion is at the beginning of the list, n iterations of the move loop will be necessary. If the insertion is at the end of the list, 0 iteration of the move loop is necessary. Since there is an equal probability that

Figure 13.6 Insert "Connie" at index 2 - detail

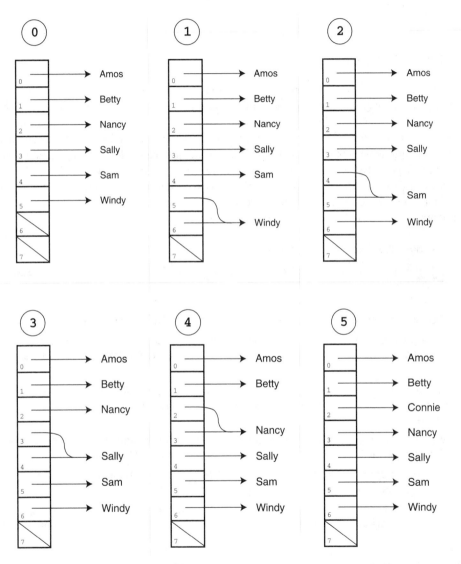

the insertion point will be between index 0 and n, the average number of elements moved is n/2, which is O(n). A formal analysis would mirror that of the sequential search in Section 11.5.1.

If the capacity of the vector is exceeded, n copy loop iterations are required to move all the elements from the old array to the new array. Again, the result is O(n).

JAVA

13.5 Arrays

In Chapter 11 we learned how to use vectors to create lists of objects. In this chapter we are investigating how to use the more primitive array construct to accomplish the same tasks. A prime benefit of using vectors and arrays is that we do not need to declare a unique identifier for every instance of an object. We can use subscripts to distinguish between various objects within a group. Thus, we do not need to know many variables we need in advance. By using a vector or array we can create as many as we need at run-time. Arrays, unlike vectors, can contain primitive values, such as ints, characters, and booleans, in addition to objects. Unlike vectors, arrays are fixed in size. Table 13.1 summarizes the differences between arrays and vectors and will help us determine when to use each.

Table 13.1 Arrays Versus Vectors

Array	Vector
Once declared it is fixed in size.	Variable size.
Elements can be objects or values.	Elements can only be objects.
Homogeneous—all elements are of the same type.	Heterogeneous—elements are any object or any element derived from the class `Object`.
Inserting or deleting elements in the middle of an array may require writing code to shift elements.	Elements are shifted automatically upon insertion or deletion.
More efficient in applications where the size of the array is stable.	Dynamic characteristics of vector require execution time overhead.
The square bracket notation can be confusing for the novice.	Operations on vectors use standard method calls.
Some objects, for example polygons, require information to be passed to them in arrays.	We can make an array do everything a vector can so we can get by without ever using vectors.

13.5.1 Creating Arrays

We will begin by looking at arrays of objects. Listing 13.10 contains an implementation of a `Star` class. It contains a constructor that creates a star at a random location, and a `paint` method that draws that star. We will use it as our example object when demonstrating how to create and manipulate an array of objects. There are three steps required to create an array of stars:

1. Create an array reference.
2. Create an array.
3. Create and assign objects to the array elements.

The first step is to declare the identifier that will reference an array. The square brackets, `[]`, in the following line indicates that `milkyWay` will reference an array of stars. Figure 13.7 illustrates what this line of code does. No objects have yet been created. The slash indicates a `null` reference—a reference to no object.

```
Star [] milkyWay;
```

The next step is to create an array. The code for doing this is shown below. The phrase `new Star[50]` creates an array that can reference 50 stars. However, it does not create any of the stars (see Figure 13.8). This array will always contain references for exactly 50 stars. It will not shrink or expand to accommodate fewer or more stars. If we need fewer stars, we can leave some of the array elements null. If we need more stars, we will have to create a new array.

```
milkyWay = new Star[50];
```

Often these first two steps are combined into one statement as shown below. They were separated above for the sake of illustration:

```
Star [] milkyWay = new Star[50];
```

The basic form for creating an array is shown below:

```
ElementClassName [] ArrayIdentifier =
        new ElementClassName [ mumberOfElements ] ;
```

Thus far we have created an array, but the array is empty. In the last step we assign objects to the array elements. The code required to accomplish this is shown below. The result is illustrated in Figure 13.9:

```
for (int i=0; i<50; i++)
  milkyWay[i] = new Star();
```

Listing 13.10 Star Class

```
1  //************************************************************
2  //
3  // title:    Star
4  //
5  // A class for creating and drawing stars at random locations.
6  //
7  //************************************************************
8
9  import java.awt.Color;
10 import java.awt.Graphics;
11 import java.awt.Polygon;
12
13 public class Star
14 {
15   Polygon myStar;
16
17   final private int MAX_X = 580;
18   final private int MAX_Y = 380;
19
20   //---------- Star -------------------------------------------
21   // pre:  none
22   // post: a star is created with a random color and location
23   public Star()
24   {
25     int x = (int)Math.floor(Math.random() * MAX_X);
26     int y = (int)Math.floor(Math.random() * MAX_Y);
27
28     myStar = new Polygon();
29     myStar.addPoint(x+10,  y);
30     myStar.addPoint(x+18,  y+16);
31     myStar.addPoint(x,     y+6);
32     myStar.addPoint(x+20,  y+6);
33     myStar.addPoint(x+2,   y+16);
34   }
35
36   //---------- paint ------------------------------------------
37   // pre:  g is a valid graphics context
38   // post: this star is drawn on g
39   public void paint(Graphics g)
40   {
41     g.setColor(Color.yellow);
42     g.fillPolygon(myStar);
43   }
44 }
```

Figure 13.7 Step 1—Declare a Reference to
an Array of Stars

milkyWay

Figure 13.8 Step 2—Create Empty Array of Stars

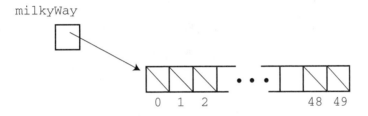

Figure 13.9 Step 3—Fill the Array with Stars

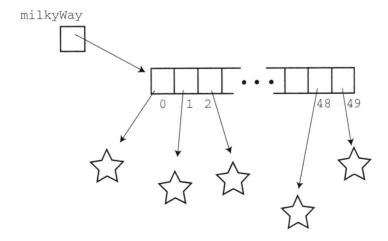

13.5.2   Accessing Array Elements

Array indices always begin at 0 and end at n − 1 where n is the number of elements in the array. Thus, the first index of the `milkyWay` array is 0 and the last index is 49. Trying to access an element outside the range of 0 to n − 1 will cause an `IndexOutOfBound-sException` to be thrown (Section 9.4.6 , page 418).

```
milkyWay [-5] = new Star();      // run-time exception
milkyWay[105] = new Star();      // run-time exception
```

Accessing an element in an array follows the general form shown below:

```
ArrayIdentifier [ integerExpression ]
```

The index is any valid integer expression. For example:

```
milkyWay [i*5-3] = milkyWay [(int)(Math.random() * 49.0)];
```

An element is assigned to an array by placing an array reference on the left side of an assignment operator, and it is retrieved from an array by placing an array reference in an expression. The following code fragment illustrates the process of creating and initializing an array without the use of a loop:

```
Star [] threeSome = new Star[3];
threeSome[0] = new Star();
threeSome[1] = new Star();
threeSome[2] = new Star();
```

These three stars are drawn with the following code:

```
threeSome[0].paint(g);
threeSome[1].paint(g);
threeSome[2].paint(g);
```

Because the only thing in the paint code that changes is the index, it can be replaced by the more general code shown below. This code illustrates a common pattern that visits all the elements of an array:

```
int n = 3;
for (int i=0; i<n; i++)
  threeSome[i].paint(g);
```

13.5.3   Swapping Array Elements

Another task that is often performed on arrays is to swap two elements. The following code shows how this is done:

```
Star temp = milkyWay [6];
milkyWay  [6] = milkyWay [23];
milkyWay [23] = temp;
```

A general purpose method for accomplishing the task is shown below:

```
public void swap (Star galaxy[], int i, int j)
{
  Star temp  = galaxy [i];
  galaxy [i] = galaxy [j];
  galaxy [j] = temp;
}
```

13.5.4   Typing Rules

The `milkyWay` array may hold only `Star` objects. The appearance of `Star` at the left side of the first line below establishes this restriction. We may not place movie reviews, strings, or colors in a `milkyWay` array.

```
Star [] milkyWay = new Star[50];
milkyWay [14] = new Thumbs ("Titanic",up,up,"12/97");//error
milkyWay [37] = "Syntax Error";                      //error
milkyWay [42] = Color.white;                         //error
```

We can create arrays that will hold any object. For example, the array `peanutButter-Jar` defined below can contain any of the above objects:

```
Object [] peanutButterJar = new Object [50];
peanutButterJar [14] =
            new MovieReview ("Titanic",up,up,"12/97");
peanutButterJar [37] = "Green Mile";
peanutButterJar [42] = Color.white;
peanutButterJar [11] = new Star();
```

This is exactly what we do when we implement a vector class with arrays. Any object retrieved from a `peanutButterJar` is an object. If we want to apply custom methods to an object retrieved from an array of `Object` instances, we must do an explicit cast, just like the ones we did with vectors.:

```
Object element = peanutButterJar [i];
if (element instanceof Star)
{
  Star alpha = (Star)element;
  alpha.paint(g);
}
```

13.5.5 Making Copies

Often we must make copies of arrays. We must do so carefully or the program will not behave as expected. We learned in Chapter 1 that we can refer to the same object with more than one name. We called this aliasing. The same holds true with array elements. More than one array index can reference the same star object. The following code illustrates:

```
milkyWay  [2] = milkyWay [23];
milkyWay [48] = milkyWay  [2];
```

The stars at index 2, 23, and 48 all reference the same star. The stars that were previously referred to by index 2 and 48 are now floating in space awaiting the garbage collector. If we had an operation to change the color of a star, changing the color of a star using any of the indices 2, 23, and 48 changes the star at the other two indices because they are the same star. Figure 13.10 illustrates.

Figure 13.10 Referencing the Same Star

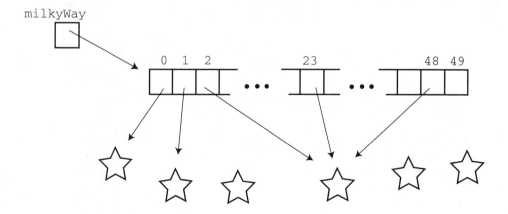

Suppose we want to make a copy of our array of stars. First we must decide what it means to make a copy of objects (stars). Does it mean that we have two arrays that reference the same objects (stars), which we call a *shallow copy*, or does it mean that we also create copies of the objects (stars) that the arrays reference, which we call a *deep copy*. We generally mean the latter but let us look at some intermediate steps to see the ramifications of the decisions we are making.

The following would not give use a copy of the `milkyWay` array. It would simply alias it as shown in Figure 13.11. Both `andromeda` and `milkyWay` reference the same array of stars. This is not what we intended.

```
Star [] andromeda = milkyWay;
```

Figure 13.11 Aliasing an Array

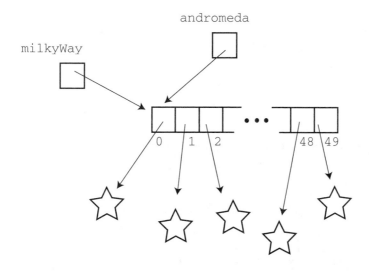

The following code would not fair much better. It would create a new array but not new stars. Although the `andromeda` and `milkyWay` identifiers reference unique arrays, they reference the same old stars. See Figure 13.12.

```
Star [] andromeda = new Star [50];
for (int i=0; i<50; i++)
   andromeda[i] = milkyWay[i];          .
```

To copy the array correctly there are several steps required:

Figure 13.12 New Array with Old Stars

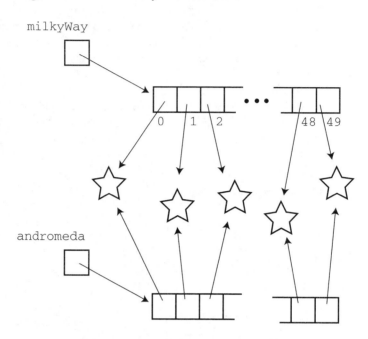

Listing 13.11 Star Copy Constructor—Insert in Listing 13.10

```
1   //---------- Star --------------------------------
2   // pre:  none
3   // post: this star is a copy of star "s"
4   public Star(Star s)
5   {
6     int [] xPoints = s.myStar.xpoints;
7     int [] yPoints = s.myStar.ypoints;
8     int numPoints = s.myStar.npoints;
9     myStar = new Polygon (xPoints, yPoints, numPoints);
10  }
```

1. Make a new array the same size as the original array.
2. Make a copy of each star and assign it to the new array.

The second step is to make a copy of a star. However, making a copy of a star is not as simple as it may appear. Using the assignment statement as we did above does not create a copy of a star—it only creates an alias for the same star. We must add a copy constructor to our Star class. A *copy constructor* creates a clone of an object. A copy constructor for the `Star` class is shown in Listing 13.11. A copy constructor contains a single parameter that references the star it will copy. The following code shows how one is used. Notice the difference between making a copy and an alias:

```
Star alpha       = new Star ();
Star alphaCopy   = new Star (alpha);    // make a copy
Star alphaAlias = alpha;                // make an alias
```

The copy constructor must make a copy of the polygon of the original star. This process is made much more difficult than necessary because the `Polygon` class does not contain a copy constructor. We are forced to make a copy of a polygon by first extracting the x values for all the points in the polygon. This in done in Line 6 (Listing 13.11). Notice that all the x points are stored in an array of ints. Next, we do the same thing for the y points in Line 7. Finally, we ask the polygon how many points it has. We can use the information gathered in Lines 6, 7, and 8 to construct a copy of our original polygon. On the other hand, if the `Polygon` class had a copy constructor, we could replace Line 6 through 9 with the following:

```
myStar = new Polygon (s.myStar);  // not supported by Polygon
```

The two steps in our copy process are shown below. This gives us the result we desire (Figure 13.13):

```
Star [] andromeda = new Star [50];
for (int i=0; i<50; i++)
  andromeda[i] = new Star (milkyWay[i]);
```

Figure 13.13 New Array with New Stars

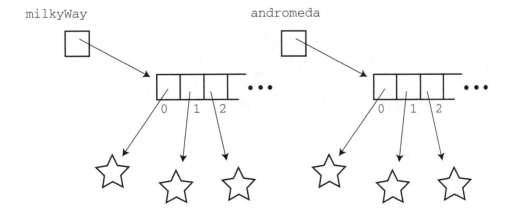

623

13.5.6 A Complete Example

Listing 13.12 puts some of the code we have discussed above together to create an applet that displays 50 stars on a black background (Figure 13.14). We need only change Line 17 to display a different number of stars.

Listing 13.12 The `Night` Class

```
1  //******************************************************************
2  //
3  // title:   Night
4  //
5  // Draw a night full stars.
6  //
7  //******************************************************************
8
9  import java.awt.Color;
10 import java.awt.Graphics;
11 import java.applet.Applet;
12 import Star;
13
14 public class Night extends Applet
15 {
16   private Star [] myMilkyWay;
17   private final int NUMBER_STARS = 50;
18
19   //---------- init -------------------------------------------
20   // create the stars
21   // called automatically
22   public void init()
23   {
24     setBackground(Color.black);
25     myMilkyWay = new Star[NUMBER_STARS];
26     for (int i=0; i<NUMBER_STARS; i++)
27       myMilkyWay[i] = new Star();
28   }
29
30   //---------- paint ------------------------------------------
31   // draw the stars
32   // called automatically
33   public void paint(Graphics g)
34   {
35     for (int i=0; i<NUMBER_STARS; i++)
36       myMilkyWay[i].paint(g);
37   }
38 }
```

13.5.7 Arrays of Primitive Values

Since vectors cannot hold primitive values, it is usually more convenient to use an array when we need a collection of primitives. Creating an array of primitives is similar to create an array of objects. For example, the code below creates an array of random integers:

```
int n = 100;
int [] numbers = new int[n];
for (int i=0; i<n; i++)
    numbers[i] = (int)(Math.random() * 100.0);
```

We can use all the patterns we learned for vectors in Chapter 11 on arrays. For example, the following shows how to find the maximum and average of our array of random numbers:

```
// finding the maximum
int max = numbers[0];
for (int i=1; i<n; i++)
    if (numbers[i] > max)
        max = numbers[i];

// finding the average
int sum = 0;
for (int i=0; i<n; i++)
    sum += numbers[i];
int average = sum / n;
```

Arrays of integers work slightly differently than arrays of objects because ints are values. A new operator is not required to create each int in an array. Thus, the following creates array elements with the same values. Indices 2, 23, and 48 are not aliases for a single object, as they were when we did this for objects. They just happen to contain the same value. Compare this result with the result we achieved with arrays of object in Figure 13.10:

```
numbers [2]  = numbers [23];
numbers [48] = numbers [2];
```

Figure 13.14 Array with the Same Values

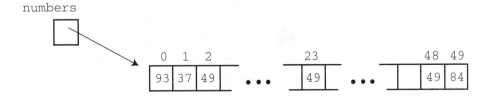

One of the easiest things to do when working with integer arrays is to confuse an index with the value stored at an index. For example, if the value of the index is 23, the expression numbers[23] has the value 49. 49 is the value stored at index 23.

Making a copy of an array of primitives is easier than making a copy of an array of objects. We do not have to worry about copy constructors. For example, we can make a copy of the numbers array using the code fragment below:

```
int [] numbersCopy = new int [n];
for (int i; i<n; i++)
  numbersCopy[i] = numbers[i];
```

In addition, there is a shortcut that can be used to create and initialize an array of primitives. It is illustrated below.:

```
int [] fourSome = {49, 46, 13, 8};
```

This code creates an array of four ints and initializes its contents to the values 49, 46, 13, and 8. It is equivalent to the following code fragment:

```
int [] fourSome = new int [4];
fourSome [0] = 49;
fourSome [1] = 46;
fourSome [2] = 13;
fourSome [3] =  8;
```

Figure 13.15 Checkers

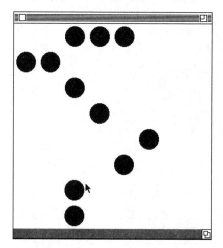

13.5.8 Two-Dimensional Arrays

Unlike vectors, arrays can have an unlimited number of dimensions. For example, we can think of about the placement of checkers on a checkerboard using two dimensions: rows and columns (Figure 13.15).

Listing 13.13 Two-dimensional Checker Pieces

```
1  import java.awt.Color;
2  import java.awt.Graphics;
3  import java.applet.Applet;
4
5  public class CheckerBoard extends Applet
6  {
7    boolean [][] myCheckerBoard;
8
9    public void init()
10   {
11     setBackground (Color.white);
12     myCheckerBoard = new boolean [8][8];
13     for (int row = 0; row < 8; row++)
14     {
15       for (int column = 0; column < 8; column++)
16       {
17         myCheckerBoard[row][column] = Math.random() < 0.2;
18       }
19     }
20   }
21
22   public void paint( Graphics g )
23   {
24     g.setColor (Color.red);
25     for (int row = 0; row < 8; row++)
26     {
27       for (int column = 0; column < 8; column++)
28       {
29         if (myCheckerBoard [row][column])
30         {
31           g.fillOval (column * 40 + 4, row * 40 + 4, 32, 32);
32         }
33       }
34     }
35   }
36 }
```

The code that creates rows of checkers in shown in Listing 13.13. To indicate that we have a two-dimensional array we use two sets of square brackets in our array declaration as shown below. The array will hold booleans. A true value indicates that a cell holds a checker and a false indicates that it is empty:

```
boolean [][] myCheckerBoard;
```

If one were creating a checker game, one would need a scheme to represent multiple values (empty, red, red king, black, and black king). One solution is to create an array of checker objects that would indicate what kind of checker is occupying a square. We could also use integers with special values that indicate the contents of a square.

Once we have declared the array, we must create it. Again we use two indices: one for the number of rows and the second for the number of columns. Thus, the array below would be 25 rows of 10 columns or 25 columns of 10 rows depending on which indices we choose to use for which dimension:

```
myCheckerBoard = new boolean [25][10];
```

Finally, we can access a particular element by using two indices. The following would make row 3 column 6 have the same value as row 4 column 0.

```
myCheckerBoard [3][6] = myCheckerBoard [4][0];
```

When we initialize all the elements of a two-dimensional array, it is convenient to use a nested loop as shown in Lines 13 through 19 of Listing 13.13. This is an example of the raster scan pattern from Section 9.3.6.

We compute the absolute location of a piece only when it is painted in Line 31. Multiplying the column index by 40 will locate a piece in the x direction. Each column will be 40 pixels wide. Adding four will offset the piece four pixels from the left column edge. Given that each piece is 32 pixels wide, it will be four pixels from the right column edge as well ($4 + 32 + 4 = 40$). We compute the y location in the same manner.

13.5.9 Using One-Dimensional Arrays for Two-Dimensional Structures

We can represent a two-dimensional checkerboard with a one-dimensional array. We can create a 64 element one-dimensional array and do some computation to determine the array index for each row and column. Figure 13.16 shows one way of implementing a map from one to two dimensions.

Our intuition tells us that using a two-dimensional array to represent a checkerboard is better than using a one-dimensional array. However, some programmers argue that many operations are easier with a one-dimensional array. For example, to determine if there is a

Figure 13.16 Map from One to Two Dimensions

0	1	2	3	4	5	6	7
8	9	10	11	12	13	14	15
56	57	58	59	60	61	62	63

checker diagonally down to the right using a one-dimensional array, we check the element at `currentIndex + 9`. For example, suppose we have a checker at index 3. We would check index 12. Looking diagonally down to the left is `currentIndex + 7` and diagonally up to the right is `currentIndex - 7`. Simple subtractions and additions to one index value may be viewed as easier than trying to manipulate two indices.

Listing 13.14 shows the one-dimensional version of Listing 13.13. Notice that the nested loops are gone and mapping from one-dimensional to two-dimensional indices is easy (Lines 26 and 27).

Using a one- or two-dimensional array for board games, such as checkers and chess, is often a matter of taste. Programmers will disagree about which is easier.

Listing 13.14 One-dimensional Version of Listing 13.13

```
1 import java.awt.Color;
2 import java.awt.Graphics;
3 import java.applet.Applet;
4
5 public class CheckerBoard extends Applet
6 {
7   boolean [] myCheckerBoard;
8
9   public void init()
10   {
11     setBackground (Color.white);
12     myCheckerBoard = new boolean [64];
13     for (int i = 0; i < 64; i++)
14     {
15       myCheckerBoard[i] = Math.random() < 0.2;
16     }
17   }
18
19   public void paint( Graphics g )
20   {
21     g.setColor (Color.red);
22     for (int i = 0; i < 64; i++)
23     {
24       if (myCheckerBoard [i])
25       {
26         int row    = i % 8;
27         int column = i / 8;
28         g.fillOval (row * 40 + 4, column * 40 + 4, 32, 32);
29       }
30     }
31   }
32 }
```

13.5.10 Passing Arrays to Methods

Passing an array to a method follows the same rules used to pass any objects. However, we must be sure to specify the type of the array elements and the number of dimensions. In Listing 13.15 we replace Lines 13 through 19 of Listing 13.13 with an initBoard method. Notice how the formal array parameter in Line 8 of Listing 13.15 is specified. When we pass the myCheckerBoard object, the actual parameters need only the array name. The compiler checks that the declaration of myCheckerBoard matches the formal parameter and OKs the transfer.

Listing 13.15 Passing a Two-dimensional Boolean Array

```
1    public void init()
2    {
3      setBackground (Color.white);
4      myCheckerBoard = new boolean [8][8];
5      initBoard (myCheckerBoard);
6    }
7
8    private void initBoard (boolean [][] checkerBoard)
9    {
10     for (int row = 0; row < 8; row++)
11     {
12       for (int column = 0; column < 8; column++)
13       {
14         checkerBoard [row][column] = Math.random() < 0.2;
15       }
16     }
17   }
```

When an array is passed to a method, changing an array element in the called method changes it in the calling method. Thus, changing the values of the checkerBoard object in Line 14 of the initBoard method in Listing 13.15 changes the element of the myCheckerBoard array in Line 5. The names checkerBoard and myCheckerBoard are aliases for the same array object.

SUPPLEMENTARY MATERIAL

13.6   Design

We stated in Section 7.5 that good design comes from experience, and experience comes from bad design. Even though the designs in this book are small, they did not appear on the page in one step. The traffic program is a case in point. During an early pass the Car class had the interface shown in Listing 13.16.

Listing 13.16   Bad Car Class Interface

```
1 public class Car
2 {
3    public Car(int location, Car carAhead, World world)
4    public int getSpeed()
5    public void paint(Graphics g)
6    public void update ()
7 }
```

The difference between Listing 13.16 and Listing 13.2 may appear subtle. The two parameters in the update method in Listing 13.2 have been moved to the constructor in Listing 13.16. Thus, when each car is created, we store as part of that car's state the car ahead and the world on which it drives.

At first it may appear natural for a car to know which car it is following and the world on which it drives. After all, when we drive down the interstate we have visual contact with the car ahead and know where we are on the map. Our update procedure is simplified, we just need to tell each car to update itself. We do not need to pass each car the car ahead and the world it is on. Compare Listing 13.6 and Listing 13.17.

Listing 13.17   Updating the Cars in Bad Design

```
1    public void update ()
2    {
3       // update all but first car
4       for (int i=MAX_CARS-1; i>=0; i--)
5       {
6          myCars[i].update();
7       }
8    }
```

Now suppose we want to expand our program so that cars can pass each other. We have information about the order of cars in two places: the array of cars is ordered and each car points to the car ahead. When we have duplicate information, we must be sure to update information in each place. Thus, when a car passes another, we must swap the cars in the array and update the `carAhead` instance variable in each car. In the design from Section 13.10 we need only to swap the cars. When we begin to think about a multiple lane highway, this simplification is important. One of the goals of a good design is to make a program easier to maintain. Therefore, a good design heuristic is that elements of arrays should not know about each other.

A question in many simulations is who should know where things are. In our traffic example each car knows where it is but the `Traffic` class holds the `car` array and thus knows the car order. The situation is different when we look at board games. For example, who should know where a checker is on a checkerboard. Does the checker know or does the checkerboard know? In this example it is probably better for the checkerboard to know. It is easy to ask a checkerboard which pieces are in adjacent squares than the checkers. Given a checker at row 3 column 5, we can ask the board if there is a checker in row 4 column 6. However, if each checker knows where it is, we must look at all the checkers before we know which checker is next to a given one. For example, if we are given a checker in row 3 column 5, we must ask each checker if it is in row 4 column 6.

13.7 Threads

13.7.1 Discrete Events

The sequence of events that govern the execution of this traffic simulation follows the basic outline of the animated Flash program described in Section 6.7. It may be helpful to look at the Flash program because it provides another example.

Recall that a thread is a single flow of control. All of the programs we have looked at thus far, with the possible exception of the animated Flash application, contain a single thread. When our programs are running, there is only one statement that is the current focus of control. In our traffic simulation we must start a second thread of execution. The original thread is responsible for painting the display, and the new thread is responsible for updating the state of each car and the speed plot. See Figure 13.17.

Execution begins in the traffic applet's `init` method (Listing 13.18). It is responsible for creating the world, the cars, and starting the animation thread. Once the `start` method has completed, the original applet thread goes into a housekeeping mode. It is responsible for handling all the events that occur in the background. For example, it repaints the display when the window is resized or if requested by the program. It also handles mouse events.

Figure 13.17 The Threads of Execution

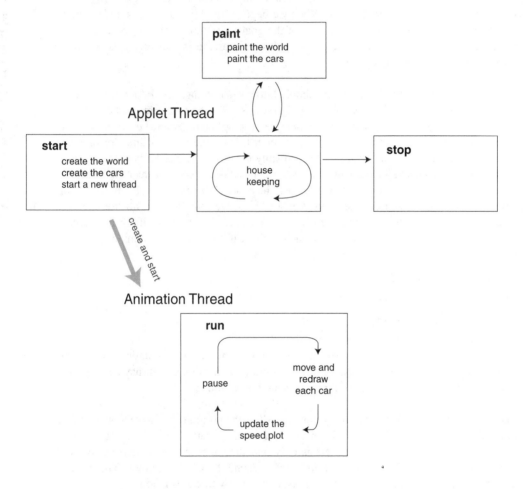

If we try to get by with one thread by moving the code from Listing 13.1 into our `init` method, the display may not get painted until the loop exits. In this case the loop is infinite, so the display will never get painted. Calling `paint` explicitly within the loop may

Listing 13.18 Starting a Thread

```
1    private Thread      myAnimation;
2    ...
3    public void init()
4    {
5      ...
6      myAnimation.start();
7      myHazardStatus  = false;
8      ...
9    }
```

not help. On some platforms painting will not occur until the original thread is free to perform some hidden housekeeping tasks.

Introducing a second thread allows our program to manage two tasks at once. One tread is for doing hidden housekeeping tasks and a second for moving cars. Multiple threads of execution are consistent with real life. We often do more than one thing at a time. For example, we may wash our car, sing, and think about tonight's date. A program, on the other hand, does not really do multiple things at once. Most computers have only one thread of execution. Multiple threads are implemented through a process called *time slicing*. The underlying Java run-time system manages a list of all program threads. It takes turns executing each active thread. By cycling through each tread many times per second it provides us with the illusion of doing more than one thing at a time. Thus, we do not get more done by adding more threads. We do more things, each at a slower pace.

13.7.2 Thread Interface

We use the `Runnable` interface to implement threads. An example occurs in Listing 13.20 on page 640. Another appears in Section 6.7 , page 249. In this section we will take a more detailed look at how we implement threads using the `Runnable` interface. Threads can also be implemented by extending the `Thread` class. We will not cover this technique in this book.

Listing 13.19 shows an example of a thread that counts down from 9 to 0. It displays a new digit every second until it reaches zero. The first thing we must do is implement the `Runnable` interface (Line 5). The `Runnable` interface requires that we implement a `run` method. We will talk more about interfaces in Section 14.4.

The `run` method is where execution will begin for the second thread. The `run` method, Lines 29 through 45, is comprised of a `for` loop that counts down from 9 to 0 displaying each digit. The call to the `pause` method within the loop causes the second thread to sleep

Listing 13.19 Using a Tread to Count down from 9

```
1  import java.awt.*;
2  import java.applet.Applet;
3
4  public class CountDown extends Applet
5                          implements Runnable
6  {
7    Thread mySecondThread;
8
9    public void init()
10   {
11     mySecondThread = new Thread(this);
12     mySecondThread.start();
13   }
14
15   public void paint( Graphics g )
16   {
17     Dimension size = getSize();
18     g.setColor (Color.red);
19     g.fillRect (0, 0, size.width, size.height);
20   }
21   public void pause (int milliseconds)
22   {
23     try
24     {
25       Thread.sleep(milliseconds);
26     }
27     catch (InterruptedException e) {;}
28   }
29   public void run ()
30   {
31     Graphics g = getGraphics();
32     Dimension size = getSize();
33     Font big = new Font ("Monospaced", Font.BOLD, 216);
34     g.setFont (big);
35
36     pause (2500);
37     for (int i = 9; i>=0; i--)
38     {
39       g.setColor (Color.blue);
40       g.fillRect (0, 0, size.width, size.height);
41       g.setColor (Color.green);
42       g.drawString (String.valueOf(i), 20, 170);
43       pause (1000);
44     }
45   }
46 }
```

for 1 second (1000 milliseconds) during each loop iteration. When a thread sleeps, it executes no code, leaving the computer free to execute other threads.

When the `run` method is done executing, it is terminated. This leaves the program with only the original thread. It takes the second thread about 12.5 seconds to execute—2.5 seconds for the pause before the loop and 10 seconds for each one second pause within the loop. The pause at the beginning of the loop allows the system enough time to completely display its window before the count down starts.

The second thread is started by the original thread within its `init` method (Lines 9 through 13). Its first task is to create the new thread in Line 11. Next, it starts it in Line 12. When the second thread starts it begins its thread in the `run` method, which we described in the previous paragraph.

Notice that `mySecondThread` is declared as an instance variable (Line 7). If we made it local to the `init` method, we would run the risk of it becoming garbage collected.

13.7.3 Preventing Flicker

We introduced the problem with animation flicker in Section 6.8 , page 255. Flicker results when the original thread responds to a paint request between an erase and a draw by an animation thread. For example, in the traffic example from Section 13.2 we can implement car motion with the following process:

```
1       loop forever
2          erase an object at its current location
3          compute it new location
4          draw it
5          pause
6       end loop
```

Flicker occurs because we do not know when the housekeeping thread will respond to our paint requests. For example, if it paints between Lines 2 and 4 in the above code, it will display an erased car. When an object is erased, it appears in the background color, which is often white. Thus, white will be displayed for a brief instant before the housekeeping thread has a chance to redraw our moving object in a new location. Depending on the length of the pause in Line 5, display of erased artifacts may not occur often. However, computers are fast. Because the computer does so many things a second, even if the chances of something happening are small, it can happen many times per second.

A trick we can use to reduce flicker is not to erase. Instead we draw over the rear of the car with the road color and redraw the car at its new location (Figure 13.18). This trick works

Figure 13.18 Drawing a Car without Flicker

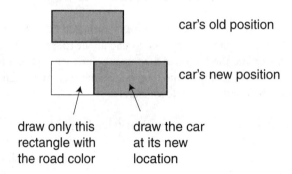

well if the background color is a single solid color. If the background is complex, this trick may not work. Another problem can occur if the housekeeping thread happens to catch us between painting over the rear of the car and drawing the car at its new location, the car may appear too short for an instant. This artifact is much less annoying than seeing periodic white flashes.

REFERENCE

13.8   Summary

The focus of this chapter is arrays. We learned how to create arrays of objects in three steps: first creating a reference to an array, next creating an empty array, and finally initializing each element. We used loops to create and access all the elements of an array. We learned how to handle arrays of objects and arrays of primitive values. We saw how to apply some of the iteration and list patterns we learned earlier to arrays.

We also learned how to manipulate two-dimensional arrays. They require two indices for access. We used the raster scan pattern to manipulate them.

Using a traffic simulation, we learned how to use arrays to implement a simulation. We implement discrete simulation by looking at the world in timed steps. At each step our world made a small change. Our timing loop was implemented in a second thread of execution, freeing the original thread to maintain the display.

By implementing a vector class, we learned how to grow a vector dynamically and insert and delete elements in the middle. We grew a vector dynamically by creating a new larger array and moving elements form our original array to our larger array. We inserted elements into a vector by moving all elements at a greater index up to make room, and then inserting the new element. We removed elements by moving all the elements at a greater index down by one to fill in the gap.

13.9   Bibliography

- Resnick, Mitchel. 1994. *Turtles, Termites, and Traffic Jams*. Cambridge, MA: The MIT Press.

PROGRAM LISTINGS

13.10 Traffic Simulation Code

Listing 13.20 Traffic Class

```
1  //*********************************************************
2  // title:   Traffic
3  //
4  // Create, update, and paint a list of cars.
5  //*********************************************************
6
7  import vista.VPlot;
8  import java.awt.Color;
9  import java.awt.Event;
10 import java.awt.Graphics;
11
12 public class Traffic
13 {
14    private final int MAX_CARS    = 100;  // number of cars
15
16    private Car[]  myCars;                // array of cars
17    private VPlot  mySpeedPlot;           // a plot of a car speeds
18
19    //---------- Traffic ------------------------------------
20    // Execution begins here with initialize.
21    // Called automatically
22    public Traffic()
23    {
24       // create the traffic
25       myCars      = new Car[MAX_CARS];
26       int x       = 0;
27       for (int i=0; i<MAX_CARS; i++)
28       {
29          myCars[i] = new Car(x);
30          x -= (int)(Math.random() * 100 + 20);
31       }
32
33       // create the speed graph
34       mySpeedPlot = new VPlot(0, Car.SPEED_LIMIT + 15, MAX_CARS,
35                               "Car Speeds");
36       mySpeedPlot.reverse();
37    }
```

Listing 13.20 `Traffic` Class

```
38    //---------- graph ----------------------------------------
39    // Graph the speed of each car.
40    public void graph ()
41    {
42      int[] speeds = new int[MAX_CARS];
43      for (int i=0; i<MAX_CARS; i++)
44      {
45        speeds[i] = myCars[i].getSpeed();
46      }
47      mySpeedPlot.setLine(speeds);
48    }
49
50    //---------- paint ----------------------------------------
51    // Draw the cars.
52    // Called automatically
53    public void paint( Graphics g )
54    {
55      for (int i=0; i<MAX_CARS; i++)
56      {
57        myCars[i].paint(g);
58      }
59    }
60
61    //---------- update ----------------------------------------
62    // Update the position of the cars.  The cars are adjusted
63    // from back to front.  As a result a car's t+1 position is
64    // based on time value of t for the car in front of it.
65    // Thus, a drivers reaction time is the time between calls
66    // to this method
67    public void update (World world)
68    {
69      // update all but first car
70      for (int i=MAX_CARS-1; i>0; i--)
71      {
72        myCars[i].update(myCars[i-1], world);
73      }
74      // first car has none in front of it
75      myCars[0].update(null, world);
76    }
77 }
```

Listing 13.21 Car Class

```
1  //*************************************************************
2  //
3  // title:   Car
4  //
5  // Hold the state of a single car.
6  //    blue  - cruising at maximum
7  //    red   - braking
8  //    green - accelerating
9  //
10 //*************************************************************
11
12 import java.awt.Color;
13 import java.awt.Graphics;
14
15 public class Car
16 {
17   public  final static int SPEED_LIMIT     = 55;  // mph
18   private final static int CAR_LENGTH      = 10;  // feet
19   private final static int CAR_WIDTH       = 5;   // feet
20   private final static int DANGER_DISTANCE = 10;  // 10 feet for
21                                                   // every 10 mph
22   private int    mySpeed;       // this car's current speed (mph)
23   private int    myMaxSpeed;    // this car's maximum speed (mph)
24
25   // location on the road (feet from an arbitrary location - the
26   // left-hand side of the display)
27   private int    myCurrentLocation;
28   private int    myPreviousLocation; // location previous time
29   private Color  myColor;              // reflects car's speed
30
31   //---------- Car -------------------------------------
32   // pre:  location is in feet, 0 is the left edge of the window
33   //       Ignore for first car (null)
34   //       The roadway on which the cars drive
35   // post: A car is created traveling at 10 mph over
36   //       the speed limit.
37   public Car (int location)
38   {
39     myCurrentLocation = location;
40     myMaxSpeed        = SPEED_LIMIT + 10;
41     mySpeed           = myMaxSpeed;
42     myColor           = Color.blue;
43   }
44
```

Listing 13.21 Car Class

```
45    //---------- getSpeed -------------------------------------
46    // pre:  none
47    // post: this car's current speed is returned.
48    public int getSpeed()
49    {
50      return mySpeed;
51    }
52
53    //---------- paint ----------------------------------------
54    // pre:  g is a valid graphics context
55    //       world knows about the road
56    // post: car is drawn on roadway.
57    public void paint(Graphics g)
58    {
59      int feetPerPixel = World.FEET_PER_PIXEL;
60
61      // feet must be converted to pixels
62      int oldX     = myPreviousLocation / feetPerPixel;
63
64      // compute display location and size of the car
65      int x        = myCurrentLocation / feetPerPixel;
66      int y        = World.ROAD_Y + World.ROAD_WIDTH /
67                     feetPerPixel / 2 + 2 / feetPerPixel;
68      int length   = CAR_LENGTH / feetPerPixel;
69      int width    = CAR_WIDTH  / feetPerPixel;
70
71      // erase the old car position
72      g.setColor(World.ROAD_COLOR);
73      g.fillRect(oldX, y, x - oldX, width);
74
75      // draw the new car position
76      g.setColor(myColor);
77      g.fillRect(x, y, length, width);
78    }
79
80
```

Listing 13.21 Car Class

```
81     //---------- update -----------------------------------
82     // pre:  none
83     // post: Given this car's speed and distance to the car ahead,
84     //           a new location, speed, and car color are computed
85     public void update (Car carAhead, World world)
86     {
87       myPreviousLocation = myCurrentLocation;
88
89       // compute space between this car and the car ahead
90       int spacing = 0;
91       if (carAhead != null)
92         spacing = carAhead.myCurrentLocation -
93                 myCurrentLocation - CAR_LENGTH;
94       else
95         spacing = Integer.MAX_VALUE;
96
97       // if we are too close, slow down
98       if (spacing < DANGER_DISTANCE * mySpeed / 10)
99       {
100        mySpeed -= 10;
101        myColor = Color.red;
102      }
103      // if we encounter a hazard, slow down
104      else if (world.isHazard(myCurrentLocation) &
105               mySpeed > SPEED_LIMIT / 2)
106      {
107        mySpeed -= 10;
108        myColor = Color.red;
109      }
110      // if none of the above, speed up
111      else
112      {
113        mySpeed += 5;
114        myColor = Color.green;
115      }
116      // keep the car under a max speed and not in reverse
117      if (mySpeed > myMaxSpeed)
118      {
119        mySpeed = myMaxSpeed;
120        myColor = Color.blue;
121      }
122      if (mySpeed < 0)
123      {
124        mySpeed = 0;
125        myColor = Color.blue;
126      }
127
128      // compute the number of feet the car has moved
129      int deltaFeet = mySpeed*5280/3600*World.DELTA_TIME / 1000;
130      myCurrentLocation += deltaFeet;
131    }
132 }
```

Listing 13.22 `World` Class

```
1  //***********************************************************
2  //
3  // title:   World
4  //
5  // Traffic simulation. Simple model of cars driving down a single
6  // lane highway.  Each driver attempts to maintain a comfortable
7  // distance behind the car ahead.  If a driver is too close then
8  // they apply the brakes.  Otherwise the drivers accelerate
9  // until a maximum speed is reached.
10 //
11 // Mitchel Resnick, "Turtles, Termites, and Traffic Jams",
12 // MIT Press, 1994, p. 68.
13 //
14 // The World class is responsible for drawing the ground, cars,
15 // and keeping track of hazards.  A second thread is used to
16 // manage animation.
17 //
18 //***********************************************************
19
20 import java.awt.Color;
21 import java.awt.Dimension;
22 import java.awt.Graphics;
23 import java.awt.event.MouseListener;
24 import java.awt.event.MouseEvent;
25 import java.applet.Applet;
26
27 public class World extends Applet
28                    implements MouseListener, Runnable
29 {
30   // milleseconds between updates
31   public final static int   DELTA_TIME     = 100;
32   public final static Color ROAD_COLOR     = Color.black;
33   public final static int   ROAD_Y         = 50;
34   public final static int   ROAD_WIDTH     = 15;    // feet
35   public final static int   FEET_PER_PIXEL = 1;
36
37   private Traffic   myTraffic;
38   private Thread    myAnimation;
39
40   private final int HAZARD_LENGTH = 75;
41   private boolean   myHazardStatus;
42   private int       myHazardX;
43
```

Listing 13.22 World Class

```
44    //---------- drawTrees -----------------------------------
45    // Draw a forest of trees.
46    // internal use.
47    private void drawTrees(Graphics g, Color color, int howMany)
48    {
49      int maxTreeDiameter = 30 / FEET_PER_PIXEL;
50      int x;
51      int y;
52      int d;
53      Dimension size = getSize();
54
55      for (int i=0; i<howMany; i++)
56      {
57        x = (int)(Math.random() * (size.width + maxTreeDiameter) -
58                                            maxTreeDiameter);
59        y = (int)(Math.random() * (size.height + maxTreeDiameter) -
60                                            maxTreeDiameter);
61        d = (int)(Math.random() * maxTreeDiameter);
62        g.setColor(color);
63        g.fillOval(x, y, d, d);
64      }
65    }
66
67    //---------- init ------------------------------------
68    // pre:  The width and height components of the display
69    //       size is greater than 0.
70    // post: A roadway is created with no hazards.
71    public void init()
72    {
73      addMouseListener (this);
74      myTraffic       = new Traffic();
75      myAnimation     = new Thread (this);
76      myAnimation.start();
77      myHazardStatus  = false;
78      myHazardX       = 0;
79    }
80    //---------- isHazard -----------------------------------
81    // pre:  none
82    // post: If x is between the start and end of the hazard,
83    //       return true.  Otherwise false.
84    public boolean isHazard(int x)
85    {
86      return myHazardStatus &
87             x > myHazardX * FEET_PER_PIXEL &
88             x < myHazardX * FEET_PER_PIXEL + HAZARD_LENGTH;
89    }
```

Listing 13.22 World Class

```
90     //---------- paint ------------------------------------
91     // pre:  g is a valid graphics context
92     // post: The world is drawn.
93     public void paint(Graphics g)
94     {
95       Dimension size = getSize();
96
97       // draw the grass
98       g.setColor(Color.green);
99       g.fillRect (0, 0, size.width, size.height);
100
101      // draw the trees
102      Color forestGreen1 = new Color(35, 142, 35);
103      drawTrees(g, forestGreen1, 75);
104      Color forestGreen2 = new Color(35, 180, 35);
105      drawTrees(g, forestGreen2, 75);
106      Color forestGreen3 = new Color(35, 210, 35);
107      drawTrees(g, forestGreen3, 75);
108
109      // draw the road
110      g.setColor(ROAD_COLOR);
111      g.fillRect (0, ROAD_Y, size.width,
112                    ROAD_WIDTH / FEET_PER_PIXEL);
113
114      // draw the cars
115      myTraffic.paint(g);
116    }
117
118    //---------- mousePressed ----------------------------
119    //    Called automatically when the mouse button is pressed.
120    // post: A hazard is added to the roadway.
121    public void mousePressed (MouseEvent e)
122    {
123      Graphics g = getGraphics();
124      myHazardStatus = true;
125      myHazardX    = e.getX();
126      g.setColor(Color.red);
127      g.fillRect(myHazardX, ROAD_Y + ROAD_WIDTH + 5,
128                    HAZARD_LENGTH, 10);
129    }
130
```

Listing 13.22 World Class

```
131    //---------- mouseReleased -------------------------------
132    //     Called automatically when the mouse button is pressed.
133    // post: A hazard is removed from the roadway.
134    public void mouseReleased (MouseEvent e)
135    {
136      Graphics g = getGraphics();
137      Color springGreen = new Color (0, 255, 127);
138      myHazardStatus = false;
139      g.setColor(springGreen);
140      g.fillRect(myHazardX, ROAD_Y + ROAD_WIDTH + 5,
141          HAZARD_LENGTH, 10);
142    }
143
144    public void mouseClicked(MouseEvent e) {;}
145    public void mouseEntered (MouseEvent e) {;}
146    public void mouseExited (MouseEvent e) {;}
147
148    //---------- pause ---------------------------------------
149    // pre:  milliseconds >= 0
150    // post: This thread of control sleeps for "milliseconds".
151    public void pause (int milliseconds)
152    {
153      try
154      {
155        Thread.sleep (milliseconds);
156      }
157      catch (InterruptedException e) {;}
158    }
159
160    //---------- run -----------------------------------------
161    // The animation thread begins execution here.  Each car is
162    // moved and painted.  A speed graph is drawn.
163    public void run ()
164    {
165      Graphics g = getGraphics();
166
167      while(true)
168      {
169        myTraffic.update (this);
170        myTraffic.paint (g);
171        myTraffic.graph ();
172        pause (DELTA_TIME);
173      }
174    }
175  }
```

13.11 MiniVector Class

Listing 13.23 MiniVector Class

```
1    //****************************************************************
2    //
3    // title:   MiniVector
4    //
5    // MiniVector is an expansible array - it grows and
6    // shrinks.
7    //
8    // An implementation of Vector subset for illustrational
9    // purposes.
10   //
11   //****************************************************************
12
13   public class MiniVector
14   {
15      private final int CAPACITY_INCREMENT = 10;
16
17      private Object[] myElements;   // the elements in this vector
18      private int      mySize;       // number of elements in this
19                                     // vector
20      private int      myCapacity;   // maximum number of elements
21                                     // this vector can hold without
22                                     // growing
23
```

Listing 13.23 MiniVector Class

```
24    //---------- addElement ----------------------------------
25    // pre:  none
26    // post: "obj" is added to the end of this vector.
27    //            Size of the vector grows by one.
28
29    public void addElement (Object obj)
30    {
31      // capacity exists to add new element
32      if (mySize < myCapacity)
33      {
34        myElements[mySize] = obj;
35        mySize++;
36      }
37
38      // capacity of this vector must be increased to accommodate
39      // new element
40      else
41      {
42        Object[] newElements = new Object[myCapacity +
43                                CAPACITY_INCREMENT];
44        for (int i=0; i<mySize; i++)
45        {
46          newElements[i] = myElements[i];
47        }
48        newElements[mySize] = obj;
49        mySize++;
50        myCapacity += CAPACITY_INCREMENT;
51        myElements = newElements;
52      }
53    }
54
55    //---------- elementAt ----------------------------------
56    // pre:        "index" >= 0 & "index" < size()
57    // post:       The element at location "index' is returned.
58    // exception: "ArrayIndexOutOfBoundsException" if pre-condi-
tion
59    //            fails
60
61    public Object elementAt(int index)
62         throws ArrayIndexOutOfBoundsException
63    {
64      if (index < 0 | index >= mySize)
65        throw new ArrayIndexOutOfBoundsException();
66      else
67        return myElements[index];
68    }
69
```

Listing 13.23 `MiniVector` Class

```
70    //---------- insertElementAt ------------------------------
71    // pre:        "index" >= 0 & "index" <= size()
72    // post:       all elements at "index" and higher are moved up
73    //             by one.  "obj" inserted at "index".
74    //             Size of the vector grows by one.
75    // exception: "ArrayIndexOutOfBoundsException" if
76    //             pre-condition fails
77
78    public void insertElementAt(Object obj, int index)
79      throws ArrayIndexOutOfBoundsException
80    {
81      // pre-conditions not met - throw exception
82      if (index < 0 | index > mySize)
83        throw new ArrayIndexOutOfBoundsException();
84
85      // capacity exists to insert new element
86      else if (mySize < myCapacity)
87      {
88        for (int i=mySize; i>index; i--)
89        {
90          myElements[i] = myElements[i-1];
91        }
92        myElements[index] = obj;
93        mySize++;
94      }
95
96      // capacity of this vector must be increased to accommodate
97      // new element
98      else
99      {
100       Object[] newElements = new Object[myCapacity +
101                             CAPACITY_INCREMENT];
102       for (int i=mySize; i>index; i--)
103       {
104         newElements[i] = myElements[i-1];
105       }
106       newElements[index] = obj;
107       for (int i=index-1; i>=0; i--)
108       {
109         newElements[i] = myElements[i];
110       }
111       mySize++;
112       myCapacity += CAPACITY_INCREMENT;
113       myElements = newElements;
114     }
115   }
116
```

Listing 13.23 MiniVector Class

```
117   //---------- MiniVector ---------------------------------
118   // pre:        none
119   // post:       An empty vector is created.
120
121   public MiniVector()
122   {
123     myElements = new Object[CAPACITY_INCREMENT];
124     mySize = 0;
125     myCapacity = CAPACITY_INCREMENT;
126   }
127
128   //---------- removeElementAt ----------------------------
129   // pre:        "index" >= 0 & "index" < size()
130   // post:       all elements at "index" + 1 are moved down
131   //             by one. Size of the vector shrinks by one.
132   // exception: "ArrayIndexOutOfBoundsException" if
133   //             pre-condition fails
134
135   public void removeElementAt(int index)
136   {
137     // exercise for the reader
138   }
139
140   //---------- setElementAt -------------------------------
141   // pre:        "index" >= 0 & "index" < size()
142   // post:     The element at location "index' is set to "obj".
143   // exception: "ArrayIndexOutOfBoundsException" if
144   //             pre-condition fails
145
146   public void setElementAt(Object obj, int index)
147     throws ArrayIndexOutOfBoundsException
148   {
149     // exercise for the reader
150   }
151
152   //---------- size --------------------------------------
153   // pre:        none
154   // post:       the number of elements in this vector is
155   //             returned.
156
157   public int size()
158   {
159     return mySize;
160   }
161 }
```

PROBLEM SETS

13.12 Exercises

Arrays—Section 13.5

1 Answer the following questions based on the declaration below:

```
int [] numbers = new int[10];
```

a. What is the maximum number of elements in the `numbers` array?

b. What is the range of allowable indices?

c. What is the range of allowable elements?

d. Write the code necessary to set the element with index 5 to 274.

e. Write the code necessary to set the first element to 4529.

f. Write the code necessary to set the last element to 32.

g. Write the code necessary to initialize all element to 99.

2 What is the output of the following code fragment:

```
char [] word = new char[8];
word[1] = '2';
word[3] = word[1];
word[2] = 'D';
word[0] = 'R';
System.out.print(word[0]);
System.out.print(word[1]);
System.out.print(word[2]);
System.out.println(word[3]);
```

3 What is the output of the following code fragment:

```
double [] numbers = new double[15];
for (int i=0; i<15; i++)
  numbers[i] = i * 2.5 - 3.0;
for (int i=5; i<10; i++)
  System.out.println(numbers[i]);
```

4   What is the output of the following code fragment:

```
int [] numbers = new int[10];
for (int i=0; i<10; i++)
  numbers[i] = i;
for (int i=1; i<10; i++)
  number[i] += number[i-1];
for (int i=0; i<10; i++)
  System.out.println(numbers[i]);
```

5   Write a code fragment that creates an array of 200 doubles and stores the square root of each index value within its corresponding element. For example, the element with index 4 will contain the value 2.0.

6   Write a code fragment that rotates the elements in an array up by an integer value i. The element at location 2 is moved to location 2 + i. The element at location n – 1 (n is the number of elements in the array) is moved to location i – 1. For example, given the following array:

| 15 | 45 | 78 | 19 | 63 | 52 | 77 | 90 | 62 |

a rotation with i=3 would result in the following array:

| 77 | 90 | 62 | 15 | 45 | 78 | 19 | 63 | 52 |

7   Write a code fragment that creates an array of 10000 random integers between the values of 1 and 100000.

8   Write a code fragment to display the array created in exercise 7

9   Modify the selection sort to sort (in order) the array created in exercise 7

10   Write a code fragment to find the following statistics about the array created in exercise 7

    a.   Compute the percent of elements that are even.

    b.   Compute the average of all numbers in the array.

    c.   Compute the percent that are between 5,000 and 6,000.

    d.   Compute the percent that are repeats (difficult).

11   Write a code fragment that creates a 10-by-10 integer array product in each element is the product of its indices. For example product[3][5] contains the value 15.

12 What does the following code fragment print?

```
int [][] numbers = new int [4][3];
int i = 0;
for (int row = 0; row<4; row++)
{
  for (int column = 0; column<3; column++)
  {
    numbers [row][column] = i;
    i++;
  }
}
for (int row = 0; row<4; row++)
{
  for (int column = 0; column<3; column++)
  {
    System.out.println (numbers [row][column]);
  }
}
```

13 What does the code in exercise 12 print if we change the print loops to the following?

```
for (int column = 0; column<3; column++)
{
  for (int row = 0; row<4; row++)
  {
    System.out.println (numbers [row][column]);
  }
}
```

14 Suppose we change the print line in exercise 12 to the following. What kind of run-time error will result and why?

```
System.out.println (numbers [column][row]);
```

MiniVector—Section 13.4

15 What is the order of complexity of the `elementAt`, `size`, and `removeEle-mentAt` methods? Support your answers.

13.13 Projects

13.13.1 Primitive Arrays

Arrays—Section 13.5

16

   a.   Create a program that has an array of 100 red balls with random locations and displays them.

   b.   Give the balls random sizes between 25 and 75 pixels.

   c.   Give the balls random colors.

Traffic—Section 13.2

17   Give drivers different characteristics and allow them to pass each other:

   a.   aggressive: drive fast (20 mph over the speed limit), follow close (`DANGER_DISTANCE = 3 feet per 10 mph`), and pass often (any car going slower than it).

   b.   moderate: drive within 5 mph of the speed limit, follow at the distance specified in the current simulation, and pass more reluctantly than aggressive drivers. They will only pass cars going more than 5 mph slower than they want to go. This group should represent the highest percentage of drivers.

   c.   conservative: drive at least 5 mph under the speed limit, leave large distance between them (20 feet per 10 mph) and the car ahead, and never pass.

A challenge will be simulating a car pass. Think about how to do this. Should there be an array for each lane of cars? How do we know it is safe for a car to change lanes?

Use a random number together with an aggressive quotient to determine whether a car passes during a given time period. Give cars with different aggressive quotients different colors.

Check for rear end collisions under the situation of sudden slowing (road hazard or slow driver).

Tweak the rule until you have a good simulation going. Create graphics tools that help you analyze the simulation. Write and justify some observations. For example, do cars have a tendency to cluster behind slower drivers? Why?

18   Add a bar graph to the world window that shows cars in various speed ranges as outlined below. If GUIs have been covered, put the bar graph in a second pop-up window. The bar graph should show the percentage of cars in various speed ranges:

   a.   bar 1—cars driving less than 10 mph below the speed limit

   b.   bar 2—cars driving from 10 mph below the speed limit to the speed limit

   c.   bar 3—cars driving over the speed limit.

VPlot

19   The plot generated by the `VPlot` class looks jagged. It can be smoothed by averaging each point with the two points on each side of it and itself. Add a method to the `VPlot` class that smooths lines. How are you going to handle special cases; the beginning and end of a line? How does this affect the minimum number of points that can now be plotted.?

20   Mismatches between the number of points in a line and the number of points specified by the constructor is a problem with the VPlot interface. How would you redesign the interface to alleviate the problem? Implement and test your new design.

MiniVector (Listing 13.23 on page 649)

21   Implement the `setElementAt` and `removeElementAt` methods in the `MiniVector` class. Be careful of the order in which elements are shifted in the `remove` method.

Option—During removal if the size of the vector is less than 1/3 of its capacity, decrease its capacity by 1/2.

22   The `Vector` class has other methods we have not implemented in the `MiniVector` class. Look up their signature and semantics in a Java reference and implement a subset of the following:

   a.   capacity

   b.   clone

   c.   contains

   d.   copyInto

   e.   ensureCapacity

f. firstElement

g. indexOf

h. isEmpty

i. lastElement

j. lastIndexOf

k. removeAllElements

l. removeElement

m. setSize

n. trimToSize

Threads—Section 13.7.2

23 Use exercise 16 as a basis. Add an animation thread and make the balls do one of the following:

a. All balls move slowly to the right.

b. Each ball moves slowly in a random direction. The random direction is determined when each ball is created and does not change. The balls may move off the screen.

c. Each ball moves in a random direction. The random direction is determined each time the ball is moved. The balls may move off the screen.

d. Just like c) except the ball bounces off the sides of the display window. When a ball hits a vertical wall the value of its delta x changes sign. When a ball hits a horizontal wall the value of its delta y changes sign.

e. Just like c) except the ball wraps around the display. For example, if it goes off the bottom, it appears at the top at the same y location.

f. Just like d) except the balls slowly grow and shrink in size.

13.13.2 Others

24 Dewdney in *The Armchair Universe* describes a world of *Sharks and Fish on the Planet Wa-Tor*. Use inheritance and arrays to implement this world (difficult assignment).

14 Event Handling

Doodling

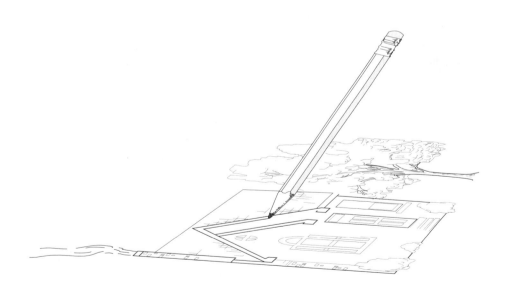

14.1   Objectives

Concepts   **Section 14.2, page 661**

This chapter is an introduction to event-based programming. Using the example of a Doodle program we will learn how to handle mouse events. Our program will respond to mouse button presses and mouse drags.

Pattern   **Section 14.3, page 669**

Java implements a callback pattern to solve the event-handling problem. We use this pattern by informing the Java runtime system to call particular methods when events occur. By using this pattern a programmer does not have to write an event loop.

Java Skills

Next, the chapter addresses how we handle events in Java:

- Implementing interfaces   Section 14.4.1, page 671
- MouseListener interface   Section 14.4.2, page 673
- MouseMotionListener interface   Section 14.4.3, page 675
- MouseEvent class   Section 14.4.4, page 676

Abilities

By the end of this chapter we should be able to do the following:

- Write programs that responds to mouse events.

CONCEPTS

14.2 Doodling

In Chapter 4 we talked about two styles of user interactions with a program. In the event-driven style the user controls the interaction. In the program-driven style the program controls the interaction. In this chapter we will learn more about writing event-driven programs.

The mouse was invented in 1965 by Douglas Engelbart and his colleagues at the Stanford Research Institute. The mouse, together with graphics displays, provided the key ingredients for the development of Graphical User Interfaces (GUIs). GUIs define a point and click method of interacting with a computer. The user of a GUI program may click on a button, select a menu item, drag an icon, type text, or do other actions. Each of these actions initiate an event to which a program may respond.

In the previous chapters we have seen programs that respond to browser-initiated events. For example, the `init` method responds to the creation of an applet object. The `destroy` method responds when a window is destroyed. The `paint` method responds when the display must be created or updated. We will now turn our attention to several methods that respond to mouse events. The first is `mousePressed`; the second is `mouseDragged`.

> An *event* is an occurrence to which a computer program may respond. Example events to which Java programs can respond include mouse movement, mouse clicks, menu selection, button presses, window movement, window scrolling, key clicks, and many others.

Responding to events is an everyday occurrence. It begins in the morning when the alarm goes off. We respond to the alarm event by turning the alarm off. We respond to a hunger event by eating an apple. We respond to a hello from a special person with a quickened heart beat and a change in skin color.

14.2.1 Doodle Requirements

In this section we will create a program that allows us to sketch on the computer display. We will accomplish this by responding to mouse events. Mouse events are generated when a user moves a mouse and presses its button.

Interactive graphics had its beginnings with Ivan Sutherland's Sketchpad. He created a program in the early 1960s that allowed users to sketch and manipulate drawings on a computer display with a light pen. It contained many innovative features that are the basis of drawing programs today. He received the ACM Turing Award in 1988 for his work. The program we will create in this chapter is much more primitive than Sutherland's.

We will write a simple doodle program that allows people to draw freehand pictures in a window using the mouse. The Doodle program will support four choices of colors: red, green, blue, and black. The program will be rather limited. We will not support saving or printing the image. An example interaction of this program is shown in Figure 14.1 .

Figure 14.1 Snapshot of the Doodle Program

14.2.2   Doodle Design

In Section 6.5 , page 219 we introduced the idea of method cohesion. We strive to write methods that have a high degree of cohesion by encapsulating highly-related ideas within a method. The methods in Chapter 6 are cohesive because each method accomplishes a single idea. This is called *functional cohesion*.

In the Doodle program we will organize actions by when they occur. For example, some actions must occur when the program starts up, and others when the mouse is manipulated. *Temporal cohesion* organizes actions into methods that are related by time.

The element of time in the Doodle program is defined by events. There are four events for which we must write code. Each event will have a corresponding method. We will give each the following responsibilities:

- Start up—responsible for creating the color palette and initializing program state.
- Painting—responsible for drawing the color palette when the drawing window is created and when the window is resized.
- Mouse down—responsible for storing the current mouse position and selecting a new drawing color.
- Mouse drag—responsible for drawing lines and updating the current mouse position.

The basic organization of the program is to create the palette at program initialization time, draw the color palette when the window is painted, select a palette color when the mouse button is pressed, and draw a line when the mouse is dragged (mouse drag means that the mouse is moved while the button is pressed). When the mouse is dragged, a line is drawn from an old mouse position to a new mouse position.

14.2.3   Doodle Implementation

The implementation of the Doodle program is shown in Listing 14.1. Rectangles are instantiated in the `init` method. They will be used in the `paint` method to create the color palette, and in the `mousePressed` method to determine which color a user has selected. For example, in Line 50 the red rectangle at location (0,170) is created. This rectangle will be drawn in the `paint` method. We make the palette rectangles instance variables because we must use the palette in the `paint` and `mousePressed` methods.

The `init` method also initializes `myLastX` and `myLastY` to 0. When we drag the mouse, a line will be drawn from the old mouse position to the new mouse position. These two instance variables determine the beginning of the doodle line. Finally, `init` sets the default drawing color to black.

Listing 14.1 Doodle Program

```
1  //*************************************************************
2  //
3  //   title:    Doodle
4  //
5  //   The doodle program allows people to draw freehand pictures in
6  //   a window using the mouse.  There are three choices of colors:
7  //   red, green, blue, and black.  The image cannot be saved or
8  //   printed.
9  //
10 //*************************************************************
11
12 import java.awt.Color;
13 import java.awt.Event;
14 import java.awt.Graphics;
15 import java.awt.Rectangle;
16 import java.awt.event.MouseEvent;
17 import java.awt.event.MouseListener;
18 import java.awt.event.MouseMotionListener;
19 import java.applet.Applet;
20
21 public class Doodle extends    Applet
22                  implements MouseListener, MouseMotionListener
23 {
24
25   private int       myLastX;              // previous mouse location
26   private int       myLastY;
27
28   private Color     myCurrentColor;    // current drawing color
29
30   private Rectangle myRedPalette;       // palette
31   private Rectangle myGreenPalette;
32   private Rectangle myBluePalette;
33   private Rectangle myBlackPalette;
34
```

Listing 14.1 Doodle Program

```
35   //---------- init --------------------------------------
36   // Initialize the mouse pointer and create the palette.
37
38   public void init ()
39   {
40     setBackground(Color.white);
41
42     // set last mouse position
43     myLastX = 0;
44     myLastY = 0;
45
46     // initialize drawing color
47     myCurrentColor = Color.black;
48
49     // create palette
50     myRedPalette   = new Rectangle (  0, 170, 50, 30);
51     myGreenPalette = new Rectangle ( 50, 170, 50, 30);
52     myBluePalette  = new Rectangle (100, 170, 50, 30);
53     myBlackPalette = new Rectangle (150, 170, 50, 30);
54
55     addMouseListener(this);
56     addMouseMotionListener(this);
57   }
58
59   //---------- paint --------------------------------------
60   // Draw the palette
61   //
62   // Note: when the drawing window is resized or covered, the
63   // image may be lost because paint cannot redraw it.
64   public void paint (Graphics g)
65   {
66     g.setColor(Color.red);
67     g.fillRect(myRedPalette.x, myRedPalette.y,
68                myRedPalette.width, myRedPalette.height);
69     g.setColor(Color.green);
70     g.fillRect(myGreenPalette.x, myGreenPalette.y,
71                myGreenPalette.width, myGreenPalette.height);
72     g.setColor(Color.blue);
73     g.fillRect(myBluePalette.x, myBluePalette.y,
74                myBluePalette.width, myBluePalette.height);
75     g.setColor(Color.black);
76     g.fillRect(myBlackPalette.x, myBlackPalette.y,
77                myBlackPalette.width, myBlackPalette.height);
78     g.drawString("Color Palette", 75, 160);
79   }
80
```

Listing 14.1 Doodle Program

```
81   //---------- mousePressed -----------------------------------
82   // Reset the mouse location and select a color from the
83   // palette.
84
85   public void mousePressed(MouseEvent e)
86   {
87     int x = e.getX();
88     int y = e.getY();
89
90     // reset last mouse position
91     myLastX = x;
92     myLastY = y;
93
94     // select a color
95     if (myRedPalette.contains(x,y))
96       myCurrentColor = Color.red;
97     if (myGreenPalette.contains(x,y))
98       myCurrentColor = Color.green;
99     if (myBluePalette.contains(x,y))
100      myCurrentColor = Color.blue;
101     if (myBlackPalette.contains(x,y))
102       myCurrentColor = Color.black;
103   }
104
105   //---------- mouseDragged ----------------------------------
106   // Draw the doodle.
107
108   public void mouseDragged(MouseEvent e)
109   {
110     int x = e.getX();
111     int y = e.getY();
112
113     Graphics g = getGraphics();
114     g.setColor(myCurrentColor);
115     g.drawLine (myLastX, myLastY, x, y);
116     myLastX = x;
117     myLastY = y;
118   }
119
120   // Unused methods from "MouseListener"
121   public void mouseReleased(MouseEvent e) {}
122   public void mouseClicked(MouseEvent e) {}
123   public void mouseEntered(MouseEvent e) {}
124   public void mouseExited(MouseEvent e) {}
125   // Unused methods from "MouseMotionListener"
126   public void mouseMoved(MouseEvent e) {}
127 }
```

The color palette is drawn within `paint` by making multiple calls to the `fillRect` method. It is surprising to find no `fillRect` method that takes a `Rectangle` object as a parameter. After all, there is a `fillPolygon` method which takes a `Polygon` object as a parameter in the `StarryNight` program (see Listing 3.1 on page 95). As a result, it is necessary to access each of the rectangle fields (`x`, `y`, `width`, and `height`) directly to draw the rectangle.

The `paint` method only draws the color palette. This has a critical effect on the program's behavior. If the drawing window is resized or covered, the user's drawing will be lost. We could avoid this by drawing into an image object and displaying simultaneously, but it would complicate the program.

Whenever a mouse button is pressed, an event is generated and the `mousePressed` method is called. The `mousePressed` method has two responsibilities. The first is to store the location of the mouse in `myLastX` and `myLastY`. These stored locations will be used as the beginning of the line to be drawn. The second responsibility of `mouse-Pressed` is to select a new color based on a click within the color palette. When the `mousePressed` method is called, we can get the location of the mouse through calls to `getX` and `getY` (see Lines 87 and 88). If the location of the mouse is in one of the rectangles, for example `myRedPalette.contains(x,y)`, the drawing color is changed.

A mouse drag event occurs when a mouse button is held down and the mouse is moved. It invokes the `mousedDragged` method. This method draws a line from the previous mouse location to the current mouse location. When the mouse is dragged, the mouse dragged event is generated many times. Thus, many short straight lines are drawn, giving the illusion of a curved line.

Once `mouseDragged` draws a line, the current location of the mouse must be saved as the last mouse location. Thus, the next time the `mouseDragged` method is called, the line will continue unbroken.

14.2.4 Testing

Programs that respond to events are difficult to test. It may be impossible to completely test an event-driven program. Events can occur in unexpected order. Even if we cannot test a program completely, we must attempt to test it as thoroughly as possible. First, we should think about each method and determine if it is working as expected. Some questions that we might ask follow:

- Does the `init` method execute? Is the window background white? Does the drawing color start out black? Is the color palette created with the correct size and location of each rectangle?

- Is the `paint` method executed? Is the color palette drawn?

- Is the `mousePressed` method executed? When the mouse button is pressed in the red rectangle, does the drawing color change to red? How about for green, blue, and black?

- Is the `mouseDragged` method executed? Do lines of the appropriate color get drawn when the mouse is dragged?

When we investigate each method, we should look at every line of code and make sure that each has been exercised. We talked more about statement testing in Chapter 8 and Chapter 9. After we have exercised the program, we should play with it. Observe how it behaves and note any problems. Giving our programs to a friend to use is a good way of testing them. People who were not intimately involved in creating a program can take a fresh look at it. They will try things that did not occur to us, and thus find problems that we cannot.

PATTERNS

14.3 Callback Pattern

blem

The `mousePressed` and `mouseDragged` methods we wrote in the previous section are callback methods. They are called when the mouse button is pressed or the mouse is dragged.

> A *callback* method is a method that is called when an event occurs. It contains code written by a programmer to respond to the event that called it.

me
lution

We first encountered the callback pattern in Section 4.2.3 , page 127. The callback pattern has been implemented in Java to solve the problem of handing events. Without callback functions, handling events would be more difficult. For example, early Macintosh and Windows programming environments did not use the callback pattern. Instead, it was necessary for programmers to do all of their event handling in an event loop. An example is shown in Listing 14.2.

sequences

When events are generated, they are placed in a queue. (A queue is much like a line of people waiting for lunch. The first one in the lunch line is the first one out. In this case the first event in the event queue is the first one out.) An event loop is an infinite loop that gets an event from the event queue and executes code based on what event was returned.

The `handleMouseDown` and `handleMouseDragged` methods in Listing 14.2 correspond to our callback methods. The problem with using an event loop is that we have to write it and we must be careful to do it correctly. The loop must be written in way to accommodate other programs that may be executing in the background. If a programmer wrote their program incorrectly, a background program may not execute or the computer may freeze.

The solution to putting the responsibility of writing a correct event loop on the programmers shoulders is to provide callback methods such as the ones used in the `MouseListener` and `MouseMotionListener` interfaces.)

Listing 14.2 Macintosh Event Loop (Stylized to Look Like Java)

```
1   public static void main (String args[])
2   {
3     EventRecord theEvent;
4     while (true)
5     {
6       GetNextEvent (everyEvent, theEvent);
7       if (theEvent.what == mouseDown)
8         handleMouseDown(theEvent.x, theEvent.y);
9       else if (theEvent.what == mouseDragged)
10          handleMouseDragged(theEvent.x, theEvent.y);
11    }
12  }
13
14  public static void handleMouseDown (int x, int y)
15  {
16    // put our mouse pressed code here
17  }
18
19  public static void handleMouseDragged (int x, int y)
20  {
21    // put our mouse dragged code here
22  }
23
```

JAVA

14.4 Interfaces

In this section we will take a closer look at what we need to do to implement Java interfaces. In particular, we will look at what we must do to implement the mouse-handling interfaces.

14.4.1 Implementing Interfaces

Recall from Chapter 7 that a class interface specifies the signature of all of a class's methods. A method's signature gives us all the information we need to know to invoke a method. A signature does not specify what a method does or how it does it. Java has a special interface construct that allows us to specify an interface. An interface will specify only how to invoke a method. But by itself, an interface does nothing because it contains no code that performs actions. The methods within an interface must be implemented in another class. One use for interfaces is to implement event handling.

When we indicate that we will implement an interface we enter a contract with Java. We have agreed to implement every method within that interface. For example, the Shape interface in Listing 14.3 specifies two methods: moveTo and paint. In Line 4 of Listing 14.4 we inform Java that we will implement the Shape interface in our Box class. Therefore, we must implement both the moveTo method and the paint method.

Listing 14.3 Shape Interface

```
1 import java.awt.Graphics;
2
3 public interface Shape
4 {
5    public void moveTo (int x, int y);
6    public void paint   (Graphics g);
7 }
```

When we implement an interface method, the signature of each method we implement must match the signature of the method in the interface. If we fail to implement an interface's method, we will get a syntax error. However, that error that the Java compiler generates may be misleading. For example, if we inadvertently change one of the ints to a double in Line 17 of Listing 14.4, the error messages returned may be something like the following:

671

Listing 14.4 Box Class

```
1  import java.awt.Color;
2  import java.awt.Graphics;
3
4  public class Box implements Shape
5  {
6    private int myX;
7    private int myY;
8    private Color myColor;
9
10   public Box ()
11   {
12     myX = 0;
13     myY = 0;
14     myColor = Color.blue;
15   }
16
17   public void moveTo (int x, int y)
18   {
19     myX = x;
20     myY = y;
21   }
22
23   public void paint (Graphics g)
24   {
25     g.setColor(myColor);
26     g.fillRect (myX, myY, 50, 50);
27   }
28 }
```

```
Error    : class Box is an abstract class. It can't be instan-
tiated.
BoxTester.java line 15    Box blueBox = new Box();

Error    : class Box must be declared abstract. It does not
define void moveTo(int, int) from interface Shape.
Box.java line 4    public class Box implements Shape
```

A similar error can be the result of a missing import statement; for example, if the `Mou-seEvent` class in not imported in Line 1 of Listing 14.5. Errors like these have sent many a beginning programmer into the ozone. They attempt to fix the problem by making the `Box` class abstract, which only leads to more problems. Attempting to fix these problems creates a cascading effect of more errors, making the situation worse. It is not until we read the second error message that the real problem becomes clear. All that is necessary is to carefully match the signatures of the interface with the signatures of their implementation. *Be warned.*

We may implement methods in addition to those in the interface. For example, we may add the following to Listing 14.4. But we must retain the moveTo method with two int parameters.

```
public void moveTo (double x, double y)
{
  myX = (int)x;
  myY = (int)y;
}
```

14.4.2   MouseListener Interface

The MouseListener interface specifies methods that respond to mouse button events and to when the mouse enters or leaves a component. There are three required steps to make a program respond to these events:

1. Promise to implement the mouse listener interface.
2. Implement the interface by writing methods that correspond to each method signature in this interface.
3. Register an instance of a class with the event listener.

The first step is to promise to implement the MouseListener interface, Line 6 in Listing 14.5. The mouseListener interface in Listing 14.6 is provided to us by Java. When we write a program that must handle mouse events, we must import it as in Line 2 of Listing 14.5.

Second, we must implement each one of the methods in the interfaces. Listing 14.5 shows an example of how this can be done and what each method does. If there is an event for which we do not have a response, we must still implement the method. We simply instruct the program to do nothing, as we have done in Lines 121 through 124 in Listing 14.1. As we mentioned in the previous section, we must be careful to match signatures and import MouseEvents. Syntax error messages that occur from oversights may be misleading.

The final step is to register our class with the Java mouse listener. This is done in Line 10 of Listing 14.5. Registering listeners tells the Java run-time system to listen for mouse events on its behalf. If a mouse event associated with the mouseTester window occurs, the runtime system will call the appropriate callback method. If we fail to register our listener, our callback methods will never get called.

Notice that many of the mouse listener methods in Listing 14.1 do not do anything. An interface requires us to implement all of methods even if we do not need them. Java provides a MouseAdapter class (not an interface) that implements all the mouse listener

Listing 14.5 Trivial Mouse Tester Applet

```
1    import java.awt.event.MouseEvent;
2    import java.awt.event.MouseListener;
3    import java.applet.Applet;
4
5    public class MouseTester extends Applet
6                            implements MouseListener
7    {
8        public void init()
9        {
10          addMouseListener(this);
11       }
12       public void mouseClicked (MouseEvent event)
13       {
14        System.out.println ("Mouse button pressed and released.");
15       }
16       public void mouseEntered (MouseEvent event)
17       {
18         System.out.println ("Mouse entered applet window.");
19       }
20       public void mouseExited (MouseEvent event)
21       {
22         System.out.println ("Mouse exited applet window.");
23       }
24       public void mousePressed (MouseEvent event)
25       {
26         System.out.println ("Mouse button pressed.");
27       }
28       public void mouseReleased (MouseEvent event)
29       {
30         System.out.println ("Mouse button released.");
31       }
32 }
```

Listing 14.6 java.event.MouseListener Interface

```
1 public abstract interface MouseListener extends EventListener
2 {
3   public abstract void mouseClicked  (MouseEvent e);
4   public abstract void mouseEntered  (MouseEvent e);
5   public abstract void mouseExited   (MouseEvent e);
6   public abstract void mousePressed  (MouseEvent e);
7   public abstract void mouseReleased (MouseEvent e);
8 }
```

methods to do nothing. In some situations it is possible to extend the `MouseAdapter` class. The benefit is that we need to override only the mouse event methods we choose to implement, and thus save some work. However, a class may extend only one other class. Thus, it is not possible to extend `Applet`, `MouseAdapter`, and `MouseMotion-Adapter` in the same class. For the sake of simplifying our discussion, we will not use adapters in this text. However, for those of us who are interested, supplementary Section 14.5 provides a an example and brief overview.

14.4.3 MouseMotionListener Interface

The `MouseMotionListener` interface specifies methods that respond to mouse move and mouse drag events. Using this interface is similar to using the `MouseListener` interface. The `MouseMotionListener` interface provided by Java is shown in Listing 14.7. An example of using it is shown in Listing 14.8 .

Listing 14.7 `java.event.MouseMotionListener` Interface

```
1 public abstract interface MouseMotionListener extends EventLis-
tener
2 {
3   public abstract void mouseDragged (MouseEvent e);
4   public abstract void mouseMoved   (MouseEvent e);
5 }
```

Listing 14.8 Trivial Mouse Tester Applet

```
1   import java.awt.event.MouseMotionListener;
2   import java.applet.Applet;
3
4   public class MouseTester extends Applet
5                            implements MouseMotionListener
6   {
7       public void init()
8       {
9         addMouseMotionListener(this);
10      }
11      public void mouseDragged (MouseEvent event)
12      {
13         System.out.println ("The mouse is being dragged.");
14      }
15      public void mouseMoved (MouseEvent event)
16      {
17         System.out.println ("The mouse is moving.");
18      }
19  }
```

14.4.4   MouseEvent Class

When an event occurs and a callback method is called, we often need information about the event. Event objects are used in Java to carry information about events to callback methods. A MouseEvent object is sent to all of the mouse callback methods. We can use this object to get information about the mouse when the event occurred. An important piece of information is where the mouse pointer was when the mouse event was generated. An example of extracting this information is shown below.:

```
public void mousePressed (MouseEvent event)
{
  int   x = event.getX();
  int   y = event.getY();
  Point p = event.getPoint();
}
```

SUPPLEMENTARY MATERIAL

14.5 Adapters and Inner Classes

The Doodle program in Listing 14.1 required that we implement all methods in the MouseListener interface. Thus, we implemented the methods in Lines 121 through 124 even though we did not need them. Java provides the MouseAdapter class, which implements these methods to do nothing already (Listing 14.9). All we need to do is inherit it and override the methods we want to have do something. However, a class may extend only one class. Because the Doodle program already extends Applet (Line 21), we are not allowed to extend MouseAdapter as well.

Listing 14.9 MouseAdapter Class—Found in java.awt

```
1 public class MouseAdapter implements MouseListener
2 {
3    public void mousePressed (MouseEvent e) {}
4    public void mouseReleased (MouseEvent e) {}
5    public void mouseClicked (MouseEvent e) {}
6    public void mouseEntered (MouseEvent e) {}
7    public void mouseExited (MouseEvent e) {}
8 }
```

We can get around the problem of inheriting more than one class by using inner classes.

Inner classes are classes defined within other classes.

Listing 14.10 shows how the Doodle program would need to be changed to use adapter classes. (Bolded areas show locations of change.) First, note that two inner classes have been defined. The first, called MouseHandler in Lines 20 through 26, is used to extend the MouseAdapter class. It overrides the mousePressed method, but it does not need to implement any of the other mouse listener classes. The code in the mouse-Pressed method will not change.

Similarly, the MouseMotionHandler extends the MouseMotionAdapter class (Lines 28 through 34). It overrides the mouseDragged method.

When we registered the event listeners in Lines 12 and 13, we replaced the keyword this with code that instantiates the new listener objects. In the original Doodle program we told

Listing 14.10 Doodle Program Using Adapters and Inner Classes

```
1  import java.awt.event.MouseAdapter;
2  import java.awt.event.MouseMotionAdapter;
3  import ...
4
5  public class Doodle extends Applet
6  {
7      ... See Listing 14.1
8
9    public void init ()
10     {
11        ... See Listing 14.1
12       addMouseListener (new MouseHandler());
13       addMouseMotionListener (new MouseMotionHandler());
14     }
15    public void paint (Graphics g)
16     {
17        ... See Listing 14.1
18     }
19
20     public class MouseHandler extends MouseAdapter
21     {
22       public void mousePressed(MouseEvent e)
23       {
24          ... See Listing 14.1
25       }
26     }
27
28     public class MouseMotionHandler extends MouseMotionAdapter
29     {
30       public void mouseDragged(MouseEvent e)
31       {
32          ... See Listing 14.1
33       }
34     }
35 }
```

the event system that it could find the mouse callback methods in this Doodle applet (see Lines 55 and 56 in Listing 14.1). We are now telling the event system that it will find the mouse callback methods in new MouseHandler and MouseMotionHandler objects, which we create in Lines 12 and 13 of Listing 14.10.

The only other changes are to import adapters instead of listeners and not to promise to implement the listeners in Line 5.

Inner classes have more benefits than allowing us to use adapters. They allow us to make modular event-handling systems that can change dynamically.

REFERENCE

14.6 Summary

In an event-driven style of programming a programmer must write programs that respond to user-initiated events such as mouse movement, mouse presses, and keyboard clicks. This style of programming is inherently different from the program-driven style, where a programmer determines how the user will interact with a program.

Mouse events are handled in Java by implementing the `MouseListener` and `MouseMotionListener` interfaces. These interfaces provide methods that are called when mouse button, mouse move, mouse enter, and mouse exit events occur. These methods are activated by registering the listeners through a `AddListener` method. When a mouse event method is called, an event object is passed to it, which can be used to extract the mouse location at the time of the event.

Java supports the callback pattern for handing events. It eliminates the need to write an event loop, and thus allows the programmer to concentrate on the methods that respond to events.

14.7 Bibliography

* Sutherland, Ivan. 1963. Sketchpad: A Man-Machine Graphical Communication System. *Massachusetts Institute of Technology, Technical Report No. 296* (January 30).

PROBLEM SETS

14.8   Exercises

Events—Section 14.2

1   Make a list of events to which you must respond in your daily life.

2   Select two events from your list in problem 1. Write an event handler for those events (a method similar to `mousePressed`).

3   About how many times can you be interrupted before you begin to lose track of what you are doing?

4   Can you think of additional events (other than mouse and keyboard events) to which a program might respond.

Callback Pattern—Section 14.3

5   Observe your instructor in class. Write a series of callback methods that describe how the instructor responds to student questions.

6   Rewrite the solution in the previous exercise using an event loop.

7   Write a series of callback methods that describe how your parents respond to an interruption in their daily routine.

14.9   Projects

Doodle—Section 14.2

8   Add four more colors to the palette bar of the Doodle program in Listing 14.1. This is an example of program maintenance. The program's function is being expanded.

9   Modify the Doodle program in Listing 14.1 to use an array of color palettes. Thus, the selection of a new color can be done with a loop.

10 Modify the Doodle program in Listing 4.1 so that it draws symmetrically horizontally and vertically, such as the drawing on the right. For example, drawing a line in one corner of the screen causes the same line to appear in the other three corners.

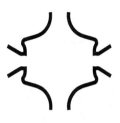

11 Modify the Doodle program in Listing 4.1 so that it draws a circle at the mouse position whenever the mouse button is pressed. Use a color palette to change colors.

12 Modify the Doodle program in Listing 4.1 so that it draws an oval. Mouse down defines one corner and mouse up defines the other corner. Draw the oval as the mouse is dragged. Include a color palette.

13 Save the drawings in the Doodle program to a file.

    a. Hard: Modify the Doodle program to draw in a scratch image. When `paint` method is called, paint the scratch image. Hint: make `mouse-Dragged` draw to both the display and scratch image at the same time.

    b. Difficult: Save the image to a file and read it back to the program. See Section 16.4.2 , page 777 for help about reading and writing objects.

14.9.1　Handling Mouse Events—Section 14.4

14 Create an applet that draws a figure (butterfly, airplane, dog, bat, etc). that follows the onscreen cursor when the mouse is dragged.

15 Modify exercise 14 so that the figure changes from a dog to a cat or something else depending on if the mouse is dragged or moved.

16 Create an applet that contains two eyeballs that look toward the onscreen cursor as the mouse moves.

17 Create a program with an image of yourself, or some other person, that winks when the mouse button is pressed. Section 3.6.5 , page 109 describes how to draw an image.

18 Create a program that draws a rectangle or circle whenever the mouse button is clicked. The rectangles and circles should be of random size, position, and color.

The following computes a random number between 0 and 5:

```
int number = (int)(Math.random() * 5.99999);
```

15 User Interfaces

Projecting Wages

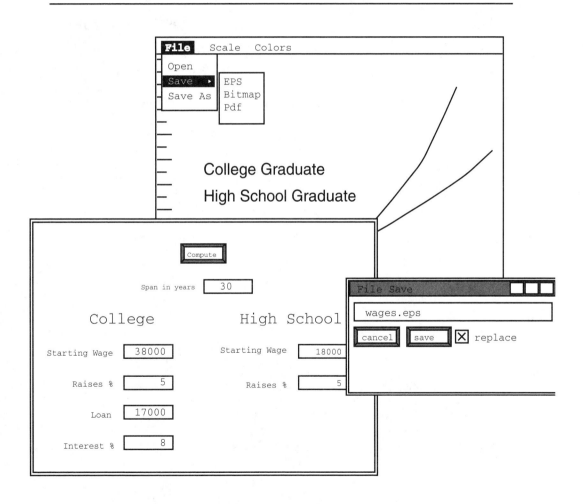

15.1   Objectives

Concepts
Section 15.2, page 685

This chapter looks at implementing graphical user interfaces. We will learn how to create, display, and respond to windows, buttons, menus, and checkboxes. We will begin with a look at a program that projects the earning power of a college graduate versus a high school graduate. In addition to demonstrating how to implement a user interface, we will use this program to demonstrate how to organize objects to create a flexible implementation.

Patterns
Section 15.3, page 692

The program described in the previous paragraph uses a simplified Model-View-Controller (MVC) pattern. It partitions a program into three kinds of objects: a model that estimates future earnings, a controller that gets user input, and an observer (view) that displays the results. We will find that this arrangement makes a program easier to understand and modify.

We will also learn how Java uses the strategy pattern to control the placement of components within a window. This pattern gives a programmer flexibility when designing an interface.

Java Skills

Next the chapter addresses in more detail the objects Java uses to create interfaces.

- Handling windows   Section 15.4.2, page 697
- Implementing buttons   Section 15.4.4, page 702
- Implementing menus   Section 15.4.5, page 705
- Implementing radio buttons   Section 15.4.6, page 708
- Handling keyboard events   Section 15.4.8, page 714

Abilities

By the end of this chapter we should be able to do the following-:

- Write graphic user interfaces with pop up windows, buttons, menus, checkboxes, and keyboard input.
- Partition a program into classes using the MVC pattern.

CONCEPTS

15.2 Wage Projections

Suppose we have just entered college and we are wondering what benefit the next years will bring. We are looking at a debt of $15,000 to $20,000 or more, a lot of hard work, and cramped living spaces. How do we know that this investment will pay itself off?

There are a lot of reasons for going to college. In addition to the hope for a better job, we broaden our understanding of the world, we learn how to teach ourselves, and we get a transition between home and the outside world; also, it is a lot of fun. But the question of whether we are getting our money's worth is a nagging one. In this section we will write a program that helps us investigate this question.

15.2.1 Requirements

We will write a program that allows us to compute our potential earnings as a college graduate versus a high school graduate. We will enter the following information::

- College starting wage and expected yearly increases.
- College debt and interest rate.
- High school starting wage and expected yearly increases.
- Time period over which to compute the results.

The program will provide us with the following:

- Graph accumulated earning over the requested time period based on our expected salary each year for the given period, minus state and federal taxes, and minus our college loan assuming a 10-year payment schedule.

The wages projection program does not take into account many items that impact our financial status. For example, it does not account for home mortgages, changes in property values, stock options, life insurance, retirement and other benefits.

For example, a high tech firm in the Portland area paid high school graduates in the $14,000 to $21,000 range in 1997. They paid college graduates in the $33,000 to $42,000 range. Given that the average debt of a University of Portland graduate is about $17,000 with an interest rate of 8%, let us project how 1997 freshmen fair after four years of college.

Figure 15.1 shows an sample input with the accompanying results displayed in Figure 15.2. Notice that the accumulated earnings of the college graduate passes those of the high school graduate about seven years after college graduation. In addition, 30 years after graduation, the difference between the earnings of the two groups is substantial.

Figure 15.1 Input for Wage Projection

Figure 15.2 Output for Wage Projections

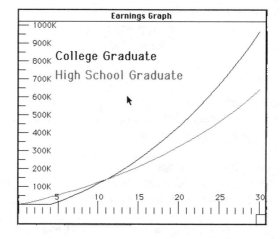

If the disparity between high school and college beginning salaries is not so great, it will take longer to recoup our expenses. For example, if the difference between the two salaries is halved to $28,000 for the college graduate, it extends the time to recoup by about eight to ten years. We may find it interesting that adding another $10,000 to our debt only delays the earnings cross-over by a couple of years. In fact, a college debt in the range of a few tens of thousands of dollars appears to have a relatively small impact on our overall earnings.

There are also the notable exceptions. Bill Gates, for example, did not graduate from college. One expects that college graduation would not have had a positive impact on his earnings. However, there are few Bill Gateses in the world. Most of us will find that college opens doors.

15.2.2 Design

The wage projection program is partitioned into three major components. We will describe them below and in Figure 15.3.

- `WagesController`: Execution begins in this class with the creation of the interface shown in Figure 15.1. The interface object waits for user input. When the "Compute" button is pressed it sends its input information to a `WagesModel` object, which computes college and high school graduate earnings.

- `WagesModel`: An object from this class is responsible for computing college and high school earnings. Once a new set of earnings is computed, a request is made to the `EarningsObserver` to update this display.

- `EarningsObserver`: An object of this class requests the latest information from the `WagesModel` object and displays it graphically.

15.2.3 Implementation

The implementation of this program is rather lengthy. It contains a little over 700 lines. The code for the entire application is found in Section 15.9, page 733. But let us not despair. We will not discuss the entire program in detail. In this section we will concentrate on the `WagesController` class.

The `WagesController` class has four important methods. They are outlined below and in Listing 15.1.

- Because we are creating an application, the `WagesController` class has a `main` method where execution begins.

- In addition, it has a constructor so that we can create an instance of the controller window.

Figure 15.3 Design of the Earning Program

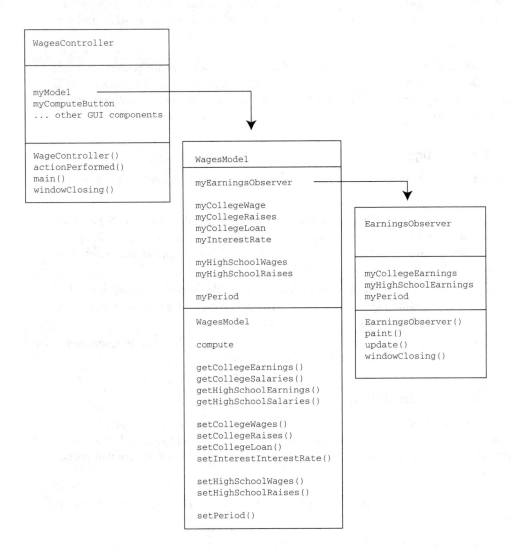

Listing 15.1 Outline of the WagesController Class

```
1    public class WagesController extends JFrame
2            implements ActionListener, WindowListener
3    {
4       ... an instance of the wages model
5       ... GUI components
6
7     public WagesController ()
8     {
9       ... create an instance of the wages model
10      ... set up the physical characteristics of this window
11      ... set up the GUI components
12           ... create them
13           ... place them in this window
14           ... register their event listeners
15      ... register this window listener
16      ... display this window
17    }
18
19    public void actionPerformed (ActionEvent e)
20    {
21      ... update the wages model when the "Compute" button is press
22    }
23
24    public static void main (String args[])
25    {
26       ... create an instance of itself
27    }
28
29    public void windowClosing(WindowEvent event)
30    {
31       ... exit the program
32    }
33  }
```

- It has an `actionPerformed` callback method, which is called whenever the "Compute" button is pressed.

- Finally, it has a `windowClosing` callback method, which is called whenever the window close icon is pressed.

Recall that the `main` method must be declared static (Section 7.6.6, page 310). As a result, when the Java interpreter begins executing the application it does so by making the following call:

```
WagesController.main();
```

No object has been created. Thus, our first responsibility is to create a `WagesController` object. This is done in the `main` method as shown in Listing 15.2.

Listing 15.2 `main` Method

```
1   public static void main (String args[])
2   {
3     WagesController controller = new WagesController();
4   }
```

In Listing 15.1 we see that the constructor, Lines 7 through 17, has a great number of responsibilities. It must create an instance of the wages model, which is responsible for performing the computations. In addition, the constructor must set up the physical characteristics of the controller window, add all the GUI components, and set up the event listeners. Once it has set up all these things, the rest of the activity is guided by user actions that generate events.

The code for the constructor can be found in Lines 56 through 64 of Listing 15.20 on page 733. The code for setting up the physical characteristics of the controller window is accomplished with a call to `setWindow`, which is found in Lines 202 through 208. This code is straightforward and explained with an example in Section 15.4.2.

The constructor also calls the addGUI method in Lines 106 through 157. This method is responsible for placing the GUI components in the window. It is a rather lengthy method, but much of its code repeats with small variations. A typical sequence of code is to create a text field or label and place it in the window.

```
label = new JLabel ("Starting Wage");
add (label, layout.RIGHT, 0, 3, 1, 1);
```

The above code creates a label with the string "`Starting Wage`" and places it right justified in column zero of row three of an imaginary grid. More information about using the `VGridBagLayout` manager is found in Section 15.4.13, page 723. Labels are discussed in Section 10.6.1, page 458.

Making our program respond to button events is similar to making it respond to mouse events. A chief difference is that we must create a button and add it to the window first. This is done in Lines 114 and 116 of Listing 15.20. We must also register our listener with the new button in Line 115. This code is summarized below:

```
myComputeButton = new JButton("Compute");
myComputeButton.addActionListener (this);
add (myComputeButton, layout.CENTER, 0, 0, 4, 1);
```

Next we promised to implement the `ActionListener` interface in Line 33.

```
public class WagesController extends JFrame
        implements ActionListener, WindowListener
```

Finally, we write the `actionPerformed` method in Lines 70 through 73. See below. More details about creating buttons is found in Section 15.4.4, page 702.

```
public void actionPerformed (ActionEvent e)
{
  makeComputations();
}
```

Whenever the "Compute" button is pressed, we must update our wages model. Thus, the `actionPerformed` method calls the `makeComputations` method, which updates the wages model with the current information that the user has entered within the controller window. The `makeComputations` method is found in Lines 175 through 196 of Listing 15.20. It consists of several statements such as the one below:

```
myModel.setCollegeWage
      (VTextFieldUtilities.getDouble(myCollegeWage));
```

Text fields contain strings. Strings are sequences of characters. They must be converted to numbers to be useful. In this example the `getDouble` method in the `VTextFieldUtilities` class converts a string in a text field to a double and returns it. The result is used to set the state of the wages model. More about the `VTextFieldUtilities` class is found in Appendix: C on page 921. Text fields are discussed in Section 10.6.2, page 459.

The last action of the `makeComputations` method is to ask the wages model to recompute wages.

The final responsibility we must fulfill is to make our application respond to window closing events. The steps by now should be familiar. We promise to implement the Window-Listener interface in Line 33 and write the `windowClosing` method in Lines 215 through 218. Finally, we register our listener with our window in Line 62. More about handling window listeners in found in Section 15.4.3, page 701.

PATTERNS

15.3   GUI Patterns

Within this chapter we use the callback pattern to make our program respond to button and window events. We are also using a couple of new object patterns to make our design and implementation easier. We will first talk about the MVC pattern that we hinted at in Section 7.5.1. This is followed by a peek at how the strategy pattern is used to help us place GUI components within a window.

15.3.1   Simplified Model-View-Controller Pattern

name

Recall that object patterns are snippets of reusable design. The Model-View-Controller (MVC) pattern is one that has been around for a long time. We will argue that using this pattern will make a program easier to modify and better communicate our intent.

solution

The MVC pattern contains three kinds of classes. See below and Figure 15.4.

- Model: The model is the set of data and actions that describes some real world object or process. For example, it can be a mathematical system such as the one that projects future income. The chaos model from Chapter 5-, which projects future population growth, is another example. Yet another example is a 3D description of a physical object.

- View: The view displays modeled information. A model may have more than one view. For example, information may be displayed graphically as we did in the Earnings- Observer class. It may also be displayed as a table or pie chart by using different viewers. The term *observer* is another term for viewer. For example, Java has an Observer interface in the util library, which corresponds to a view. In addition, it has an Observerable class, which corresponds to a model.

- Controller: The controller lets the user change the underlying model through the press of a button, menu selection, changing values in text fields, etc.

problem

A primary motivation for the MVC pattern is to decouple changes in one component from impacting any of the others. For example, we can change the user interface without impacting our model or any of its views. In addition, we can make changes to the model without breaking the user interface or the model views. Finally, this pattern simplifies the process of adding and removing views. Each view is independent of the others.

Figure 15.4 MVC Pattern

Controller

Model

View
(Observer)

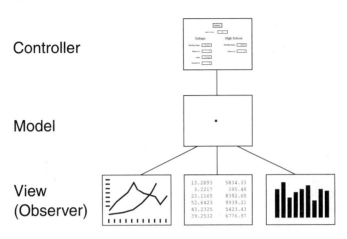

Our pattern is a simplified version of the full implementation of the MVC pattern because we have not taken advantage of inheritance. One of our goals is to easily add and remove views. When we learn how to use inheritance we will be able to put all of our views within a list. When our model changes, we can iterate through the list, updating each in turn. This basic approach is shown below. Regardless of how many views we have we will never need to change this code.

```
int count = 0;
while (count < n)
{
  view = getView(count);
  view.update(this);
  count++;
}
```

To make this work, each view must have an update method called by the model. The view's update method is responsible for getting current information from the model and updating its display. Figure 15.5 shows the sequence of method calls that supports a model with two views.

It is not possible to customize each view's update method with a custom set of parameters. Pulling views off a list, as we have above, requires each update to have the same parameters. We pass the update method this model. The update method can then ask this model for information. The problem with sending all the information through parameters to the update method is that a view may not need all the information a model has. Sending all the information is a waste of effort.

Figure 15.5 Model - Observer Sequence Diagram

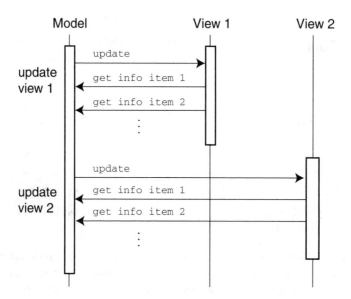

An example of a model calling `update` is shown in Line 70 of Listing 15.21 on page 739 in the `WagesModel` class. Because we do not know how to implement inheritance, we have simplified our approach by calling a single observer explicitly. Thus, the code to update our view is only one line long.

```
myEarningsObserver.update(this);
```

The `update` method is implemented in Lines 167 through 173 of Listing 15.22 on page 748 in the `EarningsObserver` class. It asks the model for a new list of college earnings, high school earnings, and the time period.

```
public void update(WagesModel model)
{
    myCollegeEarnings    = model.getCollegeEarnings();
    myHighSchoolEarnings = model.getHighSchoolEarnings();
    myPeriod             = model.getPeriod();
    repaint();
}
```

15.3.2 Strategy

Java provides several strategies for placing GUI components in a window. The strategy we used in the wages program is governed by an imaginary grid. Each component is placed at a specific location by providing its column and row. This strategy is utilized in the `addGUI` method of the wages program (Line 106 of Listing 15.20 on page 733). It uses the `VGridBagLayout` manager.

The layout manager is created in Line 109 and attached to the window in Line 110. From this point on, each time we add a component to our window, it uses the `VGridBagLayout` manager to place the component. This code is summarized below:

```
VGridBagLayout layout = new VGridBagLayout();
setLayout(layout);
add (myComputeButton, layout.CENTER, 0, 0, 4, 1);
```

However, we will discover in Section 15.4.4 that there is also a flow layout manager. Using the flow layout manager, components are placed in rows from left to right and from top to bottom in the order in which they are added. Although the flow layout manager is easy to use, it does not allow us to precisely place components within a window. When a window is resized, the GUI components are repositioned in rows to fit the entire width of a window. The result can be sloppy-looking user interfaces. Thus, Java has provided us with a choice of possible layout managers. In addition to the flow layout and grid bag layout managers, there are the `BorderLayout`, `GridLayout`, and `CardLayout` managers. We will not discuss these others.

Each layout manager embodies a strategy for placing components within a window. Thus, the name *strategy pattern*. Each strategy is implemented with its own component placement algorithm. When we set the layout manager for a window, we are changing the strategy that a window uses to place components. The basic steps for accomplishing this are shown above for the grid bag layout manager and below for the flow layout manager.

```
FlowLayout layout = new FlowLayout();
setLayout(layout);
add (myYesButton);
```

The strategy pattern allows us to change the behavior of an object on the fly. In the example above, the Java team needed to implement only one `JFrame` class. They and we can change a frame's behavior by using predefined and custom layout managers.

The strategy pattern has many other uses. For example, we can define strategies for filtering an image. One strategy may smooth an image by averaging neighboring pixels. Other strategies may convert an image to a grayscale image by averaging the three RGB components of a pixel.

Another place where the strategy pattern can be used is in text editing. Various strategies can be implemented for determining where line breaks appear. Some strategies may do an exceptional job by taking into consideration an entire paragraph at a time. However, they may require a substantial computation overhead. A more economical strategy may consider each line individually.

JAVA

15.4 Graphical User Interface Components (Java 2)

In this section we will look at the GUI components in more detail. We will demonstrate how to create windows, buttons, menus, and respond to keyboard events using Java *Swing*. Swing is one of the libraries that differentiates Java 1.1 from Java 2. It enhances the functionality of the by including split windows, tabbed frames, desktop panes, plus many other features. Unfortunately, at the writing of this text not all Java tools and development environments have been upgraded to handle Java 2. See the supplementary section for differences.

15.4.1 An Applet

We will begin by learning how to create a frame (window). We have been creating windows since we learned about applets in Section 3.5, page 99. Before we create our first frame we review the process of creating a window using an applet. Once we have created an applet we will compare its code to the code for a frame that does the same thing.

The applet that we create displays a simple message in its window (Figure 15.6). The code for accomplishing this task is shown in Listing 15.3. It should require no explanation. This program needs an accompanying HTML file, which is shown in Listing 15.4. Recall that an applet needs such a file and that the size of the window is specified within it.

Notice the use of the `JApplet` class and its corresponding import. Swing class names contain a `J` prefix. For trivial GUIs the primary difference between Java 1.1 and 2 will be simple name changes.

15.4.2 Creating a Frame

An advantage of an applet is that much of the work required to create a window is provided free. Creating the frame shown in Figure 15.7 requires more steps. We begin by extending the `JFrame` class instead of the `JApplet` class (Line 5). Because we are not extending an applet, we are creating an application that cannot be run over the web. As a result, no HTML file is required, but we must have a `main` method.

Figure 15.6 An Applet

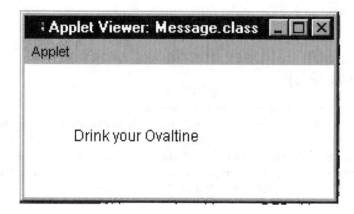

Listing 15.3 An Applet

```
1 import java.awt.Color;
1
2 import java.awt.Graphics;
3 import javax.swing.JApplet;
4
5 public class Message extends JApplet {
6
7   public void init()
8   {
9     setBackground(Color.white);
10   }
11
12   public void paint (Graphics g)
13   {
14     g.drawString ("Drink your Ovaltine", 40, 60);
15   }
16 }
```

Listing 15.4 HTML File

```
1 <title>Message</title>
2 <hr>
3 <applet code=Message.class width=250 height=100>
4 </applet>
5 <hr>
6 <a href="Message.java">The source.</a>
```

Figure 15.7 A Frame with a Message

Listing 15.5 Creating a Frame

```
1  import java.awt.Color;
2  import java.awt.Graphics;
3  import javax.swing.JFrame;
4
5  public class Message extends JFrame
6  {
7    public static void main(String args[])
8    {
9      Message message = new Message();
10   }
11
12   public Message()
13   {
14     setTitle("From your sponsor");
15     setSize(200, 100);
16     show();
17   }
18
19   public void paint (Graphics g)
20   {
21     g.drawString ("Drink your Ovaltine", 40, 60);
22   }
23 }
```

Execution begins in the `main` method (Line 7). The first order of business is to create the frame by calling its constructor in Line 9.

The constructor, Lines 12 through 17, sets the window title, its size, and tells the window to display itself. When we created applets, the HTML file specified the initial size of a window, set the window title, and displayed it.

Listing 15.6 Closing a Window

```
1  import javax.swing.JFrame;
2  import java.awt.Color;
3  import java.awt.Graphics;
4  import java.awt.event.WindowEvent;
5  import java.awt.event.WindowListener;
6
7  public class Message extends JFrame
8          implements WindowListener
9  {
10    public static void main(String args[])
11    {
12      Message message = new Message();
13    }
14
15    public Message()
16    {
17      addWindowListener(this);
18      setTitle("From your sponsor");
19      setSize(200, 100);
20      show();
21    }
22
23    public void paint (Graphics g)
24    {
25      g.drawString ("Drink your Ovaltine", 40, 60);
26    }
27
28    public void windowClosing(WindowEvent event)
29    {
30      System.exit(0);
31    }
32
33    public void windowOpened(WindowEvent event){}
34    public void windowClosed(WindowEvent event){}
35    public void windowIconified(WindowEvent event){}
36    public void windowDeiconified(WindowEvent event){}
37    public void windowActivated(WindowEvent event){}
38    public void windowDeactivated(WindowEvent event){}
39  }
```

The role of the constructor is similar to the role of the `init` method for applets. The constructor will contain all the initialization code required to set up the new window.

In general, it is good practice to place the call to the `show` method last within a constructor. If the `show` method is called before components such as buttons and labels have been added to the window, those components will not appear in the window until an event forces the window to be repainted.

15.4.3   Closing a Window

The frame we created in the previous section does not behave the same as our applet window. Although the minimize and maximize icons are functional, the window close icon does not work correctly. The window closes but the application does not quit. We cannot quit our program by clicking on the close icon. In Listing 15.6 we implement the program termination.

To make the program quit when we press the close window icon we will implement a window listener in the same way we implemented mouse listener interfaces in Chapter 14. The process of adding a window event listener requires three steps:

1. Promise to implement the `WindowListener` interface.
2. Write methods that correspond to each method signature in this interface.
3. Register the window listener with the frame.

The process begins by promising to implement the `WindowListener` interface in Line 8. We will implement the `WindowListener` interface in a similar manner to the `MouseListener` interface described in Section 14.4.2. We must implement seven methods, Lines 28 through 38. The only one we have do anything to is the `windowClosing` method in Line 28. The other methods are documented in Appendix: B on page 909. When the window closing icon is clicked, we ask the Java system to quit executing this program. If this window is one of several in an applications and we only want to destroy this one window, we can replace `System.exit()` with `dispose()`.

Before window closing will work, we must register a window listener. Line 17 states that when a window event occurs on "this" window frame, the method for responding to the window event is found in "this" class (Figure 15.8).

Figure 15.8 Syntax of Registering a Window Listener

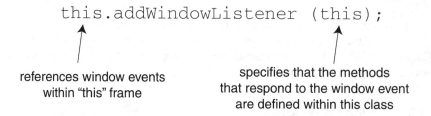

references window events
within "this" frame

specifies that the methods
that respond to the window event
are defined within this class

15.4.4   Using Buttons

Now let us move on to adding buttons. They can be added to frames and applets. The application in Listing 15.7 creates a window with two buttons. When the yes button in pressed, "yes" is displayed. When the no button is pressed, "no" is displayed. See Figure 15.9.

Figure 15.9 Yes or No but Not Maybe

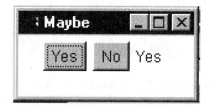

Listing 15.7 Respond to a Yes and No Button

```
1  import javax.swing.JButton;
2  import javax.swing.JFrame;
3  import javax.swing.JLabel;
4  import java.awt.Color;
5  import java.awt.Container;
6  import java.awt.FlowLayout;
7  import java.awt.Graphics;
8  import java.awt.event.ActionEvent;
9  import java.awt.event.ActionListener;
10
```

Listing 15.7 Respond to a Yes and No Button

```
11  public class Message extends JFrame
12                      implements ActionListener
13  {
14     private        JButton   myYesButton;
15     private        JButton   myNoButton;
16     private        JLabel    myResultLabel;

17     public static void main(String args[])
18     {
19        Message message = new Message();
20     }

21     public Message()
22     {
23        // set up window
24        setTitle("Maybe");
25        setSize(200, 75);
26        Container pane = getContentPane();
27        pane.setLayout (new FlowLayout ());
28        pane.setBackground(Color.white);

30        // set up "Yes" button
31        myYesButton = new JButton ("Yes");
32        myYesButton.addActionListener (this);
33        pane.add (myYesButton);

35        // set up "No" button
36        myNoButton = new JButton ("No");
37        myNoButton.addActionListener (this);
38        pane.add (myNoButton);

40        // set up result label
41        myResultLabel = new JLabel ("          ");
42        pane.add (myResultLabel);

44        // pop up this window
45        show();
46     }

47     public void actionPerformed (ActionEvent e)
48     {
49        if (myYesButton == e.getSource())
50           myResultLabel.setText("Yes");
51        else if (myNoButton == e.getSource())
52           myResultLabel.setText("No");
53     }
54  }
```

Adding a button is a five step process:

1. Create a button.
2. Add it to the frame (or applet).
3. Promise to implement the `ActionListener` interface.
4. Write an `actionPerformed` method to respond to button presses.
5. Register a listener with the button.

The `yes` button is created in Line 31. The parameter to the button constructor specifies its label. Notice that `myYesButton` is an instance variable declared in Line 14. We will need to access it in the `actionPerformed` method to determine which button caused a button event.

In the second step, the button is added to the frame, Line 33. This step makes the button visible. Each frame has a container called a contents pane, which we access in Line 27. Components are placed left-to-right and top-to-bottom within this pane because we set the layout manager to flow layout in Line 27. In our example, we have three components, two buttons and a label, that all fit in one row. If the frame is resized, components realign themselves.

To take care of step three we promise to implement the `ActionListener` interface in Line 12.

In step four we write the `actionPerformed` method (Lines 47 through 53). The `if` statement in Line 49 checks whether the action event came from `myYesButton`. If the action came from the `yes` button, we display "yes" in the frame. The second `if` statement checks whether the event was caused by `myNoButton`. We can see a general pattern here. As we add buttons and other action elements such as menu items, we add more nested `if` statements. It will not take too many action elements before the `actionPerformed` method becomes one monstrous nested `if` statement. See Section 15.5, page 727 for another approach.

Finally, in step five we register an action listener with `myYesButton` (Line 32). Thus, we have informed the Java run-time system to call the `actionPerformed` method in this `Message` class whenever `myYesButton` is pressed. We must do the same with myNoButton in Line 37.

15.4.5 Using Menus

In this section we will look at adding menus to a frame. Listing 15.8 contains an example with the resulting window shown in Figure 15.10. This figure illustrates the placement of the menus in a Windows machine. Menus will be placed in a different window on a Macintosh. Under the `Blue` menu, one can choose to create a blue box or blue oval. Under the `Red` menu, one can choose to create a red box.

Figure 15.10 Boxes and Ovals Menus

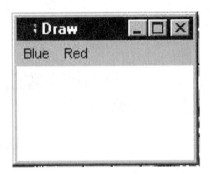

Listing 15.8 Boxes and Ovals Code

```
1 import javax.swing.JFrame;
2 import javax.swing.JMenu;
3 import javax.swing.JMenuBar;
4 import javax.swing.JMenuItem;
5 import javax.swing.JPanel;
6 import java.awt.Color;
7 import java.awt.Graphics;
8 import java.awt.event.ActionEvent;
9 import java.awt.event.ActionListener;
10
11 public class Message extends JFrame implements ActionListener
12 {
13    private       JMenuItem myBlueBoxMenuItem;
14    private       JMenuItem myBlueOvalMenuItem;
15    private       JMenuItem myRedBoxMenuItem;
16
17    public static void main(String args[])
18    {
19      Message message = new Message();
20    }
21
```

Listing 15.8 Boxes and Ovals Code

```
22    public Message()
23    {
24      // set up window
25      setTitle("Draw");
26      setSize(250, 120);
27
28      // set up menu items
29      myBlueBoxMenuItem = new JMenuItem ("Box");
30      myBlueBoxMenuItem.addActionListener (this);
31      myBlueOvalMenuItem = new JMenuItem ("Oval");
32      myBlueOvalMenuItem.addActionListener (this);
33      myRedBoxMenuItem = new JMenuItem ("Box");
34      myRedBoxMenuItem.addActionListener (this);
35
36      // set up menu bar
37      JMenu    blueMenu = new JMenu("Blue");
38      JMenu    redMenu  = new JMenu("Red");
39      blueMenu.add(myBlueBoxMenuItem);
40      blueMenu.add(myBlueOvalMenuItem);
41      redMenu.add(myRedBoxMenuItem);
42      JMenuBar menuBar  = new JMenuBar();
43      menuBar.add(blueMenu);
44      menuBar.add(redMenu);
45      setJMenuBar(menuBar);
46
47      // pop up this window
48      show();
49    }
```

Listing 15.8 Boxes and Ovals Code

```
50    public void actionPerformed (ActionEvent e)
51    {
52      Graphics g = getGraphics();
53
54      // handle blue box menu selection
55      if (myBlueBoxMenuItem == e.getSource())
56      {
57        g.setColor (Color.blue);
58        g.fillRect (100, 50, 50, 50);
59      }
60      // handle blue oval menu selection
61      else if (myBlueOvalMenuItem == e.getSource())
62      {
63        g.setColor (Color.blue);
64        g.fillOval (150, 50, 50, 50);
65      }
66      // handle red box menu selection
67      else if (myRedBoxMenuItem == e.getSource())
68      {
69        g.setColor (Color.red);
70        g.fillRect (200, 50, 50, 50);
71      }
72    }
73  }
```

Figure 15.11 Menu Parts

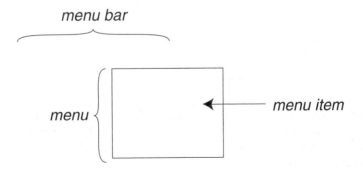

Before we can understand the code, we must learn to identify the parts of the menu system. Figure 15.11 illustrates how it is composed of a menu bar, menus, and menu items. Each window has at most one menu bar. It is a container for menus. This illustration shows four menus: `File`, `Edit`, `Blue`, and `Red`. Each menu contains menu items. For example, the `Box` and `Oval` items are shown in our illustration.

Creating an application with menus has the same five steps required to create an application with buttons. The first two steps, creating the menus and adding them to the display, are more lengthy because there are three menu classes: `JMenuBar`, `JMenu`, and `JMenuItem`. We must create the menu bar, menus, and menu items. In addition, we must add menu items to menus, add menus to the menu bar, and finally set the frame's menu bar. The rest of the steps follow closely the steps we used when creating buttons.

15.4.6   Using Radio Buttons

Radio buttons are mutually exclusive. Only one button can be set at any given time. The application in Listing 15.9 illustrates how to use radio buttons. It sets the background color of a frame (Figure 15.12). When the green button is pressed, any other button that is currently on is turned off.

Figure 15.12 Set Background Color

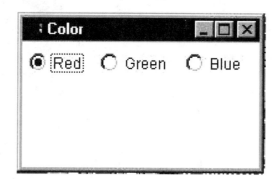

Radio buttons are created in Lines 35, 40, and 45. The boolean value specifies the group in its initial state in addition to its label. A true state indicates that the initial state of a radio button will be selected. Only one button in a group should be set true. A radio button group is defined in Line 50 and the buttons added to it in Lines 51 through 53.

Multiple radio button groups can be created. However, each check box can belong to only one radio button group.

Listing 15.9 Set Background Color

```
1 import javax.swing.ButtonGroup;
2 import javax.swing.JFrame;
3 import javax.swing.JRadioButton;
4 import java.awt.Color;
5 import java.awt.Container;
6 import java.awt.FlowLayout;
7 import java.awt.event.ItemEvent;
8 import java.awt.event.ItemListener;
9
10 public class Message extends JFrame
11                      implements ItemListener
12 {
13    private      Container    myPane;
14    private      JRadioButton myRedRadioButton;
15    private      JRadioButton myGreenRadioButton;
16    private      JRadioButton myBlueRadioButton;
17
18    public static void main(String args[])
19    {
20      Message message = new Message ();
21    }
22
23    public Message()
24    {
25      // set up window
26      setTitle("Color");
27      setSize(200, 125);
28
29      // set up content pane
30      myPane = getContentPane ();
31      myPane.setBackground (Color.red);
32      myPane.setLayout (new FlowLayout());
33
34      // set up red radio button -- the default
35      myRedRadioButton = new JRadioButton ("Red", true);
36      myRedRadioButton.addItemListener (this);
37      myPane.add (myRedRadioButton);
38
39      // set up green radio button
40      myGreenRadioButton = new JRadioButton ("Green", false);
41      myGreenRadioButton.addItemListener (this);
42      myPane.add (myGreenRadioButton);
43
```

Listing 15.9 Set Background Color

```
44      // set up blue radio button
45      myBlueRadioButton = new JRadioButton ("Blue", false);
46      myBlueRadioButton.addItemListener (this);
47      myPane.add (myBlueRadioButton);
48
49      // set up radio button group
50      ButtonGroup colorGroup = new ButtonGroup();
51      colorGroup.add (myRedRadioButton);
52      colorGroup.add (myGreenRadioButton);
53      colorGroup.add (myBlueRadioButton);
54
55      // pop up this window
56      show();
57    }
58
59    public void itemStateChanged (ItemEvent e)
60    {
61      // change the frame's background color
62      if (myRedRadioButton == e.getSource())
63        myPane.setBackground(Color.red);
64      if (myGreenRadioButton == e.getSource())
65        myPane.setBackground(Color.green);
66      if (myBlueRadioButton == e.getSource())
67        myPane.setBackground(Color.blue);
68      repaint();
69    }
70  }
```

Notice the `itemStateChanged` method in Lines 59 through 69. It is called whenever the a radio button is pressed. All we need to do is figure out which button it was in Lines 62, 64, and 66.

15.4.7   Option Dialogs

Swing provides the `JOptionPane` class for creating input dialog and message boxes. Listing 15.10 contains an application that allows a user to change the color of a frame (see top of Figure 15.13). The color menu has three items: red, green, and blue. Selecting the red item displays the dialog box in the bottom left of Figure 15.13. Entering a value and selecting OK changes the red component of a frame's background. The RGB components of the color can be displayed by selecting RGB item under the `show` menu (bottom right of Figure 15.13).

Figure 15.13 Color Applications with Input and Message Option Dialog Boxes

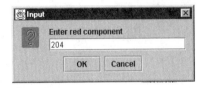

Listing 15.10 Creating Option Panes

```
1  import javax.swing.JFrame;
2  import javax.swing.JMenu;
3  import javax.swing.JMenuBar;
4  import javax.swing.JMenuItem;
5  import javax.swing.JOptionPane;
6  import java.awt.Color;
7  import java.awt.Component;
8  import java.awt.Graphics;
9  import java.awt.event.ActionEvent;
10 import java.awt.event.ActionListener;
11
12 public class SetColor extends JFrame implements ActionListener
13 {
14    private JMenuItem myRedMenuItem;
15    private JMenuItem myGreenMenuItem;
16    private JMenuItem myBlueMenuItem;
17    private JMenuItem myShowRGBMenuItem;
18
19    private int      myRedComponent;
20    private int      myGreenComponent;
21    private int      myBlueComponent;
22
23    final   int      WIDTH  = 250;
24    final   int      HEIGHT = 150;
25
```

Listing 15.10 Creating Option Panes

```
26   public static void main(String args[])
27   {
28     SetColor setColor = new SetColor();
29   }
30
31   public SetColor()
32   {
33     // set up window
34     setTitle("Set the Color");
35     setSize(WIDTH, HEIGHT);
36     myRedComponent   = 0;
37     myGreenComponent = 0;
38     myBlueComponent  = 0;
39     Component pane = getContentPane ();
40     pane.setBackground (new Color (myRedComponent,
41       myGreenComponent, myBlueComponent));
42
43     // set up menu items
44     myRedMenuItem = new JMenuItem ("Red");
45     myRedMenuItem.addActionListener (this);
46     myGreenMenuItem = new JMenuItem ("Green");
47     myGreenMenuItem.addActionListener (this);
48     myBlueMenuItem = new JMenuItem ("Blue");
49     myBlueMenuItem.addActionListener (this);
50     myShowRGBMenuItem = new JMenuItem ("RGB");
51     myShowRGBMenuItem.addActionListener (this);
52
53     // set up menu bar
54     JMenu     colorMenu = new JMenu("Color");
55     JMenu     showMenu  = new JMenu("Show");
56     colorMenu.add(myRedMenuItem);
57     colorMenu.add(myGreenMenuItem);
58     colorMenu.add(myBlueMenuItem);
59     showMenu.add(myShowRGBMenuItem);
60     JMenuBar menuBar  = new JMenuBar();
61     menuBar.add(colorMenu);
62     menuBar.add(showMenu);
63     setJMenuBar(menuBar);
64
65     // pop up this window
66     show();
67   }
68
```

Listing 15.10   Creating Option Panes

```
69    public void actionPerformed (ActionEvent e)
70    {
71      if (myRedMenuItem == e.getSource())
72      {
73        String redString =
74          JOptionPane.showInputDialog ("Enter red component");
75        if (redString.length() == 0)
76          myRedComponent = 0;
77        else
78          myRedComponent = Integer.parseInt (redString);
79      }
80      else if (myGreenMenuItem == e.getSource())
81      {
82        String greenString =
83          JOptionPane.showInputDialog ("Enter green component");
84        if (greenString.length() == 0)
85          myGreenComponent = 0;
86        else
87          myGreenComponent = Integer.parseInt (greenString);
88      }
89      else if (myBlueMenuItem == e.getSource())
90      {
91        String blueString =
92          JOptionPane.showInputDialog ("Enter blue component");
93        if (blueString.length() == 0)
94          myBlueComponent = 0;
95        else
96          myBlueComponent = Integer.parseInt (blueString);
97      }
98      else if (myShowRGBMenuItem == e.getSource())
99      {
100       JOptionPane.showMessageDialog (this,
101         "Red(" + myRedComponent +
102         "), Green(" + myGreenComponent +
103         "), Blue(" + myBlueComponent + ")");
104     }
105     Component pane = getContentPane ();
106     pane.setBackground (new Color (myRedComponent,
107         myGreenComponent, myBlueComponent));
108     repaint ();
109   }
110 }
```

Lines 73 and 74 create the red input dialog box. When this code is executed, control is not returned to Line 75 until the user selects the OK or Cancel button. The dialog is said to be *modal* because no action can occur until the dialog is dismissed. Line 75 takes the string output of the dialog and converts it to an integer. The showInputDialog method takes a single parameter which acts as a prompt.

The message dialog is created in Line 100 through 103. It is dismissed by selecting the OK button. The showMessageDialog method takes two parameters: the parent frame and message string.

15.4.8   Keyboard Input

The last event handling process we will look at is the one for capturing keyboard events. The code in Listing 15.11 responds to a key press and captures the character associated with the key. It then displays the character in a frame (Figure 15.14).

Figure 15.14 Key Display

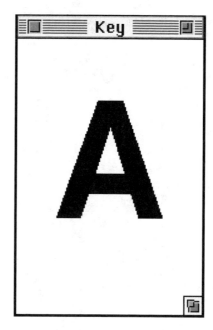

Listing 15.11 Display Key

```java
1 import javax.swing.JFrame;
2 import java.awt.Color;
3 import java.awt.Container;
4 import java.awt.Font;
5 import java.awt.Graphics;
6 import java.awt.event.KeyEvent;
7 import java.awt.event.KeyListener;
8
9 public class Message extends JFrame
10                     implements KeyListener
11 {
12   private final int WIDTH  = 150;
13   private final int HEIGHT = 200;
14
15   public static void main(String args[])
16   {
17     Message message = new Message();
18   }
19
20   public Message()
21   {
22     // set up window
23     setTitle("Key");
24     setSize(WIDTH, HEIGHT);
25     Container pane = getContentPane ();
26     pane.setBackground(Color.white);
27     show();
28
29     // set up key listener
30     addKeyListener(this);
31     requestFocus();
32   }
33
```

Listing 15.11 Display Key

```
34   public void keyPressed (KeyEvent e)
35   {
36      // clear the window and set the font
37      Graphics g = getGraphics();
38      g.setColor(Color.white);
39      g.fillRect(0,0,WIDTH,HEIGHT);
40      Font     f = new Font ("sansserif", Font.BOLD, 128);
41      g.setFont(f);
42
43      // get and display a character
44      char    c = e.getKeyChar();
45      String  s = String.valueOf(c);
46      g.setColor(Color.black);
47      g.drawString (s, 30, 140);
48   }
49
50   public void keyReleased (KeyEvent e) {}
51   public void keyTyped    (KeyEvent e) {}
52 }
```

Three steps are required:

1. We implement the KeyListener interface in Line 10.

2. We write the keyPressed method in Lines 34 through 48. Notice how we extract the character pressed from the key event in Line 44.

3. Finally we register this key listener with the frame in Line 30. There is one additional twist. The programmer must request the focus in Line 31, or the user must click in the window before we start typing. The focus determines which GUI component will respond to a keyboard event.

Notice that there are three methods associated with the KeyListener interface. We implemented the keyPressed method in Lines 34 through 48 and the other two in Lines 50 and 51.

15.4.9   Split Window Panes

We stated at the beginning of this section that Swing enhanced the Java 1.1 AWT by adding split windows, tabbed panes, and other GUI features. In these next two subsections we will demonstrate how to create a character decoding program. In one text area the characters we type are displayed. In another, their ASCII integer equivalents are displayed.

In this subsection we use a split text window. The left side contains the characters as we type them. The right side contains their ASCII integer equivalents. We can grab the center bar between the windows with the mouse and move it to the left and right (Figure 15.15).

Figure 15.15 Split Window with Moveable Center Bar

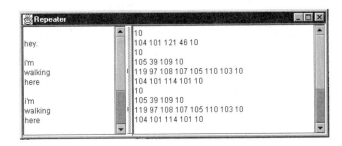

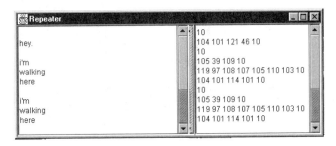

Listing 15.12 Split Window Code

```
1 import javax.swing.JFrame;
2 import javax.swing.JScrollPane;
3 import javax.swing.JSplitPane;
4 import javax.swing.JTextArea;
5 import java.awt.Color;
6 import java.awt.event.KeyEvent;
7 import java.awt.event.KeyListener;
8
```

Listing 15.12 Split Window Code

```
9 public class Decode extends JFrame
10                    implements KeyListener
11 {
12   JTextArea  myOriginalArea;
13   JTextArea  myCodedArea;
14
15   public static void main(String args[])
16   {
17     Decode decoder = new Decode();
18   }
19
20   public Decode ()
21   {
22     // set up the window
23     setBackground(Color.white);
24     setTitle("Repeater");
25     setSize(500, 200);
26     addKeyListener(this);
27
28     // create the original text area
29     myOriginalArea = new JTextArea (10,15);
30     myOriginalArea.setLineWrap (true);
31     JScrollPane leftPane = new JScrollPane (myOriginalArea);
32
33     // create the decoded text area
34     myCodedArea = new JTextArea (10, 15);
35     myCodedArea.setLineWrap (true);
36     JScrollPane rightPane = new JScrollPane (myCodedArea);
37
38     // put the text areas in a split window and put it in
39     // the frame
40     JSplitPane splitPane =
41           new JSplitPane (JSplitPane.HORIZONTAL_SPLIT,
42                           leftPane, rightPane);
43     setContentPane (splitPane);
44     requestFocus();
45     show();
46   }
```

Listing 15.12 Split Window Code

```
47    public void keyPressed (KeyEvent e)
48    {
49      // display character representation
50      char     c = e.getKeyChar ();
51      String   s = String.valueOf (c);
52
53      // display integer representation
54      myOriginalArea.append (s);
55      int      i = (int)c;
56      s             = String.valueOf(i) + " ";
57      myCodedArea.append (s);
58      if (c == '\n')
59         myCodedArea.append ("\n");
60    }
61
62    public void keyReleased (KeyEvent e) {}
63    public void keyTyped    (KeyEvent e) {}
64  }
```

The code to implement a split window is shown in Listing 15.12. Key parts are found in Lines 29 through 31 where the left text area is created and placed in a scroll pane. Objects created from the Java 1.1 `TextArea` class contain a scrolling feature. Text areas created from the Java 2.0 `JTextArea` class must be placed within a scrolling pane to implement text scrolling. In a similar manner, Lines 34 through 36 implement the right text pane. Finally, Lines 40 through 43 create the split pane and insert it into the window frame.

Figure 15.16 Tabbed Window

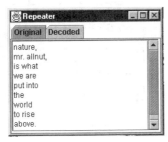
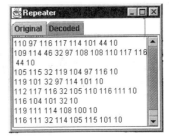

15.4.10 Tabbed Windows

In this section we reimplement the character decoding program from the previous subsection. This time we use a tabbed pane (Figure 15.16). The original characters are captured in one tab and the decoded integers are displayed within another. Listing 15.13 shows the modifications necessary to do the transformation. Lines 38 through 43 in Listing 15.12 are replaced with Lines 5 through 10 in Listing 15.13. Instead of creating a split pane, we create a tabbed pane, add two tabs to it, and set the frame's content pane to our newly created tabbed pane.

Listing 15.13 Tabbed Window Code

```
1    import javax.swing.JTabbedPane;
2    ...
3    ...
4    ...
5    // put the text areas in a tabbed window and put it in
6    // the frame
7    JTabbedPane tabbedPane = new JTabbedPane ();
8    tabbedPane.addTab ("Original", leftPane);
9    tabbedPane.addTab ("Decoded", rightPane);
10   setContentPane (tabbedPane);
```

15.4.11 Border Layout Manager

The programs above use the `FlowLay-out` manager, which places GUI components in a display row-by-row from left to right. It is easy to use but not flexible. A `BorderLayout` manager give us a little more control. It partitions a display into five areas (north, east, west, south, and center) and allows us to place a component into each.

Listing 15.14 demonstrates how to use the `BorderLayout` manager. It is created and set in Line 7. Next, each of five buttons is added to one of its partitions in Lines 12, 14, 16, 18, and 20. The result is shown in Figure 15.17.

Figure 15.17 Border Layout

Listing 15.14 Using the Border Layout

```
1    public Message()
2    {
3        // set up window
4        setTitle("Button Placement");
5        setSize(300, 150);
6        Container pane = getContentPane ();
7        pane.setLayout (new BorderLayout());
8        pane.setBackground(Color.white);
9
10       // set up buttons
11       JButton eastButton = new JButton ("East");
12       pane.add (eastButton, BorderLayout.EAST);
13       JButton westButton = new JButton ("West");
14       pane.add (westButton, BorderLayout.WEST);
15       JButton southButton = new JButton ("South");
16       pane.add (southButton, BorderLayout.SOUTH);
17       JButton centerButton = new JButton ("Center");
18       pane.add (centerButton, BorderLayout.CENTER);
19       JButton northButton = new JButton ("North");
20       pane.add (northButton, BorderLayout.NORTH);
21
22       // pop up this window
23       show();
24   }
```

Figure 15.18 Using Panels

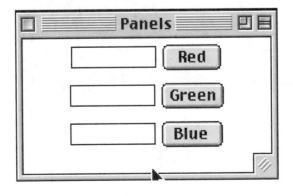

JAVA

Listing 15.15 Panels

```
1    public Message()
2    {
3      // set up window
4      setTitle("Panels");
5      setSize(200, 130);
6
7      // Create the red panel
8      JTextField redField   = new JTextField (8);
9      JButton    redButton  = new JButton ("  Red  ");
10     JPanel     redPanel    = new JPanel ();
11     redPanel.setLayout (new FlowLayout ());
12     redPanel.add (redField);
13     redPanel.add (redButton);
14
15     // Create the green panel
16     JTextField greenField  = new JTextField (8);
17     JButton    greenButton = new JButton ("Green");
18     JPanel     greenPanel  = new JPanel ();
19     greenPanel.setLayout (new FlowLayout ());
20     greenPanel.add (greenField);
21     greenPanel.add (greenButton);
22
23     // Create the blue panel
24     JTextField blueField   = new JTextField (8);
25     JButton    blueButton  = new JButton (" Blue ");
26     JPanel     bluePanel   = new JPanel ();
27     bluePanel.setLayout (new FlowLayout ());
28     bluePanel.add (blueField);
29     bluePanel.add (blueButton);
30
31     // add panels to window
32     Container pane = getContentPane ();
33     pane.setBackground(Color.white);
34     pane.setLayout (new BorderLayout());
35     pane.add (redPanel, BorderLayout.NORTH);
36     pane.add (greenPanel, BorderLayout.CENTER);
37     pane.add (bluePanel, BorderLayout.SOUTH);
38
39     // pop up this window
40     show();
41   }
```

15.4.12 Panels

The five areas of a `BorderLayout` manager are often too few. Panels give us some control by allowing us to partition an area into subareas. We can set the layout manager for each panel and place that panel within another panel. For example, in Listing 15.15, we create three panels, set their layout managers to flow layout, and place a text field and button in each one. Next we set the display to the border layout manager and place the three panels within the display. The results are shown in Figure 15.18. This strategy allows us to treat each text field and button as a single unit. We can nest panel to any depth. Thus, we can have panels within panels within panels. Each panel has its own layout manager.

15.4.13 VGridBagLayout Class

The `GridBagLayout` allows a programmer to precisely place components within a window. We will use a simplified form of this layout manager called the `VGridBagLayout`. The left window in Figure 15.19 shows how buttons can be placed in an imaginary grid. Each time a button is placed we specify its row, column, width, height, and whether the component should completely fill its cell.

Figure 15.19 `VGridBagLayout` Buttons with All Fills on the Left

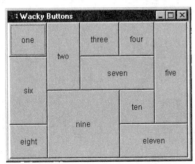
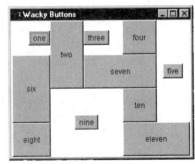

The code for creating Figure 15.19 is shown in Listing 15.16. Once we have set up the layout manager in Lines 14 and 15, we add components to our window. An example of adding a button is shown in the following two lines of code:

```
b = new Button ("five");
layout.add (b, pane,  layout.CENTER, 4, 0, 1, 3, true);
```

Listing 15.16 VGridBagLayout **Example**

```
1  import javax.swing.JButton;
2  import javax.swing.JFrame;
3  import java.awt.Color;
4  import java.awt.Container;
5  import vista.VGridBagLayout;
6
7  public class GridLayout extends JFrame
8  {
9    public GridLayout()
10   {
11     setTitle("Wacky Buttons");
12     setSize(300,240);
13     Container pane = getContentPane ();
14     VGridBagLayout layout = new VGridBagLayout();
15     pane.setLayout (layout);
16
17     JButton b;
18     b = new JButton ("one");
19     layout.add (b, pane,  layout.CENTER, 0, 0, 1, 1, true);
20     b = new JButton ("two");
21     layout.add (b, pane,  layout.CENTER, 1, 0, 1, 2, true);
22     b = new JButton ("three");
23     layout.add (b, pane,  layout.CENTER, 2, 0, 1, 1, true);
24     b = new JButton ("four");
25     layout.add (b, pane,  layout.CENTER, 3, 0, 1, 1, true);
26     b = new JButton ("five");
27     layout.add (b, pane,  layout.CENTER, 4, 0, 1, 3, true);
28     b = new JButton ("six");
29     layout.add (b, pane,  layout.CENTER, 0, 1, 1, 2, true);
30     b = new JButton ("seven");
31     layout.add (b, pane,  layout.CENTER, 2, 1, 2, 1, true);
32     b = new JButton ("eight");
33     layout.add (b, pane,  layout.CENTER, 0, 3, 1, 1, true);
34     b = new JButton ("nine");
35     layout.add (b, pane,  layout.CENTER, 1, 2, 2, 2, true);
36     b = new JButton ("ten");
37     layout.add (b, pane,  layout.CENTER, 3, 2, 1, 1, true);
38     b = new JButton ("eleven");
39     layout.add (b, pane,  layout.CENTER, 3, 3, 2, 1, true);
40
41     show();
42   }
43
44   public static void main(String args[])
45   {
46     GridLayout gridLayout = new GridLayout();
47   }
48 }
```

Notice that when we add a component to a window we are applying an `add` method to a layout object. This is different than is true for all other layout managers. In Java's layout managers the `add` method is applied to a frame's or applet's pane. (See Line 33 in Listing Listing 15.7). The discrepancy has arisen because the `add` method in the `VGridBag-Layout` manager is part of its class. The `add` method should really be packaged within the `Frame` class (more precisely the `Container` class).

The parameters of the `add` method shown above have the following meaning:

- b   Add the component named b to the window.
- pane   Add it to this window's pane.
- layout.CENTER   Center it within the cell. Other options are RIGHT and LEFT.
- 4   Place it in column 4—first column is column 0.
- 0   Place it in row 0—the first row.
- 1   It should be one cell wide.
- 3   It should be three cells high.
- true   Make it fill the entire cell.

The `add` method is overloaded. A quick look at Appendix: C on page 917 will show the signature for two methods that have default widths, heights, and fill values.

The right window in Figure 15.19 shows the impact of left alignment with no fill on the `three` button. Its call to `add` looks as follows:

```
b = new Button ("three");
layout.add (b, pane,  layout.LEFT, 2, 0, 1, 1, false);
```

WARNING: The Java `GridBagLayout` tries to size rows and columns based on how they are populated. Rows and columns may be given physical widths or heights of zero if Java determines they are not being used. Follow the rules below to prevent the disappearance of rows and columns:

- Each row should have at least one component that is one unit high. Buttons `one`, `seven`, `eight`, and `ten` fulfill this requirement.

- Each column should have at least one component that is one unit wide. Buttons `one`, `two`, `three`, `four`, and `five` fulfill this requirement.

15.4.14 Common Mistakes

Creating a GUI provides us with a lot to think about. It is easy to make mistakes. What follows are some things that can go wrong and what to do about them.

1. The frame does not show up.

   - A frame object was not created.

   - The show method was not executed.

2. GUI components do not show up in the frame or applet window.

   - The components were not added to the window's pane.

   - The show method was executed before the components were added to the window's pane.

3. The button or menu items are there but they do not do anything.

   - Its action listener is not registered (add listener method not executed).

4. There is a syntax error that says my interface class should be abstract.

   - Look at the next error message. Check all methods that are required by the interface. Make sure that each is correctly spelled and the parameters are correct.

5. There is a syntax error that says there is an incompatible type for the method that adds a listener to a component.

   - Look at the class header. Does it implement the correct listener?

SUPPLEMENTARY MATERIAL

15.5 Using Inner Classes with Buttons

In Section 14.5, page 677 we learned how to use adapters and inner classes to handle mouse events. By inheriting from an adapter we discovered that is was not necessary to implement all the methods within an interface. We could simply override the "do nothing" ones we inherited from an adapter.

The `ActionListener` does not have a corresponding `ActionAdapter`. The `ActionListener` has only one method; it is assumed it will always be implemented. Thus, we must always use a listener interface when working with buttons and menus.

In Listing 15.7 on page 702 we implemented a simple program which responds to `yes` and `no` buttons. An implementation of this program using inner classes is shown in Listing 15.17. (Bolded areas show places of change.) Notice that we have created an inner class for each button. We register these listener objects for each of these classes in Lines 13 and 18. For example, Line 13 tells the event system that when a button action event occurs for the `yes` button, execute the `actionPerformed` method found in an object of the class `YesHandler`.

In Listing 15.7, the `actionPerformed` method had to use an `if` statement to distinguish between `yes` and `no` button events. Because we have an action listener object for each button, we no longer need an `if` statement. Each `actionPerformed` method is registered with only one button.

Using inner classes is flexible. For example, we could have a single action handler class that is shared by many objects. This may reduce the need to write similar code in several `actionPerformed` methods. We may also select from several action handler objects dynamically. This would allow the action that a button performs to change.

Eliminating the need for a large `if` statement is a significant win for modular and easy-to-maintain code. However, the use of inner classes adds some complexity for small programs. Beginners may initially have problems managing the nested structures and responding to bracket mismatches.

Listing 15.17   Respond to a Yes or No Button—Inner Class Version

```
1  import ...
2
3  public class Message extends JFrame
4  {
5    ... see Listing 15.7
6
7    public Message()
8    {
9      ... see Listing 15.7
10
11     // set up "Yes" button
12     myYesButton = new JButton ("Yes");
13     myYesButton.addActionListener (new YesHandler());
14     pane.add (myYesButton);
15
16     // set up "No" button
17     myNoButton = new JButton ("No");
18     myNoButton.addActionListener (new NoHandler());
19     pane.add (myNoButton);
20
21     ... see Listing 15.7
22    }
23
24    public class YesHandler implements ActionListener
25    {
26      public void actionPerformed (ActionEvent e)
27      {
28        myResultLabel.setText("Yes");
29      }
30    }
31
32    public class NoHandler implements ActionListener
33    {
34      public void actionPerformed (ActionEvent e)
35      {
36        myResultLabel.setText("No");
37      }
38    }
39 }
```

15.6   GUIs with the AWT (Java 1.1)

For those of us caught in the world of Java 1.1, Listing 15.18 shows a rewrite of the Swing version of Listing 15.7 on page 702. Notice the absence of the J prefix for buttons, frames, and labels. In addition, notice they are all located within the AWT library (Lines 1, 4, and 6).

Listing 15.18 Respond to a Yes and No Button (Java 1.1)

```
1 import java.awt.Button;
2 import java.awt.Color;
3 import java.awt.FlowLayout;
4 import java.awt.Frame;
5 import java.awt.Graphics;
6 import java.awt.Label;
7 import java.awt.event.ActionEvent;
8 import java.awt.event.ActionListener;
9
10 public class Message extends Frame
11                      implements ActionListener
12 {
13   private       Button  myYesButton;
14   private       Button  myNoButton;
15   private       Label   myResultLabel;
16
17   public static void main(String args[])
18   {
19     Message message = new Message();
20   }
21
22   public Message()
23   {
24     // set up window
25     setLayout (new FlowLayout());
26     setBackground(Color.white);
27     setTitle("Maybe");
28     setSize(150, 75);
29
30     // set up "Yes" button
31     myYesButton = new Button ("Yes");
32     myYesButton.addActionListener (this);
33     add (myYesButton);
34
35     // set up "No" button
36     myNoButton = new Button ("No");
37     myNoButton.addActionListener (this);
38     add (myNoButton);
39
40     // set up result label
41     myResultLabel = new Label ("      ");
42     add (myResultLabel);
43
44     // pop up this window
45     show();
46   }
```

Listing 15.18 Respond to a Yes and No Button (Java 1.1)

```
47    public void actionPerformed (ActionEvent e)
48    {
49      if (myYesButton == e.getSource())
50        myResultLabel.setText("Yes");
51      else if (myNoButton == e.getSource())
52        myResultLabel.setText("No");
53    }
54 }
```

A more significant change is the absence of the container pane inside the `JFrame`. In Java 1.1 we add components directly a frame. See Lines 33, 38, and 42.

The Java 1.1 version of Listing 15.8 on page 705 is shown in Listing 15.19.

Listing 15.19 - Boxes and Ovals Code (Java 1.1)

```
1  import java.awt.Color;
2  import java.awt.Frame;
3  import java.awt.Graphics;
4  import java.awt.Menu;
5  import java.awt.MenuBar;
6  import java.awt.MenuItem;
7  import java.awt.event.ActionEvent;
8  import java.awt.event.ActionListener;
9
10 public class Message extends Frame implements ActionListener
11 {
12   private       MenuItem myBlueBoxMenuItem;
13   private       MenuItem myBlueOvalMenuItem;
14   private       MenuItem myRedBoxMenuItem;
15
16   public static void main(String args[])
17   {
18     Message message = new Message();
19   }
20
21   public Message()
22   {
23     // set up window
24     setBackground(Color.white);
25     setTitle("Draw");
26     resize(150, 120);
27
```

Listing 15.19 - Boxes and Ovals Code (Java 1.1)

```
28      // set up menu items
29      myBlueBoxMenuItem = new MenuItem ("Box");
30      myBlueBoxMenuItem.addActionListener (this);
31      myBlueOvalMenuItem = new MenuItem ("Oval");
32      myBlueOvalMenuItem.addActionListener (this);
33      myRedBoxMenuItem = new MenuItem ("Box");
34      myRedBoxMenuItem.addActionListener (this);
35
36      // set up menu bar
37      Menu    blueMenu = new Menu("Blue");
38      Menu    redMenu  = new Menu("Red");
39      blueMenu.add(myBlueBoxMenuItem);
40      blueMenu.add(myBlueOvalMenuItem);
41      redMenu.add(myRedBoxMenuItem);
42      MenuBar menuBar  = new MenuBar();
43      menuBar.add(blueMenu);
44      menuBar.add(redMenu);
45      setMenuBar(menuBar);
46
47      // pop up this window
48      show();
49    }

50    public void actionPerformed (ActionEvent e)
51    {
52      Graphics g = getGraphics();
53
54      // handle blue box menu selection
55      if (myBlueBoxMenuItem == e.getSource())
56      {
57        g.setColor (Color.blue);
58        g.fillRect (0, 50, 50, 50);
59      }
60      // handle blue oval menu selection
61      else if (myBlueOvalMenuItem == e.getSource())
62      {
63        g.setColor (Color.blue);
64        g.fillOval (50, 50, 50, 50);
65      }
66      // handle red box menu selection
67      else if (myRedBoxMenuItem == e.getSource())
68      {
69        g.setColor (Color.red);
70        g.fillRect (100, 50, 50, 50);
71      }
72    }
73 }
```

REFERENCE

15.7   Summary

In this chapter we learned how to create graphical user interfaces. We used the Model-View-Controller pattern to partition a program into classes that made the program easy to understand and modify. The *controller* is the user interface. The *model* simulates a mathematical or physical system. The *view* displays the state of the model.

A new window is created by extending the Frame class. The frame may need to be sized, titled, and have a layout manager assigned to it. Finally, a show operation must be applied to make the window visible. Window closing and other window events are handled by extending the WindowListener interface.

The basic step for adding a GUI component to a window is to create the component, add it to the window, implement the appropriate listener, write the appropriate callback methods, and register the listener.

Buttons and menus require the implementation of the ActionListener. The callback method of interest is named actionPerformed. Menus require the creation of three kinds of objects: menu items, menus, and menu bars.

Active checkboxes require that the ItemListener interface be implemented. The callback method is named itemStateChanged.

Keyboard captures are possible by implementing the KeyListener interface. We must write the keyPressed method to capture key events.

15.8   Bibliography

- Gamma, Erich, Richard Helm, Ralph Johnson, and John Fusillades. 1995 *Design Patterns: Elements of Reusable Object-Oriented Software*. Reading, MA: Addison Wesley.

SUPPLEMENTARY MATERIAL

PROGRAM LISTINGS
15.9   Wages Projection Program

Listing 15.20 `WagesController` Class

```
1  //*************************************************************
2  //
3  // title:   WagesController
4  //
5  // This program computes future earnings of college and
6  // high school graduates.  Projections are based on starting
7  // salaries, expected raises, and college loans.
8  //
9  // The program is organized around the observer pattern.
10 //    WagesController:  The user interface (Controller)
11 //    WagesModel:        The economic model that computes
12 //                       wages (Subject, Model)
13 //    EarningsObserver: Displays a graph comparing earnings
14 //
15 //*************************************************************
16
17 import javax.swing.JButton;
18 import javax.swing.JFrame;
19 import javax.swing.JLabel;
20 import javax.swing.JTextField;
21 import java.awt.Color;
22 import java.awt.Component;
23 import java.awt.Container;
24 import java.awt.Font;
25 import java.awt.event.ActionEvent;
26 import java.awt.event.ActionListener;
27 import java.awt.event.WindowEvent;
28 import java.awt.event.WindowListener;
29 import vista.VGridBagLayout;
30 import vista.VTextFieldUtilities;
31
```

Listing 15.20 `WagesController` Class

```
32 public class WagesController extends JFrame
33         implements ActionListener, WindowListener
34 {
35   public static final  Color HIGH_SCHOOL_COLOR =
36                        new Color (35, 142, 35);
37   public static final  Color COLLEGE_COLOR     = Color.red;
38
39   private       WagesModel        myModel;
40
41   private       JButton           myComputeButton;
42   private       JTextField        myPeriod;
43
44   private       JTextField        myCollegeWage;
45   private       JTextField        myCollegeRaises;
46   private       JTextField        myCollegeLoan;
47   private       JTextField        myInterestRate;
48
49   private       JTextField        myHighSchoolWage;
50   private       JTextField        myHighSchoolRaises;
51
52   //---------- WagesController -------------------------------
53   // pre:  none
54   // post: a wages interface created.
55
56   public WagesController ()
57   {
58     myModel = new WagesModel();
59     setWindow();
60     addGUI();
61     makeComputations();
62     addWindowListener(this);
63     show();
64   }
65
66   //---------- actionPerformed -------------------------------
67   // pre:  called automatically when compute button pressed
68   // post: computer new earnings and update the earnings graph
69
70   public void actionPerformed (ActionEvent e)
71   {
72     makeComputations();
73   }
74
```

Listing 15.20 `WagesController` Class

```
75    //---------- add -------------------------------------
76    //    component  - component to be added
77    //    alignment  - position constraint of the component in
78    //                 its grid cell (LEFT, CENTER, or RIGHT justify)
79    //    x          - column the component is inserted within
80    //    y          - row the component is inserted within
81    //    width      - number of cells wide component gets
82    //    height     - number of cells high component gets
83    //
84    // pre:  layout manager has been set to VGridBagLayout
85    // post: the component has been added to this frame
86    // note: this method is not necessary.  It was added to
87    //       make adding components to a window with a
88    //       VGridBagLayout manager look the same as it does
89    //       for other layout managers.  The calls to this method
90    //       may be replaced with the following:
91    //         layout.add (myComputeButton, this, layout.CENTER,
92    //                     0, 0, 4, 1);
93
94    private void add (Component component, int alignment,
95               int x, int y, int width, int height)
96    {
97      Container pane = getContentPane ();
98      VGridBagLayout layout =(VGridBagLayout)(pane.getLayout ());
99      layout.add(component,pane, alignment, x, y, width, height);
100   }
101
102   //---------- addGUI ----------------------------------------
103   // pre:  makeWindows has been called
104   // post: all the GUI components added to this window
105
106   private void addGUI ()
107   {
108     Container pane = getContentPane ();
109     VGridBagLayout layout = new VGridBagLayout();
110     pane.setLayout(layout);
111     Font bold  = new Font ("DialogInput", Font.BOLD, 18);
112
113     // add compute button and span in years text field
114     myComputeButton = new JButton("Compute");
115     myComputeButton.addActionListener (this);
116     add (myComputeButton, layout.CENTER, 0, 0, 4, 1);
117     JLabel label = new JLabel ("Span in years");
118     add (label, layout.RIGHT, 0, 1, 2, 1);
119     myPeriod = new JTextField("30", 3);
120     add (myPeriod, layout.LEFT, 2, 1, 2, 1);
121
```

Listing 15.20 WagesController **Class**

```
122        // add labels and fields for college graduate earnings
123        label = new JLabel ("College");
124        label.setFont(bold);
125        label.setForeground(COLLEGE_COLOR);
126        add (label, layout.CENTER, 0, 2, 2, 1);
127        label = new JLabel ("Starting Wage");
128        add (label, layout.RIGHT, 0, 3, 1, 1);
129        myCollegeWage = new JTextField("38000", 7);
130        add (myCollegeWage, layout.LEFT, 1, 3, 1, 1);
131        label = new JLabel ("Raises %");
132        add (label, layout.RIGHT, 0, 4, 1, 1);
133        myCollegeRaises = new JTextField("5", 3);
134        add (myCollegeRaises, layout.LEFT, 1, 4, 1, 1);
135        label = new JLabel ("Loan");
136        add (label, layout.RIGHT, 0, 5, 1, 1);
137        myCollegeLoan = new JTextField("17000", 7);
138        add (myCollegeLoan, layout.LEFT, 1, 5, 1, 1);
139        label = new JLabel ("Interest %");
140        add (label, layout.RIGHT, 0, 6, 1, 1);
141        myInterestRate = new JTextField("8", 3);
142        add (myInterestRate, layout.LEFT, 1, 6, 1, 1);
143
144        // add labels and fields for high school graduate earnings
145        label = new JLabel ("High School");
146        label.setFont(bold);
147        label.setForeground(HIGH_SCHOOL_COLOR);
148        add (label, layout.CENTER, 2, 2, 2, 1);
149        label = new JLabel ("Starting Wage");
150        add (label, layout.RIGHT, 2, 3, 1, 1);
151        myHighSchoolWage = new JTextField("18000", 7);
152        add (myHighSchoolWage, layout.LEFT, 3, 3, 1, 1);
153        label = new JLabel ("Raises %");
154        add (label, layout.RIGHT, 2, 4, 1, 1);
155        myHighSchoolRaises = new JTextField("5", 3);
156        add (myHighSchoolRaises, layout.LEFT, 3, 4, 1, 1);
157    }
158
159  //---------- main ----------------------------------------
160  // pre:  execution begins here
161  // post: this controller window is created and displayed
162
163  public static void main (String args[])
164  {
165     WagesController controller = new WagesController();
166  }
167
```

Listing 15.20 `WagesController` Class

```
168     //---------- makeComputations --------------------------
169     // pre:  the instance variable myModel has been created
170     //       addGUI has been called
171     // Update the "Wages" model with current settings from the
172     // text fields.  Then recompute salaries and earnings.  If
173     // any of the text fields are invalid, do not recompute.
174
175     private void makeComputations ()
176     {
177       int period = (VTextFieldUtilities.getInt(myPeriod));
178       if (period < 4) {
179         myPeriod.setText("***");
180         return;
181       }
182       myModel.setPeriod              (period);
183       myModel.setCollegeWage
184         (VTextFieldUtilities.getDouble(myCollegeWage));
185       myModel.setCollegeRaises
186         (VTextFieldUtilities.getDouble(myCollegeRaises)/ 100.0);
187       myModel.setCollegeLoan
188         (VTextFieldUtilities.getDouble(myCollegeLoan));
189       myModel.setInterestRate
190         (VTextFieldUtilities.getDouble(myInterestRate) / 100.0);
191       myModel.setHighSchoolWage
192         (VTextFieldUtilities.getDouble(myHighSchoolWage));
193       myModel.setHighSchoolRaises (VTextFieldUtilities.
194         getDouble(myHighSchoolRaises)/100.0);
195       myModel.compute();
196     }
197
198     //---------- setWindow -------------------------------------
199     // pre:  none
200     // post: the physical characteristics of this window are set
201
202     private void setWindow ()
203     {
204       setSize(400,250);
205       setLocation(380, 200);
206       setTitle("Wages");
207       setBackground (Color.white);
208     }
209
```

Listing 15.20 WagesController Class

```
210    //---------- windowClosing -----------------------------
211    // pre:   called automatically when window closing icon
212    //        selected
213    // post: this application is exited
214
215    public void windowClosing(WindowEvent event)
216    {
217      System.exit(0);
218    }
219
220    // window listener methods that do nothing
221    public void windowOpened(WindowEvent event){;}
222    public void windowClosed(WindowEvent event){;}
223    public void windowIconified(WindowEvent event){;}
224    public void windowDeiconified(WindowEvent event){;}
225    public void windowActivated(WindowEvent event){;}
226    public void windowDeactivated(WindowEvent event){;}
227 }
```

Listing 15.21 `WagesModel` Class

```
1 //****************************************************************
2 //
3 // title:    WagesModel
4 // update:   simplified and reorganized
5 //
6 // The economic model that computes wages.
7 //
8 //****************************************************************
9
10 import java.util.Vector;
11
12 public class WagesModel
13 {
14    // the observer
15    private EarningsObserver myEarningsObserver;
16
17    // college grad numbers
18    private double myCollegeWage;        // starting wages
19    private double myCollegeRaises;      // year percent / 100 raises
20    private double myCollegeLoan;        // amount of college loans
21    private double myInterestRate;       // interest rate on loans
22
23    // high school grad number
24    private double myHighSchoolWage;     // starting wages
25    private double myHighSchoolRaises;
26
27    // other numbers
28    private int    myPeriod;             // active wage earning period
29    private int    myCrossOver;          // period college earner
30                                         // exceed high school
31    // salary and earning tables
32    private double myCollegeSalaries[];     // yearly salaries
33    private double myCollegeEarnings[];     // total earnings
34    private double myHighSchoolSalaries[];  // yearly salaries
35    private double myHighSchoolEarnings[];  // total earnings
36
```

Listing 15.21 `WagesModel` Class

```
37    //---------- WagesModel -------------------------------------
38    //
39    // pre:  none
40    // post: A default wage model is constructed
41
42    public WagesModel ()
43    {
44      myCollegeWage        = 38000;
45      myCollegeRaises      = 0.05;
46      myCollegeLoan        = 17000;
47      myInterestRate       = 0.08;
48
49      myHighSchoolWage     = 18000;
50      myHighSchoolRaises   = 0.05;
51
52      myPeriod             = 30;
53      myCrossOver          = Integer.MAX_VALUE;
54
55      myEarningsObserver = new EarningsObserver ();
56    }
57
58    //---------- compute ---------------------------------------
59    //
60    // pre:  none
61    // post: Salaries and total wages are computed for an period
62    //        of times specified by the period.
63    //        Salaries and earnings are after taxes (they are
64    //        take home).
65
66    public void compute()
67    {
68      computeCollege();
69      computeHighSchool();
70      myEarningsObserver.update(this);
71    }
72
```

Listing 15.21 `WagesModel` Class

```
73   //---------- computeCollege -------------------------------
74   //
75   // internal use only - compute college salaries and earnings
76   private void computeCollege()
77   {
78     // handle the 4 years in college
79     myCollegeSalaries = new double[myPeriod + 1];
80     myCollegeEarnings = new double[myPeriod + 1];
81     for (int i=0; i<=4; i++) {
82       myCollegeSalaries[i] = 0.0;
83       myCollegeEarnings[i] = 0.0;
84     }
85
86     // handle the years after college
87     double wage     = myCollegeWage;
88     for (int i=5; i<=myPeriod; i++) {
89      myCollegeSalaries[i] = takeHome(wage, i) - loanPayment(i);
90       myCollegeEarnings[i] = myCollegeEarnings[i-1] +
91                               myCollegeSalaries[i];
92       wage = wage + wage * myCollegeRaises;
93     }
94   }
95
96   //---------- computeHighSchool ----------------------------
97   //
98   // internal use only - compute high school salaries & earnings
99   private void computeHighSchool()
100  {
101    // handle year zero
102    myCrossOver         = Integer.MAX_VALUE;
103    myHighSchoolSalaries = new double[myPeriod + 1];
104    myHighSchoolEarnings = new double[myPeriod + 1];
105    double wage         = myHighSchoolWage;
106    myHighSchoolSalaries[0] = 0;
107    myHighSchoolEarnings[0] = 0;
108
109    // handle the remaining years
110    for (int i=1; i<=myPeriod; i++) {
111      myHighSchoolSalaries[i] = takeHome(wage, i);
112      myHighSchoolEarnings[i] = myHighSchoolEarnings[i-1] +
113                                myHighSchoolSalaries[i];
114      if (myCrossOver == Integer.MAX_VALUE &
115          myCollegeEarnings[i] > myHighSchoolEarnings[i])
116        myCrossOver = i;
117      wage = wage + wage * myHighSchoolRaises;
118    }
119  }
120
```

Listing 15.21 `WagesModel` Class

```
121    //---------- getCollegeSalaries ---------------------------
122    //
123    // pre:  none
124    // post: Yearly salaries (after taxes) are returned for a
125    //       given period of time.
126
127    public double[] getCollegeSalaries()
128    {
129      return myCollegeSalaries;
130    }
131
132    //---------- getCollegeEarnings ---------------------------
133    //
134    // pre:  none
135    // post: Accumulated earnings (after taxes) are returned for
136    //       a given period of time.
137
138    public double[] getCollegeEarnings()
139    {
140      return myCollegeEarnings;
141    }
142
143    //---------- getHighSchoolSalaries ----------------------
144    //
145    // pre:  none
146    // post: Yearly salaries (after taxes) are returned for a
147    //       given period of time.
148
149    public double[] getHighSchoolSalaries()
150    {
151      return myHighSchoolSalaries;
152    }
153
154    //---------- getHighSchoolEarnings ----------------------
155    //
156    // pre:  none
157    // post: Accumulated earnings (after taxes) are returned for
158    //       a given period of time.
159
160    public double[] getHighSchoolEarnings()
161    {
162      return myHighSchoolEarnings;
163    }
164
```

Listing 15.21 `WagesModel` Class

```
165   //--------- getCrossOver --------------------------------
166   //
167   // pre:  none
168   // post: The year that college earnings overtake high school
169   //       earnings is returned.
170
171   public int getCrossOver()
172   {
173     return myCrossOver;
174   }
175
176   //--------- getPeriod ---------------------------------
177   //
178   // pre:  none
179   // post: The number of years over which the model is run is
180   //       returned.
181
182   public int getPeriod()
183   {
184     return myPeriod;
185   }
186
187   //--------- loanPayment --------------------------------
188   //
189   // internal use only - The yearly payment for a loan is
190   // returned. It is assumed that loan will be paid in 10 years
191
192   private double loanPayment(int year)
193   {
194     if (year > 3 & year <= 13) {
195       double ratePlus1      = myInterestRate / 12 + 1.0;
196       double ratePlus1ToM  = Math.pow (ratePlus1, 10.0 * 12.0);
197       double monthlyPayment = myCollegeLoan * myInterestRate
198                 / 12.0 * ratePlus1ToM / (ratePlus1ToM - 1.0);
199       return monthlyPayment * 12.0;
200     }
201     else
202       return 0;
203   }
204
```

Listing 15.21 `WagesModel` Class

```
205    //---------- setCollegeLoan ---------------------------------
206    //
207    // pre:  amount >= 0.0
208    // post: The loan amount is set for this model.
209
210    public void setCollegeLoan (double amount)
211    {
212      myCollegeLoan = amount;
213    }
214
215    //---------- setCollegeWage ---------------------------------
216    //
217    // pre:  wage >= 0.0
218    // post: The expected wage upon college graduation is set.
219
220    public void setCollegeWage (double wage)
221    {
222      myCollegeWage = wage;
223    }
224
225    //---------- setCollegeRaises ---------------------------------
226    //
227    // pre:  rate >= 0.0
228    // post: The fractional yearly increase in wages is set.
229
230    public void setCollegeRaises (double rate)
231    {
232      myCollegeRaises = rate;
233    }
234
235    //---------- setInterestRate ---------------------------------
236    //
237    // pre:  rate >= 0.0
238    // post: The fractional interest of college loans is set.
239
240    public void setInterestRate (double rate)
241    {
242      myInterestRate = rate;
243    }
244
245
```

Listing 15.21 `WagesModel` Class

```
246   //---------- setHighSchoolWage ---------------------------
247   //
248   // pre:  wage >= 0.0
249   // post: The expected wage upon high school graduation is
250   //       set.
251
252   public void setHighSchoolWage (double wage)
253   {
254     myHighSchoolWage = wage;
255   }
256
257   //---------- setHighSchoolRaises --------------------------
258   //
259   // pre:  rate >= 0.0
260   // post: The percent yearly increase in wages is set.
261
262   public void setHighSchoolRaises (double rate)
263   {
264     myHighSchoolRaises = rate;
265   }
266
267   //---------- setPeriod ------------------------------------
268   //
269   // pre:  time >= 4
270   // post: The period over which this model is computer is set.
271
272   public void setPeriod (int time)
273   {
274     myPeriod = time;
275   }
276
```

Listing 15.21 `WagesModel` Class

```
277    //---------- takeHome -----------------------------
278    //
279    // internal use only - given a wage, the takehome salary is
280    //    returned.  The tax brackets are adjusted over time
281    //    to match inflation.
282
283    private double takeHome (double wage, int year)
284    {
285      double FICA        = wage * 0.0765;
286      double state       = wage * 0.08;
287      double temp        = FICA + state;
288
289      double inflation   =    1.03;
290      double adjustment = Math.pow(inflation, year);
291      double bracket1    =    221.00 * adjustment;
292      double bracket2    =   2179.00 * adjustment;
293      double bracket3    =   4625.00 * adjustment;
294      double bracket4    =  10513.00 * adjustment;
295      double bracket5    =  22713.00 * adjustment;
296
297      // 0% bracket
298      double fed = 0.0;
299      if (wage < bracket1)
300        return (wage - FICA - state - fed);
301
302      // 15% bracket
303      if (wage < bracket2) {
304        fed = fed + (wage - bracket1) * 0.15;
305        return wage - FICA - state - fed;
306      }
307
308      // 28% bracket
309      fed = fed + (bracket2 - bracket1) * 0.15;
310      if (wage < bracket3) {
311        fed = fed + (wage - bracket2) * 0.28;
312        return wage - FICA - state - fed;
313      }
314
315      // 31% bracket
316      fed = fed + (bracket3 - bracket2) * 0.28;
317      if (wage < bracket4) {
318        fed = fed + (wage - bracket3) * 0.31;
319        return wage - FICA - state - fed;
320      }
321
```

Listing 15.21 WagesModel Class

```
322      // 36% bracket
323      fed = fed + (bracket4 - bracket3) * 0.31;
324      if (wage < bracket5) {
325        fed = fed + (wage - bracket4) * 0.36;
326        return wage - FICA - state - fed;
327      }
328
329      // 39% bracket
330      fed = fed + (bracket5 - bracket4) * 0.36;
331      fed = fed + (wage - bracket5) * 0.39;
332      return wage - FICA - state - fed;
333    }
334
335    //---------- toString -------------------------------------
336    //
337    // pre:  none
338    // post: string representation of this wage model returned.
339
340    public String toString()
341    {
342      String s = "";
343      for (int i=0; i<myPeriod; i++)
344       s = s + Double.toString(myCollegeSalaries[i])    + "  " +
345               Double.toString(myCollegeEarnings[i])    + "  " +
346               Double.toString(myHighSchoolSalaries[i]) + "  " +
347               Double.toString(myHighSchoolEarnings[i]) + "\n";
348      return s;
349    }
350 }
```

Listing 15.22 EarningsObserver Class

```
 1  //**************************************************************
 2  //
 3  // title:   EarningsObserver
 4  //
 5  // A "Wages" observer that graphs accumulated college earnings
 6  // versus high school earnings.
 7  //
 8  //**************************************************************
 9
10  import javax.swing.JFrame;
11  import java.awt.Color;
12  import java.awt.Dimension;
13  import java.awt.FlowLayout;
14  import java.awt.Font;
15  import java.awt.Graphics;
16  import java.awt.event.WindowEvent;
17  import java.awt.event.WindowListener;
18
19  public class EarningsObserver extends Frame
20                                     implements WindowListener
21  {
22    private double myCollegeEarnings[];
23    private double myHighSchoolEarnings[];
24    private int    myPeriod;
25
26    private final  int OFFSET = 15;  // offset of graph from top
27                                     //    and bottom
28
29    //---------- EarningsObserver ----------------------------
30    //
31    // pre:  none
32    // post: A new earnings graphic is created based on the
33    //       current wages model.
34
35    public EarningsObserver()
36    {
37      setState();
38
39      // set up this window
40      addWindowListener(this);
41      setSize(400,300);
42      setTitle("Earnings Graph");
43      setBackground (Color.white);
44      setLocation(20,20);
45      show();
46    }
47
```

Listing 15.22 EarningsObserver Class

```
48    //---------- setState -------------------------------------
49    // initialize earnings state to some bogus value so paint
50    // will not fail.  Update will provide the appropriate
51    // state values when called
52    private void setState ()
53    {
54      myCollegeEarnings     = new double[2];
55      myCollegeEarnings[0] = 0.0;
56      myCollegeEarnings[1] = 10000.0;
57
58      myHighSchoolEarnings    = new double[2];
59      myHighSchoolEarnings[0] = 0.0;
60      myHighSchoolEarnings[1] = 10000.0;
61
62      myPeriod = 1;
63    }
64
65    //---------- paint ----------------------------------------
66    //
67    // pre:  none
68    // post: This graph is drawn
69
70    public void paint (Graphics g)
71    {
72      // compute the x and y scales
73      Dimension size = getSize();
74      double xScale = size.width / myPeriod;
75
76      double maxY    = 0.0;
77      if (myCollegeEarnings    [myPeriod] >
78          myHighSchoolEarnings[myPeriod])
79        maxY = myCollegeEarnings[myPeriod];
80      else
81        maxY = myHighSchoolEarnings[myPeriod - 1];
82      double yScale = (size.height - 2 * OFFSET) / maxY;
83
84      // graph earnings
85      g.setColor(WagesController.COLLEGE_COLOR);
86      paintLine(myCollegeEarnings, xScale, yScale, g);
87
88      g.setColor(WagesController.HIGH_SCHOOL_COLOR);
89      paintLine(myHighSchoolEarnings, xScale, yScale, g);
90
91      paintLabels (xScale, yScale, g);
92    }
93
```

Listing 15.22 EarningsObserver Class

```
94    //---------- paintLabels -----------------------------------
95    //
96    // internal use only - draw this graph's labels and tick
97    //    marks.
98    private void paintLabels (double xScale, double yScale,
99                              Graphics g)
100   {
101      Dimension size = getSize();
102
103      // paint legend
104      Font f = new Font ("DialogInput", Font.BOLD, 18);
105      g.setFont(f);
106      g.setColor (WagesController.COLLEGE_COLOR);
107      g.drawString ("College Graduate", 60, 60);
108      g.setColor (WagesController.HIGH_SCHOOL_COLOR);
109      g.drawString ("High School Graduate", 60, 90);
110      g.setColor (Color.black);
111
112      // paint x axis labels
113      f = new Font ("DialogInput", Font.PLAIN, 12);
114      g.setFont(f);
115      for (int i=0; i<=myPeriod; i++)
116      {
117        int x = (int)(xScale * i);
118        if (i % 5 != 0)
119          g.drawLine (x, size.height - 10, x, size.height);
120        else
121        {
122          g.drawLine (x, size.height - 20, x, size.height);
123          g.drawString (Integer.toString(i),
124                        x - 6, size.height - 22);
125        }
126      }
127
128      // paint y axis labels
129      int i = 0;
130      for (int yTick = size.height - OFFSET; yTick > 0;
131              yTick -= (int)(yScale * 50000.0))
132      {
133        if (i%2 != 0 | i == 0)
134          g.drawLine (0, yTick, 10, yTick);
135        else {
136          g.drawLine   (0, yTick, 15, yTick);
137          g.drawString (Integer.toString (i * 50) + "K",
138                  22, yTick + 5);
139        }
140        i++;
141      }
142   }
```

Listing 15.22 `EarningsObserver` Class

```
143    //---------- paintLine ------------------------------
144    //
145    // internal use - plot one of this graph's earnings lines.
146    private void paintLine(double line[], double xScale,
147                           double yScale, Graphics g)
148    {
149      Dimension size = getSize();
150
151      for (int i = 1; i <= myPeriod; i++)
152      {
153        int leftX = (int)((i - 1) * xScale);
154        int leftY = size.height-OFFSET-(int)(line[i-1]*yScale);
155        int rightX = (int)(i * xScale);
156        int rightY = size.height-OFFSET-(int)(line[i]*yScale);
157        g.drawLine (leftX, leftY, rightX, rightY);
158      }
159    }
160
161    //---------- update ------------------------------------
162    //
163    // pre:  none
164    // post: Current values for college and high school earnings
165    //       are obtained from the wages model and this graph is
166    //       redrawn
167    public void update(WagesModel model)
168    {
169      myCollegeEarnings    = model.getCollegeEarnings();
170      myHighSchoolEarnings = model.getHighSchoolEarnings();
171      myPeriod             = model.getPeriod();
172      repaint();
173    }
174
175    //---------- windowClosing ------------------------------
176    // pre:  called when window closing icon selected
177    // post: this window is removed
178    public void windowClosing(WindowEvent event)
179    {
180      dispose();
181    }
182
183    // window listener methods that do nothing
184    public void windowOpened(WindowEvent event){;}
185    public void windowClosed(WindowEvent event){;}
186    public void windowIconified(WindowEvent event){;}
187    public void windowDeiconified(WindowEvent event){;}
188    public void windowActivated(WindowEvent event){;}
189    public void windowDeactivated(WindowEvent event){;}
190 }
```

PROBLEM SETS

15.10 Exercises

Earnings Projections—Section 15.2

1   What is the impact on a college graduate's earnings for the following situations? When do the college and high school earnings cross?

   a.   College debt doubles.

   b.   12% interest rate.

   c.   College starting salary of $28,000.

   d.   College pay raises of 7%.

GUI Components—Section 15.4

2   Do a line-by-line comparison of the code for creating a window using an Applet (Listing 15.3 on page 698) and using a Frame (Listing 15.6 on page 700). List lines side-by-side in the programs that do similar things and describe how the differ.

3   Look at the program in Listing 15.6 on page 700. The program will compile and run with the following lines missing: 12, 17, 18, 19, 20, 21, and 31. Describe the impact on program execution with each of these lines removed.

4   Look at the program in Listing 15.6 on page 700. The program has syntax errors if the following lines are missing: 8 and 34. What are the syntax errors for each missing line and why do they occur. (The syntax error for 8 is difficult to explain.)

5   Look at the program in Listing 15.7. The program will compile and run with the following lines missing: 32 and 33. Describe the impact of program execution with these lines removed.

6   Look at the program in Listing 15.7. The program will compile with Line 31 missing. However, when it runs it will generate a null-pointer exception. Why?

15.11 Projects

Earnings Projections—Section 15.2

7 The `WagesModel` class provides a `getCrossOver` method that returns the number of years that it takes for a college graduate's earnings to overtake a high school graduate's earnings. Add a second observer to the wages program that displays this value in its own window (implement the `windowClosing` callback method). Use the MVC pattern.

MVC Pattern—Section 15.3

8 Write a program that displays a Fahrenheit temperature in degrees Fahrenheit and Celsius using the MVC pattern. The model's state should be the Fahrenheit temperature. One view should display the temperature in Fahrenheit and a second view in Celsius. The controller should allow a user to change the temperature stored in the model.

```
celsius = (fahrenheit - 32) * 5 / 9
```

9 The chaos program in Listing 4.5 on page 132 does not follow the MVC pattern faithfully. Reimplement it so that it does.

10 Add a second view to the program in exercise 9 that displays the results of each generation in a table format.

11 The stock program in Chapter 9 is a primary candidate for a MVC organization. Create views that display graphs that have the following views:
- **a.** rough vs. smoothed
- **b.** stock prices
- **c.** Standard and Poor's 500
- **d.** NASDAQ
- **e.** Absolute values vs. changes

12 Use the MVC pattern to implement the program in exercise 25 of Chapter 5.

GUI Components—Section 15.4

13 Add a "maybe" button to the program in Listing 15.7.

14 Add a "Green" menu with "oval" and "box" menu options to the program in Listing 15.8.

15 (Long assignment.) Create a four-function calculator using buttons and a text field for display. It should have a single button for each digit, each function, the equal key, and clear key. Use the MVC pattern. Some of the operations included in the model are:

- appendDigit: Append a digit to the end of an input buffer by multiplying the buffer by 10 and adding the digit.
- add: Add the input buffer to the accumulator and reset the input buffer to zero.
- clear: Zero the accumulator and input buffer.

  a. Implement it for integer arithmetic only.

  b. Implement it for real arithmetic.

16 Implement a typing tutor. It should display a random letter on the screen much like the one that appears in Figure 15.14. The user must then type the letter. The process repeats. After a predetermined number of interactions, the program displays the number of correct key presses and elapsed time (Section 7.7). Include a menu that allows a user to select how many letters are displayed for each round.

17 Create a word processing program. Select from the following options. (a. is mandatory).

  a. Pop up a frame with a text area in it. See Chapter 10.

  b. Implement a "file" menu with a quit option.

  c. Implement a "font" menu for monospaced, sans serif, and serif fonts. Add a menu for BOLD, ITALIC, and PLAIN font options. Add a menu for 10, 12, 14, 18, 24, 36, 72-point font sizes. Font changes affect the entire text. In other words, only one font can be used at a time. See Chapter 10.

  d. Implement a "search" menu with a "find-" menu item. It should pop up a frame with a text field for the search string, a cancel button, and a search button. Pressing the search button should move the cursor to the first occurrence of the search string in the text area. See Chapter 10.

  e. Add a search and replace menu item to the previous part. See Chapter 10.

  f. Add a checkbox to the previous part that modifies the search so that it is not case-sensitive. See Chapter 10.

  g. Implement a file menu with an "open" and "save" menu item. They should bring up file dialog boxes that allow us to load and save the text area to and from a file.

16 Inheritance

Persistent Stores for Graphics Objects

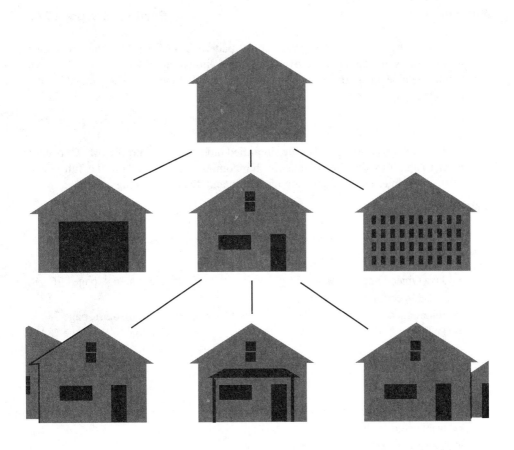

16.1   Objectives

Concepts   Section 16.2, page 757

We begin by revisiting a program for drawing a graphics image much like the one in Chapter 7. In this reincarnation, we use inheritance. Each kind of object class inherits from a shape class. We take advantage of polymorphism to store all the drawing shapes within a list. We use dynamic binding to paint each shape without knowing what specific kind of shape we have. One of the payoffs arrives when we use persistent data storage to save the drawing in a file. This file is then read in a type-safe manner and displayed.

Patterns   Section 16.3, page 772

We revisit the simplified composite object pattern from Chapter 7 and investigate some of its shortcomings. We overcome these limitations by using the full-blown composite object pattern. Polymorphism and dynamic binding are key to making the composite pattern work.

Section 16.7, page 789

In an optional section we revisit the simplified model-view-controller (MVC) pattern from Chapter 15. We investigate its shortcomings and show how the full-blown MVC overcomes them. Again, polymorphism and dynamic binding are key.

Java Skills

We address the Java language skills required to effectively implement and use inheritance.

- Java ObjectOutputStream   Section 16.4, page 776
- Java ObjectInputStream
- Inheritance   Section 16.5.1, page 780
- Packages   Section 16.5.3, page 784
- Protected   Section 16.5.4, page 786
- Design considerations   Section 16.6, page 786

Abilities

- Save and restore persistent information.
- Implement inheritance.
- Use polymorphism and dynamic binding.

CONCEPTS

16.2   Inheritance

16.2.1   Reuse

The Doodle program (Chapter 14) has several limitations. One limitation is that we can only draw lines, we cannot manipulate the geometric shapes that comprise a drawing, and another is that we cannot save and load drawings from files. If we want to save a drawing in a file, we have two major choices. One approach is to save each of the geometric shapes that comprise an image. For example, the image in Figure 16.1 is composed of rectangles, ovals, and polygons. Each one of the shapes can be saved to disk and then reloaded later. Some drawing tools call this an *object representation* of an image. In this chapter we will implement this technique.

Figure 16.1 A Background Image

The second method is to save the image as pixels. This is the technique used in many image file formats and by paint programs. However, the individuality of shapes that comprise the image are lost. For example, we cannot easily select the oval and rectangle objects that comprise the tree and move them. Many tools call this representation a *bitmap* image.

Listing 16.1 The Shape class

```
1  //**********************************************************
2  //
3  // title:    Shape
4  //
5  // This is the abstract Shape class that is inherited by all
6  // components.  The Shape class is never instantiated directly.
7  //
8  //**********************************************************
9
10 import java.awt.Color;
11 import java.awt.Graphics;
12 import java.io.Serializable;
13
14 public abstract class Shape implements Serializable
15 {
16   Color  myColor;
17
18   //---------- add -----------------------------------------
19   // pre:  none
20   // post: do nothing
21   // overridden by the composite component.
22   public void add (Shape thing)
23   {
24   }
25
26   //---------- setColor ------------------------------------
27   //
28   // pre:  none.
29   // post: the color of this component is changed to c.
30   public void setColor (Color c)
31   {
32     myColor = c;
33   }
34
35   //---------- paint ---------------------------------------
36   // pre:  none.
37   // post: do nothing.
38   // Each component must override this method.
39   public abstract void paint (Graphics g);
40 }
```

Listing 16.2 The Box class

```
1  //**********************************************************
2  //
3  // title:    Box
4  //
5  // This component is a rectangle.
6  //
7  //**********************************************************
8
9  import java.awt.Color;
10 import java.awt.Graphics;
11 import java.io.Serializable;
12
13 public class Box extends Shape implements Serializable
14 {
15    int    myX;
16    int    myY;
17    int    myWidth;
18    int    myHeight;
19
20    //--------- Box -------------------------------------------
21    //
22    // pre:  x, y, width, and height are positive.
23    // post: a rectangle component is created
24    public Box (int x, int y, int width, int height,
25                Color color)
26    {
27      myX      = x;
28      myY      = y;
29      myWidth  = width;
30      myHeight = height;
31      myColor  = color;
32    }
33
34    //--------- paint -----------------------------------------
35    //
36    // pre:  none.
37    // post: this box is painted on graphics context g
38    public void paint (Graphics g)
39    {
40      g.setColor(myColor);
41      g.fillRect(myX, myY, myWidth, myHeight);
42    }
43 }
```

In this chapter we use the first approach. We will use inheritance to make the process of saving shapes to disk easier. One of the benefits of inheritance is that it allows classes to share instance variables and methods. Thus, it is possible to build new classes by expanding classes that have been created. However, the properties of inheritance we will benefit from most are polymorphism and dynamic binding.

All shapes that comprise our drawings may have several characteristic in common: color, location, and size. We will focus on one common characteristic—color—and create a class named Shape that has a single instance variable for color and a method to change it (Listing 16.1). All graphics components such as boxes, ovals, and triangles will inherit the setColor method from Shape.

Line 16 of Listing 16.1 defines the common color instance variable. Lines 30 through 33 define a setColor method, which can be used to modify it. These are both available to all classes that inherit the Shape class. Thus, we need to write the code for color in only one place. One advantage is the economy of reuse. Because we write the code only once, we save time. A second advantage is reliability. We only need to assure that one implementation of the code is correct.

Lines 39 through 41 define a paint method. This method is also available to each class that inherits Shape. Although the code for changing the color of an item is identical for each graphic object, each object uses different code to draw it. For example, drawing a box requires using the fillRect method, while a triangle requires a fillPolygon method. Thus, the paint method has no action because it must be customized by each graphic component. Boxes, ovals, and triangles will override this method. Recall that this strategy is also used by the Applet class. The methods init, start, paint, stop, and destroy are not implemented in the Applet class with no action. We override these methods when we extend the Applet class.

Listing 16.2 shows how the Box class inherits and overrides the paint method in the Shape class. Lines 38 through 42 contain the customized code required to draw a box.

Suppose we are given the following code. The call to setColor executes the setColor method in the Shape class. The call to paint executes the paint method in Box (Figure 16.2).

```
Box top = new Box (20, 45, 50, 75, Color.red);
top.setColor(Color.blue);
top.paint(g);
```

Because top is a Box, we determine which method is to be executed by looking at all the methods in Box. If the method is found there, we execute it. If it is not found there, we

Figure 16.2 Method calls

```
class Shape                              class Box extends Shape
{                                        {
  Color myColor;                           ...
  public void setColor(Color c)            public Box()
  {                                        {
    myColor = c;                             ...
  }                                        }

  public void paint(Graphics g)            public void paint(Graphics g)
  {                                        {
  }                                          g.setColor(myColor);
}                                            g.fillRect(...);
                                           }

                                         }

            Box top = new Box (20, 45, 50, 75, Color.red);
            top.setColor(Color.blue);
            top.paint(g);
```

look at top's immediate superclass and continue the process. For example, when we execute paint, we find the overridden paint method in the Box class and execute it. However, setColor is not found in the Box class, so we look in the Shape class where we find and execute it. There is no limit to the depth of inheritance, and thus the search for the appropriate method may go through many classes.

Listing 16.22 on page 796 and Listing 16.23 on page 797 define ovals and triangles in a manner similar to boxes.

16.2.2 Polymorphism

An example of using the Box, Oval, and Triangle classes to create a drawing is shown in Listing 16.6 with the result shown in Figure 16.1. Before we look at this code we will see how we can take advantage of polymorphism to further ease our life.

Polymorphism allows one object identifier to reference objects from more than one class. The different classes are related by a common superclass.

Polymorphism allows us to declare an identifier as a shape and reference any object that inherits from it. For example:

```
Shape aShape = new Box  (35, 14, 50, 75, Color.red);
aShape       = new Oval (25, 10, 16, 23, Color.blue);
```

Notice that aShape can reference a box, an oval, or a triangle because they are all inherited from the class Shape. We use this idea in everyday life. For example, we can define an superclass called Car as an object with a gas-powered engine and four wheels. We can then define ManualCar and AutomaticCar as classes that inherit these properties from a car. An object of the ManualCar class will have all the properties of a car with a manual transmission. An object of the AutomaticCar class will have all the properties of a car with an automatic transmission. Thus, we can write:

```
Car myCar = new ManualCar();
```
or
```
Car myCar = new AutomaticCar();
```

When we talk about myCar, we could be talking about a car with a manual or an automatic transmission. The wonderful thing about polymorphism is that we do not have to specify what kind of object we have. For example, if we say, "I am going to get into myCar and head for the mall," it has meaning no matter which kind of car we have. The operation "head for the mall" will be implemented slightly differently in a manual versus an automatic car. When we get into our manual car, the operation "going to the mall" will involve pushing in the clutch, shifting into first, hitting the gas, and popping the clutch. The same operation in an automatic car will involve shifting into drive and hitting the gas. Thus, the idea of going to the mall is an operation that can be applied to both our automatic car and manual car, but it is implemented differently in each case.

There is a parallel situation with Shapes. Painting a box requires a different set of operations than painting an oval. Java will execute the appropriate code based on what kind of object we give it. For example, in Line 6 of Listing 16.3, the paint method for Oval is called once in a blue moon and the paint method for Box is called the rest of the time. This example takes advantage of dynamic binding.

Listing 16.3 Dynamic Binding

```
1 Shape aShape;
2 CelestialObject moon = new CelestialObject ();
3 if (moon.isBlue())
4   aShape = new Oval (25, 10, 16, 23, Color.blue);
5 else
6   aShape = new Box (35, 14, 50, 75, Color.red);
7 aShape.paint(g);
```

Dynamic binding is a mechanism that waits to bind a method call to a method implementation until runtime.

When the compiler sees `aShape.paint(g)`, it cannot determine whether the `Box` or the `Oval` `paint` method should be called. The Java runtime system will have to figure out whether `aShape` is a `Box` or an `Oval` and then make the appropriate call. Because the binding between call and code is done at runtime and not at compile time, it is called dynamic binding.

We take advantage of polymorphism and dynamic binding in the `Composite` class shown in Listing 16.4. As the name implies, a `Composite` object is a collection of `Shape` objects. It allows us to treat many `Shape` objects as a single unit. For example, in the following, `flag` contains a blue box and red box. We can paint and pass these boxes to methods using only one name: `flag`.

```
Box blue = new Box ( 0,  0, 25, 30, Color.blue);
Box red  = new Box (25,  0, 25, 30, Color.red);
Composite flag = new Composite ();
flag.add (blue);
flag.add (red);
flag.paint (g);
```

The `Composite` class contains little code. The constructor creates a list. The `add` method adds a `Shape` object to this list. Finally, the `paint` method paints all the objects that have been added to the `Composite` object. Let us focus on the `paint` method.

Line 40 in Listing 16.4 can look a little overwhelming. Below, we break it down into three steps to make how it works clearer:

```
Object anyOldThing      = myList.elementAt (i);
Shape aGraphicThing = (Shape)anyOldThing;
aGraphicThing.paint(g);
```

The `paint` method has only two lines. These two lines illustrate the key benefits of polymorphism and dynamic binding. Polymorphism allows us to add any kind of shape to `myList`. When we extract them from `myList`, the `paint` operation can be applied to each and the appropriate paint method will be called. To clarify, an example follows:

Listing 16.4 The `Composite` Class

```
1  //***************************************************************
2  //
3  // title:    Composite
4  //
5  // This is a composite of other components.
6  //
7  //***************************************************************
8
9  import java.awt.Color;
10 import java.awt.Graphics;
11 import java.io.Serializable;
12 import java.util.Vector;
13
14 public class Composite extends Shape implements Serializable
15 {
16    Vector myList;
17
18    //---------- Composite ----------------------------------------
19    // pre:  none;
20    // post: a new composite object is created
21    public Composite ()
22    {
23       myList = new Vector();
24    }
25
26    //---------- add ----------------------------------------------
27    // pre:  none
28    // post: "thing" is add to this composite
29    public void add (Shape thing)
30    {
31       myList.addElement (thing);
32    }
33
34    //---------- paint --------------------------------------------
35    // pre:  none.
36    // post: this composite is painted on graphics context g
37    public void paint (Graphics g)
38    {
39       for (int i=0; i<myList.size(); i++)
40          ((Shape)(myList.elementAt(i))).paint(g);
41    }
42 }
```

```
Composite aBunchOfThings = new Composite ();
Shape thing;
thing = new Box (10, 20, 40, 30, Color.red);
aBunchOfThings.add (thing);
thing = new Oval (30, 20, 10, 10, Color.blue);
aBunchOfThings.add (thing);
thing = new Box (40, 25, 55, 15, Color.green);
aBunchOfThings.add (thing);
thing = (Shape)(aBunchOfThings.elementAt (0);
thing.paint (g);     // dynamic binding - paint for Box called
thing = (Shape)(aBunchOfThings.elementAt (1);
thing.paint (g);     // dynamic binding - paint for Oval called
```

When we apply the `paint` method to `thing` above, `thing` could be a box, oval, or triangle. Dynamic binding is helping us. Without it, we would have to write code like the code in Listing 16.5.

Listing 16.5 Painting without polymorphism

```
1 public void paint (Graphics g)
2 {
3   for (int i=0; i<myList.size(); i++)
4   {
5     Object aShape = myList.elementAt(i);
6     if (aShape instanceof Box)
7     {
8       Box aBox = (Box)aShape;
9       aBox.paint(g);
10    }
11    else if (aShape instanceof Oval)
12    {
13      Oval anOval = (Oval)aShape;
14      anOval.paint(g);
15    }
16    else if (aShape instanceof Triangle)
17    {
18      Triangle aTriangle = (Triangle)aShape;
19      aTriangle.paint(g);
20    }
21  }
22 }
```

These examples should help us understand why we had to put a `paint` method in the `Shape` class even though it does not do anything and is never called. If we do not put `paint` in the `Shape` class, the following second line below will not compile.

```
Shape thing = (Shape)(aBunchOfThings.elementAt(1);
thing.paint (g);
```

The compiler will say "syntax error, there is no paint method defined for Shape." We know that aGraphicThing must be a Box, Oval, or Triangle, each of which has a paint method. However, the compiler is not smart. It does not know that.

Polymorphism and dynamic binding make adding new types of shapes easy. All we need to do when we add a new kind of shape is to make sure it inherits Shape, create it where it is needed, and everything else takes care of itself. The exercises at the end of the chapter provide some practice.

16.2.3   Object Files

Now let's get back to the problem we posed at the beginning of this chapter—the problem of saving and loading shapes. Using the IO classes we learned in Chapter 12 presents a problem. We would be required to create a tag for each kind of shape we have and create a method that writes the tag to a file and all the instance variables for the shape. Then when we load the shape from the file, we would have to read the shape's tag and, based on that tag, create an appropriate shape object and call the appropriate read methods that we also wrote to read each shape. This is a lot of work.

The major drawback of the file IO we did in Chapter 12 is that it does not maintain type information across saves and restores. For example, we can save the string "Java" to a particular location on a disk file and then read those same four bytes as the integer 1,247,901,281 (see Figure 16.3). The IO schemes in Chapter 12 allow use to violate typing information. It is easy to make mistakes when reading untyped information because we can save it as one type of thing and read it as another.

Figure 16.3 Violating Type with File IO

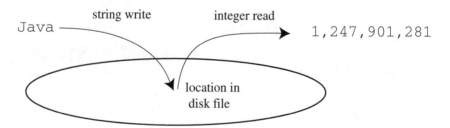

F or example, suppose we want to write the drawing of a tree to a file. First we could write a rectangle to the file representing its trunk. Next we could write an oval to the file representing its leaves. The trick comes when we read the drawing back. We must know that the

Figure 16.4 A Composite of Composites of Shapes

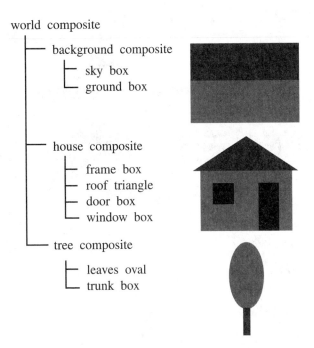

world composite
- background composite
  - sky box
  - ground box
- house composite
  - frame box
  - roof triangle
  - door box
  - window box
- tree composite
  - leaves oval
  - trunk box

first item in the file is a rectangle and read it. Next, we must know that the next item is an oval and read it. Our program would work only for files that contain a single tree.

We could solve this problem by saving the word `rectangle` before we write the rectangle and saving the work `oval` before we store the oval. These words are called tags because they provide labels for the type of object which is going to be saved. When we read a shape from the file, we first read the tag so we know whether to do a rectangle or oval read. Tags add a lot of complexity to our code.

Using persistent stores solve this problem. It stores the name of classes and instance variables with the data automatically. This information is automatically checked when the information is read from the file. The IO classes that implement persistent stores are `ObjectOutputStream` and `ObjectInputStream`. Listing 16.6 shows how to use `ObjectOutputStream` to create a persistent image store.

In a *persistent store*, type information is stored in addition to data information.

Listing 16.6   Creating a Persistent Store

```
1  //*****************************************************************
2  //
3  // title:    Create
4  //
5  // Create a graphic drawing and save it in an object file.
6  //
7  //*****************************************************************
8
9  import java.awt.Color;
10 import java.io.ObjectOutputStream;
11 import java.io.IOException;
12 import java.io.FileOutputStream;
13
14 public class Create
15 {
16   public static void main (String args[])
17   {
18     try
19     {
20       // open the object output file
21       FileOutputStream   out        = new
22                                 FileOutputStream("house.obj");
23     ObjectOutputStream objectOut =new ObjectOutputStream(out);
24
25       // create a few colors
26       Color brick         = new Color (230, 35,35);
27       Color brown         = new Color (166, 42, 42);
28       Color forestGreen   = new Color(35, 142, 35);
29       Color springGreen   = new Color (0, 255, 127);
30
31       // background
32       Shape background = new Composite ();
33       Shape sky        = new Box (0, 0, 400, 150, Color.blue);
34       background.add (sky);
35       Shape ground     = new Box (0, 150, 400, 150,
36                                     springGreen);
37       background.add (ground);
38
39       // tree
40       Shape tree       = new Composite ();
41       Shape leaves     = new Oval (40, 30, 50, 100,
42                                     springGreen);
43       tree.add (leaves);
44       Shape trunk      = new Box (60, 130, 10, 40, brown);
45       tree.add (trunk);
46
```

Listing 16.6 Creating a Persistent Store

```
47        // house
48        Shape house       = new Composite ();
49        Shape frame       = new Box (200, 100, 140, 90, brick);
50        house.add (frame);
51        Shape roof        = new Triangle (190, 100, 350, 100,
52                                          270, 50, forestGreen);
53        house.add (roof);
54        Shape door = new Box (290, 120, 30, 70, Color.black);
55        house.add (door);
56        Shape window = new Box (220, 120, 30, 30, Color.black);
57        house.add (window);
58
59        // world
60        Shape world = new Composite();
61        world.add (background);
62        world.add (tree);
63        world.add (house);
64
65        // save the world
66        objectOut.writeObject(world);
67        System.out.println ("Graphic saved");
68      }
69    catch (IOException e)
70    {
71        System.out.println("Could not open output file");
72    }
73  }
74 }
```

There is nothing unusual in this code. Lines 21 through 23 open the object output file. We create a `world` composite object which contains a `background`, house, and tree composite object. Each of these composite objects is composed of several shapes. Figure 16.4 shows how this composite drawing is organized. Finally, Line 66 writes the `world` object to a file. Notice that we needed to write only one line of code to write a composite object to a file.

Once we have the objects in a file, we can create another program that reads this file and displays the result. This is shown in Listing 16.7. It looks long, but most of it is used to create and handle a window and catch exceptions. There are only four lines of code of real interest. Lines 37 through 39 read the composite object. Line 72 draws it. Notice that this drawing code does not depend on knowing anything about the individual shapes. When we add new types of shapes we do not need to modify this code as long as each shape inherits from our `Shape` class.

Listing 16.7 The `Draw` Class—Read From Persistent Store

```
1  //*************************************************************
2  //
3  // title:    Draw
4  //
5  // This program draws what the Create application save in an
6  // object file.
7  //
8  //*************************************************************
9
10 import java.awt.Color;
11 import java.awt.Frame;
12 import java.awt.Graphics;
13
14 import java.io.FileInputStream;
15 import java.io.ObjectInputStream;
16 import java.io.FileNotFoundException;
17 import java.io.IOException;
18
19 import java.awt.event.WindowListener;
20 import java.awt.event.WindowEvent;
21
22 public class Draw extends Frame implements WindowListener
23 {
24   private static Draw myDrawingWindow;
25   private Shape myDrawing;
26
27   //---------- Draw -----------------------------------------
28   // pre:  none.
29   // post: a drawing window and drawing a component are
30   //       created
31   public Draw ()
32   {
33     addWindowListener (this);
34
35     try
36     {
37       FileInputStream in = new FileInputStream("house.obj");
38       ObjectInputStream objectIn = new ObjectInputStream(in);
39       myDrawing = (Shape)(objectIn.readObject());
40
41       setSize (400, 300);
42       show();
43     }
44
```

Listing 16.7 The `Draw` Class—Read From Persistent Store

```
45     catch (FileNotFoundException e)
46     {
47       System.out.println("File not found");
48     }
49
50     catch (IOException e)
51     {
52       System.out.println("File IO error");
53     }
54     catch (ClassNotFoundException e)
55     {
56       System.out.println("Input object not found");
57     }
58   }
59
60   //---------- main -------------------------------------------
61   // Execution begin here.  A drawing is created.
62   // Called automatically.
63   public static void main (String args[])
64   {
65     myDrawingWindow = new Draw();
66   }
67
68   //---------- paint ------------------------------------------
69   // Paint the drawing in the window.
70   // Called automatically.
71   public void paint (Graphics g)
72   {
73     myDrawing.paint (g);
74   }
75
76   //---------- windowClosing ----------------------------------
77   // Handle close windows.
78   // Called automatically.
79   public void windowClosing (WindowEvent event)
80   {
81     System.exit(0);
82   }
83
84   public void windowOpened (WindowEvent event){;}
85   public void windowClosed (WindowEvent event){;}
86   public void windowIconified (WindowEvent event){;}
87   public void windowDeiconified (WindowEvent event){;}
88   public void windowActivated (WindowEvent event){;}
89   public void windowDeactivated (WindowEvent event){;}
90 }
```

PATTERNS

16.3 Composite Pattern

problem

We introduced the *simplified composite object pattern* in Section 7.4. Without inheritance we needed to create an instance variable for each shape. For example, a program to create our house using the simplified pattern is shown in Listing 16.8. Each time we add a shape to our drawing we must change our code in three places. For example, if we wish to add a window to the door we must add a new instance variable, instantiate it in the constructor, and add a command to paint it. This would make it impossible to create a doodle program in which users add shapes to the drawing at runtime.

Listing 16.8 Using the simplified composite object pattern

```
1  public class Draw extends Applet
2  {
3      private Box      myFrame;
4      private Triangle myRoof;
5      private Box      myDoor;
6      private Box      myWindow;
7
8      public Draw ()
9      {
10         myFrame  = new Box (200, 100, 140, 90, Color.red);
11         myRoof   = new Triangle (190, 100, 350, 100,
12                                  270, 50, Color.green);
13         myDoor   = new Box (290, 120, 30, 70, Color.black);
14         myWindow = new Box (220, 120, 30, 30, Color.black);
15     }
16
17     public void paint (Graphics g)
18     {
19         myFrame.paint (g);
20         myRoof.paint (g);
21         myDoor.paint (g);
22         myWindow.paint (g);
23     }
24 }
```

772

The create and draw graphics application in the previous section takes advantage of the full-blown version of the *composite object pattern*. We use inheritance to make it easier to add new graphics components. Listing 16.9 shows how we use the composite pattern to accomplish the same drawing.

Listing 16.9 Using the composite object pattern

```
1   public class Draw extends Applet
2   {
3     private Shape myDrawing;
4
5     public Draw ()
6     {
7       myDrawing = new Composite ();
8       myDrawing.add (new Box (200, 100, 140, 90, Color.red));
9       myDrawing.add (new Triangle (190, 100, 350, 100,
10                                   270, 50, Color.green));
11      myDrawing.add (new Box (290, 120, 30, 70, Color.black));
12      myDrawing.add (new Box (220, 120, 30, 30, Color.black));
13    }
14
15    public void paint (Graphics g)
16    {
17      myDrawing.paint (g);
18    }
19  }
```

If we want to add a window to our door we only need to add a single line to the constructor. All other code stays the same. It also allows us to add shapes to our drawing dynamically. For example, we can conceive of responding to some GUI action event as follows: (With some imagination and the use of inheritance we can remove the if statements and create a general-purpose drawing program.)

```
public void actionPerformed (ActionEvent e)
{
  if (myBlueBoxMenuItem == e.getSource())
  {
    myDrawing.add (new Box (...));
  }
  else if ...
  ...
}
```

The flexibility provided by the composite pattern comes at a cost. Our code is more complex than the simplified version. We must have an abstract base class and create a composite shape. However, once the pattern is implemented future enhancements are so simplified that the initial cost pays for itself many times. Adding complexity to pay for ease of enhancement and maintenance is typical with many object patterns.

The structure of the composite object pattern is shown in Figure 16.5. We can use it as a guide for creating and modifying programs that use it. Suppose we want to add a new shape to the `Create` program in Listing 16.6.

1. Create a new class that inherits from `Shape`. Use the `Box` class in Listing 16.2 as a model. The `paint` method is key. It overrides the one in the `Shape` class.

2. Instantiate a new shape in the `main` method of the `Create` class (Listing 16.6).

3. Add the new shape to one of the composites.

4. Make no changes to the `Draw` class in Listing 16.7.

Figure 16.5 The Composite pattern

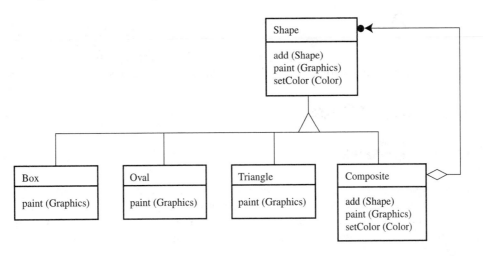

 We begin with the abstract Shape class at the top of the diagram. Its purpose is to create a common interface from which all other shapes inherit. We indicate a subclass relationship with the triangle between the superclass and all its subclasses.

 The diamond to the right of the Composite class indicates that it is an aggregate. It is a mixture of various types of objects. For example, a house composite is a mixture of frame, roof, door, and window.

 The arrow from the Composite box to the Shape indicates that the Composite is a mixture of shapes. Since Composite inherits from Shape, a Composite can contain another Composite.

● The black circle at the end of the arrow from the Composite to the Shape box indicates that the composite can hold many shapes. Arrow heads without the black circle reference only one item.

JAVA

The programs in the previous sections relied on several Java features. They include object IO and inheritance. In the following sections we explore these features.

16.4   Object Stores

16.4.1   Serializable

There is one small change needed for each class before we can perform object IO. The class must be serializable. Serializable refers to a property in which an object can be transformed into a series of bytes that can be sent to a file or network stream. All that is necessary to make a class serializable is to promise to implement the `Serializable` interface.

Figure 16.6 Dump of the file created by the program in Listing 16.6

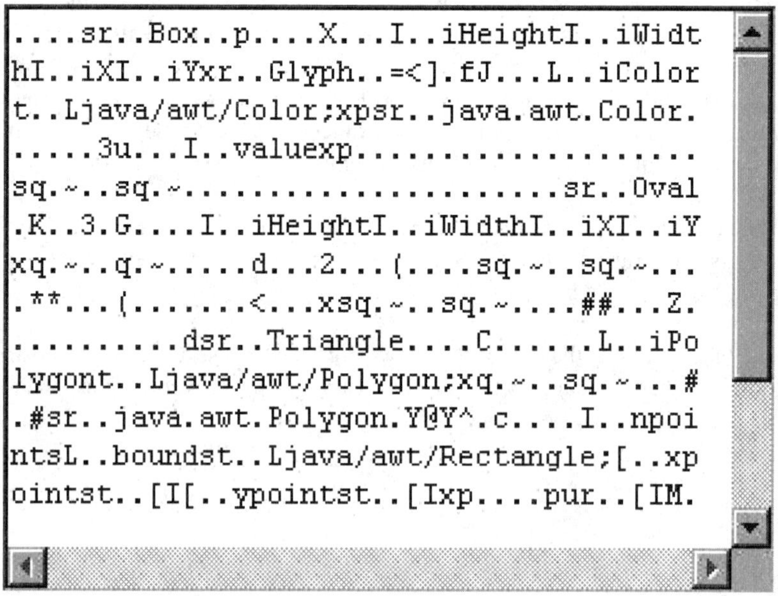

```
....sr..Box..p....X...I..iHeightI..iWidt
hI..iXI..iYxr..Glyph..=<].fJ...L..iColor
t..Ljava/awt/Color;xpsr..java.awt.Color.
.....3u...I..valuexp....................
sq.~..sq.~.....................sr..Oval
.K..3.G....I..iHeightI..iWidthI..iXI..iY
xq.~..q.~......d...2...(....sq.~..sq.~...
.**...(.......<...xsq.~..sq.~....##...Z.
.........dsr..Triangle....C......L..iPo
lygont..Ljava/awt/Polygon;xq.~..sq.~...#
.#sr..java.awt.Polygon.Y@Y^.c....I..npoi
ntsL..boundst..Ljava/awt/Rectangle;[..xp
ointst..[I[..ypointst..[Ixp....pur..[IM.
```

To make the `Box` shape in Listing 16.2 serializable we add the phrase `implements Serializable` to Line 13 as shown below:

```
public class Box extends Shape implements Serializable
```

As a result, Java adds code to the class, which makes it write appropriate information to an output stream. That information includes class and instance variable names. Using our snoop program (Figure 16.6) we can see how this information is included within the output stream.

16.4.2   Reading and Writing Objects

Listing 16.10 and Listing 16.11 show two additional classes that have been serialized. They will serve as examples for our discussion about object input and output in this section.

Listing 16.10 `Address` Class

```
1  import java.io.Serializable;
2
3  public class Address implements Serializable
4  {
5     private String myName;
6     private String myCity;
7     private int     myZip;
8
9     public Address (String name, String city, int zip)
10    {
11       myName = name;
12       myCity = city;
13       myZip  = zip;
14    }
15
16    public String getCity ()
17    {
18       return myCity;
19    }
20
21    public String toString ()
22    {
23       return myName + ", " + myCity + " " + myZip;
24    }
25 }
```

Listing 16.11 `Stats` class

```
1  import java.io.Serializable;
2
3  public class Stats implements Serializable
4  {
5      private String myName;
6      private int    myAtBats;
7      private int    myRuns;
8      private int    myHits;
9      private double myAverage;
10
11     public Stats (String name, int atBats, int runs,
12                      int hits, double average)
13     {
14         myName    = name;
15         myAtBats  = atBats;
16         myRuns    = runs;
17         myHits    = hits;
18         myAverage = average;
19     }
20
21     public int getAtBats ()
22     {
23         return myAtBats;
24     }
25
26     public String toString ()
27     {
28         return myName + ": at Bats " + myAtBats +
29             ": runs " + myRuns + ": hits " + myHits +
30             ": batting average " + myAverage;
31     }
32 }
```

Once we have made a class serializable, it is a simple matter to read and write it to a file. Listing 16.12 demonstrates. Lines 15 and 16 open our object output file. Line 18 creates an `Address` object and Line 19 writes it to the output file. Reading them in is just as easy. Lines 25 and 26 open the object input file. Line 28 reads an object   .

Notice that the code that reads the object assigns the object to the identifier `thing`. The `thing` object must be of type `Object` because `readObject` returns something of type `Object`. Although we know that `thing` is an `Address` object, the compiler is not sophisticated enough to deduce this from the program code. As a result, we must cast `thing` to an `Address` object in Line 30 before we can apply the `getCity` method to it. Recall our discussion in Section 11.4.5. We are telling the compiler, "trust me, I know

Listing 16.12 `ObjectIODemo` class

```
1  import java.io.FileInputStream;
2  import java.io.FileOutputStream;
3  import java.io.ObjectInputStream;
4  import java.io.ObjectOutputStream;
5  import java.io.FileNotFoundException;
6  import java.io.IOException;
7
8  public class ObjectIODemo
9  {
10    public static void main(String args[])
11    {
12      try
13      {
14        // output phase
15      FileOutputStream out = new FileOutputStream("things.obj");
16      ObjectOutputStream objectOut =new ObjectOutputStream(out);
17
18       Address elmer=new Address("Elmer Snid","Portland",97212);
19        objectOut.writeObject (elmer);
20        Stats zeile = new Stats ("Zeile", 3, 0, 2, 0.333);
21        objectOut.writeObject (zeile);
22        objectOut.close();
23
24        // input phase
25        FileInputStream in = new FileInputStream ("things.obj");
26        ObjectInputStream objectIn = new ObjectInputStream (in);
27
28        Object thing = objectIn.readObject();
29        System.out.println(thing);
30        System.out.println("City: "+((Address)thing).getCity());
31        thing = objectIn.readObject();
32        System.out.println (thing);
33        System.out.println ("At bats: " +
                             ((Stats)thing).getAtBats());
34        objectIn.close();
35      }
36    catch (FileNotFoundException e) {;}
37    catch (IOException e) {;}
38    catch (ClassNotFoundException e) {;}
39    }
40 }
```

JAVA

Listing 16.13 `ObjectIODemo` Output

```
Elmer Snid, Portland 97212
City: Portland
Zeile: at Bats 3: runs 0: hits 2: batting average 0.333
At bats: 3
```

what I am doing." I know that `thing` is an `Address` so let me do the cast. If `thing` is not an `Address`, the program will abort with a `ClassCastException`.

We do not have to cast `thing` into an `Address` to print it in Line 29. Line 29 is equivalent to the following:

```
System.out.println (thing.toString());
```

The `Object` class has a `toString` method. All classes inherit `Object`, and thus inherit this method. We chose to overwrite it in the `Address` class (Lines 21 through 24 of Listing 16.10). Because of dynamic binding the appropriate `toString` method is called when `thing` is an `Address` in Line 29 and a `Stats` in 32. See Listing 16.13. When we call the `getAtBats` method on `thing` in Line 33 we must cast `thing` into a `Stats` object. No other `Object` supports the `getAtBats` method.

Some languages, for example Smalltalk, do not do all the type checking that Java does. Thus, casts are not needed.

16.5   Implementing Inheritance

16.5.1   Inheritance

Now let us take a closer look at inheritance. Suppose we are writing classes for an employee database. We have salaried employees that are paid on a fixed yearly salary, and we also have hourly employees that are paid based on the number of hours they work. We could create two classes, one for each employee type. However these classes would have much in common. They would both have employee names, addresses, dependents, departments, plus many other fields.

One strategy is to share common information through inheritance. Listing 16.14 shows a rather contrived example of a base class that has been greatly simplified to make our investigation easier. All the information and methods in the Employee class are shared by salaried and hourly employees.

Listing 16.14 `Employee` class

```
1 public abstract class Employee
2 {
3    private String myName;
4    private int    myDependents;
5
6    private  final double UNIT_DEDUCTION = 2000.0;
7    protected final double TAX_RATE       = 0.28;
8
9    public Employee (String name, int dependents)
10   {
11      myName       = name;
12      myDependents = dependents;
13   }
14
15   private double deductions ()
16   {
17      return UNIT_DEDUCTION * myDependents / 12.0;
18   }
19
20   public double monthlyNet (double gross)
21   {
22      double adjusted = gross - deductions();
23      double taxes    = adjusted * TAX_RATE;
24      return gross - taxes;
25   }
26
27   public double computeMonthlyCheck ()
28   {
29      return 0.0;
30   }
31 }
```

In addition to being called the superclass, the class from which we inherit is also called the *base* class. Its subclasses are also called *derived* classes.

Notice that the `Employee` class is abstract (Line 1 contains the `abstract` keyword). Making a class abstract prevents us from instantiating an object from it. It does not make sense to create `Employee` objects because it does not completely specify what kind of employee. Similarly, it does not make sense to instantiate the `Shape` class. We always instantiate components that are derived from a shape, for example, a `Box`, `Oval`, or `Triangle`. Thus, because `Employee` is abstract, the following is not possible.

```
Employee sally = new Employee ("Sally", 2); // error
```

Listing 16.15 `SalariedEmployee` Class

```
1 public class SalariedEmployee extends Employee
2 {
3   private double mySalary;
4
5   public SalariedEmployee (String name, int dependents,
6                            double salary)
7   {
8     super (name, dependents);
9     mySalary = salary;
10  }
11
12  public double computeMonthlyCheck ()
13  {
14    double gross = mySalary / 12.0;
15    return monthlyNet (gross);
16  }
17 }
```

Listing 16.16 `HourlyEmployee` class

```
1 public class HourlyEmployee extends Employee
2 {
3   private double myHourlyRate;
4   private double myWeeklyHours;
5
6   public HourlyEmployee (String name, int dependents,
7                          double rate, double hours)
8   {
9     super (name, dependents);
10    myHourlyRate  = rate;
11    myWeeklyHours = hours;
12  }
13
14  public double computeMonthlyCheck ()
15  {
16    double gross = myHourlyRate * myWeeklyHours * 4.3;
17    return monthlyNet (gross);
18  }
19 }
```

An *abstract* class is one that may never be instantiated directly. Its purpose is to be a base class from which other classes can be derived.

We create two additional employee classes (Listing 16.16 and Listing 16.15). Because the SalariedEmployee class inherits the Employee class, it will have myName and myDependents instance variables in addition to a mySalary instance variable. It will also inherit the monthlyNet and the computeMonthlyCheck method.

The computeMonthlyCheck method is different for the two types of employees. For a salaried employee we must divide their salary by 12 before we compute their take-home pay. For an hourly employee we must multiply the number of hours times the hourly pay. Thus, we must override the computeMonthlyCheck method from the Employee class with custom ones in the SalariedEmployee and HourlyEmployee classes. However, both classes share much of the computation. Once we compute their monthly gross, we compute their taxes and take home pay in the same way. Thus, both classes share the monthlyNet method. The code below shows how we can use our employee classes.

```
Employee elmer = new HourlyEmployee ("Elmer Snid", 5, 40.0,
6.25);
Employee emmalou = new SalariedEmployee ("Emma lou", 2,
45000.0);
System.out.println
        ("Elmer's check:   " + elmer.computeMonthlyCheck());
System.out.println
        ("Emma Lou's check: " + emmalou.computeMonthly-
Check());
```

When we override the computeMonthlyCheck method we must be careful to make the method signature the same as the one in the base class. The computeMonthly-Check in Line12 of Listing 16.15, Line 14 of Listing 16.16, and Line 27 of Listing 16.14 all have the same signature.

Notice the call to super in Line 8 of Listing 16.15. It calls the constructor for the Employee class. Good design dictates that the implementation of the Employee class be hidden. Thus, the Employee class's instance variables myName and myDependents are private. The SalariedEmployee and HourlyEmployee classes cannot access the Employee class's instance variables. The constructors for these two classes must call the Employee class constructor explicitly so that its instance variables are initialized. (We will discuss private and public variables in more detail in Section 16.5.4.)

16.5.2   Things That Cannot be Inherited

We cannot inherit from Java's primitive types because they are not classes. Therefore, we never extend `int` or `boolean`. This is yet another example of the differences between Java's primitives and objects.

We may also not inherit the classes `Integer` and `Boolean` because they and other arithmetic classes are defined as `final`. The final keyword on a class stipulates that no class can extend it.

16.5.3   Packages

The Java package statement allows us to assemble classes into libraries. *Libraries* are collections of related classes that can be used within a program. The `vista` class library is distributed with this book. It contains some commonly used utilities. The `java.awt` library is an example of a collection of classes provided by Java. Let us create a library for our employee classes. We will name our library after the name of our company: Banner Investors Group (BIG).

To place a class in a library we only need to add the `package` statement before any other statements. The following line is inserted at the beginning of each of the employee classes.

```
package big;
```

The compiler will create a directory named `big`, if one does not exist, and place the generated `Employee.class`, `SalariedEmployee.class`, and `HourlyEmployee.class` files within this directory.

When we want to use the employee classes within a class that is not a part of the `big` package, we must import it. For example, our new payroll program is shown in Listing 16.17. Notice the imports in Lines 1 through 3.

Figure 16.7 illustrates the directory structure that is created. Compilers contain settings that inform them where to look for libraries. One location is typically the current directory. The Java libraries are placed in a location where the compiler is instructed to look. In addition, most compilers allow the user to specify additional locations. Thus we could place the `big` directory anywhere as long as we can specify to the compiler where it can be found.

Java uses the following rule. Classes that are not in the same package (directory) of the class that needs them must be explicitly imported (or their name must be fully specified,

Listing 16.17 `Payroll` Class

```
1 import big.Employee;
2 import big.HourlyEmployee;
3 import big.SalariedEmployee;
4
5 public class Payroll
6 {
7    public static void main(String args[])
8    {
9      Employee elmer = new HourlyEmployee("Elmer Snid", 5, 40.0,
6.25);
10     Employee emmalou = new SalariedEmployee ("Emma lou", 2,
45000.0);
11     System.out.println
12          ("Elmer's check:   " + elmer.computeMonthlyCheck());
13     System.out.println
14         ("Emma Lou's check: " + emmalou.computeMonthlyCheck());
15   }
16 }
```

Figure 16.7 `big` directory structure

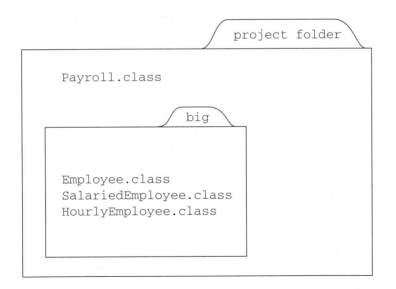

for example, `java.awt.Color`). All classes in the same package (directory) are available by default.

16.5.4 Public, Protected, and Private Modifiers

We made a side trip into packages because Java treats classes in the same package differently than classes in different packages. Let us take another look at the `Employee` class in Listing 16.14. Line 20 makes the `monthlyNet` method public. If it is not public, its derived classes could not access it. Because it is public, every class can access it. For example, the payroll program could do the following.

```
Employee elmer = new HourlyEmployee ("Elmer Snid", 5, 40.0,
6.25);
System.out.println (elmer.monthlyNet (3000));  // bad idea
```

The `monthlyNet` method was written to share common code between the `SalariedEmployee` and `HourlyEmployee` class. It was not designed to be called by any other classes. To prevent the above, we can make the `monthlyNet` class protected as shown below. The protected attribute will allow its derived class to access it but not payroll.

```
protected double monthlyNet (double gross)
```

The following summarizes method and instance variable access privileges:

- private: Accessible only within the class in which it is defined.
- protected: Accessible by all classes that inherit the class in which it is defined and within all classes in the same package.
- public: Accessible by all classes that have access to this class.

Once we have made `monthlyNet` protected, there are two reasons why `SalariedEmployee` and `HourlyEmployee` can access it. These two classes inherit the `Employee` class and all these classes are in the same package. However, the`Payroll` class cannot access monthlyNet because it does not inherit it and is not in the same package. The following is no longer possible from the `Payroll` class:

```
System.out.println (elmer.monthlyNet (3000));  // error
```

16.6   Design

In this section we will summarize some design issues that are illustrated in the examples above. They are from *Object-Oriented Design Heuristics* by Reil. Before we put these design heuristics to memory, let us remind ourselves why we are bothering. Recall in Section 7.5 that good design supports a program's requirements, makes maintenance easier, partitions the code effectively, and supports incremental development. The purpose of each heuristic is to support good design.

- (Reil Heuristic 5.1) Inheritance should be used to model a specialization hierarchy. For example, a salaried employee is a specialized employee. It is everything an employee is plus it has a yearly salary. A box is a specialized shape. All shapes have color. In addition, a box has height and width. An applet is a specialized container. It can hold components such as labels and buttons. However, it is more specialized; it also contains a window and it works over the web.

- (Reil Heuristic 2.1 and 5.3) All instance variables in a superclass should be private. Do not make them protected or public. This allows us to reorganize a class's state without breaking clients of this class.

- (Reil Heuristic 5.2) Subclasses know something about their superclasses. However, a superclass should know nothing about any of its subclasses. We do not want to modify a base class every time we add or alter a derived class. The whole point of inheritance is to make enhancement and modification easier.

- (Reil Heuristic 5.5) Inheritance should be no deeper than the number of classes we can keep in our short-term memory. This number is about six. For example, in Java we have `Object: Component: TextComponent: TextArea` and `Object: Component: Container: Panel: Applet:` *ourApplet.*

- (Reil Heuristic 5.7) A base class should be an abstract class. For example, `Employee` in Listing 16.14 and `Shape` in Listing 16.1.

- (Reil Heuristic 5.12) Code that uses a selection statement to execute different code based on an object's type is usually a mistake (Listing 16.5). Use polymorphism instead (Listing 16.4). One of the big advantages of implementing employees and shapes using inheritance is polymorphism. When we print monthly checks or paint shapes we do not need to add code that distinguishes between salaried and hourly workers or between boxes and ovals.

- (Reil Heuristic 5.18) Do not use inheritance when containment is needed.

We take a look at the last heuristic in more detail. Inheritance is often called an "is-a" relationship. For example, a salaried employee "is an" employee. A box "is a" shape. An applet ""is a" container (it holds buttons, text areas, etc.). These are all good examples of using inheritance.

An employee is not a name. An employee "has a" name. Therefore `name` should be an instance variable of the `Employee` class. The `Employee` class does not inherit the `String` class. An employee is not a department. An employee "has a" department.

Therefore the employee could contain a reference to a department. An employee should not inherit a department. Containment defines a "has a" relationship.

Using inheritance where containment is needed can result in a proliferation of classes. For example, a house is not a furnace. But suppose we decided that it was. We could make a house inherit furnace. If it had a gas furnace it would inherit gas furnace. Thus, we would have `GasFurnaceHouse`. In a similar manner we would have a `WoodFurnaceHouse` and a `OilFurnaceHouse`. When we add water heaters we would need to inherit from electric water heater, gas water heater, and solar water heater. Thus, we would need a `GasWaterHeaterGasFurnaceHouse` class, `GasWaterHeaterWoodFurnace-House` class, and so on until we have created all nine combinations. If we add three types of air conditioners, we suddenly end up with 27 classes of houses. This becomes hard to manage. What we want to say is that a house contains a furnace, water heater, and air conditioner. Each of these is part of a house's state and thus is an instance variable.

SUPPLEMENTARY MATERIAL

16.7 Model-View-Controller Pattern

Inheritance gives us an opportunity to fully implement the model-view-controller (MVC) pattern we saw in Section 15.3. Let us quickly review the simplified version to understand its limitations.

Figure 15.4 on page 693 shows the relationship of controller, model, and view objects.

- Model: The model is the set of data and actions that describes some real-world object or process.
- View (Observer): displays the modeled information.
- Controller: provides for user input.

We determined that one of the advantages of the MVC patterns is that it partitions code in model, view, and controller components. This makes our code easier to manage. In this section we will enhance our ability to manage a program by using inheritance in our MVC pattern. In particular, we want to make it easier to manage multiple views of a program's model.

It is often desirable to view the model information it provides in many different forms. Sometimes a graph expresses the results most clearly. Other times a table of numbers or a pie chart is most useful. Sometimes we need to see all of the information and other times we want to focus on only a subset of the information produced by the model. Each one of these benefits from the implementation of a unique view. For example, in our wages program we may choose to have a crossover view that displays the year when college earnings overtake high school earnings.

Our implementation in Chapter 15 makes it more difficult to add views than is necessary. Listing 16.18 shows how the code for creating a view is distributed within the model. When we add a view we must change the code in three places. We must add a new instance variable for each view, add the code to create each view in the model constructor, and add code to paint each view after the model is recomputed. We will not be able to make these changes at runtime.

Listing 16.18 Outline of the Chapter 15 Simplified Model

```
1   public class WagesModel
2   {
3     private EarningsObserver myEarningsObserver;
4     ...
5     public WagesModel ()
6     {
7       ...
8       myEarningsObserver = new EarningsObserver ();
9     }
10
11    public void compute()
12    {
13      ...
14      myEarningsObserver.update(this);
15    }
16  }
```

Using the full-blown model-view-controller, we can write code that allows us to add a new view at the click of a button. Our strategy is to create a list of viewers managed by the model. The controller will create new views and ask the model to add them to its list. To process a list of arbitrary views, we must take advantage of polymorphism and dynamic binding. Its structure in illustrated in Listing 16.8.

First, we will implement an abstract observer class. It will be used as a base class for all observers. The key method that we will override is update (Listing 16.19). Now we can reimplement the EarningsObserver class to inherit from Observer (Line 1 in Listing 16.20).

Listing 16.19 The Abstract Observer Class

```
1  import java.awt.Frame;
2  public abstract class Observer extends Frame
3  {
4    public void update (WagesModel wm) {;}
5  }
```

Listing 16.20 The New EarningsObserver Class

```
1  public class EarningsObserver extends Observer
2                                implements WindowListener
3  {
4    ...
5  }
```

Listing 16.21 The new `WagesModel` class

```
1   import java.util.Vector;
2   public class WagesModel
3   {
4      private Vector myObserverList;
5      ...
6
7      public WagesModel ()
8      {
9         ...
10
11        myObserverList = new Vector ();
12     }
13
14     public void add (Observer observer)
15     {
16        myObserverList.addElement (observer);
17     }
18
19     public void compute()
20     {
21        ...
22        notify ();
23     }
24
25     public void notify ()
26     {
27        for (int i=0; i<myObserverList.size(); i++)
28           ((Observer)(myObserverList).elementAt(i)).update(this);
29     }
30     ...
31     ...
32     ...
33  }
```

We must make the model work with a list of observers. Listing 16.21 outlines this code.

- First, we declare an instance variable for a list of observers in Line 4.

- The constructor in Line 11 creates an empty list of observers.

- The controller is responsible for creating and adding observers to the model. We must implement an `add` method that allows the controller to add observers to the list (Lines 14 through 17).

Figure 16.8 MVC Sequence Diagram

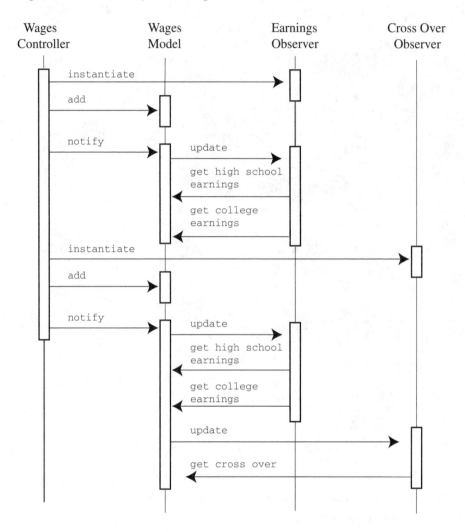

- We write the `notify` method, which updates all observers in the observer list (Lines 25 through 29). This is the code that relies on polymorphism and dynamic binding. Each item in the list could be any kind of observer as long as it inherits `Observer`. Notice the cast to `Observer` in Line 28.

- Finally, the `compute` method updates all observers by calling `notify` (Line 22).

Figure 16.8 on page 792 shows a sequence of events in which the controller creates and adds two observers to the model. It demonstrates how these objects interact.

1. The controller begins by creating an earnings observer.
2. The new observer is added to the model's list. The model now has a list of one observer.
3. The controller asks the model to update all of its observers. The model finds a list of a single earnings observer. The model tells this observer to update itself. As a result, the observer gets the latest earnings information from the model and redraws itself.
4. The controller creates a second observer.
5. The new observer is also added to the model's list. The model now has a list of two observers.
6. The controller asks the model to update all of its observers. The model finds a list of two observers. The model tells each observer to update itself. As a result, each observer gets the latest earnings information from the model and redraws itself.

Notice how each observer makes specialized requests to the model. One of the advantages of the MVC pattern is that each view only gets the information it needs from the model. For example, the crossover observer only needs to know the crossover year, so that is the only information it requests.

Now all we need to do is modify the controller class to create observers and add them to the model. In Figure 16.9, two new observers have been added. One displays the crossover year—the year when college earnings pass the high school earnings. The second displays the difference between college and high school earnings.

Our application is more flexible. Adding additional kinds of observers is easy. All we need to do is create a new observer that inherits the abstract `Observer` class (Listing 16.24 on page 798). The key is to implement the `update` method so that it requests any information it needs from the model. Finally, the controller must create an instance of our new observer and add it to the list of observers maintained by the model. The code in the model is not changed.

Figure 16.9 Many Views

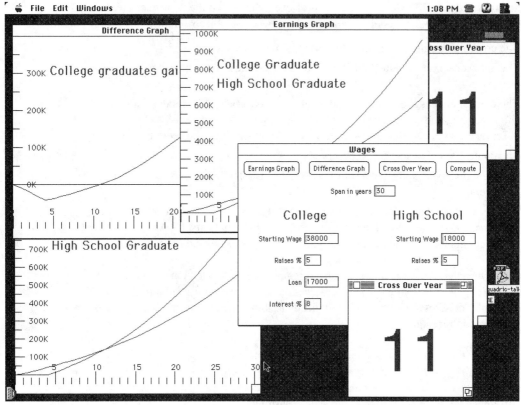

REFERENCE

16.8   Summary

The key ideas covered in this chapter are inheritance, polymorphism, dynamic binding, and persistent store. By using inheritance, we were able use the composite object pattern to organize shapes of a drawing into a simple inheritance structure. Since the shapes have a common superclass, we were able to use polymorphism to refer to these shapes without needing to know to which class a shape belongs. Dynamic binding allowed us to apply operations to these objects without knowing their exact type. The composite pattern simplified added new shapes to our drawing.

We also took advantage of inheritance to implement the model-view-controller pattern with similar results.

We learned to use the `ObjectOutputStream` and `ObjectInputStream` to store and load objects from a persistent store. The benefit of a persistent store is that type information is preserved and checked during file input.

We learned how to use the `protected` modifier in combination with packages to control the visibility of methods and create libraries.

16.9   Bibliography

- Gamma, Erich with Richard Helm, Ralph Johnson, and John Vlissides. 1995. *Design Patterns: Elements of Reusable Object-Oriented Software*. Reading, MA: Addison Wesley.
- Riel, Arthur J. 1996. *Object-Oriented Design Heuristics*. Reading, MA: Addison Wesley.

PROGRAM LISTINGS

Listing 16.22 The `Oval` Class

```
1  //****************************************************************
2  //
3  // title:    Oval
4  //
5  // This component is an oval.
6  //
7  //****************************************************************
8
9  import java.awt.Color;
10 import java.awt.Graphics;
11 import java.io.Serializable;
12
13 public class Oval extends Shape implements Serializable
14 {
15    int    myX;
16    int    myY;
17    int    myWidth;
18    int    myHeight;
19
20    //---------- Oval -----------------------------------------
21    // pre:  x, y, width, and height are positive.
22    // post: an oval component is created
23    public Oval (int x, int y, int width, int height,
24                 Color color)
25    {
26      myX      = x;
27      myY      = y;
28      myWidth  = width;
29      myHeight = height;
30      myColor  = color;
31    }
32
33    //---------- paint ----------------------------------------
34    // pre:  none.
35    // post: this oval is painted on graphics context g
36    public void paint (Graphics g)
37    {
38      g.setColor(myColor);
39      g.fillOval(myX, myY, myWidth, myHeight);
40    }
41 }
```

Listing 16.23 The Triangle Class

```
1  //*************************************************************
2  //
3  // title:    Triangle
4  //
5  // This component is a triangle.
6  //
7  //*************************************************************
8
9  import java.awt.Color;
10 import java.awt.Graphics;
11 import java.awt.Polygon;
12 import java.io.Serializable;
13
14 public class Triangle extends Shape implements Serializable
15 {
16    Polygon myPolygon;
17
18    //---------- Triangle ------------------------------------
19    // pre:  x, y, width, and height are positive.
20    // post: a triangle component is created
21    public Triangle (int x1, int y1, int x2, int y2,
22                     int x3, int y3, Color color)
23    {
24      myPolygon = new Polygon();
25      myPolygon.addPoint(x1, y1);
26      myPolygon.addPoint(x2, y2);
27      myPolygon.addPoint(x3, y3);
28      myColor  = color;
29    }
30
31    //---------- paint ---------------------------------------
32    // pre:  none.
33    // post: this triangle is painted on graphics context g
34    public void paint (Graphics g)
35    {
36      g.setColor(myColor);
37      g.fillPolygon(myPolygon);
38    }
39 }
```

Listing 16.24 CrossOverObserver Class

```
1  //**********************************************************
2  //
3  // title:    CrossOverObserver
4  //
5  // A "Wages" observer that displays when college earnings
6  // overtake high school earnings.
7  //
8  //**********************************************************
9
10 import java.awt.Color;
11 import java.awt.Dimension;
12 import java.awt.FlowLayout;
13 import java.awt.Font;
14 import java.awt.Frame;
15 import java.awt.Graphics;
16 import java.awt.event.WindowListener;
17 import java.awt.event.WindowEvent;
18
19 public class CrossOverObserver extends Observer
20                                   implements WindowListener
21 {
22   private int         myCrossOver;
23
24   //---------- EarningsGraph --------------------------------
25   //
26   // pre:  none
27   // post: A new crossover graph is created based on the
28   //         current wages model.
29
30   public CrossOverObserver()
31   {
32     addWindowListener(this);
33     setBackground (Color.white);
34     setSize(200, 150);
35     setTitle ("Cross Over Year");
36     setLayout(new FlowLayout());
37     setLocation (430, 20);
38     show();
39   }
40
```

Listing 16.24 CrossOverObserver Class

```
41    //---------- paint --------------------------------------
42    //
43    // pre:  none
44    // post: This crossover year is displayed
45
46    public void paint (Graphics g)
47    {
48      g.setColor(Color.red);
49      Font f = new Font ("sansserif", Font.PLAIN, 96);
50      g.setFont(f);
51      if (myCrossOver == Integer.MAX_VALUE)
52        g.drawString ("**", 50, 125);
53      else
54        g.drawString (Integer.toString(iCrossOver), 50, 125);
55    }
56
57    //---------- update --------------------------------------
58    //
59    // pre:  none
60    // post: Current cross over year is obtained from the
61    //       wages model and this year is redrawn
62
63    public void update (WagesModel model)
64    {
65      myCrossOver = model.getCrossOver();
66      repaint();
67    }
68
69    public void windowClosing (WindowEvent event)
70    {
71      dispose();
72    }
73
74    // window listener methods that do nothing
75    public void windowOpened (WindowEvent event){;}
76    public void windowClosed (WindowEvent event){;}
77    public void windowIconified (WindowEvent event){;}
78    public void windowDeiconified (WindowEvent event){;}
79    public void windowActivated (WindowEvent event){;}
80    public void windowDeactivated (WindowEvent event){;}
81 }
```

PROBLEM SETS

16.10 Exercises

Inheritance—Section 16.5

1 List the advantages of inheritance.

2 What is printed by the following code fragments? See Listing 16.25.

a.
```
Father dad = new Father(42);
dad.mayIBorrowTheCar();
```

b.
```
Mother mom = new Mother(40);
int    age = mom.getAge();
System.out.println(age);
```

c.
```
Parent oldOne = new Father(39);
oldOne.mayIBorrowTheCar();
oldOne = new Mother(41);
oldOne.mayIBorrowTheCar();
```

d.
```
Parent oldOne = new Parent(45);
oldOne.mayIBorrowTheCar();
```

e.
```
int day = 2;
Parent oldOne;
switch (day) {
  case 0: oldOne = new Parent(52); break;
  case 1: oldOne = new Mother(35); break;
  case 2: oldOne = new Father(42); break;
  case 3: oldOne = new Parent(48); break;
}
oldOne.mayIBorrowTheCar();
System.out.println(oldOne.getAge());
```

f. Do the above if day is 3.

Listing 16.25 `Parent, Father,` a nd `Mother` classes

```
1 public class Parent
2 {
3   private int iAge;
4   public int getAge()
5   {
6     return iAge;
7   }
8   public void mayIBorrowTheCar()
9   {
10     System.out.println("NO");
11   }
12   public Parent (int age)
13   {
14     iAge = age;
15   }
16 }
17
18 public class Father extends Parent
19 {
20   public Father (int age)
21   {
22     iAge = age;
23   }
24   public void mayIBorrowTheCar()
25   {
26     System.out.println("Ask mom");
27   }
28 }
29
30 public class Mother extends Parent
31 {
32   public void mayIBorrowTheCar()
33   {
34     System.out.println("Yes");
35   }
36   public Mother (int age)
37   {
38     iAge = age;
39   }
40 }
```

3   If the `Parent` class in Listing 16.25 is made abstract, which of the following is illegal?

```
Parent oldOne     = new Parent(52);
Parent numberOne  = new Mother(35);
Parent otherOne   = new Father(42);
```

4   Given the following code, which operations are legal?

```
in Base.java
public class Base
{
   private   void base1 () {;}
   protected void base2 () {;}
   public    void base3 () {;}
}
in Derived.java
public class Derived extends Base
{
}
in Client.java
public class Client
{
   public static void main (String args[])
   {
      Derived d = new Derived ();
   }
}
```

a.   `d.base1 ();`

b.   `d.base2 ();`

c.   `d.base3 ();`

5   Given the following code, which operations are legal?

```
in Base.java
package pack;
public class Base
{
  private   void base1 () {;}
  protected void base2 () {;}
  public    void base3 () {;}
}
in Derived.java
package pack;
public class Derived extends Base
{
}
in Client.java
import pack.Derived;
public class Client
{
  public static void main (String args[])
  {
    Derived d = new Derived ();
  }
}
```

a.   `d.base1 ();`

b.   `d.base2 ();`

c.   `d.base3 ();`

Patterns—Section 16.3 and Section 16.7

6   Create a sequence diagram for the following sequence of events for the implementation of composite pattern in Section 16.2. See Figure 16.8 on page 792 for an example.

```
Shape leaves   = new Oval (40, 30, 50, 100, Color.green);
leaves.paint (g);
```

7   Create a sequence diagram for the following sequence of events for the implementation of composite pattern in Section 16.2. See Figure 16.8 on page 792 for an example.

```
Shape tree     = new Composite ();
Shape leaves   = new Oval (40, 30, 50, 100, Color.green);
tree.add (leaves);
Shape trunk    = new Box (60, 130, 10, 40, Color.black);
tree.add (trunk);
tree.paint (g);
```

8   Create a sequence diagram for the following sequence of events for the implementation of the MVC pattern in Section 16.7. See Figure 16.8 on page 792 for an example.

- create an earnings observer
- add it
- update
- change input values and compute
- update

16.11   Projects

Inheritance—Section 16.2, Section 16.5

9   Add three trees to the `Create` application in Listing 16.6.

10   Add a line shape to the `Create` and `Draw` programs (Listing 16.6 and Listing 16.7).

11   Add a star shape to the create and draw programs (Listing 16.6 and Listing 16.7).

12   Modify the classes from Section 16.2 so that all the shapes are part of a shapes package. The create and draw programs should not belong to any package.

13   Combine the create and draw programs (Listing 16.6 and Listing 16.7). Modify them so they can save and restore images using the `FileDialog` class.

14   Combine the ideas of the Doodle program in Chapter 14, the create program in Listing 16.6, and the drawing program in Listing 16.7 to create a general-purpose drawing programming. Include tools that let the user to select line, oval, or rectangle drawing tools. Add buttons and/or menus to make your program able to save and load arbitrary drawings.

Object Stores—Section 16.4

15   Write a program that reads the movie review file from Chapter 11 and Chapter 12 and saves it as an object file.

16   Write a program that reads the stock price file from Chapter 9 and Chapter 12 and saves it as an object file.

17   Write one application that saves the story template from Listing 10.1 on page 441 in an object file. Next modify Listing 10.1 so that it reads the template from the object file.

18   Reimplement the editor from exercise 17 in Chapter 15 so that it saves and restores from an object file.

19   Write a program that maintains a list of all your CDs. It should contain a CD class that contains a field for the name of the CD, the name of the performers, and a rating from one to five stars (five stars is the highest rating). It should be able to save and load your list from an object file.

Create another class which is a list of CDs. It should support the operations of sort and search.

Create an interface that asks for each CD's name, performer, and rating. Include support menus, buttons, and text fields for input, searching, and sorting.

A   HTML

A Web Page

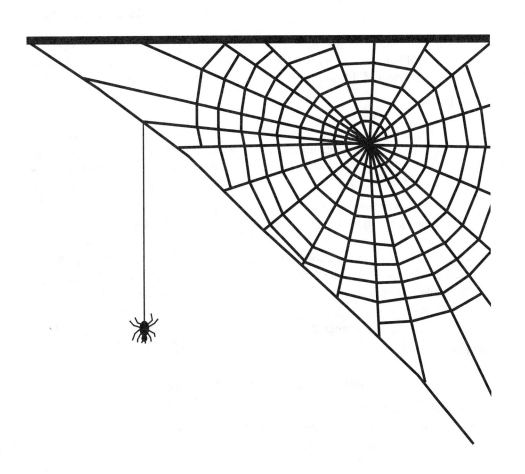

A.1   Objectives

Concepts   **Section A.2, page 809**

This appendix focuses on how information is represented in a web document and how that organization differs from other computer word processing systems. We begin with a brief look at how formatted text is represented using a WYSIWYG (What-You-See-Is-What-You-Get) word processor and a markup language.

Section A.3, page 810

We then move on to a brief look at how the web came about. This is followed by a look at an example web page written with HTML.

Section A.5, page 834

Finally, an optional section looks at the underlying representation of text files and how they differ from binary files. Knowing the difference will help us understand why they are treated differently on the web and within text editors.

HTML Skills

This chapter takes a look at a small subset of HTML. Some knowledge of HTML is required to make Java programs available over the web. In addition, learning HTML can serve as a gentle introduction to using the various computer components required to write a Java program.

- HTML document organization   Section A.4.2, page 822
- Writing paragraphs   Section A.4.3, page 823
- Using headers   Section A.4.4, page 825
- Working with fonts and special characters Section A.4.5, page 826
- Anchors and linking to other web pages   Section A.4.8, page 828
- Embedding images   Section A.4.11, page 831
- Creating lists   Section A.4.12, page 832
- Embedding a Java program   Section A.4.13, page 833

Abilities

By the end of this chapter we should be able to do the following:

- Create a web page.
- Using the local software tools to edit and save files. (Must be provided by the local institution.)

CONCEPTS

A.2   Type Setting and Word Processing

Tex (pronounced "tech"), designed by Donald E. Knuth, is example of a markup language that uses printable characters to embed formatting commands. Knuth invented Tex as a typesetting language for his series of books entitled *The Art of Computer Programming.* Tex and its LaTex variant are used heavily for computer science publications. To place the word "Zod" in italics one enters the sequence {\em Zod} in LaTex. In HTML, a markup language used to represent web documents, it appears as <i> Zod </i>.

> *Markup* is a metaphor derived from the annotations that editors make in documents to describe how they should be typeset. Rules are included to describe how titles will be placed, where images appear, font sizes, links to other documents, background colors, and much more.

An annoyance of markup languages is that document preparation is a multistep process. For example, in LaTex the document is first edited with the special markup commands embedded within the text. Next it is run through a LaTex translator one or more times to create a device-independent representation. This device-independent representation is sent through another translator, which converts it to a device-specific representation such as PostScript. Finally, it is sent to the printer. This process is time-consuming, and it requires great skill on the writer's behalf to first learn the formatting commands and then to imagine their impact on the final document. For those who have learned LaTex, they find it an expressive environment that provides extensive control over a final document. For the casual user, a word processor is much easier to use.

Another approach to document preparation is the word processor. Word processing was invented by IBM as a means to market their Selectric typewriter system. It included a magnetic tape system for recording, editing, and playing back documents. This market expanded with the introduction of computers dedicated to word processing. Wang Laboratories got a foothold in the computer market through this medium. The market changed with the introduction of the IBM PC. Word processors changed from machines dedicated to one specific task, to word processing programs that are added to a general-purpose computer.

Compared with today's word processing packages, these early systems were difficult to learn because they required memorizing special key sequences. This changed with the development of the graphical user interface (GUI) at Xerox PARC (Palo Alto Research Center). Apple popularized GUIs with the introduction of the Macintosh in 1984. The chief advantage of GUIs is that they are easy to learn. To print a document, it is sufficient to pull down a menu and select Print. No messy translators. Another advantage is the WYSIWYG (What-You-See-Is-What-You-Get) display. In earlier word processors characters were displayed monospaced on the screen. Typically a display would contain 24 lines of 80 evenly spaced characters. As a result, the display did not match the printed output. This problem was corrected with the GUI interface. Documents appeared on the screen as they would appear after printing.

In WYSIWYG word processing, commands for formatting are not entered using printable sequences of characters as they are in markup languages. Instead, they are encoded by sequences of nonprintable characters. For example, to italicize the word Zod, one highlights Zod by double-clicking on it and then choosing the italic icon from the tool bar. In WordPerfect 5.0 the italicized Zod is stored as the following character sequence:

```
195 8 195 90 111 100 196 8 196
```

The first three numbers indicate the start of italicized text, the next three encode the characters "Zod," and the final three indicate the end of italicized text. The standard set of printable characters have values between 32 and 126. Notice that 195 and 196 are out of that range. Most word processors encode formatting information by taking advantage of the 256 possible values for a byte of information. This may cause problems if these documents are transmitted over a modem. Many modems are set up to transmit numbers no larger than 127. Thus, the numbers from 128 to 255 are not transmitted correctly. Special software must be used to encode and decode word processing documents to get around this problem. (See Section A.5 , page 834 for details about the representation of text.)

A.3   The World Wide Web

A.3.1   A Little History

In the 1950s, the U.S. Congress authorized the National Science Foundation (NSF) to "foster an interchange of scientific information among scientists in the United States and foreign countries." Scientific experiments produce a lot of information. The communication of that information to colleagues is critical. By sharing information, researchers can build on other's work.

The Internet has its roots in ARPANET (Advanced Research Projects Agency Network). ARPANET was funded by the Department of Defense (DoD) in the late 1960s to provide communication between DoD-funded projects in academia and industry. In the 1980s NSF funded a project, called NSFNET, to make networking available to a broader constituency. This network has grown and became known as the Internet. In 1969 ARPANET had four computers connected to it. This slowly grew to 200 in 1983. In January of 1996 there were more than 80,000 networks connected to the Internet worldwide, with the number doubling every 12 months. In the U.S., the Internet is supported by a network of high-speed connections provided by such companies as MCI, Sprint, AGIS, UUNet/AlterNet, ANS, and PSI. Since these high-speed connections support traffic between distant locations, they are collectively called the "Internet Backbone." Some have also used the term the "Information Superhighway" to draw an analogy between the Internet and the Interstate Highway System (Figure A.1).

Figure A.1 Internet

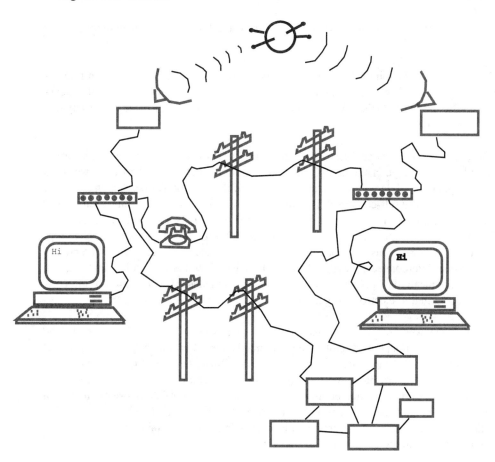

A *network* is a set of computers that are connected together by twisted pairs of copper wire, cable, optical fibers, modems, microwave radio, and satellite links. These computers communicate with each other by sending *packets*, chunks of information. These packets follow a *protocol*, which describes how information is organized in the packet. An important piece of information within the protocol is the destination address.

The web was started by Tim Berners-Lee in 1989 while at CERN, the European Laboratory for Particle Physics. He was interested in managing all the information he and his colleagues around the world had gathered about accelerators and accelerator experiments. He was concerned that important information may be lost. His solution is based on a distributed hypertext system.

A *hypertext* document includes text with electronic links to other hypertext documents.

This project has grown into the World Wide Web (WWW, or web), which is an international interconnected collection of electronic documents managed by governments, industry, schools, and individuals. The web does not belong to and is not managed by any one person or organization.

The web has many of the characteristics of a book. It is a medium for recording information with the advantage of including sound and motion. What makes the web powerful is that it is dynamic, while a book is static. What is printed in a book does not change with time and is typically self-contained. References to other books or documents often require trips to a local library. In contrast, information on the web can be easily changed and electronically linked. A single page may have links to supporting information and related topics all over the world. This additional information can be accessed with a click of a button. This dynamic interconnectedness is changing how we view and manipulate information. This does not mean that books will disappear. It simply means that some kinds of information is more suited to electronic organization.

We access the web by running a web browser that is connected to the Internet. The browser reads documents with embedded commands that determine how the page should appear and how it links to other documents. The web illustrates one of the important uses for a network: to share data. Another reason for networking computers is for sharing resources. For example, computers in faculty offices and student laboratories can share a single printer. In addition, a super computer at one site can be shared by scientists at other locations. An additional use for networks is electronic mail. Electronic mail allows quick communications among people all over the world.

A.3.2 The Starry Night—A Web Page Design

Vincent van Gogh is a well-known post-impressionist painter of the late 19th century. Our task is to create a web page that illustrates his artistry by focusing on The Starry Night painting. The following describes how the web page is to look and the information it is to contain:

> Requirements for the van Gogh web page: The goal of this page is to illustrate the artistry of Vincent van Gogh. Use his painting *The Starry Night* to illustrate his impact both visually and in text. The web page is to be entitled "The Starry Night." It will contain a small rendition of *The Starry Night* painting and a brief historical outline. Include a visual interpretation followed by a few notes about the painter. Illustrate the painting's impact by providing an audio clip of Don McLean's song *Vincent*. Provide a link to a larger rendition of *The Starry Night*. Links should also be provided to the Paris WebMuseum which has a large collection of van Gogh's work. See Figure A.2 for a sketch of the final web page.

Figure A.2 Rough Sketch of The Starry Night Web Page

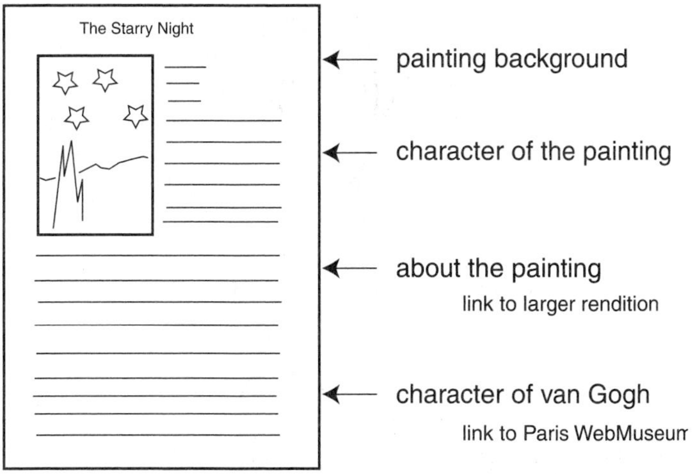

A.3.3 Web Page Implementation

Hypertext Markup Language (HTML) describes a set of rules for expressing the layout and links for pages on the web. Hypertext has its roots with Ted Nelson, who coined the term in 1965. Hypertext became popular in 1987 when Apple released HyperCard, which was developed by Bill Atkinson. *Hypermedia* refers to the incorporation of sound, video, and graphics into hypertext documents.

The text formatting used in HTML is expressed by annotating the text with commands. Web browsers, such as Netscape, Explorer, and Mosaic, translate HTML documents into the final representation we seen in a computer window.

A *translator* is a computer program that converts one computer language to another. For example, a web browser converts HTML documents to the computer commands needed to display a document (e.g., PostScript and True Type, Figure A.3). In Chapter 1 we describe how a translator is used to convert Java programs to byte-code instructions.

Figure A.3 Translation Process—Latin to English & HTML to Display

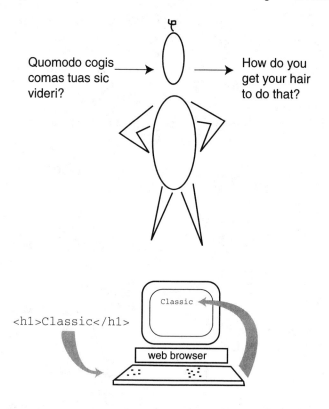

Unlike books, hypertext documents are not constrained to be a linear sequence of pages. Hypertext organizes text by interconnecting documents. For example, in the document describing *The Starry Night* painting there is a link to a document that describes other van Gogh paintings at the Paris WebMuseum. A *link* is a pointer from one web page to another. When a link is selected, the web page to which the link points is retrieved. At the Paris WebMuseum there are other links that point to yet other web pages.

Listing A.1 is the HTML document for The Starry Night web page shown in Figure A.4. This page illustrates how HTML commands can be used to create a web page. The remainder of this section will outline how HTML source code in Listing A.1 achieves the display in Figure A.4. More details about HTML are found in Section A.4.

> *Note:* The screen image captured in Figure A.4 is annotated with numbers to make it easier to match the description with the image. Within this section, when a number appears in square bracket, such as [1], it refers to annotation 1 in Figure A.4. In addition, the numbers placed in front of each line in Listing A.1 are not part of the HTML document. They are placed there to make it easier to reference each line of code.

The Starry Night HTML source program in Listing A.1 begins with comments (Lines 1 through 11). Comments are ignored by a web browser. They are inserted into a document to provide information to a person reading the HTML program. It is information that is generally of no interest to the person browsing the web, and thus should not appear within the browser display window. In this example, the comments state who authored the web page and briefly why the web page was written.

An HTML document is composed of two parts: the header and the body. The browser window title [1] is described within the header part (Lines 13 through 17 of Listing A.1). The body part describes how the text within the browser window will appear (Lines 19 through 72).

The title [2] that appears within the web window is placed between heading tags (Line 21). The `h1` tag corresponds to the largest header.

The `hr` (horizontal rule) tag, which appears in Line 23, creates a horizontal line at [3]. It is used to visually partition the heading from the main part of the text.

The image tag in Line 25 describes the location and placement of the image that appears at [4]. The name of the image file is `starry-night.small.jpg`. In this case, the image is to be left justified (`align=left`). Since the image is left aligned, text will squeeze in on the right side of the image if there is room.

Figure A.4 Translated Web Page for The Starry Night

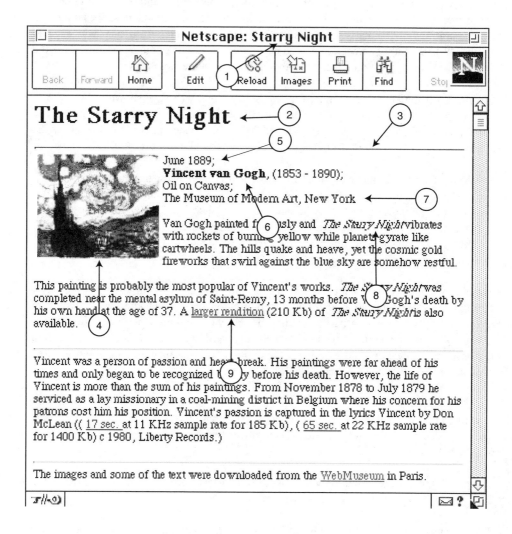

Listing A.1 HTML Code for The Starry Night

```
1  <!----------------------------------------------------------
2  --
3  -- title:   The Starry Night
4  -- author:  Ed C. Epp
5  -- date:    5-28-96
6  --
7  -- A web page that illustrates the artistry of Vincent van Gogh
8  -- using his painting The Starry Night to illustrate its impact
9  -- both visually and in verse.
10 --
11 ----------------------------------------------------------------
>
12
13 <head>
14
15 <title> Starry Night </title>
16
17 </head>
18
19 <body>
20
21 <h1> The Starry Night </h1>
22
23 <hr>
24
25 <img align=left src="gogh.starry-night.small.jpg">
26
27 June 1889; <br>
28 <b>Vincent van Gogh</b>, (1853 - 1890); <br>
29 Oil on Canvas; <br>
30 The Museum of Modern Art, New York <p>
31
32 Van Gogh painted furiously and <i>The Starry Night</i>
33 vibrates with rockets of burning yellow while planets gyrate
34 like cartwheels.
35 The hills quake and heave, yet the cosmic gold fireworks that
36 swirl against the blue sky are somehow restful.
37 <p>
38
39 This painting is probably the most popular of Vincent's works.
40 <i>The Starry Night</i> was completed near the mental asylum
41 of Saint-Remy, 13 months before Van Gogh's death by his own hand
42 at the age of 37.
43 A <a href="gogh.starry-night.jpg">larger rendition</a> (210 Kb)
44 of <i> The Starry Night </i> is also available.
45 <p>
46
47 <hr>
48
```

Listing A.1 HTML Code for The Starry Night

```
49 Vincent was a person of passion and heart-break.
50 His paintings were far ahead of his times and only began to be
51 recognized briefly before his death.
52 However, the life of Vincent is more than the sum of his paint-
ings.
53 From November 1878 to July 1879 he serviced as a lay missionary
54 in a coal-mining district in Belgium where his concern for his
55 patrons cost him his position.
56 Vincent's passion is captured in the lyrics Vincent
57 by Don McLean  ((
58  <a href="vincent11-17.aiff"> 17 sec.  </a>
59  at 11 KHz sample rate for 185 Kb), (
60  <a href="vincent22-65.aiff"> 65 sec. </a>
61  at 22 KHz sample rate for 1400 Kb)
62  c 1980, Liberty Records.)
63 <p>
64
65 <hr>
66
67 The images and some of the text were downloaded from the
68 <a href="http://watt.emf.net/wm//paint/auth/gogh/">WebMuseum</
a>
69 in Paris.
70 <p>
71
72 </body>
```

The br tag in Line 27 creates a line break at [5]. Any text that follows appears on the next line.

Text between b tags in Line 28 is bolded. Thus, Vincent van Gogh at [6] appears in bold. Another tag that changes the type font is the italics tag (i). Text in Line 32 between i tags appears in italics as shown at [8].

The p tag signals the beginning of a paragraph (see [7] and Line 30). Inspection of Listing A.1 shows how several additional paragraphs are specified using the paragraph tag. Notice that the line endings in Listing A.1 do not match the line endings in the browser window. Text fills the entire width of the window unless a break or paragraph tag is found. Each word could be placed on its own line without changing the appearance of the browser window. The blank lines are included to make the HTML source code easier to read; they communicate nothing to the browser. Resizing the browser window causes the line breaks to occur at different locations. Since line breaks in the HTML document have no affect on the browser, the author chose to start each sentence on a new line. This makes it easier to move sentences around by cutting and pasting entire lines.

Anchors allow us to link to other documents. The anchor tag from Line 43 shown below.

```
<a href="gogh.starry-night.jpg">larger rendition</a>
```

It is used to create a link to a large rendition of *The Starry Night* painting. The href attribute defines the location of that image. In this case it is located in a file named gogh.starry-night.jpg. The text between the beginning and ending anchor tag, larger rendition, defines the *hot text*. Clicking on hot text at [9] activates the link. In this example, clicking on larger rendition in the browser window will load the larger image. The jpg extension tells the browser that an image is to be loaded. By contrast, an html extension loads a web page and an aiff extension loads an audio clip.

```
<a href="vincent11-17.aiff"> 17 sec. </a>
```

Above is an example of a link to an audio file (see Line 58). When the hot text 17 sec is selected, a portion of the song *Vincent* by Don McLean is played. (This may require some special hardware or software on the user's computer. Do not be surprised if you do not hear anything. Since audio clips are large files, it may take a while for the sound to start.)

It is a common courtesy to indicate the file size if a link to an audio or image file initiates downloading of a large file. If a file is too large, a user may decide not to download it. A 1400 Kb file will take a long time to load.

The final anchor in Line 68 creates a link to the Paris WebMuseum, where other paintings of van Gogh can be found. This link illustrates how HTML documents can be used to tie together information from around the world. This link will always point to the most recent information at the Paris WebMuseum.

HTML

A.4   HTML

This section takes a closer look at a subset of HTML. There is a lot more to HTML than appears here. This introduction is designed to provide us with the tools to set up a minimal web page with Java applets.

HTML commands are written with tags. Each *tag* describes something about how the text that follows should be formatted within a browser window. Many tags are followed by an ending tag that informs the browser to end the previous format command. HTML commands are generally of the form:

```
<tag ID > intervening text </tag ID >
```

Notice that the tag begins a format action in the first set of arrow brackets and ends it with a second set of arrow brackets. The ending tag is identical to the beginning tag except for a single forward slash (/) character. There are several tags that break this general HTML rule. Four of those tags are the `hr`, `img`, `br`, and `p` tags. They may not have an ending tag.

Tag IDs are not *case sensitive*. It does not make a difference whether uppercase or lowercase letters are used. Thus, the tag IDs `head`, `hEaD`, and `HEAD` are identical in HTML.

A.4.1 Comments

Comments are useful for making notes in an HTML document without having them appear in the browser display. Comments begin with < ! - - and end with - ->. Everything between these character sequences is ignored.

For example:

```
<!-- The following line was added to meet federal guidelines
title 18.7 for the disposal of pencil sharpener waste.  Before
making any changes please refer to page 3764 paragraph 7. -->
```

The above comment would be important to programmers assigned to modify this web page. It would inform them to look carefully at title 18.7 requirements before making any modifications to the next line. However, this information will probably not be of interest to the person browsing the web page. Comments can appear anywhere within the HTML source code. See Figure A.5.

Figure A.5 Comments

```
I can see the great effort <!-- but it
turned out poor --> you placed on your
term paper.  <!-- Consider a change
in major. -->
```

I can see the great effort you placed on your term paper.

A.4.2   Sections

An HTML document is composed of two parts: a header and the body. The browser window title is described within the header part. The body part describes how the text within the browser window will appear.

The header section begins with <head> and ends with </head>. The text that is between the head tags specifies the name of the browser window. Figure A.6 shows an example with a window titled "Buzz Lightyear" and a body which contains "To infinity and beyond."

Figure A.6 Page Sections

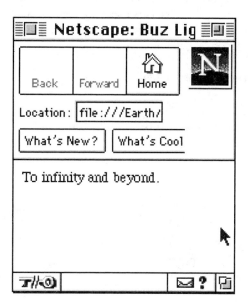

```
<head>
<title> Buzz Lightyear </title>
</head>

<body>
To infinity and beyond.
</body>
```

A.4.3   Line Control

A web browser formats a web page without regard to carriage returns and tabs. The following describes how to control ends of lines, new paragraphs, and turn off formatting.

```
<br>           break: starts a new line.
<p>            Starts a new paragraph
<pre> </pre> Preformatted text: do not format it.
```

Indicating the beginning of a paragraph automatically means that any previous paragraph must have ended. A paragraph need not have an ending tag, but it may be included. We can simply place paragraph tags between paragraphs. Web authors use various styles of placement. Some put them so they appear at the ends of paragraphs. Others place them so they appear at the beginnings or between paragraphs. The style generally used in this text is to place them at the end of paragraphs. This placement is less obtrusive. Other styles are equally valid; for example, the following three examples accomplish the same thing:

```
Paragraph one. <p>   │ Paragraph one.        Paragraph one.
                     │ <p>
Paragraph two.       │ Paragraph two.        <p> Paragraph two.
```

An example of how line control tags work is show in Figure A.7.

Figure A.7 Line Control

```
One fish <br> Two fish <br> Red fish <br> Blue fish. <p>   Edward Bear,
known to his friends
as
Winnie-the-Pooh for short,
was walking


through the forest one day, humming proudly to himself.   He had made up
a little hum that very morning, as he was doing his
Stoutness Exercises in front of the glass.
<p>

<pre>
                                                  Dr. Seuss
                  A. A. Milne
</pre>
```

One fish
Two fish
Red fish
Blue fish.

Edward Bear, known to his friends as Winnie-the-Pooh for short, was walking through the forest one day, humming proudly to himself. He had made up a little hum that very morning, as he was doing his Stoutness Exercieses in front of the glass.

                                          Dr. Seuss

                  A. A. Milne

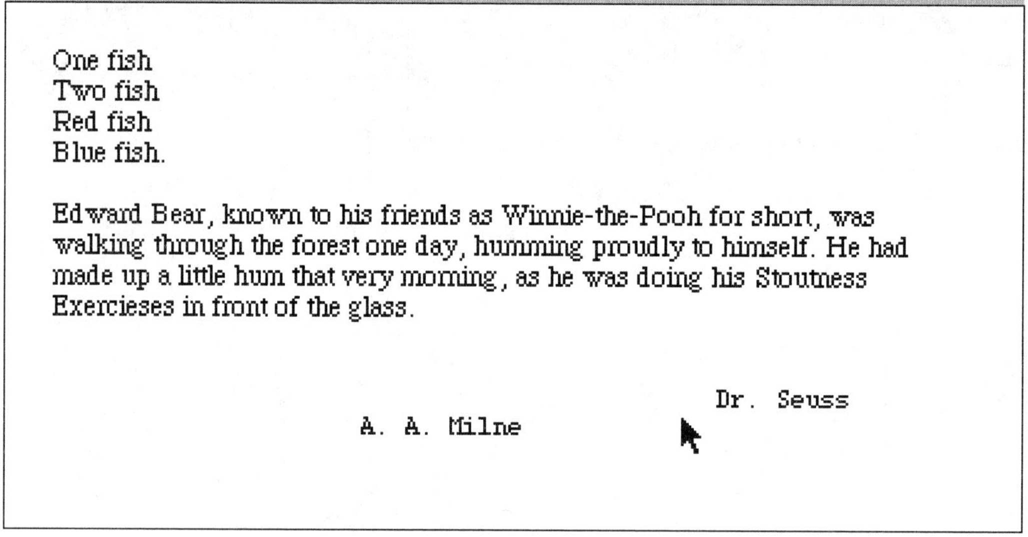

A.4.4 Headings

There are six possible heading tags: h1, h2, h3, h4, h5, and h6. Each represents a different level of heading where h1 is the highest level. The higher the level the larger the font used to display the head. Headers can be placed throughout a web page. Figure 1.8 shows an example.

Figure A.8 Headings

```
<h1> I'm Falling </h1>
<h2> I'm Falling </h2>
<h3> I'm Falling </h3>
<h4> I'm Falling </h4>
<h5> I'm Falling </h5>
<h6> I'm Falling </h6>
<h1> Splat! </h1>
```

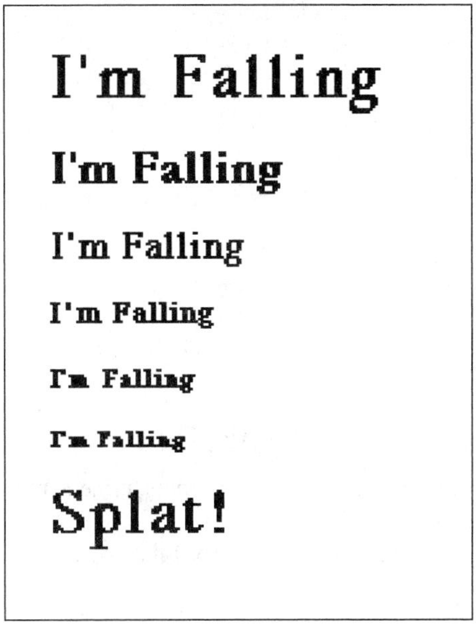

A.4.5   Font Styles

Font styles can be specified with the follow tags:

```
<b>   </b>   Bold font style.
<i>   </i>   Italics font style.
<tt>  </tt>  Typewriter font style - monospaced: used for code.
```

An example is shown Figure A.9.

Figure A.9 Font Styles

```
The following will be said
<b> boldly </b>,
with great
<i> emphasis </i>.
<tt> Using too many font styles makes a
     document hard to read. </tt>
```

> The following will be said **boldly** ,
> with great *emphasis*. Using too
> many font styles makes a
> document hard to read.

A.4.6   Horizontal Rules

A horizontal rule tag, hr, puts a line across a web page (Figure A.10).

Figure A.10 Horizontal rule

<hr><hr><hr>

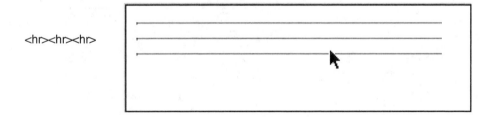

A.4.7 Special Characters

Printable characters such as <, >, and " have special meaning in HTML. Therefore, these characters cannot appear directly in text. If they are needed, special character sequences must be used to display them (Table A.1). An example of using special characters is shown in Figure A.11.   :

Table A.1 Special Characters

character sequence	what is displayed
&lt;	Left arrow bracket (<).
&gt;	Right arrow bracket (>).
&amp;	Ampersand (&).
&quot;	Double quote mark (").
	Nonbreaking space - forced spaces.

Figure A.11 Special Characters

```
The anchor for   
  The White House
    is <br>
<tt>
&lt;a href = &quot;
http://www.whitehouse.gov
&quot;&gt; </tt>
```

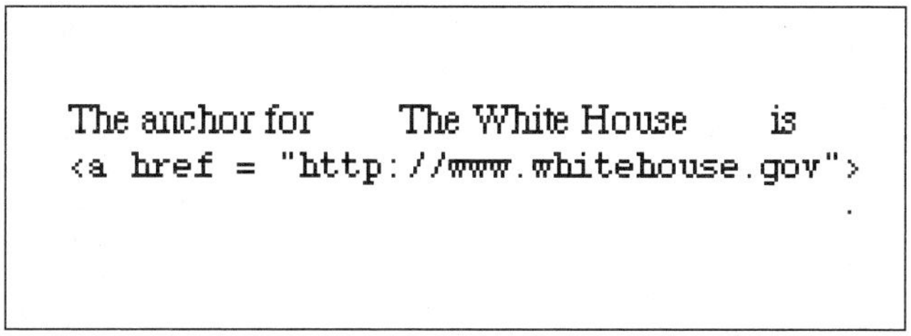

The anchor for   The White House   is
<a href = "http://www.whitehouse.gov">

A.4.8   Anchors and Links

One of the functions of an anchor is to provide a link to another document. The `href` attribute specifies the destination of the link. Clicking on the hot text associated with an anchor will fetch the web page at the given location. In many browsers, hot text is under-lined and colored.

```
<a> </a>                        Anchor tag.
  href          = "address"     Link destination attribute.
  name          = "source"      Link source attribute.
```

Href is an example of a *tag attribute*. They provide additional specifica-tions for a tag in the same way that an adjective modifies a noun or an adverb might modify a verb.

An example of using an anchor is shown in Figure A.12.

Figure A.12 Anchors

```
<a href = "http://www.whitehouse.gov">
White House </a>
```

White House

A.4.9 Anchor URL Extensions

In most of our examples, the web browser will locate a file with the name ending in ".html" such as "index.html". Given the html extension, the browser will treat the file as a web page. Other file extensions, shown in Table A.2, will have different impacts on a browser.

Table A.2 File Name Extensions

extension	file type
aiff	Sound in another audio format
au	Sound in basic audio format
gif	Image in Graphics Interchange Format
jpg, jpeg	Image in compressed jpeg format
html, htm	Hypertext page
mov	Video clip in Macintosh QuickTime format
mpg, mpeg	Video in compressed mpeg format
pict	Image in Macintosh format
xibm	Image in IBM format

A.4.10 Anchors URL Prefixes

An anchor can also be used to create a hot text item for sending mail. Such an anchor is often placed on a home page to make it easy for a reader to send mail to the page owner. Notice that the only change in an anchor from a page link is to replace `http` with `mailto` in the anchor. Other options are listed in Table A.3. An example of an email link is shown in Figure A.13.

Table A.3 Types of Anchors

URL prefix	anchor type
file	Grab a plain text file.
ftp	Transfer the specified document using ftp.
http	A web page link as described above.
gopher	Access the given Gopher server.
mailto	Send mail to the specified address.
news	Access the given news group.
telnet	Start a telnet session at the given address.

Figure A.13 Mail Link

```
Ed C. Epp <a href =
  "mailto:epp@rainier.uofport.edu">
&lt;epp@rainier.uofport.edu&gt;
</a>
```

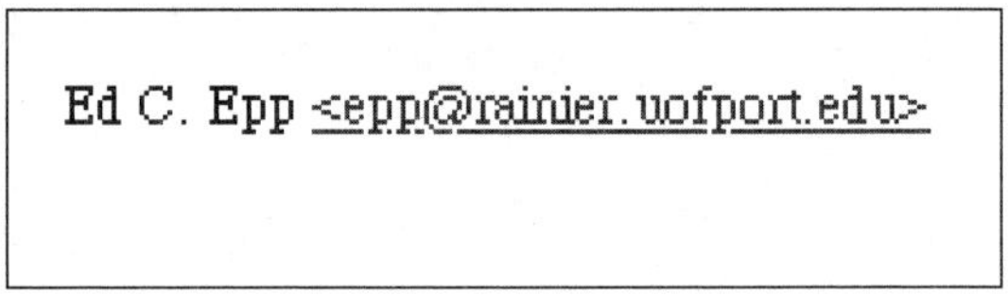

Ed C. Epp <epp@rainier.uofport.edu>

A.4.11   Images

Image tags serve to position an image on the left and right side of a page. There is an additional attribute that allows text to replace the picture for those readers who cannot or choose not to display images.

```
<img> </img>                       Image tag.
  src          = "address"         Attribute determines image location.
  align        = placement         Attribute to specify the placement of an
                                   image on a page: top, bottom, left,
                                   right, middle.
  alt          = "string"          Attribute determines the alternative
                                   string to be displayed in lieu of an im-
                                   age.
```

An example of an image is show in Figure A.14. Notice how the text wraps around the images.

Figure A.14 Images

```
The White House. The White House.
The White House. The White House.
The White House. The White House.
<img align=left src="pin_kids2.jpg">
<img align=right src="pin_kids2.jpg">
Washington DC. Washington DC.
Washington DC. Washington DC.
Washington DC. Washington DC.
Washington DC. Washington DC.
Washington DC. Washington DC.
Washington DC. Washington DC.
```

The White House. The White House. The White House. The White House. The White House. The White House. Washington DC. Washington DC.

 Washington DC. Washington DC. Washington DC. Washington DC. Washington DC.

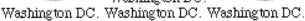

Washington DC. Washington DC. Washington DC. Washington DC. Washington DC.

A.4.12 Lists

Items can be placed in an ordered list, in which each item is numbered, or in an unordered list, in which each item has a bullet.

```
<ol> </ol>    An ordered list.
<ul> </ul>    An unordered list.
<li>          A list item.
```

An example of using lists is shown inFigure A.15.

Figure A.15 Lists

```
Today's Jobs

<ol>
  <li> Brush teeth
  <li> Go to the store for:
    <ul>
      <li> Candy bar
      <li> Gum
      <li> Soda
    </ul>
  <li> Sit in the sun
  <li> Watch TV
    <ol>
      <li> Friends
      <li> Seinfeld
      <li> Mash
    </ol>
  <li> Skip homework
</ol>
```

Today's Jobs

1. Brush teeth
2. Go to the store for:
   o Candy bar
   o Gum
   o Soda
3. Sit in the sun
4. Watch TV
   1. Friends
   2. Seinfeld
   3. Mash
5. Skip homework

A.4.13 Java

The whole purpose for putting information about HTML in this text is because we can use an `applet` tag to attach Java programs to a web page. Many of the programs we write in this text can be attached to a web page and run by web users all over the world.

The process of attaching Java code to a web browser is described in Chapter 1 (Section 1.8.2 , page 27). We provide a description of the `applet` tag here so that this chapter can be used as an HTML reference.

The various attributes of the `applet` tag are shown in Table A.4.

Table A.4 Applet Tag

```
<applet> </applet>Java applet tag.
  code = "file"Location attribute of the J-Code applet class.
  width = valueWidth attribute of the applet display.
  height = valueHeight attribute of the applet display.
  align      = placement  Attribute to specify the placement of
                          an applet on a page: top, bottom, left,
                          right, middle.
  alt = "string"Attribute determines the alternative string to be
                          displayed in lieu of an applet.
<param>         Parameter tag.
  name = "string"Attribute determines the parameter's name
  alt  = "string"Attribute determines the parameters value
```

An example use of an `applet` tag is shown below. The `code` attribute specifies that the Java code is to be found in a file named `LanderSimulation.class` and that the program will run in a window 240 by 120 pixels wide on the web page. The `param` attribute specifies that a parameter named `fuel` with value `100` is sent to the applet.

```
<applet code=LanderSimulation.class width=240 height=120>
  <param name="fuel" value="100">
</applet>
```

SUPPLEMENTARY MATERIAL

A.5   Bits, Bytes, and Text

In Section A.3 we saw how an HTML document can be used to format text within a browser. In this section we will look at how text and text files are represented. Looking at the underlying representation of files will help us understand how information is passed between computers.

A.5.1   Binary Numbers

Within a computer, programs and data are represented as numbers. At the lowest level these numbers are binary (base two with only 1s and 0s). Binary bits can be represented by the flow of electricity, by the direction that iron particles are magnetized, or by the position of a switch. Binary bits are usually clumped together in units of eight bits, called a byte.

> A *bit* is a single piece of information that can represent a 1 or 0. Eight bits are a *byte*. Sometimes half a byte, four bits, is called a *nibble*.

Since each bit can represent one of two numbers, each byte can represent one of 256 numbers (2^8). For example, the binary number `00101101` is the binary representation for the decimal number `45`.

$$0*2^7 + 0*2^6 + 1*2^5 + 0*2^4 + 1*2^3 + 1*2^2 + 0*2^1 + 1*2^0 = 45$$

The smallest eight-bit number is zero. The largest eight-bit number is 255.

$$1*2^7 + 1*2^6 + 1*2^5 + 1*2^4 + 1*2^3 + 1*2^2 + 1*2^1 + 1*2^0 = 255$$

A.5.2   ASCII Character Encoding

We stated above that all information within a computer is represented as numbers. Representing characters as numbers can be viewed as a cipher, much like those we used in grade school to pass secret messages. The American Standard Code for Information Interchange (ASCII) is the most common encoding scheme in use today. It uses seven bits for encoding characters. Thus, there are 128 possibilities (2^7). A character is often stored within a single byte. The eighth bit is either ignored or used for error checking. Of the 128 characters, 62 are used for upper- and lowercase letters and the 10 digits. For example, the string R2D2 is encoded with the following integer sequence: 82, 50, 68, 50. The remaining ASCII character codes are used for punctuation and special nonprintable control characters. Table A.5 shows each of these characters with its ASCII decimal representation.

The first 32 ASCII characters are special control characters and are not printable. Each has a special meaning even though that meaning may be obsolete. On a keyboard, these control characters can be created by using the Control key together with a letter. Control-A (^A), for example, is encoded by the number 1, ^B by a 2, ^C by a 3, and so on. The special characters of particular interest include the bell (7 or ^G), backspace (8 or ^H), horizontal tab (9 or ^I), line feed (10 or ^J), and carriage return (13 or ^M). Control C (3) terminates a program on Unix and MS-DOS platforms. Control-S may stop transmission and therefore should be avoided in documents that are transmitted. Null, which is encoded with a 0, is generally ignored.

Java uses the character sequences in Table A.6 to represent several of the nonprintable characters.

A.5.3   Text and Binary Files

ASCII was used heavily as a standard means for communicating information over telephone and telegraph wires. For example, a local news station could rent a teletype machine and get regular news flashes. Teletype machines also became printers for early computers. As a result, the standards used for teletype machines made their way into computers. On teletype machines, the line feed character advances the paper one line and the carriage return moves the printing head to the beginning of the line. Both characters are needed to advance to a new line even though a person at the keyboard may have only pushed the Return key. Thus, one key press is mapped to two characters. Unfortunately, computer vendors have used different strategies for representing an end-of-line. Some have chosen the two characters used by teletype machines, while other vendors have chosen one of the two characters.

Listing A.2 shows four lines of text adapted from Dr. Seuss. This listing depicts how the text would appear on a Unix, Macintosh, or Windows platform. Listing A.3 shows how that text is encoded on a Unix platform. Notice that the end of each line is encoded with a line feed character (10). The Macintosh uses the carriage return (13) (see Listing A.4), and MS Windows uses a carriage return and line feed. Fortunately, many file transfer programs, such as ftp, take these differences into consideration. These programs convert end-of-line representations from one vendor into the representation used by another. Occasion-

Table A.5 ASCII Codes

decimal	character	decimal	character	decimal	character	decimal	character
0	null	32	space	64	@	96	`
1		33	!	65	A	97	a
2		34	"	66	B	98	b
3		35	#	67	C	99	c
4		36	$	68	D	100	d
5		37	%	69	E	101	e
6		38	&	70	F	102	f
7		39	'	71	G	103	g
8	backspace	40	(	72	H	104	h
9	hor. tab	41	)	73	I	105	i
10	line feed	42	*	74	J	106	j
11		43	+	75	K	107	k
12	form feed	44	,	76	L	108	l
13	carriage ret	45	–	77	M	109	m
14		46	.	78	N	110	n
15		47	/	79	O	111	o
16		48	0	80	P	112	p
17		49	1	81	Q	113	q
18		50	2	82	R	114	r
19		51	3	83	S	115	s
20		52	4	84	T	116	t
21		53	5	85	U	117	u
22		54	6	86	V	118	v
23		55	7	87	W	119	w
24		56	8	88	X	120	x
25		57	9	89	Y	121	y
26		58	:	90	Z	122	z
27		59	;	91	[	123	{
28		60	<	92	\	124		
29		61	=	93	]	125	}
30		62	>	94	^	126	~
31		63	?	95	_	127	delete

Table A.6 Special Character in Java

decimal	character sequence	meaning
8	\b	backspace
9	\t	horizontal tab
10	\n	line feed
12	\f	form feed
13	\r	carriage return
34	\"	double quote
39	\'	single quote
92	\\	backslash

ally a file in the wrong format appears on one's desktop. When writing a program it is important not to depend on a particular new line character sequence. If one does, a program may not work correctly on other platforms.

Listing A.2 The Dr. Seuss Text File

```
1 fish,
2 fish,
red fish,
blue fish.
```

In Listing A.3 through Listing A.5, the first column specifies the location of the character in the file. The next 10 columns are the characters as they are encoded by a number. The last column holds those 10 characters printed as they would be displayed. A dot (.) either represents a period or an unprintable character.

Listing A.3 UNIX Text File Format

```
 0     49   32  102  105  115  104   44   10   50   32     1 fish,.2
10    102  105  115  104   44   10  114  101  100   32     fish,.red
20    102  105  115  104   44   10   98  108  117  101     fish,.blue
30     32  102  105  115  104   46   10                     fish..
```

Listing A.4 Macintosh Text File Format

```
 0     49   32  102  105  115  104   44   13   50   32     1 fish,.2
10    102  105  115  104   44   13  114  101  100   32     fish,.red
20    102  105  115  104   44   13   98  108  117  101     fish,.blue
30     32  102  105  115  104   46   13                     fish..
```

Listing A.5   MS Windows Text File Format

```
 0     49  32 102 105 115 104  44  13  10  50      1 fish,..2
10     32 102 105 115 104  44  13  10 114 101       fish,..re
20    100  32 102 105 115 104  44  13  10  98      d fish,..b
30    108 117 101  32 102 105 115 104  46  13      lue fish..
40     10                                          .
```

Files are called *text files* if they use seven bits to encode only the ASCII characters. If a file contains numbers that encode program instructions, images, or audio, they are called *binary files*. Binary files typically use eight bits, and thus they may not be transferred properly between computers if the transfer programs thinks it is a text file. For example, when a text file is transferred from a Unix machine to a Macintosh using the ASCII mode in ftp, all the line feeds (10s) are changed to carriage returns (13s). This will mess up an image file where the 10s and 13s represent colors and not new lines. It is important to put file transfer programs, such as ftp, into the `binary` mode when transferring images, but not when transferring text.

Modems can be particularly devastating to binary files if they are not transferred using the correct programs. Many modems are set up to send and receive 7 bits. Information in the eighth bit is thrown away. Thus, any byte with a value greater than 127 will be corrupted.

CHAPTER REFERENCE

A.6 Summary

The Internet grew out of a need to share information. It started with a few government agencies and universities and developed into a system that stretches across the entire world. One medium for sharing information over the Internet is the web.

Web documents are created using HTML (Hypertext Markup Language). A markup language uses embedded ASCII characters to describe how a document is to be formatted. In HTML, an author specifies formatting by placing tags within arrow brackets. Typically each beginning tag has an identical ending tag with a "/" character.

WYSIWYG (What You See Is What You Get) word processors embed nonprinting information within a document to specify formatting. This information is embedded automatically by the word processor when the user selects menu options and chooses formatting options.

A byte is eight binary bits (1 or 0). Text files are encoded with ASCII characters using seven-bit integers. This encoding allows 128 possible characters. The characters include letters, digits, punctuation, and special control characters. One of the functions of control characters is to encode end-of-line. Different platforms use different sequences to represent end of lines. Binary files use all eight bits of byte to represent information.

A.7 Bibliography

- `http://www.w3.org/`

  Additional information about the web can be found at this location.

- `http://www.boutell.com/faq/`

  One of the documents you will find at the above site contains answers to frequently asked questions (FAQ) about the web. Many news groups and web pages point to FAQs to help new users.

- `http://home.netscape.com/home/about-the-internet.html`

  This site as general information about the Internet.

- `http://www.yahoo.com/`

If you are looking for something on the web, Yahoo! is a good place to start. It has an index and a search engine for quickly finding information by category or by keyword.

- `http://www.yahoo.com/Science/Computer_Science/`

  One of the Yahoo! categories in computer science. This is an excellent location to look for additional information about a computer science topic. Use it to track down information about networking.

- Larry Aronson. 1994. *HTML Manual of Style*. Emeryville, CA: Ziff-Davis Press.

  This is a nice, manageable reference to HTML. Since it is only 132 pages long, it is not overwhelming or expensive. In addition, it contains some good example pages.

PROBLEM SETS

A.8   Exercises

Type Setting and Word Processing—Section A.2

1   Using a word processor of your choice, describe the steps required to make a word bold.

2   Compare the process of making the word "scratch" bold in a typical word processor with the process of entering the character sequence `<b> scratch </b>` in a text-processing system. How do they compare relative to their ease of use, time to learn, and time for a writer to use each command?

The Web—Section A.3

3   Many public schools have a policy that limits the personal information a student is allowed to display on a web page. For example, last names, phone numbers, and addresses are not allowed. These policies are motivated to protect students against sexual predators. Given the environment of your school, which items do you feel are appropriate on your home page? Should such items include your image and phone number? What do you suspect the dangers are to predatory behavior such as stalking or crank phone calls? Does it make a difference if you are male or female? Does it make a difference if your page is accessible by the whole campus or the whole world?

4   Is it appropriate for students to place nude images on their web pages? Does it make a difference who owns the computer on which the web page resides; for example, if it is a University's computer or a personal computer in your home? Does it make a difference if the computer is owned by a state or private institution?

5   Find and report on a newspaper or magazine account of inappropriate web activity. What is your view of the incident?

6   What do you suspect the impact of the web will be on publishing? Will paper magazines and books become obsolete or diminished? Would you read a novel on a hand-held computer if you could buy it electronically? Why or why not? Is the web an enhancement to current technologies or will it replace some?

HTML—Section A.4

7   Write a complete HTML program to display a page that says "Hello world."

8   Write an HTML code fragment that will reference this book. Include the author's name in plain text, the title in italics, the publisher in bold, and the copyright date in plain text.

9   Write an HTML code fragment that lists what you had for dinner last night. Use the list element.

10   Find a web page with a colored background. Look at the HTML source code for the web page. Locate a tag that makes it have a background. Write down the HTML tag to make the background blue. Write down the HTML tag for putting an image in the background.

ASCII—Section A.5

11   Translate the your name into a sequence of ASCII decimal integers.

12   What does the follow sequence of integers say?
- **a.**   34 76 101 116 32 105 116 32 98 101 32 115 111 46 34
- **b.**   51 46 49 52 49 53 57

A.9   Projects

HTML—Section A.4

13   Create your home page. Include the page title, a header, your name, your major, and a paragraph that describes you.

14   Add the following to your home page (you may choose not to add some of these items for privacy reasons):
- **a.**   Link to the course home page, your instructor, and/or this book.
- **b.**   Your class schedule using the HTML list element.
- **c.**   A list of your favorite web sights (use Yahoo!).
- **d.**   Mail anchor.
- **e.**   Your image (photograph).

15   Learn how to use the electronic mail system. Send a message to the instructor or teacher's assistant listing your favorite movies.

B Java Class Reference

Standard Classes

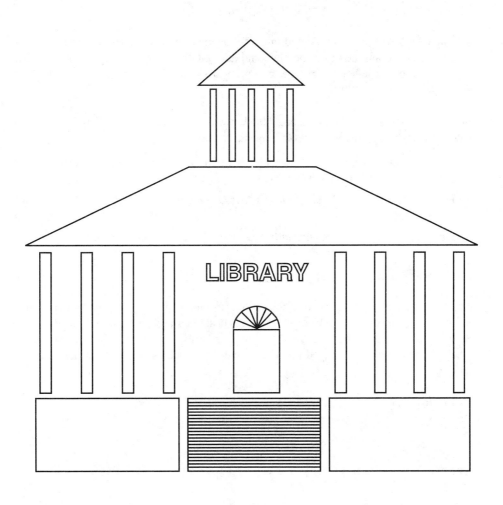

Introductory Comments

This appendix contains a few highlights of the class libraries. The most useful methods from selected classes are summarized by providing an abbreviated class interface, short description, and a few examples. Each class has a pointer to the main text where further information and examples can be found.

Classes with the J prefix are part of Java's Swing library (version 2.0). For tools that work only with version 1.1 some of the AWT GUI components are also included. For example, JFrame and Frame, JButton and Button, ...

Additional information can be found in the following references. The references by Chan, Lee, and Kramer are the most complete and authoritative. They are part of the Java Sun team. However, these books are large and pricy. Together they include about 3700 pages and cost a little over $100.

Flanagan's book is much more manageable but with less detail. It lists all JDK 1.1 classes and methods. It does this in about 600 pages for about $20.

- Patrick Chan, Rosanna Lee, Douglas Kramer, *The Java Class Libraries Second Edition, Volume 1*, **Addison Wesley**, 1998.
- Patrick Chan, Rosanna Lee, *The Java Class Libraries Second Edition, Volume 2*, **Addison Wesley**, 1998.
- David Flanagan, *Java in a Nutshell: A Desktop quick Reference*, **O'Reilly**, 1997.

ActionEvent Class - java.awt.event

The ActionEvent class is used to respond to button presses and menu selection. It makes its first appearance in Chapter 15 and is described in Section 15.4.4, page 702 and Section 15.4.5, page 705. The getActionCommand methods can be used to get the label of the component initiated this event. See ActionListener interface, Button and Menu classes.

Listing B.1 ActionEvent Class

```
1 public class ActionEvent extends AWTEvent
2 {
3   public String getActionCommand();
4 }
```

ActionListener Interface - `java.awt.event`

The `ActionListener` interface is used to respond to button presses and menu selection. The `actionPerformed` method must be implemented to be useful. It makes its first appearance in Chapter 15 and is described in Section 15.4.4, page 702 and Section 15.4.5, page 705. See `ActionEvent`, `Button`, and `Menu` classes.

Listing B.2 ActionListener Interface

```
1 public abstract interface ActionListener extends EventListener
2 {
3   public abstract void actionPerformed (ActionEvent e);
4 }
```

The `actionPerformed` method is called whenever a button is pressed or menu item selected.

Applet Class - `java.applet`

The `Applet` class is described in Section 3.5, page 99. The `Applet` class inherits from `Panels` which inherits from `Containers` (page 858) which inherits from `Component` (page 854) which inherits from `Objects` (page 891.) (See Figure 3.3 on page 100.) As a result, everything that can be done by an Object, Component, Container, or Panel can be done with an Applet. See these classes to find additional methods provided by the `Applet` class than those listed in this section.

Listing B.3 `Applet` Class

```
1  public class Applet extends Panel
2  {
3     public void destroy ();
4     public AudioClip getAudioClip (URL url, String name);
5     public URL getCodeBase ();
6     public URL getDocumentBase ();
7     public Image getImage (URL url, String name);
8     public void init ();
9     public void resize (int width, int height);
10    public void resize (Dimension d);

11    public void showStatus (String s);
12    public void start ();
13    public void stop ();
14 }
```

Table B.1 Applet Methods

method	description
destroy	Callback method called automatically when a browser has closed this applet's page. It is normally overridden by a programmer. See Section 3.5, page 99.
getAudioClip	Audio clip at "url" with "name" is returned. If the audio clip cannot be found, null is returned. ```AudioClip scream =` ` getAudioClip (getDocumentBase(),` `"scream.au");` `scream.play(); // play it once` `scream.loop(); // play it over and over` `scream.stop(); // stop playing it``` This applet will attempt to locate an audio file named "scream.au" at the same URL where the HTML document is located that references this applet. The only sound format supported is the 8,000 Hz mono 8-bit ULAW format.
getCodeBase	The URL prefix that contains the code (*.class file) for this applet is returned. ```AudioClip scream =` ` getAudioClip (getCodeBase(), "scream.au");``` This applet will attempt to locate an audio file named "scream.au" at the same URL where the *.class code file for this applet is located.
getDocumentBase	The URL prefix for the HTML document that contains this applet is returned. See getAudioClip and Section 3.6.5, page 109 for an example.
getImage	An image at "url" with "name" is fetched. This method works similar to getAudioClip. However, control returns immediately from this call. The pixels in the image are not returned until they are needed, for example, for the graphics context drawImage method. The GIF and JPEG image formats are supported. See Section 3.6.5, page 109.
init	Callback method called automatically when a browser creates this applet's page. It is normally overridden by a programmer. See Section 3.5, page 99.

Table B.1 Applet Methods

method	description
resize	The applet window is resized to width and height. This method may be ignored by the applet context. Typically, applet viewers respond to it and web browsers, such as Netscape, ignore it. `resize (400, 300);`
showStatus	The status message is typically displayed in a status bar at the lower left of the applet window. `showStatus ("initialization is complete");`
start	Callback method called automatically when this applet's display becomes visible in a browser's window. It is normally overridden by a programmer. See Section 3.5, page 99.
stop	Callback method called automatically when this applet's display becomes invisible in a browser's window. It is normally overridden by a programmer. See Section 3.5, page 99.

Boolean Class - `java.lang`

Briefly introduced in Section 2.6, page 60. Used as a wrapper class for boolean primitive values.

Listing B.4 Boolean Class

```
1 public final class Boolean
2 {
3    public Boolean (boolean value);
4    public static boolean valueOf (String s);
5    public Boolean booleanValue ();
6    public boolean equals (Object obj);
7    public String toString ();
8 }
```

BorderLayout Class - `java.awt`

The border layout manager places components in a window's left, top, right, bottom, or center location. A demonstration of its use is in Section 15.4.11, page 720. An example of setting the layout manager is shown below.

```
pane.setLayout (new BorderLayout());
pane.add (abutton, BorderLayout.NORTH);
```

Listing B.5 BorderLayout Class

```
1 public class BorderLayout
2 {
3    public static final int CENTER;
4    public static final int EAST;
5    public static final int NORTH;
6    public static final int SOUTH;
7    public static final int WEST;
8    public BorderLayout ();
9 }
```

BufferedInputStream Class - `java.io`

The `BufferedInputStream` class is described in Section 12.7.1, page 572. It is used in conjunction with the FileInputStream. Input is buffered for efficiency. See `FileIn-putStream`, Table B.12 on page 862, for the description of its operations. A file can be opened as follows.

```
BufferedInputStream f = new BufferedInputStream
                    (new FileInputStream("image.gif"));
```

Listing B.6 BufferedInputStream Class

```
1 public class BufferedInputStream extends FilterInputStream
2 {
3    public BufferedInputStream (InputStream in);
4    public int available () throws IOException;
5    public void close () throws IOException;  // inherited
6    public int read () throws IOException;
7    public long skip (long count) throws IOException;
8 }
```

BufferedOutputStream Class - `java.io`

The `BufferedOutputStream` class is used in conjunction with the FileOutputStream class. Output is buffered for efficiency. See `FileOutputStream`, Table B.13 on page 863, for the description of its operations. It works similarly to the `BufferedInputStream` described in Section 12.7.1, page 572.

Table B.2 FileOutputStream Methods

operations	description

BufferedOutputStream	If possible, this file is opened for writing. For example:
	
	`BufferedOutputStream f = new`
	`    BufferedOutputStream`
	`        (new FileOutputStream("image.gif"));`

close	This file is closed.
flush	This file is closed. For example: `f.flush();`
write	The least significant byte of "data" is written to this file. For example: `f.write(123);`

Listing B.7 BufferedOutputStream Class

```
1 public class BufferedOutputStream extends FilterOutputStream
2 {
3    public BufferedOutputStream (OutputStream out);
4    public void close () throws IOException;   // inherited
5    public void flush () throws IOException;
6    public void write (int byte) throws IOException;
7 }
```

BufferedReader Class - `java.io`

The BufferedReader described in Section 12.4.1, page 554. It is used in conjunction with the `FileReader` class for reading characters from a text file. Input is buffered for efficiency. A major benefit of this class is the provision of the readLine method.

Table B.3 BufferedReader Methods

operations	description
BufferedReader	If possible, this file is opened for reading.
close	This file is closed.
read	If not end of file, the next character is returned and the file point advances by one character. If end of file, -1 is returned.
readLine	if not end of file, a string is returned containing characters form the current file pointer to line terminating character(s): line feed, carriage return, or carriage return/line feed. The line terminating characters are consumed but not placed in the returned string. If end of file, null is returned.
skip	The file pointer for this file is moved "count" characters ahead. It returns the number of characters actually skipped which may be less than "count" if we are at end-of-file.

Listing B.8 BufferedReader Class

```
1 public class BufferedReader extends Reader
2 {
3    public BufferedReader (Reader in)
4    public void close () throws IOException
5    public int read () throws IOException
6    public String readLine () throws IOException
7    public void skip (long count) throws IOException
8 }
```

BufferedWriter Class - `java.io`

The BufferedWriter class is described in Section 12.4.3, page 560. It is used in conjunction with the `FileWriter` class for writing text to a file.

Table B.4 BufferedWriter Methods

operations	description
`BufferedWriter`	If possible, this file is opened for writing.
`close`	This file is closed.
`flush`	Write all the bytes in the buffer that have not been written to this file.
`newLine`	A line separator is sent to this file. What specific characters it sends depends on the platform.

`write`	Write a byte or string to a file.
	
	`// The following do the same least significant`
	`// byte to a file.`
	`out.write('A');`
	`out.write(65);          // same as above`
	
	`// "Mag" written to this file`
	`String title = new String("Jerry Maguire");`
	`out.write(title);`
	`out.write(title, 6, 3);`

Listing B.9 BufferedWriter Class

```
1 public class BufferedWriter extends Writer
2 {
3    public BufferedWriter (Writer out);
4    public void close () throws IOException;
5    public void flush () throws IOException;
6    public void newLine () throws IOException;
7    public void write (int data) throws IOException;
8    public void write (String s) throws IOException; // inherited
9    public void write (String s, int offset, int length)
10            throws IOException;
11 }
```

Button Class - `java.awt`

See the `JButton` class and Section 15.6, page 728.

ButtonGroup Class - `javax.swing`

The `ButtonGroup` class is used to tie radio buttons together. It makes its first appearance in Chapter 15 and is described in Section 15.4.6, page 708. See `JRadioButton`..

Listing B.10 ButtonGroup Class

```
1 public class ButtonGroup
2 {
3   public ButtonGroup();
4   public void add (AbstractButton button);
5 }
```

Color Class - `java.awt`

The `Color` class is described Section 3.6.6, page 112. Each color has three components: red, green, and blue. Thus the initials RGB. Each component can be between 0 and 255. Colors can also be represented as real numbers between 0.0 and 1.0 and as hue, saturation, and brightness components (HSB.) The real number and hue representations are not covered here.

Listing B.11 Color Class

```
1   public class Color
2   {
3     public static final Color black;
4     public static final Color blue;
5     public static final Color cyan;
6     public static final Color darkGray;
7     public static final Color gray;
8     public static final Color green;
9     public static final Color lightGray;
10    public static final Color magenta;
11    public static final Color orange;
12    public static final Color pink;
13    public static final Color red;
14    public static final Color white;
15    public static final Color yellow;
16    public Color (int red, int green, int blue);
17    public Color (int rgb);
18    public Color brighter ();
19    public Color darker ();
20    public int getBlue ();
21    public int getGreen ();
22    public int getRGB ();
23    public int getRed ();
24    public String toString ();
25  }
```

Table B.5 Color Methods

method	description
Color	The color summer blue can be created in the following two ways.

	`Color summerBlue = new Color(56, 176, 222);`
	`g.setColor(summerBlue);`
	`Color summerBlue = new Color(3715294);`
	$3{,}715{,}294 = 56 * 256^2 + 176 * 256^1 + 222$ where 56 is the red, 176 green, and 222 blue values.

brighter	A new brighter version of this color is returned.
	`Color lightSummerBlue = summerBlue.brighter();`
darker	A new darker version of this color is returned.
	`Color darkSummerBlue = summerBlue.darker();`

Table B.5 Color Methods

method	description
getBlue	The blue component of this color is returned.
	`Color summerBlue = new Color(56, 176, 222);` `int blue = summerBlue.getBlue();   // blue is 222`
getGreen	The green component of this color is returned.
	`Color summerBlue = new Color(56, 176, 222);` `int green = summerBlue.getGreen(); // green is 176`
getRGB	The RGB integer representation of a color is returned.
	`Color summerBlue = new Color(56, 176, 222);` `int RGB = summerBlue.getRGB();   // RGB is 3,715,294`
getRed	The red component of this color is returned.
	`Color summerBlue = new Color(56, 176, 222);` `int red = summerBlue.getRed();   // red is 56`
toString	a string representation of this color's RGB values is returned.

Component Class – `java.awt`

The `Component` class is abstract. We never instantiate it directly. The Component class is a superclass of most GUI components. Thus, the operations described here are common to many classes. For example, some of the GUI component that inherit it are `Checkbox`, `Button`, `Canvas`, `Label`, `TextComponent`, `TextArea`, and `TextField`. In addition, it is inherited by `Container`, `Panel`, `Applet`, `Window`, and `Frame` classes.

Table B.6 Example Colors with RGB Values
http://www.infi.net/wwwimages/colorindex.html

color	r	g	b	color	r	g	b
white	255	255	255	lime green	50	205	50
red	255	0	0	mandarin orange	228	120	51
green	0	255	0	maroon	142	35	107
blue	0	0	255	medium aquamarine	50	205	153
magenta	255	0	255	medium blue	50	50	205
cyan	0	255	255	medium forest green	107	142	35
yellow	255	255	0	medium goldenrod	234	234	174
black	0	0	0	medium orchid	147	112	219
aquamarine	112	219	147	medium sea green	66	111	66
baker's chocolate	92	51	23	medium slate blue	127	0	255
blue violet	159	95	159	medium spring green	127	255	0
brass	181	166	66	medium turquoise	112	219	219
bright gold	217	217	25	medium violet red	219	112	147
brown	166	42	42	medium wood	166	128	100
bronze	140	120	83	midnight blue	47	47	79
bronze II	166	125	61	navy blue	35	35	142
cadet blue	95	159	159	neon blue	77	77	255
cool copper	217	135	25	neon pink	255	110	199
copper	184	115	51	new midnight blue	0	0	156
coral	255	127	0	new tan	235	199	158
corn flower blue	66	66	111	old gold	207	181	59
dark brown	92	64	51	orange	255	127	0
dark green	47	79	47	orange red	255	36	0
dark green copper	74	118	110	orchid	219	112	219
dark olive green	79	79	47	pale green	143	188	143
dark orchid	153	50	205	pink	188	143	143
dark purple	135	31	120	plum	234	173	234
dark slate blue	107	35	142	quartz	217	217	243
dark slate gray	47	79	79	rich blue	89	89	171
dark tan	151	105	79	salmon	111	66	66
dark turquoise	112	147	219	scarlet	140	23	23
dark wood	133	94	66	sea green	35	142	104
dim gray	84	84	84	semi-sweet chocolate	107	66	38
dusty rose	133	99	99	sienna	142	107	35
feldspar	209	146	117	silver	230	232	250
firebrick	142	35	35	sky blue	50	153	204
forest green	35	142	35	slate blue	0	127	255
gold	205	127	50	spicy pink	255	28	174
goldenrod	219	219	112	spring green	0	255	127
gray	192	192	192	steel blue	35	107	142
green copper	82	127	118	summer sky	56	176	222
green yellow	147	219	112	tan	219	147	112
hunter green	33	94	33	thistle	219	191	216
indian red	78	47	47	turquoise	173	234	234
khaki	159	159	95	very dark brown	108	64	51
light blue	192	217	217	very light gray	205	205	205
light gray	168	168	168	violet	79	47	79
light steel blue	143	143	189	violet red	204	50	153
light wood	233	194	166	wheat	216	216	191
				yellow green	153	204	50

Figure B.1 Component Class Hierarchy

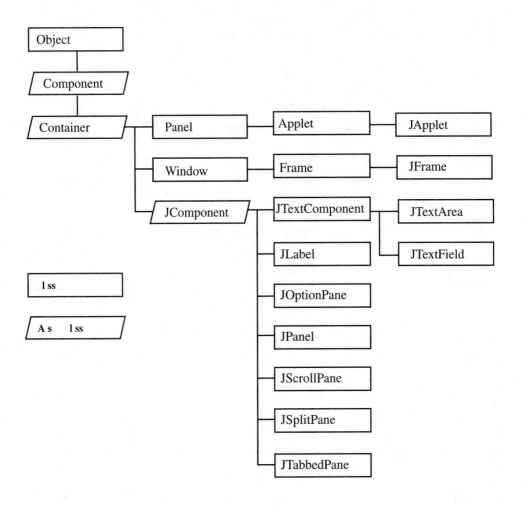

Table B.7 Component Methods

method	description
addKeyListener	A key listener is added to this component. See Section 15.4.8, page 714 for an example.

Table B.7 Component Methods

method	description
addMouseListener	A mouse listener is added to this component. See Section 14.4.2, page 673 for an example
addMouseMotionListener	A mouse motion listener is added to this component. See Section 14.4.3, page 675 for an example
getGraphics	The graphics context for this component is returned. See the `mouseDragged` method in Listing 14.1 on page 664.
paint	Callback method called automatically when this component needs to be repainted. It is normally overridden by a programmer. See Section 3.5, page 99.
repaint	Repaint typically calls `update` which in turn calls `paint`. See `update` below. See Section 6.8, page 255.
setBackground	This component's background color is set to c. See Listing 3.4 on page 105.
setFont	This component's font is set to f. See Section 10.6.5, page 465.
setForeground	This component's foreground color is set to c.
setLocation	This component's top-left corner is moved to the given location.
update	This method is called automatically by `repaint`. By default `update` does the following: ```public void update (Graphics g)\n{\n g.setColor(getBackground());\n g.fillRect(0, 0, width, height);\n g.setColor(getForegrouind());\n paint(g);\n}``` Thus, when `repaint` is called the drawing area is first cleared and then `paint` is called. This can cause flicker during animation. It is often advantages to override the `update` method. See Section 6.8, page 255.

Listing B.12 Component Class

```
1   public abstract class Component
2   {
3     public void addKeyListener (KeyListener listener);
4     public void addMouseListener (MouseListener listener);
5     public void addMouseMotionListener (MouseMotionListener
6                                                   listener);
7     public Graphics getGraphics ();
8     public void paint (Graphics g);
9     public void repaint ();
10    public void setBackground (Color c);
11    public void setFont (Font f);
12    public void setForeground (Color c);
13    public void setLocation (int x, int y);
14    public void setLocation (Point p);
15    public void update (Graphics g);
16  }
```

Container Class - `java.awt`

The `Container` class is abstract. We never instantiate it directly. The `Container` class serves as a base class for applets and frames (Figure B.1.) The primary benefit of the `Container` class is to hold objects derived from the `Component` class.

Table B.8 Container Methods

method	description
add	Add a component to this container, for example, a button. See Section 15.4.4, page 702. An optional constraint may specify where the component is to be placed, for example, "EAST" in the `BoarderLayout` manager.
remove	Remove a component from this container.
removeAll	Remove all components from this container.
setLayout	Set the layout manager for this container. See Section 15.4.4, page 702 and Section 15.4.13, page 723.

DecimalFormat - `java.text`

The `DecimalFormat` class is used to format base ten numbers for output. It is described in Section 12.4.4, page 562. `DecimalFormat` extends `NumberFormat`. See `NumberFormat` for additional operations.

Listing B.13 Container Class

```
1 public abstract class Container extends Component
2 {
3   public void add (Component comp);
4   public void add (Component comp, Object constraints);
5   public void remove (Component comp);
6   public void removeAll ();
7   public void setLayout (LayoutManager mgr);
8 }
```

Listing B.14 DecimalFormat Class

```
1 public class DecimalFormat extends NumberFormat
2 {
3   DecimalFormat ();
4   DecimalFormat (String pattern);
5   public void applyPattern (String pattern);
6 }
```

Table B.9 Decimal Format Patterns

character	description
0	if 0, show a 0 else show a digit
#	if 0, show nothing else show digit
.	decimal place holder
,	placement of grouping separator
-	negative sign
%	multiply by 100 and show as percentage
;	separates positive format on left and optional negative on right
'	quote for literal inclusion
other	appears literally

Dimension Class - `java.awt`

The primary use for this class is to package a width and height value into a single object. An example is show in Listing B.16.

Table B.10 Dimension Methods

method	description
`equals`	Returns true if this dimension equals d.
`setSize`	Set the size of this dimension.
toString	The string representation of this object is returned.

Listing B.15 Dimension Class

```
1 public class Dimension
2 {
3    public int height;
4    public int width;
5    public Dimension (int width, int height);
6    public boolean equals (Object d);
7    public void setSize (int width, int height);
8    public void setSize (Dimension d);
9    public String toString ();
10 }
```

Listing B.16 Example of Using the Dimension Class

```
1 Dimension d = new Dimension(300,200);
2 this.setSize(d);
3 Dimension e = this.getSize();
4 int width  = e.width;          // width is 300
5 int height = e.height;         // height is 200
```

Double Class - `java.lang`

A wrapper class for the `double` primitive. Objects of the `Double` class are immutable. See the `Integer` class for examples of what these methods do. Examples of using the Double class can be found in Section 12.4.2, page 558. The following shows how to convert a string to a double.

```
String s = "123.456";
Double D = Double.valueOf(s);
double d = D.doubleValue();
```

Listing B.17 Double Class

```
1 public final class Double extends Number
2 {
3   public static final double MAX_VALUE;
4   public static final double MIN_VALUE;
5   public Double (double value);
6   public Double (String s) throws NumberFormatException;
7   public double doubleValue ();
8   public boolean equals (Object obj);
9   public String toString ();
10   public static Double valueOf (String s)
11                         throws NumberFormatException;
12 }
```

EventObject Class - `java.util`

Objects of the `EventObject` class are typically created by the underlying run-time system. They are seldom created by a programmer explicitly. Events are introduced in Chapter 14 and Chapter 15. All events inherit this event object class. The `getSource` method determines which component generated an event.

Table B.11 EventObject Methods

method	description
EventObject	An event object is created where "source" is the component that generated it
getSource	The object that initiated this event is returned

Listing B.18 EventObject Class

```
1 public class EventObject
2 {
3   public EventObject (Object source);
4   public Object getSource();
5 }
```

Figure B.2 EventObject Class Hierarchy

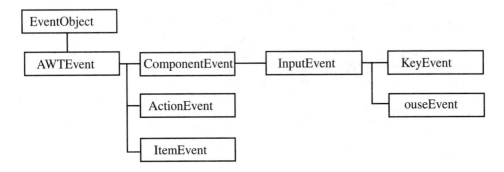

FileDialog Class - `java.awt`

The FileDialog class is described in Section 12.7.3, page 575.

Listing B.19 FileDialog class

```
1 public class FileDialog extends Dialog
2 {
3    public FileDialog (Frame parent, String title);
4    public String getDirectory ();
5    public String getFile ();
6 }
```

FileInputStream Class - `java.io`

The FileInputStream class is described in Section 12.7.1, page 572 and Section 12.7.2, page 574. It is used for reading individual bytes from a file.

Table B.12 FileInputStream Methods

operations	description
`FileInputStream`	If possible, this file is opened for reading.
`available`	The number of remaining bytes to be read in this file is returned.
`close`	This file is closed.

Table B.12 FileInputStream Methods

operations	description
read	If not end of file, the next byte is returned and the file pointer advances by one. If end of file, -1 is returned.
skip	The file pointer for this file is moved "count" bytes ahead. It returns the number of characters actually skipped which may be less than "count" if we are at end-of-file.

Listing B.20 FileInputStream Class

```
1 public class FileInputStream extends InputStream
2 {
3    public FileInputStream (String fileName)
4         throws FileNotFoundException
5    public int available () throws IOException
6    public void close () throws IOException
7    public int read () throws IOException
8    public long skip (long count) throws IOException
9 }
```

FileOutputStream Class - `java.io`

The FileOutputStream class is described in Section 12.7.1, page 572. It is used for writing individual bytes to a file.

Table B.13 FileOutputStream Methods

operations	description
FileOutputStream	If possible, this file is opened for writing. For example: `FileOutputStream f = new FileOutputStream("report.txt");`
close	This file is closed. For example: `f.close();`
write	The least significant byte of "data" is written to this file. For example: `f.write(123);`

Listing B.21 FileOutputStream Class

```
1 public class FileOutputStream extends OutputStream
2 {
3    public FileOutputStream (String fileName)
4       throws IOException;
5    public void close () throws IOException;
6    public void write (int data) throws IOException
7 }
```

FileReader Class - `java.io`

The FileReader class is described in Section 12.4.1, page 554. We use it primarily in conjunction with `BufferedReader` for opening files.

Listing B.22 FileReader Class

```
1 public class FileReader extends InputStreamReader
2 {
3    public FileReader (String fileName)
4          throws FileNotFoundException;
5 }
```

FileWriter Class - `java.io`

The FileWriter class is described in Section 12.4.3, page 560. We use it primarily conjunction with `BufferedWriter` for opening files.

Listing B.23 FileWriter Class

```
1 public class FileWriter extends OutputStreamReader
2 {
3    public FileWriter (String fileName) throws IOException;
4    public FileWriter (String fileName, boolean append)
5          throws IOException;
6 }
```

Float Class - `java.lang`

A wrapper class for the `float` primitive. Objects of the `Float` class are immutable. See the `Integer` class for examples of what these methods do. The following shows how to convert a string to a float.

```
String s = "123.456";
Float  F = Float.valueOf(s);
```

```
        float  f = F.floatValue();
```

Listing B.24 Float Class

```
1 public final class Float extends Number
2 {
3   public static final float MAX_VALUE;
4   public static final float MIN_VALUE;
5   public Float (float value);
6   public Float (String s) throws NumberFormatException;
7   public boolean equals (Object obj);
8   public float floatValue ();
9   public String toString ();
10  public static Float valueOf (String s)
11                            throws NumberFormatException;
12 }
```

FlowLayout Class - `java.awt`

The flow layout manager places components in rows left-to-right and top-to-bottom. A demonstration of its use is in Section 15.4.4, page 702. Applets use the flow layout by default. Frames have no default layout. An example of setting the layout manager is shown below.

```
        this.setLayout (new FlowLayout());
```

Listing B.25 FlowLayout Class

```
1 public class FlowLayout
2 {
3   public FlowLayout ();
4 }
```

Font Class - `java.awt`

A font determines how displayed text looks. Section 10.6.5, page 465 shows an example setting the font of a text area to 18 point bold SansSerif. Figure B.3 shows examples of three of the available fonts. Fonts contain three properties:

- logical name
- style
- point size

The `setFont` method is defined within the Component class which is inherited by many other classes. As a result, it is possible to set the font of text areas and text fields.

Fonts can be one of the following:

- `"DialogInput"`
- `"Monospaced"`
- `"SansSerif"`
- `"Serif"`

Listing B.26 Font Class

```
1 public class Font extends Object
1 {
2    public Font (String name, int style, int size);
3    public static final int BOLD;
4    public static final int ITALIC;
5    public static final int PLAIN;
6 }
```

Figure B.3 Examples of Three Fonts

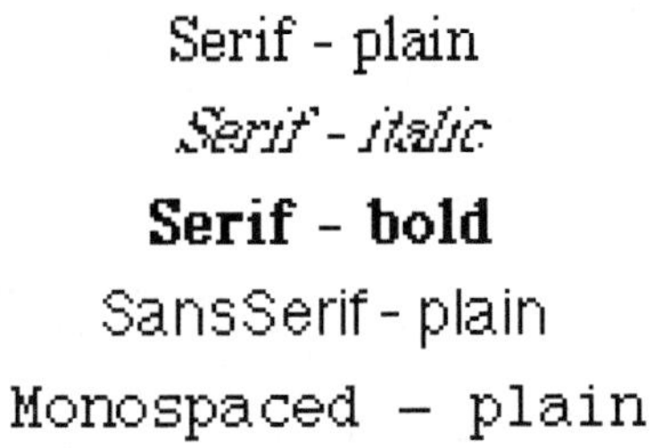

Serif - plain

Serif - italic

Serif - bold

SansSerif - plain

Monospaced — plain

Frame Class - `java.awt`

The Frame class is described in Section 15.6, page 728. See `JFrame`.

Graphics Class - `java.awt`

The `Graphics` class is described Section 3.6, page 104. Objects from the Graphics class are used for device-independent drawing of rectangles, lines, strings, etc. Graphics objects are not created directly, but obtained from a component or an image. For example, the paint method has a Graphics parameter that is used for drawing images on a display.

Several of the `Graphics` methods come in two forms: `drawXXX` and `fillXXX`. An example is `drawOval` and `fillOval`. The `drawXXX` methods draw an outline of the shape with their inside unchanged. The `fillXXX` methods fill the inside of the shape with the current drawing color.

Listing B.27 Graphics Class

```
1   public abstract class Graphics
2   {
3     public void drawArc (int x, int y, int width, int height,
4                          int startAngle, int arcAngle);
5     public boolean drawImage (Image image, int x, int y,
6                          ImageObserver observer);
7     public void drawLine (int x1, int y1, int x2, int y2);
8     public void drawOval (int x, int y, int width, int height);
9     public void drawPolygon (int[] xPoints, int[] yPoints,
10                         int nPoints);
11    public void drawPolygon (Polygon p);
12    public void drawRect (int x, int y, int width, int height);
13    public void drawRoundRect (int x, int y,
14                         int width, int height,
15                         int arcWidth, int arcHeight);
16    public void drawString (String str, int x, int y);
17    public void fillArc (int x, int y, int width, int height,
18                         int startAngle, int arcAngle);
19    public void fillOval (int x, int y, int width, int height);
20    public void fillPolygon (int[] xPoints, int[] yPoints,
21                         int nPoints);
22    public void fillPolygon (Polygon p);
23    public void fillRect (int x, int y, int width, int height);
24    public void fillRoundRect (int x, int y,
25                         int width, int height,
26                         int arcWidth, int arcHeight);
27    public Color getColor ();
28    public Font getFont ();
29    public void setColor (Color c);
30    public void setFont (Font f);
```

Listing B.27 Graphics Class

```
31    public void setPaintMode ();
32    public void setXORMode (Color c);
33    public void translate (int x, int y);
34    public String toString ();
35 }
```

Table B.14 Graphics Methods

method	description
drawArc fillArc	An arc is drawn. • The arc is a portion of an oval defined by x, y, width, and height (see drawOval.) • "startAngle" and "arcAngle" are in degrees. Counterclockwise is positive. • "startAngle" is the beginning of the arc with 0 the oval's right most point. • "arcAngle" is the number of degrees the arc spans. For example `g.drawArc(20, 10, 200, 150, 45, 135);` 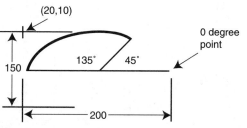
drawImage	The "image" is drawn with its upper left corner at (x,y). See Listing 3.6 on page 109 for an example.
drawLine	A line is drawn from (x1,y1) to (x2,y2). For example: `g.drawLine(150,30,50,60);` 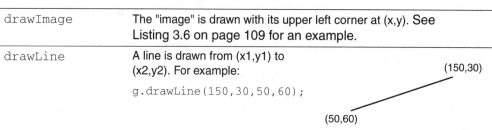

Table B.14 Graphics Methods

method	description
`drawOval` `fillOval`	An oval drawn with its upper-left corner at (x,y) that is `width` wide and `height` high. For example: `g.drawOval` `      (50,30,150,75);` 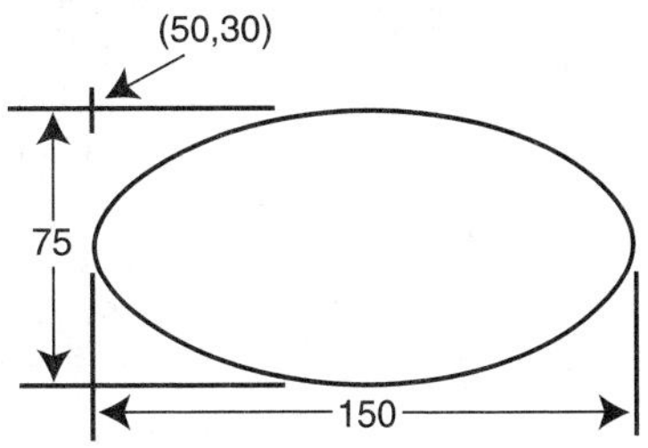

`drawPolygon`
`fillPolygon`
	A polygon is drawn. Points are drawn in the order they are entered into a polygon. Two examples for drawing the same polygon are shown below. 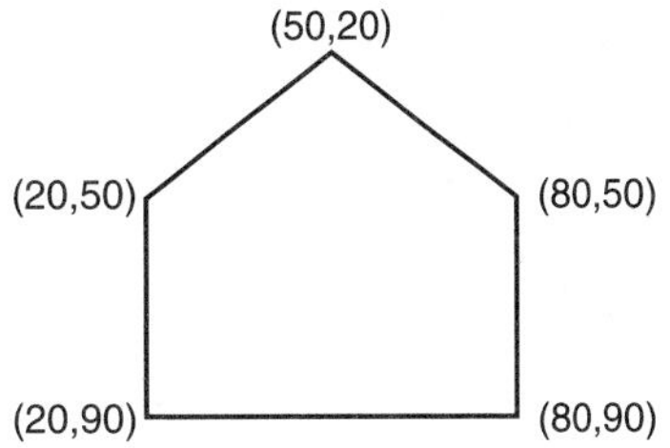
	
	`int[] xPoints =`
	`   {50, 80, 80, 20, 20};`
	`int[] yPoints =`
	`   {20, 50, 90, 90, 50};`
	`g.drawPolygon`
	`   (xPoints, yPoints, 5);`
	
	`Polygon pentagon = new Polygon();`
	`pentagon.addPoint(50,10);`
	`pentagon.addPoint(86,38);`
	`pentagon.addPoint(74,82);`
	`pentagon.addPoint(26,82);`
	`pentagon.addPoint(14,38);`
	`g.drawPolygon(pentagon);`

`drawRect` `fillRect`	A rectangle drawn with its upper-left corner at (x,y) that is `width` wide and `height` high. For example: `g.drawRect` `      (50,30,150,75);` 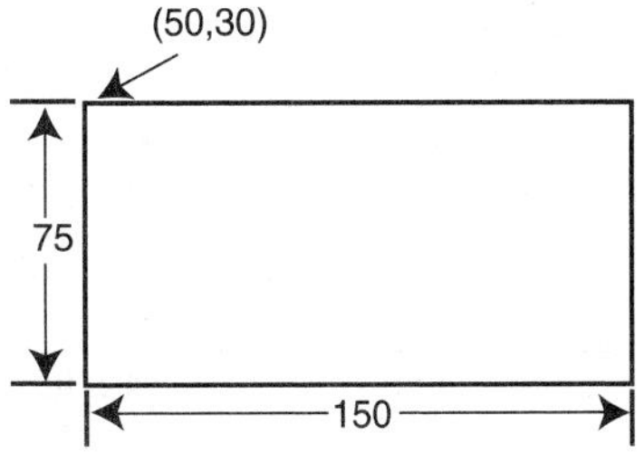

Table B.14 Graphics Methods

method	description

drawRoundRect
 	
fillRoundRect
	A rounded rectangle is drawn with its upper-left corner at (x,y) and width wide and height high. The first four parameters of a rounded rectangle are the same as those of a rectangle. The last two parameters describe how the corners are to be rounded. They specify an ellipse that one can imagine being quartered and each quarter placed in the four corners of the rectangle. The example below describes the rounded rectangle and an ellipse that fits into one of its corners.
	
	`g.drawRoundRect(50,30,250,125,150,75);`
	`g.drawOval     (50,30,        150,75);`
	
	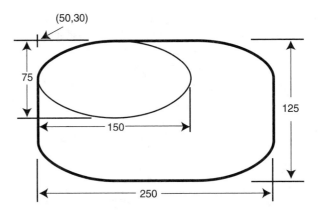

drawString	A string with its lower-left corner at (x,y) is drawn. For example: `g.drawString ("Pez", 24, 40);`

getColor	The foreground color of this graphics context is returned. In the following example c gets the value for the color blue.
	
	`g.setColor(Color.blue);`
	`Color c = g.getColor();`

getFont	The font for this graphics context is returned. The value of f in the example below is courier 12 point plain font.
	
	`Font courier = new Font("Courier", Font.PLAIN, 12);`
	`g.setFont(courier);`
	`Font f = g.getFont();`

Table B.14 Graphics Methods

method	description
setColor	The foreground color of this graphics context is set to c. See Section 3.6.2, page 104.
setFont	The font for this graphics context is set to f. See `getFont`.
setPaintMode	Set this graphics context to normal paint mode Undoes `setXOR-Mode`. For example: `g.setPaintMode();`

setXORMode	Set this graphics context to xor paint mode. Drawing the same object at the same location in same color twice has the net effect of doing nothing. For example:
	
	`g.setXORMode(Col-or.black);`
	`g.fillRect(50, 50, 150, 75);`
	`g.fillOval(70, 70, 150, 75);`

translate	The origin of this graphics context is moved by "x" and "y". If the origin of the graphics window was the upper left corner and "width" is the width and "height" is the height of the window, in the example below the new origin is the middle of the window.
	
	`g.translate(width/2, height/2);`
	To move the origin back to its original location do the following.
	
	`g.translate(-width/2, -height/2);`

Integer Class - `java.lang`

The `Integer`, `Long`, `Float`, and `Double` classes have many similar operations. Because the methods in these classes are similar, only the Integer class is described in detail within this section. Table B.15 contains a snapshot of the Integer, Long, Float, and Double classes.

Table B.15 Integer, Long, Float, and Double Methods (NA=Not Available)

		methods			
purpose	static	Integer	Long	Float	Double
object constructor	no	Integer	Long	Float	Double
equality check	no	equals	equals	equals	equals
get value	no	intValue	longValue	floatValue	doubleValue
string to primitive type	yes	parseInt	parseLong	NA	NA
primitive type to binary string	yes	toBinaryString	toBinaryString	NA	NA
primitive type to hex string	yes	toHexString	toHexString	NA	NA
primitive type to octal string	yes	toOctalString	toOctalString	NA	NA
primitive type to string	yes/no	toString	toString	toString	toString
string to numerical object	yes	valueOf	valueOf	valueOf	valueOf

The `Integer` class is a wrapper for the `int` primitive. Objects of the `Integer` class are immutable. Examples of using the `Integer` class can be found in Section 12.4.2, page 558. The following shows how to convert a string to an int.

```
String  s = "123";
int     i = Integer.parseInt(s);
```

or

```
String  s = "123";
Integer I = Integer.valueOf(s);
int     i = I.intValue();
```

Table B.16 Integer Methods

method	description

`MAX_VALUE`
 	
`MIN_VALUE`
	```Integer.MAX_VALUE // returns 2,147,483,647```
	```Integer.MIN_VALUE // returns -2,147,483,648```

`Integer`	Create an integer. For example:
	
	```Integer j = new Integer(123);```
	```Integer k = new Integer("123");```
	```if (j.equals(k)) // returns true```

`equals`	returns true if this integer and i have the same value. For example:
	
	```Integer j = new Integer(42);```
	```Integer k = new Integer(42);```
	```j.equals(k) // returns true```

`intValue`	The int value of this Integer is returned. For example:
	
	```Integer I = new Integer(93);```
	```int i = I.intValue(); // i is 93```

`parseInt`	Convert a string to an integer. Same as using the combination valueOf and intValue. It is not available for `double` and `float`. For example:
	
	```// the following prints 1234```
	```String r = new String("1234");```
	```System.out.println(Integer.parseInt(r));```
	
	```// the following prints 180```
	```String s = new String("B4");```
	```System.out.println(Integer.parseInt(s,16));```
	
	```// the following prints 13```
	```String t = new String("1101");```
	```System.out.println(Integer.parseInt(t,2));```

Table B.16 Integer Methods

method	description

toBinaryString	An important difference between `toString` and `toBinaryString` is how they treat negative numbers. `toBinaryString` uses two's complement notation. For example:
	
	```// the following prints 10110100```
	```String s = Integer.toBinaryString(180);```
	```System.out.println(s);```
	
	```// the following prints 11111111111111111```
	```String t = Integer.toBinaryString(-1);```
	```System.out.println(t);```

toHexString	An important difference between `toString` and `toHexString` is how they treat negative numbers. `toHexString` uses two's complement notation. For example:
	
	```// the following prints b4```
	```String s = Integer.toHexString(180);```
	```System.out.println(s);```
	
	```// the following prints ffffffff```
	```String t = Integer.toHexString(-1);```
	```System.out.println(t);```

toOctalString	An important difference between `toString` and `toOctalString` is how they treat negative numbers. `toOctalString` uses two's complement notation. For example:
	
	```// the following prints 264```
	```String s = Integer.toOctalString(180);```
	```System.out.println(s);```
	
	```// the following prints 37777777777```
	```String t = Integer.toOctalString(-1);```
	```System.out.println(t);```

Table B.16 Integer Methods

method	description

toString	An important difference between the method toString and the methods toBinaryString, toHexString, and toOctal-String is how they treat negative numbers. toString uses sign and magnitude notation. For example:
	
	``
	Integer i = new Integer(180);
	String q = i.toString(); // q is "180"
	String r = Integer.toString(180); // r is "180"
	String s = Integer.toString(180,16); // s is "b4"
	String t = Integer.toString(180,8); // t is "264"
	String u = Integer.toString(-1); // u is "-1"
	``

valueOf	The Integer representation of this string is returned. Note: this is a static method. For example:
	
	``
	String r = new String("1234");
	Integer a = Integer.valueOf(r);
	int x = a.intValue(); // x is 1234
	
	String s = new String("B4");
	Integer b = Integer.valueOf(s, 16);
	int y = b.intValue(); // y is 180
	
	String t = new String("1101");
	Integer c = Integer.valueOf(t, 2);
	int z = c.intValue(); // z is 13
	``

ItemEvent Class - java.awt.event

The ItemEvent class is used to respond to radio button selection. It makes its first appearance in Chapter 15 and is described in Section 15.4.6, page 708. See ItemListener interface and JRadioButton class.

Listing B.28 Integer Class

```
1  public final class Integer extends Number
2  {
3    public static final int MAX_VALUE;
4    public static final int MIN_VALUE;
5    public Integer (int value);
6    public Integer (String s) throws NumberFormatException;
7    public boolean equals (Object obj);
8    public int intValue ();
9    public static int parseInt (String s)
10                       throws NumberFormatException;
11   public static int parseInt (String s, int radix)
12                       throws NumberFormatException;
13   public static String toBinaryString (int i);
14   public static String toHexString (int i);
15   public static String toOctalString (int i);
16   public String toString ();
17   public static Integer valueOf (String s)
18                       throws NumberFormatException;
19 }
```

Listing B.29 ItemEvent Class

```
1  public class ItemEvent extends AWTEvent
2  {
3    public Object getItem();
4  }
```

Table B.17 ItemEvent Methods

method	description
getItem	Return the object that initiated this event.

ItemListener Interface - `java.awt.event`

The `ItemListener` interface is used to respond to radio button selection. The `item-StateChanged` method is called whenever checkbox item is changed. It makes its first appearance in Chapter 15 and is described in Section 15.4.6, page 708. See `ItemEvent` and `JRadioButton` classes.

Table B.18 ItemListener Methods

operation	description
itemStateChanged	Callback method called when a checkbox is selected.

Listing B.30 ItemListener Interface

```
1 public abstract interface ItemListener extends EventListener
2 {
3   public void itemStateChanged (ItemEvent e);
4 }
```

JApplet Class - `javax.swing`

See Section 15.4.1, page 697 and the Applet class in this Appendix. JApplets may have menus but Applets may not.

Table B.19 Some Methods Added to Applet by JApplet

method	description
`getContentPane`	Returns the content pane of this frame
`getMenuBar`	Return this frame's menu bar. If it has no menu bar, return null.
`setMenuBar`	Set this frame's menu bar. If one already exist, it is removed.

Listing B.31 JApplet Class

```
1 public class JFApplet extends Applet
2 {
3   ...
4   public Container getContentPane ();
5   public JMenuBar getJMenuBar ();
6   public void setJMenuBar (JMenuBar menuBar);
7 }
```

JButton Class - `javax.swing`

The `JButton` class is used to create buttons. It makes its first appearance in Chapter 15 and is described in Section 15.4.4, page 702. The constructor creates a button with the given label and the `addActionListener` registers and action listener with this button. See `ActionEvent` class and `ActionListener` interface.

JFrame Class - `javax.swing`

The JFrame class is described in Section 15.4.2, page 697. It is used for creating windows. `JFrame` (Java 2.0) inherits from `Frame` (Java 1.1) which inherits from `Window`. `Window` inherits from `Container`. `Container` inherits from `Component`. See

Listing B.32 JButton Class

```
1 public class JButton extends AbstractButton
2 {
3   public JButton (String label);
4   public void addActionListener
5             (ActionListener listener);  // inherited
6 }
```

Figure B.1 on page 856. Component contains methods such as addKeyListener, addMouseListener, addMouseMotionListener, getGraphics, paint, repaint, setBackground, setFont, setForeground, and update.

Table B.20 Frame Methods

method	description
JFrame	An invisible Frame instance is created. If the constructor has a String parameter, the window get the title of the text. Otherwise the frame is untitled
dispose	Destroy this frame and free all of the resources it used.
getContentPane	Returns the content pane of this frame
getMenuBar	Return this frame's menu bar. If it has no menu bar, return null.
setMenuBar	Set this frame's menu bar. If one already exist, it is removed.
setTitle	Set the title of this frame.

Listing B.33 JFrame Class

```
1 public class JFrame extends Frame
2 {
3   public JFrame ();
4   public JFrame (String title);
5   public void dispose ();
6   public Container getContentPane ();
7   public JMenuBar getJMenuBar (); // J's gone in Frame class
8   public void setJMenuBar (JMenuBar menuBar);
9   public setTitle (String title); // inherited from Frame
10 }
```

JLabel Class - `javax.swing`

Works just like the Label class only for Java 2.0. See Section 15.4.4, page 702 for an example.

JMenu Class - `javax.swing`

The `JMenu` class constructor creates a menu with the given label. We can add menu items to a menu using the `add` method. Additional methods not listed add separators, remove items, and perform other tasks. An example of using the J enu class is shown in Section 15.4.5, page 705. See also `JMenuBar` and `JMenuItem` classes.

Listing B.34 JMenu Class

```
1 public class JMenu extends JMenuItem
2 {
3    public JMenu (String label);
4    public JMenuItem add (JMenuItem item);
5 }
```

JMenubar Class - `javax.swing`

The `JMenuBar` class constructor creates a menu bar. We can add menus to a menu bar using the `add` method. Additional methods not listed remove menus and perform other tasks. An example of using the J enuBar class is shown in Section 15.4.5, page 705. See also `JMenu` and `JMenuItem` classes.

Listing B.35 JMenubar Class

```
1 public class JMenuBar extends JComponent
2 {
3    public JMenuBar ();
4    public JMenu  add (Menu m);
5 }
```

JMenuItem Class - `javax.swing`

The `JMenuItem` class constructor creates a menu item with the given label. A menu item is enabled by default. We can disable a menu item by sending the `setEnabled` method a false value and enable it by sending `setEnabled` a true value. When a menu item is disabled, it appears as light gray and it cannot be selected. An example of using the JMenu-Item class is shown in Section 15.4.5, page 705. See also JMenu and JMenuBar classes.

Listing B.36   JMenuItem Class

```
1 public class JMenuItem extends AbstractButton
2 {
3   public JMenuItem (String label);
4   public void addActionListener
5             (ActionListener listener);      // inherited
6   public void setEnabled (boolean status);
7 }
```

JOptionPane Class - javax.swing

The JOptionPane class is a flexible and easy to use class for creating input and message dialog boxes. One of the easiest ways to create a dialog is to use its static methods. An example can be found in Section 15.4.7, page 710. Listing B.37 shows only two of the dozens of methods JOptionPane supports.

Listing B.37   JOptionPane Class

```
1 public class JOptionPane extends JComponent
2 {
3   public static String showInputDialog(Object message);
4   public static void showMessageDialog(Component parent,
5                                         Object message)
6 }
```

JPanel Class - javax.swing

Objects from the JPanel class can be nested to create panels within panels. Panels can be used to group components into logical groups and control how they are placed within a frame. Use the add operation inherited from Container (through JComponent) to add components to a panel. An example is shown in Section 15.4.12, page 723.

Listing B.38   JOptionPane Class

```
1 public class JPanel extends JComponent
2 {
3   public JPanel ();
4   public JPanel(LayoutManager layout)
5 }
```

JRadioButton Class - `javax.swing`

The JRadioButton class is used to create radio buttons. It makes its first Button-Group and ItemEvent classes and ItemListener interface.

Table B.21 JRadioButton Methods

method	description
JRadioButton	The "state" parameter allows us to set the initial state of the checkbox.
addItemListener	An item listener is added to this button.

Listing B.39 JRadioButton Class

```
1 public class JRadioButton extends JToggleButton
2 {
3    public JRadioButton (String label);
4    public JRadioButton (String label, boolean state);
5    public void addItemListener
6                   (ItemListener listener); // inherited
7 }
```

JScrollPane Class - `javax.swing`

The JScrollPane class is used as a containing for things we want to scroll. An example can be found in Section 15.4.9, page 716.

Listing B.40 JScrollPane Class

```
1 public class JScrollPane extends JComponent
2 {
3    public JScrollPane(Component view)
4 }
```

JSplitPane Class - `javax.swing`

The JSplitPane class is used to create split windows. An example can be found in Section 15.4.9, page 716.

Listing B.41 JSplitPane Class

```
1 public class JSplitPane extends JComponent
2 {
3    public static final int HORIZONTAL_SPLIT;
4    public static final int VERTICAL_SPLIT;
5    public JSplitPane(int orientation,  Component leftComponent,
6                     Component rightComponent)
7 }
```

JTabbedPane Class - javax.swing

The JTabbedPane class is used to create tabbed windows. An example can be found in Section 15.4.10, page 719.

Listing B.42 JSplitPane Class

```
1 public class JTabbedPane extends JComponent
2 {
3    public JTabbedPane ();
4    public void addTab(String title, Component component)
5 }
```

JTextArea and JTextField Class - javax.swing

Unlike the TextArea class, JTextArea must be placed in a JScrollPane to get scroll bars. See Section 15.4.9, page 716 for an example. Use JTextArea and JText-Field with the JApplet and JFrame classes. See the TextArea and TextField classes.

KeyEvent Class - java.awt.event

The ItemEvent class is used to respond to checkbox selection. It makes its first appearance in Chapter 15 and is described in Section 15.4.8, page 714. See KeyListener interface.

Listing B.43 KeyEvent Class

```
1 public class KeyEvent extends InputEvent
2 {
3    public char getKeyChar();
4 }
```

KeyListener Interface – `java.awt.event`

The `KeyListener` interface is used to respond to key presses. It must be inherited. Typically one or more of its methods is overridden to be useful. It makes its first appearance in Chapter 15 and is described in Section 15.4.8, page 714. Its methods are described in Table B.22. See `KeyEvent` class.

Table B.22 KeyListener Methods

method	description
keyPressed	Callback method called automatically when a key is pressed. It is normally overridden by a programmer.
keyReleased	Callback method called automatically when key is released. It is normally overridden by a programmer.
keyTyped	Callback method called automatically when a character is generated. It is normally overridden by a programmer.

Listing B.44 KeyListener Interface

```
1 public abstract interface KeyListener extends EventListener
2 {
3    public abstract void keyPressed (KeyEvent e);
4    public abstract void keyReleased (KeyEvent e);
5    public abstract void keyTyped (KeyEvent e);
6 }
```

Label Class – `java.awt`

The `Label` class is used to create text messages in a window. It makes its first appearance in Chapter 15 and is described in Section 10.6.1, page 458.

Table B.23 Label Methods

method	description
Label	A new label with the message "text" is created. Alignment can hold the values LEFT, CENTER, or RIGHT. For example. `Label msg = new Label ("Compute", Label.RIGHT);`
setText	The message on this label is set to "text".

Listing B.45 Label Class

```
1 public class Label extends Component
2 {
3   public static final int LEFT;
4   public static final int CENTER;
5   public static final int RIGHT;
6   public Label (String text);
7   public Label (String text, int alignment);
8   public void setText (String text);
9 }
```

Long - java.lang

A wrapper class for the long primitive. Objects of the Long class are immutable. See the Integer class for examples of what these methods do. Examples of using the Long class can be found in Section 12.4.2, page 558. The following shows how to convert a string to a double.

```
String  s = "123";
long    i = Long.parseLong(s);
```

or

```
String  s = "123";
Long    L = Long.valueOf(s);
long    l = L.longValue();
```

Listing B.46 Long Class

```
1  public final class Long extends Number
2  {
3    public static final long MAX_VALUE;
4    public static final long MIN_VALUE;
5    public Long (long value);
6    public Long (String s) throws NumberFormatException;
7    public boolean equals (Object obj);
8    public long longValue ();
9    public static long parseLong (String s)
10                        throws NumberFormatException;
11   public static long parseLong (String s, int radix)
12                        throws NumberFormatException;
13   public static String toBinaryString (long i);
14   public static String toHexString (long i);
15   public static String toOctalString (long i);
```

Listing B.46 Long Class

```
16    public String toString ();
17    public static Long valueOf (String s)
18                            throws NumberFormatException;
19 }
```

Math Class - `java.lang`

What follows is a summary of a subset of the operations provided by the math class library. All angles are in radians.

1 radian = 180 / ¼ degrees = approximately 57 degrees.

Listing B.47 Math Class

```
1    public class Math
2    {
3      public final static double E;
4      public final static double PI;
5      public static double abs (double a);
6      public static float abs (float a);
7      public static int abs (int a);
8      public static long abs (long a);
9      public static double acos (double a);
10     public static double asin (double a);
11     public static double atan (double a);
12     public static double ceil (double a);
13     public static double cos (double a);
14     public static double exp (double a);
15     public static double floor (double a);
16     public static double log (double a);
17     public static double max (double a, double b);
18     public static double max (float a, float b);
19     public static int max (int a, int b);
20     public static long max (long a, long b);
21     public static double min (double a, double b);
22     public static double min (float a, float b);
23     public static int min (int a, int b);
24     public static long min (long a, long b);
25     public static double pow (double a, double b);
26     public static double random ();
27     public static double rint (double a);
28     public static long round (double a);
29     public static int round (float a);
```

Listing B.47 Math Class

```
30    public static double sin (double a);
31    public static double sqrt (double a);
32    public static double tan (double a);
33 }
```

Table B.24 Math Methods

operation	description
E	`Math.E` yields `2.7182818284590452354`
PI	`Math.PI` yields `3.14159265358979323846`
abs	Absolute value is returned. If a number is negative, return its positive counterpart. If it is positive, return it unchanged. For example: `Math.abs(-32.5)` yields `32.5`
ceil	Round up. For example: `Math.ceil(3.24)` yields `4.0`
cos	Cosine is returned. For example: `Math.cos(.5236)` yields `0.86603`
exp	Computes e^a. For example: `Math.exp(1.0)` yields `2.718`
floor	Round down. For example: `Math.floor(3.74)` yields `3.0`
log	Returns natural log (base e.) For example: `Math.log(2.178)` yields `1.0`
max	Returns the maximum of two numbers. For example: `Math.max(32.5, 75.1)` yields `75.1`
min	Returns the minimum of two numbers. For example: `Math.min(32.5, 75.1)` yields `32.5`
pow	Computes a^b. For example: `Math.pow(3.0, 5.0)` yields `243.0`

Table B.24 Math Methods

operation	description
random	An arbitrary number between 0.0 and 1.0 is returned. The number that is returned is different each successive call. Although there is a predictable pattern to the results, the pattern is so obscure that for all practical purposes the numbers are random. The pattern eventually repeats but the number of doubles in the cycle is so large that it should have no impact on our programs. For example. `Math.random()` yields some number
rint	Round to nearest whole real number. For example: `Math.rint(3.74)` yields `4.0`

round	Round to the nearest integer. For example:
	
	`Math.round(3.74)` yields `4L`
	
	`Math.round(3.74F)` yields `4`

sin	Sine is returned. For example: `Math.sin(.5236)` yields `0.50`
sqrt	Square root is returned. For example: `Math.sqrt(25.0)` yields `5.0`
tan	Tangent is returned. For example: `Math.tan(.5236)` yields `0.5774`

Menu, Menubar, MenuItem Classes - `java.awt`

See J enu, J enubar, and enuItem and Section 15.6, page 728.

MouseEvent Class - `java.awt.event`

A ouseEvent object is sent to all of the mouse callback methods. We can use this object to get information about the mouse when the event occurred. A description of how to use it and examples can be found in Section 14.2, page 661 and Section 14.4.4, page 676. See also `MouseListener` and `MouseMotionListener`.

Listing B.48 MouseEvent Class

```
1 public class MouseEvent extends InputEvent
2 {
3    public Point getPoint();
4    public int   getX();
5    public int   getY();
6 }
```

MouseListener Interface - `java.awt.event`

By implementing the ouseListener interface we can create programs that respond to mouse button events and events generated when the mouse pointer enters of leaves a components. The interfaces is shown in Listing B.49. A description of how to use it and examples can be found in Section 14.2, page 661 and Section 14.4.2, page 673. See also `MouseMotionListener` and `MouseEvent`. Table B.25 describes when the mouse methods are called.

Listing B.49 MouseListener interface

```
1 public abstract interface MouseListener extends EventListener
2 {
3    public abstract void mouseClicked  (MouseEvent e);
4    public abstract void mouseEntered  (MouseEvent e);
5    public abstract void mouseExited   (MouseEvent e);
6    public abstract void mousePressed  (MouseEvent e);
7    public abstract void mouseReleased (MouseEvent e);
8 }
```

Table B.25 MouseListener Methods

method	description
mouseClicked	Callback method. This method is called when the mouse button is pressed and released. The coordinates for when the mouse was pressed and release must be close together.
mouseEntered	Callback method. This method is called when the mouse pointer enters this component.
mouseExited	Callback method. This method is called when the mouse pointer leaves this component.
mousePressed	Callback method. This method is called when the mouse button is pressed.

Table B.25 MouseListener Methods

method	description
`mouseReleased`	Callback method. This method is called when the mouse button is released.

MouseMotionListener Interface - `java.awt.event`

By implementing the ouse otionListener interface we can create programs that respond to mouse move and drag events. The interfaces is shown in Listing 2.50. A description of how to use it and examples can be found in Section 14.2, page 661 and Section 14.4.3, page 675. See also `MouseListener` and `MouseEvent`. Table B.26 describes when the mouse motion methods are called.

Listing 2.50 - MouseMotionListener Interface

```
1 public abstract interface MouseMotionListener
2                             extends EventListener
3 {
4   public abstract void mouseDragged (MouseEvent e);
5   public abstract void mouseMoved   (MouseEvent e);
6 }
```

Table B.26 MouseMotionListener Methods

method	description
`mouseDragged`	Callback method. This method is called when the mouse is moved with the mouse button held down.
`mouseMoved`	Callback method. This method is called when the mouse is moved.

NumberFormat Class - `java.text`

The `NumberFormat` class is used to format numbers for output. It is described in Section 12.4.4, page 562. `DecimalFormat` extends `NumberFormat`. See `DecimalFormat`.

Listing B.51 NumberFormat Class

```
1 public class NumberFormat extends Format
2 {
3    public String format (double number);
4    public String format (long   number);
5    public void setMaximumFractionDigits (int value);
6    public void setMaximumIntegerDigits  (int value);
7    public void setMinimumFractionDigits (int value);
8    public void setMinimumIntegerDigits  (int value);
9 }
```

Table B.27 NumberFormat Methods

operation	description
format	Format a number to produce a string based on the current pattern and digit width settings.
setMaximumFractionDigits	Sets the maximum number of digits allowed in the fractional part of a number. If the number has more digits than the maximum, the least-significant digits are truncated.
setMaximumIntegerDigits	Sets the maximum number of digits allowed in the integer part of a number. If the number has more digits than the maximum, the most-significant digits are truncated.
setMinimumFractionDigits	Sets the minimum number of digits allowed in the fractional part of a number. If the number has less digits than the minimum, the remaining places are filled with zeros.
setMinimumIntegerDigits	Sets the minimum number of digits allowed in the integer part of a number. If the number has less digits than the minimum, the remaining places are filled with zeros.

Object Class - `java.lang`

The `Object` class is the superclass of all classes in Java. Thus, all classes inherit its operations.

Listing B.52 Object Class

```
1 public class Object
2 {
3    public clone () throws CloneNotSupportedException
4    public boolean equals (Object obj);
5    public Class getClass ();
6    public String toString ();
7 }
```

Table B.28 Object Methods

operation	description
clone	Creates a copy of an object. Its default implementation creates a new instance of the object in which each instance variable is a copy of the original. If the instance variable holds an object, the new object references the instance objects. In other words, it makes a shallow copy. See Section 13.5.5, page 620.)
equals	The default implementation determines that two objects are equal if they refer to the same object.
toString	Converts this object to its string representation. It is typically used for debugging purposes. This operation is automatically called in certain situations when an object appears where a string is expected. For example, in `System.out.println` and when a string concatenation operator (+) appears.

ObjectInputStream Class - `java.io`

The ObjectInputStream class is described in Section 16.4, page 776. It is used for reading persistent stores. Type information is preserved and checked at run-time.

Table B.29 ObjectInputStream Methods

operations	description

ObjectInputStream	If possible, this file is opened for reading. For example:
	
	`ObjectInputStream f = new ObjectInputStream`
	`                (new FileInputStream("picture.obj"));`

close	This file is closed.
read	If not end of file, the next byte is returned and the file pointer advances by one. If end of file, -1 is returned.
readBoolean	Boolean primitive is read from this file.
readChar	Character primitive is read from this file.
readDouble	Double primitive is read from this file.
readFloat	Float primitive is read from this file.
readInt	Integer primitive is read from this file.
readLong	Long primitive is read from this file.
readObject	An object is read from this file.

Listing B.53 objectInputStream Class

```
1   public class ObjectInputStream extends InputStream
2   {
3     public ObjectInputStream (InputStream in)
4          throws IOException, streamCorruptedException;
5     public void close () throws IOException;
6     public int read () throws IOException;
7     public boolean readBoolean () throws IOException;
8     public char readChar () throws IOException;
9     public double readDouble () throws IOException;
10    public float readFloat () throws IOException;
11    public int readInt () throws IOException;
12    public long readLong () throws IOException;
13    public boolean readObject () throws IOException;
14         ClassNotFoundException, OptionalDataException;
15  }
```

ObjectOutputStream Class - `java.io`

The ObjectOutputStream class is described in Section 16.4, page 776. It is used for writing to persistent stores. Type information is preserved and checked when the object is read in.

Listing B.54 ObjectOutputStream Class

```
1  public class ObjectOutputStream extends OutputStream
2  {
3     public ObjectOutputStream (OutputStream out);
4     public void close () throws IOException;
5     public void write (int data) throws IOException;
6     public void writeBoolean (boolean state) throws IOException;
7     public void writeBytes (String words) throws IOException;
8     public void writeChar (int letter) throws IOException;
9     public void writeDouble (double data) throws IOException;
10    public void writeFloat (float data) throws IOException;
11    public void writeInt (int data) throws IOException;
12    public void writeLong (long data) throws IOException;
13    public void writeObject (Object obj) throws IOException;
14 }
```

Table B.30 ObjectOutputStream Methods

operations	description

ObjectOutputStream	If possible, this file is opened for reading. For example:
	`ObjectOutputStream f = new ObjectOutputStream`
	`                  (new FileOutputStream("picture.obj"));`

close	This file is closed.
write	The least significant byte of "data" is written to this file. For example: `f.write(123);`
writeBoolean	A boolean primitive is written to this file.
writeBytes	A byte primitive is written to this file.
writeChar	A character primitive is written to this file.
writeDouble	A double primitive is written to this file.
writeFloat	A float primitive is written to this file.
writeInt	An integer primitive is written to this file.

Table B.30 ObjectOutputStream Methods

operations	description
writeLong	A long primitive is written to this file.
writeObject	An object is written to this file.

Point Class – `java.awt`

The primary use for this class is to package a x and y value into a single object. For example:

```
Point p = new Point(50,25);
this.setLocation(p);
Point q = this.getLocation();
int x  = q.x;
int y  = q.y;
```

Table B.31 Point Methods

operation	description
equals	Returns true if the x and y values of two points are equal.
setLocation	Gives this point new values for x and y.

Listing B.55 Point Class

```
1 public class Point
2 {
3   public int x;
4   public int y;
5   public Point();
6   public Point (int x, int y);
7   public boolean equals (Object obj);
8   public void setLocation (int x, int y);
9   public void setLocation (Point p);
10 }
```

Polygon class - `java.awt.Polygon`

The `Polygon` class is described Section 3.6.4, page 107 and demonstrated in Listing 3.1 on page 95.

Table B.32 Polygon Methods

operation	description
addPoint	Add a point to this polygon.
contains	Return true it the points is within this polygon.
getBounds	Return the smallest rectangle that includes all the points of this polygon.

Listing B.56 Polygon Class

```
1 public class Polygon
2 {
3    public Polygon ();
4    public void addPoint (int x, int y);
5    public boolean contains (int x, int y);
6    public boolean contains (Point p);
7    public Rectangle getBounds ();
8 }
```

An example polygon is shown in Figure B.4. Code for creating the triangle and illustrating the `contains` and `getBounds` methods is shown in Figure B.57. The heavy lines define the polygon. The rectangle enclosing it is called the bounding rectangle.

Figure B.4 A Polygon (Triangle)

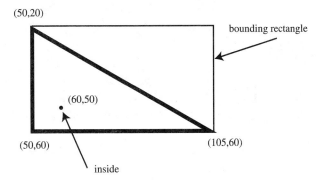

Listing B.57 Polygon Example

```
1  // create a triangle
2  Polygon rightTriangle = new Polygon();
3  rightTriangle.addPoint ( 50, 20);
4  rightTriangle.addPoint ( 50, 60);
5  rightTriangle.addPoint (105, 60);
6
7  // the following if statement is true
8  if (rightTriangle.contains (60,50)
9     System.out.println("Inside");
10
11 // r will have the following characteristics:
12 //    x     = 50, y      = 20
13 //    width = 55, height = 40
14 Rectangle r = rightTriangle.getBounds();
```

RandomAccessFile - `java.io`

The RandomAccessFile object is designed to read and write information at arbitrary locations within a file. A example appears in Section 12.7.6, page 581.

Listing B.58 RandomAccessFile Class

```
1  public class RandomAccessFile
2  {
3    public RandomAccessFile (String name, String mode)
4            throws IOException;
5    public void close () throws IOException;
6    public long getFilePointer () throws IOException;
7    public long length () throws IOException;
8    public int read () throws IOException;
9    public boolean readBoolean () throws IOException;
10   public byte readByte () throws IOException;
11   public char readChar () throws IOException;
12   public double readDouble () throws IOException;
13   public float readFloat () throws IOException;
14   public void readFully () (byte[], int offset, int length)
15           throws IOException;
16   public int readInt () throws IOException;
17   public String readLine () throws IOException;
18   public long readLong () throws IOException;
19   public short readShort () throws IOException;
```

Listing B.58 RandomAccessFile Class

```
20    public void seek (long position) throws IOException;
21    public void write (int b) throws IOException;
22    public void writeBoolean (boolean b) throws IOException;
23    public void writeByte (int b) throws IOException;
24    public void writeBytes (String s) throws IOException;
25    public void writeChar (int c) throws IOException;
26    public void writeDouble (double d) throws IOException;
27    public void writeFloat (float f) throws IOException;
28    public void writeInt (int i) throws IOException;
29    public void writeLong (long l) throws IOException;
30    public void writeShort (int s) throws IOException;
31 }
```

Table B.33 RandomAccessFile Methods

operations	description
RandomAccessFile	If possible, open this file. "r" for read mode. "rw" for read/write mode.
close	This files is closed.
getFilePointer	The position of the file pointer is returned.
length	The number of bytes in this file is returned.
read	Read a single byte from this file. -1 returned if end-of-file.
readBoolean	Read a boolean from this file. Exception is thrown at end-of-file.
readByte	Read a boolean from this file. Exception is thrown at end-of-file.
readChar	Read a 16 bit character from this file. Exception is thrown at end-of-file.
readDouble	Read a double from this file. Exception is thrown at end-of-file.
readFloat	Read a float from this file. Exception is thrown at end-of-file.
readFully	Read "length" bytes from this file. Put them into the "byte" array starting at "offset". Exception is thrown at end-of-file.
readInt	Read an int from this file. Exception is thrown at end-of-file.

Table B.33 RandomAccessFile Methods

operations	description
readLine	Read a string of characters from this file terminated with \n or end-of-file. Reads the 8 bit form of characters.
readLong	Read a long from this file. Exception is thrown at end-of-file.
readShort	Read a short from this file. Exception is thrown at end-of-file.
seek	Move the file pointer to "position".
write	Write a byte to this file.
writeBoolean	Write a boolean to this file.
writeByte	Write the least-significant byte to the int to this file.
writeBytes	Write the least-significant byte of each character in a string to this file. Recall that strings have 16 bit characters.
writeChar	Write a 16 bit character to this file.
writeDouble	Write a double to this file.
writeFloat	Write a float to this file.
writeInt	Write a int to this file.
writeLong	Write a long to this file.
writeShort	Write a short to this file.

Rectangle Class - `java.awt`

A subset of the rectangle operations are summarized here. An example of using it can be found in Listing 14.1 on page 664.

Listing B.59 Rectangle Class

```
1   public class Rectangle
2   {
3       public int x;
4       public int y;
5       public int width;
6       public int height;
7       public Rectangle (int x, int y, int width, int height);
8       public Rectangle (Rectangle r);
9       public Rectangle (Point p, Dimension d);
10      public void add (int x, int y);
```

Listing B.59   Rectangle Class

```
11    public void add (Rectangle r);
12    public boolean contains (int x, int y);
13    public boolean contains (Point p);
14    public boolean equals (Object r);
15    public Point getLocation ();
16    public Dimension getSize ();
17    public void grow (int hor, int vert);
18    public Rectangle intersection (Rectangle r);
19    public boolean intersects (Rectangle r);
20    public void setLocation (int x, int y);
21    public void setLocation (Point p);
22    public void setSize (int width, int height);
23    public void setSize (Dimension d);
24    public void translate (int hor, int vert);
25 }
```

Table B.34   Rectangle Methods

operation	description
add	This rectangle is just large enough to contain its original self and the point (x,y) or rectangle r (depending on its parameters.)
contains	Returns true if Point (x,y) or p is inside this rectangle.
equals	returns true if the x, y, width, and height values of this rectangle and r are equal.
getLocation	The upper left corner of this rectangle is returned.
getSize	A dimension corresponding to this rectangles width and height is returned.
| grow | ```
x      = x - hor
y      = y - vert
width  = width + 2 * hor
height = height + 2 * vert
``` |
intersection	A new rectangle which is the intersection of this rectangle and r is returned.
intersects	Returns true if this rectangle and r intersects.
setLocation	Gives this rectangle new x and y values.
setSize	Gives this rectangle new width and height values.
```

Table B.34 Rectangle Methods

operation	description
translate	Moves this rectangle by a relative distance.
	`x = x + hor` `y = x + vert`

Runnable Interface - `java.lang`

The `Runnable` interface is used to create another thread of execution. Execution of the new thread begins in the `run` method. It is described in Section 6.7, page 249 and Section 13.7.2, page 635. An additional example can be found in Section 13.2, page 599.

Listing B.60 ActionListener Interface

```
1 public abstract interface Runnable
2 {
3   public abstract void run ();
4 }
```

StreamTokenizer Class - `java.io`

The `String` class is described Section 12.6, page 569 and demonstrated in Listing 4.11 on page 150 and Listing 10.11 on page 470. It is well suited for tokenizing source program. However, it can be used to read simple data files.

Listing B.61 String Class

```
1  public class StreamTokenizer
2  {
3    public final static int TT_EOF;
4    public final static int TT_EOL;
5    public final static int TT_NUMBER;
6    public final static int TT_WORD;
7    public double nval;
8    public String sval;
9    public int ttype;
10   public StreamTokenizer();
11   public void eolIsSignificant (boolean eolSign);
12   public int nextToken() throws IOException;
13   public void whitespaceChars (int low, int h);
14 }
```

Table B.35 String Methods

operation	description
TT_EOF	end-of-file type constant- see ttype
TT_EOL	end-of-line type constant- see ttype
TT_NUMBER	number type constant- see ttype
TT_WORD	word type constant- see ttype
nval	numeric value for TT_NUMBER tokens
sval	string value for TT_WORD and string tokens

ttype	This fields holds the type of token parsed by nextToken. For example:
	
	`StreamTokenizer in = new StreamTokenizer`
	`(...);`
	`if (in.ttype = in.TT_WORD)`
	`  String word = in.sval;`
	`else if (in.ttype = in.TT_NUMBER)`
	`  double number = in.nval;`

eolIsSignificant	Specifies whether the end-of-line is recognized as a token. Pass it "true" if end-of-line should be recognized. For example:
	
	`StreamTokenizer in = new StreamTokenizer`
	`(...);`
	`in.eolIsSignificant (true);`

nextToken	Parse the next token from the stream. Return its ttype. For example:
	
	`StreamTokenizer in = new StreamTokenizer`
	`(...);`
	`int type = in.nextToken ();`
	`if (type == in.TT_WORD)`
	`  System.out.println (in.sval);`

whitespaceChars	Specifies the range of white space characters. For example: `in.whitespaceChar (0, 32);  // set it to default`

String Class - `java.lang`

The `String` class is described Section 10.5, page 449 and demonstrated in Listing 10.1 on page 441. Character indices are counted starting at zero.

Listing B.62 String Class

```
1   public class String
2   {
3     public String();
4     public String (String s);
5     public char charAt (int index);
6     public int compareTo (String s);
7     public boolean equals (Object s);
8     public boolean equalsIgnoreCase (Object s);
9     public int indexOf (String s, int offset);
10    public int length ();

11    public String substring (int beginIndex, int endIndex);
12    public String toLowerCase ();
13    public String toUpperCase ();
14    public static String valueOf (boolean b);
15    public static String valueOf (char c);
16    public static String valueOf (int i);
17    public static String valueOf (long l);
18    public static String valueOf (float f);
19    public static String valueOf (double d);
20  }
```

Table B.36 String Methods

operation	description

String	Create a new string. For example:
	
	```String a = new String();```
	``` // creates an empty string```
	```String b = new String("Shine");```
	``` // creates the string "Premium"```
	```String c = new String(b);```
	``` // string w is identical to b```

charAt	Return character at "index." For example:
	
	```String s = new String("Fried Green Tomatoes");```
	```char c = s.charAt(2); // c is 'i'```

Table B.36 String Methods

operation	description
`compareTo`	Return a negative number if this string proceeds string 's" alphabetically (Unicode ordering).
	Return zero if this string is identical to string "s".
	Return a positive number if this string follows string "s" alphabetically (Unicode ordering).
	For example:

	<pre>String r = new String ("pizza");
	r.compareTo("pizza") // returns 0
	r.compareTo("pizzaPie") // returns negative
	r.compareTo("Pizza") // returns positive
	r.compareTo("pixel") // returns positive</pre>

`equals`	Returns true if this string is equal to "s". For example:

	<pre>String r = new String ("pizza");
	r.equals("pizza") // returns true
	r.equals("Pizza") // returns false</pre>

`equalsIgnoreCase`	Returns true if this string is equal to "s" regardless of case. For example:

	<pre>String r = new String ("pizza");
	r.equals("pizza") // returns true
	r.equalsIgnoreCase("PiZZa") // returns true</pre>

`indexOf`	The index of the first occurrence of string "s" in this string after the given offset. If the offset is missing, it is given the default 0. If "s" is not found, -1 is returned. For example:

	<pre>String r = new String("When We Were Kings");
	int i = r.indexOf ("We") // i is 5
	int j = r.indexOf ("We", 0) // j is 5
	int k = r.indexOf ("We", 6) // k is 8</pre>

`length`	The length of this string is returned. For example:

	<pre>String r = new String();
	String s = new String(" ");
	          // one space between quotes
	String t = new String("123456");
	int i = r.length() // i is 0
	int j = s.length() // j is 1
	int k = t.length() // k is 6</pre>

Table B.36 String Methods

operation	description

substring	Return a substring of this string. For example:
	
	``java
	String s = new String ("Return of the Jedi");
	String t = s.substring(2, 6);
	        // t is a new string "turn"
	``

toLowerCase	A new string is returned in which all upper case letters in this string are converted to lower case. For example:
	
	``java
	String s = new String("R2D2!");
	s.toLowerCase() // s is "r2d2!"
	``

toUpperCase	A new string is returned in which all lower case letters in this string are converted to upper case. For example:
	
	``java
	String s = new String("12 Monkeys");
	s.toUpperCase() // s is "12 MONKEYS"
	``

valueOf	A primitive data value is converted to a string. Note: this is a static method. For example:
	
	``java
	String.valueOf(false) // "false" returned
	String.valueOf('X') // "X" returned
	String.valueOf(48) // "48" returned
	String.valueOf(3.13159) // "3.14159" returned
	String.valueOf(123.45e30) // "1.2345e32"
	``

StringTokenizer Class - `java.util`

A string tokenizer is used for parsing strings into tokens. The `StringTokenizer` class is described 12.4.2 on page 558 and demonstrated in Listing 12.28 on page 588.

Table B.37 StringTokenizer Methods

operation	description
hasMoreTokens	Returns true if this tokenizer has more tokens.
nextToken	The next token is returned. `NoSuchElementException` raised if there is not a next token.

Listing B.63 StringTokenizer Class

```
1 public class StringTokenizer
2 {
3   public StringTokenizer (String s, String delimiters)
4   public boolean hasMoreTokens ()
5   public String nextToken ()
6 }
```

System Class - `java.lang`

The `System` class contains several methods used to access system resources such as memory and perform program exit. In addition, provides methods for standard input and output.

Listing B.64 System Class

```
1 public class System
2 {
3   public static PrintStream out;
4   public void exit (int status);
5 }
```

TextArea Class - `java.awt`

A text area contains multiple lines of text with vertical and horizontal scroll bars. The `TextArea` class is described Section 10.6.3, page 460 and demonstrated in Listing 10.1 on page 441. TextArea inherits from TextComponent.

This is a Java 1.1 component that should be used with the Applet and Frame class. Use JTextArea and JTextField with the JApplet and JFrame class.

Listing B.65 TextArea Class

```
1 public class TextArea extends TextComponent
2 {
3   public TextArea ();
4   public TextArea (String s);
5   public TextArea (String s, int rows, int columns);
6   public void append (String s);
7   public void insert (String s, int index);
8   public void replaceRange (String s, int start, int end);
9 }
```

Table B.38 TextArea Methods

operation	description
append	The string s is concatenated to the end of this text area's text.

insert	The string s is inserted at location "index" in this text area's text. For example:
	
	`TextArea title = new TextArea ("The Wife");`
	`title.insert ("Preacher\'s ", 4);`
	
	This text area now contains "The Preacher's Wife".

replaceRange	The selected text in this text area is replaced.
	
	`TextArea title = new`
	`        TextArea ("The Empire Strikes Back");`
	`title.replaceRange ("Killer Tomato", 4, 10);`
	
	The title now contains "The Killer Tomato Strikes Back".

TextComponent class – `java.awt`

The primary purpose of the TextComponent class is to encapsulate the functionality that is common to the TextArea and TextField classes. The `TextComponent` class is described in Section 10.6.4, page 462.

Listing B.66 TextComponent Class

```
1 public class TextComponent extends Component
2 {
3    public String getSelectedText ();
4    public int getSelectionEnd ();
5    public int getSelectionStart ();
6    public String getText ();
7    public void select (int start, int end);
8    public void selectAll ();
9    public void setEditable (boolean editable);
10    public void setSelectionEnd (int end);
11   public void setSelectionStart (int start);
12   public void setText (String s);
13 }
```

Table B.39 TextComponent Methods

operation	description
getSelectedText	The selected text in this text component is returned. If no text is selected, a null string is returned.
getSelectionEnd	The end of the user selected text is returned.
getSelectionStart	The beginning index of the user selected text is returned
getText	All of the text in the text component is returned.
select	A string beginning at "start" index through "end" index - 1 is selected.
selectAll	All the text in this text component is selected.
setEditable	If "editable" is true this text component is user editable. The editable property determines whether the text component can be modified by the program user. For example, if a text component's editable property is set to false, a program user can only read the text component. They may not enter new or modify existing information within it. Regardless of the editable setting, a programmer is free to modify the contents of the text component.
setSelectionEnd	The end of the selected text is set to the value of the "end" parameter.
setSelectionStart	The start of the selected text is set to the value of the "start" parameter.
setText	This text component contains only the text in "s".

TextField Class - java.awt

TextField inherits from TextComponent, thus, it may be editable by the program and user. A text field contains one line of text. It is often used for text input. The Label class also displays a single line of text. It is not editable by the user so it is used primarily for output. The TextField class is described in Section 10.6.2, page 459.

This is a Java 1.1 component that should be used with the Applet and Frame class. Use JTextArea and JTextField with the JApplet and JFrame class.

Listing B.67 TextField Class

```
1 public class TextField extends TextComponent
2 {
3   public TextField ();
4   public TextField (String s);
5   public TextField (String s, int columns);
6   public void addActionListener (actionListener listener)
7 }
```

Vector Class - `java.util`

Vectors are expandable, heterogeneous lists of items. A description of a subset of the methods in the vector class follows. The `Vector` class is described in Section 11.4, page 504 and demonstrated in Listing 11.13 on page 521.

Listing B.68 Vector Class

```
1  public class Vector
2  {
3    public Vector ()
4    public void addElement (Object item)
5    public Object elementAt (int index)
6    public void insertElementAt (Object item, int index)
7    public boolean isEmpty ()
8    public void removeAllElements ()
9    public void removeElementAt (int index)
10    public void setElementAt (Object item, int index)
11   public int size ()
12 }
```

Table B.40 Vector Methods

operation	description
`addElement`	"item" is added to the end of this vector. The capacity of the vector grows automatically to accommodate the new item
`elementAt`	The element at location "index" is returned.
`insertElementAt`	All element at "index" and above are moved up by one index. "item" is inserted at "index".
`isEmpty`	True is returned if this vector is empty, false is returned if this vector has at least one item in it.

Table B.40 Vector Methods

operation	description
removeAllElements	This vector is made empty
removeElement	All element at "index" and above are moved down by one index. The old item is at "index" is lost.
setElementAt	Element at "index" is "item".
size	The number of elements in this vector is returned.

Window Class - `java.awt`

Frame inherits from Window. See Frame.

Listing B.69 Window Class

```
1  public class Window extends Container
2  {
3    public Window ()
4    public void addWindowListener (WindowListener listener)
5  }
```

WindowListener Interface - `java.awt.event`

Implementing the WindowListener interface allows a program to respond to window events. One of the most common events to listen for is window closing. We typically respond to this event by quitting an application or destroying the window. An example is shown in Section 15.4.3, page 701. The specification for this interface in shown in Listing B.70 with a description in of each in Table B.41. WindowEvent is not documented within this text.

Listing B.70 WindowListener Interface

```
 1 public abstract interface WindowListener extends EventListener
 2 {
 3    public abstract void windowActivated    (WindowEvent e);
 4    public abstract void windowClosed       (WindowEvent e);
 5    public abstract void windowClosing      (WindowEvent e);
 6    public abstract void windowDeactivated  (WindowEvent e);
 7    public abstract void windowDeiconified  (WindowEvent e);
 8    public abstract void windowIconified    (WindowEvent e);
 9    public abstract void windowOpened       (WindowEvent e);
10 }
```

Table B.41 Window Methods

method	description
windowActivated	This callback method is called when a window is activated. For example, the requestFocus() method can activate a window.
windowClosed	This callback method is called if the application applied the dispose() method to a window. In other words, it is called after a window has been destroyed.
windowClosing	This callback method is called when a user requests that a window is closed by using a platform-specific gesture such as clicking on a close icon. A typical action is to quit an application or to dispose of a window within this method.
windowDeactivated	This callback method is called when a window is deactivated. For example a user gesture or method call moves the focus to another component.
windowDeiconified	This callback method is called when a user performs a platform-specific gesture to deiconify a window.
windowIconified	This callback method is called when a user performs a platform-specific gesture to iconify a window.
windowOpened	This callback method is called when a window is shown for the first time.

C Vista Reference

Custom Classes

VActionButton Class

The `VActionButton` class is designed to work together with the `VApplet` framework to create simple GUI interfaces. Whenever a `VActionButton` is pressed, the `action` method in the `VApplet` class is called. See Listing 4.5 on page 132 for an example. See also the `VField` and `VLabel` classes.

Table C.1 VActionButton Methods

operations	description
VActionButton	The action button constructors are the only methods needed.
	• applet - The buttons need to know the applet in which they are to reside.
	• label - The `label` parameter will provide a label for the button. If no label is given the button will get the default label: "Action"
	`public VActionButton (Applet applet);`
	`public VActionButton (String label,` `                        Applet applet);`

Listing C.1 VActionButton Class

```
1 public class VActionButton extends Button
1 {
2   public VActionButton (Applet applet);
3   public VActionButton (String label, Applet applet);
4 }
```

VApplet Class

The `Vapplet` class is identical to the `java.applet.Applet` class with one exception. The `VApplet` class provides an `action` method which is meant be overridden. It is designed to work with the `VActionButton`, `VField`, and `VLabel` classes. See Listing 4.5 on page 132 for an example.

Listing C.2 VApplet Class

```
1 public class VApplet extends Applet
1 {
2   public void action ();
3 }
```

Table C.2 VApplet Methods

operation	description
action	Callback method. Overwrite this method. It will be called when a VActionButton object is pressed or a return in pressed in a VField object.

VField Class

The VField class is designed to work together with the VApplet framework to create simple GUI interfaces. It is used to input and output integers, doubles, and strings. Whenever the return key is pressed, the action method in the VApplet class is called. See Listing 4.5 on page 132 for an example. See also VActionButton and VLabel classes.

Table C.3 VField Methods

operations	description
VField	There are five constructors for creating a field. The first two create a blank field. The first one uses the default width of 16 characters. The second allows the field width to be specified. The last three constructors provide an initial string, integer, or double value for the field. When we specify an initial string value, the field is as wide as the string. When the initial values are numbers, the field width must be specified. Each of these constructors need to get passed an applet object so that it knows where to display this field.
getDouble	Returns the double representation of the string stored in this field. If that string cannot be converted to a double, a zero is returned and this field becomes "***".
getInt	Returns the integer representation of the string stored in this field. If the string cannot be converted to an int, a zero is returned and this field is set to "***".
getString	Returns the string stored in this field.
setDouble	Set this field to the string representation of d.
setInt	Set this field to the string representation of i.
setString	Set this field to s.

Listing C.3 VField Class

```
1  public class VField implements KeyListener
1  {
2    public VField (Applet applet);
3    public VField (int width, Applet applet);
4    public VField (String s, Applet applet);
5    public VField (int initValue, int width, Applet applet);
6    public VField (double initValue, int width, Applet applet);
7    public double getDouble ();
8    public int getInt ();
9    public String getString ();
10   public void setDouble (double d);
11   public void setInt (int i);
12   public void setString (String s);
13 }
```

VGraph Class

The VGraph class is used for drawing line graphs. Line graphs are created by following these steps.

1. Create a `VGraph` object
2. Start a new line
3. Add the leftmost point to the new line
4. Add successive points to the right of the previous point
5. If additional lines are needed, repeat lines 2 through 4

The `VGraph` class is used in the chaos program (Listing 5.1 on page 168). The simple example in Listing C.4 produces the plot in Figure C.1.

Listing C.4 VGraph Example Listing

```
1  import java.awt.*;
2  import java.applet.*;
3  import vista.VGraph;
4
5  public class Graph extends Applet {
6
7    public void paint (Graphics g)
8    {
9      setBackground(Color.white);
10     VGraph plot = new VGraph (-10, 10, -1, 1, this);
11     plot.addLine(Color.blue);
```

Listing C.4 VGraph Example Listing

```
12      plot.addPoint(-8,-0.8);
13      plot.addPoint( 0, 0.8);
14      plot.addPoint( 8,-0.8);
15      plot.addLine(Color.red);
16      plot.addPoint(-7,-0.5);
17      plot.addPoint( 7, 0.5);
18      plot.paint();
19    }
20  }
```

Figure C.1 VGraph Example Plot

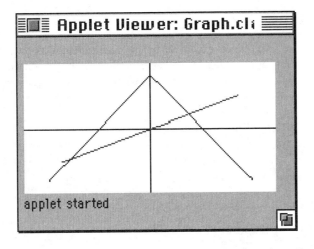

Listing C.5 VGraph Class

```
1  public class VGraph
2  {
3    public VGraph (double minX, double maxX,
4                   double minY, double maxY, Applet applet)
5    public void addLine (Color lineColor)
6    public void addPoint (double x, double y)
7    public void paint ()
8  }
```

Table C.4 VGraph Methods

operations	description
VGraph	An empty line graph is created that will plot lines in the "applet" window. "minX" and "maxX" define the range of numbers plotted horizontally. "minY" and "maxY" define the range of number plotted vertically.
addLine	Sets the color and starting point for a line graph.
addPoint	The point (x,y) is added to the current line
paint	This line graph is drawn in the "applet" window.

VGraphFrame

Works just like VGraph objects except VGraphFrame creates its own display window. Thus, it can be used in applications as well as in applets. VGraph, on the other hand, displays in an applet window only. An example of using VGraphFrame appears in Section 9.2 , page 393. See also VGraph.

Listing C.6 VGraphFrame Class

```
1 public class VGraphFrame extends Frame
2 {
3   public VGraphFrame (double minX, double maxX,
4                 double minY, double maxY)
5   public void addLine (Color lineColor)
6   public void addPoint (double x, double y)
7   public void paint ()
8 }
```

VGridBagLayout

The VGridBagLayout manager class makes it easier to take advantage of the Grid-BagLayout manager. It's use is described in Section 15.4.13 , page 723. An additional example can be found in Listing 15.20 on page 733.

Table C.5 VGridBagLayout Methods

operations	description
CENTER LEFT RIGHT	Possible component alignment values.
VGridBagLayout	Create a layout manager.
add	Add a component to a window.

- component   - component to be added to the "window".
- window   - window in which the "component" should be added.
- alignment   - position constraint of the component within its grid cell (LEFT, CENTER, or RIGHT justify)
- x   - column the component is inserted within.
- y   - row the component is inserted within.
- width   - number of cells wide component gets (default is 1.)
- height   - number of cells high component gets (default is 1.)
- fill   - make the component completely fill its allocated space (default is false.)

Listing C.7 VGridBagLayout Class

```
1   public class VGridBagLayout extends GridBagLayout
2   {
3     public static final int CENTER = GridBagConstraints.CENTER;
4     public static final int LEFT   = GridBagConstraints.WEST;
5     public static final int RIGHT  = GridBagConstraints.EAST;
6     public VGridBagLayout ()
7     public void add (Component component, Container window,
8                       int alignment, int x, int y,
9                       int width, int height, boolean fill)
10    public void add (Component component, Container window,
11                      int alignment, int x, int y,
12                      int width, int height)
13    public void add (Component component, Container window,
14                      int alignment, int x, int y)
15  }
```

VLabel Class

The VLabel class is designed to work together with the VApplet framework to create simple GUI interfaces. It is used to label GUI components. See Listing 4.5 on page 132 for an example. See also the VField and VActionButton classes.

Table C.6 VLabel Methods

operations	description
VLabel	The VLabel class contains only a single constructor. It creates a label specified by s which is display in "applet".

Listing C.8 VLabel Class

```
1 public class VLabel extends Label {
2   public VLabel (String s, Applet applet);
3 }
```

VPlot Class

The VPlot class creates its own window. Thus, it can be used for applets and applications. It is used for plotting automobile speeds in Section 13.2.5 , page 604.

Table C.7 VPlot Methods

operations	description
VPlot	A new graph is created
	• minY - Minimum y value that will be displayed.
	• maxY - Maximum y value that will be displayed.
	• numberPoints - number of points in this graph. They will be equally spaced along the x-axis.
	• title - title of this graph.
forward	Set graph to plot points for each line from left to right.
paint	This line graph is drawn on the frame's window.
reverse	Set graph to plot points for each line from right to left.
setLine	Add a line to this graph. It is represented as an array of integer y values. The points will be equally spaced along the x-axis.

Listing C.9 VPlot Class

```
1 public class VPlot extends Frame
2 {
3    public VPlot (double minY, double maxY, int numberPoints,
4                  String title)
5    public void forward ()
6    public void paint (Graphics g)
7    public void reverse ()
8    public void setLine (int line[])
9 }
```

VRead Class

Simple text IO is not trivial in Java. The VRead class is used to read from the keyboard goes to the display. VRead is introduced in Section 4.2.1 , page 123 and explained in Section 4.4.3 , page 144.

Listing C.10 VRead Class

```
1   public class VRead
2   {
3      public Read ();
4      public Read (String fileName);
5      public char readChar ();
6      public double readDouble ();
7      public int readInt ();
8      public String readString ();
9      public void waitForCR(VWrite out);
10  }
```

Table C.8 VRead Methods

operations	description
VRead	A standard keyboard input object is created. `VRead io = new VRead();`
VRead	A file input file object is created `VRead in = new VRead ("aFile.txt");`
readChar	A character is returned.
readDouble	If a legal double is entered, its value is returned. If the double is illegal, a new value is requested.
readInt	If a legal integer is entered, its value is returned. If the int is illegal, then the program asks for a legal integer.
readString	The entered string, less end of line, is returned
waitForCR	Control will not return until the return key is pressed. For example, when a Java application terminates in Symantec Cafe V1.8, it returns immediately to the IDE. When this method is placed at the end of the program, it allows us to read the results printed to standard output before control returns to the IDE. `in.waitForCR(out);`

VTextFieldUtilities

The VTextFieldUtilities class makes it easier to get int and double values out of the system. An example of using it appear in Section 15.2.3 , page 687.

Table C.9 VTextFieldUtilities Methods

operations	description
getDouble	If "field" contains a valid string representation of a double, the string is extracted and its corresponding double value is returned. If its string cannot be converted to a double, "***" is displayed in the text field and 0.0 is returned. Note, this is a static method.
getInt	If "field" contains a valid string representation of an int, the string is extracted and its corresponding int value is returned. If its string cannot be converted to an int, "***" is displayed in the text field and 0 is returned. Note, this is a static method.

Listing C.11 VTextFieldUtilities Class

```
1 public class VTextFieldUtilities
2 {
3    public static double getDouble (TextField field)
4    public static int getInt (TextField field)
5 }
```

VWrite Class

Simple text IO is not trivial in Java. The VWrite class is used to create a console object making interactive I/O easier for the novice. Output goes to the display. VWrite is introduced in Section 4.2.1 , page 123 and explained in Section 4.4.2 , page 142.. The VWrite class combines many of the functions found in the Java DecimalFormat, NumberFormat, and io classes. Additional information about how the output formatting works can be found in Appendix B on page 858 and page 889 and in Section 12.4.4 , page 562.

Listing C.12 VWrite Class

```
1   public class VWrite
2   {
3     public VWrite ();
4     public VWrite (String fileName);
5     public void applyPattern (String pattern);
6     public void write (char c);
7     public void write (String s);
8     public void write (long i);
9     public void write (double d);
10    public void writeln ();
11    public void writeln (char c);
12    public void writeln (String s);
13    public void writeln (long i);
14    public void writeln (double d);
15    public void setFractionDigits (int i);
16    public void setIntegerDigits (int i);
17    public void setNumberStringLetters (int i);
18    public void spaces (int n);
19  }
```

Table C.10 VWrite Methods

operations	description
VWrite	A standard console output object is created.
	`VWrite out = new VWrite();`
VWrite	A standard output file object is created.
	`VWrite out = new VWrite("aFile");`

Table C.10 VWrite Methods

operations	description

applyPattern	The new "pattern" is used to print numbers. It uses the `Deci-malFormat` class in Appendix B on page 858 and described in Section 12.4.4 , page 562.
	
	``
	double aValue = 12345678.9012;
	io.applyPattern("$#,##0.00;($#,##0.00)");
	io.println(template.format(aValue) + " " +
	          template.format(-aValue));
	``
	
	The result is shown below.
	
	``
	$12,345,678.90 ($12,345,678.90)
	``
	
	Other possible patterns:
	
	``
	0.0 no commas and no "$"
	0.0;-0.0 same as above
	``

write	A character, string, integer, or real is printed. The output buffer is flushed.
writeln	Same as `write` except for a "new line".

setFractionDigits	The number of digits on the right side of the decimal is set to i. It uses the `NumberFormat` class in Appendix B on page 889 and described in Section 12.4.4 , page 562. For example:
	
	``
	double aReal = 12.3;
	out.setIntegerDigits(4);
	out.setFractionDigits(3);
	``
	
	The resulting output follows.
	
	``
	0,012.300
	``

setIntegerDigits	The number of digits on the left side of the decimal is set to i. See `setFractionDigits` for an example.
setNumberStringLetters	The maximum number of characters in a string is set to i. If i < minimum number of characters, the minimum is also set to i.
spaces	n spaces are printed. If n <= 0 then 0 spaces are printed.

Glossary

Abstract class: One that may never be instantiated directly.

Abstraction: The process of focusing on the essential details of a system.

Actual parameters: Parameters that appear in a method call.

Aliasing: Giving a single object more than one name.

Algorithm: A step-by-step procedure to accomplish a particular task. These steps must be carried out in a finite amount of time and must give the identical answers given identical initial conditions.

Algorithmic analysis: Classifies algorithms by placing them in broad order of complexity categories.

Alphabetic character: In English the character in the range from "A" through "Z" and "a" through "z."

Alphanumeric character: Alphabetic and numeric characters.

Applet: A Java program that extends Applet. They can be run from a web browser, contain a window, and respond to paint events.

Appletviewer: A stripped down web browser. Its purpose is for viewing local Java applets.

Application: A program that does not inherit from the `Applet` class. Application do not have a framework to automatically pop up a window, communicate over the web, or handle paint events.

ASCII: (American Standard Code for Information Interchange) a common encoding scheme for characters.

Assignment statement: A statement used to give an object an identity.

Associativity: Determines the order in which operators with the same precedent are evaluated.

Base class: A class from which we inherit.

Binary files: Files use 8 bits to encode program instructions, images, audio, and many other types of data.

Bit: A single piece of information that can represent a 1 or 0.

Branch coverage: Test cases must be provided until the conditional in every `if` statement evaluates to true and to false at least once.

Bug: An error of logic in a computer program.

Byte: Eight bit.

Byte-code: A special number code designed to be easy to interpret by computers.

Callback method: A method that is called by an event handler. It contains code written by a programmer to respond to the event that called it.

Chaos: Numerical models that have a sensitive dependence on initial conditions.

Checked exception: An exception in which the compiler insists that the programmer provide an exception handler.

Class: Describes the behavior and possible states of an object. Behavior is defined by the operations a class provides.

Class variables: Stores the internal state of an object that is shared with all instances of its class.

Client: Someone or something that makes use of services of something else.

Code fragment: A subset of a program.

Cohesion: A measure of how the actions in the method are related. Strong cohesion often signifies good design. A class in which all the methods and instance variables that compose it are related. In a strongly cohesive class all instance variables and methods are necessary for the support of a single idea.

Concatenation: The process of combining several strings to create a new string.

Conditional: Flow of control constructs that execute other statements if special conditions hold.

Conditional body: The statements embedded within a conditional.

Constant: Identifiers with values that cannot be changed.

Constructor: Operation (method) that creates an object when the `new` operator is applied to it.

Copy constructor: Creates a clone of an object.

Coupling: Indicates the interconnectedness of methods or objects. Low coupling often indicates a good design.

Delimiters: Token separators.

Derived class: A class that inherits another class.

Design: The process of decomposing a system into components and determining how those component interact with each other.

Discrete event simulation: Modeling the world in discrete time steps.

Dynamic binding: A mechanism that waits to bind a method call to a method implementation until run-time.

Encapsulation: The process of hiding information that is not useful to a programmer.

Exception handler: Code that responds to an exception.

Exception: Occurrences that violates a Java language constraint.

Explicit type cast: A type conversion requested by a programmer.

event: An occurrence to which a computer program may respond.

Event-driven: A style of programming in which a program must respond to user requests.

File path: The name of a file that uniquely identifies it. It includes its name, the directories that embed it, and the disk on which it can be found.

Flag: A special boolean value used to control the flow of a program. It is set in one location and checked in another.

Flow of control: Defines an execution path through a sequence of statements. Each statement, except the first, is preceded by the execution of a single statement.

Formal parameters: Parameters that appear in a method definition.

Frame: A structure designed to hold all the local variables associated with a method.

Framework: A set of interacting classes that are designed to support the construction of a particular kind of software system. They can be customized to solve a particular problem by creating custom subclasses of the framework classes.

Functional cohesion: The principle that a method should accomplish a single idea.

Garbage collection: An action taken automatically by a program to return the resources required to maintain an object.

Hypertext: Document includes text with electronic links to other hypertext documents.

Identifier: A name given to an object, class, or method (operation.)

Identity: An object's name.

Immutable object: An object with no operations which will change its state.

Implicit type cast: A type conversion done automatically by the Java compiler without the programmer giving instructions to do so.

Inheritance: A mechanism that allows one to create a new class by adding functionality to an existing class.

Inner classes: Classes defined within other classes.

Instance variables: An object or value used to implement an object's state

Instantiating: The process of creating an object.

Integers: Numbers without a fractional part.

Interface: All the signatures that define the operations on an object.

Interpreter: A program that executes a program that has not been converted into the native language of the computer.

IO: An abbreviation for input/output. It can refer to input from a user's keyboard and output to a CRT display and it can refer to input from and output to a file.

Iteration: The process of repetitive execution.

Java compiler: A translator that converts Java programs to byte-code instructions.

Keyword: Special words that look like identifiers but have special meaning to the Java compiler.

List: A sequential ordering of items. Each element in a list, except for the first, has a predecessor and each element has a successor, except for the last.

Literals: Text representations of numbers.

Local variable: An object or value declared within a block.

Loop: Are flow of control constructs that execute statements repeatedly.

Loop body: The statements embedded within a loop.

Markup: Commands readable and created by a writer are included in a document to describe how titles will be placed, where images appear, font sizes, links to other documents, background colors, and much more.

Mesh: A decomposition of a geometric form into polygons. It may also be called a **polygonal mesh**.

Method: A Java mechanism for doing operations. Methods may change or access the state of an object.

Nesting: Embedding one statement within another.

Network: A set of computers that are connected together by twisted pairs of copper wire, cable, optical fibers, modems, microwave radio, and satellite links.

Null: An identifier that does not refer to an object.

Numeric character: Character in the range from 0 through 9.

Object: Have an identity, state, and operations.

Object oriented design: Decomposing a system into class and determining how those classes interact.

Object oriented language: A programming language that supports objects and class inheritance.

Object pattern: Describes a commonly used structure for organizing objects and classes to help solve a general design problem.

Off-by-one errors: A category of errors in which a value is too large or too small by single unit.

Operation: Actions that change or report on an object's state.

Optimization: The process of making a system more efficient. In a computer program, that may entail making it run faster or run with less memory.

Order of complexity: Defines the efficiency category to which an algorithm belongs. It is described by a polynomial term that dominates the function that computes the time require to execute the algorithm.

Overflow: Computations that result in values that are larger than a value can hold.

Overloading: The ability of a programming language to distinguish methods by their signature.

Override: A method that is inherited from a superclass may be re-implemented in the subclass. This new method is said to override the inherited method.

Packets: Chunks of information sent between computers.

Parameter: A mechanism for passing data (information) from the current method to another method.

Pass by reference: A parameter passing technique in which we transmit an access path to the object itself.

Pass by value: A parameter passing technique in which the actual parameter value is copied to a method and initializes the new value for a formal parameter.

Path: A unique sequence of statements.

Path coverage: Test cases must be provided until every executable path is executed at least once.

Pattern: A commonly used structures for describing a general solution to a common problem. It contains four parts: a name, a problem, a solution, and a consequence.

Persistent store: Type information is stored in a file in addition to data information.

Polymorphism: Allows one object identifier to reference objects from more than one class. The different classes are related by a common superclass.

Profiler: A program that counts the number of times each unit, for example a statement or method, is executed.

Program-driven: A style of programming in which the program controls how the user interacts with a program.

Precision: The accuracy with which a real number can represent a value. Precision is determined by the number of significant digits a number contains.

Protocol: Describes how information is organized within the packet.

Random access file: A file in which we can read and write to arbitrary location within the file.

Reals: Numbers with a fractional part

Robot: Machines that link stimulus to actions. They use devices called *sensors* to check their surroundings and use the information sensors gather to control *actuator* which manipulate world.

Selection: The process of conditional execution.

Semantics: Describes what that statement means.

Sentinel: A condition that governs when a loop should be exited.

Signature: The order, number, and kind of parameters a method has in addition to the method's name, return type, and to the class to which it belongs.

Simulation: A methodology that employs computers to model the important features of a physical system.

State: An object's current conditions.

Statement: Communicates instructions to a computer. It is a sequence of tokens that collectively express an action. a sequence of tokens that collectively have meaning.

Statement coverage: Test cases must be provided until every statement has been executed at least once.

Stepwise refinement: A *top-down* design methodology that begins by taking a problem and partitioning it into smaller subproblems. Each of these smaller pieces can be further partitioned.

String: A fixed length sequence of characters. Each character within a string has a character that precedes it, except the first character, and a character that succeeds it, except the last character.

Subclass: When one class inherits from another, the new class is called the subclass.

Superclass: When one class inherits from another, the original class is called the superclass.

Syntax: Describes the form that a programming language statement must take.

Temporal cohesion: The principle that a methods should accomplish actions that are related by time.

Test harness: A program that executes a piece of code under test. By executing the test code under various conditions our confindence in the code is raised.

text files: Files that use 7 bits to encode only the ASCII characters.

Thread: Each flow of control in a program.

Token: A sequence of characters that have a collective meaning.

Translator: A computer program that converts one computer language to another.

Type cast: The conversion of one type a value from one type to another type.

Type coercion: A process that forces a value of one type to be converted into a value of another type.

Unchecked exception: An exception for which an exception handler is not required.

Walk-through: A process in which a human plays the role of the computer. Each statement in the code under investigation is executed by hand and the result placed in a table.

White space: Spaces, tabs, and new lines.

Wrapper: A class with the purpose of providing a new interface for an existing set of classes or primitive values.

WYSIWYG (What-You-See-Is-What-You-Get): documents appear on the screen as they will appear after printing.

Index

C

callback method 130, 926
carriage return 449
catch clause 420
ceil 885
CENTER 848
chaos 161, 926
char 448
character 448
  alphabetic 448, 925
  alphanumeric 448, 925
  numeric 448, 928
charAt 902
Checkbox class 881
CheckboxGroup class 852
class 5, 926
  base 925
  defining 277, 305
  derived 781, 926
class variable 313, 926
client 305, 926
clone 891
close 561, 848, 849, 850, 851,
    863, 864, 892, 893,
    896
code fragment 175, 926
cohesion
  class 299
  functional 663, 926
  methods 221, 926
  temporal 663, 930
Color class 112, 853
command line arguments 578
comment 24, 115
compareTo 454, 902
comparison operator 60
compiler 26, 928
Component class 858
compound statement 65
concat 451
concatenate 451, 926
conditional 40, 65, 926
conditional body 65
constant 195, 926
constructor 21, 282, 285, 309,
    926
container 704
Container class 294, 859

contains 667, 895, 899
controller 692
convertion
  number to string 466
  string to number 466
copy
  deep 621
  shallow 621
copy constructor 622, 926
cos 885
coupling
  methods 221, 926
  objects 300

D

DataInputStream class 552,
    579
DataOutputStream class 552,
    579
debugging 76
DecimalFormat class 562, 859
declaration 20
declaring integers 178
declaring real numbers 186
delimiter 17, 545, 926
design 296, 926
  object inheritance 786
  object oriented 296, 928
destroy 101, 845
dialog 710
Dialog font 466
DialogInput font 866
Dimension class 860
discrete event simulation 599,
    926
discrete numbers 176
dispose 701, 878
divide and conquer 172
do statement 416
double 186
double buffering 258
Double class 861
double quote 449
doubleValue 468, 559, 861
drawArc 867
drawImage 110, 867
drawLine 867
drawOval 867

drawPolygon 107, 867
drawRect 867
drawRoundRect 867
drawString 867
dynamic binding 763, 926

E

EAST 848
elementAt 507, 508, 908
else clause 66
encapsulation 211, 926
Engelbart, Douglas 661
equals 454, 847, 860, 861,
    865, 876, 884, 891,
    894, 899, 902
equalsIgnoreCase 902
err 566
escape character 449
event 661, 927
event-driven
           programming 127,
    927
EventObject class 861
exception 419, 927
  checked 419, 926
  handler 398, 419, 926
  raising 419
  unchecked 419, 930
exit 701
exp 885
experimental procedure 315
extends 99, 782

F

false 60
file path 538, 927
FileDialog class 576, 862
FileInputStream class 552,
    573, 862, 863
FileOutputStream class 552,
    573
FileReader class 552, 554, 864
FileWriter class 552, 560, 864
fillArc 867
fillOval 107, 867
fillPolygon 107, 867
fillRect 105, 667, 867